Melusine's Footprint

D1637373

Explorations in Medieval Culture

The titles published in this series are listed at *brill.com/emc*

Melusine's Footprint

Tracing the Legacy of a Medieval Myth

Edited by

Misty Urban, Deva F. Kemmis, and
Melissa Ridley Elmes

BRILL

LEIDEN | BOSTON

Cover illustration: Melusine expelled from the castle. In John Ashton, *Romances of Chivalry Told and Illustrated in Fac-simile* (London: Unwin, 1890), 65.

The Library of Congress Cataloging-in-Publication Data is available online at http://catalog.loc.gov

Names: Urban, Misty, editor. | Kemmis, Deva, editor. | Elmes, Melissa Ridley, editor.
Title: Melusine's footprint : tracing the legacy of a medieval myth / edited by Misty Urban, Deva F. Kemmis, and Melissa Ridley Elmes.
Other titles: Explorations in medieval culture.
Description: Leiden ; Boston : Brill, 2017. | Series: Explorations in medieval culture
Identifiers: LCCN 2017041351 | ISBN 9789004315082 (hardback : alk. paper)
Subjects: LCSH: Melusine (Legendary character) in literature. | Melusine (Legendary character) | Women in literature. | Mythology in literature. | Literature, Medieval–History and criticism.
Classification: LCC PN57.M39 M459 2017 | DDC 809/.93351–dc23
LC record available at https://lccn.loc.gov/2017041351

Typeface for the Latin, Greek, and Cyrillic scripts: "Brill". See and download: brill.com/brill-typeface.

ISSN 2352-0299
ISBN 978-90-04-31508-2 (hardback)
ISBN 978-90-04-35595-8 (e-book)

Contents

PART IV
Melusines Medieval to Modern

Acknowledgements

This project began as a happy circumstance. After casting about for something to work on together, Melissa and Deva gave a paper on the German and French Melusine traditions at the 2014 International Congress on Medieval Studies at Kalamazoo, where Misty was also presenting on Melusine in a session on Middle English romance. In the chance meeting and conversations that followed, we agreed there was a need for more interdisciplinary scholarship on Melusine, and decided we ought to do something about that. We would therefore like to extend appreciation to those session organizers for bringing us together.

Our contributors have been delightful to work with, and we thank them for their professionalism and generosity. We extend deep gratitude to Kat Tracy for recommending the book for Brill's *Explorations in Medieval Culture* series and guiding the drafting of our initial proposal, to the EMC editorial board for improving the proposal with their perceptive advice, and to the anonymous reviewer who recommended the completed volume for publication. Marcella Mulder, our volume editor at Brill, was a gracious and expert guide at every stage of production, and we owe a great debt of thanks to our typesetter Malathy Chandrasekaran and to the entire production team for producing a beautiful volume and answering our every request with patience and great style.

Misty would like to thank Jane Burns for her expertise on all things Melusine, and Kat Tracy, Amy Vines, and Alison Gulley for being terrific role models in all things to do with medieval women. Special thanks go to David F. Johnson, Andrew Galloway, and Thomas D. Hill for being phenomenal mentors, guides, and friends who are not at all afraid of monstrous women.

Deva would like to thank Fr. Ronald Murphy, her *Doktorvater*, whose guidance made her homecoming to the world of medieval poetry possible. She is also grateful to Kat Tracy, Tina Boyer, Astrid Weigert, and Kristin Cole for showing the way, but mostly for their friendship, and to Elaine and Bill Shea, Daniel Kemmis and Jean Larson, Francie Shea, Jill Kohler, Jeanne Koester, Arthur, Walter, and all of her brothers, for their love.

Melissa's gratitude goes out to Amy Vines, at the time her dissertation advisor, who made the initial introduction to Misty and enthusiastically supported the idea of doing the book ("But *after* you finish your dissertation!"), to the MEARCSTAPA editorial board (Ana Grinberg, Tina Boyer, Renee Ward, Kat Tracy, Asa Mittman, Stefanie Goyette, Mary Leech, Thea Tomaini, Jeff Massey, and Derek Newman-Stille) for their fellowship, advice, and encouragement, and to Nicholas, Anna, and Fallon Elmes, Kristie and Patricia Ridley, and Don and Ellen and Dixie Elmes for their support and love.

List of Illustrations

Notes on Contributors

Jennifer Alberghini

is a PhD candidate at the Graduate Center, CUNY. She specializes in late Middle English literature, particularly the works of Chaucer and Gower and romance. She is currently working on a project on the intersections of marital and familial relationships and their impact on female autonomy.

Anna Casas Aguilar

is Assistant Professor at the Department of French, Hispanic, and Italian Studies at the University of British Columbia. Her research and teaching focus on peninsular literature, gender, and cultural studies. She has published articles in the *Journal of Spanish Cultural Studies*, *Revista de Estudios Hispánicos*, *Romance Quarterly*, and *Celestinesca*. She is currently finishing a book manuscript on masculinity, paternity, and self-writing in Spain.

Frederika Bain

has published on monstrous births, fairy spells, and early modern executions and murder. She is employed by the University of Hawai'i—Mānoa.

Anna-Lisa Baumeister

is a PhD candidate in the Department of Comparative Literature at the University of Oregon. She specializes in *Goethezeit* literature, translation studies, and feminist theory.

Albrecht Classen

is University Distinguished Professor of German Studies at The University of Arizona, where he researches and teaches medieval and early modern literature and culture. His publications deal with topics including gender, xenology, friendship, rural and urban space, mental health, hygiene, crime and punishment, the forest, triviality, bestsellers, and women writers. In 2010 he published the *Handbook of Medieval Studies* (3 vols), and in 2015 the *Handbook of Medieval Culture* (3 vols). He is the editor of *Mediaevistik* and *Humanities Open Access*.

Chera A. Cole

teaches writing and literature at Texas Woman's University. She specializes in Middle English romances and the supernatural in medieval texts.

Tania M. Colwell

is a Visiting Fellow and Sessional Lecturer at ANU College of Arts and Social Sciences. She is a historian of late medieval and early modern Europe, specializing in the cultural and social history of France and England, with a special interest in the ways cultural production, especially manuscript and early book culture, contributed to identity formation across the period.

Melissa Ridley Elmes

is Assistant Professor of English at Lindenwood University. She has published articles and essays on the Arthurian legend, Chaucer, and teaching topics in medieval literature and medievalism, and has work forthcoming on the Robin Hood legend. She is currently working on two book manuscripts: one on violence at the feast in medieval British texts, and one specifically on violence at the Arthurian feast.

Zoë Enstone

works as Programme Leader/Teaching Fellow in Arts and Humanities at the University of Leeds. Her PhD thesis explored the development of Morgan le Fay in Arthurian romance and she is currently finalizing research for a monograph on this topic. Her broader research interests include magic and identity in the middle English romances and transitions and boundaries.

Stacey L. Hahn

is Associate Professor of French at Oakland University in Rochester, Michigan, where she teaches French language and literature. Her field of research interest is medieval French prose romance, particularly the *Lancelot-Grail* Cycle and Jean d'Arras' *Roman de Mélusine*.

Deva F. Kemmis

is an instructor of German language and culture at the Goethe-Institut in Washington, DC. Her publications include an essay on the female prophetic in the *Nibelungenlied*, the entry for "German Courtly Epic" in the *Classical and Medieval Literature Criticism Series*, and a forthcoming article in the *Yearbook of the Society for Medieval German Studies*. She is preparing a translation of a recent German monograph on political philosophy.

Ana Pairet

is Associate Professor in the Department of French of Rutgers University-New Brunswick. She is the author of *Les mutacions des fables: figures de la métamorphose dans la littérature française du Moyen Âge* (Champion, 2002). She has written on mythography and mythmaking in the vernacular Ovidian tradition and in Christine de Pizan's works, and on the reception and transformations of chivalric romance across Europe.

Pit Péporté

is an associate lecturer at the University of Luxembourg. He has published in the fields of late medieval history, historiography, and medievalism, notably *Constructing the Middle Ages: Historiography, Collective Memory and Nation-Building in Luxembourg* (Brill, 2011).

Simone Pfleger

is a PhD candidate in the Department of Germanic Languages and Literatures at Washington University in St. Louis. Her research interests include twentieth- and twenty-first-century German-language literature, film, and culture, gender and queer theory, political subjectivity, affect, intimacy, precarity, and futurity.

Caroline Prud'Homme

is an expert in medieval and early modern French manuscript culture. Her publications include *Le discours sur le voyage chez les écrivains de la fin du Moyen Âge* (Champion, 2012). She recently curated the Newberry Library's French Renaissance Paleography website. She teaches French literature in Canada.

Renata Schellenberg

is Associate Professor of German at Mount Allison University in Canada. Her specialization is German literature and culture of the long eighteenth century. She has published on Goethe, Herder, and Alexander von Humboldt and on scientific literacy and material and print culture of the epoch. Her monograph on museum studies and cultures of remembrance in post-Enlightenment Germanophone Europe was published in 2016.

Misty Urban

teaches writing at Muscatine Community College. She has published books and articles on medieval literature, world authors, medieval feminism, teaching medieval literature, and medieval romance, including *Monstrous Women in Middle English Romance* (Edwin Mellen, 2010).

Angela Jane Weisl

is Professor of English at Seton Hall University. Her most recent book is *Medievalisms: Making the Past in the Present,* with Tison Pugh (Routledge, 2012).

Lydia Zeldenrust

is Associate Lecturer in Medieval Literature at the University of York. Her dissertation studied the Western European translations of the *Mélusine* romance and she has published articles on dragon women, translation strategies in the Castilian *Melosina,* and cross-cultural influences among the images of early *Mélusine* editions.

Zifeng Zhao

is studying Art History at McGill University. His research pursues the intercultural exchange between China and Central Europe in the early modern period in literature and visual art.

Introduction

> Et lors fist un moult doulereux plaint et un moult grief souspir, puis sault
> en l'air et laisee la fenestre et trespasse le vergier, et lors se mue en une
> serpente grant et grosse et longue de la longeur de.xv. piéz. Et sachiéz que
> la pierre sur quoy elle passa a la fenestre y est encores, et y est la fourme
> du pié toute escripte.[1]

> Thenne she bygan to gyue a sore syghe, & therwith flawgh in to thayer
> out of the wyndowe, transfigured lyke a serpent grete & long in xv foote
> of length. And wete it well that on the basse stone of the wyndowe apa-
> reth at this day themprynte of her foote serpentous.[2]

Melusine's footprint, which Jean d'Arras swore in his own day was yet visible
on a certain windowsill in the castle of Mervent, was only the first of many
impressions this fairy woman would go on to make on late medieval literature,
symbolism, and visual culture. Her figure draws on the archetype of the supernatural woman, well-attested in art and myth among the ancient and classical
worlds of the Mediterranean basin and Near and Middle East, where primordial goddesses and other munificent and terrible beings could assume a part-
serpent, part-bird, or part-piscine form.[3] The medieval Melusine shares much
with legendary water-women who proliferate through former Celtic-speaking
lands and who may have evolved from lamiae, mermaids, naiads, oceanids,
and other figures of Greek and Roman myth.[4] Tales of these extraordinary females persist through the early Middle Ages. Medieval Latin collections such
as Walter Map's *De Nugis Curialium* [*Courtiers' Trifles*] (ca.1200) and the *Otia
Imperialia* [*Recreation for an Emperor*], compiled by Gervase of Tilbury in the
early thirteenth century, offer tales of fairy women who sought noble marriages but, when exposed to the holy rites of the Eucharist, changed shape and
disappeared from human purview. Thus it is not entirely remarkable that, at

---

1   Jean d'Arras, *Mélusine ou La Noble Histoire de Lusignan,* ed. Jean-Jacques Vincensini (Paris: Le
    Livre de Poche, 2003), 704.

2   A. K. Donald, ed., *Melusine: Compiled (1382–1394 AD) by Jean D'Arras, Englisht about 1500,*
    Part I, Early English Text Society ES. 68 (London: Kegan Paul, Trench, Trübner & Co., 1895,
    rpt. 2002), 320.

3   Gillian M. E. Alban, *Melusine the Serpent Goddess in A. S. Byatt's* Possession *and in Mythology*
    (Lanham: Lexington Books, 2003).

4   Diane Purkiss, *At the Bottom of the Garden: A Dark History of Fairies, Hobgoblins, and Other
    Troublesome Things* (New York: New York University Press, 2000), 50–51.

© KONINKLIJKE BRILL NV, LEIDEN, 2017 | DOI 10.1163/9789004355958_002

some point in the Poitou region of western France, this story pattern is imposed on a local nymph or goddess figure, *la mére Lusine*, and allies her with the fortunes of the mighty Lusignan family, a medieval dynasty whose sons controlled fortresses including Lusignan and Parthenay, fought in the Crusades, and served as kings of Cyprus and Jerusalem.[5] What is remarkable is that in the lengthy historical romance of Jean d'Arras, completed in 1393, Melusine springs to life as a vividly realized half-fairy woman who is also an impressive medieval chatelaine, matriarch, and foundress of the Lusignan line. When discovered in the form of a monstrous half-serpent, after many years of happy marriage and the birth of several sons, she assumes the dragon-like form described above and, in so doing, burns herself indelibly into the medieval European imagination.

The fascination with Melusine rests in large part on her parallels with other shape-shifting, water- or earth-associated females who have made persistent appearances in literature and legend worldwide. Women with ophidian, piscine, or other features reminiscent of dragon-kind slither through the foundational stories of any number of cultures, from the islands of Japan to the creation myths of the first peoples of the Americas.[6] The snake- or fish-woman (sometimes both together) has occupied a salient strand of Western literature and myth from the first recorded instances, including the Sumerian Tiamat in her dragon form, the half-viper Echidna mentioned in Hesiod, and the Greek

5   Léo Désaivre explores her origins in "Le mythe de la mère Lusine (Meurlusine, Merlusine, Mellusigne, Mellusine, Mélusine, Méleusine): Étude critique et bibliographique," in *Mémoires de la Société de statistique, sciences, lettres et arts du département des Deux-Sèvres*, 2nd series, vol. 2, no. 1 (1882): 81–302; so does Josef Kohler, *Der Ursprung der Melusinensage: Eine ethnologische Untersuchung* (Leipzig: E. Pfeiffer, 1895), 1–10, and Robert L. Nolan, "An Introduction to the English Version of *Melusine*," (PhD diss., New York University, 1971).

6   Mary Pope Osborne, *Mermaid Tales from Around the World* (New York: Scholastic, 1993) collects several examples. The mermaid is a popular and personal subject of investigation, as demonstrated by, in a very small sampling of recent works, Theodore Gachot, *Mermaids: Nymphs of the Sea* (London: Aurum Press, 1996), Amanda Adams, *A Mermaid's Tale: A Personal Search for Love and Lore* (Nanoose Bay: Greystone Books, 2006), and Syke Alexander, *Mermaids: The Myths, Legends, and Lore* (Avon, MA: Adams Media, 2012). The pervasiveness of this image lends itself to psychoanalytical exploration, most memorably by Carl Jung, *The Archetypes and the Collective Unconscious*, trans. R. F. C. Hull (New York: Pantheon Books, 1959); see, as just one recent example, Gillian Pothier, "The Submerged Feminine: The Symbol of the Mermaid in the Human Psyche" (master's thesis, Pacifica Institute, 2011). The bibliography to this volume offers a list of studies on Melusine and her analogues that have been fundamental to critical scholarship on her texts and her legacy.

Python living beneath the sacred ancient Greek oracle at Delphi. Early Greek art depicts the classical sirens as women with bird forms from the neck down, luring men to shipwreck with their hauntingly beautiful voices. Naiads and nereids course through Ovid's first-century Latin works, often transforming into brooks or other bodies of water to escape life-threatening situations or again in consequence of the curse of an offended deity. These seminal texts, among others,[7] are thought to have provided inspiration for the generations of mythological water-women that appear in world literature, art, and culture to the present day.

But among these many iterations, Melusine is original and distinct, crystallizing several unusual features into one memorable if ever-changing form. While popular legends, epics, and medieval romances privileged the exploits of marvelous heroes such as Arthur, Charlemagne, and Alexander, and the cultural imaginary credited the dispersed heroes of Troy as the founders of European civilization, the *Roman de Mélusine* by Jean d'Arras and a French poem appearing a short time later, the *Roman du Parthenay* by Coudrette (ca.1401), foreground a mythical woman as the origin of a powerful medieval dynasty that will make its way into several royal and ruling houses across Europe and the Near East. The notion of a civilization or house founded by a monstrous woman is not unique to Jean d'Arras; the near-contemporary *Brut* legend in England invented a first wave of colonization by a set of fifty murderous Greek sisters who procreated with demons and populated the island with monsters which the Trojan hero Brutus had to defeat.[8] But, unlike other fairies of the romance tradition who frequently have malevolent intentions, or who are exiled from their human marriages when their true origins are revealed, Melusine's European authors and translators cast her as a respected medieval matriarch.

---

7 Ovid, *Metamorphoses* Books VII and XV, trans. Michael Simpson (Amherst: University of Massachusetts, 2001). Sirens appear in numerous texts and fragments in the post-Homeric period, including the works of Pliny the Elder, Hesiod, Euripides, and Virgil and his commentators. See for example Jacqueline Leclerc-Marx, *La Sirène dans la pensée et dans l'art de l'Antiquité et du Moyen Âge: du mythe païen au symbole chrétien* (Brussels: Academie Royale de Belgique, 1997); Leofranc Holford-Strevens, "Sirens in Antiquity and the Middle Ages," in *Music of the Sirens*, ed. Linda Phyllis Austern and Inna Naroditskaya (Bloomington: Indiana University Press, 2006), 16–51; Jenifer Neals, "Les Femmes Fatales: Skylla and the Sirens in Greek Art," in *The Distaff Side: Representing the Female in Homer's Odyssey*, ed. Beth Cohen (Oxford: Oxford University Press, 1995), 175–184. See also Frederika Bain's contribution to this volume for a discussion of how sirenic imagery influences depictions of Melusine.

8 Friedrich W. D. Brie, ed. *The Brut, or The Chronicles of England*, 2 vols, The Early English Text Society, os 131, 136 (London: Oxford University Press, 1906, 1908).

She endows chantries and chapels, builds several castles, manages great estates, advises her husband on how to restore his broken patrimony, and counsels her elder sons in chivalrous behavior before funding their expeditions to fight the Saracens and rescue threatened kingdoms ranging from Cyprus and Armenia to Bohemia and Luxembourg. She is an eminent foremother whose descendants can be justly proud of bearing her heraldic insignia on their arms. Yet the form that most prominently invokes Melusine is an unmistakable combination of the female, ophidian, and aerially equipped, as seen in the Germanic heraldic symbol that bears her name, the oft-reproduced woodcut that serves as the frontispiece to this volume, or the much-admired illumination in the Duc de Berry's *Tres Riches Heures* that depicts a dragon circling the castle of Lusignan.

Melusine's serpentine eruption is not, like that of her immediate predecessors in the texts of Map and Gervase, a revelation of some essentially Othered nature residing under the masquerade of human beauty, or at least not obviously so. Despite and in part because of her royal, if mixed, descent from King Elinas of Albany and his fairy wife, Presine, Melsuine is fated to undergo a weekly transformation into the form that her audiences find most memorable: as a consequence of a curse laid upon her by her mother, she turns once a week into a serpent from the waist down, a latent monstrousness she must keep hidden from the world—or, more urgently, from her husband, for only in successful human marriage can the half-fairy Melusine hope to acquire a human soul and die within the compass of Christian salvation. Six days a week, she maintains the form of an ordinary human woman, the form into which she was presumably born and in which she may reproduce in the customary manner. Hers is not a sudden reversion to non-human form brought upon by the shock of discovery, like the legend told of Roger de Château Rousset or the fabled ancestor of the Plantagenets,[9] but a ritual seclusion and a weekly rest from her labors, in the manner recommended by the Hebrew Yahweh.

---

9   Caroline Prud'Homme discusses the marital adventures of Roger de Château Rousset and its analogues in other medieval collections in her chapter "Mermaid, Mother, Monster, and More," in this volume. Gerald of Wales records the myth that an early count of Anjou took a fairy wife of this type, who because of her demonic affiliations could not endure the elevation of the Eucharist (see, for one instance, Elizabeth Hallam, ed., *The Plantagenet Chronicles* [New York: Crescent Books, 1995], 22). Later this serpent-wife made her way down the Angevin line to replace Eleanor of Aquitaine; in the metrical romance *Richard Coer de Lyon*, Henry II's fairy wife Cassodorien experiences a similar transformation, and this ancestry explains Richard's larger-than-life abilities. See Peter Larkin, ed., *Richard Coer de Lyon*, TEAMS Middle English Texts (Kalamazoo, MI: Medieval Institute Publications, 2015).

The motif of the woman imbued with a serpentous aspect as the result of a supernatural curse surfaces elsewhere in medieval European literature: a serpent with a woman's mouth, lips, and teeth menaces the unnamed hero in the French poem *Le Bel Inconnu* [*The Fair Unknown*],[10] and the Italian poem *Pulzella Gaia* [*Merry Maiden*], which pre-dates Jean's romance, features a maiden released from her serpent form by the brave knight Gawain, only to be betrayed by and subsequently forced to depart from him and return to her mother, Morgan.[11] But, uniquely in Melusine's case, both stages of her transformation—or translation—from half fairy to half serpent to a dragon fifteen feet long are connected to moments of betrayal by men who were supposed to protect her. Her father's violation of his promise not to see his wife Presine in childbed—trespassed in his excitement and perhaps apprehension at learning she has presented him with triplet girls—leads to her upbringing on Avalon in the company of an unhappy mother, on whose behalf Melusine plots revenge against her forgetful father and which results in her curse. Making the resolution of Melusine's curse dependent on the fidelity of her own husband, Raymond, Presine in effect condemns her daughter to worse torment than she herself was forced to undergo, for the fleeing Melusine must not only relinquish her husband, her castle, and her rights and powers as a respected medieval noblewoman, but she is also forced to leave behind her youngest two children, who have not yet been weaned. In Jean d'Arras' original account and most of the subsequent adaptations, Melusine's suffering, as a result of these multiple betrayals, provides the narrative with a strong affective thread. A folkloric tradition found across Europe that attributes the haunting sound of a female cry produced by gusts of wind to the *cri de Mélusine*—documented in French and Czech territories if not others—testifies to this.

Despite being anchored in an agenda of political legitimization and image-enhancement by which Jean d'Arras furnished his patron, the Duc de Berry, with claims to Poitou—and, more specifically, Lusignan—through a mythologized (though not wholly invented) descent from the rulers of Luxembourg, Armenia, Cyprus, and Bohemia,[12] Melusine eventually slipped free of these genealogical

10   Renaud de Beaujeu, *Le bel inconnu*, ed. Michèle Perret, trans. Michèle Perret and Isabelle Weill (Paris: Champion, 2003.). See Ana Pairet's chapter, "Polycorporality and Heteromorphia," for a discussion of this scene.

11   Zoë Enstone discusses this poem in her chapter, "Melusine and Purgatorial Punishment: The Changing Nature of Fays," in this volume.

12   See Donald Maddox and Sara Sturm-Maddox's introduction to their translation *Melusine: Or, the Noble History of Lusignan by Jean d'Arras* (University Park Pennsylvania State University Press, 2012), 3–16.

and dynastic ties and found her way into the hearts and minds of a broad audience. Following Jean d'Arras' prose narrative, the verse rendition of the *Roman de Lusignan* by Coudrette expanded Melusine's patronage to the lords of Parthenay,[13] a move which paved the way for many future adaptations. The French story in both forms enjoyed huge popularity. More than ten manuscript copies were made of Jean's romance alone, and in the century following the *editio princeps* printed at Geneva in 1478, over twenty editions of the French romance found their way into print, most accompanied by extensive illustrations.

Thüring von Ringoltingen translated Coudrette into the German prose novel *Melusine* in 1456, and the German chapbook *Die schöne Melusine* (ca.1484), based on Thüring's version, enjoyed a huge reception in German-speaking regions, spreading the story through northern and eastern Europe and as far afield as Russia.[14] *Historia de la linda Melosina*, a Castilian version based on Jean d'Arras' romance, appeared in 1489, with another edition printed in Seville in 1526. Translations into Middle English of the prose and verse French stories appeared shortly after 1500, with traces of a print run in England dated to 1510. Gheraert Leeu printed his Middle Dutch *Meluzine* in 1491, with later editions appearing in 1510 and 1602.

The figure of the serpent woman, sometimes winged or sometimes bathing, proliferated in visual art in company with Melusine's travels across Europe. The Swiss polymath Paracelsus incorporated *melusines* into his meticulous classification of elemental spirits, water-affiliated creatures who quested for a soul through human marriage, and the twin-tailed siren or mermaid gained currency as a potent alchemical symbol as well as a motif appearing in visual art, painting, and architectural features.[15] Various noble families, including the counts of St. Pol, the Dukes of Burgundy, and Plantagenet kings all incorporated Melusine into their own bloodline, not to be outdone by the lords of Lusignan.[16]

---

13   Maddox, *Melusine*, 14.

14   Thüring's *Melusine* is referred to as a *Prosaroman* [prose novel] or *Feenroman* [fairy novel] in the Germanic tradition, among other generic terms for long narratives of the medieval and early modern periods. In the English and French traditions, "romance" is the conventional generic term.

15   See Melissa Ridley Elmes's chapter, "The Alchemical Transformation of Melusine," for discussion of this phenomenon.

16   Philippa Gregory, David Baldwin, and Michael Jones discuss the various royal houses that claimed Melusine in *The Women of the Cousin's War: The Duchess, the Queen, and the King's Mother* (New York: Touchstone, 2011); so do Maddox and Sturm-Maddox in the introduction to their translation, as does Pit Péporté in his chapter, "Melusine and Luxembourg: A Double Memory," in this volume.

Depictions of Melusine in woodcuts and paintings tend to emphasize her human qualities by putting her in relationship with other characters, but architectural features and sculpture more freuqently portray an independent Melusine with her monstrous features—fish-like tail and, often, dragon's wings—undeniably on display. She came to embody a visual metaphor for any number of complexities: the supposed duality of women's nature; a meta-critique of the values of chivalry, aristocracy, or medieval romance; and a warning of the ever-permeable boundaries between the perceived world and the world unseen.

Melusine's popularity is not limited to the medieval and early modern world. Editions of her story continued to circulate through the seventeenth and eighteenth centuries, particularly in Germany and France, where the romance matter filled two books: one devoted to the history of Melusine and a second to the exploits of her most infamous son, Geoffrey Great-Tooth. The Romantics of German and then English literature found the figure of the serpent woman evocative of a larger interest in the supernatural realm, and several variations of the otherworldly woman taking and then being betrayed by a human bridegroom appeared, among them the tale of "Herr Peter Dimringer von Staufenberg" (1818) by the brothers Grimm, the German literary fairy tale *Undine* by Friedrich de la Motte Fouqué (1811), "Die neue Melusine" [The New Melusine] appearing in Johann Wolfgang von Goethe's *Wilhelm Meisters Wanderjahre* [*Wilhelm Meister's Journeyman Years*] (1807), and the poem "Lamia" by John Keats (1820). Melusine migrated to other artistic genres, taking a title role in German dramatist Jakob Ayrer's *Von der schönen Melusina* (1598), Felix Mendelssohn's overture "The Fair Melusina" (1834), and Julius Hübner's oil painting "Die schöne Melusine" (1844), among other incarnations.

To document the resurgence of Melusine and her avatars in recent years would be to generate an extensive and hugely varied list. Melusine lends her name to publications ranging from a journal on surrealism to Belgian graphic novels chronicling the adventures of an adolescent witch. English readers have re-encountered the fairy woman through A. S. Byatt's bestselling novel *Possession* (1990) and the Cousin's War novels of Philippa Gregory (2009—15). French audiences too busy to read the entire romance can hear the adventures encapsulated in the lyrics to "Mélusine" by popular singer-songwriter Nolwenn Leroy. The Mélusine and the People of Lusignan Association in southwestern France preserves memories of Melusine's influence through tours, exhibits, and literature, including a walking trail that follows the heroine's footsteps. In Luxembourg, where she is celebrated as the founder of the duchy through her marriage to Siegfried, the Luxembourg City Tourist office uses Melusine in their branding, and she features in a commemorative postage stamp as well as the name of a popular nightclub. Drinkers of Starbucks™ coffee interested in the logo of the flowing-haired woman sporting a crown and a large double fishtail can consult the company's website to find they borrowed the siren from a sixteenth-century woodcut, another enduring reinvention of Melusine.

Scholarship on Melusine has likewise gained purchase as modern readers discover the lasting appeal of this medieval story. For reasons explored below, French and German scholarship has outpaced studies in Spanish, English, and Dutch, which are nevertheless beginning to accumulate. At the turn of this century, the Bibliothèque Mélusine series published a collection of scholarship that surveyed Melusine's evolution in Francophone traditions,[17] and Claudia Steinkämper compiled a history of German evolutions of this figure.[18] As Melusine has cropped up increasingly in English scholarship of recent years, including in Corinne Saunders' *Magic and the Supernatural in Medieval English Romance* (2010), Angela Florscheutz's *Marking Maternity in Middle English Romance* (2014), and Kristina Pérez's *The Myth of Morgan La Fey* (2014), these evolving appearances suggest a need for work in English that collects and analyzes this figure's multiple appearances and multivalent meanings as a companion to and extension of the French and German overviews.

Following the achievements of Donald Maddox and Sara Sturm-Maddox in establishing Melusine as a subject worthy of study in their volume of collected essays, *Melusine of Lusignan: Founding Fiction in Late Medieval France* (1996)—a volume to which the scholars collected here owe a clear debt, along with their accessible and engaging English translation of the French romance by Jean d'Arras (2012), another work consulted frequently by the authors here represented—this volume attempts to capture, and follow through in its many forms and incarnations, the enduring spell that Melusine casts on audiences. While unable to be comprehensive, this volume aims to be broadly representative in scope, tracing Melusine's changing role in the French, Germanic, Dutch, Spanish, and English literary traditions, with reference to her sisters in the Far East. The essays below study Melusine's iconography in woodcuts, illustrations, and as an alchemical symbol, investigate the many modes and meanings invested in medieval and post-medieval iterations of her narrative, and trace the transmission and reception of this multivalent, multi-faceted hybrid figure from the medieval period through the present day. Contributors hail from the United States, Canada, Europe, and China, working in the disciplines of art

---

17   Arlette Bouloumié, ed., *Mélusine: moderne et contemporaine* (Lausanne: L'Age d'homme, 2001).

18   Claudia Steinkämper, *Melusine – vom Schlangenweib Zur "Beauté mit dem Fischschwanz": Geschichte einer literarischen Aneignung* (Göttingen: Vandenhoeck & Ruprecht, 2007).

history, literature and languages, manuscript studies, comparative literature, and film, ensuring a diverse theoretical and methodological approach to the subject.

Taken together, the chapters in this volume discover a wide and fascinating range of implications embedded in the manifold forms this serpent/fairy/dragon/woman manifests. Melusine functions as a bridge between the natural and supernatural realms; a remarkably accomplished courtly lady with a hidden dimension that reflects concerns about the Christian soul; exemplar of the problematic nature of a female body; or simply an endlessly mutating metaphor for whatever anxieties and preoccupations the reader brings to the text. The following chapters employ a range of theoretical frameworks for better understanding Melusine's multiple roles, making use of critical lenses including gender, monstrosity, queerness, material culture, race, and various hybrids thereof. Others employ unexpectedly rich and original approaches, such as reading the poetic encounter with Melusine as an epistemological avenue for transformational knowing; thinking about her transformation as a process, rather than a moment; challenging the normative terms of happiness; and reading Melusine in modern visualizations of the abject. Given her proliferation across contemporary media, particularly in the graphic arts, and her growing status as both tourist attraction and nationalistic icon—not to mention her ubiquitous global presence as the face of the Starbucks corporation—a volume of scholarship that devotes thorough and sustained critical attention to the meanings of Melusine and her marvelous afterlives seems both timely and necessary. This book endeavors not only to trace the various footprints that Melusine has left since she first surfaced in the medieval imagination, but also to illuminate her divergent semantic possibilities and cultural relevance for medieval audiences as well as those of the present day.

The organization of this volume is designed to illuminate, characterize, and connect these many incarnations of Melusine in a way that captures the legend's developments and appropriations across time and place. The first section, Bodies and Texts, establishes the wide circulation of the Melusine legend and maps her appearances in medieval visual and textual traditions across Europe, suggesting the points at which the figure both adapts and articulates cultural fears, values, apprehensions, and beliefs.

Frederika Bain's opening essay examines Melusine's relationship with the fish-tailed sirens of legend to provide a detailed textual and iconographic tradition for reading Melusine's slippery body, exploring what she inherits from Western traditions reaching from Homer's sirens and the *Liber monstrorum* to medieval marginalia and the female centaurs evoked by King Lear. Her survey grounds the investigations to follow and also hints at a trend to tame, or

attempt to contain, the problematic form of the piscine woman. Ana Pairet
follows with a reconsideration of how Melusine has been embodied and received in the critical tradition. She questions the crucial definitions of hybridity and monstrosity that have typically been applied, and in so doing opens
a new line of inquiry into this multi-faceted figure and offers a more expansive vocabulary of terms that prove truer to the complex medieval vision of
her. At the same time, Pairet's investigation reflects on key moments in the
story—particularly Melusine's animalistic transformations—that most influence later translations in art and print.

Caroline Prud'Homme then focuses on late medieval manuscript and print
translations of the French prose and verse romances to investigate how these
authors and their audiences perceived Melusine. Her study reveals each work
as an intricate literary masterpiece in its own right, but she also compares crucial scenes across the textual tradition to explore how Jean d'Arras seems to
intentionally complicate his heroine with her fairy parallels, how the Spanish
renditions attempt to fit her into a native tradition of courtly romance, how the
English authors nervously downplay Melusine's serpentine and potentially demonic aspects, and how the Swiss author Thüring, in defiance of all, seems to
emphasize, indeed celebrate her Otherness. Albrecht Classen goes on to examine the significant editions of Thüring's tale and compare the textual Melusine
to the program of pictorial illustration. Classen's descriptive overview of the
popular and widely reproduced woodcuts of the earliest German printings,
alongside Feyerbrand's *Buch der Liebe* (1587), observes how the increasingly
wealthy, urban patrons of the romance adapted Melusine and her concerns to
their own circumstances, and gestures toward the breadth of cultural information contained in these depictions. In conclusion, Classen makes the hitherto
unobserved connection that the popular Lüsterweibchen, or female-figured
chandeliers, sustain Melusine as a household furnishing, keeping her ever in
view.

Concluding this section on bodies and texts, Melissa Ridley Elmes turns
to a different tradition that embraced the figure of Melusine, exploring how
Paracelsus employs her not just as an element of his mystical world but as a
potent alchemical symbol. His Melusine becomes a crucial feature in the alchemical wedding that yielded the apex of all such experiments, immortal life
in the form of the philosopher's stone. His use of Melusine in this process resonates with her literary origins as a transformed entity but also, as Ridley Elmes
shows, incorporates her into a complex "chemical theology" that recasts her
as a firmly Christian metaphor for union with the divine, while imbuing her
with a mysterious allure that would go on to inspire Romantic poets such as
Goethe and Keats. Together, these essays in section one present a vibrant map

of Melusine's reach and establish the influence she would exert on the late medieval European imagination and centuries beyond.

The second section turns from Melusine as an icon to the ways in which she is recruited more specifically as an emblem of national identity. Anna Casas Aguilar reads the empire-building Melosina of the Castilian *Historia de la linda Melosina* as endorsing the architectural and political ambitions of her historical counterpart, Isabel I of Castile, noting the parallels in construction projects and Christian achievement that were endorsed by the Catholic Monarchs. At the same time, Casas Aguilar picks up on the subtle reflections in the text on the exercise and reach of female influence, suggesting that Melusine's latent non-humanity expresses a contemporary anxiety about a female body in a typically male position of power. Turning northwards, Lydia Zeldenrust discovers an ease with the notions of hybridity in the earliest Dutch text, one unusual among translations in that it embeds episodes from Coudrette's poem seamlessly into Jean d'Arras' prose. Zeldenrust suggests this fluency might reflect a culture characteristic of the Low Countries, where Melusine in her half-serpent form, like her French sibling, can function as marker and monument.

Pit Péporté next explores Melusine's special relationship with the Grand Duchy of Luxembourg, beginning with the way Jean d'Arras pays tribute to his patron the Duc de Berry's Luxembourgian ties in his genealogical romance. Melusine's valorous elder sons all conquer lands and found noble houses from which Jean de Berry could claim descent, thus legitimizing his position as the rightful owner of Lusignan, Melusine's favorite castle. In recent centuries, Melusine has been more directly adopted as the founding foremother of the capital city, and Péporté explores how the frequent and hearty recuperation of this serpentine woman marks the Luxembourgian sense of identity. In contrast, Jennifer Alberghini deals with a different incarnation across the Channel, the Middle English *Romans of Partenay*, to examine how the opening treatise on translation inserted by the anonymous redactor reflects a project of reclaiming Melusine as a representative of English identity. She locates this text and its effort to render Melusine in the "mother tongue" within larger efforts to endorse English nationality, on a level with Caxton's use of Malory's Arthurian material, though English audiences did not adopt Melusine as a national heroine the way that Luxembourgians did.

Following these contributions outlining Melusine's varied political meanings, the essays in section three offer theoretically grounded readings of the textual traditions of Melusine that explore her many refigurations as a cultural metaphor. Stacey L. Hahn makes a case for reading Jean d'Arras' narrative as instructional literature for chivalric youth. She observes the many ways that adolescent rebellions provide pivotal moments in the plot, including the parental conflicts that propel Melusine and Raymond toward one another, and the ways in which the maturation of Melusine's sons furnishes the bulk of the middle portion of the prose romance. From issues of sibling rivalry to raising the next generation, she notes the prevalence of family dynamics as a theme that tightly knits the narrative action and provides a template for chivalrous conduct for its audience. In comparison, Simone Pfleger considers the conflicts in Thüring's version of Melusine in light of recent theoretical work on happiness, noting that Melusine rather fulfills a promise of unhappiness due to her inability to conform to the heteronormative requirements of the courtly world.

Angela Jane Weisl continues this interrogation of the essential courtly structures of the romance, reading Melusine's hybrid and changeable body as reflecting the inherent conflicts between the conventions of *fin'amors*, which ascribe erotic power to the desired damsel, and the anxieties about female influence and agency embedded in the chivalric romance. Chera A. Cole takes up these anxieties as they are exhibited in the Middle English prose version of Melusine, reading the work through modern race and monster theory to investigate how Melusine's ability to "pass" as a human depends on, but ultimately thwarts, her desire to integrate into the human world and its promise of Christian salvation. Zoë Enstone extends this theme to chart a larger movement across the medieval romance in both its French and English iterations of granting fairy agents a greater role in doling out Christian punishments. She specifically examines the parallels between depictions of purgatory and the torments inflicted by fairy women to suggest that their participation in Christian punishment was a way to more firmly integrate these figures into a Catholic framework, and perhaps neutralize their more troubling associations.[19]

Concluding this third section, Zifeng Zhao brings together several of the strands established in previous essays, including the role of maternal advisement and Melusine's function as a blended Mary-and-Eve figure, in his analysis of Thüring's use of the theme of metamorphosis. He stretches Melusine's influence outside of Europe to note the many parallels her story shares with Lady White Snake, or Madam White, a legendary Chinese serpent woman who is likewise deprived of her husband and her humanity, suffering not exile but

---

19   Richard Firth Green examines this process of integration in *Elf Queens and Holy Friars: Fairy Beliefs and the Medieval Church* (Philadelphia: University of Pennsylvania Press, 2016).

imprisonment. His comparative analysis extends Melusine's influence into new realms and broadens the cultural paradigms from which her story draws. Altogether, the essays in section three demonstrate how the story of Melusine continues to yield new insights into the social values and tensions visible to medieval and early modern audiences.

The concluding section samples Melusine's many afterlives, discovering recognizable rearticulations of her medieval incarnations along with subtler resonances of the serpent/fairy/dragon/woman in the post-medieval world. Renata Schellenberg analyzes the Melusine reconfigured by Goethe, who reinvented the medieval legend as a princess of the dwarven world whose fate depends on an indifferent barber who narrates a sort of fractured fairy tale about his failure to live up to heroic ideals. Deva F. Kemmis casts a light back on the long and vibrant Germanic tradition of depicting water women as sources of revelation and instruction by positioning Ingeborg Bachmann's short story "Undine Geht" [Undine Goes] (1961) within an epistemological framework that rests on postures of attentive listening reminiscent of moments in Thüring's *Melusine*. Her chapter returns to the mythological water woman the voice long deprived her. Rounding out the perspective of recent Germanic influences, Anna-Lisa Baumeister considers how three very different late twentieth-century artworks refigure and respond to the crucial moments of the Melusine myth while updating the differently bodied, specularly captured woman into a figure of the abject.

Misty Urban's chapter concludes the section and the volume by offering a survey of English Melusines up to the present moment, arguing that the reappearances of powerful and not always inimical half-serpent women in modern novels, art, and film engage contemporary audiences with the medieval Melusine's flexibility and multivalence as metaphor and message. As a whole, this volume traces a sweeping legacy of fascination, provocation, and challenge that generates new insights into Melusine's meanings to medieval audiences and signals her continued relevance to the present. This collection aims to cement the foothold the medieval Melusine has gained as a subject for critical scholarship in English, initiate diverse strands of inquiry that can propel this scholarship in new directions, and introduce the previously unknowing reader to one of medieval Europe's most powerful and popular myths.

A note on usage: throughout the volume, English forms of proper names are generally relied upon (Melusine, Raymond, etc.). Non-English spellings will typically indicate the title of a work or the proper name of a literary character, and all quotations remain faithful to their source. Unless otherwise noted, all translations into English are rendered by the author of the chapter in which the passage appears.

PART I

Bodies and Texts:
Mapping Melusine in Art and Print

∵

CHAPTER 1

The Tail of Melusine: Hybridity, Mutability, and the Accessible Other

Frederika Bain

> Let each judge for himself the following material, because throughout I shall paint a little picture of a sea-girl or siren, which if it has the head of reason is followed by all kinds of shaggy and scaly tales.[1]

The *Liber monstrorum*, an eighth-century compendium of fantastic beasts, is generally accepted as the first instance[2] in which sirens are described as having "the body of a maiden, but [...] scaly fishes' tails, with which they always lurk in the sea."[3] However, this relatively straightforward description is coupled, as the epigraph shows, with ambiguous descriptors that associate the siren with both "shaggy and scaly" [*hispidae squamosaque*][4] characteristics, as though she were potentially mammalian or reptilian as well as or instead of piscine. In this passage the narrator figures the siren's biformity as a metaphor for his own work, which he promises will combine reason—that which is clearly visible and comprehensible, like the human half above the water—with the strange and phantasmal—that which mysteriously hides in the deep, like the fish's tail. This metaphoric use of female hybridity, as well as the characterization of that hybrid as half fish—and yet not quite—mark an early point in the medieval European tradition of half-piscine biform women to which the romance *Mélusine* is heir and to which it contributes.

A wide variety of male and female monsters appears in the Middle Ages, yet the specific category of the monstrous as predicated upon hybridity is primarily the realm of the female; there are many more animal–woman than

---

1 Andy Orchard, ed. and trans., *Liber monstrorum*, in *Pride and Prodigies: Studies in the Monsters of the* Beowulf-*Manuscript* (Toronto: University of Toronto Press, 1995), 254–317, at 257.

2 The *Liber* was first so identified by Edmond Faral, "La Queue de Poisson des Sirènes," *Romania* 74 (1953): 433–506, at 441. There are far earlier visual depictions of the siren as fish-tailed, but if coupled with textual descriptions these are of the older half-avian form.

3 Orchard, *Liber*, 263.

4 Orchard, *Liber*, 256.

animal–man biforms. At the same time, hybridity is frequently used in the medieval misogynist tradition to figure human women's negative traits: duplicity, mutability, and the unequal yoking of rationality or control to the lack thereof. A compelling evocation of this trope appears in Shakespeare's *King Lear* (ca.1605), in which the old king rages of his daughters, and by extension all women: "Down from the waist they are centaurs, / Though women all above. / But to the girdle do the gods inherit; / Beneath is all the fiend's" (4.6.120–3).[5] While centaurs are one of the few animal–human hybrids generally imagined as male, here the association of femininity and biformity is strong enough to drive the shift towards women. In this speech, the lower bodily stratum of women, be they fully human or part animal, is figured as bestial and infernal, at the same time that the upper portion may be reasonable and amenable to virtue. This metaphorizing movement points to a common conception of woman as Other—yet not wholly other.

Like the siren in the *Liber monstrorum* earlier in the Middle Ages and Lear's centaur-associated daughters in the early modern period, Melusine, the snake / fish / dragon / fairy-woman introduced in Jean d'Arras' romance of the same name and elaborated in multiple traditions thereafter, is an exemplar of what may be termed the accessible Other. She herself is comprised of known and unknown parts, and the components of her hybrid nature are similarly unstable and mutable. Like other female biforms such as the siren, the mermaid, and the sea monster Scylla, as well as the grotesque (though not hybrid) Sheela-na-gig, her representation displays a tendency towards the piscine.[6] All these figures in their earliest incarnations are shown or described as having other than a fish's form but over time tend towards fishtails, a movement that appears early in the history of Melusine's visual representation but lags behind in her textual depiction. Illustrations and descriptions of Melusine's changing forms, and those of earlier and later "melusinian" variants,[7]

---

5   William Shakespeare, *The Tragedy of King Lear*, 2nd ed., ed. Jay L. Halio (Cambridge: Cambridge University Press, 2005).

6   Françoise Clier-Colombani also examines such possible iconographic antecedents as mermaids, sirens, lamiae, Scylla, Echidna, winged dragons, and other creatures in *La fée Mélusine au Moyen Âge: Images, mythes et symboles* (Paris: Le Léopard d'Or, 1991).

7   In *Les fées au Moyen Âge: Mélusine et Morgane* (Geneva: Editions Slatkine, 1984), Laurence Harf-Lancner identifies "melusinienne" tales as those that combine the elements of a union between a human and a supernatural being / fairy contingent upon a taboo or condition, which is subsequently contravened, leading to the downfall of the mortal partner (83–4). Another excellent discussion of Melusine's literary antecedents can be found in Jacques Le Goff and Emmanuel Le Roy Ladurie, "Mélusine maternelle et défricheuse," *Annales: Économies, Sociétés, Civilisations* (1971): 587–622.

are shaped by iconographic tradition and symbolism surrounding the question of just how "other" women are. The representations, and their symbolic import, display a trend towards integration of their disparate parts into a form closer to human, or at least towards the possibility of increased sexual and social access to these hybrid creatures by males, primary creators of the depictions. These ends are furthered by, among other things, the use of the fishtailed form.

There are marked variations in Melusine's representation, between accounts and between text and image in the same account. In the first romances by Jean d'Arras (ca.1393) and Coudrette (ca.1401),[8] Melusine is cursed to assume a woman's shape above the waist coupled with a huge serpent's tail below, but Giovanna Giudicini points out that a very early Coudrette manuscript already shows Melusine not only flying in the shape of a winged dragon and in the bath with a snake's tail, but also nursing an infant "as a siren in an upright position." Giudicini notes:

> In the various texts she is often said to be transforming into a serpent from the waist down or flying away, but is also referred to as a marine creature, a marine fairy and a marine portent. This kind of confusion is not unique to the tale of Melusine. In Celtic and Northern European folklore there is often confusion between aerial and aqueous nature of these half-fairies.[9]

Such confusion can be seen in Thüring von Ringoltingen's translation of the romance (1456); in that tale, Melusine is called "Schlang" [serpent], but the

---

8   Jean d'Arras, *A Bilingual Edition of Jean d'Arras's* Mélusine *or* L'histoire de Lusignan, ed. and trans. Matthew W. Morris (Lewiston, NY: Edwin Mellen Press, 2007); Coudrette, *A Critical Edition of Coudrette's* Mélusine *or* Le Roman de Parthenay, ed. and trans. Matthew W. Morris (Lewiston, NY: Edwin Mellen Press, 2003).

9   Giovanna Giudicini, "The Political and Cultural Influence of James V's Court on the Decoration of the King's Fountain in Linlithgow Palace," in *Art and Identity: Visual Culture, Politics and Religion in the Middle Ages*, ed. Sandra Cardarelli, Emily Jane Anderson, and John Richards (Newcastle-upon-Tyne: Cambridge Scholars Publishing, 2011), 167–92, at 171–2. By "siren," it is well to note, she means "mermaid." This image in the BNF MS Fr 12575 fol. 89 has been identified by François Eygun as the oldest representation of Melusine "en sirène"; see "Ce qu'on peut savoir de Mélusine et de son iconographie," *Bulletin de la Société des Antiquaires de l'Ouest et des Musées de Poitiers* (3rd trimestre de 1949): 56–95, at 56. It shows her as a land-bound fish-woman, surrounded by pillars in a hall, her tail resting uneasily upright on a checkered floor.

commentary references her as a "Merfaÿm" [mermaid].[10] Another variation identified by Lydia Zeldenrust is in the transformation Melusine undergoes when she is reproached by Raymondin and flies away from Lusignan.[11] While she is described in the manuscript and incunable editions of Jean and Coudrette, and the Dutch and Spanish versions that follow them, as transforming into a winged serpent or dragon[12] upon flying out of the house, in German versions she is said to be a winged serpent only from the navel down,[13] minimizing the ophidian form if not yet moving towards the piscine. Both descriptions, however, are frequently coupled with illustrations of her as a half-dragon woman. In the sixteenth century, the Swiss alchemist and physician Paracelsus describes a category of elemental beings called melusines who are wholly human in shape, though lacking the human spiritual principle.[14] The next significant changes to Melusine's iconography appear in the nineteenth century, when elements of her story are incorporated into that of Undine, a human-shaped sea-sprite who becomes a spring of water, and Goethe's *Die neue Melusine* (1807), whose title character is human but tiny in size.[15] The German literary tradition of the nineteenth century generally figures Melusine and Undine characters as human in appearance, while the related Little Mermaid of Denmark is fish-tailed yet enabled by a spell to take on human form.

The number of Melusine's tails, when she is tailed, also varies. In the cover-sheet illustration of Estienne de Chypre de Lusignan's *Les Genealogies de Soixante et sept tresnobles et tresillustres maisons, partie de France, parti estrágeres,*

---

10   Schneider, Karin, ed., *Thüring von Ringoltingen: Melusine* (Berlin: Erich Schmidt Verlag, 1958).

11   Lydia Zeldenrust, "Serpent or Half-Serpent? Bernhard Richel's *Melusine* and the Making of a Western European Icon," *Neophilologus* 100:1 (January 2016): 19–41. See also Zeldenrust's contribution to this volume.

12   Clier-Colombani notes the extensive similitude of medieval serpents and dragons: "au Moyen Âge, les figures du serpent et du dragon sont étroitement liées. En effet, chaque fois que dans un texte médiéval, nous avons rencontré la mention d'un serpent, l'illustration correspondante a montré un dragon ailé jetant du feu" [in the Middle Ages, the figures of the serpent and the dragon are closely linked. In effect, each time in a medieval text we encountered the mention of a serpent, the corresponding illustration showed a winged dragon spouting fire], *Les fées*, 184.

13   Zeldenrust, "Serpent or Half-Serpent?," 22.

14   See Melissa Ridley Elmes's contribution to this volume for a discussion of Paracelsus' use of Melusine.

15   See Renata Schellenberg's contribution to this volume for a discussion of how Goethe reinvents his Melusine.

etc. (1586), Melusine is pictured with two snake tails.[16] A similar variant, with two fishtails, can be seen in late medieval and early modern alchemical texts such as *The Azoth* (1624), attributed to Basilius Valentinius,[17] in which a figure identified as Melusine appears with breasts spurting blood and milk, as well as in some of the German editions of the romance such as Johannes Bamler's 1480 *Buch von einer Frawen genant Melusina*.[18] By the seventeenth century, "melusine" or "melusina" appears as a generic term, primarily in Germanic heraldry, denoting a female figure with two fishtails.[19]

Before discussing in greater depth the animal portions of the hybrid Melusine, it is instructive to look at her human aspect. Whatever form her lower body later takes, and regardless of the iconographic traditions from which it derives and the significations of which it partakes, Melusine appears first in the narratives as a stunningly beautiful and fully human woman. This feature is critical to her representation in the romance and in all melusinian precursors to and later adaptations of it, although it has drawn far less scholarly comment than her mutable biformity. Melusine's alluring female form does the narratological work of captivating her potential husband and dispelling his initial disquiet at her otherworldly nature to the extent that he accedes to the stipulations placed on their joining, thus setting in motion the events of the marriage plot.

Symbolically, her beauty has the effect of revealing her essential nature, whether good or evil. In the two most commonly cited early melusinian variants, Walter Map's story of Henno cum Dentibus in *De nugis curialium* (ca.1200) and Gervase of Tilbury's account of Count Raymond in the *Otia imperialia* (ca.1211), the supernatural or fairy woman is aligned with the demonic, unable to attend Mass or receive the Host.[20] It is her beautiful human

---

16 Reproduced in Pit Péporté, *Constructing the Middle Ages: Historiography, Collective Memory and Nation-Building in Luxembourg* (Leiden: Brill, 2011), 88. See also Péporté's contribution to this volume.

17 Basilius Valentinus, *Les douze clefs de philosophie de frere Basile Valentin ... plus l'Azoth, ou, Le moyen de faire l'or caché des philosophes: traduction francoise*, eds. Jean Gobille and Clovis Hesteau Nuisemen (Paris: Chez Pierre Moët, 1660), 151.

18 Reproduced in Jean Cirlot, *Dictionary of Symbols,* 2nd ed., trans. Jack Sage (Mineola: Dover Publications, Inc., 2002), 297.

19 Arthur Charles Fox-Davies, *The Art of Heraldry: An Encyclopedia of Armory* (London: T. C. and E. C. Jack, 1904), 162, 303.

20 Walter Map, *De nugis curialium: Courtiers' Trifles*, ed. and trans. M. R. James, rev. C. N. L Brooke and R. A. B. Mynors (Oxford: Clarendon Press, 1983), 347; Gervase of Tilbury, *Otia imperialia: Recreation for an Emperor*, ed. and trans. S. E. Banks and J. W. Binns (Oxford: Clarendon Press, 2002).

form, as much as her later-discovered hybrid nature, that illustrates her moral depravity, serving as a sign of her hypocrisy and duplicity. Henno, upon seeing the "most lovely girl [...] the fairest of things," both desires her and fears a trap, though he sees none; when her nature is revealed, the fairy wife is termed a "brilliant pestilence."[21] While Melusine's beauty retains the same narratological function—captivation and the assuaging of uneasiness—in later variations in which she is a positive character, it takes on an alternate symbolic function. In Jean d'Arras, Coudrette, Ringoltingen, and others, her appearance accords with the medieval commonplace that physical loveliness, particularly in women, is an outward and visible sign of inward, invisible grace and truthfully signals her essentially devout and beneficent nature. Thus her fully human female beauty is as unstable and multivalent as her various hybrid forms.

The influence of iconographic tradition on illustrations and descriptions of Melusine also appears in other instances unrelated to her caudal appendage. For example, Françoise Clier-Colombani notes that the episode of Melusine's return to care for her children after flying away is illustrated in all of the Coudrette manuscripts by her nursing her youngest sons, rather than by any of the other instances of care described in the text: she "chauffoit, alaistoit, recouchoit" [warmed, nursed, put (them) to bed]. Clier-Colombani argues that this preference on the part of the illustrators is "vraisemblablement dicté par le poids du mythe de la nourriture surnaturelle des héros" [surely dictated by the weight of the myth of the supernatural nourishment of heroes],[22] such as the suckling of Romulus and Remus by a wolf. However, the "weight" of traditions regarding nursing is iconographic as much as narrative. At one end of the spectrum exists the large and varied visual tradition of the *Madonna lactans*, images of the Virgin Mary's nursing Jesus, rather than caring for him in other ways, an emphasis not attested in textual sources.[23] At the other end is the variety of images of breastfeeding mermaids and sirens that appear in manuscript illustration and church decoration,[24] such as in the margins of the Alphonse

---

21   Map, *De nugis*, 347.

22   Clier-Colombani, *Les fées*, 70.

23   Margaret Miles notes that the *Madonna lactans* trope is related to that of the Virgin of Humility, itself used to heighten the sense of the Madonna's accessibility to common people, because highborn women did not usually breastfeed their own children; see *A Complex Delight: The Secularization of the Breast, 1350–1750* (Berkeley: University of California Press, 2008), 202–4.

24   Such images may easily explain the BNF image of Melusine as a mermaid nursing her child.

Psalter[25] or in carvings on the Strasbourg Cathedral or at the Iglesia de San Vicente de Serrapio in Spain. Together, they create a body of influence surrounding the visual depiction of nursing that could easily have been persuasive to illustrators seeking to picture instances of maternal care.[26]

The greatest amount of visual influence is seen in the varying representations of Melusine's tail or tails. The preponderance of images of other half-fish creatures, particularly women, constitutes a strong visual tradition moving the depiction of Melusine and other female biforms towards the piscine. An almost bewildering variety of creatures in the medieval European imaginary combines the bottom half of a fish with the top half of a land creature, whether human or animal. Such aquatic hybrids as sea-bishops, sea-pigs, marine calves, sea-dogs, tritons, and many others appear on maps, in carvings, in bestiaries, and elsewhere. A relatively late sampling of this variety may be seen in the chapter "Concerning Marine Monsters" in Ambroise Paré's *Des monstres et prodiges* (1573), which includes a sea-devil, a marine monk, and many others. Paré argues, "It must not be doubted that just as one sees several monstrous animals of diverse shapes on the earth, so also are there many strange sorts of them in the sea."[27] The understanding that every land creature has an aquatic equivalent was, as Chet Van Duzer comments, "a fruitful generator of exotic sea creatures" in illustrations.[28] While it is attested by Pliny and in the bestiary tradition and endorsed by Augustine of Hippo, Isidore of Seville, and Gervase of Tilbury, this theory is far less evidenced in textual sources in contrast with its fecund and varied presence in image.

If among biform creatures the animal half most commonly constituting the lower portion is the fish, then among the half-piscine biforms that combine a human top with the fish bottom, the vast majority are female. The best-documented of these female figures, and the one whose visual image Melusine's most

25   London BL MS Add. 24686 fol. 13.
26   It may also be noted that the act of nursing necessarily emphasizes the breasts, clearly a concern of many of the romance's illustrators in other contexts, as when Melusine is in the bath and flying away, though such emphasis is not present in the text. A desire to highlight her breasts may also account for the change to the half-female, half-dragon form in the German variants. It is also possible that this early iconographic emphasis on nursing influenced the later representation of the alchemical Melusine producing blood and milk from her breasts.
27   Ambroise Paré, *On Monsters and Marvels*, trans. Janis L. Pallister (Chicago: University of Chicago Press, 1982), 107–136, at 107.
28   Chet Van Duzer, *Sea Monsters on Medieval and Renaissance Maps* (London: British Library, 2013), 9.

resembles, is the siren in her fish–woman form. While sirens are not described physically in the *Odyssey*, where they first appear, early visual representations of them show varying combinations of bird and human, while later versions combine fishtails with human heads and torsos.[29] The word's first use in English, according to the *Oxford English Dictionary* (n. 2), is in Chaucer's *Romaunt of the Rose* (1366), where its relation to fish–women is clearly in evidence: "Though we mermaydens clepe hem here [...] Men clepen hem sereyns in Fraunce" [Though we call them mermaids here (...) Men call them sirens in France].[30] The OED entry notes the labile nature of the term, prefacing the definition with the disclaimer, "In early use frequently confused with the mermaid." It is not, however, only in early use that such confusion occurs. Misty Urban comments, "Medieval artists often interchange the serpent–woman or mermaid and her close cousin the bird–woman or siren, sometimes even combining the two as in the relief of the 'transitional mermaid, with fishtail, claws, and feathers' which Sir Arthur Waugh observed on a misericord in Carlisle Castle."[31] As with Melusine, textual and visual depictions of the siren are frequently at odds. As Debra Hassig points out, many bestiaries that *describe* the siren as a bird–woman *show* her as a fish–woman.[32] Eleanor Sachs remarks that the earliest manuscript of the *Physiologus*, circa the second century, shows and describes a siren as half woman, half bird, "but in a ninth-century version [...] the siren is illustrated [though presumably not described] in the form of a mermaid, half woman half fish."[33]

---

29   The siren's changes in shape have been documented by generations of sirenologists, whose ongoing interest has been to discover precisely when she first began to be represented as avian and then when as piscine. Wilfred Mustard's 1908 "Siren-Mermaid" may be the earliest of these genealogies, offering an ample listing of depictions from Euripides to Lyly (Mustard, "Siren-Mermaid," *Modern Language Notes* 23, no. 1 [January 1908]: 21–4.) Edmond Faral's classic "La Queue de Poisson des Sirènes" is invaluable, identifying the importance of the *Liber monstrorum* mentioned above. De Rachewiltz's exhaustive study *De Sirenibus* devotes most of a chapter to the exploration of the fish-tailed siren's development, while Leofranc Holford-Strevens updates the scholarship in "Sirens in Antiquity and the Middle Ages" in *The Music of the Sirens*, ed. Linda Phyllis Austern and Inna Naroditskaya (Bloomington: Indiana University Press, 2006), 16–51.

30   Geoffrey Chaucer, *The Romaunt of the Rose*, in *The Riverside Chaucer*, ed. Larry G. Benson (Boston: Houghton Mifflin, 1987), ll. 682–4.

31   Misty Urban, *Monstrous Women in Middle English Romance* (Lewiston, NY: Edwin Mellen Press, 2010), 60.

32   Debra Hassig, *Medieval Bestiaries: Text, Image, Ideology* (Cambridge: Cambridge University Press, 1995), 105.

33   Eleanor Sachs, "Some Notes on a Twelfth-Century Bishop's Mitre in the Metropolitan Museum of Art," *The Bulletin of the Needle and Bobbin Club* 61:1&2 (1978): 3–52, at 6.

In contrast, the description of "Meremaides" in Arthur Golding's 1567 translation of Ovid's *Metamorphoses* as having "Both feete and feathers like to Birdes" while they "beare / The upper partes of Maidens still" (5.686–687) is one of the very few instances in which the siren's older part-bird shape is coupled with the mermaid's name rather than the reverse.[34]

The siren's corporeal ambiguity may extend beyond the more familiar bird and fish shapes into other animal figures: Siegfried de Rachewiltz points out that some pictures of bird–woman sirens are labeled *lamiae* in the late Middle Ages, though a lamia is more frequently understood to be a snake woman. In Caxton's *Mirrour of the Worlde* (1489), the section "Off Bakbytyng" describes "[l]osengiers and evilseiers" [deceitful flatterers and evil-sayers] as "ii mere-meidynes." The first kind, who sings sweetly to sailors and then eats them, "hatthe bodye of a womman / and tayle of a fisshe and cleys liche an egle" [has the body of a woman and tail of a fish and claws like an eagle], associating it with the "transitional" siren. The second "rennyth as an hors, some- / tyme fleith, the which hatthe soo stronge venym that noo / triacle maye avayle, for dethe cometh or that a man felith / the bytynge" [runs as a horse, sometimes flies, which has so strong a venom that no antidote may avail, for death comes before a man feels the biting].[35] However, the bird and fish shapes are by far the most common variants, and though the bird shape recurs intermittently, even as late as William Browne's description in the *Inner Temple Masque* (1614) of sirens as having "upper parts like women, to the navel, and the rest like a hen,"[36] the fish dominates almost exclusively by the early modern period.

The two-tailed mermaid–siren, with which Melusine becomes associated by the sixteenth century and increasingly thereafter, does not arise directly from the bird-bodied form but may instead arise from the iconography of the sea monster Scylla. One of the many aquatic dangers faced by Odysseus along with Charybdis and the sirens, she is another female biform whose verbal and visual depictions vary over the centuries of her representation but move progressively closer to a mermaid shape. Sachs argues of her appearance on funerary monuments, "The relationship between these Etruscan Scyllas and

---

34   Ovid, *Metamorphoses*, trans. Arthur Golding, ed. John Frederick Nims (Philadelphia: Paul Dry Books, 2000), 131.

35   Siegfried de Rachewiltz, *De Sirenibus: An Inquiry into Sirens from Homer to Shakespeare* (New York: Garland Publishing, 1987), 175. Robert R. Raymo, Ruth E. Sternglantz, and Elaine E. Whitaker, eds., *The Mirroure of the Worlde: A Middle English Translation of the Miroir de Monde* (Toronto: University of Toronto Press, 2003), 11. 5918, 5921–22, 5927–30.

36   William Browne, *The Inner Temple Masque*, in *The Works of British Poets, with Prefaces*, vol. 4, ed. Robert Anderson (London: John and Arthur Arch, 1795).

the twelfth-century double-tailed mermaid with her frontal pose with the tails spread out or rising on each side is obvious," a connection also drawn by Terry Pearson and Clier-Colombani.[37] Mercedes Aguirre Castro discusses the disconnect between Scylla's description and visual depiction, explaining that while Scylla is described in the *Odyssey* as entirely monstrous and not at all human, having six dogs' heads on six necks, each with an excessive amount of teeth, she is instead pictured, as early as the fifth century BCE, as "a hybrid creature, half woman half fish, frequently with one or more dog heads protruding from her waist"; the fishtail is occasionally a "sea snake tail."[38] This visual image of Scylla is echoed later in verbal description, in the same way that textual sources identify Melusine and the siren as fish–women later than do the images. Similarly, images of a two-tailed Scylla appear later, though they do not replace the single-tailed version but exist side by side with it;[39] they may also occasionally have wings,[40] strengthening their association with representations of sirens. Scylla's appearance becomes not only more like a conventional mermaid's over time but also progressively less fearsome; it may even be alluring, in a further example of the increasing potential for access characteristic of representations of female hybrids.

This turn from the alien to the accessible can also be seen in two other possible precursors to the double-fishtailed form. According to Pearson, the *sirène bifide* may derive from the *Rankenfrau*, the Roman and Greek floriated fertility figure whose legs end in long vines or acanthus leaves, frequently held up by her human hands.[41] Both narrative and iconographic pressures are evidenced in the medieval European turn away from vines and towards tails, similar to the turn from snake to fishtail discussed below. The idea of human-to-plant metamorphosis, common in Greek and Roman tradition, is far less available in the literature and oral tradition of the Middle Ages, and other forms of animal–vegetable hybridity, aside from the Green Man figure and a few other isolated instances, are also scarce, while the possibility of animal–human hybridity remains strongly viable. Thus such floriated figures are much less common than human–animal figures, whether anguipedal

---

37   Sachs, "Some Notes," 10; Terry Pearson, "The Mermaid in the Church," *Profane Images in Marginal Arts of the Middle Ages: Proceedings of the VI Biennial Colloquium Misericordia International* (2009): 105–121, at 107; Clier-Colombani, *Les fées*, 100.

38   Mercedes Aguirre Castro, "Scylla: Hideous Monster or Femme Fatale? A Case of Contradiction between Literary and Artistic Evidence," *Cuadernos de Filología Clásica: Estudios griegos e indoeuropeos* Vol. 12, 2002, 321–2.

39   Aguirre Castro, "Scylla," 322.

40   Aguirre Castro, "Scylla," 325

41   Pearson, "The Mermaid", 119–20.

or fishtailed.[42] Another splayed figure found on Romanesque churches and cathedrals is the Sheela-na-gig; though she is not a hybrid, several scholars, including Jørgen Andersen and Anthony Weir and James Jerman, argue that she may be a precursor to or associated with the two-tailed siren due to her appearance in similar contexts and her gesture of holding apart her legs and labia in the way that the latter holds apart her tails.[43] The Sheela's apotropaic sexual import may be muted in images of double-tailed sirens, who frequently veil the split between their tails with a girdle, belt, or skirt, though Weir and Jerman also identify an "exhibitionist siren" at Zamora who clearly shows her vulva between her tails.[44] Even the veiled split, however, implies the existence of something requiring veiling; Pearson calls such double-tailed figures "so much more overtly sexual than the more subtly suggestive [single-tailed] woman–fish hybrid."[45]

The Zamora siren also points to the possibility that the single fishtail might have been represented as split to create the aquatic equivalent of legs, perhaps as a conscious or unconscious attempt to address the paradox of both single-fishtailed and single-serpent-tailed figures: sexual tempters whose bodily conformation is both a lure towards and a negation of the possibility of sex with the human men they tempt. As Silvio Bernardini comments, obliquely, "[T]he concave attribute of the female sex is difficult to place on a single-tailed mermaid."[46] Jean Cirlot also alludes to this dilemma, arguing that both single-tailed sirens and "French viper-fairies—as exemplified by Melusina in particular" symbolize "the torment of desire leading to self-destruction, for their abnormal bodies cannot satisfy the passions that are aroused by their enchanting music and by their beauty of face and bosom."[47] Such a paradox may be nullified by imagining the possibility of sexual approachability embodied in the spreading of the nether appendages; as Bernardini amplifies, "[T]he two tails act as a sort of sexual declaration."[48] From whatever direction the *sirène bifide*

---

42   Anthony Weir and James Jerman note the existence of a variety of animal–human–foliage figures at Auvergne and Melbourne, which they identify as "extension[s] of the exhibitionist"; see *Images of Lust: Sexual Carvings on Medieval Churches* (London: B. T. Batsford Ltd., 1986), 44.

43   Jørgen Andersen, *The Witch on the Wall: Medieval Erotic Sculpture in the British Isles* (Copenhagen: Rosenkilde and Bagger, 1977), 47; Weir and Jerman, *Images of Lust*, 44, 48–53.

44   Weir and Jerman, *Images of Lust*, 51.

45   Pearson, "The Mermaid," 119.

46   Silvio Bernardini, *The Serpent and the Siren: Sacred and Enigmatic Images in Tuscan Rural Churches*, trans. Kate Singelton (Siena: San Quirico d'Oricia, 2000), 52.

47   Cirlot, *Dictionary of Symbols*, 297–8.

48   Bernardini, *Serpent and the Siren*, 52.

derives, then, the figure exemplifies human-like conformation in, and thus greater accessibility to, the female half-piscine biform.

It is not difficult to establish that an ample tradition of fishtailed women was available to illustrators of the romance of Melusine. In comparison, the only widespread tradition in medieval Europe of beautiful or even superficially appealing snake–woman figures was that of the woman-headed Eden-serpent.[49] Following Petrus Comestor's inference in the *Historia scholastica* (ca.1173) that the seducer in the Garden must have taken on the semblance of a woman in order to allay Eve's fears, a significant portion of the tempting snakes portrayed between the thirteenth and seventeenth centuries bear the head, and often the upper body, of a woman combined with their serpentine tail.[50] This dracontopede, or "virgin-faced dragon,"[51] is identified by Nona Flores as "an image [...] largely unsupported by authority [...] that was developed so creatively by artists and writers for over four hundred years."[52] Such development was hence influenced by considerations other than the transmission of the biblical story, including the aesthetic and symbolic usefulness of the female hybrid form as "a sign of moral duplicity."[53] At least one fishtailed Eden serpent exists as well: a sculpture from Île-de-France (ca. fourteenth century) shows the Virgin Mary standing on and triumphing over a mermaid rather than the traditional serpent.[54] The negative symbolism of the mermaid–siren by this date was consistent with such a tableau, itself widespread in image though not attested in any textual sources. Nonetheless, the fish–woman must have been a compelling image to have tempted the artist to abandon the snake form, against the strong counter-pressure of the Bible's text.

Both iconographic and symbolic considerations oppose Melusine's continuation as a serpent–woman in her later representation. In the *Otia*, the demonic melusinian character takes on the semblance of a snake, while in *De nugis* she is discovered in the bath in the form of a dragon.[55] Both creatures are linked

---

49   The lamia, of Greek origins, was often represented as female and snakelike but was usually hideous and terrifying.

50   Nona C. Flores, "'Effigies Amicitiae … Veritas Inimicitiae': Antifeminism in the Iconography of the Woman-Headed Serpent in Medieval and Renaissance Art and Literature," in *Animals in the Middle Ages*, ed. Nona C. Flores (New York: Garland, 1996), 167–195.

51   Flores, "Effigies Amicitiae," 168.

52   Flores, "Effigies Amicitiae," 169.

53   Flores, "Effigies Amicitiae," 174.

54   Flores, "Effigies Amicitiae," 173.

55   In Gervase of Tilbury's story as referenced in the Middle English translation of *Melusine*, the fairy wife turns into a serpent *when*, not before, the betrayal occurs: after Sir Robert du Chastel Roussel sees his wife naked, violating his nuptial promise, she "putte her heed

in the Bible and in medieval Christian iconography with Satan and the Antichrist—most influentially with the snake in the Garden of Eden—and by extension with temptation, guile, hypocrisy, lust, and vanity. Denise Jalabert emphasizes this connection throughout medieval art, and Flores concurs that "a serpent's tail associates a creature with not only the serpent but also Satan and all his connotations: evil, death, and sin."[56] In his discussion of Melusine in *Liber de Nymphis, sylphis, pygmaeis et salamandris*, Paracelsus makes this association explicit, commenting, "[O]n Saturdays she had to be a serpent. This was her pledge to the devil for his helping her in getting a man,"[57] a plot element that does not appear in any previous textual sources. Although Paracelsus does not reference the Devil's previous choice of the serpent in the Garden of Eden, Melusine's ophidian shape likely influenced his association of her with the Devil. While Gillian Alban, and to a lesser extent Sonia Saporiti,[58] argue for the possibility that prehistoric ophidian goddesses and other fertility figures influenced Melusine's representation, the snake shape has far more negative than positive associations in medieval and early modern European literature. Even Weir and Jerman, who argue that "the snake in antiquity often had a beneficent role," conclude, "The negative aspect of the serpent is the one that prevails in Romanesque art."[59] There is some difficulty, therefore, in maintaining the positive character of a figure identified as a snake—or with maintaining a snake identification in a figure not coded as wholly negative.

This, however, is what Jean d'Arras' and Coudrette's Melusine narratives attempt to do. While retaining much of the original structure of the earlier

---

in to a watre and was tourned in to a serpent," A. K. Donald, ed., *Melusine* (London: Kegan Paul, Trench, Trübner & Co., 1895), 5–6.

56   Denise Jalabert, "De l'art oriental antique à l'art roman. Recherches sur la faune et la flore romane. II. Les sirènes." *Bulletin monumental* 95 (1936): 433–71, esp. 454–7; Flores, "Effigies Amicitiae," 173.

57   Paracelsus, *A Book on Nymphs, Sylphs, Pygmies, and Salamanders, and on the Other Spirits*, trans. Henry E. Sigerist, in *Four Treatises of Theophrastus von Hohenheim Called Paracelsus*, ed. Henry E. Sigerist (Baltimore: Johns Hopkins Press, 1941; paperback ed. 1996), 246.

58   Gillian M. E. Alban, "The Serpent Goddess Melusine: From Cursed Snake to Mary's Shield" in *The Survival of Myth: Innovation, Singularity and Alterity*, ed. Paul Hardwick and David Kennedy (Newcastle-upon-Tyne: Cambridge Scholars Publishing, 2010), 23–43, and *Melusine the Serpent Goddess in A.S. Byatt's* Possession *and in Myth* (Lanham: Lexington Books, 2003); Sonia Saporiti, "Melusine and the Ophidian Feminine," in *Myth and Symbol: A Psychoanalytic Study in Contemporary German Literature* (Newcastle-upon-Tyne: Cambridge Scholars Publishing, 2013), 59–76, at 67.

59   Weir and Jerman, *Images of Lust*, 63.

stories, they figure Melusine as a virtuous and noble character, in keeping with her role as genetrix of a powerful dynasty and ancestress of the patrons of the authors. In pursuit of this goal, while they do not go so far as to praise her periodic metamorphoses into snake form, they attempt to distance her ophidian nature as much as possible from negative connotations. As James Wade notes in *Fairies in Medieval Romance,* Jean d'Arras and those who translate his romance situate Melusine's periodic snake nature as a curse, a plot element which does not appear in Gervase's and Map's tales and which "functions as a useful narrative device whereby the author can maintain a certain fidelity with other supernatural-bride legends without implying any diabolical origins."[60] This recuperation of Melusine's character and of her snake form is also achieved by Raymondin's reaction to her secret shape. Immediately after seeing her, he makes no mention of her physical body but instead mourns his projected loss of her in a lament serving as an extended moral blazon on her myriad virtues: "'Farwel beaute, bounte, swetenes, amyablete / Farwel wyt, curtoysye, & humilite / Farwel al my joye, al my comfort & myn hoop / Farwel myn herte, my prowes, my valyaunce,'" etc.[61] Seeming to ignore her serpentine shape entirely, he berates himself for contravening the condition placed upon their marriage and upbraids Fate for leading him to do so. Even when later, maddened by grief, Raymondin calls her "fals serpente,"[62] he again attempts to negate his words, immediately smothering them with a similar torrent of abuse against himself and praise of Melusine.

Such attempts to recuperate the snake figure may have found a more receptive audience in France, where Melusine is first given this name, than in the British Isles, where the *Otia* and *De nugis* were written. Snakes are comparatively uncommon in England; in *The Life-History of British Serpents*, Gerald Leighton comments, "In very few countries of the world are the members of the class Reptilia so sparsely represented as in the British Isles."[63] In comparison, France has at least eleven species of snakes, and George Boulenger refers to the "extraordinary abundance" of vipers in parts of this country.[64] In areas with few or no snakes, snake symbolism would be received primarily

---

60   James Wade, *Fairies in Medieval Romance* (New York: Palgrave Macmillan, 2011), 125.

61   Donald, *Melusine,* 298.

62   Donald, *Melusine,* 314.

63   Gerald Rowley Leighton, *The Life-History of British Serpents and Their Local Distribution in the British Isles* (Edinburgh: William Blackwood and Sons, 1901), 3.

64   George Albert Boulenger, *The Snakes of Europe* (1913; repr., London: Forgotten Books, 2013), 136–7.

from outside sources, of which the Bible was the most accessible and influential, while places in which snakes were often encountered might have a
wider range of empirically based symbolic associations. A similar process can
be seen in medieval bestiaries and in their later offshoots, such as Edward
Topsell's natural histories of animals, birds, and snakes. Those animals with
which the author might have been familiar, such as swine and dogs, receive a
more naturalistic discussion than animals that would have been unfamiliar,
such as crocodiles and panthers, which are frequently described in wholly
imaginary or symbolic, rather than realistic, terms. Accordingly, in none of
the many Irish melusinian variants identified by Bo Almqvist does the positively coded (and unnamed) Melusine analogue have any sort of snake-like or
draconian characteristics.[65]

Even in France the snake figure, naturalistic or combined with a female
head and upper body, nevertheless remained associated with the devil and
must have influenced Melusine's representation. Flores points to the deceptive
nature of the female-headed serpent in the fifteenth-century *Mistère du Viel
Testament*, whose snake tail is "poignante et mortelle" [sharp and deadly] in
comparison with its sweet face;[66] in *The Medieval Popular Bible*, Brian Murdoch
quotes the French Prose Bible's dictum, "Li serpenz senifie le deable" [The serpent signifies the devil].[67] Clier-Colombani shows that Melusine is associated
with the demonic even in the early French versions, arguing that Melusine's
reaction to Raymondin's denunciation in Coudrette "laisse clairement enten-
dre que pour l'auteur, les fées sont à la fois les instruments et les victimes de
Satan" [clearly implies that for the author, fairies are at the same time the instruments and the victims of Satan].[68] Joanna Pavlevski claims of the depiction
of Melusine in the fifteenth century, "[S]a queue de serpent lui ferme la porte
de l'espèce humaine, crée a l'image de son Createur" [her serpent's tail closes
the door for her to the human race, created in the image of its Creator].[69] Even

---

65   Bo Almqvist, "The Mélusine Legend in Irish Folk Tradition," in *Mélusines continentales
      et insulaires*, ed. Jeanne-Marie Boivin and Proinsias MacCana (Paris: Champion, 1999),
      263–279.

66   Flores, "Effigies Amicitiae," 171.

67   Brian Murdoch, *The Medieval Picture Bible: Expansions of Genesis in the Middle Ages*
      (Cambridge: D.S. Brewer, 2003), p. 20 n. 3.

68   Clier-Colombani, *Les fées*, 183.

69   Joanna Pavlevski, "Une esthétique originale du motif de la femme-serpent: recherches
      ontologiques et picturales sur Mélusine au XVe siècle," *L'Humain et l'animal dans la France
      médiévale (XIIe–XVe s.): Human and Animal in Medieval France, (12th–15th c.)* (Leiden:
      Brill, 2014), 73–94, at 92.

with Melusine's repeated assurances that she is "par Dieu" [of God], the serpent's negative associations are never entirely eclipsed.[70]

However, Melusine's strong and continued connection with the physical and cultural geography of France provides for an alternate form of accessibility to her character here. As Emmanuel Le Roy Ladurie has shown, in the French oral tradition as it developed after the first written romances, Melusine remains tied to the land, becoming increasingly associated with agricultural as well as dynastic fertility. She enables farmers to foretell the size of the harvest by means of the water level in a fountain associated with her and is even responsible for the introduction of the haricot bean, beloved in French cuisine.[71] Le Roy Ladurie conjectures that when Melusine moved back into the realm of oral tradition after her emergence from it into the world of letters, the elements of her legend that continued to be emphasized were those of interest to the storytellers, often peasants: agricultural work and wonder tales.[72] In this verbal tradition, she remains almost exclusively a snake. The narratological work she does is not hindered by snake symbolism; while associated with fountains, she is not a water sprite but remains largely connected to the earth, even in one story striking the ground with her heel and disappearing into it.[73] Being ophidian is not a bar to her role as genetrix of a dynasty, an association that remains highly salient in this tradition. Rather, snakes could have been more easily aligned with this role than fish, which are not viviparous, while among the snakes found specifically in the Poitou region, where the Melusine tales were first collected by Jean d'Arras, at least one species, the asp viper (*Vipera lastei*), gives birth to live young.[74]

In Germany, where Melusine appears beginning with Thüring von Ringoltingen's translation (1456) of Coudrette, the melusinian oral and written tradition tends towards aqueity, while variants beyond the original translation

---

70   This, as well as the iconographic pressure towards nursing mermaids, may be a reason that even in the early French versions she is at least once illustrated with a fish's rather than a snake's tail.

71   Emmanuel Le Roy Ladurie, "Mélusine Down on the Farm: Metamorphosis of a Myth," in *The Territory of the Historian* (Chicago: University of Chicago Press, 1979), 203–220, at 211.

72   Le Roy Ladurie, "Mélusine," 212.

73   Le Roy Ladurie, "Mélusine," 210.

74   Daniel G. Blackburn and James R. Stewart, "Viviparity and Placentation in Snakes," in *Reproductive Biology and Phylogeny of Snakes*, ed. Robert D. Aldridge and David M. Sever (Boca Raton: A. K. Peters/CRC Press, 2011), 121.

that retain the snake form use it as an occasion of horror rather than aid.[75] Thüring remains for the most part close to his source;[76] however, while he describes Melusine in the bath as snake-tailed, his prologue promises a tale about a mermaid, apparently a character more calculated to appeal to his potential audience. And although in France the coats of arms of the families that claim descent from Melusine, such as the Lusignans, remain closely aligned to the textual sources, portraying a snake-tailed woman frequently in a tub, it is in the German tradition that "melusine" enters the language as a heraldic term denoting a two-tailed mermaid, as seen in the arms of Die Ritter of Nuremberg. Later German characters based on Melusine, such as Undine and Lorelei, are explicitly associated with water; though they are not described as piscine biforms in the first texts in which they appear, these names are subsequently often associated with fishtailed women.

While Melusine is figured in the first English translation of the romance (ca.1500) as a snake, she is not embraced in this shape in England, as Urban has pointed out.[77] After the early sixteenth-century translations of Jean's romance and of Coudrette, into the *Romans of Partenay*, Melusine essentially disappears, save for scattered references in relation to French history and geography; because she is firmly associated with the French tradition, any descriptions of her feature a snake's tail. It is not until the first English translation (1818) of the German *Undine* (1811) by Friedrich de la Motte Fouqué, in which she is a sea spirit, that the biform woman gains a wider anglophone audience. In the undine form she proved immensely popular, such that almost a hundred translations and variants of the story appeared in English within the next 150 years, estimates Burton Pollin.[78] Also arising out of later Germanic and more water-associated traditions are Luxemborgian versions of Melusine's story. Pit Péporté traces the beginning of this tradition, sparked by a renewed

---

75   This appears in a variant of the Peter Diemringer von Stauffenberg cycle from Baden in which a beautiful fairy woman named Melusine addresses a knight, Sebald, asking that he deliver her from torment by kissing her three times. No sooner does he attempt to do so than she appears with the tail of an enormous snake and arms like elephants' trunks, whereupon he leaps from her embrace and dooms her to her fate; see Jérémie Babinet, *Mélusine, Geoffroy à la Grand'Dent: légendes poitevines* (Paris: Chez Techener, 1847), 55–6, and Le Roy Ladurie, "Mélusine," 218.

76   Albrecht Classen, *The Forest in Medieval German Literature: Ecocritical Readings From a Historical Perspective* (Lanham: Lexington Books, 2015), 184.

77   Urban, *Monstrous Women*, 47–56.

78   Burton R. Pollin, "'Undine' in the Works of Poe," *Studies in Romanticism* 14:1 (Winter, 1975), 59–74, at 60–1.

interest in the storyline throughout Europe in the early nineteenth century, in the first two versions published in Luxembourg; in both, he notes, Melusine is described as having a fishtail when she is discovered in the bath, an alteration which is consistent throughout the Luxembourgian tradition.[79]

If the primary association with snakes in the Middle Ages is demonic, the import of the fish form is more ambiguous. Fish, or fishtails, might be Christian or anti-Christian and might symbolize sexlessness or sexual sin. The fish was an early Christian sign for Jesus, based on the initial letters of the phrase "Ἰησοῦς Χριστός, Θεοῦ Υἱός, Σωτήρ" [Jesus Christ, son of God, savior], which spell "ΙΧΘΥΣ" [fish]; and fish might, by extension, symbolize the human (Christian) soul, especially in the context of the disciples' identification as fishers of men and, for some, as fishermen as well. Pavlevski argues that the developing tail of the fish on the siren enhances its Christological symbolism in comparison to the bird–siren of Greco-Roman antiquity.[80] Hassig also notes that fish were praised for their association with chastity in the bestiary tradition, based on their supposed ability to reproduce without sex.[81] However, the piscine siren–mermaid herself has multiple demonic or at least negative significations, figuring both visually and textually as a symbol of lust, pride, vanity, and the temptations of idleness or earthly pleasure. De Rachewiltz suggests that the siren's iconographic representation reflects the allegorical use to which she is put: "the Siren became 'fishy' when the notion of woman as either-harlot-or-angel started to take foot in the preachings of the Church"[82]—when it became necessary to distinguish the winged messenger of God from the winged temptress.

If sirens were denied wings, lest they be mistaken for angels, and Melusine in many traditions sheds her serpent's tail along with its satanic associations, the question of the alternate choice of fishtail remains. It is a visual cue of the importance of the water, uniquely penetrable and yet ungraspable, in the understanding of these creatures. As the two-fishtailed form opens the possibility of greater accessibility to the female biforms that wear it, so too is water figured as more humanly penetrable than fire, with its destructive burning, or air, through which only birds and spirits could fly. Paracelsus tacitly assumes humans' greater connection to water creatures than to other elementals; only

---

79   Péporté, *Constructing the Middle Ages*, 93. However, one Luxembourgian author, the
      Chevalier l'Evêque de la Basse-Mônturie, does have Melusine return to the home she had
      been forced to abandon every seven years in the shape of a snake, 92–3.

80   Pavlevski, "Une esthétique," 92.

81   Hassig, *The Mark of the Beast: The Medieval Bestiary in Art, Life, and Literature* (New York:
      Routledge, 1997, 2013), 76.

82   De Rachewilz, *De Sirenibus*, 89.

water and earth spirits—nymphs and pygmies—are able to speak like humans, while air and fire spirits—sylphs and salamanders—are not; and only nymphs look like humans, while pygmies are small, sylphs elongated, and salamanders burning. And while the earth is likewise penetrable and frequently itself linked with femaleness, metaphorized in terms of fertility and generation, it lacks the second term of the formulation, the sense of elusiveness and alienness. The Otherness and dangers of the water, particularly the ocean, are salient in the symbolism of mermaid–sirens. Aguirre Castro argues that the transformations of both Scylla and the sirens into fish–women are related to folkloric traditions concerning the perils of the sea, and in her discussion of sea monsters, Rosemary Wright suggests that peoples who lived close to the sea might have had a particular apprehension of "the powers of darkness conjured up by the untamed ocean," leading to the creation of symbols of evil in the shape of sea monsters or to the addition of fishtails to existing images of evil.[83] But although Van Duzer calls sea monsters "one of the most potent symbols of the wildness and dangers of the ocean," he shows elsewhere that they are also used to delight and instruct viewers, "suggesting in a general way that the sea can be dangerous, but more emphatically indicating and drawing attention to the vitality of the oceans and the variety of creatures in the world."[84]

The addition of a fishtail to a female hybrid is also a means by which to invoke the assumed likeness of women to water. What is hidden in the water, like the fishtail, is elusive, dangerous, titillating, and potentially graspable, characteristics long assumed to be female. Humorally speaking, women were moister than men; like water, they were mutable and easily diverted; like water, both potentially useful and potentially perilous. Representations of Melusine and related female biforms parallel the larger representation of women and their fluctuating proportions of Otherness and access, from the demonic fairy wife, untamable and unredeemable at the height of the twelfth-century misogynist tradition, to the Victorian ideal of the wholly tamed and self-abnegating Little Mermaid, who gives up her life for love for a human man and the Christian God at the same time that she irrevocably sheds her fishtail in favor of legs. By contrast, present-day melusinian mermaids may switch back and forth between tails and legs at will, showing their Otherness while providing for the possibility of its mitigation, retaining only enough difference to titillate but not enough to threaten.

---

83   Aguirre Castro, "Scylla," 327; Rosemary Wright, "The Rider on the Sea-Monster," in *The North Sea World in the Middle Ages,* ed. Thomas R. Liszka and Lorna E. M. Walker (Cornwall: Four Courts Press, 2001), 70–87, at 70.

84   Van Duzer, *Sea Monsters,* 52, 11.

CHAPTER 2

Polycorporality and Heteromorphia: Untangling Melusine's Mixed Bodies

Ana Pairet

The reception of the late medieval tale of Melusine across early modern Europe attests to the long-lasting appeal of the central theme of cyclical transformation and a shared fascination for the heroine's corporality. As captured in Jean d'Arras' prose romance *Roman de Mélusine ou La Noble Histoire de Lusignan* (ca. 1393), which provides the first known written rendition of the Melusine legend, and in Coudrette's narrative poem *Roman de Parthenay* (1401), the eponymous character is defined by her double nature and the contradictory social roles she performs.[1] Condensing the paradoxes of the founding mother figure, her hidden, mixed body is subject to a visual prohibition that ultimately brings about the ruin of the lineage.[2]

As if transfixed by the seductive mixed-body trope, modern critics have lavished attention on Melusine's corporeal hybridity and celebrated her

---

1 All references are to Jean d'Arras, *Mélusine ou La Noble Histoire de Lusignan*, ed. Jean-Jacques Vincensini (Paris: Le Livre de Poche, 2003) and to Coudrette, *Le Roman de Mélusine ou Histoire de Lusignan*, ed. Eleanor Roach (Paris: Klincksieck, 1982). Page numbers corresponding to the French original and English translation respectively are given in parentheses. Translations of Jean d'Arras come from *Melusine; or the Noble History of Lusignan*, trans. Donald Maddox and Sara Sturm-Maddox (University Park: Pennsylvania State University Press, 2012).

2 The sources, structural elements, and contexts at work in Jean d'Arras' and Coudrette's romances have been surveyed in abundant detail, beginning in the 1880s. Léo Desaivre first studied the sources of the myth in Poitou folklore, its transmission and its iconography: "Le mythe de la mère Lusine (Meurlusine, Merlusine, Mellusigne, Mellusine, Mélusine, Méleusine). Étude critique et bibliographique," in *Mémoires de la Société de statistique, sciences, lettres et arts du département des Deux-Sèvres*, 2nd series, vol. 2, no.1 (1882): 81–302. For the historical contexts and structural components of the genealogical myth, see Jacques Le Goff and Emmanuel Le Roy Ladurie, "Mélusine maternelle et défricheuse," in *Annales: Économies, Sociétés, Civilisations* 26 (1971): 587–622, and Claude Lecouteux, "La structure des légendes Mélusiniennes," *Annales: Économies, Sociétés, Civilisations* 2 (1978): 294–306. Laurence Harf-Lancner surveys antecedents to Melusinian tales in twelfth- and thirteenth-century Latin literature in *Les Fées au Moyen Âge: Morgane et Mélusine, La naissance des fées* (Geneva: Droz, 1984), 119–154.

---

in-betweenness: "If ever there was an exemplary case of the meaning of lim-inality—that zone of marginality and permeability—the *Roman de Mélusine* would appear to be it," writes Gabrielle Spiegel.[3] The heroine's distinctive "poly-corporality,"[4] as well as the birthmarks borne by Melusine's sons, are routinely folded into the category of monstrosity by scholars, whereas rarely is trans-formation as theme and as process adequately addressed. Indeed, present-day commentators arguably conflate discursive categories that in the medieval worldview were understood to be distinct, with the result that Melusine's fluid corporality finds itself stabilized discursively through ahistorical or otherwise anachronistic notions that run contrary to medieval tropes of transformation. Notions of hybridity, in particular as defined by contemporary postcolonial theory, may speak to nothing so much as our desire to suffuse the past with ideas of our own design.[5]

Archetypal and symbolic readings of Melusine are common, from "phallic mother" to serpent goddess.[6] This selective attribution of meaning to a given scene (that of Melusine bathing) or feature (her dragon wings or serpentine tail) comes at the expense of narrative context and the dynamic quality of

---

3   Gabrielle Spiegel, "Maternity and Monstrosity: Reproductive Biology in *The Roman de Melu-sine*," in *Melusine of Lusignan: Founding Fiction in Late Medieval France*, ed. Donald Maddox and Sara Sturm-Maddox (Athens, GA: University of Georgia Press, 1996), 100.

4   Kevin Brownlee, "Mélusine's Hybrid Body and the Poetics of Metamorphosis," *Yale French Studies* 86 (1994): 18–38, reprinted in *Melusine of Lusignan*, 76–99. In Brownlee's reading Melusine's "polycorporality" is a powerful narrative construct involving the tension between "three bodies" (female, mixed body, fantastic animal).

5   To the extent that the Old French term *muance* encompasses not only bodily change per se, but also changes in fortune as well as territorial transfers, it resonates in ways that hybridity and monstrosity could not with themes central to the genealogical and geopolitical dimen-sions of Jean d'Arras' and Coudrette's romances.

6   In discussing Melusine's mythical undertones, Marina S. Brownlee reads the heroine's aveng-ing of her mother as an appropriation of phallic attributes: "Melusine is a phallic mother in that she entombs her father in a womb-like cavern," "Interference in *Mélusine*," in *Melusine of Lusignan*, 229. For a reading of Melusine's phallic imagery as referenced by Sigmund Freud, see Erin Felicia Labbie, *Lacan's Medievalism* (Minneapolis: University of Minnesota Press, 2006), 85–87. Maria Frangos analyzes Melusine's phallic legacy in *"The shame of all her kind": A genealogy of Female Monstrosity* and *Metamorphosis from the Middle Ages Through Early Modernity* (PhD diss., University of California, Santa Cruz, 2008). Jean Markale, *Mélusine ou l'androgyne* (Paris: Retz, 1983) is an extreme example of Jungian archetypal reading. For modern variations on the chthonic thematics, see for example Gillian M. E. Alban, *Melu-sine the Serpent Goddess in A.S. Byatt's* Possession *and in Mythology* (Lanham, MD: Lexington Books, 2003).

literary myth.[7] Instead of reducing Melusine's textual and visual representation to an arbitrarily composed set of attributes and analogous meanings, the heroine's transformations can first be approached as process, and her multiple, mixed bodies as polysemic marvels. Beyond the confines of the medieval romances, transmission of the Melusine story in early printed editions provides further material through which to explain the fascination the shape-shifting founding-mother figure continues to exert. This text-based approach helps identify what is at stake in the representation of Melusine's metamorphic body, and how the fairy's marvelous footprint is reconfigured, literally and figuratively, from the late medieval to the early modern period.

Melusine is routinely referred to as a monster. To be sure, monstrosity provides a powerful framework from which to analyze medieval and early modern cultural representations.[8] Recent scholarship that builds on the methodology of "monster theory"[9] has approached Melusine's monstrous maternity as a genealogical trope, with particular focus on the Middle English versions of the romance.[10] In such readings, Melusine's

---

7   Claude Lévi-Strauss, "La Structure des mythes," in *Anthropologie Structurale* (Paris: Plon, 1958), 227–255.

8   On medieval and early modern descriptions of monsters, see Rudolf Wittkower, *Allegory and the Migration of Symbols* (London: Thames and Hudson, 1977), 46–74; Claude-Claire Kappler, *Monstres, demons et merveilles à la fin du Moyen Âge Paris* (Paris: Payot 1980); John Block Friedman, *The Monstrous Races in Medieval Art and Thought* (Cambridge, MA: Harvard University Press, 1981); Marie-Hélène Huet, *Monstrous Imagination* (Cambridge, MA: Harvard University Press, 1993); David Williams, *Deformed Discourse: The Function of the Monster in Medieval Thought and Literature* (Montreal: McGill-Queen's University Press, 1996); Francis Dubost, *Aspects fantastiques de la littérature médiévale (XIIe-XIIIe siècles): L'Autre, l'Ailleurs, l'autrefois* (Paris: Champion, 1991), 426–625; *The Monstrous Middle Ages*, ed. Bettina Bildhauer and Robert Mills (Toronto: University of Toronto Press, 2003); and Dana M. Oswald, *Monsters, Gender and Sexuality in Medieval English Literature* (Rochester, NY: Boydell & Brewer, 2010).

9   Jeffrey Jerome Cohen, "Monster Culture (Seven Theses)," in *Monster Theory: Reading Culture*, ed. Jeffrey Jerome Cohen (Minneapolis: University of Minnesota Press, 1996), 3–25.

10   On medieval views of reproductive biology that identified matter "supplied by the maternal *menstruum*" as the cause of monstrosity, see Gabrielle Spiegel, "Maternity and Monstrosity," 104. Secondary sources on the Middle English *Melusine* have explored the genealogical implications of the monstrous mother trope. See in particular Tania M. Colwell, "Mélusine: Ideal Mother or Inimitable Monster?," in *Love, Marriage, and Family Ties in the Later Middle Ages*, ed. Isabel Davis et al. (Turnhout: Brepols, 2003), 181–203, and Angela Florschuetz, *Marking Maternity in Middle English Romance: Mothers, Identity and Contamination* (New York: Palgrave Macmillan, 2014), 155–185. Misty Urban provides a comprehensive analysis of "metaphorical female monstrosity" in *Monstrous Women in*

"hybridizing"[11] body reveals anxieties related to the marginalization of women in patrilineal genealogical transmission. However relevant to the analysis of genealogical romance this line of thinking may be, it folds the theme of transformation into the notion of monstrous hybridity in a way that arrests the narrative and thematic coherence of bodily change. Descriptive or interpretative use of the monstruous category should be greeted with caution given the fluid boundaries between marvels and monsters for medieval and early modern readers.

The intertwining of discourses on marvels and of transformation as theme in medieval Melusinian narratives merits further philological and discursive analysis.[12] Monstrosity and transformation were rarely associated in theological, encyclopedic, or other literary works of the Middle Ages, which examined the two phenomena independently, following Augustine of Hippo and Isidore of Seville.[13] Deriving from distinct written traditions, medieval bestiaries, books of marvels, encyclopedic works, and moralizations of Ovid's *Metamorphoses* all featured a variety of theriomorphic monsters with a human trunk and animal upper or lower body parts, including dog-headed men, centaurs, satyrs, and sirens.[14] Yet few classical or medieval accounts of monstrous beings identified the composite human-animal body as the result of a process of transformation.[15]

In Isidore of Seville's *Etimologiae* XI ("De homine et portentis") [Of men and prodigious beings], metamorphic and partially transformed bodies are categorized as aberrations; in apparent defiance of the natural order ("contra

---

Middle English Romance (Lewiston, NY: Edwin Mellen Press, 2010). The analysis of gendered monstrosity continues to elicit doctoral research, including Maureen Smith, "Gender, Monstrosity, and *Le Roman de Mélusine*" (MSc diss., University of Edinburgh, 2013).

11 Florschuetz, *Marking Maternity*, 155.

12 On the vocabulary of bodily transformation in the Old French vernacular, see Ana Pairet, *"Les mutacions des fables": figures de la métamorphose dans la littérature française du moyen âge* (Paris: Champion, 2002), 20–28.

13 Narratives of humans taking on animal form are common in the Celtic, Greco-Roman, and Scandinavian tales that medieval European writers employed as sources or intertexts. For an overview of diverse mythological and religious traditions in representing metamorphosis, see Cristina Noacco, *La métamorphose dans la littérature française des XIIe et XIIIe siècles* (Rennes: Presses Universitaires de Rennes, 2008), 25–39.

14 Kappler, *Monstres*, 147–157.

15 Two such examples, both involving a female subject, are the tales of Medusa and the sea-monster Scylla. Citing examples from the eighth- or ninth-century *Book of Monsters*, Philippe Walter traces a direct genealogy between Melusine and hybrid mythological sea-monsters in *La Fée Mélusine, le serpent et l'oiseau* (Paris: Imago, 2008), 108.

naturam"), such portents are created by God and thus are part of nature.[16] Isidore borrows from the Greek "heteromorphia," the term by which he designates composite bodies. After describing the monstrous races found in remote lands and a variety of fictional mixed-body creatures from the Greco-Roman tradition, including the Gorgons and the sirens, Scylla, centaurs of various kinds, and the Minotaur, Isidore devotes a separate section to transformations per se ("De transformatis"), in which he quotes *exempla* nearly identical to those provided by Augustine in *City of God* XVIII, 18.[17]

Augustine and Isidore strongly reject the prospect that humans can be partly or totally transformed into animals. They associate such narratives with the poetic fictions of pagan poets as well as the allegorical tradition. In *City of God*, which provided medieval clerics with an influential theoretical and doctrinal framework for dealing with mythological and folk narratives of transformation, Augustine adamantly refutes the notion of actual change, namely via the theory of delusional metamorphosis in which the illusion of the senses is induced by demons. For his part, Isidore explains most narratives of transformation in evemerist terms and presents mythical creatures as poetic fictions, although he does include in his *Etymologies* examples of prodigious heteromorphic creatures living in the East, with animal faces, heads, or bodies such

---

16   Isidorus Hispalensis, *Etimologiae* XI, ed. Fausto Gasti (Paris: Les Belles Lettres, 2010), 132–159. Isidore distinguishes *portenta, ostenta, monstra* and *prodigia*, according to what such phenomena predict or tell. The typology of prodigious beings includes those who experience partial transformations ("in parte tranfigurantur") resulting in an animal face or body, and total transformation into an animal, a phenomenon Isidore illustrates with the example of a woman who gave birth to a calf. He opposes prodigious beings ("portentum") where transformation is complete (as in Plinius' account of a woman giving birth to a snake) and prodigious things ("portentuosum") where only minor deformity is found (such as six fingers). Prodigious beings are categorized according to their size or the size of body part or of a superfluous member; uneven body parts or lack of a body part; partial transformation including animal face or body ("heteromorfia"); total transformation into an animal; organs in the wrong place; excess in one part of the body and lack in the other; premature development; conjunction of such aberrations; hermaphroditism; the monstrous races of faraway lands; and imaginary beings such as sirens, Cerberus, the Chimera or the Hydra.

17   Isidore, *Etimologiae* XI, 160–163. In particular, he references Circe's transformation of Ulysses' men into swine, the legend of the Arcadian wolves, and the birds of Diomedes. See Augustine, *City of God*, Book XVIII, 17, in *City of God*, vol. V, trans. William Chase Green (Cambridge, MA: Harvard/Loeb Classical Library, 1960). To these Augustinian fables, Isidore adds the anecdote of criminals who change their appearance into that of witches or wild beasts, to further rationalize transformation as intentional delusion.

as the dog-headed Indian "cynocephali."[18] If Isidore's taxonomy of natural aberrations hints at metamorphosis as one possible cause for composite bodies, the causal link is never made. Ultimately, in medieval representations, the bodies of prodigious beings and those of monstrous races presumed to inhabit the periphery of the Western world must be stable: their primary function is to signify God's designs and metaphorically to represent cultural Alterity, including multiple conflicting collective identities.[19]

To approach Melusine's corporality with some clarity, it is crucial to disentangle historically, philologically, and conceptually the theme of transformation from the composite female body with which it is associated in Jean d'Arras' and Coudrette's narratives. In classical and medieval literature, human-to-animal transformation can be either the expression of an ontological hiatus, where moral and rational attributes disappear with the vanishing human form as is the case of the werewolf (*versipelles*) in Petronius' *Satyricon,* or, on the contrary, a trope for an essential double nature, in reference to the animal side of mankind.[20] However, bodily change rarely results in composite or mixed bodies, as is the case in the Melusine romances. Combining the motif of human-to-animal transformation with multiple figures of composite bodies is a rhetorical move that destabilizes the exemplarity of most animal transformation narratives that were available to medieval readers, including Ovid's *Metamorphoses,* Walter Map's *De Nugis Curialium* (ca.1181–1193), Gerald of Wales' *Topographia Hibernica* (ca.1188), and Gervase of Tilbury's *Otia Imperialia* (ca.1210).[21]

---

18   Mentioned by Augustine of Hippo who doubts their existence (*City of God* XVI, 8), dog-headed creatures are a recurring expression of the *topos* of the monstrous race. Since Greek antiquity, *cynocephali* were associated with violence, bloodthirstiness, and cannibalism.

19   On hybridity as figure for mixed collective identities, see Jeffrey Jerome Cohen, *Hybridity, Identity, and Monstrosity in Medieval Britain: On Difficult Middles* (New York: Palgrave MacMillan, 2007).

20   As told in *Satyricon* chapter 62, trans. by E. H. Warmington (Cambridge, MA: Harvard University Press, 1969). Visual representations of composite bodies often depict a stage in a transformation process, such as Daphne partially changed into the bay tree. Ovid's *Metamorphoses* offers endless variations of the suffering human conscience trapped in animal (Calixto, Io) or vegetal form (Myrrha), staging the slow dissolution of distinctive human features such as speech. Likewise, most human-to-animal or animal-to-human transformations in medieval narratives play on the idea of double nature: either the human being loses its nature when assuming animal form (such as Petrone's *versipelles*) or, as is more frequent, it retains some or all of its moral features under animal appearance.

21   On mutability as theme in the context of the late twelfth-century revival of Ovid's *Metamorphoses*, see in particular Caroline Walker Bynum, *Metamorphosis and Identity* (New York: Zone Books, 2001), 86–98.

The search for shape-shifting predecessors in the clerical and courtly literature of the Middle Ages is a circular quest that takes us back to the very same
"merveilles" from Gervase of Tilbury, whom Jean d'Arras' prologue quotes.[22] At
the heart of medieval depictions of marvels we rarely find fear, but more often
a suspension of judgment that may serve rhetorical and poetic ends, as is the
case in Jean d'Arras' prologue and epilogue.[23] Melusine's name, which according to the intradiegetic gloss given by the Count of Poitiers signifies "merveilles"
(218), calls for more detailed intertextual exploration of marvelous transformations in courtly literature.[24] Marvels serve to structure medieval romance as a
series of repeated encounters with multiple forms of Alterity, more often that
not in a parodical or otherwise playful mode,[25] as is the case in the thirteenth-
century romance *Le Bel Inconnu,* in which one notorious shape-shifting predecessor of Melusine is featured. At the narrative midpoint, out of a closet comes a
shimmering and luminescent *wivre,* described as *dyable,* whom the Bel Inconnu
readies himself to fight.[26] The serpentine creature avoids the blows by humbling
itself before the knight, much like the werewolf in Marie de France's *Bisclavret.*
The marvelous beast has the lips of a woman: "Hom ne vit onques sa parelle, /
Que la bouce ot tote vermelle: / parmi jetoit le feu ardant" [never had he seen
anything of the sort: from its scarlet mouth came burning fire] (ll. 3133–3135).[27]

---

22   Rupert T. Pickens, "The Poetics of Paradox in the *Roman de Mélusine,*" in *Melusine of
      Lusignan,* 48–75.

23   Marvelous creatures, objects, and phenomena are not necessarily supernatural, for the
      term *merveilles* merely denotes an inability to comprehend on the part of the witness,
      much like the Old English *wundor,* "object of astonishment." Practices and phenomena
      that challenge cultural, social, and emotional boundaries, inspiring terror or disgust, are
      more often denoted by the term *estrane.* See *De l'étranger à l'étrange ou la conjointure de
      la merveille, Senefiance* 25 (1988).

24   In Latin and vernacular works, the marvelous lexical spectrum ranges from natural and
      manmade wonders to phenomena, creatures, and abilities that defy the natural order or
      exceed known human ability. On the many meanings of medieval marvels in Old French
      literature, see Francis Dubost's lexical inventory in *Aspects fantastiques* (Paris: Champion,
      1991), 61–92; for the distinction between marvelous, monstrous and fantastic elements,
      see Dubost, 426–625.

25   On the ways marvelous motifs in medieval romances contribute to parodic rewriting
      of courtly conventions, see in particular Christine Ferlampin-Acher, *Merveille et topique
      merveilleuse dans les romans médiévaux* (Paris: Champion, 2003) and Isabelle Arseneau, *Par-
      odie et merveilleux dans le roman dit réaliste au XIIIe siècle* (Paris: Classiques Garnier, 2012).

26   On the Dragon Maiden motif, see Lydia Zeldenrust, "When a Knight Meets a Dragon Maiden:
      Human Identity and the Monstrous Animal Other," (master's thesis, Utrecht University, 2011).

27   Renaud de Beaujeu/Renaut de Bage, *Le bel inconnu,* ed. Karen Fresco (New York: Garland,
      1992).

Fascinated by this *mervelle*, the knight fails to prevent the snake from kissing him before it disappears into the closet. As the Bel Inconnu thinks himself the victim of a diabolic ploy, an otherworldly voice tells him he has prevailed and reveals his identity and lineage. At daybreak, the marvel and nocturnal terrors theatrically vanish. Waking up in a sun-drenched room, Guiglain, now cognizant of his identity, discovers at his side a maiden whose spell he has broken by enduring the *fier baisier*: the shimmering infernal beast is now a beautiful lady dressed in a green gown who will give him her hand and a kingdom. This prefiguration in Renaud de Beaujeu's poem of Melusine's transformations simultaneously provides one of the earliest vernacular renditions of the marvelous motif of the Dragon Maiden, and a compelling example of shape-shifting as an elaborately theatricalized process. The deliberate hiatus that allows reverse transformation from beast to maiden in *Bel Inconnu* may even be seen as a playful narrative transposition of the clerical discourse on marvels, a parodic dimension that possibly resurfaces in the comic overtones of the voyeuristic bath scene in medieval renderings of Melusine. [28]

Each of Melusine's three mixed bodies—the half-woman half-snake; the ambiguously gendered flying "serpent(e)" that leaves behind a human footprint; and the motherly Dragon Maiden—has been subjected to intense scrutiny. Missing is an analysis of transformation as process, rather than as a series of discontinuous liminal states. Indeed, the narrative articulation of paradoxical bodily representations has major implications for the romance's exemplarity. Readings of Melusine's mixed corporality are most often based on the well-known transgression scene in which Raymondin discovers his spouse bathing, transformed into a snake from the navel down, and, to a lesser extent, on the more complex narrative sequence in which Melusine jumps from Lusignan's castle tower and changes into a dragon, leaving on the windowsill "la fourme du pied toute escripte" [the form of her foot inscribed therein] (704, 194).[29] Both scenes thematically connect transformation and composite corporeality even as they frame, depict, and implicitly moralize metamorphosis in strikingly different ways.[30]

28   On parodic animal transformation see Christine Ferlampin-Acher, "Guillaume de Palerne: une parodie," in Élisabeth Gaucher, ed., *La tentation du parodique dans la littérature médiévale, Cahiers des recherche médiévales et humanistes* 15 (2008): 59–72.

29   Laurence De Looze, "'La fourme du pie toute escripte': Melusine and the Entrance into History," in *Melusine of Lusignan*, 125–136.

30   Kevin Brownlee identifies "the discursive components of the composite figure of Melusine in their dynamic (and unstable) juxtapositions and interrelations," and distinguishes "two different kinds of metamorphosis, each resulting from a different type of transgression," "Mélusine's Hybrid Body," 77.

In the voyeuristic bath scene, Raymondin does not witness Melusine's transformation but rather gazes in horror at her serpentine lower body. Presine's curse, at the opening of the romance, tames the pathos of transformation, conferring on Melusine's body a cyclical nature and a moral exemplarity. Melusine's full human-to-animal metamorphosis as she departs Lusignan, by contrast, carries a different moral lesson. Her slow-paced, elaborate transformation into a flying snake is the outcome of her husband's visual and oral transgression, which is recalled as she leaves the courtly stage by a dissonance between what is seen and what is heard: "et ne sçorent que penser, car ils voient la figure d'une serpente et oÿent la voix d'une dame qui yssoit de lui" [Everyone up in the fortress and the townsfolk below were utterly confused to hear a lady's voice issuing from the mouth of a dragon] (706, 195). While Melusine's weekly partial transformation represents penance, her full transformation into a winged dragon vividly illustrates her failed trajectory towards humanity, which is brought about by her husband's shortcomings and announces the ruin of the Lusignan line.

The definitive quality of the human-to-animal transformation is amplified by a third scene of transformation in the romance's epilogue. There, the English sergeant Cersuelle and his mistress witness a "serpente grande et grosse merveilleusement" [a dragon that was extrordinarily large] (810, 227) changing into a tall lady, then back to a dragon. Jean d'Arras provides this nearly contemporary account the better to establish the historical veracity of his subject matter: "comme je vous ay cy dessus retrait en l'hystoire, quant la dicte forteresse doit changier seigneur, la serpente s'appert trois jours devant" [as I have told you already, the dragon always appeared three days before the fortress was to change hands] (810, 227). The scene takes place at night by the fire, recalling both nocturnal terrors such as those described in *Bel Inconnu*, and Melusine's nightly visits to breastfeed her younger sons. The very movements of the unnamed spectral lady express restlessness: "et l'autre heure retournoit le visaige devers le feu et gueres detemps ne se tenoit en un moment" [at other times, she turned toward the fire and was very restless] (812, 228). Jean d'Arras reports three additional eyewitness accounts by men of different conditions who claim to have seen "la serpente de Lusignan" [the dragon of Lusignan]. At the close of the romance, the fairy's transformations come full circle, trapping the founding mother of the Lusignan line in her mythical animal form.

In Jean d'Arras, and Coudrette's narratives, Melusine's mixed bodies and her sons' anatomical anomalies are for the most part described as marvels, with the notable exception of Horrible, whom she orders to be killed. Evolving notions of *prodigia* in the early modern period may have prompted a shift from marvel to monster in the ways such figures were reinterpreted and rewritten.[31] The shift from polysemic marvel to exemplary monster was facilitated by the fact that the Melusine story simultaneously thematized transformation and unions between human beings and supernatural creatures. However, neither Jean d'Arras' nor Coudrette's romance draws a direct link between mixed bodies and mixed ancestry, which is essential to their respective genealogical programs. Jean's prologue firmly associates thematic transformation with alliances between humans and fairies. This is framed by Gervase of Tilbury's account of unions with dragon ladies that come to a sudden end when the spouse breaks his promise: "et aucuns convertissoient en serpens un ou pluseurs jours de la semaine" [Once or even several times a week, some of these women turned into serpents]; "tantost la fae bouta sa teste dedans l'eaue et devins serpente n'onques puis ne fu veue" [she plunged her head into the water, became a serpent and was never seen again] (118, 21). While they prefigure the Melusinian narrative in that breaking the pact brings about the transgressor's ruin, such unions remain childless. Jean d'Arras and Coudrette refocus the tale on the fairy's progeny in a way that prompts critical speculation about the means by which the mother's ontological Alterity may be transmitted. Jean d'Arras in particular experiments with human-fairy intercourse, carefully recording the different outcomes of such encounters, a slippery territory that Coudrette leaves uncharted.[32] To some extent, such narrative case-studies are consistent with medieval theories of generation, for as Douglas Kelly points out, in natural philosophy women were thought to transmit blood, which "carries the order to which one belongs," whereas men preserved and transmitted seed.[33]

---

31   Increasingly restricted to the natural world, prodigious beings and events lost most of their allegorical meaning as naturalists developed a new focus in taxonomies and classification. See Brian M. Ogilvie, *The Science of Describing: Natural Science in Renaissance Europe* (Chicago: University of Chicago Press, 2006), 1–8; Wittowker, *Marvels of the East*, 185.

32   Coudrette's prologue does not include references to unions with supernatural beings, and he only tells the story of Elinas and Presine later in the tale. For a comparison, see Matthew W. Morris, "Les deux Mélusines," in *Écriture et réécriture du merveilleux féerique: autour de Mélusine*, ed. Matthew Morris and Jean-Jacques Vincensini (Paris: Classiques Garnier, 2012), 115–118.

33   Douglas Kelly, "The Domestication of the Marvelous," 42. Kelly references Peter Lombard's *Sententiae* and Nicole Oresme's *Le Livre du ciel et du monde*. See also Williams, *Deformed Discourse*, 117. Gabrielle Spiegel analyzes Melusine's twinship from the perspective of Aristotelian biological thinking and takes up the wider structural issue of the transgression and eventual abolition in the romance of major cultural categories such as "form and nature, body and spirit, human and animal, history and myth, appearance and reality"

It can be argued that Melusine's composite body and her weekly metamorphosis result not from her mixed ancestry but rather from her rebellion against gender roles and patriarchal hierarchy. Cursing her "faulses et mauvaises" daughters, Presine reveals their biological make-up, and the missed opportunity to live their lives as mortals:

> La vertu du germe de ton pere, toy et les autres, eust attrait a sa nature humaine et eussiés esté briefment hors des meurs nimphes et faees sans y retourner. Mais, desormais, je te donne le don que tu seras tous les samedis serpente du nombril en aval. Mais si tu treuves homme qui te veulle prendre a espouse que il te convenance que jamais le samedy ne te verra, non qu'il te descuevre ne ne le die a personne, tu vivras cours naturel comme femme naturelle et mourras naturelment. (134–35)
>
> [The power of your father's seed would eventually have drawn you and your sisters towards his human nature, and you would soon have left behind the ways of nymphs and fairies forever. But I proclaim that henceforth every Saturday you shall become a serpent from the navel down. If, however, you find a man who wishes to marry you and will promise never to look upon you or seek you out on Saturday and never to speak of this to anyone, you shall live out your life as a mortal woman and die naturally.] (25)

If Melusine's moral transgression will be written on her cyclically composite body from this point on, it is important to note that this weekly metamorphosis does not preclude her from living and dying as a mortal.

The complex terms of Presine's curse warn against the temptation to naturalize Alterity through categories of monstrosity, whether medieval or modern. Indeed, as tempting as it may be to see in the composite bodily features and moral flaws of the Lusignans the weakened product of maternal "hybridity," an interpretive move such as this arrests the narrative trajectory of Alterity that lies at the heart of the genealogical romance.[34] The term "hybridity" ultimately

---

("Maternity and Monstrosity," 107). While Spiegel analyzes the ways in which Melusine's "transgressive doublenesss" both figures and undermines cultural categories such as form and spirit, or human and animal, she falls back into a juxtaposition of dualistic readings of Melusine's successive bodies: "by the end of the tale she is further transmogrified into a dragon, initially chthonic and finally aerien, an additional mixing of categories that suggest that, ultimately, Melusine is best understood as a figure of the hybrid *tout court*" (107).

34   Angela Florschuetz discusses "maternal bodies as sites of danger and contamination" in *Marking Maternity*, 155.

underscores the paradoxes underlying the depiction of Melusine and her off-spring.[35] Eight of the Lusignan sons are afflicted by physical or moral deformities yet do not pass on these "mother's marks" to their offspring, a fact that both reaffirms medieval theories of generation and meets the etiological and political purpose of the genealogical narrative.[36] While Melusine's half-woman, half-snake avatar and the lion's claw on Regnault's face are clearly theriomorphic, few narrative cues identify them as monstrous.

Defining hybridity as the mixing of bodily features correlated to general categories such as animal, non-human, or sub-human ultimately presupposes an essentialist framework. To label Melusine and her offspring as monstrous hybrids is to arrest the trajectory of Alterity and to put the reader sensibly in the same position as that of the fascinated voyeur of the Melusine tale. Useful here is the exemplary nature of the central voyeuristic scene, for Raymondin ultimately misreads his spouse's composite body, causing his own misfortune and her transformation into a "serpente" as she leaves the Lusignan domain. If Melusine and her progeny can be described at all as *hybrida*, it is only with respect to their mixed origins.[37] Indeed, when used metaphorically to describe the Lusignans' composite bodies, the term may be anachronistic in that

---

35   Rupert T. Pickens, "The Poetics of Paradox," 48–75.

36   Critics have proposed different interpretations of the fact that the last two children have no monstrous features, from a sign of the fairy's evolution towards humanity and a weakening of "mother-marks," (Kelly, "Domestication of the Marvelous," 42) to parthenogenesis, as suggested by Joanna Pavlevski, "Naissances féeriques et fondation de lignée dans *La Noble Histoire de Lusignan* et *Le Roman de Parthenay* de Coudrette," *Questes* 27 (Jan. 2014): 125–52. On asymmetry in the series see in particular Jane H. M. Taylor, "Melusine's Progeny: Patterns and Perplexities," in *Melusine of Lusignan*, 165–84. On Geoffrey, see Suzanne Roblin, "Le sanglier et la serpente", in *Métamorphose et bestiaire fantastique*, ed. Laurence Harf-Lancner (Paris: Collection de l'Ecole Normale Supérieure de Jeunes Filles, 1985), 246–285; Sophie Roubaud, "La mort de Fromont et d'Horrible: l'apport de Coudrette," in *550 Jahre deutsche Melusine-Coudrette und Thüring von Ringoltingen,* ed. André Schnyder et al. (Bern: Peter Lang, 2008), 237–50.

37   The Latin terms *hybrida* or *ibrida* (mongrels) commonly referred to mixed-breed animals or born of different species (*animalia ambigena* or *bigenera*), as in Isidore of Seville, *Etymologiae* XII, quoted in Minton Warren, "On the Etymology of Hybrid (lat. Hybrida)," *The American Journal of Philology* 5, no. 4 (1884): 501. According to Alexander Adam, the word *hybridae* was also used, with a derogatory meaning, for the offspring of people of different origin, "the children of a Roman Citizen, whether man or woman, and a foreigner, were accounted spurious, and their condition little better than that of slaves," *Roman Antiquities* (London: T. Cadell et al., 1830), 428. As recorded by *Dictionnaire Le Robert* the first known use of the term *hybride* in French dates from 1596.

bodily hybridity does not fit the categories at work in medieval taxonomies of prodigious beings, nor is there a direct causal connection between cross-mating and monstrosity in medieval teratology or in courtly narratives.[38] A complex, historically constructed category, hybridity can hardly be used neutrally as a descriptive term.[39] The figures that the modern reader identifies as "hybrids" are better understood as sites of exploration of what Jeffrey Jerome Cohen calls "difficult middles" placed at the interstices of ethnic and religious boundaries.

Following Melusine's transformations in print will help clarify the cultural trajectory of the fairy's metamorphic corporality in its dynamic tension with the stable monstrosity of her offspring. Rubrication and iconography generated in the transmission of Jean d'Arras' and Coudrette's romances point to diverse rhetorical, poetical, and symbolic functions of marvelous motifs, as well as to their progressive reinterpretation or clarification as they migrate through space, time, and social strata. Of particular interest are the textual and visual reconfiguration of Melusine's polycorporality from the 1478 French *editio princeps* of Jean d'Arras' romance to its Spanish 1526 translation.

The printed trajectory of the Melusine legend is particulary complex due to the two competing Old French versions. During the fifteenth century, Coudrette's poem exerted a lasting influence in Northern Europe, thanks to the German prose version produced by Thüring von Ringoltingen in 1456.[40] The Old German version was the first to be printed in 1467 and was quickly

---

38   There seems to be a clear break between classical and medieval explanations of human-animal mixed bodies. Both Pliny and Plutarch attribute theriomorphic monstrosity to intercourse between humans and animals (Kappler, *Monstres*, 147). Rare are the medieval texts that explicitly present theriomorphic monsters as resulting from *contra naturam* unions. One of the few examples is the ox-man described by Gerald of Wales in *Topographia Hibernica* and in *Expugnatio Hibernica*; see Cohen, *Hybridity, Identity, and Monstrosity in Medieval Britain*, 88–90. More frequently, theriomorphic body parts are attributed to the mother's excessive lust. See Williams, *Deformed Discourse*, 179–197.

39   The Latin term strictly referred to crossbred animals, or, by extension and in derogatory fashion, to people of mixed origins. In its modern usage it denotes either heterogeneity in origin or nature, as in Latin, or mixture. As Jeffrey Jerome Cohen puts it, to describe the paradoxical aspects of mixed collective identities in Medieval England, "hybridity is a fusion and a disjunction, a conjoining of differences that cannot simply harmonize," *Hybridity, Identity, and Monstrosity*, 2.

40   *Thüring von Ringoltingen, Melusine nach den Handschriften kritisch herausgegeben*, ed. Karin Schneider (Berlin: E. Schmidt, 1958); *The Romans of Partenay, or of Lusignen: Otherwise Known as the Tale of Melusine: translated from the French of La Coudrette (before 1500 A. D.)*, rev. ed. by Walter W. Skeat (London: Trübner for the Early English Text Society), 1899.

translated into other vernaculars.[41] The success of the richly illustrated 1474 German edition may have prompted French-speaking printers to dust off the French prose version, first printed in Switzerland by Adam Steinschaber in August 1478, with colored woodcuts loosely inspired by those in Richel's incunabula.[42] While subsequent editions in Lyons and Paris followed the text printed by Steinschaber, they reused or copied Richel's woodcuts in an interesting process that visually reduced the disparities in Jean d'Arras' and Coudrette's treatment of marvelous and magic elements. In both series of woodcuts, the iconographic program underscores the central role of Melusine's sixth son, Geoffrey. The contrast between the cyclical half-snake and Geoffrey, who permanently displays a boar tusk, eventually shaped the early printed trajectory of the romance in France. As first noted by Laurence Harf-Lancner, Renaissance printers such as Michel Le Noir resolved the thematic and generic tensions at work in the genealogical romance by splitting Jean's narrative into two tales, featuring respectively Melusine (*Histoire de la belle Melusine,* 1517), and Geoffrey Big-Tooth (*Histoire de Geoffroy la Grant Dent,* ca.1530).[43]

Jean's prose was translated into Castillian Spanish and printed in Toulouse by Johann Parix and Etienne Cléblat under the title *Historia de la linda Melosina* (1489) and printed again in Seville in 1526 by Jacob Cromberger. The Spanish *editio princeps* tends to reduce the ambiguity of marvelous signs.[44]

---

41   Thüring von Ringoltingen, *Melusine (1456). Nach dem Erstdruck Basel: Richel um 1473/74,* ed. André Schnyder and Ursula Rautenberg (Wiesbaden: Reichert, 2006). On the dissemination of Richel's woodcuts, see Lydia Zeldenrust, "Serpent or Half-Serpent? Bernhard Richel's *Melusine* and the Making of a Western European Icon," *Neophilologus* 100, no. 1 (2016): 19–41.

42   *La première édition de l'Histoire de la Belle Mélusine de Jean d'Arras, imprimée par A. Steinschaber à Genève en 1478,* ed. Wilhelm Joseph (Paris: Champion, 1923). On the choice by French-speaking printers of Jean d'Arras' version over that of Coudrette, see Matthew W. Morris, "Political Expediency and Censorship in Fifteenth-Century France," *Postscript* 18–19 (2002): 35–44 and "Les deux Mélusines," 107.

43   Laurence Harf-Lancner, "*L'Histoire de Mélusine* et *l'Histoire de Geoffroi à la grant dent*: les éditions du roman de Jean d'Arras au XVIe siècle," *Bibliothèque d'Humanisme et Renaissance* 50 (1988): 349–366. For an in-depth analysis of French editions of Jean d'Arras' romance, see Hélène Bouquin, "Éditions et adaptations de *l'Histoire de Mélusine* de Jean d'Arras (XVe-XIXe siècle): Les aventures d'un roman médiéval" (PhD diss., École nationale des chartes, 2000).

44   *Historia de la linda Melusina,* ed. Ivy A. Corfis (Madison: University of Wisconsin Press, 1986). For the progressive erasure of marvelous features in the two Castillian editions, see Ana Pairet, "Intervernacular Translation in the Early Decades of Print: Chivalric Romance and the Marvelous in the Spanish *Melusine* (1489–1526)," in *Translating the Middle Ages,* ed. Karen L. Fresco and Charles D. Wright (Burlington, VT: Ashgate, 2012), 86–101.

In a striking example, the lion's claw that graces the cheek of Anthoine, Melusine's fourth son, becomes a simple birthmark, as comparison with the text of the first French printed edition shows:

> mais au naistre il apporta en la joue ung grif de lyon, de quoy moult furent ceulz qui le visrent esbahys (117)
>
> [at birth he bore on his cheek a lion's claw, which astonished all those who saw him]
>
> Et auia en la quijxada vna señal como vna pata de leon, de lo qual eran todos muy maravillados (50)
>
> [And on his cheek he had a birthmark that looked like a lion's claw, which amazed everybody]

The two Spanish translations derive from the early Lyons edition, which itself follows the text of the Geneva 1478 imprint.[45] Translation of specific phrases reveals how particular motifs were reinterpreted and culturally adapted over a span of four decades. One telling example is the ellipsis in the depiction of Melusine as she jumps out of the castle window that has framed her courtly existence, and into the space of legend:

> et lors se mua en forme de serpent moult grande, grosse et longue comme de xv. piés; et sachiés que en la pierre sur quoy elle passa au partir de la fenestre, demoura et encores est empraint la forme du piet d'elle (359)[46]
>
> [and then she changed into the shape of a very big fat snake, about 15 feet long; and you should know that on the stone on which she stepped as she jumped out of the window was left and is still imprinted the shape of her foot]
>
> E luego se mudo en figura de sierpe muy grande et gruesa e luenga como de.xv. pies. E sabed que en la piedra do ella paso a partir de la ventana, queda avn la forma de su pie (162)[47]

---

45   For the genealogy of the Castilian translations see Donatella Gagliardi, "La historia de la linda Melosina: una o due versioni castigliane del romanzo di Jean d'Arras?," Medioevo romanzo 22, no. 1 (1998): 116–41.

46   Quotes from the French editio princeps (Geneva, 1478) come from Jean d'Arras, Melusine: Nouvelle édition conforme à celle de 1478, ed. Charles Brunet (Paris: Jannet, 1854). Quotes from the Castillian editions follow Corfis, Historia de la linda Melusina. Translations of the French and Castillian are the author's.

47   Toulouse: Parix et Cléblat, 1489, fol. 134.

[And then she changed into the figure of a snake very large and fat and about 15 feet long. And you should know that on the stone where she stepped as she left the window, still remains the shape of her foot]

salto de la ventana y va por el ayre volando en figura de sierpe muy grande (163)[48]

[she jumped out the window, flying through the air in the shape of a very large snake]

The retelling of Melusine's flight in the 1526 edition provides a spectacular example of how her marvelous footprint was redrawn in early modern editions. The second Castilian translation attenuates the fairy's terrifying liminality by silencing her sighs after she reminds her husband to put their son Horrible to death. This omission anticipates the fairy's transformation from mother and spouse into a fantastic flying beast, a process that is also omitted. Emphasizing the hiatus between human and beast, the second Castilian translation literally erases Melusine's footprint, the metonymy of the humanity the flying snake has left behind.

The textual and visual Melusinian archive is rich, diverse and complex. And yet, the analysis of Melusine's mixed corporality often comes up short, as if the reader's first impulse were to arrest diegetic instability by superimposing metaphorical, exemplary, or allegorical meanings onto fluid, anamorphic figures. One could argue that this gap between representation and interpretation is by design, for at the heart of the medieval narrative lies a tension between the tale of transformation and its moral or allegorical significance. Studying transformation as a process both intratextually and intertextually, as well as across a variety of media, provides the means to grasp the fluidity and multiplicity of Melusine and to account for the fascination that this elusive figure continues to exert.

---

48   Seville: Cromberger, 1526, fol. 53b-53d.

CHAPTER 3

Mermaid, Mother, Monster, and More: Portraits of the Fairy Woman in Fifteenth- and Sixteenth-Century *Melusine* Narratives

Caroline Prud'Homme

The story of a beautiful fairy who transforms into a serpent has long been known in France. Early on, the tale was associated with the *pays de Linges*, or Saintonge; in an *exemplum* by Geoffrey of Auxerre (ca.1180), as well as in the story recorded by Vincent de Beauvais in his *Speculum naturale* [*The Mirror of Nature*] (ca.1250), the fairy is surprised in the bathtub by one of her female servants.[1] A similar tale appears in Gervase of Tilbury's *Otia Imperialis* [*Recreation for an Emperor*] (ca.1210), where the mortal husband of the fairy woman is named Raymond, or Roger, de Château Rousset, lives near Aix-en-Provence, and sees his wife with a serpent tail, bathing.[2] In Pierre Bersuire's *Reductorium morale* [*Redaction of Morals*] (ca.1342), the fairy and her husband are unnamed, but their story in essence is that of Melusine and Raymondin: the founder of the fortress of Lusignan and of the Lusignan-Parthenay lineage, a fairy woman is caught in the bathtub by her mortal husband, at which time she transforms into a serpent, only to return in this guise when the fortress changes hands.[3] An expanded Latin narrative may have existed ca.1375 in the

---

[1]   There appears to have been confusion between *Linge* (*Lingonica dioecesis, Lingonensi provincia*), another name used for Saintes, and *Langres* in certain versions of the story. See Jacques Le Goff and Emanuel Le Roy Ladurie, "Mélusine maternelle et défricheuse," *Annales Économies, Sociétés, Civilisations* 26, no. 3–4 (1971): 589. Walter Map's "Henno cum dentibus," another fairy-serpent tale, is rather set in Normandy. See *De nugis curialium*, ed. Montague Rhodes James (Oxford: Clarendon Press, 1914), 176–9. Geoffrey of Auxerre, "Sermo XV," in *Super apocalypsim*, ed. Ferrucio Gastaldelli (Rome: Ed. di Storia e letteratura, 1970), 186–7. Vincent of Beauvais, *Speculum naturale* II, 127. See Jacques Le Goff, "Mélusine maternelle et défricheuse," 590. This story is based on a now-lost narrative by Hélinand de Froidmont (ca.1200).

[2]   Gervase of Tilbury, *Otia Imperialia: Recreation for an Emperor*, ed. S.E. Banks and J.W. Binns (Oxford: Clarendon Press, 2002), 88–91 (1.15 "De oculis apertis post peccatum").

[3]   Pierre Bersuire, "Prologue to Book 14," in *Reductorium morale* (Paris: Claude Chevallon, 1521). Quoted by Laurence Harf-Lancner, *Les fées au Moyen Âge. Morgane et Mélusine. La naissance des fées* (Paris: Champion, 1984), 57.

library of Duc Jean de Berry.[4] It likely attributed the name Melusine to the fairy woman and was the source for Jean d'Arras' *Mélusine ou la noble histoire de Lusignan* (composed ca.1387–93) and Coudrette's *Le roman de Mélusine ou histoire de Lusignan* (written ca.1401).

Both narratives circulated in manuscript and print during the fifteenth and sixteenth centuries and were adapted in European languages during the same period. The Swiss patrician Thüring von Ringoltingen translated Coudrette's romance in 1456. This German *Melusine* was printed for the first time in Basel in 1473–4 by Bernard Richel, even before Jean d'Arras' text first appeared in print in 1478, in Geneva. The German *Melusine* was undoubtedly a hit: printed 27 times from 1473–4 to 1587,[5] it circulated extensively as a chapbook, which, in turn, formed the basis for translations in Dutch (1500), Czech (1555), Polish (1569), Danish (1667), and Russian (1677), among others. A Spanish adaptation of Jean d'Arras appeared in Toulouse in 1489, printed by Jean Parix, known for having introduced the printing press to Spain, and his associate, Étienne Clébat.[6] Jacob and Juan Cromberger printed another Spanish edition in Seville in 1526.[7] An edition of the *Historia de Melosina* printed in Valencia in 1512 has not survived.[8] Jean d'Arras was also adapted to Dutch in print in 1491 by Gheraert Leeu, and to English, in manuscript, ca.1500; small fragments of an English printed *Melusine* exist.[9] An anonymous translator introduced Coudrette to English readers,

---

4   Jules Guiffrey, *Inventaires de Jean duc de Berry: 1401–1416* (Paris: Ernest Leroux, 1894): I, 264–5 (items 980 and 981 are a two-volume Latin manuscript titled *Istoire de Lesignen*).

5   Laurence Harf-Lancner, "Du manuscrit à l'imprimé: l'illustration du *Roman de Mélusine* de Thüring von Ringoltingen à Jean d'Arras," in *550 Jahre deutsche Melusine – Coudrette und Thüring von Ringoltingen. 550 de Mélusine allemande – Coudrette et Thüring von Ringoltingen, actes du colloque organisé par les universités de Berne et de Lausanne en août 2006*, ed. André Schnyner and Jean-Claude Mühlethaler (Bern: Peter Lang, 2008), 151.

6   See Anna Casas Aguilar's contribution to this volume for a discussion of the Spanish *Historia de la linda Melosina*.

7   According to Miguel Ángel Frontón Simón, the edition of 1526 is a stylistic revision of the 1489 edition rather than an independent new edition. "*La historia de la linda Melosina*. Edicion y estudio de los textos españoles" (PhD diss., Universidad Complutense de Madrid, 2002), 157.

8   Alan D. Deyermond, "*La historia de la linda Melosina*: Two Spanish versions of a French Romance," in Alan D. Deyermond, ed., *Medieval Hispanic Studies Presented to Rita Hamilton* (London, Tamesis Books, 1976), 62.

9   Six fragments of an English printed *Melusine* attributed to Wynkyn de Worde ca.1510 are held at Oxford's Bodleian Library (Vet. Al d. 18.) See Tania M. Colwell, "The Middle English Melusine: Evidence for an early printed edition of the prose romance in the Bodleian

ca.1500–1525.[10] Interestingly, no Italian adaptation of Melusine is known for the premodern period.

From the late fourteenth to the sixteenth century, a variety of European authors chose to bring to their audience the story of Melusine. Depicting the character posed a challenge due to her multiple facets: human and otherworldly, daughter and fairy, good Christian and criminal, wife yet serpent, founder of a lineage and yet mermaid, exemplary citizen yet monster, mother and dragon. While essentially the same story is told in the medieval and early modern *Melusine* narratives, each author reinvents the character and makes her unique. Each calls attention to specific details that support his interpretation of the fairy woman. Jean d'Arras regularly underlines his character's complexity as a way to distance his work from folk legends. The two anonymous Spanish translators reinterpret Jean's narrative to meet the expectations of *libros de caballerías* readers; they portray Melusine as a courtly lady. The English translators of Jean d'Arras and Coudrette constantly erase from their texts magical and otherworldly elements that English readers of the sixteenth century would likely have associated with the devil; Melusine's monstrous nature is glossed over and her role as a good wife and an exemplary Christian are the focal points. In Coudrette, Melusine is both a romance character in the Arthurian fashion and a being that inspires fear and fascination. The Swiss writer Thüring von Ringoltingen conceives of Melusine as Other first, human second; he responds to his readers' fascination for the monstrous by depicting an otherworldly character who is still accessible due to her Christian faith.

Each author's approach to Melusine is revealed through the manner in which he portrays her in his narrative. Close textual readings of seminal passages—in particular, the introduction of Melusine in the prologue, the encounter between King Elinas and the fairy Pressine, Melusine and Raymondin's first meeting, the bath scene, and the final transformation—illustrate how the character subtly changes with each different *Melusine* narrative.

Authors find in prologues a unique place to introduce their fictional universe to their audience. They use strategies to entice readers to continue

---

Library", *The Journal of the Early Book Society for the Study of Manuscripts and Printing History* 17 (2014): 254–82. See Lydia Zeldenrust's contribution to this volume for a discussion of Leeu's Dutch prose *Meluzine* and Zoë Enstone's chapter for an analysis of the English prose translation.

10 See Jennifer Alberghini's contribution to this volume for a discussion of the English translator's project.

reading and guide their interpretation of the main character within a familiar framework that makes her acceptable and captivating. Jean d'Arras and Coudrette likely wrote for a public already familiar with the legend of the fairy serpent and her connection to Lusignan, but each approaches the material quite differently. Jean chooses to evoke fairy legends to set apart his own narrative, while Coudrette omits them entirely and rather sets his text within the tradition of romances of chivalry. Jean uses prolepsis, where Coudrette prefers spectacular turns of events.

In his prologue, Jean d'Arras connects with his audience by recounting stories about fairies. These tales are used as prolepsis of his own narrative and as tools to highlight the complexity of his literary character. He first recalls a tale circulating in Poitou: fairies and other similar creatures appear as tricksters who play pranks on children at night, warm the latter by the fire ("les bestournent ou ardent"),[11] and leave them unharmed, as if they had never visited. Fairies inspire mixed feelings; they are associated with the marvelous, with strange events that people are aware of, yet cannot explain. *Mirabilia*, in the Middle Ages, elicit astonishment, fear, fascination, and admiration, according to Daniel Poirion.[12] Jean emphasizes trickery and deceit, suggesting a darker side to fairies, an aspect that is much more developed in Thüring von Ringoltingen's narrative. In Jean d'Arras, such visits echo the episode of Melusine's magical return to nurse her two youngest children, once she has fully transformed into a serpent and has departed from the castle of Mervent. This is one of numerous passages in the romance that have a proleptic function, announcing events that will unfold later in the narrative.

After having recalled fairy legends, Jean d'Arras continues his discussion by introducing two short tales from an *auctoritas*, Gervase of Tilbury: in the first, a beautiful fairy enters marriage with a mortal on the condition that he will not see her on Saturdays. She brings him happiness and fortune, as long as he keeps his word, but will transform into a serpent and disappear if he breaks his vow. The second story differs from the first only in the taboo imposed by the

---

11   Jean d'Arras, *Mélusine ou la noble histoire de Lusignan*, ed. Jean-Jacques Vincensini (Paris: Librairie Générale Française, 2003), 116. Hereafter Vincensini, *Mélusine*. In the printed edition of 1478 by Adam Steinschaber, the passage about *bestourner*, a word that was no longer in use, is replaced with "et ostent et emportent aulcunes fois les enfants des berceaux" [and sometimes snatch and carry infants away from their cradles], Jean d'Arras, *Mélusine. Nouvelle édition conforme à celle de 1478, revue et corrigée*, ed. Charles Brunet (Paris: P. Jannet, 1854), 12.

12   Daniel Poirion, *Le merveilleux dans la littérature française du Moyen Âge* (Paris: Presses Universitaires de France, 1982), 4.

fairy to her husband, that of not seeing her during childbirth. The two tales correspond to the two main narrative patterns of Jean d'Arras' romance, the story of Melusine and that of her mother, Pressine.[13] Jean again foretells moments of his narrative and traces a portrait of fairies as complex beings who could be both benevolent and maleficent.

Towards the end of his prologue, Jean d'Arras finally introduces his main character by her greatest achievement: "La noble fortresse de Lisignen en Poictou fu fondee par une faee" [the noble fortress of Lusignan in Poitou was founded by a fairy].[14] It is the only moment in which Melusine is clearly defined as a fairy; the word *faée* itself is very sparingly used within the narrative, as Laurence Harf-Lancner has shown.[15] Jean d'Arras limits the fairy label associated with Melusine to the margins of his text as a way to bring the reader in with more familiar notions, but also as a strategy to make a legendary figure into a complex romance character. Jean anchors his heroine within a certain lineage, as is the case for many heroes of romances of chivalry, and he uses the well-known device of delayed naming. It is noteworthy that the founder of the Lusignan fortress, who is also the beautiful woman from the fountain, receives the name Melusine d'Albanie[16] at her wedding ceremony, when she officially enters the public sphere and integrates into the human world.[17]

As is to be expected, the Spanish, English, and Dutch adaptations generally abridge Jean d'Arras' prologue, and are not always faithful to his approach to the material. Copies of the 1491 Antwerp edition circulated without a prologue, opening *in media res* with the story of King Elinas of Albany;[18] other copies bore a short prologue expunging almost everything from the source, apart from the story of the knight of Château Rousset (albeit without the name

---

13   See Sara Sturm-Maddox, "Crossed Destinies: Narrative Programs in the *Roman de Melusine*," in *Melusine of Lusignan: Founding Fiction in Late Medieval France*, ed. Donald Maddox and Sara Sturm-Maddox (Athens, GA: University of Georgia Press, 1996), 12–31.

14   Vincensini, *Mélusine*, 122.

15   Harf-Lancner, *Les fées au Moyen Âge*, 41. The few occurrences include the "faée condicion" [fairy nature] of Melusine and her sisters, and "la fontaine de Soif, la fontaine faee" [the fountain of Thirst, the fairy fountain] (Vincensini, *Mélusine*, 134, 158).

16   Vincensini, *Mélusine*, 196.

17   In the opening narrative about Elinas and Pressine, Melusine is called by her name, but the connection between her and the lady whom Raymondin encounters at the *Fontaine de Soif* is only suggested. The Seville edition of 1526 names Melusine from the beginning.

18   Jean d'Arras, *De schoone historie van Melusina* (Antwerp: Gheraert Leeu, 1491), fol. 1ʳ.

of its author, Gervase). The word *alvinne*, fairy, frequently occurs without any elaboration,[19] as if the word itself were enough to situate the reader within the chosen frame of reference. The two Spanish translations, on the contrary, bring the material closer to the reader with local references and connections. In these translations, fairies are tied to a regional legend of a vampire-like creature, known in Spain and Portugal as *xorguinas*.[20] Fairies, here, do not poke fun at children; rather, they suck their blood.[21] The words "nuestros ancianos" [our ancestors] and "nuestros padres"[22] [our elders], while taken directly from Jean d'Arras, are coupled with the repeated words "los dizen" [they say] and the reference to imaginary visions;[23] they suggest that these legends are not imports from faraway Poitou, but are part of the public's own folk tradition. In the Spanish editions, the strategy is to integrate the Melusine narrative within a certain framework familiar to the audience, in this case folk tales, elsewhere, *libros de caballerías* with their courtly characters.

In sixteenth-century England, fairy tales would have been seen in a different light: magic and prophecy are associated with the devil.[24] It is not surprising that the English translator of Jean d'Arras abridges the passage about fairy pranks. He rather focuses his discussion on Gervase of Tilbury. He stresses the latter's status as an *auctoritas* ("a man worshipfull & of credence," "he saith for certayn," "recounted for trouth")[25] and his interpretation of fairyhood as a punishment from God. There is an intention here to distance Melusine from any

---

19   See G. Ru, "La traduction néerlandaise de Jean d'Arras" (Master's thesis, University of Ghent, 2008), 66–74.

20   See Fabiàn Alejandro Campagne, "Witch or Demon? Fairies, Vampires, and Nightmares in Early Modern Spain," *Acta Ethnographica Hungarica* 53.2 (2008): 381–410.

21   "[…] y dizen que sean xorguinas" (vampires), "E aun dizen las viejas que los tuestan al fuego y les beuen la sangre" [and they said that they were vampires; and the elders said that they threw the children in the fire and drank their blood] (Toulouse, 1489). Jean d'Arras, *Historia de la linda Melosina*, ed. Ivy A. Corfis (Madison: The Hispanic Seminary of Medieval Studies, 1986), 3 (Seville, 1526.) Hereafter Corfis, *Melosina*.

22   Corfis notes the usage of "Nuestros mayores" instead of "nuestros padres" in the 1526 edition (*Melosina,* 3–4.)

23   "Cada dia oymos dezir a nuestros padres que ay algunas gentes que de muchas maneras de visiones aparecieron" [every day we hear from our elders that there are people who have had different kinds of visions (about fairies)] (Corfis, *Melosina,* 3).

24   Misty Urban, *Monstrous Women in Middle English Romance* (Lewiston, NY: Edwin Mellen Press, 2010), 88.

25   *Melusine compiled (1382–1394 A.D.) by Jean d'Arras, Englisht about 1500*, ed. Alexander K. Donald (London: Kegan Paul, Trench, Trübner & Co. Early English Text Society, 1895), 4. Hereafter Donald, *Melusine.*

demonic associations, so that she can be perceived by the reader in a positive light and integrated into a Christian framework.

Unlike Jean d'Arras and his translators, Coudrette obliterates fairy lore and immediately sets his text within the realm of romance: Lancelot, Perceval, and Gawain are named,[26] and the heroine is introduced by name and lineage. Though Melusine is presented as a fairy,[27] there is no mention of her transformation into a serpent until the bathing scene. Where Jean d'Arras opts for prolepsis, Coudrette prefers spectacular turns of events. Melusine appears as a conventional romance character with a certain magical dimension rather than as a well-known legendary figure. As such, her identity is concealed beyond the prologue, until she takes Raymondin as husband.[28]

The anonymous English translator of Coudrette follows his source very closely in the prologue and elsewhere. Yet he also adds his own touch, playing on the proximity between the words *fair* and *fairy* in his language: "Thys castell was made with on of faire" [29] [This castle was made by one of the fairies]; "The fair Melusigne men gan hire to call" [30] [The fair Melusine as men began to call her]; "This fayrie woman";[31] "thys fayr layde."[32] The medieval *topos* of the fair lady, noble in rank, beauty and character, finds new resonance here, where the fair lady is also a fairy.

Thüring von Ringoltingen's romance significantly departs from the other *Melusine* narratives when it comes to the introduction of his character. Rather than creating a sense of familiarity for the public with allusions to folk tales, Christian values, conventional romance characters, or literary types, Thüring appeals to his readers' fascination for monsters, beasts, and other magical creatures[33] by presenting them with Otherness:

---

26   Coudrette, *Le roman de Mélusine ou histoire de Lusignan*, ed. Eleanor Roach (Paris: Klinck-sieck, 1982), 107, lines 21 and 23. Hereafter: Roach, *Roman de Mélusine*.

27   "Melusine fut appellee / La fee que vous ay nommee" [Melusine she was called, the fairy whom I just named] (Roach, *Roman de Mélusine*, 109, lines 75–6).

28   Corfis, *Melosina*, 144, line 1095.

29   Coudrette, *The Romans of Parthenay or of Lusignen: otherwise known as the Tale of Melu-sine. Translated from the French of La Coudrette (about 1500–1520)*, ed. Walter W. Skeat (London: N. Trübner, Early English Text Society, 1866), 5, line 142. Hereafter Skeat.

30   Skeat, *Romans of Parthenay*, 5, line 147.

31   Skeat, *Romans of Parthenay*, 6, line 148.

32   Skeat, *Romans of Parthenay*, 20, lines 365 and 381.

33   Classen, "Love and Fear of the Foreign: Thüring von Ringoltingen's *Melusine* (1456). A Xenological Analysis," *Daphnis* 33, no. 1–2 (2004): 97–113, at 103.

Düss aventürlich buoch bewiset unss von einer frowen genant Melusine, die ein merfaye und darzuo ein geborne küngin und uss dem berge
Awalon komen wass, der selbe berg lit in Franckenrich. Und wart düsse
merfaye alle samstag vom nabel hinunder ein grosser langer würm, dan
sü ein halb gespönste was.

[This book of adventures reports of a woman called Melusine, who
was a mermaid and born a queen. She came from the mountain Avalon,
which is located in France. Every Saturday this mermaid transformed
into a big long snake from her navel down because she was half a ghost.][34]

Thüring's character is the epitome of hybridity and difference. Where his
source omits Melusine's hybrid body in the prologue, he chooses to describe
her tail with the adjectives "big" or "tall" and "long" ("grosser," "langer"). He
features her otherworldliness: a mermaid who transforms into a serpent and
comes from Avalon,[35] the legendary resting place of Arthurian heroes, and is a
ghost.[36] In Thüring's literary aesthetics, Melusine's difference is to be celebrated as an object of curiosity, both frightening and fascinating. The word *gespönste* is frequently used to highlight unusual, otherworldly events or features: the
wedding attendants think that they must be seeing a mirage, an illusion; the
erection of the fortress of Lusignan is so uncanny that witnesses do not know
what to make of it; and the various physical oddities of Melusine's sons are
signs of her ghostly nature.[37]

More than other authors who play up Melusine's humanity, Thüring performs a balancing act between *monsterizing* and humanizing his character, so

---

34   Thüring von Ringoltingen, *Melusine*, ed. Karin Schneider (Berlin: E. Schmidt, 1958), 36.
      Hereafter Schneider, *Melusine*. English translation by Albrecht Classen, "Love and Fear of
      the Foreign", 103. "Wurm" can be translated as "worm," "dragon," or "snake."

35   In Coudrette, the mention of Avalon appears much later in the narrative, when Geof-
      frey Great-Tooth discovers the tomb of his grandfather Elinas (Roach, *Roman de Mélusine*,
      272, line 4945).

36   In Coudrette, Raymondin says of Melusine "Je croy que ce n'est que fantosme" ["I believe
      this is only a fantasy"] (Roach, *Roman de Mélusine*, 235, line 3810) when he learns of the
      tragedy of Maillezais abbey. The mermaid and Avalon references may have been taken
      from Jean d'Arras for their striking effect: Pressine's voice is compared in beauty to that
      of a mermaid, and Melusine and her sisters imprison their father in a mountain in North-
      umberland, which is not on the island of Avalon *per se* (Vincensini, *Mélusine*, 122, 134).
      For an in-depth study of Thüring's style and translation, see Elisabeth Pinto-Mathieu, *Le
      roman de Melusine de Coudrette et son adaptation dans le roman en prose de Thüring von
      Ringoltingen* (Göppinger: Kummerle, 1990).

37   Schneider, *Melusine*, 50, 54.

that she is both fascinating and relatable, frightening and familiar to his audience. The human and the non-human are thus often associated in his text. Above, Melusine is a ghost; yet she is also a woman, a queen, and the founder of a noble lineage. Below, ghost and mother are associated again:

> Und das ist von eyner frowen genant Melusine, die ein merfrowe gewesen un noch ist, dass sü nit gantz nach mönschlicher natur ein wib gewesen ist; besunder hat sü von Gottes wunder ein andre gar frömde und selczne usszeichnung gehebt, und wie das sige, das ir wandel sich etwas eynem vast grossen Gottes wunder oder gespönst glichete, so hat sü natürliche und eliche kint gelassen.
>
> [And (the story speaks of) a woman named Melusine, who was a fairy and still is, and she was not completely of human nature. She was marked through the power of God with very strange and curious characteristics, and although her nature was more like that of a miraculous being created by God or of a ghost, she left behind natural and legitimate children.][38]

Melusine, as a literary character, evolves in a human fictional universe, and her status as mother ties her to this world, as does her faith. Throughout the narrative, the heroine appears as an exemplary Christian. She introduces herself as being of God to Raymondin; she establishes several monasteries in Poitou and encourages her husband to have faith and trust in God upon hearing of the tragedy of Maillezais.[39] Melusine's faith stands out in Thüring's narrative because it seems in contradiction with her Otherness, so frequently evoked with the word "gespönste."

In Thüring as in other *Melusine* narratives, the integration of the fairy serpent into a Christian framework contributes to guiding the readers' interpretation; she cannot be a creature of the devil since she acts as a true Christian. Furthermore, her condition as a fairy comes from God: it is a divine gift for Thüring, but a divine punishment for Jean d'Arras.[40] In both cases, Melusine can be seen as a Christian *mirabilium*, a marvel of God to be admired and reflected upon.

The prologues in the *Melusine* narratives introduce a character within a frame of reference familiar to readers, be it fairy tales, romances of chivalry, courtly literature, or contemporary Christian culture. They prepare readers for the story to unfold and they place signposts to guide their interpretation. They

---

38 Schneider, *Melusine,* 36. English translation by Classen, "Love and Fear," 105.
39 Schneider, *Melusine,* 51, 91.
40 Vincensini, *Mélusine,* 118.

do so within the narrative as well, including in the story of King Elinas of Albany and the fairy Pressine. This episode contributes to making Melusine a complex literary character by adding a backstory, an explanation for her weekly transformation into a half serpent. It also introduces the reader to a fairy who echoes the heroine, but also has individual traits.

Jean d'Arras approaches Pressine in a fashion similar to that of the prologue; certain elements signal to readers that they are within the realm of romance, while others refer to common or learned ideas. The meeting between Elinas and Pressine takes place during a hunt in a forest, near a well, elements that set the scene for chivalric adventure or lovers' encounters. At the same time, Jean recalls fairies from the prologue by identifying Pressine as such: "celle qui tousjours chantoit si melodieusement que oncques seraine, faee ne nimphe ne chanta tant doulcement" [she was singing so melodiously that no mermaid, fairy nor nymph ever sung so sweetly].[41] Akin to a mermaid, Pressine bewitches Elinas with her voice, so much so that he momentarily loses his bearings.[42]

Jean d'Arras also connects with his readers' horizon of expectations by evoking a common idea about fairies: their beauty cannot be surpassed, as the French expression "plus belle que fée" [more beautiful than a fairy] suggests.[43] When Elinas gazes at the singer, he is taken by her beauty; she is the most beautiful woman he has ever seen.[44] After about fifteen lines, Jean reiterates the beauty of singer and song in almost identical terms: every time, the noun *beauté* is used, yet there is no further description, as if the use of the superlative renders any descriptive attempt unnecessary.

This idea of the beautiful fairy may have influenced a shift in the title of the *Melusine* narratives from manuscript to print. In late fourteenth- and fifteenth-century manuscripts, the Lusignan lineage prevails, as seen in those used by Jean d'Arras, *Mélusine ou la noble histoire de Lusignan*; Coudrette, *Le roman de Mélusine ou histoire de Lusignan*; and the English translation of Coudrette, *The Romans of Parthenay or of Lusignen: otherwise known as the Tale of Melusine*. In fifteenth- and sixteenth-century printed editions, the character is dissociated

---

41   Vincensini, *Mélusine,* 122.

42   Elinas is bewitched ("repeuz et abusé"), he does not know whether it is day or night nor if he is sleeping or awake: "il ne scet s'il est jour ou nuit, ou s'il dort ou veille" (Vincensini, *Mélusine,* 122.)

43   Harf-Lancner, *Les fées au Moyen Âge,* 37. See also Roach, *Roman de Mélusine* 124, lines 502–3.

44   "Et a l'approuchier de la fontaine, apperceust tresplus belle dame que il eust oncques jour veu, a son adviz" [and as he approached the fountain, he saw the most beautiful maiden he had ever seen] (Vincensini, *Mélusine,* 122). See also Melusine and Raymondin's encounter in Vincensini, *Mélusine,* 162.

from a specific place and her positive qualities, embodied in her beauty, are now the focal point: *Histoire de la belle Mélusine, Die Schöne Melusine, Historia de la linda Melosina*.[45] The Spanish title contains another layer of meaning with the adjective *linda*: the sounds "l" and "n" are doubled, as if to mimic the flow of water, the primary element associated with Melusine.

The choice of this Spanish title could also have to do with an affirmation of courtly values, particularly in the Seville edition of 1526.[46] In the encounter of Elinas and Pressine, this courtliness appears in the depiction of the lady, the downplaying of her magical attributes, and the amplification of the *voyeur* motif. The translator uses typical vocabulary of *libros de caballerías* to describe his character: richly adorned,[47] Pressine is not only "fermosa y apuesta" [beautiful and elegant], she possesses "fermosura," "gentileza," and "gracia" [beauty, nobility, grace].[48] Where Jean d'Arras compares her voice to that of a mermaid, the translator makes her a simple maiden ("donzella"), recasting the initial impression of Otherness:

[...] oya una boz que tan dulcemente cantava *mas parescia ser* angelica que umana [...] Ni [Elinas] pensava [...] que en contemplar y oyr aquella donzella que *apenas creya ser umana* por la gracia que en ella veya.[49]

[heard a voice who sang so sweetly that it appeared more angelic than human [...] and (Elinas) thought [...] that looking at this maiden and listening to her, it would be difficult to believe that she was human because of the grace he saw in her.]

---

45   The demise of the Lusignan house may have also contributed to this shift.

46   Fernando Gomez Redondo speaks of a "consciencia caballeresca affirmada" [affirmed chivalric consciousness], *Historia de la prosa de los reyes católicos: el umbra del Renascimiento* (Madrid: Ediciones Càtedra, 2012). Quoted by Laura Baquedano, "*Paz, amor e buena ventura*. Les mots, la sagesse et la subtilité des femmes au service de la paix dans l'*Historia de la linda Melosina* à la fin du XVᵉ siècle," *E-Spania* 20 (February 2015): par. 19.

47   "Tan adornada donzella, assi en belleza como en tan grande riqueza como sobre ella traya" [Such an adorned maiden, who displayed her beauty and riches so elegantly] (Corfis, *Melosina*, 5).

48   So does Melusine, who is addressed by Raymondin as "linda señora" [beautiful lady] (Corfis, *Melosina*, 16).

49   Corfis, *Melosina*, 5. Emphasis added. In Jean d'Arras: "et quant il approucha de la fontaine, il oyt une voix qui chantoit si melodieusement qu'il ne cuida pas pour vray / que ce ne feust voix angelique; mais touttefoiz il entendy assez pour la grand doulçour de la voix que c'estoit voix femenine" [and when he approached the well, he heard a voice singing so sweetly he could not doubt this must have been the voice of an angel; but after listening for a while, he realized that because of its softness, the voice was that of a woman] (Vincensini, *Mélusine*, 120).

The scene of the secret observer not only prefigures the famous one where Raymondin spies on Melusine through a hole,[50] but is reframed here into a courtly episode. Elinas is "embevescido" [absorbed] by the sweet song of Pressine, but he takes on the role of the lover observing his lady from afar. His faculties still intact, he gets down from his horse, ties its lead to a tree branch, and approaches the singer as quietly as he can. Elinas deliberately hides behind trees so that he will not be heard or seen.[51] When he finally glances at the lady, he rejoices that he can appreciate the entertainment while being hidden from the view, thanks to branches and leaves.[52] Elinas is cast here in the leading role, whereas he is more passive in Jean's text, where Pressine is the one who bewitches and attracts him to her. The Seville edition of 1526 highlights and develops the elements of its source that match most closely its audience's frame of reference, the *libros de caballerías*.

In Jean d'Arras' narrrative, the story of Elinas and Pressine blends romance conventions and fairy material while foretelling the first encounter between Raymondin and Melusine and the transgression of the taboo. The episode is also crucial in transforming a legendary figure into a fully fledged romance character by making sense of her being and her actions. Once Elinas breaks his covenant never to see his wife during childbirth and Pressine retires to Avalon with her daughters, the latter imprison their father in a mountain, and Pressine crafts a special curse for each of them to avenge him.[53] Jean d'Arras leads his audience to approach Melusine's weekly transformation as a curse from her fairy mother,[54] not as a devilish feat; he shows that her actions to integrate the

---

50 In this sense, Elinas and Pressine are duplicates of Raymondin and Melusine. According to Gabrielle M. Spiegel, Geoffrey Great-Tooth may also be seen as a double of Melusine. See "Maternity and Monstrosity: Reproductive Biology in the *Roman de Melusine*," in *Melusine of Lusignan*, 100–124.

51 "Y passo a passo, quanto secretamente que pudo por entre los arboles se acerco a la fuente" [and step by step, as quietly as he could, he approached the well between the trees] (Corfis, *Melosina*, 5.)

52 "Pues assi cubierto de las ramas y fojas de aquellas arboles que alli eran, lo mejor que pudo porque no pudiesse ser visto" [In this fashion, covered by the leaves and branches of the trees nearby, in the best way be could, so he could not be seen] (Corfis, *Melosina*, 5).

53 Vincensini, *Mélusine*, 122–136.

54 According to Catherine Gaullier-Bougassas, Pressine could be seen as the instrument of divine will, and her curse, the divine punishment alluded to in the prologue. See "La fée Présine: une figure maternelle ambiguë aux origines de l'écriture romanesque," in *550 Jahre deutsche Melusine*, ed. André Schnyder and Jean-Claude Mühlethaler (Berlin: Peter Lang, 2008), 111–128, at 113. This idea is also explored by Zoë Enstone in her contribution to this volume.

human world through marriage are actually an attempt to escape her destiny and leave her fairy nature behind.

Jean also renders his main character more complex by juxtaposing her with her mother. Pressine is portrayed as a vindictive kind of fairy; unlike Melusine, she has no pity for her children who commit crimes, nor does she turn to God, as her daughter does when she hears of Geoffrey Great-Tooth's destructive actions. She punishes her children for robbing her of her only pleasure in life.[55] Furthermore, she sets Melusine up to fail. She imposes conditions on her daughter's union with a mortal that are even more restrictive than the ones that ruled her own marriage,[56] restrictions that make transgression all the more likely: the taboo recurs every week, and Melusine's fairy nature is made clearly visible in her physical appearance on Saturdays. Pressine is angry when her husband breaks his promise and vents her wrath on him. Melusine's response to a similar situation is at the opposite end of the spectrum: she gives her husband a chance, as long as he keeps her secret to himself, and when he breaks this second covenant, she is filled with grief and sadness. Pressine's portrait makes Melusine shine *a contrario*: it highlights her humanity, her ability to be compassionate, loving, and forgiving. In this sense, it shapes the reader's overall positive interpretation of the main character.

When it comes to the story of Elinas and Pressine, Coudrette differs again from Jean d'Arras in his spectacular turns of events. The audience discovers Melusine's story as it unfolds in a series of *coups de théâtre*: a mysterious and beautiful woman encounters Raymondin at a well; she builds fortresses as if by magic and gives birth to children with odd physical features; she turns into a half-serpent on Saturdays and later transforms fully into a dragon. Readers learn of Melusine's curse only when Geoffrey Great-Tooth uncovers his grandfather Elinas's tomb and reads the inscription-letter left by Pressine.[57] In it, she explains that she punished her daughters by *faerie* out of love for her husband.[58]

---

55   "C'estoit ou je prenois toute la plaisance que j'avoie en ce monde mortel et vous me l'avez tollue" [It was all my pleasure in this mortal world, and you took it from me] (Vincensini, *Mélusine*, 134).

56   The causes of which are not explained by Jean d'Arras or Coudrette.

57   Roach, *Roman de Mélusine*, 271–5, lines 4919–5050.

58   "Desquelles ainsi me vengay / [...] Pour leur pere Helinas le roy / [...] Car par foy, je l'aymoye moult; / Combien qu'eüst mespris vers moy, / Je l'aymoye de bonne foy" [I got revenge against them [...] for their father Elinas the King [...] for, by God, I loved him much, even though he did me wrong, I loved him in good faith] (Roach, *Roman de Mélusine*, 275, lines 5043, 5045, 5048–50).

The story of Elinas and Pressine frames the reader's interpretation of Melusine as more than a one-dimensional legendary figure: it makes her a literary character with a past, a family, and motivations for her actions. The meeting of Melusine and Raymondin is a defining moment, much like the prologue and the Elinas-Pressine episode, in the sense that it sets the scene for the central story to unfold. It introduces the main character anew, first through Raymondin's perception in his half-dream state, and then by her emergence as his savior.

In Jean d'Arras, when Raymondin arrives at the Fontaine de Soif, he is grief-stricken from having accidentally killed his beloved maternal uncle, the Count of Poitiers, during a hunting expedition. He flees the scene and lets his horse guide him. He is absorbed by his despair, in a state akin to sleep. Melusine holds his rein and deliberately provokes him, calling him "Sire vassaulx" and "Sire musars" [Sire vassal, sire absent-minded or idiot].[59] When she touches his hand, he imagines that he is under attack and fights. He finally awakens and looks at Melusine, who seems to be the most beautiful woman he has ever seen.[60]

Raymondin responds to the trauma of his uncle's death by first fleeing, then freezing and fighting. His reactions to the discovery of Melusine's serpent tail have a similar pattern: he flees the scene, then freezes, having no emotional response to what he just saw, then fights the facts by revealing his wife's secret to the whole court. Jean d'Arras deflects Melusine's uniqueness by focusing on Raymondin's response to a terrible loss and by using humor in the bathing scene. He chooses to suggest Melusine's Otherness rather than depict this quality directly; one could argue that he lets his readers fill in the blanks with their imagination, since they are already familiar with Melusine's story.

As Coudrette does not refer to folktales about fairies, he is more direct than Jean d'Arras in this scene, guiding his readers to recognize that Otherness is central to his version. Raymondin initially perceives Melusine as a ghost: "Tressault et la dame apperçoit / Lors cuide que fantosme soyt, / Il ne scet s'il veille ou s'il dort" [he jumps and sees the maiden; he thinks she is a ghost; he

---

59   Vincensini, *Mélusine*, 162. Similarly, Melusine says in Coudrette: "Par Dieu! vassault, ne monstrez mie / Que soyez de noble lignie" [By God! Vassal, you do not appear to be of noble lineage!] (Roach, 124, lines 511–2).

60   "Ne lui semble mie qu'il eust oncques mais veu si belle" [It did not seem he had ever seen someone so beautiful] (Vincensini, *Mélusine,*164).

does not know whether he is awake or asleep].[61] He then recasts his first impression almost immediately: "Mais quant il vit le corps humain / De la dame qui le tenoit, / Où si grant beauté avoit, / Il entr'oublia ses enuis / Et ne scet s'il est mors ou vis" [But when he saw the body of the lady holding him and her exquisite beauty, he forgot his woes; he does not know whether he is alive or dead].[62] The double symmetrical structure, Raymondin's sleep state and his response of fear and fascination in the presence of Melusine, all signal an encounter with the Otherworld, similar to the meeting of the mortal and the fairy in "Lanval" and the discovery of the uninhabited city in *Partonopeu de Blois*.[63]

The English translator of Coudrette rewrites the scene so that the otherworldly, which could be associated with the devil, is downplayed, if not erased. In this case, Raymondin does not think Melusine a ghost; he rather deems her a figment of his imagination ("There he trowed that fantesie it were" [he believed that it was a fantasy]), a fleeting thought, only to be forgotten when the thought of his sorrow returns.[64] The sight of her beautiful living body does not quickly reassure him, as in Coudrette, but renews the thought of his dead uncle's body: "Moche the more troubled his noysance heuye" [his heaviness of heart troubled him more].[65] Melusine is not particularly mysterious, nor does she stand apart from other women; she simply has "gret beaute [...] presynted freshlye" [great beauty, freshly presented].[66]

Thüring von Ringoltingen stands on the opposite end of the spectrum, highlighting Melusine's Otherness. The double symmetrical structure used by Coudrette is merged into one sentence: "wüste nit, ob er lebendig oder tod was, oder ob dis sein gespenst oder sust ein frowe were" [he does not know whether he is alive or dead, nor whether it is a ghost or a real woman.][67] Thüring reinterprets the scene so that Melusine's two aspects, human and ghost, are placed on

---

61   Roach, *Roman de Mélusine*, 124, lines 517–519. Melusine's wedding apparel also signals her otherness: "La demoiselle fut tant belle / Et si richement atournee / Que trestouz ceulx qui la journee / La virent, distrent pour certain / Que ce n'estoit point corps humain, / Mais sembloit mieulx corps angelique" [The maiden was so beautiful and so richly adorned that all those who saw her throughout the day said that for certain her body was not that of a human, but appeared like that of an angel] (Roach, *Roman de Mélusine*, 145, lines 1126–31).

62   Roach, *Roman de Mélusine*, 125, lines 538–541.

63   Michel Stanesco, "La fée amante et le chevalier: de l'interdit au premier rite sacrificiel," in *Transgression et contestation*, ed. Russell King (University of Nottingham: Nottingham Modern Languages Publications Archive, 2000), 3–12.

64   Skeat, *Romans of Parthenay*, 19, line 358; 20, lines 361–4.

65   Skeat, *Romans of Parthenay*, 20, line 383.

66   Skeat, *Romans of Parthenay*, 20, line 382.

67   Schneider, *Melusine*, 42.

equal footing. Thüring not only draws his readers in by portraying a fascinating monster, he also challenges his audience's notions as to the nature of human and otherworldly by suggesting that they coexist in this figure.

In the *Melusine* narratives, the largely mysterious woman from the well emerges as the hero's savior and the romance's main character, characteristics evident in the dialogue that forms the second part of the scene. Here, the distressing impression created by Melusine's knowledge of Raymondin's misfortunes is counterbalanced by several reassuring mentions of God and of her Catholic faith.[68] She leads Raymondin to postulate a correlation between inner and outer beauty, in harmony with medieval physiognomy;[69] even before she guides him, he is already half-persuaded and believes she will bring him good fortune: "Car de si belle creature / Ne puet fors bonne aventure / Venir, eur et trestous biens" [of such a beautiful creature could only come good adventure, happiness and richness.][70] Melusine gives instructions to resolve his situation; the medieval motif of the damsel-in-distress rescued by the brave knight in shining armor undergoes a gender reversal wherein the male victim is counseled by a female protagonist, which calls attention to Melusine's overall positive influence on Raymondin and their community. Her role as a guide might also be more palatable to a medieval audience given Raymondin's half-dream state; the scene can be viewed as something of an *oraculum*, a vision in which a dreamer receives guidance from a figure who speaks to him or her.[71]

In Jean d'Arras' narrative, Melusine is Raymondin's guide and savior, but she also mirrors him in many respects. At the time of their meeting, both have committed a crime against a father figure; Melusine has imprisoned her father in a mountain, and Raymondin accidentally killed his maternal uncle. According to Jean Markale, the first crime is the equivalent of usurping a father's place, and in the process, the daughter appropriates her father's masculine qualities and abilities, which include building fortresses, founding a lineage, and taking charge of her destiny.[72] Raymondin, on the other hand, takes on

---

68 Among others: Roach, *Roman de Mélusine,* 127, lines 595, 609–10, and 615.

69 See for instance *The Secrets of Secrets (Secreta Secretorum): A Modern Translation with an Introduction of the "Governance of Princes",* ed. Lin Kerns (Lewiston, NY: Edwin Mellen Press, 2008).

70 Roach, *Roman de Mélusine,* 126, lines 575–6. This initial opinion of Melusine is completely reversed later in the narrative, when Raymondin accuses her being a traitorous serpent.

71 Macrobius, *Commentary on the Dream of Scipio.* See Steven F. Krueger, *Dreaming in the Middle Ages* (Cambridge: Cambridge University Press, 1992), 40.

72 Jean Markale, *Mélusine ou l'androgyne* (Paris: Retz, 1983), 28. See also Spiegel, "Maternity and Monstrosity," 106.

a stereotypically feminine role by publicly displaying his grief. Melusine approaches him as a cursed fairy woman attempting to integrate into the human world; Raymondin flees this world and needs a guide to negotiate his re-entry into society. The mirror device and play between the masculine and the feminine echo the portrait of the fairy Pressine in the sense that they function as part of Jean d'Arras' strategy to portray Melusine as a complex literary character.

The meeting of the two main characters by the well is a significant moment in the *Melusine* narratives that likewise attributes specific roles to each. One follows when the other leads. One is the victim, the other the savior. One is easily persuaded, and the other embodies the wisdom of the guide. When Raymondin reveals Melusine's secret to the world, he recalls the critical moment when it all began with spite. He blames Melusine for having so easily bewitched him.[73] With this scene, the various authors manage to present Melusine's Otherness and to discount it at the same time, using dream vision references. The same could be said of the bathing scene and of the fairy's final transformation.

The moments leading to the end of her relationship with Raymondin—the accusations of the Count of Forez, the first transgression of the taboo, and the fairy woman's departure—are likewise striking in how Melusine's Otherness is both put forward and negated by the author at the same time.

The conversation between Raymondin and his brother, which leads to the discovery of Melusine's serpent tail, exemplifies traits already documented in the previous versions. In Jean d'Arras' and Coudrette's versions, the Count of Forez reports two rumors about his sister-in-law: one that she is unfaithful to her husband, the other that she is a fairy doing penance for a crime on Saturdays. In the Spanish translations, the first option is given a more courtly twist, as Melusine is accused of loving a man more than Raymondin.[74] In the English *Romans of Parthenay*, Melusine's Otherness is minimized; the fairy accusation appears in passing, without any mention of penance, whereas the theme of adultery is developed.[75] The unfaithful wife brings shame to her husband,

---

73 In Jean d'Arras, Raymondin blames himself for not having been more discerning when he first met Melusine (Vincensini, *Mélusine*, 668). In Thüring, he deems Melusine a ghost that should inspire fear ("Es is gantz ein gespönst und diss wib," Schneider, *Melusine*, 91).

74 "Quando de vos se esconde, es por que a un otro que mas ama, con quien el tal tiempo se ayunta" [When she parts from you, it is to see a man whom she loves more, with whom she spends her time enjoying herself] (Corfis, *Melosina*, 148).

75 "That day hir body anothir man shall have, / To you trayteresse, other so to crave; / And som other sayn she is off the fayry. [...] I beleve she doth you shame and outrage." (Skeat, *Romans of Parthenay*, 99, lines 2769–2771, 2778).

conduct in direct opposition to the ideal wife portrayed in conduct manuals of sixteenth-century England.[76] In Thüring, both charges are present, though the otherworldly is put forward: the Count of Forez reports that some consider Melusine a ghost and a strange creature ("ein gespönste und ein ungehür wesen.")[77] In the chapbook, he rather suggests that Melusine is a monster who returns weekly to her true nature.[78]

In Jean d'Arras, the transgression scene opens with a certain erotic tone, as Raymondin pierces a hole through a wall with his sword, mimicking a maiden's defloration. The act of lovemaking and the moments leading to a culmination are reverberated by narrative suspension: rubrics, analepsis, evocations of the time of the reader, and repetitive instances all break the linearity of the scene and defer the moment where Raymondin finally gazes at his wife's naked body.[79] Jean's initial depiction of Melusine's upper body is reminiscent of the mermaid combing her hair, as she appears in medieval bestiaries. But the scene suddenly turns comical. Melusine's tail is "aussi grosse comme une tonne où on met harenc, et longue durement, et debatoit de sa coue l'eaue tellement qu'elle faisoit saillir jusques a la voulte de la chambre" [as thick as a herring barrel, and very long, and she was splashing her tail in the water so much that she made it shoot up to the ceiling.][80] The eroticism of the metaphoric penetration and of the seductive mermaid sharply contrasts with the workaday barrel of salted fish. Jean completely deflects Melusine's Otherness; he defuses any frightful response or a devilish interpretation by amusing his readers. In doing so, he also leaves a certain amount of space for his reading public to imagine the scene and match it to the stories they have heard.

The English translator of Jean d'Arras follows his source almost word for word, though he guides his reader's interpretation by presenting the scene as one of penance: Melusine's weekly bathing is a purification ritual akin to a

---

76   For a discussion on this topic, see David M. Turner, *Fashioning Adultery: Gender, Sex and Civility in England, 1660–1740* (Cambridge: Cambridge University Press, 2002).

77   Schneider, *Melusine*, 80.

78   See Claude Lecouteux, "Introduction," in Thüring von Ringoltingen, *Mélusine et autres récits*, ed. Claude Lecouteux (Paris: Champion, 1999), 7–30, at 13.

79   For a more complete analysis of this narrative device, see Kevin Brownlee, "Melusine's Hybrid Body and the Poetics of Metamorphosis," *Yale French Studies* 86 (1994): 21–23. Similarly, in Coudrette, 25 verses separate Raymondin's explosion of rage following his conversation with his brother and his gazing at his wife's body.

80   Vincensini, *Mélusine*, 660.

baptism,[81] with which she cleanses herself of her crime against her father. The translator dismisses any potentially evil interpretations of the scene. He negates Melusine's Otherness by the humorous herring barrel comparison and the words "in lykness of a grete serpent."[82] This could be simply a visual analogy for the general shape of the tail; this "lykness" may also be read as an outward appearance of something that is different in reality, or in Raymondin's perception. In this case, the translator would be concealing the true aspect of Melusine's lower body, which could be another strategy to erase the monstrous from his narrative.

Coudrette signals Melusine's Otherness in a scene that inspires both desire and horror in Raymondin. Melusine's skin is as white as snow, her body firm and attractive. No woman could equal her in beauty. Then Coudrette adds: "Maiz queue ot dessoubz de serpent, / Grande et orrible vrayement: / D'argent et d'asur fut burlee; / Fort s'en debat, l'eaue a croulee" [But below she had a serpent's tail, large and truly horrible, chiseled in silver and blue; she moved it and splashed water all over].[83] Terrified, Raymondin makes the sign of the cross, as if to ward off evil,[84] and prays to God. The scene recalls Raymondin's initial response to Melusine upon their encounter: he first thought she was a ghost, then realized she was a woman. Here, he first sees the woman, her otherworldly body afterwards. In Coudrette, Melusine's hybridity is fully recognized, rather than deflected; it even possesses aesthetic qualities, considering the tail appears engraved in the colors of the Lusignan arms.

Thüring von Ringoltingen expands the scene by developing the idea that there could be beauty in the monstrous: Melusine's exceedingly beautiful body from the belly button upwards can only be matched by a jewel-like, silver-incrusted tail:

> Aber vom nabel hin der under teil ein grosser langer fyentlicher wurms schwantz von blawer lasur mit wiser silbrin farbe und rundern silberin tropfen gesprenget.

---

81   "And therin she bathed herself, making there her penytence as ye shal here herafter" [and therin she bathed herself, performing her penance, as you shall hear hereafter] (Donald, *Melusine*, 296). See also Urban, *Monstrous Women*, 103.

82   Donald, *Melusine*, 297.

83   Roach, *Roman de Mélusine*, 211, lines 3073–6.

84   Roach, *Roman de Mélusine*, 211, lines 3077–85. The absurd juxtaposition of the two parts of Melusine's body would have been seen as an offense to divine creation. See Françoise Clier-Colombani, "Le beau et le laid dans le *Roman de Mélusine*," in *Le beau et le laid au Moyen Âge* (Aix-en-Provence: Presses Universitaires de Provence, 2000), par. 44.

[But below she had a terrifying, long and ghastly tail of a snake with
blue and white colors sprinkled and interspersed with drops of silver, as
is commonly the appearance of a snake.][85]

Of all the depictions of the serpent tail in *Melusine* narratives, this is certainly
the most detailed and the most visually suggestive.[86] As he does elsewhere in
the narrative, Thüring balances Melusine's s Otherness and humanity, but he
adopts a strategy similar to that of Jean d'Arras in the same scene: he deflects
the culminating point of the scene with a comment about the common appearance of snakes. The introduction of a piece of everyday life disrupts the
accumulation of frightful yet beautiful elements and compels the reader to
re-integrate the familiar human world.[87]

The English translator of Coudrette meets Jean d'Arras with the use of humor to minimize the potentially frightening effect of the depiction of Melusine's tail on his audience. His portrait of an admirable and courteous lady
elicits laughter when it reaches its end with an unexpected rhyme pairing
("reverent" and "serpent"): "To properly speke off hir faccion, / Never non fairer
ne more reverent: / But a tail had beneth of serpent!" [To properly describe her
phsycial appearance, there was never one fairer nor more attractive, but she
had beneath the tail of a serpent!].[88] The readers then approach the "gret and
orrible" tail chiseled in blue and silver, which appears in the next lines, with
lightheartedness, rather than fear. The playful rhyme "reverent/serpent" gives
prominence to Melusine's hybridity, simultaneously summing up her humanity in her faith, and her monstrosity in her tail.

The crucial transformation of Melusine into a flying creature, another culminating moment of Otherness, is given far less textual space then the bathing
scene. Most authors prefer to focus on the moments leading up to it, where her
very human grief is expressed. In Coudrette, the anaphoric *adieux* between
Melusine and Raymondin are marked by a courtly vocabulary in line with the
previous depiction of Melusine's upper body.[89] Coudrette then softens the

---

85   Schneider, *Melusine,* 81; English translation by Classen, "Love and Fear," 111.

86   See Classen's analysis for more details ("Love and Fear," 111).

87   The illustrated and abridged chapbook reframes Thüring's scene, toning down Melusine's
      Otherness but highlighting her magical abilities: the scene is set in a marvelous grotto
      near a well, created by the fairy herself for her weekly bathing. The scene then resonates
      with the magical erection of the Lusignan fortress. See Claude Lecouteux, "Introduction,"
      13.

88   Skeat, *Romans of Parthenay,* 100, lines 2805–7.

89   Roach, *Roman de Mélusine,* 246–7, lines 4171–4200 and 248, lines 4232–4252.

impact of the metamorphosis by using a phrase already familiar to the reader, "D'argent et d'asur [...] burlee" [silver and blue ... incised]; in her final transformation, a little part of Melusine's old self is still present, and her true fairy nature acknowledged: "celle faée, / Qui devenue estoit serpente" [this fairy, who was changed into a serpent].[90]

Thüring does not miss the opportunity to portray Otherness and here he explicitly casts Melusine as a frightening monster: "Und was zu stund eins ougenblickes wider vom gürtel nider ein vyendtlicher unghürer grosser und langer wurm worden" [and from that moment on she was right away transformed into a horrifying monster with the shape of a snake down from her navel].[91] In Thüring, the sinister, otherworldly aspects of Melusine seem to completely take over her humanity, unlike what happens in Jean d'Arras, in which hybridity still defines her. When she returns in Jean's narrative, people see a serpent but hear a woman's voice; to the English knight Cresewell, she appears as a serpent who transforms briefly into a woman before becoming a serpent again.[92] In Jean, Melusine is exiled from society by the public revelation of her fairy nature, but she no longer needs to conceal her hybridity. In private, she remains a mother who visits her two newborns, Thierry and Raymonnet, at night. Jean recalls the fairy-trickster legend from the prologue, writing that the mother warms her two children by the fire.[93] He does not specify the form in which Melusine appears, but the two Spanish translations and the English manuscript, which significantly downplay Melusine's serpentine nature and develop her humanity, are more explicit: she returns as a woman.[94]

It is striking that the moments in the *Melusine* narratives in which the eponymous character's Otherness comes most clearly into focus—the bathing scene and the final transformation—are also the ones in which humor, absurd juxtapositions, and workaday elements defuse frightful interpretations. Even Thüring von Ringoltingen chooses to counterbalance his suggestive depiction of the serpent's tail with a comment taken from daily life.

---

90   Roach, *Roman de Mélusine,* 247, line 4211; 247, lines 4213–4. The same phrase is found in Jean d'Arras (Vincensini, *Mélusine,* 771, 811.)

91   Schneider, *Melusine,* 96. English translation by Classen, "Love and Fear," 117.

92   Vincensini, *Mélusine,* 707, 811.

93   "Les tenoit au feu" [held them near the fire] (Vincensini, *Mélusine,* 704). For a discussion on Melusine's return to breastfeed in Coudrette and the possible choice of a wet-nurse in Jean d'Arras, see Catherine Léglu, "Nourishing lineage in the earliest French versions of the *Roman de Mélusine*," *Medium Aevum* 74, no. 1 (2005): 71–85, esp. 71–74.

94   Corfis, *Melosina,* 164; Donald, *Melusine,* 322.

The authors of fourteenth-, fifteenth-, and sixteenth-century *Melusine* narratives essentially tell the same story, but they each have their own inter- pretation of the main character. Writing for different publics with different expectations, they adapt the portrait of the fairy woman so that she was relat- able and fascinating. Jean d'Arras evokes fairy lore to draw readers in but also to set his work apart. His use of prolepsis creates echoes in the narrative and highlights the complexity of his literary character. He prefers to suggest more than to emphasize Melusine's Otherness. The two Spanish translations pull the narrative into their own tradition of *libros de caballerías*, making Melusine a courtly lady and a loving mother much more than a magical being. The English translator of Jean d'Arras also makes his character's humanity his focal point: she is a good mother and a devout Christian. The monstrous is consciously deflated so that Melusine may not be perceived as an evil creature.

Coudrette plays with the literary conventions of his time: he associates his character with legendary Arthurian heroes, proceeds by way of *coups de théâtre* as if his readers had no prior knowledge of fairy legends, and signals the otherworldly as something to be feared and fascinated by. Thüring von Ringoltingen revels in constantly reiterating Melusine's monstrous features. His character has the dark, frightening side of a ghost, but she is also pious and conforms to social mores. The English *Romans of Parthenay* is often in opposi- tion to Thüring with its focus on the fairy woman's humanity: Melusine is a fair lady who does penance for her crimes and whose magical aspects are almost always downplayed. The portrait of the fairy woman subtly changes focus in the *Melusine* narratives, making her a different character in each instance, but in every case, it ultimately reminds readers of their own human nature, and of human curiosity in the face of mystery.

CHAPTER 4

The Melusine Figure in Fifteenth- and Sixteenth-Century German Literature and Art: Cultural-Historical Information within the Pictorial Program

With a Discussion of the Melusine-Lüsterweibchen Connection

Albrecht Classen

Modern investigations have increasingly turned to the text-image relationship, especially in pre-modern narratives. An analysis of this relationship in the many reprints of the Melusine novel reveals a wealth of cultural-historical information hidden in woodcuts from the late fifteenth and sixteenth centuries and beyond. How the artists contextualized the central events through pictorial means reflects their attitudes toward the monstrous or hybrid nature of the female protagonist.

Only a few decades ago, research reflected fairly little of the long tradition of the *Melusine* myth, which saw its full light first by the late fourteenth century with Jean d'Arras' prose *Mélusine* (ca.1393) and then ca.1400 with Coudrette's verse rendering.[1] In 1456 the Bernese patrician Thüring von Ringoltingen created a German translation which spawned a whole series of manuscript copies and then, by the 1470s, many printed versions. These incunabula and early modern prints ranked among the most popular literary texts of their time, making *Melusine*, either in its French or German version, a bestseller, or, perhaps more appropriately, a steadyseller.[2] Despite a lack of interest shown by

---

1 Jean d'Arras, *Melusine, or, The Noble History of Lusignan*, ed. and trans. Donald Maddox and Sara Sturm-Maddox (University Park: Pennsylvania State University Press, 2012).

2 For a review of the research history, combined with interpretative approaches, see Albrecht Classen, *The German Volksbuch: A Critical History of a Late-Medieval Genre*, Studies in German Language and Literature 15 (Lewiston, NY: Edwin Mellen Press, 1995, reissued 1999), 141–162; for an insightful study, see Kurt Ruh, *Die 'Melusine' des Thüring von Ringoltingen*, Sitzungsberichte, Philosophisch-historische Klage (Munich: Verlag der bayerischen Akademie der Wissenschaften, 1985). See also the contributions to *550 Jahre deutsche Melusine – Coudrette und Thüring von Ringoltingen: Beiträge der wissenschaftlichen Tagung der Universitäten Bern und Lausanne vom August 2006*, ed. André Schnyder and Jean-Claude Mühlenthaler, Tausch 16 (Berlin Peter Lang,

© KONINKLIJKE BRILL NV, LEIDEN, 2017 | DOI 10.1163/9789004355958_006

older scholarship,[3] the *Melusine Stoff* evolved into many different new versions, including dramas (Hans Sachs 1556 and Jakob Ayrer 1598) and other literary media throughout the subsequent centuries,[4] and it gained true fame once the Romantics rediscovered it.[5] Justus Friedrich Wilhelm Zachariae reprinted the text for the first time in 1772 (*Von der schönen Melusinen: einer Meerfey*), followed by Ludwig Tieck in 1800 and 1807 (*Melusine*).[6]

Today the situation has changed radically, since many scholars have discovered both the genre of early modern prose novels at large and the *Melusine* novels in particular.[7] Recent emphasis has rested on the visualization of the narrative. The relationship between text and image in the *Melusine* print editions of Thüring's novel is the topic of Kristina Domanski's article, whereas

2008); *Eulenspiegel trifft Melusine: Der frühneuhochdeutsche Prosaroman im Licht neuer Forschungen und Methoden. Akten der Lausanner Tagung vom 2. bis 4. Oktober 2008*, ed. Catherine Drittenbass and André Schnyder, together with Alexander Schwarz, Chloe 42 (Amsterdam: Rodopi, 2010). The text itself is well-edited and commented in *Romane des 15. und 16. Jahrhunderts*, ed. Jan-Dirk Müller, Bibliothek der Frühen Neuzeit (Frankfurt a. M.: Deutscher Klassiker-Verlag, 1990), 9–176, and 1012–87. For a bibliography of all incunabula and early modern prints until 1600, see Bodo Gotzkowsky, *"Volksbücher": Prosaromane, Renaissancenovellen, Versdichtungen und Schwankbücher: Bibliographir der deutschen Drucke*. Part I: *Drucke des 15. und 16. Jahrhunderts* (Baden-Baden: Verlag Valentin Koerner, 1991), 105–25, Part II: *Drucke des 17. Jahrhunderts*, 39–41.

3   See, for instance, Hans Rupprich, *Die deutsche Literatur vom späten Mittelalter bis zum Barock*. Part One: *Das ausgehende Mittelalter, Humanismus und Renaissance 1370–1520*, Geschichte der deutschen Literatur von den Anfängen bis zur Gegenwart 4.1 (Munich: C. H. Beck, 1970), 71–72. He briefly introduces the text and offers a succinct plot summary.

4   Even most recent literary histories tend to ignore the entire *Melusine* tradition; see, for instance, *A New History of German Literature*, ed. David E. Wellbery and Judith Ryan (Cambridge, MA: The Belknap Press of Harvard University Press, 2004); for a critique, see Classen's review in *The German Quarterly* 79, no. 2 (2005): 256–58. Peter Nusser, *Deutsche Literatur: Eine Sozial- und Kulturgeschichte. Vom Mittelalter bis zur Frühen Neuzeit* (Darmstadt: Wissenschaftliche Buchgesellschaft, 2012), 274, mentions the text only in one sentence.

5   Classen, *The German Volksbuch*, 161–62; Hans-Jörg Künast and Ursula Rautenberg, *Melusine/ Die Überlieferung der 'Melusine' des Thüring von Ringoltingen: Kommentierte Quellenbibliographie, buchwissenschaftliche, sprachwissenschaftliche und kunsthistorische Aufsätze* (Berlin: de Gruyter, 2013); *Mélusine: moderne et contemporaine*, ed. Arlette Bouloumié, Bibliothèque Mélusine ([Lausanne]: L'Age d'homme, 2001). See also the useful survey by Charles Lecouteux, "Melusine," *Enzyklopädie des Märchens*, ed. Rolf Wilhelm Brednich, vol. 9, no. 2 (Berlin De Gruyter, 1998), 556–61.

6   Classen, *The German Volksbuch*, 161.

7   Xenia von Ertzdorff, *Romane und Novellen des 15. und 16. Jahrhunderts in Deutschland* (Darmstadt: Wissenschaftliche Buchgesellschaft, 1989), 63–70.

Catherine Drittenbass studies the evolution of time in the text. Martin Behr and Mechthild Habermann investigate the print history from 1473/74 until 1516, work which Hans-Jörg Künast continues with a study of the print history in the second half of the sixteenth century. Ursula Rautenberg focuses on the *Melusine* prints from the workshops by Hermann Gülfferich (1549), his son-in-law Weigand Han (1556 and ca.1560), and his heirs (1564, 1571, and 1577). Editions by Christian Eggenolfs Erben (ca.1575 and 1580) and Sigmund Feyerabend (in his *Buch der Liebe*, 1587), which appeared in octavo size, were to become characteristic of the typical *Volksbuch* in the following centuries. The Baroque author Johan Michael Moscherosch in 1640 still seems to have known *Melusine*, which he includes derogatorily in a list of popular works that ordinary people tended to read instead of the Bible and other uplifting works, in his two-volume *Les Visiones De Don De Quevedo, Satyrische Gesichte Philanders vom Sittewalt*.[8] André Schnyder's investigations have yielded around twenty additional editions from the early modern period, and he focuses specifically on Baroque versions from 1776 and 1788.[9]

Nicolas Bock has studied in detail how the illustration program in the *Melusine* incunabula correlates with the structural organization of the text, highlighting the transformation of the visual elements that in the fifteenth century still somewhat served the purpose of depicting the monstrous aspects represented by Melusine, her sisters, and her sons, but which nevertheless underscored the exemplary nature of Melusine's love for Reymond.[10] Some of the *Melusine* prints contain a large number of illustrations, especially the *editio princeps* produced by Johann Bämler in 1474 in Augsburg (72 illustrations), the edition that appeared in Basel in 1475/76 (68 illustrations), and in Straßburg in 1477/78 (67 illustrations). Anton Sorg similarly included 71 illustrations in his Augsburg print from 1485.[11] These publishers understood well how to

---

8   Felix Bobertag, ed., *Gesichte Philanders von Sittewald von Hanß Michael Moscherosch*, Deutsche National-Literatur 32 (1800; Berlin: W. Spemann, 1883), 93; the sixth and probably last edition of this work appeared in 1665 (vol. 2) and 1677 (vol. 1). The author acknowledges a debt for this reference to Bernd Bastert, ed., *Herzog Herpin: Kritische Edition eines spätmittelalterlichen Prosaepos*, Texte des späten Mittelalters und der frühen Neuzeit 51 (Berlin: Erich Schmidt, 2014), XXI.

9   All these articles are included in *Eulenspiegel trifft Melusine*.

10   Nicolas Bock, "Im Weinberg der Melusine: Zur Editions- und Illustrationsgeschichte Thürings von Ringoltingen," *550 Jahre deutsche Melusine*, 31–45.

11   Backes, Martina, *Fremde Historien: Untersuchungen zur Überlieferungs- und Rezeptionsgeschichte französischer Erzählstoffe im deutschen Spätmittelalter*, Hermaea, NF, 103 (Tübingen: Niemeyer, 2004), 136–54. III; Bock, "Im Weinberg," 32–33, but he seems to confuse the print tradition, providing wrong dates and numbers of woodcuts; cf. Gotzkowsky, "Volksbücher", 106–25.

promote this text among their wealthy audiences—or they knew how to influence their audience with these well-illustrated volumes—and could afford to take the risk of embellishing their editions so lavishly because their customers, rich and high-ranking individuals among the aristocracy and well-to-do urban dwellers, obviously cared little about the costs and welcomed such impressive copies of the *Melusine* narrative.

The great popularity of Thüring's novel-translation far into the seventeenth and even eighteenth centuries, and the rich illustration programs in a good number of the printed versions, invite a closer investigation of the cultural-historical information contained in the images, which often prove to be opulent and luxurious.[12] Recent scholars have examined, for instance, the narrative and its reception history, the arrangement of the texts in the various editions, and the relationship between text and image.[13] The present purpose, however, cannot be to summarize what details can be found in those images; instead the intention is specifically to examine how the artist(s) represented the world in which Melusine, Reymond, and their children operate, what concepts of mythical creatures existed in visual terms, how, if at all, the natural environment was reflected, and whether we can observe noteworthy differences between the woodcuts in the fifteenth-century prints and those in Sigmund Feyerabend's famous *Buch der Liebe* from 1587, which also includes a version of Thüring's novel.

Jan-Dirk Müller had already reprinted, in small black-and-white format, the woodcuts of the 1474 edition by Johann Bämler (Munich, Bayerische Staatsbibliothek, c.a.295) when he published his volume *Romane des 15. und 16. Jahrhunderts* (1990). The edition by Bernhard Richel published 1473/74, today held in the Universitäts- und Landesbibliothek Darmstadt, allows an investigation in much greater detail, since he reproduced the images in large format

---

12   The number of copies of some prose novels such as *Melusine* sold through catalogues of the book sellers in Frankfurt a. M. and at other places is known; see Hans-Joachim Koppitz, "Zur Verbreitung unterhaltsamer und belehrender deutscher Literatur durch den Buchhandel in der zweiten Hälfte des 16. Jahrhunderts," *Jahrbuch für internationale Germanistik* 7 (1975): 20–35. See also Thomas Vertschegger, "'Das abenteürlich buch bewyset uns von einer frawen genandt Melusina': Beobachtungen zur deutschen Drucküberlieferung der 'Melusine' im 15./16. Jahrhundert," *Gutenberg-Jahrbuch* 69 (1994): 108–21.

13   See the contributions to *Zeichensprachen des literarischen Buchs in der frühen Neuzeit: die 'Melusine' des Thüring von Ringoltingen*, ed. Ursula Rautenberg, Hans-Jörg Künast, Mechthild Habermann, and Heidrun Stein-Kecks (Berlin: De Gruyter, 2013). The approach here in part pursues quite similar aspects, but the focus will rest on iconographic details and their cultural-historical significance.

(177 mm x 135 mm) and in color.[14] By the same token, with the help of digitalization technology, Feyerabend's massive volume from 1587 is now accessible online, which significantly facilitates a comparison, here focusing on the respective illustration program.

Dealing with this genre, several factors urge that these woodcut images be approached with considerable care. The printers often used the same woodstock for different scenes, so the illustration program does not necessarily correspond closely with the text. Sometimes the woodcuts were simply transferred from one text to another to save costs. Moreover, these incunabula and early prints were intended for the book market and so were strategically placed in order to enhance the book's selling points. And the material itself, wooden plates, did not allow for highly detailed images and forced the artist to focus on central motifs, figures, buildings, and objects, leaving out most of the common embellishments and marginal details familiar from later centuries.

Nevertheless, as Heidrun Stein-Kecks emphasizes, "Die einmal gefundene Ikonographie bleibt prägend, Änderungen betreffen stilistische Neuerungen und Modernisierungen des Beiwerks bzw. ganzer Bildkonzepte" [The once invented iconography remains dominant; changes only concern stylistic innovations and modernizations of the marginal aspects or of the whole picture concept].[15] Altogether, the woodcuts included in Bernhard Richel's (1473/74) and Johannes Bämler's (1474) incunabula maintained a profound influence over the next two hundred years.[16] Changes concerned the increasingly eroticized body of Melusine, whose pudenda suddenly become visible when she is depicted in the bath, and the increasingly ethical and moral interpretation of this mythical figure. But sixteenth-century illustrations, though still woodcuts ("Textholzschnitte"), essentially continued with the same tradition, dramatizing the narrative events by visual means.[17]

---

14   *Die schöne Melusine: Ein Feenroman des 15. Jahrhunderts in der deutschen Übertragung des Thüring von Ringoltingen. Die Bilder im Erstdruck Basel 1473/74 nach dem Exemplar der Universitäts- und Landesbibliothek Darmstadt*, ed. Heidrun Stein-Kecks, together with Simone Hespers and Benedicta Feraudi-Denier (Darmstadt: Wissenschaftliche Buchgesellschaft, 2012).

15   Stein-Kecks, *Die schöne Melusine*, 19.

16   Stein-Kecks, *Die schöne Melusine*, 19

17   John L. Flood, "Sigmund Feyerabends 'Buch der Liebe' (1587)," in *Liebe in der deutschen Literatur des Mittelalters: St. Andrews Colloquium 1985*, ed. Jeffrey Aschroft, Dietrich Huschenbett, and William Henry Jackson (Tübingen: Max Niemeyer, 1987), 204–20; Gotzkowsky, *"Volksbücher"*, 67–70.

The following discussion could rely on many parallel book illustrations, since the intention is to explore the iconographic horizon to which late medieval readers, especially of the *Melusine* novel along with many others of the same genre, would have been exposed on a daily basis. This prose novel traverses the world of the illustrated incunabulum and then the early modern book, and readers expected attractive texts at that time, which often required colored book illustrations. The cultural-historical information that the woodcuts convey sheds light on the common concepts determining the lives of the wealthier sections of late-medieval urban societies, where this novel enjoyed the greatest popularity.

Bernhard Richel included sixty-seven large-format illustrations in his edition from 1474, which accompany two hundred folio pages of text. Those illustrations serve as a kind of chapter introduction, with the chapter title at the top of each picture. The type area consists of 208 x 134 millimeters with twenty-seven to thirty-five lines, which leaves generous margins. Altogether, Richel aimed at a wealthy audience with his impressive print run, one copy of which is housed today in Darmstadt. Although the space of the individual scenes in the illustrations is often vague and little defined, the artist regularly created an excellent composition and included very common elements of fifteenth-century life and culture.[18]

The cultural-historical project is amply demonstrated by the initial illustration, which reflects on the book's origins as a result of Count Jean de Parthenay's having ordered his chaplain to collate a chronicle of his own family. The illustration depicts three persons, two of authority and rank, the third apparently a younger man. The older figures wear specific hats, have valuable collars decorating their long coats, and seem to debate with each other in a learned fashion. The chaplain sits behind an elevated desk, with an open book resting on it, evidently ready to embark on the task of creating an account of the Lusignan family.

The group is situated in a curiously open space with no real frame, though one can assume that the artist took it as a given that the viewer would understand that the setting is in an interior room. In the Basel print by Johann Bämler, the prince is much more clearly marked through his larger size, his standing position, and his unique headgear, while the scribe sits in the corner of a room in front of a table on which two books are placed. The prince holds another book in his hand. A further comparison would yield multiple differences, since various artists were probably involved. But the following analysis will focus on the Darmstadt incunabulum, then turn to the famous *Buch der*

---

18   Stein-Kecks, *Die schöne Melusine*, 28–30.

Liebe printed by Sigmund Feyerabend in 1587,[19] which also includes *Melusine*, in an effort to explore the differences in the cultural-historical approach pursued by the artist(s) around one hundred years after Thüring's novel had been first printed.

Each illustration serves, as the name implies, as a reading aid, offering a visual representation of a central theme. The artist naturally tried to give an idea of characteristic features in clothing, headgear, armors, shoes, and the like. The woodcut on fol. 5r presents, for instance, young Reymond and his benefactor, Count Emmerich, who is reading the configuration of the stars, predicting a catastrophe soon to happen. Unbeknownst to him, he will be that victim, which will subsequently make room for Reymond to rise to high influence with the help of his future wife, Melusine.

The spectator's view is directly aimed at the two horsemen, arrayed with distinctive clothing, swords, hats, and long-tipped shoes. Both their pants are painted in yellow, whereas Reymond's top is divided into red and blue. Both have put on galoshes to protect their pants from mud. The artist carefully outlined the bridles, saddles, and straps of the horses, obviously demonstrating a solid familiarity with these animals as they were used for transportation. Reymond's horse even has a docked tail. Later, on fol. 6v, Reymond rides away without holding the bridle because he is so shocked about Emmerich's sudden death, which he brought about himself. This time the horse is riding to the left in the exactly same direction as the boar. This configuration only changes on fol. 10r when Reymond takes leave of Melusine and her sisters, which forced the artist to present him from behind, and this time in full gallop, though he is still turned to Melusine and her two sisters, while the horse races ahead.

Quite commonly, the men wear overcoats divided into two parts dyed in two kinds of colors, irrespective of their social class. Only figures of authority and the courtly ladies do not display such a fashion. Their long dresses are held together by a belt, while the top part splits open, exposing their necks. Melusine, her sisters, and other ladies don elaborate headdresses, so-called "templettes."[20] To perform the marriage service for Melusine and Reymond, a

19   Thomas Veitschegger, *Das Buch der Liebe: Ein Beitrag zur Buch- und Verlagsgeschichte des 16. Jahrhunderts,* Studien zur Geschichtsforschung des Mittelalters 1 (Hamburg: Verlag Dr. Kovač, 1991). Feyerabend's collection contains the following prose novels: *Kaiser Octavian, Magelone, Ritter Galmy, Tristrant und Isalde, Camillo und Emilia, Florio und Bianceffora, Theagenes und Chariclia, Gabriotto und Reinhart, Melusine, Ritter vom Turn, Pontus und Sidonia, Herzog Herpin,* and *Wigoleis.*

20   Albert Racinet, *The Historical Encyclopedia of Costume* (1988; New York: Facts On File, 2000), 156–57.

bishop appears in his typical vestments and wearing his mitre (fol. 16v). Subsequently, during the wedding feast, Reymond serves everyone as their host. As many cultural historians have already noted, there are no forks on the table, and the guests have only knives available.[21] The room where they enjoy their meal has no windows, but the walls seem to be well-fitted with wooden panels, while the floor is covered by a kind of green carpet. As was the norm for courtly festivals throughout the Middle Ages, a tournament follows the meal, as seen in fol. 18v. Two knights battle against each other while their squires watch them from behind, an important focus especially in light of later renderings of this scene in the *Buch der Liebe* (1587). Illustrations follow of the wedding night (fol. 19v) and of the scene with the guests leaving (fol. 19v).[22] There are some elements reflecting outdoor natural spaces, but the artist focuses primarily on the various groups of people, their dresses and accoutrements, their hairstyles, headgear, and horses.

The artist understood well that one of Melusine's significant abilities consisted of creating new castles and erecting fortresses, drawing from a seemingly infinite amount of wealth, so many woodcuts contain walls (fol. 21v), towers, cityscapes (fol. 24v, 36v, 39r), and gates (fol. 29v., 31r, 33v, 35v). One woodcut shows a monastery in the back, though the individual features do not help distinguish it as such. The scene deals with Froymond joining the monastic community, being welcomed by two monks, who are fully grown men, whereas he still seems to be a child, judging by his small size, as if he were an oblate, though this is not part of the text. The background on the right side shows a church behind a wall, while a tall gate rises behind the two monks. Without this image, it would be difficult to recognize the building complex as a monastery. Later illuminations give many more details of the monastic ensemble, including a group of buildings which underscores how much money Geffroy donated to rebuild the monastery after he burned down the old one, killing his brother, all the other monks, and the abbot (fol. 83r).

Again a church stands in the middle, with a strong and tall gate, accompanied by a cluster of other buildings, but this time the lack of monks makes it rather difficult to identify the complex truly as a monastery. Nevertheless, prior

---

21 For this phenomenon, see the famous study by Norbert Elias, *Über den Prozeß der Zivilisation: Soziogenetische und psychogenetische Untersuchunge,* vol. 1: *Wandlungen des Verhaltens in den weltlichen Oberschichten des Abendlandes* (1939; Frankfurt a. M.: Suhrkamp, 1981), 170–76. For a historical approach, see Bee Wilson, *Consider the Fork: A History of How We Cook and Eat* (New York: Basic Books, 2012).

22 This must be an error in the reprint, since fol. 20v is missing, whereas 19v is repeated once.

to that image, fol. 8or depicts the earlier scene, in which the craftsmen are working, raising walls, pulling up stones, carrying mortar up a ladder, and mixing the mortar in a big container. Stein-Kecks bemoans the crude arrangement of the entire setting in which the building process seems already to have been completed, whereas the workmen are still performing their usual tasks, as unnecessary as those still seem to be.[23] But irrespective of the progress in erecting the buildings, the images give a clear concept of how masons and other craftsmen carried out their work. On fol. 83r the artist emphasizes the wealth on which the monastery could pride itself after Geffroy's rich endowment by way of painting the various gabled roofs in different colors and by including many windows.

Other illustrations regale readers with the image of a ship upon which Uriens, Melusine's firstborn, stands, together with his brother Gyot, both ready to depart, saying good-bye to their mother, who stands at the shore with her head and eyes lowered, obviously mournful at seeing two of her sons leaving her for knightly adventures in far-away Cyprus. Even though the artist has drawn the ship disproportionately, both the mast and the stern indicate its mighty size and splendor.

As often as outdoor scenes are portrayed throughout the entire text, the artist also endeavors to convey how the indoor settings are arranged. When Reymond visits Pope Leo and confesses his sins, he kneels before him next to an elegant altar, which is covered with a chalice and a candle holder. The pope sits on a massive throne, while the back wall is broken up by three windows. Even though the central perspective does not work here at all, it is obvious that the viewer is expected to recognize the elaborate architecture. Despite the private atmosphere, one recognizes the pope's central function by his vestments and his papal tiara, while Reymond has taken off his hat (still the same as in the beginning, decorated with a feather or a green branch and a red band) and extends his hands toward the pope, who blesses him.

In this scene the windows are closed, seemingly covered by glass panes. In fol. 82r, where Geffroy kneels in front of the same pope, also confessing his sins, there are now four windows, all open and showing the world outside. The pope sits on a different throne and there is no altar to be seen, but instead a kind of a couch in the background covered by a green blanket and a red pillow.

Although significant events take place in the forest throughout the romance, the artist mostly refrains from depicting that natural space. Instead he includes only a few trees in the background each time a major event happens

---

23   Stein-Kecks, *Die schöne Melusine*, 154.

in the forest, such as in fol. 5r, 6v, 7v, 10r, 12v, 52r, 53v, etc. One cannot expect much more from a woodcut, though contemporary artists working in other media certainly had begun to explore ways to reflect much more specifically on the forest and other natural environments. The genre of Books of Hours comes to mind, on which ecocritical perspectives truly abound, and where natural elements including the forest emerge in a quite sophisticated manner. But that is not the case in the illustrations for *Melusine*.[24]

Thüring's prose novel is, like the texts by his two French predecessors, strongly determined by emotional responses to specific events. Reymond accidentally kills his benefactor Emmerich and is completely distraught. He is shocked or terrified by the appearance of three mysterious women; later, when he discovers his wife's true nature, he worries that she might have noticed his transgression of his oath. Once he has revealed her secret in public, she must depart for good, which affects them both in extremely emotional terms; in fact, she collapses, while he breaks down psychologically. Earlier, Geffroy killed all the monks, and that woodcut (fol. 57v) gives a compelling impression of the horrible death the miserable monks endure. But when Reymond and subsequently his son, Geffroy, confess their guilt to the pope, the emotional affliction is not noticeable in the images.

One can realize, therefore, how important those illuminations are for the further elaboration of the narrative features involving the various protagonists, Reymond and Melusine above all. The medium of a woodcut was neither easy to handle nor flexible, and yet the artist makes an effort to convey the feelings experienced by those figures. When Reymond learns about the astrological reading by Emmerich, he gestures with his left arm across his body, signaling his puzzlement (fol. 5r). After he has accidentally killed his uncle, he rides off with both hands crossed in front of his chest, portraying his grief (fol. 6v). When he encounters Melusine and her two sisters, Reymond's great surprise is expressed through his two arms held up wide apart, while he gazes directly at Melusine (fol. 7v). Melusine's sadness when she says goodbye to her sons Uriens and Gyot is indicated by her arms crossed before her hips and her

---

24   Albrecht Classen, "Rural Space in Late Medieval *Books of Hours*: Book Illustrations as Looking-Glass into Medieval Mentality and Mirrors of Ecocriticism," *Rural Space in the Middle Ages and Early Modern Age: The Spatial Turn in Premodern Studies*, ed. Albrecht Classen, with the collaboration of Christopher R. Clason, Fundamentals of Medieval and Early Modern Culture 9 (Berlin: De Gruyter, 2012), 529–59; Classen, *The Forest in Medieval German Literature: Ecocritical Readings from a Historical Perspective,* Ecocritical Theory and Practice (Lanham: Lexington Books, 2015), which includes a whole chapter on *Melusine*.

downcast eyes (fol. 23r). The monks' horror when they are bured alive is vividly displayed, their arms held wide open, though their faces hardly reveal any
emotions, apart from one monk who has his mouth open screaming, or perhaps praying loudly to God (fol. 57v).

When Reymond and Melusine collapse on their bed as a result of their emotional distress over her enforced departure, the bystanders demonstrate their
empathy through the hands held together, or a hand held up, and by the heads
bent sideways or downwards (fol. 60r). As Melusine, already on her way out
of human society, dictates last instructions, her crossed hands at her left hip
and her curved body signal her grief, while a sorrowful facial expression as her
husband rests on the bed shows that she is entirely powerless and profoundly
distraught (fol. 61r). The artist's habit of using gestures rather than facial features to suggest emotions is typical of late-medieval woodcuts.

This does not diminish the high quality of these art works illustrating one of
the most popular prose novels from the middle of the fifteenth century. Most
importantly, irrespective of numerous shortcomings in the artistic design, the
faulty perspectives, and the lack of awareness about or interest in the natural
environment, the artist fully succeeds in providing very poignant illuminations
highlighting the central theme of the various sections. When Reymond departs
from the death scene in the forest, the cut in the side of the boar is paralleled
by the cut in Count Emmerich's left chest just above the heart. The spear with
which Reymond had tried to kill the boar but instead hit his uncle lies on the
ground, the shaft of which the dead count holds in his hand. Whether the boar
is alive cannot be determined, but its eyes are still open, and it seems to rush
away in the same direction as the one Reymond's horse is taking.

Reymond's encounter with Melusine in the forest—though the latter does
not exist as a natural entity, since we only notice a small green slope at the
foot of the three ladies and a tiny enclosure for the well—is superbly arranged,
powerfully expressing how shocked Reymond is, how magisterially Melusine
has orchestrated the scene to meet her future husband, and how superior she
is in comparison to Reymond. Even though she stands on the ground, his horse
only reaches to her hip, and Reymond seems tiny in contrast to her. The establishment of the new dynasty by means of the rope cut out of a deer hide
is clearly illustrated, with Reymond standing by and watching the workmen
encircling the land around the well. Part of the rope still consists of the deer's
legs, so that we understand its origin. Curiously, however, Reymond does not
seem to give any directions and stands quietly on the side, with his arms folded, while the other men are hard at work.

The many scenes reflecting the marriage festivities, the subsequent wars
fought by Melusine's sons, the scene with the badly wounded king of Cyprus,

and others can be ignored here since they do not contribute essentially to the argument. The central turning point in the narrative proves to be the moment when Reymond spies on his wife and then realizes both Melusine's truly hybrid nature as a fairy figure and the fact that he has transgressed his oath upon his brother's instigation. The artist created a characteristically simultaneous image, with various events taking place at the same time in the same picture (fol. 49r). Reymond has already cut a hole into the door and is holding his sword in his right hand. Melusine, still in her bath, can be seen from the side as if behind a glass wall. Reymond, however, is now turning his head away, looking at his brother who is rushing away on his horse, disappearing on the left behind a rocky slope, obviously aware of his guilt. Significantly, Reymond has raised his left hand toward him, and his entire body is half turned to the left, as if getting ready to pursue this brother whom he blames for having urged him to spy on his wife. At the same time, Melusine gazes at Reymond, since she knows what he has done. Her facial expression is neutral, but she crosses her arms and hands in front of her. The picture clearly hints that the future will be grim for the married couple, and things will change very soon.[25]

Later, when Reymond has exposed Melusine's true nature in public by openly maligning her as a monstrous creature, she collapses and faints, as illustrated on fol. 57r. Reymond stands above her while a servant throws water on Melusine to revive her. Another man and woman stand in the background, looking directly at Reymond, perhaps reproachfully. Later, shortly before Melusine has to depart, the couple lies stretched out on the bed (fo. 6or), she already half-removed from him, resting on the bed only with her upper torso, while Reymond has both of his arms resting flat next to his body. Melusine turns her head away from him, whereas he stares straight ahead. The three people behind the bed convey the scene's heavy emotions, one of them turning his head toward the couple, while the woman and another servant stare at each other.

One of the most famous scenes, which the artists generally enjoyed depicting, concerns Melusine's flying away, having jumped out of the window (fol. 62v). As in the bath scene, she is nude from the waist up, and she still wears her fanciful headgear, but now two large wings extend from her back while her turquoise tail twirls, apparently giving her enough of a spin to fly away. She does not make any effort to move forward, but instead holds her extended hands together. Reymond stands on the wall behind the crenellation next to another person, and both seem to be engaged in conversation, judging by their hand gestures.

---

25   For parallel woodcuts showing the same scene, see Stein-Kecks, *Die schöne Melusine* (2012), 17–19.

This scene is intriguingly paired by a later image of Melusine back in the bedroom at night, suckling her youngest child, while two wet nurses, lying in bed, watch from a distance but do not dare to get up and greet her (fol. 65v). All three women are explicitly gender-identified because of their naked breasts. One of the small children lies in the cradle, tightly wrapped. Typical for the style, there is hardly any furniture in the room, so the viewer focuses exclusively on the people, especially Melusine, re-emphasizing her maternal function, bringing her back into the human community, and removing entirely, at least in this situation, the monstrous features that had forced her to leave her husband and family.

A reader might also note as a peculiarity the way in which the artist presents the giant against whom Geffroy is fighting in Northumberland (fol. 67r). Even though the giant carries the usual club, he also wears sophisticated armor, although this does not protect him from Geffroy's mortal attack with his lance. Even though beards are not completely absent in any of the woodcuts, the giant has a very bushy beard and long hair, which underscore his uncivilized existence. The giant appears only slightly taller than his opponent, but his entire body shape is much bigger, especially his head. This element becomes much more vivid in another woodcut (fol. 75v) which depicts the transportation and public display of the defeated giant to the people whom he had terrorized for such a long time.

Granted, the artists included relatively few details in their images, but the cultural-historical information contained in them is impressive. Moreover, the visual theme highlights many of the truly critical moments in the narrative and begins to tell a story parallel to Thüring's account. Gestures, mimicry, postures, clothing, rocks, weapons, buildings, horses, tools, and many other aspects come into play and assist the narrative in developing fully in the printed version. Additionally, the woodcuts fully satisfy the general demand to shed light on the important events as described by the narrator. Little wonder then that they became model illustrations commonly imitated or copied by succeeding woodcutters, especially for those also working in Straßburg.[26]

At the end of the sixteenth century, the Frankfurt book editor and seller Sigmund Feyerabend offered a huge collection of erotic novels, which his cousin Johann Feyerabend had printed for him in 1587, along with woodcuts created by Jost Amman. It was a costly enterprise and did not witness a second

---

26   Benedicta Feraudi-Denier, "Drucke für die Kunst und Drucke für den Kunden: Wandlungen der 'Melusine'-Illustrationen während vier Jahrhunderten," in *Zeichensprachen des literarischen Buchs*, 263–90. She offers more of a survey of the changes which affected the woodcuts over four hundred years of *Melusine* reception.

edition, probably because Feyerabend died in 1590.[27] Nevertheless, the *Buch der Liebe* seems to have sold well and can be regarded as a major success on the book market. Feyerabend begins his printed version with an emblematic image showing Melusine in her bath, naked from her navel up, barely covering her breasts with the left arm while deftly displaying her female body, making the viewer a voyeur.[28] Feyerabend compiled and published this volume to provide illustrative reading material to teach his audience how to differentiate, as the subtitle suggests, between "was recht ehrliche / dargegen auch was vnordentliche Bulerische Lieb sey" [what is virtuous and what is, by contrast, inappropriate adulterous love].[29] The image is included as a signatory emblem and provides a number of allegorical messages about Melusine's monstrous nature, as represented by her enormous, strongly swirling tail, a griffin outside of the bath, which itself is quite elaborate, and by the rather complex natural background, in which Melusine's two sisters appear on both sides of a valley, the one squatting on rocks, the other standing on the walls of a castle holding a falcon in her hand. Melusine's headgear is marked by an even fancier design than in the woodcuts from the 1474 edition, equipped with a wide curtain-like fabric flowing down onto her shoulders. It proves to be more important, however, that Melusine stands in an open-air bath, with no wall or roof over her head. Reymond is nowhere to be seen, and there is no indication of the

---

27 Flood, "Sigmund Feyerabends 'Buch der Liebe' (1587)," 220, gives the year of 1592, but Ilse Ilse O'Dell specifies his death date with April 22, 1590. See O'Dell, *Jost Ammans Buchschmuck-Holzschnitte für Sigmund Feyerabend: Zur Technik der Verwendung von Bild-Holzstocken in den Drucken von 1563–1599*, Repertorien zur Erforschung der frühen Neuzeit 13 (Wiesbaden: Otto Harrassowitz, 1993), 18. This seems to be the correct date; see Rudolf Schmidt, *Deutsche Buchhändler. Deutsche Buchdrucker*, vol. 2 (Berlin/ Eberswalde: Weber, 1903), 240–46. See also Tina Terrahe, "Frankfurts Aufstieg zur Druckmetropole des 16. Jahrhunderts: Christian Egenolff, Sigmund Feyerabend und die Frankfurter Buchmesse," *Frankfurt im Schnittpunkt der Diskurse: Strategien und Institutionen literarischer Kommunikation im späten Mittelalter und in der frühen Neuzeit*, ed. Robert Seidel and Regina Töpfer, Zeitsprünge 14, no. 1–2 (Frankfurt a. M.: Klostermann, 2010), 177–94. For an analysis of the woodcuts, see O'Dell, *Jost Ammans Buchschmuck-Holzschnitte*. Unfortunately, O'Dell does not discuss the *Buch der Liebe*, apart from two fleeting references.

28 *Das Buch der Liebe* (Frankfurt a. M.: Sigmund Feyerabend, 1587). For a modern reprint, see Thüring von Ringoltingen, *Melusine. In der Fassung des Buchs der Liebe (1587)*, ed. Hans-Gert Roloff (Stuttgart: Reclam, 1969). In the digital version available online at http://dx.doi.org/10.3931/e-rara-21652, the reprinted images can be studied much more closely by way of zooming in and enlarging them. The copy used for the digitization is held by the Universitätsbibliothek Basel, Switzerland, Wack 688.

29 Feyerabend, *Buch der Liebe*, 1587.

transgression which her husband will commit. Moreover, Melusine does not look up, perhaps because there is no one to gaze at, and she almost seems to frolic in the water, undisturbed by any unwelcome visitor. In a subtle way, the artist has cast her in a much more erotic fashion than is typically seen in fifteenth-century woodcuts and has substituted Reymond with the reader as the voyeurs attracted by this hybrid, naked female body in the bath.

The emblem for chapter four shows a hunting scene far removed from the woodcut in the incunabulum. In a medallion setting, a group of knights holds spears or lances upwards with their right hand and shields with the left, while a hunter and two greyhounds race by them in pursuit of a deer. The vista opens to a hilly landscape with ancient ruins dotting the background. The deer runs up a slope, which is supposed to represent a forest, but there is no boar to be seen, as one would expect from the narrative and, by comparison, the late-fifteenth-century woodcuts. The motif of the medallion is only faintly related to the *Melusine* text, and we can assume that the woodstock derived from a different context. When chapter six opens, by contrast, the woodcut corresponds closely with the content again, since here Melusine stops Reymond and addresses him, while her two sisters stand in the background next to a well.

The variance from the older woodcuts is remarkable, since now Melusine kneels on the ground, holding the bridle of the horse with one hand and Reymond's hand with the other. He has taken off his hat to pay her respect, and he does not seem as confounded and shocked as in the older images. All four persons are dressed in elegant, sumptuous clothing, reflecting a drastic change of fashion that signals the coming of the Baroque period. The trappings for the horse and the fountain are considerably more elaborate and more realistic than in the earlier woodcuts.

This visual reflection of the progression from the late medieval to the Baroque period finds further corroboration in the subsequent illustrations, which are increasingly filled with more details and display a highly realistic scenery, both within the building and outside. The woodcut depicting an interior room, with the dying lord lying in bed in the background, while two men, Reymond obviously one of them, debate the signed letter in the foreground, presents an elaborate space with a richly modeled bed covered by a canopy and equipped with a wrapped curtain to the side (265). The central perspective is clear here, as the lines indicating the tiled floor run correctly from the front left to the back right. Two windows in the distance stand open.

The woodcuts depicting the wedding and the tournament following the ceremonies (266r) are similar to those in the Basel incunabulum in the general setting, but they markedly differ in the way the courtly crowd is presented both in quantity and quality. Clothing, headgear, weapons, horse equipment, background structures and environments, and many other details occupy the images, almost to a point where it is difficult to grasp what constitutes the central event. Battle scenes, such as in the woodcut for chapter eight (267v, which is repeated on 271r for chapter 32) intensify this crowd mentality, though it is still clear that the Christians arrive from the left and are met by the Turks on the right, who are identified by their turbans, lack of helmets, and the crescent moon on their shields.

A wedding scene on 277r (chapter 25) re-emphasizes the overall impression that these artists were deeply informed by early Baroque style. The festive dinner company in the left front are dressed sumptuously, while servants carry in food from the kitchen. Musicians placed on a balcony on the top right entertain the wedding guests. A heavy curtain hanging above their heads opens the view toward a distant landscape of what appears to be barren rocks. Completing the detail, a pet dog sits in front of the guests, with its back turned to the viewer. Similarly, the funeral of the King of Bohemia in chapter 34 is highly elaborate, showing two groups of people, with women on the left all turned away from the viewer, while a group of men on the right are shown frontally. A third group in the background carries the bier while a dog runs along the procession. Altogether, this iconography is a departure from those characteristic of the late-medieval woodcuts for the early *Melusine* prints. Ilse O'Dell, in her discussion of the artistic style embraced by Jost Amman, who worked for Feyerabend, reaches the conclusion that the artist created "üppige Bilder" [abundant images] determined by their "detailliert-erzählende[n] Art" [detailed-narrative manner].[30]

Chapter 38, which addresses Reymond's transgression of the taboo, returns to familiar ground, but this time the woodcut is the same as the one on the very first page, showing Melusine in the bath with her long tail (273r). Geffroy's battle against the giant appears in a much livelier, almost dramatic scene (274r, chapter 39), already showing the moment at which the protagonist, in full gallop, has with his lance pushed down to the ground the giant, who helplessly holds on to his long stick (not a club). The woodcut displaying Melusine returning from her banishment to nurse her child is contained in a much smaller space, but the wet nurses are shown in dramatic movement, one of them sitting up and pointing at the ghostly appearance (277r; chapter 46). Once again, the interior space is filled with objects such as the bed, a curtain, and a small desk with a night pot on it. The eye is also invited to wander into the background and observe glass windows. While Melusine is focused on the act of nursing, gazing intently at her child, which makes it almost impossible to recognize her

---

30 O'Dell, *Jost Ammans Buchschmuck-Holzschnitte*, 31.

face, the Basel print from 1474/74 leaves much more open space, since there is no other furniture but the bed, and the wet nurses do not move.

Similarly, in another battle scene involving Geffroy and a second giant (278v, chapter 48), the artist invested much energy in showing how both combatants swing their swords against each other, barely relying on their shields for defense. A major castle situated on the hilltop in the background provides an important vantage point for the spectator. Both fighters are apparently modeled after ancient Roman soldiers, wearing classical armor and barefoot. There are only sketchy indications of the natural background, which allows the artists to bring the fighting most drastically into the foreground.

Overall, these woodcuts reflect a new era in the history of art, while the text, as reprinted for Feyerabend, closely follows the original text of the fifteenth-century manuscripts and incunabula. Considering the small size of the woodcuts, the focus has shifted to the text, to the disadvantage of the illuminations.[31] Feyerabend aimed primarily at a reading audience which apparently needed less motivation to approach the narrative through visual cues; nevertheless, the woodcuts that he included prove to be extensively elaborate and detailed. Their inclusion demonstrates how much the *Melusine* narrative continued to appeal to contemporary taste and justified a heavy financial investment in the book's production, which for its part kept the Melusine legend in the public eye.

A final example that reflects on the popularity of *Melusine*, again from an art-historical perspective, comes from an unexpected source that has not yet been considered by Melusine researchers. Anyone visiting Burg Eltz [Castle Eltz] near Cochem, Germany, in the Mosell district near the border with Luxembourg and France, can discover a most unusual lantern, or chandelier, hanging above one of the dinner tables in a festive room. The guide labels it the "Lüsterweibchen," a female attached to a chandelier, because the front is made up of the figure of a noble lady whose lower body ends in a tail. Antlers also extend from her back, and the entire arrangement serves to hold candles. The etymology of the term associates the female figure with the candelabrum exclusively, not with "voluptuousness" or "Lüsternheit"[32] (note the 'n' after

---

31   Feraudi-Denier, "Drucke für die Kunst und Drucke für den Kunden," *Zeichensprachen*, 286.

32   The best-known example of this kind of figurative chandelier allegedly dates from 1392, when Ghese Lambrachting from Lemgo donated it to the local St. Mary's Church together with the St. Mary's altar. For the discussion of an example held in Wiesbaden (Sammlung Nassauischer Altertümer, Museum Wiesbaden), see Juliane von Fircks, *"Lieben diener v[nd] dinerinne, pfleget mit steter trewen minne*: Das Wiesbadener Leuchterweibchen als Minneallegorie," *Nicht die Bibliothek, sondern das Auge. Westeuropäische Skulptur und Malerei an der Wende zur Neuzeit: Beiträge zu Ehren von Hartmut Krohm,*

FIGURE 4.1   *An example of a Lüsterweibchen or female-figured chandelier bearing*
a Melusine-like tail, Castle Etz, Germany

"Lüster," which appears only in this word). In the sixteenth, and perhaps also in the seventeenth century, many aristocratic patrons apparently enjoyed purchasing such lanterns, such as the one in Burg Eltz, in the parish church of St. Mary in Lemgo,[33] Germany, or in the House Supersaxo in Sitten, Canton Wallis, Switzerland.[34]

The Irish castle of Bunrutty near Limerick, which houses many medieval art pieces from the Continent, holds numerous such "Lüsterweibchen," one of

<hr />

ed. Tobias Kunz (Petersberg: Michael Imhof, 2008), 98–110. See also http://de.wikipedia .org/wiki/L%C3%BCsterweibchen; http://de.wikipedia.org/wiki/lüsterweibchen, and, for an extensive list of further examples, see http://www.larsdatter.com/leuchterweibchen .htm (last accessed on July 14, 2016).

33   Iris Herpers and Götz J. Pfeiffer, "'vyf waslecht up dat hartestwych'. Der figürliche Gewei-hleuchter aus der Pfarrkirche St. Marien," in *Wie Engel Gottes: 700 Jahre St. Marien Lemgo*, ed. Jutta Prieur-Pohl and Jürgen Scheffler, Schriften des Städtischen Museums Lemgo 6 (Bielefeld: Verlag für Regionalgeschichte, 2006), 144–55.

34   Dione Flühler-Kreis and Peter Wyer, *Die Holzskulpturen des Mittelalters: Katalog der Sammlung des Schweizerischen Landesmuseums Zürich* (Zürich: Schweizerisches Landes-museum, 2007), vol. 2, 24–25. See also Erich von Beckerath, *Die unerkannte astrologis-che Symbolik der Sirenen und der mit ihnen verwandten sogenannten Leuchterweibchen* (*Lüsterweibchen*). Schriftenreihe der OARCA, Freie Akademie, Omnia Arcana (Munich: OARCA, Freie Akademie (Omnia Arcana) e. V., 1971).

FIGURE 4.2   *A Lüsterweibchen appearing in Germanisches Nationalmuseum in Nuremberg,*
Germany

which even displays a male figure. The motif had apparently become univer-
sally available, but this does not change anything in the identification of the
original type with the Melusine character. Famous artists such as Tilman Rie-
menschneider (1460–1531) and Albrecht Dürer (1471–1528) were involved in
producing such chandeliers,[35] and they all obviously demonstrate a close familiarity with a whole group of hybrid creatures commonly discussed in epic poems, fairy tales, and prose novels, such as sirens, fairies, nixies, and other strange
mythological figures. There is no doubt that the artists were as familiar with the
Melusine material as they were with other fictional characters associated with
water. Thüring's novel enjoyed tremendous popularity particularly in the early
modern age, and many artists, editors, and printers were involved in the dissemination process of this work, which obviously appealed strongly to the aristocratic and other audiences. Little wonder, then, that the Lüsterweibchen can
be closely associated with Melusine, and in fact can be identified with her specifically. Over time, the connection between this light fixture and the literary
figure was forgotten, but it is time to bring both together, since the Lüsterweibchen prove to be an important reflection of the figure's long-lasting reception.

---

35   http://crafthaus.ning.com/profiles/blogs/luesterweibchen-chandeliers (last accessed on
      July 14, 2016). For a very good historical discussion of that castle, see https://en.wikipedia
      .org/wiki/Bunratty_Castle (last accessed July 14, 2016).

It would be very easy to extend this investigative analysis further to discover many other media in which this famous figure was represented, from the late Middle Ages far into the modern age, including stone sculptures on capitals or as part of fountains, such as in the West Plaza of the famous Burgos cathedral in Spain.[36] As revealed here, early book printers made great efforts to incorporate woodcuts, which at first were fairly simple but soon became highly sophisticated art works, underscoring the tremendous cultural respect that Melusine has enjoyed throughout the ages. The woodcuts in the early printed version of Thüring's novel 1473/1474 and those contained in Sigmund Feyerabend's *Buch der Liebe* demonstrate a steady flow of art works strongly focusing on the Melusine myth. The Lüsterweibchen continue this tradition, and it is highly likely that the Melusine figure found representation in many other venues throughout the centuries.[37]

---

36   Stein-Kecks, *Die schöne Melusine*, 10. For print editions of the *Melusine* in the eighteenth century, see Hans-Jörg Künast, "'Auf ein Neues übersehen, mit reinem Deutsch verbessert und mit schönen Figuren gezieret': Beobachtungen zur Drucklegung der 'Melusine' im 18. Jahrhundert," *Zeichensprachen des literarischen Buchs*, 53–72. For other print editions in the nineteenth century, see Flood, "Drei 'Londoner' Spätausläufer der 'Melusine'-Überlieferung," 33–51.

37   Françoise Clier-Colombani, "Die Darstellung des Wunderbaren: zur Ikonographie der Illustrationen in den französischen und deutschen Handschriften und Wiegendrucken des 'Melusine'-Romans," *Zeichensprachen des literarischen Buchs*, 321–46; Feraudi-Denier, "Drucke für die Kunst und Drucke für den Kunden," 263–90.

CHAPTER 5

The Alchemical Transformation of Melusine

Melissa Ridley Elmes

The fairy Melusine, developed in the eponymous dynastic French romance by Jean d'Arras and, as attested in this volume's essays, reiterated alternately as a legitimizing political symbol and a subversive romance figure in the literatures and material cultures of many countries throughout the medieval period and beyond, isn't readily associated with Christianity. Yet, in a strange turn of fate, the figure of Melusine is appropriated not only for literary and political aims, but also as an alchemical symbol of transformation. Through her place in the alchemical lexicon, a tradition with pagan beginnings but, ultimately, developed and dominated by clerics of the Church and, later, physicians in the Middle Ages and Renaissance—like Paracelsus (1493–1541), with whose work she is especially associated—Melusine becomes a form imbued with the promise of enlightenment and salvation, a dual figure representing the union of the natural and supernatural worlds. Like the figure of Christ in the *imitatio Christi*, the alchemical Melusine serves as a bridge between the visible and invisible, between the explicable and the inexplicable, between immortality and humanity, and between the sacred and the profane. In representing the mingling of the natural and supernatural worlds and the fairy and the ordinary, Melusine ultimately figures both the union of pagan and Christian beliefs and the transformation of the pagan symbol of the siren into a Christian one of duality and enlightenment.

The alchemical iteration of the Melusine figure is especially significant in terms of understanding her later English literary representations. While the Melusine legend appears to enter English literary history at the opening of the sixteenth century and then disappear until the nineteenth century, when she undergoes a seeming reversal of fortune and re-emerges as a literary figure of considerable popularity, in fact the nineteenth-century Romantics who featured her in their writings were influenced far less by the earlier literary versions of Melusine than by her alchemical figuration. The transformation of Melusine from folktale, legend, and literary figure into alchemical symbol is primarily the work of Paracelsus, a sixteenth-century doctor living and working not in England, but in Germany. His development of Melusine into an alchemical symbol as part of what Phillip Ball calls his "chemical theology"[1] was recorded in the many unpublished writings he left behind. These writings were posthumously published and disseminated by late sixteenth-century alchemists, who in turn were studied and appreciated in the nineteenth century both by occultists and by poets.

This alchemical textual tradition, as much as if not more so than her literary representation, is what brought Melusine into the Romantic consciousness—a development attained not primarily through her traditional literary presentation as a dynastic, foundational fairy figure in the romance traditions of France and, later, Germany and England, but rather as a part of the nineteenth-century fascination with the occult, represented in the poetry of the time through its appropriation of alchemical symbolism and figures for literary purposes. The nineteenth-century English literary Melusines,[2] and their twentieth-century descendants, are a fusion of the literary and alchemical Melusines of the sixteenth century received through Continental texts and their admirers. To understand this, it is necessary to understand who Paracelsus was, how he conceptualized and developed Melusine as an alchemical figure, and how in turn that alchemical Melusine found her way into the writings of the later English poets.

Philip Theophrastus Aureolus Bombast von Hohenheim, who styled himself "Paracelsus" in the period fad of renaming oneself in association with a Roman thinker,[3] lived and worked most of his life in Germany after being exiled from his native Switzerland.[4] As a child, Paracelsus received a humanist and theological education at school, and was further educated in botany, medicine, mineralogy, mining, and natural philosophy by his father, a physician and chemist.[5] Paracelsus put all of these elements of his education to work in the development of his hermetic philosophy, to which his alchemical writings featuring Melusine belong. In this idiosyncratic tradition, Melusine begins as a figure in natural philosophy, and then becomes infused with magical and alchemical meaning in Paracelsus's hermetic medicinal writings.

His initial understanding of the Melusine figure came from her pagan folkloric representation in various cultures. Paracelsus traveled widely between

---

1   Phillip Ball, *The Devil's Doctor: Paracelsus and the World of Renaissance Magic* (New York: Farrar, Strauss, and Giroux, 2006), 258.

2   In this essay, the capitalized use of the word Melusine, singular, describes the general received fairy figure; Melusines, plural, acknowledges the many different iterations of that general figure; and melusine(s) described with a lowercase "m" refer to the pagan figures of the natural world that serve as the influence and inspiration for the formally named Melusine.

3   Ball, *The Devil's Doctor*, 69–70.

4   Andrew Wear, *The Western Medical Tradition* (Cambridge: Cambridge University Press, 1995), 311.

5   Wear, *The Western Medical Tradition*, 311.

1517 and 1523. Although his exact itinerary during these voyages is unknown, he gave as their purpose the statement that "diseases wander hither and thither throughout the breadth of the world [...] If a man wishes to recognize many diseases, let him travel."[6] During these travels, he collected both natural lore through his own observations and folklore from anyone willing to speak with him about medicine, both those trained in medical arts and those who gained their knowledge through passed-down oral traditions, family lore, and experience. As he writes in his Credo, "Wherever I went, I eagerly and diligently investigated and sought after the tested and reliable arts of medicine. I went not only to the doctors but also to barbers, bathkeepers, learned physicians, women, and magicians who pursue the arts of healing; I went to alchemists, to monasteries, to noble and common folk, to the experts and the simple."[7] During these journeys, he also heard and recorded local superstitions and folktales, among these likely stories of melusines, the water nymphs, as well as other elemental figures that the Church considered to be devilish in nature.[8] Importantly, as his translator Henry Sigerist notes:

> Paracelsus collected the various popular traditions about the elemental and other spirits that had come down from pagan antiquity. He did not render them the way he found them, and did not accept the official view that they were devils. He pondered over them and tried to determine their place and function in the system of nature. Since personal observations were hardly available to him, he had to rely on traditions; but he analyzed them as he did other phenomena of nature, other creatures of God. And he found a place for them in nature where their existence and function had meaning and significance.[9]

---

6   Sigerist, H. E., trans., "Seven Defensiones," in *Paracelsus: Four Treatises* (Baltimore: The Johns Hopkins University Press, 1941), 1–41, at 26. Hereafter, *Four Treatises*.

7   Jolande Jacobi, *Paracelsus: Selected Writings* (Princeton: Princeton University Press, 1951), 4.

8   Ball, *The Devil's Doctor*, 79. For a full-length study on the relationship between folkloric fairy beings (including Melusine) and the medieval Church—which influences the sixteenth-century reception of such beings and sets the stage for why Paracelsus's work in recovering, appropriating, and incorporating folk figures like Melusine into his "chemical theology" was at once experimental and innovative, and highly criticized, in his time—see Richard Firth Green, *Elf Queens and Holy Friars: Fairy Beliefs and the Medieval Church* (Philadelphia: University of Pennsylvania Press, 2016).

9   Sigerist, H.E., trans., "Liber de Nymphis, Sylphis, Pygmaeis et Salamandris et de Caeteris Spiritibus Theophrasti Hohenheimensis," in *Four Treatises*, 223–253, at 221.

Along his way to developing a chemically oriented and theologically informed understanding of the humors that he believed were responsible for human health, Paracelsus began by writing out his ideas about how the natural world featured in his new conception of the relationship between natural, supernatural, and human. This undated treatise, *On Nymphs, Sylphs, Pygmies and Salamanders*, is where his consideration of the melusine's relationship to other beings in the spirit and natural world, and development of a highly unorthodox theological understanding of that world with Melusine as an example, first appears. He begins by describing elemental beings associated with water, earth, air, and fire in general terms as "spirit-men," claiming that "We consider them to be men, although not from Adam, but other creatures, apart from man and all other animals, in spite of the fact that they come among us and children are born from them, although not of their own kind, but of our kind," and adds that although "in the Scriptures nothing special is written of these things [...] there are some remarks about the giants only."[10] He then boldly claims that "although these things are treated outside the Scriptures, their exploration is justified by the fact that they appear and exist."[11] Ultimately, he concludes that although "people find them unnecessary and find that it is useless to talk about them,"[12] since they have not been adequately discussed and explained in terms of their relation to the world, yet exist and therefore have been created, it is in fact necessary to explore, discover, and figure out what their role is. The remainder of the treatise discusses the similarities and differences between humans and these creatures as creations of God,[13] before turning to actual description of the creatures themselves—where they live, and their cosmic significance. Paracelsus therefore appears to be the earliest philosopher to bring these elemental beings, Melusine among them, out of their theological exile as devils in order to reintegrate them into a Christian view of the world in which

---

10   Sigerist, *Four Treatises*, 226.

11   Sigerist, *Four Treatises*, 226.

12   Sigerist, *Four Treatises*, 227.

13   Paracelsus's discussion of the similarities between humans and the elemental beings that form the subject of his treatise is familiar to those who have studied Melusine's literary representation, especially in terms of her desire to marry a human to gain a soul. According to Paracelsus's view of the world, God is God; humans are made in God's image and have Soul, but are not God because of their sinfulness, and the elemental beings are not humans because they are made in humanlike form, but lack Souls. Thus, Paracelsus writes, "[...] man cannot boast that he is God, but a creation of God, thus made by God, and God wants it thus—in the same way these people cannot boast that they have a soul like man, although they look like him [...] And so the one lacks God, the other the soul. Thus God alone is God, and Man alone is Man" (Sigerist, *Four Treatises,* 230).

they hold great significance for their human counterparts, however unorthodox that view might have been. Ultimately, he creates a mirror trinity to the
Holy Trinity, this one comprised of deity, human, and spirit-man: three separate entities united in God,[14] a significant point that is prominent in his later
alchemical writings featuring Melusine.

Their significance lies in the dual role these beings play as warnings for humans "to understand what we are on earth, and in what strange ways the devil
deals with us and is after us in every corner"[15] and as guardians of nature whose
presence conceals the treasures of the earth until "the time has come for the
treasures to be revealed."[16] In Paracelsus's discussion of the roles of these beings,
the specific figure of Melusine breaks out of the general mold, singled out as an
example of a *nympha* who is mislabeled a witch or devil for her desire to acquire
a soul by marrying a human being and bearing his children. Paracelsus warns
that she is "not what the theologians considered her"—that is, not a devil—
but that she "was possessed by the evil spirit, of which she would have freed
herself if she had stayed with her husband to the end" and that consequently,
a "superstitious belief resulted, that on Saturdays she had to be a serpent. This
was her pledge to the devil for his helping her in getting a man. Otherwise, she
was a nympha, with flesh and blood, fertile and well built to have children."[17] As
throughout the treatise, although theological questions of sin, temptation, and
possession by evil spirits arise with his discussion of Melusine, Paracelsus's focus remains on describing her relationship to the natural world and to humans.

He follows this description of Melusine's nature with the disdainful comment that "it is stupid [...] to consider such women ghosts and devils on the
basis of such happenings and because they are not from Adam" because "it is
holding God's works in low esteem to assume they are rejected because they
have *superstitiones*."[18] Folding these observations into his unorthodox theological views, he concludes that "there are more *superstitiones* in the Roman
church than in all these women and witches. And so it may be a warning that
if *superstitio* turns a man into a serpent, it also turns him into a devil. That is,

---

14   The best and clearest explanation of this process can be found in chapter four, "Paracelsus
     and the Renewed Image of God," in Remo F. Roth, *Synchronicity Quest: The Common
     Depthpsychological Background of Alchemy, Christian Mysticism and Quantum Physics* (Zu-
     rich, 1996), trans. Boris Matthews, accessed August 29, 2017, http://paulijungunusmundus
     .eu/rfr/gs4htm.htm.

15   Sigerist, *Four Treatises*, 246.

16   Sigerist, *Four Treatises*, 251.

17   Sigerist, *Four Treatises*, 246.

18   Sigerist, *Four Treatises*, 246.

if it happens to nymphs, it also happens to you in the Roman Church. That is, you too will be transformed into such serpents [...] in the end, you will be a serpent and dragon, like Melusine and others of her kind."[19] His clear Protestant disdain for the Roman Catholic Church notwithstanding, in these writings, Paracelsus characterizes Melusine as a nymph, associates her with other water figures like the siren, singles her out for her similarity to humans and her desire to acquire a human soul, presents her story as one born of superstition rather than devilry, and shows great concern that people not mischaracterize her as a devil or a witch rather than a natural spirit-human. This rather complex and disorganized presentation of the Melusine figure preserves some of the elements that later are shaped into her alchemical presentation: her relationship to water and the beings associated with the other elements (air, fire, and earth), her dual form as humanoid and serpentine female, her fertility, and her desire to perfect herself through the acquisition of a soul, which ultimately would permit her ascension into heaven.

It is not possible to trace the exact path this (super)natural Melusine described in his natural writings takes in Paracelsus's mind towards her final position in the alchemical writings, but by 1562 she was fully established within his view of the process leading to *opus alchymicum*, or ultimate alchemical work, often described as the philosopher's stone and promising longevity (conventionally, immortality). In his *De vita longa* [On Long Life], Paracelsus describes the process by which the *coniunctivo*, or chemical wedding, is achieved: through first the separation of, and then union of, Iliaster and Aquaster into the hermaphroditic Primordial Man, whom Paracelsus equates with the astral man in order to unify the hermetic and Christian traditions with which he is concerned.[20] In this alchemical process, which is fundamentally theoretical

---

19   Sigerist, *Four Treatises*, 246.

20   The Iliaster is the fiery, active, and aggressive masculine principle of the *prima materia*; Paracelsus associates it with the figure of Mercurius and the fiery substance of sulfur. The Aquaster is the watery, passive, sexual and feminine principle of the *prima materia*, and Paracelsus associates it with Melusine, who stands in for a combination of Aphrodite and Venus principles, and the dissolvable, and thus integrable, substance of salt. Together in the form of *prima materia*, these principles form the hermaphrodite, an androgynous, unified male-female which Paracelsus characterizes as a melusinian Ares-Mars. This complicated symbolism is recorded in the *De longa vita*, and a more detailed explication of the process is found in Carl Jung's commentary on "Paracelsus as a Spiritual Phenomenon," in *Alchemical Studies*, trans. R. F. C. Hull (Princeton, NJ: Princeton University Press, 1967), 109–188, and in his longer work on the alchemical wedding, *Mysterium Coniunctionis*, trans. Gerard Adher and R. F. C. Hull (Princeton, NJ: Princeton University Press, 1977).

rather than practical in nature,[21] Melusine is presented as the female form of Mercurius, and the *aqua permanens* or transforming substance in the alchemical wedding, in contrast to the Ares/Mars masculine aspect of Mercurius. What is significant here is Paracelsus's substitution as Aquaster of the pagan, folkloric, half-human hybrid Melusine figure for the human Aphrodite-Venus form that typically mirrors the Arian figure of the Iliaster. Because in his earlier writings Paracelsus had brought Melusine into the Christian cosmos as one of the members of the spirit-men races found in the natural world, and thus tied into his mirror trinity, she here becomes fundamental to the alchemical process as a figure in that theological belief system. As Roth notes, "in contrast to many of his alchemist colleagues, he took the path of differentiating the unknowable unity into a trinity by subjecting his *prima materia*, the Melusinian Ares-Mars, to a process of transformation."[22] Applying fire to the Melusinian Ares-Mars figure separates the dual form into two: at this point, represented as sulfur (the Ares/Mars figure) and salt (Melusine). To these separated forms then is applied the quicksilver, or Mercury. This combination creates a trinity of forms that Paracelsus equates with the Holy Trinity: sulfur/God, quicksilver/the Holy Spirit, and salt/the Son. The trinity of forms is also simultaneously fire/creation and perfection, blood/sacrifice and salvation, and water/transformation and union. This trinity, unified through the fire of the athanor (the alchemical furnace used in such experiments), produces the hermaphroditic Primal man form that means longevity and is the goal of this transformational process. Melusine is essential to this process both in her hybrid form, as the female, sexual, unifying aspect that brings together human and nature, and in her separated Aquaster form, which is integral to the unification of water, blood, and fire into the perfected Primal Man, *opus alchymicum*. Melusine remains elemental in nature, the water nymph of folklore and legend preserved in Paracelsus's earlier treatise, now transformed also into an alchemical symbol of duality and longevity aligned with esoteric Christian beliefs concerning salvation, redemption, and union. Through her participation in the chemical wedding, she brings to the alchemist the light of knowing, or understanding, that is at the heart of human conceptions of immortality via a union with God,

---

21   That is, as much or more about contemplating the experiment as actually performing it.

22   Roth, *Synchronicity Quest*, chapter four. A translation and edition of *De vita longa* from which to quote at length does not yet exist, and the Latin text is too long to be reproduced in full here. To render this extremely complex process comprehensible to a wide audience, what follows is a description of the alchemical process that is informed by Roth's, and Jung's, descriptions as well as by the summary and quoted passage of Paracelsus's *De vita longa* which is found in Jung, "Paracelsus as a Spiritual Phenomenon," 134–144 and 173–175.

the all-knowing—the same light of understanding that Paracelsus claims the spirit-men bring to humans in his natural writings.

Paracelsus's Melusine, in particular in her alchemical iteration, is at least in part the foundation for the Melusine that Johann Wolfgang von Goethe features in his short story *Die neue Melusine* [The New Melusine], part of the longer work *Wilhelm Meister's Journeyman Years* (1807).[23] This text is often de-scribed as a fairy tale, but it is certainly also an alchemical story.[24] Goethe's knowledge of the hermetic tradition and alchemical texts including those of Paracelsus is well-attested in his own autobiography,[25] in a magisterial mono-graph by Ronald Gray,[26] and especially in scholarship on Part One of his fa-mous alchemical tragedy, *Faust* (1808); however, beyond chapter two in Gray's study, there seems to be no critical tradition in English concerning the earlier short story. Gillian Alban credits Goethe with giving names to the elements in *Die neue Melusine*—"Salamander for fire, Undine for water, Sylphe for air, and Kobold for earth"[27]—and while it is not explicitly stated, suggests that there is a connection between Goethe's names and the writings of Paracelsus, although she claims that the 1811 *Undine*, by Friedrich de la Motte Fouqué, more closely follows Paracelsus's definition and placement within the aquatic tradition of the water nymph associated with Melusine.[28]

However, while Fouqué certainly retains most clearly the figure's association with water, Goethe's rendering of the world-within-a-world, both present and hidden from human sight, his association with and combination of the Melu-sine with another spirit-people, the dwarves, and the human's desire to enter into a union with the Melusine, suggests greater associations with Paracelsian

---

23   See Renata Schellenberg's essay in this volume for a critical study of this text.

24   In *Analytic Psychology and German Classical Aesthetics: Goethe, Schiller and Jung*, Vol. 2 (New York: Routledge, 2009), Paul Bishop also notes this point and registers surprise that Jung, who worked so closely with Paracelsus's texts, did not appear to pick up on this Goe-the tale's debt to Paracelsus's alchemy when writing "Paracelsus as a Spiritual Phenom-enon" (87), although it is mentioned in passing in *Mysterium Coniunctionis*, in which Jung describes the shadowy region of the psyche as being reminiscent of "the race of dwarfs in a casket described in Goethe's poem 'The New Melusine'" (301). Ronald Gray also sees alchemical associations in the story, as discussed below.

25   Johann Wolfgang von Goethe, *Autobiography*, vols. 1–2 (Chicago: University of Chicago Press, 1976).

26   Ronald Gray, *Goethe the Alchemist* (1952; rpt. Cambridge University Press, 2010); see chapter two for his discussion of the "mignon" or Melusine figure in *Die neue Melusine*.

27   Gillian M. E. Alban, *Melusine the Serpent Goddess in A.S. Byatt's* Possession *and in Mythol-ogy* (Lanham: Lexington Books, 2003), 48.

28   Alban, *Melusine the Serpent Goddess*, 48.

writings in Goethe's short story. In a lecture discussing Goethe's mysticism delivered on March 2, 1905, Rudolf Steiner notes a further alchemical element in this short story, specifically as regards the casket in which the dwarves are located:

> What is the small box? A world, a small world, indeed, but an entire world. The human being is a microcosm, a small world in a big one. The small box is nothing but a picture of the human soul. [...] What is summarised in the human soul as the sum of the thoughts? It is the spiritual spark. If we saw into the human soul, we would discover the spiritual spark with the seeds of the future stages. This spark was enkindled in distant past in the human being who was only gifted with a vague dream consciousness. This spiritual spark which smoulders in the human soul preceded all physical states. Compared with the future size, with the perfection of the human being is that which lives today in him only seed, only something dwarfish.[29]

While Steiner is speaking from the perspective of a psychoanalytical interpretation of the story, that interpretation is grounded in the understanding of alchemy as a theoretical, psychological activity. This passage of his lecture speaks to the same ideas of the elemental spirit-people as both mirror and warning of the invisible world that exists and needs to be seen and understood in order for humans to fully grasp God's work that are the basis of Paracelsus's natural, and later alchemical, writings featuring Melusine. Goethe alters the story in many ways, but Paracelsian ideas remain at the foundation of his short story as much as that by Fouqué. In turn, both men's writings were read by the Romantics in England, and their Melusines are mingled with the original Melusine from Paracelsian writings in the English Romantic tradition.

That Paracelsus was as popular a historical figure in his own right with English Romantics as he was with their German counterparts is evident in both the penning and reception of Robert Browning's epic poem about his life in five acts, published to critical acclaim in 1835.[30] Christina Pollock Denison, an early twentieth-century critic of the poem, explains that Browning's choice of Paracelsus as its subject is tied to his interest in the scientific spirit and mysticism, and that Browning is firmly with the Romantics in supporting Paracelsus against his critics:

---

29   "Goethe's Secret Revelation, Part III: 'The New Melusine' and 'The New Paris.'" Available
       online at http://wn.rsarchive.org/Lectures/GA053/English/UNK2014/19050302p01.html
30   Boyd Litzinger and Donald Smalley, eds., *Robert Browning: The Critical Heritage* (London:
       Routledge, 1996); see esp. "Introduction," 3–4 and "Paracelsus," 38–49.

In choosing this subject for his first mature poem, Browning was guided first of all by his intense sympathy with the scientific spirit. Realizing as he did, long before the scientific minds of our time, Paracelsus' true worth, and recognizing the value of the noble work done for mankind by him, Browning set himself the glorious task of restoring to his proper place in the scientific world this great benefactor of humanity. Paracelsus' name had been covered with infamy by his enemies and biographers. Browning thrust aside all pettiness of the physical, and laid bare to us the soul of this great mystic. The mysticism associated with the name of Paracelsus was probably another reason for the choice of this subject. Browning was fond of the mystical, and is acknowledged to be its subtlest interpreter in the English language.[31]

Phillip Ball claims that Paracelsus was "a noble hero" for Goethe and the Romantics, with specific reference to William Blake's admiration of his work.[32] It is evident from these examples that Paracelsus's biography, at least, if not his alchemical writings, were read by and served as inspiration for several of the English Romantics. Even more widespread among the English Romantics than the figure of Paracelsus himself was his alchemical Melusine, who appears to have been developed in the English tradition both from Paracelsian writings and from the German Romantic tales of Melusine and Undine, which were widely read and appreciated.

John Keats, who wrote "La Belle Dame Sans Merci" in 1819 and "Lamia" in 1820, is the major English Romantic poet who clearly reworked the Melusine figure from a position informed by Paracelsian writings or their distillation into the German romantic texts by Goethe and Fouqué; Keats certainly read and was influenced by *Undine*.[33] He was also heavily interested in the hermetic

---

31   Christina Pollock Denison, *The 'Paracelsus' of Robert Browning* (New York: The Baker and Taylor Company, 1911), 61–62. Denison demonstrates clear sympathy with the Romantics' view of Paracelsus as a "great benefactor of humanity" who is not yet appreciated by his detractors; Phillip Ball notes that in fact most of the scientific community, from the Renaissance down to present-day, finds little credibility in Paracelsus's writings, although he adds that "Paracelsus simply cannot be dismissed as a credulous fool (at least, not all of the time)" (12–14, at 14).

32   Ball, *The Devil's Doctor*, 14.

33   Adriana Cracium, *Fatal Women of Romanticism* (Cambridge: Cambridge University Press, 2003), 209. Misty Urban discusses Keats's "Lamia" along with other nineteenth-century English texts featuring a Melusinian figure in her essay in this volume.

tradition, which found its way into a number of his poems.[34] In turn, although her Melusine figure is arguably closer to that of Jean d'Arras, Letitia Landon read and was influenced by Keats's "Lamia" in the writing of her "The Fairy of the Fountains" (1835).[35] That both Keats's and Landon's Melusine figures are informed not by the earlier English translations of the French Melusine legend, but rather on the part of Keats, entirely, and on the part of Landon, at least partially, by Paracelsian understandings of Melusine as an elemental being and an alchemical figure of duality, sexual union, and enlightenment is underappreciated and underexamined. It leads to a question beyond the scope of this study but evidently as a result of it worth pursuing: if there are alchemical associations between these Melusine figures, what of the other water nymphs of the British Romantic tradition? Might some of them, also, be alchemical as well as folkloric and literary in nature? If so, that expands the presence of Renaissance alchemical and hermetic writings in later British literature beyond its already evident influence.

Paracelsus's influence on certain circles fascinated with the occult during the English Romantic period is also a well-known, if underexamined, phenomenon. A. S. Byatt capitalizes on it in her novel *Possession*, in which the fictitious Victorian poets Randolph Henry Ash and Christabel LaMotte exchange letters on the subject of the myth of Melusine as she appears in Paracelsus's natural writings.[36] These letters lead to LaMotte's developing an epic poem about Melusine, and her poem, like those of her actual Victorian counterparts, is heavily imbued with the alchemical symbolism Paracelsus developed in the sixteenth century.[37] The nineteenth- and twentieth-century English literary representations of Melusine as a symbol of duality, sexuality, union, enlightenment, and wisdom do not, then, stem from the literary tradition begun by Jean d'Arras and filtered through vernacular romance into the English imaginary. Rather, the later English Melusine derives from the strange dual trajectory formed by the biography of Paracelsus's life and his own writings as they are passed down through the hermetic and alchemical traditions, and the reception, reappropriation, and development of his alchemical Melusine figure by the German Romantics, whose poetry in turn influenced some of their English counterparts. Melusine's English literary presence is a fragmented one, and in fact

---

34   Jennifer N. Wunder, *Keats, Hermeticism, and the Secret Societies* (New York: Routledge, 2016), esp. chapter 3.

35   Cracium, *Fatal Women of Romanticism*, 219.

36   A. S. Byatt, *Possession* (London: Chatto and Windus, 1990), 172.

37   As an aside, it is possible that LaMotte's last name is an homage to Baron de la Motte Fouqué, whose *Undine* influenced Keats *et al.*

might be better characterized as "presences"; like her alchemical figuration, she is at once none and all of her origins. It is, perhaps, this complex set of origins that render her so endlessly fascinating and frustrating for writers, readers, and scholars alike.

PART II

Mother, Muse:
Melusine and Political Identity

∵

CHAPTER 6

Architecture and Empire in *Historia de la linda Melosina*

Anna Casas Aguilar

Translated in 1489 from the French text *Mélusine* by Jean d'Arras, *Historia de la linda Melosina* is a chivalrous and marvelous romance in Castilian that has been mostly forgotten by critics.[1] Throughout this book, geography (such as rivers, mountains, and seas), architecture, and physical spaces are of great importance. This world of physicality not only is found in the rich imagery of buildings, in landscape description, and in the numerous spatial references, but also extends to the beauty of the fairy, the deformity of Melosina's children, the courtly manners and outfits, and the hybrid body of the protagonist, thus creating a world with a very distinctive physical economy.

The presence of architectural elements in the Castilian translation of *Mélusine* allows for a new interpretation of key problems in this text, such as the importance of boundaries and their transgression, how gender expectations are broken and reformulated in the story, and the juxtaposition between the fairy and Queen Isabel I of Castile. The links between the figure of Melosina, her constructions—that is, the erection of physical buildings[2]—and the time of conquest and expansion under the rule of the Catholic Monarchs, Isabel I of Castile and Fernando II of Aragon, suggest different ways in which the book was read in the Iberian Peninsula during the reign of the Catholic Monarchs. Scholars such as Isidro J. Rivera, Ivy A. Corfis, and Ana Pairet have already commented on the double imagery between Isabel I of Castile and Melosina. In their works, these scholars highlight the juxtaposition of these two figures as a way to understand how Melosina influenced Aragonese and Castilian readers in favor of having a queen. However, the multiple ambivalences at play when

---

1   Alan Deyermond points out this neglect in "The Lost Genre of Medieval Spanish Literature," *Hispanic Review* 43 (1975): 241. Other medieval texts in Castilian from a similar time period, such as *La Celestina*, have received much more interest and critical attention from Hispanic literary scholars. The reason for this might be that Melosina is a translation and that the chivalric genre did not belong to a strong tradition in Castilian literature.

2   The term "constructions," as used here, alludes to the erection of physical buildings and not to the literary, rhetorical, or sociocultural construction of a concept or figure.

reading Melosina as a proto-feminist figure, especially when considering architectonic and spatial elements, illuminate how, in fact, this text might have highlighted anxieties and doubts about having a female ruler.

The following pages examine the puzzling juxtaposition between the character of Melosina and Queen Isabel I of Castile, particularly when envisioning fairy and Queen as positive figures for Aragonese and Castilian inhabitants. In her groundbreaking book *Isabel Rules: Constructing Queenship, Wielding Power*, Barbara Weissberger studies how Isabel of Castile was a problematic figure in terms of gender expectations and the Queen's influence on Iberian literary culture. Weissberger affirms that "the representation of gender and sexuality in late fifteenth-century literature, whether in nonfictional works addressed to or commissioned by Isabel, or in prose fiction and poetic works in which gender representations appear to have little relationship to the Queen, is deeply affected by the presence on the throne of an absolutist monarch who is also a woman."[3] Weissberger demonstrates that the image of the Queen is a central shadow on the literary production of the time period in which she reigned and contends that Isabel I was related in numerous literary works, in an explicit or implicit way, with a distorted woman, as the Virgin, a whore, or a virago, a result of the anxiety caused by having a woman as a queen. Similarly, Melosina's hybrid attributes show ambivalence in terms both positive and negative, which has important implications if the Aragonese and Castilian readership did, indeed, interpret this character in relation to Queen Isabel I.

There is no doubt that the translator of the French text had the Queen in mind when translating *Mélusine* to Castilian. Nonetheless, while scholars have mostly considered Melosina as a figure that put Castilian and Aragonese readers in favor of Isabel I, Melosina's descriptions are tinged with the anxieties that surround a strong woman in a masculinist society: Melosina as a constructor embodies ambiguities that link her to supernatural powers and provoke resentment. Moreover, her ability to build is coupled with having children, which highlights that her desire to gain more land and construct new buildings is often outplayed by her maternal reality and the desire to give her children a material inheritance. In the text, Melosina's identity as a wife and as a mother is linked to her identity as a builder. Fecundity and building are persistent parallels, and every time Melosina has a son, she erects new buildings. Ultimately, Melosina as a constructor represents a strong and powerful woman, but the way buildings, architecture, spaces, and territories are defined and characterized in relation to the novel's protagonists, particularly by looking at Melosina's

---

3   Barbara F. Weissberger, *Isabel Rules: Constructing Queenship, Wielding Power* (Minneapolis: University of Minnesota Press, 2003), XIV.

sons, is a strategy by which the text ultimately perpetuates a patriarchal structure by reinforcing traditional gender expectations.

Several interpretations of *Melosina*,[4] including those by Rivera, Corfis, and Pairet, draw parallels between the expansion processes, land conquest, and the spread of religion in this book and the Castilian crusades, the situation of Flanders, and the encounter with America during the reign of the Catholic kings. Rivera considers that chivalric romances such as *Melosina* "assumed the literary task of explicating the aims, aspirations, and authority of knightly society." Rivera argues that *Melosina* "authenticates a system of values, prerogatives, and functions which came to be promoted by the aristocracy of the late middle ages [sic] under the ideology of chivalry" and speaks to the importance of legitimizing power through a noble action and the book's necessity of offering a "foundation story," which illustrates how events in the past give legitimacy to future governance. This legitimating move, according to Rivera, reflects a vision of power similar to the one promoted by the Catholic Monarchs.[5]

Rivera also focuses on the politics of printing that could have motivated translators Juan Parix and Esteban Clebat to render this French text into Castilian. Parix and Clebat published the first edition of *Melosina* in 1489 and this edition was printed in Toulouse.[6] Although the direct influence of the Catholic kings is never suggested, Rivera affirms that Parix and Clebat's translation was

---

4   All quotations from Ivy A. Corfis, ed., *Historia de la linda Melosina* (Madison: Hispanic Seminar for Medieval Studies, 1986) and the translation of 1489. The edition of 1526 is outside the thematic concerns of this project.

5   Isidro J. Rivera, "The *Historia de la linda Melosina* and the Construction of Romance in Late Medieval Castile," *MLN* 112 (1997): 138–142.

6   Juan Cromberger published another translation in Seville in 1526. According to Miguel Ángel Frontón Simón, these translations might have been written after a French version published between 1478 and 1489: "parece asimismo evidente que la edición francesa que sirvió de texto base para la traducción no fue la princeps ginebrina, sino alguna edición lionesa posterior: la de Gaspard Ortuin y Pierre Schenk, fechable hacia 1486, la de Guillaume Le Roy, de hacia 1489, o bien alguna de las dos ediciones de Mathieu Husz, impresa una entre 1478 y 1484, y la otra en 1480 según unos bibliógrafos o en 1490 según otros" [It seems clear that the French edition that served as the main text for the translation was not the princeps ginebrine, but a later edition from Lyon: Gaspard Ortuin and Pierre Schenk's edition from 1486, Guillaume Le Roy's edition from around 1489, or one of the two editions by Mathieu Husz. One of those was printed between 1478 and 1484, and the other one in 1480 according to some bibliographers and 1490 according to others]. See Frontón Simón, Miguel Ángel, "*La Historia de la linda Melosina*: Edición y estudio de los textos españoles" (PhD diss., Universidad Complutense, Madrid, 1996), 157.

intended to appeal to the Castilian market[7] and that the text "appeared during a period in which the concept of knighthood and chivalry was undergoing reassessment and redefinition in the Iberian Peninsula."[8] Rivera stresses that "this interest in the chivalric was coupled with the dynastic vision of the Catholic Monarchs."[9] Thus, Parix and Clebat were aware of the tastes of their potential Aragonese and Castilian public and the will of the ruling classes. In "Empire and Romance," Corfis also considers that romances such as *Melosina* were key in the processes of creating an imagined community that put the population in favor of the crown. For her part, Pairet comments on the union of the crowns of Aragon and Castile, the end of Muslim Spain, the shifting focus toward the Atlantic, and the equal power of Queen Isabel and King Fernando as ideas that the readers of the Castilian *Melosina* would have had in mind while reading the text.[10] The work of these scholars is a first step towards thinking of *Melosina* as a propaganda piece that could cause Castilian and Aragonese readers to support the Catholic kings. Thus, *Melosina* is part of a larger campaign to influence public opinion in favor of the Crown and a text in which the female protagonist, a powerful female figure, might have encouraged Aragonese and Castilian readers to favor Queen Isabel I.

These scholars have also pointed to the role of architecture, geography, and the text's mythical tone as being central to the Castilian translation and to this promotion and creation of public opinion, as these are important references in the text that would be familiar to the Castilian and Aragonese public. The opening page of *Melosina* affirms that the aim of the book is to declare "como la noble e muy fuerte fortaleza de Leziña[n] fue fundada por vna fada" [how Lusignan's noble and powerful fortress was founded by a fairy].[11] The text also gives the name of the translator and calls the reader's attention to the foundation process: "maestre Juan Patrix, que la presente obra con grand diligençia puso en enprenta, por que las presentes ystorias y fundaçion de tan noble castillo fuese no menos en el nuestro eçelente rreyno de España manjfestada" [master Juan Patrix, who printed this work with great diligence, so that the present tales and creation of such a noble castle were manifested in our excellent

---

7   Rivera, "Construction of Romance," 137.

8   Rivera, "Construction of Romance," 138.

9   Rivera, "Construction of Romance," 138.

10   Ivy A. Corfis, "Empire and Romance: *Historia de la linda Melosina*," *Neophilologus* 82 (1998): 559–575; Ana Pairet, "Historie, métamorphose et poétique de la réécriture: les traductions espagnoles du *Roman de Mélusine* (XV-XVI e Siègles)," in *Mélusine: Moderne et contemporaine*, ed. Arlette Bouloumié (Angers: L'Age d'Homme, 2001), 48.

11   Corfis, *Melosina*, 4.

kingdom of Spain].[12] Rivera observes that, while the Castilian preface retains clear references to dynasty, lineage, and foundation, the French text seems more intent on convincing the reader of the historical veracity of the story than promoting an ideological discourse: "The Castilian translation dwells on foundation and lineage. The use of "fundar" [to found or to build] (twice), "castillo" [castle] (three times), and "fundación" [creation] (twice) stands out in comparison to the French original which refers less often to these."[13] Pairet has a similar observation and explains that the translator was not trying to seem historical in the Castilian version: "le traducteur ne cherchait pas à passer pour le dépositaire direct d'un témoignage oculaire, qui était dans les genres historiques un moyen privilégié d'authentification" [the translator did not seek to pass for a direct depository of an ocular testimony, which was a preferred method of authentication in historical genres].[14] These two scholars agree in finding more of a mythical tone than a historical one in the Castilian translation, which could add to the propagandist effect.

In addition, several references are made to Aragonese and Catalan geography throughout the original French text, which also appear in the Castilian translation and which would strongly resonate with the Aragonese and Castilian readership. Mélusine's sister Palestine is imprisoned in Mount Canigo by her mother,[15] and Remondin retires to the monastery of Montserrat after his pilgrimage from Rome through Perpignan, Figueras, Girona, and Barcelona. These references to a geography familiar to the Aragonese and Castilian readers, which both Pairet and Corfis consider key in the strategy of the translators,[16] would unify the Aragonese and Catalan geography with the spaces of France, central Europe, and the Middle East. The emphasis on the spaces as well as the mythical tone would make the text more appealing to the Aragonese and Castilian readership and help create an imagery that favored the Catholic Monarchs, especially when conveying ideas of expansion and conquest like the ones endorsed by Isabel I of Castile and Fernando II of Aragon.

Corfis strongly agrees that Jean d'Arras' references to Aragonese and Catalan locations are important in order to connect with the Aragonese and Castilian readers. Jean d'Arras had firsthand knowledge of Catalonia from his visit to Barcelona in 1380 as part of the entourage of the Duchess Violant de Bar,

12   Corfis, *Melosina*, 4.
13   Rivera, "Construction of Romance," 143.
14   Pairet, "Historie, métamorphose et poétique de la réécriture," 51.
15   Corfis, *Melosina*, 10.
16   Pairet, "Historie, métamorphose et poétique de la réécriture," 50; Corfis, "Empire and Romance," 568.

who married John, Duke of Gerona, and ascended to the throne with him on the death of his father, Pere the Ceremonious, ca.1387.[17] In addition, the king of Aragon is referred to when Palestina is imprisoned in Canigó, and the writer chooses to mention that the King does appear in the original text: "do fue despues de muchos vista e maiormente del rrey de Aragon, segun cuenta el que la presente ystoria conpuso en françes que lo oyo dezir al mesmo rrey de Aragon que ende lo vido" [where she (Palestina) was seen by many and most importantly by the same king of Aragon, as the narrator of the present story tells us in French. The narrator heard it from the Aragon king himself, who also saw it]. [18] These details regarding Catalan geography and the reference of the king of Aragon would turn a foreign text into a story with familiar references, thus enforcing the double imagery between Melosina and Remondin and the figures of Isabel and Fernando.

Scholars have also pointed out Melosina's juxtaposition with Isabel. Rivera, Corfis, and Pairet all view the figure of Melosina as a possible image that the Castilian readership might have related to the figure of the female monarch. Corfis considers that "elements of Melusina's role as a founder may well be germane to Spanish literary and historical development during the Isabelline period: a time of governance by a woman of considerable skill; a time of expansion, crusade, and empire-building in the Peninsula under the guiding hand of Queen Isabel. The importance of Melusina's figure as powerful female leader may bear on the date of her first appearance in Castilian letters."[19] Corfis maintains that the image of a powerful woman who holds her authority by reigning and building could be read as a manifestation of the interest in legitimizing the power of Isabel, at the same time putting her in contact with the Aragonese crown through her husband. This would work in two ways: first, through the characterization of Remondin and Melosina as figures in an equal partnership and second, through the Aragonese connections, which relate the Aragonese territory with the French dynasty. The tale would therefore support the expression "tanto monta" [it amounts to the same], commonly used at the time and which appears in the Code of Arms of the Catholic Monarchs. This expression referred to the image of dual governance between Isabel and Fernando, in which the illusion of a powerful woman who creates a large empire

---

17   Corfis, "Empire and Romance," 569. See also Alan Deyermond, "La *Historia de la linda Melosina*: Two Spanish Versions of a French Romance," in *Medieval Hispanic Studies Presented to Rita Hamilton* (London: Tamesis, 1976), 62 and Amédée Pagès, *La poésie française en Catalogne du XIIIe siècle à la fin du XV* (Toulouse: Privat-Didier, 1936), 71.

18   Corfis, *Melosina*, 10.

19   Corfis, "Empire and Romance," 569.

is interchangeable with the figure of the male leader. The discursive strategy of equal governance would be helpful in making the figure of Isabel appealing to the Aragonese crown and making the Aragonese territories attractive to the Castilian inhabitants.

Melosina contributed to an imagery of feminine courtly governance, empire-building, and crusades that took place during the reign of the Catholic monarchs. Corfis maintains that "[a]lthough at the time of *Melosina's* first appearance in 1489 neither the imperial expansion in the Americas nor the Mediterranean Crusade had yet begun, the Catholic Monarchs had passed through the war of succession (1474–79), fending off other contenders' claims to Henry IV's throne of Castile, pacifying contentious nobles from other factions, and winning them over to support Ferdinand and Isabella's claim to power."[20] While, as Corfis explains, it is correct that the expansion to the Americas had not begun in 1489, the expansion and colonization of the Atlantic was a reality in 1489 through the colonization of the Canary Islands. The archipelago was a central geographical step that allowed for travel to the Americas, as it strategically connected the two continents and was pivotal for sailors to learn to navigate back to Europe.[21] The Canary Islands were also part of the creation of an American imaginary and discourse of colonization. As David Abulafia wonderfully explains in *The Discovery of Mankind*, "Not for nothing did the earliest printed accounts of Columbus' first voyage to the Caribbean refer to his discoveries as the 'New Canaries'."[22] Abulafia identifies July 1341 as the moment in which "two sizable ships accompanied by a smaller vessel set out for the Canaries from Lisbon, carrying, as was common at the time, a mixed crew composed of Portuguese, Castilians, Catalans and Italians."[23] Similarly, the *Reconquista* process had begun in the ninth century, and this process culminated in the war with the emirate of Granada begun in 1482. Thus, when *Melosina* was translated and published in 1489, there were already important events that related Isabel and Fernando to geographical expansionist projects. Melosina's desire for spatial expansion would thus resonate with an Aragonese and Castilian readership that could see in Melosina a parallel to Isabel 1 of Castile.

---

20   Corfis, "Empire and Romance," 569.

21   See Felipe Fernández-Armesto, *The Canary Islands After the Conquest: The Making of a Colonial Society in the Early Sixteenth Century* (Oxford: Oxford University Press, 1992).

22   David Abulafia, *The Discovery of Mankind: Atlantic Encounters in the Age of Columbus* (New Haven: Yale University Press, 2008), 5.

23   Abulafia, *Mankind*, 37.

It is important, nonetheless, to consider which parallels might have been drawn by readers and to question whether the translation in fact could have enforced certain ambivalences towards the Queen. Uses of architecture and space that highlight hesitancies over the character of Melosina could be translated into doubts about the value of having a female ruler in Aragon and Castile. Architecture and space are fertile avenues to explore the question of gender expectations and subversions in *Melosina*, as one of the most striking characteristics of Melosina is how often, how fast, and how greatly she builds. In her introduction to *Melosina*, Corfis points out that the origin of this construction myth can be found in the Gallo-Roman tradition of the text as well as in Celtic beliefs, and explains that "Mére Lusine was thought to build her castles and churches at night by the light of the moon. Not only did she build up edifices but also dropped large stones from her apron as she carried them to the building site [...] She also was responsible for accidents during the making of buildings, and builders cited her for all mishaps and delays."[24] Corfis highlights Melosina's positive and valuable characterization associated with her strength and with her power of building, but also the negative and doubtful aspects associated with her supernatural powers and with accidents and delays.

The idea of building as a magical or marvelous process appears repeatedly throughout *Melosina*. After marrying Remondin, Melosina builds the fortress that will serve as their home. Even when a detailed description of how Melosina pays carpenters and builders is provided, the narrator suggests there is something strange in these constructions:

> E obravan aquellos maestros tan presto e sotilmente que paresçia fuessen toda su vida ende estado a edificar lo que en muy breue tienpo fue edificado. E ella les pagava el sabado toda la obra de la semana syn nada les faltar ninguno [...] E verdad es que njnguno savia do estos maestros e obr[eros] eran venidos, los quales dentro de muy breve tienpo edificaron dos muy fuertes pla[ç]as, todas çercadas de muy fuertes muros e torres muy altas al deredor e ha muj fuertes bareras de la mesma rroca viua [p] icadas que no ay honbre viuiente que la pudiesse por fuerça tomar.[25]
>
> [And those masters were working so fast and delicately that it seemed like they had spent their whole lives building what was in fact finished in a very short period of time. Every Saturday Melosina paid the workers for all their work, without forgetting anyone [...] And what is true is that no one knew where these workers came from. These workers built in a very

---

24   Corfis, *Melosina*, 11.
25   Corfis, *Melosina*, 32.

short period of time two squares, enclosed by very strong walls and very high towers and surrounded by very strong gates from the same rock that no living man could lift with his strength.]

The details about how the builders were paid and what the constructions looked like give the text a sense of reality that contrasts with the ambiguous origin of the workers. The appearance of builders is similar to the appearance of other magical elements, for example, the vassals in Melosina's castle or the money and jewels of the fairy. In fact, these sumptuous objects as well as the builders have the same unknown origin as the fairy. The constructions are therefore part of the marvelous world that surrounds Melosina and that represents her as different from humans. Remondin, even when curious about where all this richness comes from, prefers not to ask Melosina, which adds to her secretive reality.

In addition to the unclear origin of the workers, part of the strangeness in the construction process is that Melosina is continuously making new buildings in a seemingly unrestrained way, which makes readers wonder about the uncontrolled powers of the protagonist. The insistence on the construction of buildings shows an anxiety toward these edifices. If, as Kent Bloomer and Charles Moore contend in *Body, Memory, and Architecture,* men have dominated nature through architecture and imposed culture and its forms,[26] Melosina's constructions could be considered an expression of her desire to dominate not only her surroundings, but also to control or conquer the nature of her body. In this sense, the hybrid body of Melosina, her supernatual powers, and her extraordinary capacity of building are presented as ambivalent elements and as elements that she aims to control.

It cannot be forgotten that Melosina's physical characteristics were likely placed in parallel to the Queen's body. In *Isabel Rules*, Barbara Weissberger explains that "because *woman* in medieval gender ideology was identified with the body, the very notion that a being who was perceived as naturally libidinous, irrational, and polluted might cure the nation's sickness was almost as disturbing as those feminized external and internal enemies who were the cause of its diseased state."[27] Following Weissberger's explanation, Melosina's non-human being and her power could have reflected suggestively on the figure of the Queen. The question is whether this juxtaposition could strengthen or legitimize the power of Isabel I or, on the contrary, suggest that the Queen was a distorted or problematic leader.

---

26   Corfis, *Melosina,* 5.
27   Weissberger, *Isabel Rules,* XVII.

In this sense, it is important to observe how the text stresses the function of the fortresses, walls, and constructions as protective, as if these fortresses and buildings were representing, in a metaphorical way, Melosina's need to protect her own dubious reality. An example of this is when Remondin is in Brittany and Melosina builds the villa of Leziñán. In this passage the strength of Melosina's constructions is stressed:

> [E]n el tienpo que esto pasava en Bretaña, Mel[o]sina hizo hedificar la villa de Leziñan e fundar los muros sobre vna rrica viña do hizo muy fuertes torres e los muros eran todos cuviertos por defender la gente que en llos serian. E dentro la villa hizo torres muy fuertes que avian bien xvj o xx pies de hancho.[28]

> [During the time in which this was happening in Brittany, Melosina had the town of Leziñán built and the walls created in a rich vineyard. She built strong towers and walls that were intended to protect the people who would be in them. And inside the town she constructed strong towers of xvj or xx feet long.]

Melosina's projects map her body onto an external surface and refashion her identity in a material way. In so doing, Melosina tries to hide her reality as a fairy. In the text, there is a parallel between how protective and strong her constructions are and her desire to protect and cover her hybrid reality. By building, Melosina on the one hand shows off her wealth and power, but on the other hand, she appears to be trying to defend herself from her own body and truth. Afraid of the dual state she inhabits,[29] walls, towers, and fortresses preserve her ambiguous body and her monstrosity. This need for protection reinforces the ambivalence of this figure as both a positive and a negative being: positive because she creates wealth and buildings for her family and subjects, but negative in the sense of doing so in a dubious way, using her supernatual, superhuman, and uncommon powers.

The geography in which Melosina is situated is also relevant, as Gabriele Spiegel observes. It is an area with woods and fountains, the space where the supernatural meets the natural "that anthropologists have taught us to recognize as sites of exchange between the world of humans and creatures of the

---

28   Corfis, *Melosina*, 42.

29   Gabriele Spiegel, "Maternity and Monstrosity: Reproductive Biology in the *Roman de Mélusine*," in *Melusine of Lusignan: Founding Fiction in Late Medieval France*, ed. Donald Maddox and Sara Sturm-Maddox (Athens, GA: University of Georgia Press, 1996), 100–124, at 102.

uncertain realms."[30] Melosina's constructions reflect her relation between the two worlds that she inhabits as an extension of this liminal geography: a bridge between the natural and wild, on the one hand, and the courtly and feudal, on the other. It is clear that, once married, Melosina "civilizes large stretches of wild, uninhabited forests with the constructions that are the source of the family's name and geographical mark of its establishment, importance and durability."[31] However, this "domesticating effect,"[32] following Douglas Kelly's term, both toward the natural space and the animal body, is always in tension with the reality of the fairy, as Melosina cannot control her changes and her buildings completely. The text often allows the reader to see that Melosina is constructing by using supernatual powers and magic. In this sense, as suggested by Pairet, the reader ends up having a feeling of instability[33] when reading about Melosina's building projects. The ever-changing spaces that Melosina creates represent, in this sense, the fear of a body in metamorphosis. These characteristics, again, could speak to Aragonese and Castilian readers about an ambivalence and double characterization of the Queen Isabel I of Castile, as a possibly hybrid and untrustworthy person who possessed more than ordinary powers.[34]

In *Body, Memory, and Architecture*, Bloomer and Moore explain that, at its core, all architecture derives from a body-centered sense of space and place[35] and that "experiences of life, especially experiences of movement and settlement in three-dimensional space, are dependent on the unique form of the ever-present body." [36] The relation Melosina has with spaces could also be read as an extension of her perception of her own body. Melosina is strong, prolific, active, and dynamic. She can organize any space and achieve immense dimensions without difficulty; she builds and improves cities including Parthenay, Melle, Vouvent, Mervent, Saint-Maixent, Catelaillon in La Rochelle, Poiters, Saintes, Talmont, and Niort.[37] Melosina's body has uncommon, magical, and supernatural characteristics, not only because of her ability to occupy

---

30   Spiegel, "Maternity and Monstrosity," 100.

31   Douglas Kelly, "The Domestication of the Marvelous in the Melusine Romances," in *Melusine of Lusignan*, 32–47, at 36.

32   Kelly, "Domestication of the Marvelous," 36.

33   Pairet, "Historie, métamorphose et poétique de la réécriture," 47.

34   For further discussion of the meanings of metamorphosis and hybridity to medieval audiences, see Ana Pairet's chapter, "Polycorporality and Heteromorphia: Untangling Melusine's Mixed Bodies," in this volume.

35   Kent Bloomer and Charles W. Moore, *Body, Memory, and Architecture* (New Haven: Yale University Press, 1977), 5.

36   Bloomer and Moore, *Body, Memory*, 37.

37   Corfis, "Empire and Romance," 564.

vast extensions of space in a very short period of time, but also because she turns into a mermaid once a month. This extensive reach of space allows her to create a lineage through both her building projects and her descendants. This feeling of easy movement through space is inherited by her children, who will also travel around vast territories of land in a short time. Nonetheless, Melosina's children do not need to hide their strangeness as Melosina does, and their expansionist desires are less subtle and more closely linked to military expansion. This gendered reality makes it evident that the feminine figure contrasts with the masculine characters in terms of how they relate to space and architecture.

Another central element is how architecture is a language that operates through sight. Using patterns of visibility and invisibility, showing and hiding, architecture is a way of evidencing the truth of the fairy and thus a form of language. With her constructions, Melosina creates a strong tension between discourse and reality. While she is protecting her hybrid body with her buildings, what she builds ends up making her deformity and difference evident. Indeed, architecture evokes and makes explicit a monstrosity that cannot hide behind the walls. In this sense, Melosina's walls work as silences and, as silences, even when they want to hide, they evoke the truth. Her buildings function as communication, both hiding and showing Melosina's truth. A key passage in the text that illustrates how language and architecture are bound together is Remondin's discovery of Melosina's hybrid body.

Remondin penetrates a physical construction, a door, while his wife is bathing in secret, and thus Remondin sees his wife transformed into a serpent. This passage shows that Remondin has access through architecture to both his wife's body and her truth, and that all three are penetrated at the same time. The door is a sort of skin for the fairy as well as a door towards her reality, a door that Remondin penetrates with his sword:

> E toma su espada que era colgada de vn pilar de la camara, e asy se va al logar do Melosina se lavaua. E hallo ende una puerta muy fuerte. E con la punta de su espada el comjiença a foradar. E hizo vn agujero tan grande que del podia bien ver lo que hazia dentro.[38]
>
> [And (Remondin) took his sword that was hanging from a pillar in the room, and went to the place where Melosina was cleaning herself. He found a very strong door. And with the sharp end of his sword he started to make a hole. And he did a hole that was so big that he could see well what (Melosina) was doing inside.]

---

38   Corfis, *Melosina*, 148.

The scene is both an image of masculine power in which the husband discovers the wife's secret—a power symbolized by the sword—as well as a castrating vision, since Remondin will lose his wealth after this discovery in which he transgresses the wife's taboo.[39] Remondin's fortune turns into a form of misfortune and is tied to the discovery that his wealth in fact comes from a hybrid being. In addition, and as Brownlee and Spiegel explain,[40] Remondin's silent transgression needs to be verbalized so that he can be punished, again highlighting the importance of language and silences in the text and their connection to physical constructions—in this case, the door penetrated by the sword. Remondin calls his wife a serpent[41] and his words are as hurtful as the sword: "E cuando Melosina oyo esta palabram uvo tan grand dolor en estas palabars que ella cayo quasi muerta del otro costado" [And when Melosina heard this word she felt such pain for what was said that she felt almost dead from the other side].[42]

Melosina's final transformation takes place in relation to architecture as well: jumping through the window, she leaves at the same time both her human body and her house.[43] Nonetheless, this final transformation is by no means liberating. Melosina will inhabit eternally the liminal space between the outside and the inside of her house as her mother condemned her to do, and thus, voicing her pain, she will remain bound to her walls and her truth: "E tu aparesçeras tres dias delante la fortaleza que tu llamaras de tu nonbre e tu haras ende grandes gemjidos quando sera que ella deva canviar e mudar su señor. E lo mismo haras quando alguno de tu linage querra morir" [And you will appear during three days in front of the fortress that you will call following your name and you will moan every time that the fortress changes owner. And the same thing will happen when someone of your lineage dies].[44] While the conclusion of *Melosina* gives an eternal space of observance and presence to the fairy in the fortress that she once built, it also ties her to a repetitive and

---

39   This image of Remondin seeing his wife's naked body in the form of a serpent recalls
       Freud's psychoanalytical theory of the male child viewing for the first time the woman's
       genitals, and how this creates the fear of castration. As Brooks considers, "Freud repeatedly posits an equivalence of blinding and castration, notably in his reading of the *Oedipus*" in Peter Brooks, *Body Work, Objects of Desire in Modern Narrative* (Cambridge, MA: Harvard University Press, 1993), 12.
40   Kevin Brownlee, "Melusine's Hybrid Body and the Poetics of Metamorphosis," in *Melusine of Lusignan,* 76–99, at 78; Spiegel, "Maternity and Monstrosity," 101.
41   Corfis, *Melosina,* 158.
42   Corfis, *Melosina,* 158.
43   Corfis, *Melosina,* 162.
44   Corfis, *Melosina,* 10.

imprisoned existence. In fact, this final imprisonment of Melosina contrasts with her sons' lives of conquests and procreation, which ultimately demonstrates that Melosina is in many ways just a link in a chain of masculine domination. Through architecture, the text shows the existing connection between Melosina and her descendants, a connection that places her in contrast with her masculine descendants, who are able to conquer freely. Thus, Melosina's expansion is terminated in a final situation in which she is imprisoned in her own fortress.

Melosina's hybrid and transgressive body and her ability to build are repetitive elements in the story that very often appear interwoven. Building and having children are connected to Melosina's identity as a wife and as a mother. From the beginning of Melosina and Remondin's relationship, she tells her husband that she will enrich him through her power and she will ensure that his "generaçion e li[n]age sea aumentado en valor, en fuerça e rriqueza" [generation and lineage shall increase in value, in strength and wealth].[45] As Douglas Kelly explains, "Melusine assumes two principal roles: she is a mother of sons and a builder of buildings."[46] Fecundity and building are persistent parallels, and every time Melosina has a son, she erects new buildings. When the first son is born, the narration makes explicit that there is a correlation between having the child, celebrating, and building:

> [E] dize la ystoria que despues de su parto, hizo Melosina muy grand fiesta do fueron convidados grand multidad de muy nobles gentes. E departida la fiesta, en el año mesmo hizo la linda Melosina vn muy fuerte castillo en la villa de Melle. E hizo hazer no menos Bovante e Marmante. E despues hizo hazer la villa e la torre de Sant Maxian e começo una abadia.[47]
>
> [And the story says that after giving birth, Melosina organized a very large celebration where many noble people were invited. And once the party was over, the beautiful Melosina had a solid castle built in the town of Melle in the same year. And she ordered no less in Bovante and Marmante. And after this she had the tower Sant Maxian built and she started an abbey.]

---

45   Corfis, *Melosina*, 18.
46   Corfis, *Melosina*, 32.
47   Corfis, *Melosina*, 50.

The same happens when the second son, Guyon, is born; just after the birth and without rest, Melosina creates castles and towers. The description of physical elements works simultaneously both for Melosina's children and her buildings:

> [E]l año segundo despues uvo Melosina vn hijo que uvo nonbre Gujon [...] E en este tienpo hizo Melosina fundar muy nobles logares por toda su tierra que ellos avian en las marcas del conde de Pujtiers e del ducado de Gujana. Ella hizo hazer el castillo de Paranaj muy fuerte e muy hermoso, casy syn comparaçion. E fundo las torres de la Rochela e el castillo, e en el comienço de la villa avia vna grand torre de tres carros que Julio Cesar havia hecho hazer.[48]
>
> [And the year after Melosina had a son whose name was Gujon [...] During this time Melosina had noble places built all over her land that belonged to them near the confines of the count of Pujtiers and the duchy of Guijana. She had the castle of Paranak built very solidly and very beautiful, almost without comparison. And she built the tower of Rochela and the castle, and at the entrance of the town there was a tower of with three carriages that Julius Caesar had had built.]

The parallelism between having children and building castles, bridges, and fortresses is evident in the text, which often describes the buildings' characteristics and the sons' deformities at the same time. In total, Melosina has eight sons, and alongside those births she builds numerous structures in new spaces that are now part of her husband's dynasty. It is important to note that what could seem to be a natural process, having children, is deeply connected to assimilationist projects—the spread of cultural homogeneity—and to the arrival of governance over wild spaces. The act of having children is integrated with the creation of a civilized or conquered space in the narrative. Moreover, the sons highlight the practical need of finding further territories and lands.

With her powers of building houses and castles and creating wealth, Melosina challenges the traditional model of a docile and passive woman. The text never loses the opportunity to clarify her dynamism, proving that Melosina is in many ways a positive model who could dispose the Aragonese and Castilian readership in favor of having a female ruler. Melosina is the one who decides the name of Luziñán[49] for her lineage and first building projects after her marriage. As Spiegel points out, these activities, especially giving the name for her

---

48   Corfis, *Melosina*, 50.
49   Corfis, *Melosina*, 34.

"agnatic lineage," had been, since the twelfth century at least, "the principal and exclusive genealogical task for males."[50]

Nevertheless, there is a tension in the story between the positive and negative effects of a powerful and female figure. During the tale, Remondin appears sometimes as a secondary character in the wife's shadow, and one could consider to what extent he can be seen as a demasculinized figure for medieval readers; in several passages, he lacks initiative and follows his wife's orders. While it is true that as Melosina builds, Remondin recovers his land,[51] in other cases, he cannot recognize the spaces that his wife has changed. This happens the second time Remondin comes to the fountain to meet Melosina, and also when he returns from fighting for his inheritance. In both cases, because of her edifications, Remondin does not know where he is: "E vio de lexos la torre obrada que Melosina avia hecho e no connosçia do fuesse ca a causa de las hedificaçiones e nouedades que Melosina avia hechas, no conosçia sy era aquella su tierra o non" [And he saw from far away the tower that Melosina had built and he did not recognize it because of all the buildings and novelties that Melosina had made. He did not recognize whether this was his land or not].[52] Melosina built so much that his house is unrecognizable and the husband finds himself alienated.

Remondin's feeling of being lost underlines Melosina's power vis-à-vis her husband's power, her activity versus his helplessness. In many senses, buildings speak of Melosina's superiority over Remondin—a superiority that he is unhappy with, as proven when Remondin decides to uncover his wife's secret despite having been warned of the consequences of doing so. Thus, Melosina's power to build invokes an ambivalence towards this figure and calls into question the extent to which Remondin feels subordinated to his wife's powers.

The ambivalent characterization of a female builder and the fact that Melosina possesses a hybrid body have important implications when thinking about a political agenda behind this text's translation for an Aragonese and Castilian audience. Those processes of building feudal spaces for which Melosina is responsible could be—for a Castilian reader—connected to the politics of Isabel and Fernando. Aurea de la Morena explains that there was an architectural fever during the time of the Catholic Monarchs,[53] due to the interest of nobles, aristocracy, and "hidalgos" [sons of somebody] in building

---

50   Spiegel, "Maternity and Monstrosity," 107.

51   Corfis, *Melosina*, 46 and 48.

52   Corfis, *Melosina*, 48.

53   Aurea de la Morena Bartolomé, "La arquitectura en la época de los Reyes Católicos: identidad y encrucijada de culturas," *Anales de historia del arte* 9 (1999): 55–66, at 56.

chapels and adding ornate details to their houses that would assert their noble lineage.[54] It is also important to keep in mind that, just before the reign of
Isabel and Fernando, there was a competition between two architectural styles
in the Peninsula, the Visigoth style and the Mozarabic architecture. The former was identified with Christianity and the latter with Islam.[55] Jerrilyn Dodds
explains that in early medieval Spain, "architecture became, then, a parallel
language of expression, of bearing witness to faith, and of differentiation from
a stronger culture: a means of creating, in as overt a way possible, an identity
of group that saw its very cultural existence threatened."[56] In his research on
Renaissance architecture in Rome and the Castilian-Aragonese Crown, Jack
Freiberg studies the architectural projects that were commissioned by Isabel
and Fernando in Rome. Such studies suggest that Castilian and Aragonese
readers would be especially aware of the fact that Melosina was building monasteries and chapels and other religious constructions, and very probably connect these constructions—as well as the ambivalence they bring to the female
protagonist—to the construction fever of the time of the Catholic Monarchs,
their crusades, and expansionism towards the Atlantic.

It is essential to consider the importance that is given to Melosina's descendants, as well as the fact that Melosina's power, gained through building projects, is never mistaken for another masculine pattern: military competence,
which is a characteristic given to her sons. Although the image of Melosina as a
builder imbues her with agency, how buildings, architecture, spaces, and territories are defined and characterized in relation to the novel's protagonists is, as
a matter of fact, a strategy by which the text perpetuates a patriarchal structure
by reinforcing certain gender expectations. Melosina builds for the husband
and sons and to perpetuate a masculine lineage, as an in-between figure of
male ascendency. In this sense, the text of *Melosina* could have relieved certain anxieties for the Castilian and Aragonese readership by suggesting that
having a Queen does not interrupt a masculine line of descent.

In fact, while Melosina is an uncommonly strong female character, there is
an important reinforcement of traditional gender expectations in the book. To
start with, Pressina, Melosina's mother, and her three daughters are exiled from
their land[57] because Melosina's father saw his wife giving birth. As revenge,

---

54   Bartolomé, "Arquitectura," 56.
55   Jerrilyn Dodds, *Architecture and Ideology in Early Medieval Spain* (University Park: Penn-
      sylvania State University Press, 1989), 71.
56   Dodds, *Architecture*, 81.
57   Corfis, *Melosina*, 8.

Melosina imprisons her father in a mountain of Northobelan.[58] When Melosina punishes her father, she not only disciplines him, but she also changes her own future, imprisoning herself in paternal law: her mother penalizes her and she will be a hybrid being for eternity. In the end, Melosina, not her father, is the one punished because of the father's and her own acts.

Continuing with this pattern, Pressina confines the three daughters in castles, thus imprisoning them eternally within a physical space while she gives a nice tomb full of rich elements and images to her husband.[59] In the succeeding generation, Melosina is the one who urges Remondin to go to Brittany and recuperate his father's legacy, the fortress of Quemjgante, and Melosina also explains to Remondin the history of his father.[60] In this sense, she initiates the restitution of Remondin from his exile and the masculine recovery of lost space. As Spiegel explains, there are numerous parricides in the book, such as Melosina's,[61] that should be considered processes of the de-symbolization of patriarchy.[62] However, the function of the woman in relation to them is very complex. On the one hand, Melosina is an exceptional female, but on the other hand, she is a figure that also reinforces masculine genealogy by constructing and starting an empire for her masculine descendants.

Melosina's sons' expansionism, wars, and battles enhance a masculine economy, especially when one pays attention to the described edifications and fortifications. Of course Melosina's sons are the sons of the mother and they represent her desire and power to conquer. However, as Jacques Le Goff comments, Mélusine's *nature* emerges through her *function* in the legend, and in this sense, the fairy is the instrument of masculine ambition.[63] Throughout her generous masculine primogeniture, Melosina creates a world of masculine domination. The continuous images and narratives of the sons overcoming the limits of the mother's empire present them as men who, despite their deformity, fight for a Western Christian tradition over the Muslim space, something that would clearly resonate for the Castilian readership. It is important to notice that these sons end up conquering new countries through marriage with the daughter of an old monarch, who dies shortly thereafter. The first two sons, Urian and Guyon, defeat a Sultan and become kings of Cyprus and Armenia

---

58   Corfis, *Melosina*, 8.

59   Corfis, *Melosina*, 10.

60   Corfis, *Melosina*, 36.

61   Spiegel, "Maternity and Monstrosity," 106.

62   Spiegel, "Maternity and Monstrosity," 107.

63   Jacques Le Goff, *Time, Work and Culture in the Middle Ages* (Chicago: Chicago University Press, 1980), 218–220.

after marrying the respective princesses. Antonio and Renaud marry the duchess of Luxemburg and the Queen of Vienna, respectively, also appropriating the spaces of these kingdoms. These alliances are the culmination of their crusades and the concluding act that reinforces a patriarchal structure through the strengthening of a military character—Melosina's sons—who will take their places as the kings to these crowns.

Melosina's sons connect space, architecture, masculinity, and wars. The descriptions of the sons defeating Moors, conquering new lands, and appropriating built spaces are tightly bound to masculine ideals: while a main aim of the battles of Melosina's sons is to defeat the Moors and "defender la Fe Cristiana" [to defend the Christian faith],[64] another motive is to conquer new spaces. Before they start their adventure, Urian and Guyon comment that they are part of a large group of descendants. Because their inheritance will be not sufficient, they need to invade new land: "Por ende, consideremos que sy nuesra heredad deve ser repartida en ocho partes, no es posible que nos podamos, segun nuestro estado, en tan poqueño condado morar" [Finally, we should consider that if our inheritance needs to be divided in eight fractions, it is impossible that we can, given our situation, live in such a small county].[65] The practical necessity of their crusades is due to the need to spread the Christian faith as well as the urge to gain new territories where they can reign. The sons are thus central for Melosina's expansionism, questioning the possibility of her working without the help of men. This is another example of how the figure of Melosina was not necessarily legitimizing Isabel I of Castile's power as a female monarch, but in fact highlighting and reinforcing the fact that the Queen was in need of several men to carry out her expansionist projects.

In the descriptions of Melosina's sons, architectural elements, villages, and fortresses are crucial as a way to characterize her descendants. Urian and Guyon arrive at the isle of Cyprus, where the king asks them if they have come to help him. When the two sons assent, the king opens his doors and castles: "Pues asy es, señor, nuestras villas e castillos vos seran todos abiertos, syn contradiçion, al entrar y salir. E plega a Dios traya vuestras naos a buen puerto" [It is like this, lord, that our towns and castles will be open to you, without impediment, to enter and leave. And pray to God that your ships arrive in a good port].[66] In the first battle in Cyprus, the Moors are winning and they attack the walls of the village: "E vinjeron çerca de los muros de la villa e començo de nuevo la escaramuça, do fueron muchos heridos y muertos. Mas con todo,

---

64   Corfis, *Melosina*, 70.
65   Corfis, *Melosina*, 50.
66   Corfis, *Melosina*, 56.

los xpistianos hizieron hujr los moros. E visto el destroço, hizo el soldan to-
car la trompeta" [And they came close to the town's walls and so the skirmish
started again, where many were wounded and died. But ultimately, the Christians made the Moors flee. And having seen the damage, he made the soldier
play the trumpet].[67] Architecture and empire-building are central elements
for the text to show Melosina's sons' strength and expansionism. However, the
sons' expansionist projects and their relation to architecture are tinged with a
militarist character not found in the descriptions of the fairy's architecture and
spaces, thus highlighting central gender differences between mother and sons.

An important battle in this respect is the one that takes place on a bridge,
where the Christians, led by Urian, defeat the Moors by making them fall from the
bridge: "E fue la vatalla grande, mas fynalmente los mores perdieron la puente e
cajeron muchos en la rriuera. E asy pasaron los xpistianos la puente ligeramente"
[And the battle was big, but finally the Moors lost the bridge and many of them
fell onto the riverbank. And so the Christians crossed the bridge easily].[68] Once
the Christians defeat the Moors, Urian asks the king to open the door of his castle and he comes into the palace where the princess lives: "E entro el cavallro do
era la ynfanta" [And the horse entered where the Princess was].[69] However, the
sultan's troops attack again. The sultan wants to enter the village because that
would mark the defeat of the king and the sultan's victory. The acquisition of a
new village and crown goes hand-in-hand with a marriage to a beautiful young
princess, and the conquest of lady and land are interconnected. Urian's reasons
for helping the king of Cyprus give readers some indication: a Moorish sultan
asked for the hand of the daughter of the king, but the king refuses to give it. The
sultan attacks Cyprus to conquer both the space and the daughter of Armenia.
Yet Urian defeats the sultan's troops and marries the king's daughter instead.

It is not difficult to establish a connection between the fortress and the
young princess's body, a correlation that is delicately and ingeniously suggested throughout the text. In fact, in discussing the medieval allegory of the body
as a building, David Cowling explains that the defensive aspect of the body-as-
building metaphor is developed extensively through religious allegories, but
also that the notion of siege "with the concomitant emphasis on the means
and moment of entry to the fortress plays an essential role in secular texts."[70]
Cowling's analysis is dedicated to the *Roman de la Rose,* where he studies the

---

67   Corfis, *Melosina,* 60.

68   Corfis, *Melosina,* 62.

69   Corfis, *Melosina,* 64.

70   David Cowling, *Building the Text. Architecture as a Metaphor in Late Medieval and Early
      Modern France* (New York: Oxford University Press, 1998), 26–27.

identification of a vulnerable part of the castle with a part of the woman's anatomy.[71] This interpretation could certainly be extended to these passages of *Melosina* where the metaphor of the body-as-building works to suggest the masculine victory over both the lady's body and the kingdom.

Clearly, when Urian and Armenia get married, Urian accedes both to the body of the princess and to the body of the crown. After defeating the Moors and after his marriage to Armenia, Urian visits his new territories and puts his new land in order: "E en esta manera paso Vrian todo su rreyo. E todo lo que era bien ordenado, el lo dexava en su orden, e lo malordenado ordenava. E las tierras que eran en buenas manos entre gente de su rrazon, el las dexava" [And so Vrian spent his entire reign. And everything that was in good order, he would leave it alone, and he organized what was disorganized. And the land that was in good hands with people of his side, he left alone].[72] Rivera observes that the word "rreyno" in the Spanish *Melosina* would have carried a particular resonance in Castile, given the activities of Isabel and Fernando. Readers would find it difficult to distance themselves from the contemporary political situation of the "rreyno de Espana" [Kingdom of Spain].[73] This reference, moreover, invites readers to meditate on the process taken by the Catholic kings to build their kingdom and to legitimize their rule, and in particular consider how Remondin had access to the lands conquered by Melosina.

Coming back to Weissberger's study, the masculine and martial characterization of the sons of Melosina was a latent problem for the Aragonese-Castilian crown. It is true that both Isabel and Fernando were fighting enemies of the Christian faith, and they were both annexing lands to their realm. However, according to Weissberger, the personal and political union of Isabel and Fernando as co-equal and harmonious was only a romanticized view[74] and she later adds that:

> Emilia Salvador Esteban rejects what she calls the assumption of total reciprocity of rule. She insists that to maintain the monarchs' strict reciprocity would be an erroneous interpretation of the "tanto monta" emblem (320), and that the monarchs' power sharing needs to be understood instead as a rhetorical construct of the intense propaganda

---

71   Cowling, *Building the Text*, 31.
72   Corfis, *Melosina*, 76.
73   Rivera, "Construction of Romance," 143.
74   Weissberger, *Isabel Rules*, 47.

campaign initiated by Isabel herself and carried out by her court writers in order to legitimize her contested succession.[75]

Weissberger studies how the motto "Tanto monta" [it amounts to the same] that Nebrija incorporated into the heraldic emblem of his patrons is thus a shortened translation of a classical epigram applied to Fernando alone[76] and explains that certain expectations, such as the role of the warrior, were only fulfilled by the figure of Fernando: "such imperialist associations could not so readily be applied to Isabel, whose gender barred her from the role of warrior prince."[77] Similarly, Melosina is not a warrior, but a builder. In this sense, while the text could have legitimized the figure of Isabel, Melosina's masculine descendants also reveal some of the ways in which Isabel's power was perceived as unacceptable. In the text only her sons—like Fernando of Aragon—were the ones embodying the military characteristics necessary for the expansionist project.

Architecture and space are an avenue of fertile analysis of the Castilian translation of Melusine, as these are central elements to exploring the superposition between the fairy and Queen Isabel I of Castile. While several scholars have highlighted this superposition as a way to understand how Melosina influenced an Aragonese and Castilian readership in favor of having a female ruler, the multiple ambivalences at play when reading Melosina as a proto-feminist figure, especially when considering architectonial and spatial elements, illuminate how this text might have highlighted anxieties and doubts behind having a female queen. In fact, there is a puzzling juxtaposition between the character of Melosina and Queen Isabel I of Castile. To start with, Melosina's materialization of the self through her buildings embodies an essential ambiguity conditioning her being. While she projects her maternal, fecund power in a way that is unapologetically phallic in its erection of towers and buildings, these buildings speak to the doubtful truth that surrounds her and ultimately enable her family's economic, social, and political power, thus reinforcing a masculine lineage. The expansionist program of an ambiguously gendered woman would have without doubt resonated in Isabelline Spain, but Melosina's distorted gender status would have also aptly described Isabel's perceived lack of "normal" femininity, thus creating an ambivalent perception towards the Queen. Ultimately, Melosina's power is limited by her inability to

---

75   Weissberger, *Isabel Rules,* 54.
76   Weissberger, *Isabel Rules,* 49.
77   Weissberger, *Isabel Rules,* 50.

embody the most prized masculine mark of identity, that of military aggression, which her sons embody.

Architecture and space are related to tropes of both masculinity and femininity in the text. Melosina's magical constructions are a consequence of her mixed body as well as a way of mapping her reality onto an external surface; architecture incorporates Melosina's wild powers and her desire to control both her body and the spaces she inhabits. The fairy's fertility and her fecund architecture relate to one another, and the text presents having children and building as parallel acts. Both actions underline Melosina's active role in the narrative as well as her final objective of lineage creation. The dual characterization of Melosina as a strong female character but also as a problematic, hybrid being coincides with Weissberger's analysis of other female figures written at the time of the Catholic Monarchs that transgress the traditional limits of gender expectations and have to be understood under the shadow of Isabel I. Although the image of Melosina as a builder presents her as a strong and powerful woman, the way buildings, architecture, spaces, and territories are defined and characterized in relation to the novel's protagonists, particularly by looking at Melosina's sons, is a strategy by which the text perpetuates a patriarchal structure by reinforcing certain gender expectations. Architecture and space show a tight tension in the *Melosina* story where gender assumptions are concerned, and this tension can help modern readers understand the image of Isabel I as a prolific builder and defender of the crown but never a warrior figure, something that is especially pertinent for Peninsular readers of the time.

CHAPTER 7

The Lady with the Serpent's Tail: Hybridity and the Dutch *Meluzine*

Lydia Zeldenrust

One of the most intriguing historic attractions of the Flemish city of Ghent is Het Toreken, a large stone house that once belonged to the medieval tanners' guild. Although the building's rich history alone is reason enough for a visit, most visitors are drawn not to the building itself but to the peculiar mermaid-shaped statue that stands atop its highest turret. The statue, which functions as a weather vane, represents the beautiful half-serpent Meluzine, who is seen holding a mirror and combing her long, flowing hair. The local guides tell of several legends that surround this statue. It is said, for instance, that Meluzine's descendants carried it to the Holy Land, where it was lost and later recovered by Flemish crusaders, who took the statue to Ghent. It is also said that Meluzine was the protector of the tanners' guild, and that the guild received the statue as a reward for their role in the city's rebellion against the French during the Hundred Years' War. Although such origin stories were undoubtedly embellished over the centuries, it is certain that a statue of Meluzine has been on Het Toreken since the late fifteenth century, when the turret was added to the main building.[1]

Meluzine's appearance on top of a guild house in the center of one of the most important cities of the southern Low Countries is a fitting testament to how, in the second half of the fifteenth century, her story was already transforming from its original incarnation as a local French legend into what would eventually become an early European bestseller. Not only had the *Mélusine* romance already been translated into German and Castilian, but the story travelled to the Low Countries as well.[2] This move northwards is already attested by the number of fifteenth-century manuscripts of Jean d'Arras' *Mélusine or*

---

1 Leen Charles and Marie Christine Laleman, *Het Gent Boek* (Zwolle: Waanders, 2006), 362.

2 Thüring von Ringoltingen's German *Melusine* is dated to 1456. The earliest witness to the anonymous Castilian *La historia de la linda Melosina* is the edition printed by Juan Parix and Estevan Cleblat in Toulouse in 1489. See Anna Casas Aguilar's contribution to this volume for a study of how *La linda Melosina* related particularly to her Castilian and Argonese audiences.

La Noble Histoire de Lusignan and Coudrette's *Roman de Parthenay* that originate from, or were illustrated in, the Burgundian Low Countries.[3] However, it
was the romance's translation into Middle Dutch, or "Diets," that contributed
significantly to the spread of the Melusine legend in the late medieval Low
Countries.

The earliest known witness to the anonymous Middle Dutch *Historie van
Meluzine* is the incunable printed by Gheraert Leeu, dated to February 9, 1491.[4]
Two more editions appeared later: Hendrick Eckert van Homberch printed a
Meluzine in January 1510, and the romance was printed again by Hieronymus
I Verdussen in 1602.[5] All three surviving editions were printed in Antwerp. In-
terestingly, the later Dutch editions do not represent separate translations but
rather duplicate the text of Leeu's incunable. Homberch and Verdussen reprint
Leeu's text with only some minor variation in spelling and abbreviations. This
means that there is really only one Dutch translation, of which there are three
surviving printed editions. The two later editions also copy Leeu's iconography.
The only surviving copy of Leeu's edition has several missing folios and now
features 46 woodcuts, but it is almost certain that the edition originally contained 50 woodcuts.[6] Leeu's iconography is reproduced in total in Homberch's
edition, while 17 of the 25 woodcuts that illustrate Verdussen's edition are derived from Leeu's set.

---

3   See, for instance, the examples listed in Jean d'Arras, *Mélusine ou La Noble Histoire de Lusig-
    nan*, ed. and trans. Jean-Jacques Vincensini (Paris: Librairie Générale Française, 2003), 44–
    46, 50–52; Eleanor Roach, "La tradition manuscrite du *Roman de Mélusine* par Coudrette,"
    Revue d'histoire des textes 7 (1977): 192–94, 207–208.

4   *Incunabula Short Title Catalogue* (hereafter ISTC): ij00218420, *Universal Short Title Cata-
    logue* (hereafter USTC): 436129. The only surviving exemplar is found in Brussels, Royal Li-
    brary of Belgium, INC B 1.369.

5   Homberch: USTC 436815. The USTC has a separate entry for a *Meluzine* printed in 1510 by
    Govaert Bac (no. 441997). This edition does not exist; the 1510 *Meluzine* was printed by
    Homberch, not Bac. The only surviving copy of Homberch's edition is now in the Library
    of Congress in Washington, DC, in the Lessing J. Rosenwald Collection no. 1118, shelfmark
    PQ1486 J25 M413. There is no catalogue listing for Verdussen's edition. Its only surviving
    copy is now in Göttingen, Niedersächsische Staats- und Universitätsbibliothek, 8 FAB III,
    2011.

6   Since Homberch is known to have copied Leeu's iconography and his edition contains 50
    woodcuts, it is likely that Leeu's edition originally featured the same number. This hypoth-
    esis is supported by Ina Kok's conclusion, based on a reconstruction of the woodcuts that
    could have appeared on the missing folios of the Brussels exemplar, that Leeu's edition would
    have contained 49 to 51 woodcuts. Kok, *Woodcuts in Incunabula Printed in the Low Countries*
    (Houten: Hes & De Graaf, 2013), 268.

Although most Melusine scholars seem to be aware of the existence of at least one edition of the romance in Dutch, almost no one has examined this translation in detail. Moreover, those few scholarly works devoted to the Dutch translation rarely mention that there are three editions, as the 1602 edition by Verdussen has so far escaped scholarly attention.[7] This is rather unfortunate, since the Dutch *Meluzine* represents a fascinating branch of the transcultural tradition, not least because it is the only version which translates parts of both Jean d'Arras' prose and Coudrette's verse redaction of the French *Mélusine*. In other words, much like Meluzine herself, the Dutch translation is a hybrid.

The concept of hybridity is central to the Dutch *Meluzine*. Not only is the translation an amalgam of different sources, but the translator also greatly emphasizes Meluzine's role as a hybrid figure. Meluzine's hybridity also plays a vital role in the iconography of the Dutch editions, to the extent that they open with a woodcut depicting Meluzine's half-serpent form, drawing the reader's attention to her unnatural combination of animal and human right from the start. This focus on Meluzine's hybrid body often comes at the cost of her serpent form, but through it she also loses some of her associations with the fairy realm. As a result, for the reader of the Dutch editions, Meluzine is not primarily a serpent or a fairy but an alluring hybrid monster. As illustrated by the statue on top of Het Toreken, this hybrid form was to become so emblematic that one can, even today, recognize the lady with the serpent's tail as Meluzine.

The Dutch translation is written in prose and is based predominantly on one of the incunabula of Jean's *Mélusine*, most likely Adam Steinschaber's *editio princeps*, printed in Geneva in 1478.[8] However, towards the end of the romance the translator also adds two episodes unique to Coudrette's version:

---

7 Verdussen's edition is mentioned by Karl Schorbach and Luc Debaene, but neither scholar examines it in any detail. Schorbach, "Eine Buchanzeige des Antwerpener Druckers Geraert Leeu in niederländischer Sprache (1491)," *Zeitschrift für Bücherfreunde* 9 (1905): 147; Debaene, *De Nederlandse volksboeken. Ontstaan en geschiedenis van de Nederlandse prozaromans, gedrukt tussen 1475 en 1540* (Antwerp: De Vlijt, 1951; repr. Hulst, 1977), 121. The author has recently discovered another *Meluzine* edition, which was likely printed in the eighteenth century by a printer known only as van Soest. This edition also goes back to Leeu's *editio princeps*, but the text undergoes several changes. As not much is known about this edition at this point—even the printer and the date are uncertain, as the first and last pages are missing—it is not included in the current discussion. However, the author hopes to determine its place within the Dutch *Meluzine* tradition in more detail in future.

8 Bob Duijvestein, "Der niederländische Prosaroman von Meluzine; eine Orienterung," in *Melusine. Actes du Colloque du Centre d'Études Médiévales de l'Université de Picardie, 13–14 janvier 1996*, ed. Danielle Buschinger and Wolfgang Spiewok (Greifswald: Reineke-Verlag, 1996), 42.

that of the English knight who tries to obtain the treasure guarded by Meluzine's sister Palestine, and that detailing the death of Meluzine's most famous
son, Godefroy. These episodes are inserted between the episode of Melior and
the king of Armenia at the Sparrowhawk Castle and the romance's epilogue.
So far, scholars discussing the Dutch translation have not noted that parts of
this translation are based on Coudrette's version, possibly because the change
in sources is rather difficult to spot.[9] This is because the Dutch translator carefully integrates the additional episodes within the structure of Jean's version,
creating a true hybrid narrative.

To give an example, the translator makes several modifications to the ending of the Melior episode in order to facilitate a smooth transition to the first
of the Coudrette episodes. In Jean's version, the Melior episode is followed directly by the epilogue, and the narrator has already given several indications
that the story is about to end. For instance, the narrator explains that "cy me
tairay des roix d'Armenie et en est conclue l'istoire" [here I cease to speak of the
kings of Armenia, and here my history is concluded], then gives the date when
the romance was finished, and finally commends Mélusine's descendants to
God, ending with an "amen."[10] These concluding passages are not repeated in
the Dutch translation, where the narrator explains only that the kings of Armenia are descendants of Meluzine. The story then continues with a heading
announcing the subject of the next episode: "hoe Palestine, die derde suster
van Melusinen, haers vaders scat bewaert op eenen hooghen berch in Arrago-
nien" [how Palestine, the third sister of Meluzine, guards her father's treasure
on a high mountain in Aragon].[11] This heading matches the pattern of earlier
headings introducing episodes translated from Jean's version, which also tend
to start with the word "hoe," or how. This means that the shift from one French
source to the other is not only made smoothly in the text, but is not discernible
on the page, either.

---

9   Only Debaene notes that the translation contains an episode about Palestine and one
     where Godefroy dies, but he does not observe that they are unique to Coudrette's version;
     see Debaene, *De Nederlandse Volksboeken*, 119.

10   Jean d'Arras, "Histoire de la belle Mélusine (Geneva: Steinschaber, 1478)," in *Incunabula:
     the Printing Revolution in Europe. Unit 64 - Romances Part II*, ed. Lotte Hellinga (Reading,
     UK: Research Publications International, 2011), RM 125: folio 189r-v. Subsequent refer-
     ences to this microfiche copy are given in parentheses.

11   "Meluzine: Leeu 1491," ed. Willem Kuiper, *Bibliotheek van Middelnederlandse Letterkunde*,
     Leerstoelgroep Historische Nederlandse Letterkunde UvA (Amsterdam, 2008—present),
     folio Z2rb. Subsequent references to this diplomatic edition will follow in parenthesis in
     the main text.

The shift from the episode of Godefroy's death back to the epilogue of Jean's version also appears quite natural. After relating the details of Godefroy's burial, the narrator explains that Diederic, one of Meluzine's youngest sons, inherits the Lusignan lands, and that many great men are descended from him. In Coudrette's version, the discussion on Thierry and his descendants forms a bridge to the narrator's own time, as he then explains that the verse romance's patron—Guillaume de Parthenay, another supposed descendant of Thierry—has died.[12] The Dutch translator devotes only a few lines to Diederic, summarizing Coudrette's lengthy discussion of the descendants by simply stating that Diederic is the ancestor of "noch vele heerlicker ridderen" [many more noble knights] (Z4vb). The episode then ends just before Coudrette's narrator shifts to his own time and mentions his patron, and the story returns to Jean's version in the next paragraph. Since the translator again removes any telltale signs that he is working from a different source, a reader unfamiliar with the differences between the two French redactions would likely not observe this shift.

Of course, one question which immediately springs to mind is why the translator added these episodes. Since Coudrette's version largely follows the same narrative as Jean's version—and since the translator clearly had access to a copy of Coudrette's version—it seems odd that the verse account was not simply translated in its entirety. If the translator specifically wanted to include the episodes of Palestine and Godefroy, then why not opt for Coudrette's version? The likely answer is that the translator did not just want to include episodes unique to Coudrette's account but also the episodes unique to Jean's. If the translator had followed the structure of Coudrette's version, then the Dutch translation would not have featured, for instance, the episodes describing the meeting of Meluzine's parents, Raymondijn's reclaiming of his inheritance, Meluzine's giving advice to her sons before they go abroad, Godefroy's adventures in Ireland, and Godefroy's meeting with the knight of the Poitevin tower. By supplementing Jean's detailed prose account with the Coudrette episodes, the translator presents us with a more complete version of the Melusine story than that found in either French redaction.

Because the translator heavily abbreviates the Coudrette episodes and introduces some significant modifications, it is difficult to determine exactly which source he used based on philological grounds alone. In fact, to add a little intrigue, it is even possible that the episodes were not derived from Coudrette's version at all. Although the translator may have worked from a Coudrette manuscript, one may wonder whether, as with the episode based on Jean's

---

12   Compare Coudrette, *Le roman de Mélusine ou histoire de Lusignan*, ed. Eleanor Roach (Paris: Klincksieck, 1982), lines 6671–6786.

version, he was not working from a printed source instead. As Coudrette's version was not published until 1854, the only printed accounts available when the first Dutch edition was printed were those of Thüring von Ringoltingen's German *Melusine*, of which at least ten editions were published before 1491.

It is tempting to suppose that the Coudrette episodes were mediated through the German version, especially since the iconography of Leeu's edition is almost certainly based on that of one of the early German incunabula.[13] Most of Leeu's woodcuts match the setting of woodcuts depicting the same scenes in the German incunabula. Moreover, the three images that illustrate the Coudrette episodes must have been copied from a German exemplar, as these same scenes do not appear in the incunabula of Jean's version or the illuminated manuscripts of Coudrette's version.[14] If the Coudrette episodes were indeed mediated through a German edition, along with the images, then the Dutch translation is even more of a hybrid than first thought, as it not only combines episodes from different redactions, but was also influenced by more than one branch of the multilingual *Melusine* tradition.

Turning to the romance itself, it is apparent that the translator makes a number of significant modifications to its main character, so that the Dutch Meluzine is not quite the same figure as the Melusine of the French versions. One of the most important differences is that Meluzine's weekly hybrid form becomes an even more important focal point than in the source material. Oddly, part of the reason why Meluzine's hybridity emerges much more strongly in this translation is because the translator intervenes mostly at the beginning and end of the romance, in scenes where Meluzine does not appear in hybrid form at all. This is because the translator creates a greater contrast between Meluzine's initial humanity and her eventual transformation into an animal, thereby highlighting the abnormal mixture of Meluzine's hybrid form even more.

---

13   On the relationship between Leeu's woodcuts and those of the German *Melusine* incunabula, and on Leeu's connections to various German printers, see Lydia Zeldenrust, "Serpent or Half-Serpent? Bernhard Richel's *Melusine* and the Making of a Western European Icon," *Neophilologus* 100, no. 1 (2016): 33–37. For a reading of the cultural-historical information conveyed in the early German woodcuts, see Albrecht Classen's contribution to this volume.

14   These woodcuts depict Palestine with the monsters that guard her treasure, the English knight being eaten by one of Palestine's monsters (missing from the surviving copy of Leeu's edition but in place in Homberch's edition), and Godefroy on his deathbed. There is one Coudrette manuscript that contains an image depicting one of these scenes: Paris, Bibliothèque nationale de France, MS. fr. 12575 features an image of Palestine and her monsters on folio 123v. However, only the German incunabula contain images of all three scenes.

At the start of the narrative, the translator suppresses Meluzine's associations with the fairy realm, so that she appears more human than fairy. In Jean's version, from which the translator is working at this point, the prologue and the romance's opening episodes are vital in setting up Melusine's supernatural background and her origins as a half-fairy. Although the translator largely follows Jean's narrative in that Meluzine is still the daughter of King Elinas and Queen Presine, he removes several crucial links between Meluzine and the fairy realm.

It would be excessive to list all of the translator's modifications here, but there are a few interesting examples worth mentioning. For instance, while a large section of Jean's prologue is devoted to stories about unions between fairy women and mortal men, which function as analogues to the main narrative, the Dutch prologue contains only one such story. The translator completely removes Jean's detailed discussion on supernatural women, in which he pays special attention to the benevolent "faees" [fairies] (2v) who, like Melusine, are betrayed by their mortal lovers and forced to disappear or transform into serpents. Instead, the translator includes only the story of Rocher van Roussel Casteele, who one day meets a beautiful "alvinne" [fairy] (A2rb) who marries him on the condition that he never see her naked. When Rocher later breaks his promise and sees her bathing, the lady disappears under the water and "terstont wart sy verwandelt in een serpent/ ende en was noyt sindert gesien" [she immediately turned into a serpent, and was never seen since] (A2rb). Although this story still forms an obvious parallel to that of Raymondijn and Meluzine, it is the prologue's only fairy story. Whereas in Steinschaber's edition, two-thirds of the prologue is devoted to listing various stories that set up Melusine's fairy origins and shape the reader's expectations of the main narrative, these fairy elements are a far less significant component in the Dutch prologue.

More importantly, it is never made clear that Meluzine is a fairy, too. While in Steinschaber's edition the long list of stories of various fairy women ends with the narrator's announcement that he will now turn to another fairy, the one who founded the castle of Lusignan, in the Dutch translation the link between Meluzine and the only other fairy mentioned in the prologue is tenuous at best. This is because the sentence that links Meluzine to other fairy women in Steinschaber's edition has been moved forward in the translation, so that it appears before the story about Rocher and his fairy lover. The Dutch narrator first says that his story is about how Lusignan "ghesticht is by eenre alvinnen" [was founded by a fairy] (A2ra-b) and then tells us about Rocher and his lady, which almost gives the impression that it is this fairy who founded the castle. Even more confusing is the statement that follows this story, when the narrator explains that he will tell "vanden edelen geslachte dat van deser alvinnen

ghecomen is" [of the noble lineage that came from this fairy] (A2rb). In Steinschaber's edition, this sentence clearly refers to Melusine, but the only fairy the
Dutch narrator could possibly be referring to at this point is Rocher's wife. To
make matters even more confusing, in the last lines of the prologue the narrator finally introduces Meluzine by name, and explains that his story is about
"Meluzinen, der selve alvinnen dochtere" [Meluzine, the daughter of this same
fairy] (A2rb). At this point, it is no longer clear at all which fairy is which. Is
Meluzine the daughter of Rocher's wife, who is also the fairy who built Castle
Lusignan? Although the confusion is later resolved, its most important result
is that Meluzine is here never directly referred to as a fairy.

This avoidance of any direct links between Meluzine and other fairies continues in the rest of the translation. For a start, while Jean occasionally calls
his Melusine a "faee," the Dutch narrator never refers to Meluzine as a fairy. In
fact, the narrator generally avoids using this term altogether; whereas in Steinschaber's edition the words "fae," "faeez," or "faees" occur sixteen times, the
term appears only twice in the translation. Both times, the French word is not
replaced by a Dutch equivalent, but the translator uses the term as if it were a
name.[15] The only term the translator sometimes uses to refer to characters described as fairies in Jean's version is the word "alvinne," a word commonly used
to refer to a female elf or fairy.[16] The word is found almost exclusively in the
prologue, with one notable exception: just before Meluzine transforms into
a serpent, she tells the members of her court that her children were not born
"van eenre alvinnen" [of a fairy] (T6ra). In other words, the only time the term
"alvinne" is used in connection to Meluzine is when she emphatically denies
being one. Moreover, not only is Meluzine never referred to as an alvinne by
the authoritative voice of the narrator, but her mother and sisters are never
referred to as such either, so that Meluzine's familial link with the fairy race is
gone, too.[17]

The overall effect of the removal of Meluzine's associations with fairies is
that she consistently appears far more human at the beginning of the romance

---

15   For instance, the fountain where Raymondijn meets Meluzine is known as "die fonteine
      Faeeze" [the fountain Faeeze] (B3va). Because it is not translated, "faeeze" becomes the
      name of the fountain rather than an indication of its links with the fairy realm, as in Jean's
      version.

16   See the entry "alvinne" – which redirects to "alf II" – in *De Geïntegreerde Taalbank. In-
      stituut voor de Nederlandse Lexicologie* <http://gtb.inl.nl> (accessed February 6, 2017).

17   The translator also does not mention the name Avalon, famously associated with fairies,
      when referring to the place where Meluzine and her sisters grow up; see Steinschaber (5v)
      and Leeu (A5ra).

than she does in Jean's version. After all, without Jean's not-so-subtle hints at Melusine's fairy nature, the reader of the translation is never led to suspect that Meluzine is anything other than human. However, towards the end of the romance the translator suddenly changes tactics and begins to suppress Meluzine's human qualities. This shift occurs around the moment when Raymondijn publicly reveals his wife's secret half-serpent form, after which Meluzine is forced to transform into a serpent completely. While in Jean's version Melusine remains an ambiguous, hybrid figure even after she transforms, the Dutch Meluzine undergoes a more definitive metamorphosis into an animal, as virtually all hints at her remaining humanity disappear.

One of the clearest ways in which the translator dehumanizes Meluzine is through a reduction of her emotional displays. The translator already reduces the intensity of Meluzine's emotions in the scenes leading up to her transformation, but the most rigorous reductions occur after Meluzine becomes an animal. In Jean's version, Melusine the serpent utters countless cries of despair. Jean's narrator also details that the serpent flies to Lusignan with "si grant effroy en sa furieuseté qu'il sambloit par tout en terre que la fouldre et tempeste y deut cheoir du ciel" [such great terror in her ferocity that it seemed to all on the ground as if storm and lightning came out of the sky] and that she later begins to "menant telle douleur et faisant si grant effroy que c'estoit grant douleur a veoir" [express such sadness and make such great terror that it was very sad to see] (156v). In the Dutch translation, the serpent's emotional turmoil is reduced to just one rather meager statement, which states only that Meluzine flies off while making "groten gecrijsende ende tempeeste" [great screaming and tempest] (T6rb). Jean's narrator tries to elicit sympathy from the reader by explaining repeatedly how much Melusine's forced departure pains her, but there is no such sympathy for the Dutch Meluzine.

This reduction in Meluzine's human-like emotions is not the only sign that she is presented more clearly as an animal after she transforms. The translator also removes several of Jean's other reminders that, although Melusine takes on the form of an animal, she is really still human inside her serpent suit. Each time Jean's narrator mentions the serpent, he explains that it is actually Melusine "transmuee *en guise* de serpent" [transformed into *the guise* of a serpent] (156v; emphasis added). Similar reminders are not found in the translation. For instance, Jean's narrator explains that, immediately after her metamorphosis, "se'n ala Melusine, *samblant de serpent*, vollant par l'air vers Lusignen" [Mélusine, *in the guise of a serpent*, flies through the air to Lusignan] (156v; emphasis added). The Dutch narrator, however, comments only that "doen nam sy haren wech na Lusignen toe" [then she went on her way to Lusignan] (T6rb), without noting her appearance or how she travels. Another important sign of Melusine's residual humanity—that the people who witness her departure "veoient la figure d'une serpente et oyoient la voix d'une dame" [saw the figure of a serpent and heard the voice of a lady] (156v)—has similarly been removed. Although the Dutch Meluzine still leaves behind a footprint when she jumps from the windowsill, this is but a rare reminder that she was once human. From the moment Meluzine leaves the window and transforms, any lingering traces of her humanity disappear.

The changes introduced at the beginning and end of the romance have the effect of highlighting Meluzine's hybrid form even more clearly than in the source material. Because the translator suppresses Meluzine's fairy nature in favor of her human side at the start, and later subdues this same humanity when she turns into an animal, Meluzine's animal-human hybrid form becomes a clear middle point in her overall transition from human to animal. The increased contrast between the two sides of Meluzine's character also emphasizes that her bodily combination of human and animal is an unnatural, monstrous mixing, the problematic tension of which must be resolved.

Another reason why Meluzine's hybridity emerges more clearly in the Dutch translation is because the episode in which her half-serpent form is described for the first time—that fateful Saturday when Raymondijn spies on his wife as she is taking a bath—is translated almost word for word. Considering that the translator regularly intervenes at the beginning and end of the romance, it is striking that he introduces no substantial changes to the episode of Meluzine in the bath. In particular, the passage describing Meluzine's hybrid body closely follows that of Steinschaber's edition:

> Melusine [...] estoit en la cuve, jusques au nombril en signe de femme, et peignoit ses cheveulx, et du nombril en bas en signe de la queue d'une serpente, grosse comme ung quaque a harenc et moult longuement, debatoit sa queue en l'eaue tellement qu'elle le faisoit bondir jusques a la voulte de la chambre. (141V)
>
> [Mélusine [...] was in the tub, in the form of a lady down to the navel and she was combing her hair, and from the navel down she had the form of a serpent's tail, as large as a barrel of herring, and very long, and with her tail she hit the water so hard that she made it bound up to reach the ceiling of the chamber.]
>
> sij sat in de cuype, tot haren navele toe inder figueren van eenre schoonder vrouwen, hair haer kemmende, ende vanden navele voerts neder waert so was sy inder formen van een groot serpents steert, ende dien steert sloech seer lanc ende herdelic in 't water alsoe dattet dwater boventegens 't gehemelte vander cameren spranc. (S2vb)

[she sat in the tub, and she was in the figure of a beautiful woman
down to her navel, combing her hair, and from her navel downwards she
was in the form of a large serpent's tail. And her tail beat very long and
fervently in the water, so that the water jumped up against the ceiling of
the chamber.]

The only detail not repeated is that Melusine's tail is as fat as a barrel of herring. The rest of the episode is also remarkably similar to Jean's version: Raymondijn gives the same angry speech to his brother, the count of Forette, who
convinced Raymondijn to spy on his wife, and he gives the same lengthy monologue to express his sorrow at having betrayed Meluzine. The narrator also details that Meluzine later joins her husband in bed, and that she comforts him
even though she knows that he saw her half-serpent form. That the translator
here follows Jean's descriptions in detail suggests that, contrary to the passages
altered at the beginning and end of the romance, this episode was considered
such a key part of the narrative that it had to remain intact. The translator may
have no qualms adjusting Meluzine's degree of humanity or animality, but her
hybrid form remains an immutable feature.

Finally, Meluzine's hybridity also takes center stage in the iconographies of
the Dutch editions. For a start, none of the editions contain an image depicting Meluzine as a complete serpent; she is only ever depicted as a serpent from
the waist down. Even in the woodcuts illustrating Meluzine's transformation,
she is not an animal but a hybrid figure. Although this is due to the influence
of the iconography of the early German editions—as the German version is
the only translation in which Melusine becomes a half-serpent after her final
transformation—its result is that, on the iconographic side of the Dutch translation, Meluzine's hybrid form eclipses her serpent form.[18]

Furthermore, unlike in Steinschaber's edition, the manuscripts of Coudrette's version, and most German incunabula, the Dutch editions feature
an image of Meluzine in hybrid form on their opening pages.[19] In all three

---

18   Zeldenrust, "Serpent or Half-Serpent?," 22, 35.
19   The only other incunable printed before 1491 that features an image of Meluzine's hy-
      brid body on its title page is Johann Bämler's 1480 German *Melusine* edition. However,
      Bämler's opening woodcut is very different from that of the Dutch editions, as it does
      not depict Raymondijn or the count, but Melusine is surrounded by a family tree. On
      Bämler's opening woodcut, see Christian Vöhringer, "Monster, Bilder und Beweise: Die
      Bedeutung der Holzschnitte in Johannes Bämlers 'Melusine' von 1474 und 1480," in *550
      Jahre deutsche Melusine - Coudrette und Thüring von Ringoltingen. Beiträge der wissen-
      schaftlichen Tagung der Universitäten Bern und Lausanne vom August 2006. 550 ans de*

FIGURE 7.1   *The Dutch Meluzine at her bath. Royal Library of Belgium INC B 1.369*

editions, this woodcut is the same as that used to later illustrate the episode
of Raymondijn's discovery of Meluzine's half-serpent form.[20] The image shows
Meluzine in the bathhouse on the left and Raymondijn in the middle, who is
looking at the count of Forette riding away on his horse on the right. The moment of discovery has passed for Raymondijn, but the reader directly observes
Meluzine's naked hybrid body. She is human from the waist up, but she also
has a long serpent's tail, which rises from the bath as if it is about to come
down and splash water up to the ceiling.

---

*Mélusine allemande - Coudrette et Thüring von Ringoltingen. Actes du colloque organisé par
les Universités de Berne et Lausanne en août 2006*, ed. André Schnyder and Jean-Claude
Mühlethaler (Bern: Peter Lang, 2008), 340–42.

20   Because the title page of the Brussels exemplar is missing, it is not entirely certain that
Leeu's edition featured an opening image of Meluzine in the bath. However, since the
opening page of Homberch's edition features the bathing woodcut—and since Homberch copied Leeu's iconography—it is highly likely that Leeu's title page also featured
this woodcut. For a possible reconstruction of Leeu's title page, see Schorbach, "Eine
Buchanzeige," 146.

By opening with an image of Meluzine in the bath, the Dutch editions highlight Meluzine's hybridity from the start, marking the bathing episode as a, if
not *the*, key moment in the romance. When the reader later comes across the
same image at the start of this episode, just before the description of Meluzine's hybrid body, they know that they are about to encounter a crucial scene.
The appearance of Meluzine's hybrid body on the front page further suggests
that her problematic half-serpent form becomes the romance's main selling
point. Since most early printed editions were sold unbound, the title page was
the best place for a printer to highlight a book's contents. Placing Meluzine's
emblematic hybrid form on the front page was a very effective marketing tool,
especially when trying to get an already familiar story to appeal to readers from
a different linguistic or sociocultural background. After all, even if a potential
buyer had not yet heard of this particular story, surely the visual spectacle of
Meluzine's monstrous body would have piqued their interest.

That Meluzine's hybrid figure could function as a selling point is supported by the appearance of the same bathing woodcut in a contemporary sales
prospectus advertising Leeu's 1491 edition. In fact, this prospectus—which
proudly announces that the edition is decorated "met schoonen personagen
ende figueren" [with beautiful characters and figures]—uses the depiction
of Meluzine's hybrid body not only to convince the buyer to pick up Leeu's
Meluzine but also to get them interested in "vele meer andere niewe boecken"
[many other new books] published by the same printer.[21]

As if to make absolutely certain that the significance of Meluzine's hybrid
form is not overlooked, the bathing woodcut in Verdussen's edition is repeated
again at the end, as the edition's final image. Although this later edition only
contains half the number of woodcuts of Leeu's and Homberch's editions,
there are nonetheless four illustrations of Meluzine's hybrid body: one at the
start, two in the middle, and another at its closing point.[22] This repetition and
careful framing of the visual narrative stresses yet again that Meluzine's hybridity is a vital and representative part of the romance.

It is perhaps no wonder, then, that the statue on top of Het Toreken in Ghent
shows Meluzine in that hybrid form which became her most crucial and defining characteristic. While in many other fifteenth-century reincarnations of the
Melusine figure outside the boundaries of her romance she typically appears

---

21   The quotations are from the reproduction in Schorbach, "Eine Buchanzeige."

22   Verdussen's iconography is another example of mixing and hybridity, as its woodcuts are
      derived from various sources. For example, the woodcuts on folios A6v, B3r, and E5v are
      copies of cuts originally created by Hans Brosamer for an edition of the German *Melusine*,
      printed by Herman Gülfferich in Frankfurt in 1549.

as a serpent—think only of Philippe le Bon's Feast of the Pheasant in 1454, which featured a *tableau vivant* of Castle Lusignan with Melusine the serpent on top of one of its towers, or of the miniature of the month March in the *Très Riches Heures du duc de Berry*, which also depicts a serpentine Melusine flying over Lusignan—the Dutch Meluzine is known more for her complicated hybridity than her eventual transformation into an animal.[23]

Unfortunately, as so often happens, the Meluzine now gracing Het Toreken is not the original, as the fifteenth-century statue was removed when the building had become so ruinous that it had to be partly broken down in the 1830s. After about a century and a half of neglect, the building eventually passed into the hands of the city council and was finally restored in the early 1980s. When the restoration work had finished, Het Toreken was again crowned with a statue of Meluzine. Almost five hundred years after the original statue was put in place, Meluzine the half-serpent was given back her rightfully prominent position. One can only hope that the Dutch *Meluzine* editions will similarly be brought back from neglect, so that more scholars may discover their unique position within the Melusine tradition.

---

23   On Melusine's presence at the Feast of the Pheasant, see Tania M. Colwell, "Reading *Mélusine*: Romance Manuscripts and their Audiences c.1380-c.1530" (PhD diss., Australian National University, 2008), 310. For a reproduction of the miniature depicting the month March, see Jean Longnon, Raymond Cazelles, and Millard Meiss, *Les Très Riches Heures du Duc de Berry* (London: Thames and Hudson, 1969), plate 4.

CHAPTER 8

Matriarchs and Mother Tongues: The Middle English *Romans of Partenay*

Jennifer Alberghini

The figure of Melusine stands as both the imagined progenitor of many medi-eval noble families and the heroine of medieval texts in numerous European languages. Yet her status in the British Isles is relatively unexplored, in part because few copies of a Middle English translation survive. There are only two known manuscripts: one that closely follows Jean d'Arras' 1393 prose romance and the other of Coudrette's 1401 verse text.[1] The dearth of surviv-ing English manuscripts, in comparison to the twenty French copies, could be because England in the Middle Ages was a special linguistic case, where multiple languages were spoken and read.[2] French, sometimes called Anglo-Norman—although this term is often rejected for its inaccuracy— was one of the country's major vernaculars, making the original romance legible to an English audience without translation.[3] There is evidence of the English circu-lation of at least one French manuscript, BnF MS. fr. 12575 (which may have

---

The author would like to thank the following for their help in preparing this article: Alex-ander Baldassano, Esther Bernstein, Marguerite Birrell, Stephanie Grace Petinos, Christina Katopodis, Micheal Angelo Rumore, Michael Sargent, and Karl Steel, and the editors for their feedback. Translations from Middle English are the editors'.

1 Matthew W. Morris, introduction to *A Bilingual Edition of Jean d'Arras's Melusine, or, L'histoire de Lusignan* by Jean d'Arras (Lewiston, NY: Edwin Mellen Press, 2007), 1.

2 Eleanor Roach, introduction to *Le Roman de Mélusine, ou, Histoire de Lusignan*, by Coudrette, ed. Eleanor Roach (Klincksieck and Paris: Librairie des Méridiens, 1982), 77.

3 Ardis Butterfield has noted that the term is more "historical" than "linguistic," and more accurately describes the eleventh century than later periods. Butterfield, "3I Roundtable: Did Chaucer Have a Mother Tongue? In Memory of David Trotter" (response presented at the New Chaucer Society Congress, July 11–14, 2016). Jocelyn Wogan-Browne, who has studied the subject extensively, prefers the term "French of England" as the most encom-passing, although still not entirely accurate. Jocelyn Wogan-Brown et al., ed., *Language and Culture in Medieval Britain: The French of England c.1100–1150* (York: York Medieval Press, 2013), 12.

belonged to Marie de Clèves, wife of Charles d'Orléans), and it is possible that others circulated as well.[4]

Despite the availability of French copies, there were those who did think that both the verse and the prose romances could be commercially valuable enough to translate them specifically into Middle English. This is especially clear for the verse translation, known as *The Romans of Partenay, or of Lusignan,* found in Cambridge, Trinity College Library MS R.3.17, conventionally dated to the early part of the sixteenth century.[5] Its translator was particularly interested in accuracy, including a prologue and an epilogue that contain a detailed discussion of his decisions. While occasionally found in secular works, including the printings of William Caxton, these sorts of discussions are best known from early fifteenth-century texts which belong to what Michael Sargent calls the "vernacularity debate."[6] This debate, usually associated with the Lollards, followers of John Wyclif, centered on whether the Bible should be translated into English.

In discussing their methodology, many vernacularity debate texts share with *The Romans of Partenay* a common trope, that of the "moder tonge" or "mother tonge" (6573).[7] Ruth Evans and others describe this term as "a language with immediate access to people's feelings and easily comprehensible—as Latin is not, even to those who can understand it. Writing in English can thus do rather more than pose a practical vernacular means of access to knowledge; it can signify clarity and open access and do so even in texts whose projected audience is relatively narrow."[8] This phrase, both in the debate texts and *The Romans of Partenay,* gives English connotations of personal meaning for their audiences and describes making accessible texts that are valuable for those audiences to be, as the translator says in his "Epilogue," "understande And knowin" [understood and

---

4   Matthew W. Morris, "Jean d'Arras and Coudrette: Political Expediency and Censorship in Fifteenth-Century France," *Postscript* 18–19 (2009): 35–44, 38.

5   M. R. James, *The Western Manuscripts in the Library of Trinity College, Cambridge: A Descriptive Catalogue* (Cambridge: Cambridge University Press, 1900–4), R.3.17.

6   Fiona Somerset and Nicholas Watson, "Preface: On 'Vernacular,'" in *The Vulgar Tongue: Medieval and Postmedieval Vernacularity,* ed. Fiona Somerset and Nicholas Watson (University Park: Pennsylvania State University Press, 2003), ix. Michael Sargent adapts the term from a March 1999 conference on "Vernacularity: The Politics of Language and Style;" personal communication with the author, December 15, 2014. Used by permission.

7   All quotations from the main text come from Coudrette, *The Romans of Partenay, or of Lusignan: Otherwise Known as the Tale of Melusine,* ed. Walter W. Skeat (Middletown, DE: Elibron Classics, 2005); line numbers follow in parenthesis.

8   Ruth Evans et al., "The Notion of Vernacular Theory," in *The Idea of the Vernacular: An Anthology of Middle English Literary Theory, 1280–1520,* ed. Jocelyn Wogan-Browne et al. (University Park: Pennsylvania State University Press, 1999), 314–330, at 325.

known]: in these cases, the Word of God and, apparently, a secular romance (6572).

Besides the generic difference, *The Romans of Partenay* is an unusual member of this conversation because, normally, the mother tongue trope was used to compare the vernacular to Latin, the primary learned language of medieval Europe. This text, however, is not a translation from Latin but from French, which complicates matters. The translator falsely paints English as the primary mother tongue of England, which could reflect French's changing status in the country during that time period. His desire for a translation of a popular text, and in particular a romance centered on Melusine, a legendary figure, could also imply a need for that type of work that is almost equivalent to the need to translate religious material. In fact, this is the type of advertising that the printer William Caxton uses in his translated books, particularly for his edition of Sir Thomas Malory's *Le Morte Darthur*. An examination of the Middle English *Romans of Partenay* in the context of the mother tongue trope, as discussed in both the vernacularity debate and Caxton's preface to that text, suggests that the translator merges language and country around this legend of the popular matriarch Melusine to create an ideal of a single-vernacular land with its own written tradition, following a pattern set by other late medieval Englishmen with their own English Bibles and Arthurian romances.

To understand the use of this trope in *The Romans of Partenay* in its immediate context, it is important to know the history of the vernacularity debate. The text most often linked to this debate is Nicholas Love's *Mirror of the Blessed Life of Jesus Christ*, which responds to a pivotal moment in its history: the passing of the *Lambeth Constitutions* by Archbishop Arundel of Canterbury in 1409.[9] As part of an anti-Lollard action, these *Constitutions* declare that no translations of the Bible or another work of devotional literature could be circulated without expressed approval from a religious authority.[10] But these rules were less powerful in their time than they might seem, not least because the Wycliffite Bible was, according to Sargent, "the most popular single text in Middle English."[11] In fact, the required approval was solicited and received for only the *Mirror* and one other text.[12] Additionally, Fiona Somerset has found that concerns

---

9   Michael Sargent, introduction to *The Mirror of the Blessed Life of Jesus Christ* by Nicholas Love (London: Garland Publishing, Inc., 1992), XVII-XVIII.

10   Sargent, *Mirror*, XVIII.

11   Sargent, *Mirror,* XX.

12   Nicholas Watson, "Censorship and Cultural Change in Late Medieval England: Vernacular Theology, the Oxford Translation Debate, and Arundel's Constitutions of 1409," *Speculum* 4 (1995): 822–864, at 831.

over Lollardy had less impact on the issue of biblical translation than previous-ly believed.[13] This can be seen particularly in a 1401 University of Oxford *de-terminacio* in which, surprisingly, Richard Ullerston, a non-Lollard participant, determines that having a vernacular Bible was acceptable.[14] Anne Hudson ar-gues that this should not be taken as an orthodox person spouting heretical views, but rather as a reminder that "so many opinions later identified with Lollardy could be questions of neutrality in the early years of the movement."[15] Furthermore, as Somerset has also noted, "For Arundel, controlling access to clerical learning by restricting vernacular translation is just one dimension of an overall concern with attaining greater control over every aspect of the cler-gy's education and professional activities," and thus "limiting [the] possibilities [of lay vernacular education] is far from his main target."[16] Therefore, it is not surprising that Ullerston's views were not criticized as heretical.

Although it is still unusual, with this dissociation from religious polemic, the entry of the translator of *The Romans of Partenay* into this debate makes more sense in that context. By bringing questions about translation to a more secular genre, *The Romans of Partenay* suggests that concern over translation could be held by writers of other genres. This concern includes an emphasis on accuracy. In his "Epilogue," the translator begins with one of the primary translation choices discussed in the debate: whether a translator should match up words in the same order as the original, that is, to translate literally, or to convey the meaning in a looser translation. One of his major concerns is "to conserve mater and substance" [preserve subject and meaning] (6581). This worry may reflect that of another major writer who took part in the vernacu-larity debate, John Trevisa, best known for translating incredibly long works.

One of these works is Ranulf Higden's history, the *Polychronicon*, translated by Trevisa in the late fourteenth century and printed by Caxton in 1482 (and therefore possibly circulating when *The Romans of Partenay* was being trans-lated).[17] This history contains two discussions of translation methodology:

---

13   Fiona Somerset, "Professionalizing Translation at the Turn of the Fifteenth Century: Ul-lerston's Determinacio, Arundel's Constitutiones," in *The Vulgar Tongue: Medieval and Postmedieval Vernacularity*, 145–158, at 146.

14   Anne Hudson, "The Debate on Bible Translation, Oxford 1401," *English Historical Review* 90 (1975): 1–18, at 9.

15   Hudson, "The Debate on Bible Translation," 17.

16   Somerset, "Professionalizing Translation," 152.

17   John Trevisa, *Dialogue Between the Lord and the Clerk on Translation (Extract) and the Epistle to Thomas, Lord Berkeley, on the Translation of Higden's Polychronicon*, in *The Idea of the Vernacular*, 131.

the *Epistle to Thomas, Lord Berkeley* and the *Dialogue Between the Lord and the Clerk on Translation*. In the *Epistle*, Trevisa explains his preference in the choice of exact words versus meaning. He notes that he may need to shift some words, "But for alle siche chaunging, the menying shal stonde and nought be ychaunged" [But for all such changes, the meaning shall remain and not be changed] (147–148).[18] Trevisa shows that he is sacrificing the original word order of the text in order to retain its message. This is naturally consistent with the methods described by others, as a biblical translator would not want to tamper with the meaning of Scripture. Although Trevisa does not specifically translate a Bible here, the idea of biblical translation is mentioned in the *Dialogue*, so it is clearly on his mind (82–90).

The translator of *The Romans of Partenay* follows Trevisa's line of thought. He elaborates on his earlier statement by saying, in his "Epilogue," that he is translating "Preseruing, I trust, mater and substance / Vnwemmed, vnhurt, for any excesse, / Or by menusing don by violence" [Preserving, I hope, the matter and substance, unmarred and unhurt by any excess or excising done in violence] (6568–70). The translator promises that meaning will be retained without too much adding or "menusing," that is, subtracting, a word Caxton also uses in his *History of Jason*, though not Malory's work.[19] In this, the translator is successful in changing neither any major details of the plot nor the text at the sentence level—or, at least, he does not change it "As ny as meter can conclude sentence," meaning that, at most, he alters words and structure for metrical purposes but otherwise makes few drastic changes (6553). Surprisingly, he achieves this through a different stylistic path, translating in verse, not prose, which Trevisa says is "more pleyn to knowe and understonde" [clearer to know and understand] (125–6). But even with this difference, Trevisa's influence is shown directly after this passage. The *Partenay* translator continues, describing "intelligens, / That will vnderstande And knowin may be / In our moder tonge, spoken in contre" [comprehension that will be made understood and known through our mother tongue, spoken in this country] (6571–3). The second line of this quotation inverts the order of Trevisa's verbs describing prose. This could be a coincidence, but it is also possible that the translator is making a direct allusion to the *Epistle* here.

Even if not connected to Trevisa, these lines are highly significant because they use the mother tongue trope. As Evans et al. have shown, the use of the

---

18   Quotations from Trevisa come from the *Dialogue* and *Epistle*; line numbers follow in parentheses.

19   William Caxton, *The History of Jason*, ed. John Munro (London: Trench, Trübner & Co. Ltd., 1914), 1.

term automatically conveys an affective resonance.[20] The translator shows a personal investment in the translation here; it is not just in any vernacular, but his own, even if he is capable of reading French as well. Notably, for this, he uses the plural: he specifies "*our* moder tonge," not just "my," which implies that this emotional connection is not unique to the translator himself, but is shared with others (6573, emphasis added). Although the text's patron is likely included in this pronoun, he may not have been the only English speaker to whom the translator is referring, but instead the translator may be anticipating (or hoping for) an even larger audience of those English people whose linguistic skills were limited and aiming for a personal connection with them.

This plurality could also be another inheritance from the vernacularity debate. An important modifier that the translator adds, suggesting that "our" refers to more than just himself and his patron, is "spoken in contre" (6573). Here, he connects the vernacular to a geographical and, especially, political entity, the "contre" or "country." L. O. Aranye Fradenburg has tracked the history of this word elsewhere in Middle English writing, finding that, by the fourteenth century, the word was used both in the sense of homeland and nation.[21] With this definition, the *Partenay* translator seems to be saying that the first—and therefore, the most important and natural—language that a person speaks is related to a singular geographic identity (which, of course, overstates the case and doesn't take into account multilingualism).

This connection between the mother tongue and country is also made by the vernacularity debate, particularly "First Seiþ Bois" (1400–1414), a defense of biblical translation taken loosely from Ullerston's *determinacio*.[22] The anonymous author uses the concept of the mother tongue to compare English and England to other languages and other countries on a European-wide scale. He says of the Bible, "it was translatid into Spaynesche tunge, Frensche tunge and Almayne, and oþer londes also han þe Bibel in þer modur-tunge" [it was translated into the Spanish, French, and German languages, and other lands also have the Bible in their mother tongue] (66–7).[23] The author argues that there have already been biblical translations in multiple European vernaculars, and England is in fact behind other countries in this: since other "londes," or "lands,"

---

20   Evans et al., "The Notions of Vernacular Theory," 325.

21   L. O. Aranye Fradenburg, "Pro Patria Mori," in *Imagining the Middle English Nation*, ed. Kathy Lavezzo (Minneapolis: University of Minnesota Press, 2003), 3–38, at 3.

22   Mary Dove, introduction to *The Earliest Advocates of the English Bible*, ed. Mary Dove (Exeter: University of Exeter Press, 2010), XLIX.

23   Quotation from "First Seiþ Bois," in *The Earliest Advocates of the English Bible*; line numbers follow in parentheses.

are allowed to have a translated Bible, then so should England. This is despite the fact that, according to Margaret Deanesly, the verse translations circulating at the time, which he may be referring to, "had not the same value" as ones in prose, presumably because they were too loose according to the standards that Trevisa and others set.[24]

The author of "First Seiþ Bois" shows a particular devotion to his land through this concept of the mother tongue, differentiating England as an individual geographic and cultural entity which needs writing in its own language, just as other lands have. With his addition of "in contre," the translator of *The Romans of Partenay* seems to be doing something similar (6573). These words potentially show strong ties to his fatherland. Or, in his case, perhaps it is better to say motherland, because his emphasis is not on a father but a mother with this highly gendered portrayal of language as well as his female protagonist. Both the trope and the text's matriarchal family emphasize the role of mothers in the formation of identity, whether it is linguistic or dynastic, and associate power with birth, not conquest, which was particularly important for the Hundred Years' War, the major conflict that formed the backdrop of the *Melusine* tradition.

In light of present-day conceptions of "England," the nationalism exhibited in these cases seems unremarkable. But both the translator of *The Romans of Partenay* and the author of "First Seiþ Bois" make their country's linguistic situation much simpler than it actually was in the fifteenth century. This is particularly clear in the romance since it is a translation from French. The translator distinguishes English as his mother tongue and French as not, saying, in his "Prologue," "I not aqueynted of birth naturall / With fre[n]she his verray trew parfightnesse" (8–9). He does not know French from birth; that is, it is literally not his native language. Walter W. Skeat, publishing in 1866, hypothesized that the translator was lying, based on his numerous errors, and that he was actually from Poitou.[25] But most modern critics have dismissed this argument, including Brenda Hosington, who calls it "hardly convincing."[26] Donald Marshall Schull, in fact, cites this and the mother tongue passage as proof that the author "explicitly claims" that he is a native English speaker and "[j]ust as explicitly [...] claims not to be a native speaker of French," finding

---

24   Margaret Deanesly, *The Lollard Bible* (Cambridge: Cambridge University Press, 1966), 146.

25   Walter W. Skeat, preface to *The Romans of Partenay*, xx.

26   Hosington, "From Theory to Practice," 409.

that there is no reason to disbelieve him.[27] These firm declarations are of the utmost importance because they show that the anonymous translator clearly identifies himself as an English speaker and that English, not French, is his, and his country's, native language.

Though not a definitive answer, this romance could serve as a place to explore a question that has puzzled scholars for years: what was the status of French in England? Particularly in studies of the late fourteenth and fifteenth centuries, the French language's role in government and everyday life has been greatly disputed. According to the late John Fisher, from around the 1410s and 20s, Henry v replaced French with English for official business.[28] As such, French has often been described as being in "decline" during that period. Christopher Cannon continues that thought with respect to medieval education, stating that "competence in French, even among the aristocracy in England, is already declining by the middle of the thirteenth century, when texts designed to teach French to the children of the nobility began to appear."[29] Ardis Butterfield, however, argues the opposite. She notes that, while Henry v was the first king to use English, it was only for specific documents, his signet correspondence; others remained in French.[30] And, with respect to education, she finds that "rather than viewing French as a language that had gone into an irreversible decline, uniquely for a vernacular language, French was given school status and thus treated not so differently from Latin."[31] Therefore, French is not degraded by not being a mother tongue, but rather is elevated. Literature further confuses the issue, with William Calin finding that most of the 95 to 115 Middle English verse romances came from both continental and insular French sources, sometimes in direct translations.[32] The translator of *The Romans of Partenay* thus reflects French's tricky status by making this declaration about the language, distinguishing it as a "foreign" one for himself and his country.

---

27   Donald Marshall Shull, "The Effect of the Theory of Translation Expressed in the Anonymous *Romans of Partenay* (T.C.C. MS R. 3.17) Upon the Language of the Poem" (PhD diss., University of North Carolina at Chapel Hill, 1984), 43.

28   John Fisher, "A Language Policy for Lancastrian England," *PMLA* 107, no. 5 (1992): 1168–80, at 1178.

29   Christopher Cannon, "From Literacy to Literature: Elementary Learning and the Middle English Poet," *PMLA* 129, no. 3 (2014): 349–64, at 351.

30   Ardis Butterfield, *The Familiar Enemy: Chaucer, Language, and Nation in the Hundred Years War* (Oxford: Oxford University Press, 2009), 323.

31   Butterfield, *The Familiar Enemy*, 330–1.

32   William Calin, *The French Tradition and the Literature of Medieval England* (Toronto: University of Toronto Press, 1994), 427.

Rather than emphasizing a decline in French, the Middle English translator seems to have particular reasons for making this claim that he does not know that language from "birth naturall" (8). First, it is a stylistic choice, an instance of the humility topos. Even if modern readers may find his language strange at times, he is still exaggerating his incompetence in this statement. Talking of an early Anglo-Norman example, William Rothwell argues that usage of this trope "has nothing whatsoever to do with supposed deficiencies in Anglo-Norman."[33] This can be extended to a variety of examples in medieval texts in multiple languages that describe translators' professed feelings about their own lack of skill. The translator of *The Romans of Partenay* follows a tradition here, much as he does when discussing his process, and his alleged insufficiency is not limited to French. In fact, with an almost perverse pride in his humility, he later declares in the "Epilogue" that he will make mistakes in whatever language he uses: "Be it latyn, frensh, or our tonge to-bore" [be it Latin, French, or our to-born (that is, native) tongue] (6558). The translator claims humility even for the mother tongue, so this is not a signal that his French is particularly bad; he suggests he is just inept generally. Additionally, the translator, at this moment, does elevate French to a high standard, describing it with the word "parfight-nesse" [perfection] (9). He is not qualified, but the language is more than fine; it's perfect, and sophisticated enough that not everyone knows it.

By elevating French, then, he is suggesting why a translation of *The Romans of Partenay* is necessary: for comprehension, just as someone might need a translation from a Latin text, biblical or otherwise. As the translator explains in the mother tongue passage, he is doing this so "That [the text] vnderstande And knowin may be" [so that (the work) may be known and understood] (6572). With regards to the Bible, this desire for access exhibited by the "First Seiþ Bois" author and others in the vernacularity debate, of course, carries a spiritual importance for vernacular readers. But why would someone want accessibility for the story of Melusine? Why does the translator try to promote this specific story in this way? A desire for understanding this legend, at first, does not make logical sense. *The Romans of Partenay*, as a romance, does not have the sort of moral significance of a biblical translation, which the translator was most likely aware of. So what could explain this anomaly?

One possible answer could be found in the work of Trevisa. In his *Dialogue*, the Lord and the Clerk discuss the issue of "need" as it comes to writing and translation. While Higden's *Polychronicon* does not fit his first two types of need—for God and for sustenance—the Lord explains that "in the third maner

---

33   William Rothwell, "Playing 'follow my leader' in Anglo-Norman studies," *Journal of French Language Studies* 6 (1996): 177–210.

to speke of thing that nedith, al that's profitable nedith, and so far to speke alle men nedith to knowe the cronicles" (56–58). Somerset interprets this type as "whatever is beneficial," and as such, he is saying that "*everyone* needs to read Higden's *Polychronicon*."[34] While this seems like a convenient plug for the circulation of his book—and it likely is—Trevisa's concept of need perhaps resonated with other translators whose works' "historical" bents could have been used to increase their demand. Certainly, the *Melusine* legend fits into that category as a quasi-historical/mythological text used to legitimate holdings won in the Hundred Years' War. Thus the translator could have been thinking of his translation with respect to a possible historical importance of *The Romans of Partenay* for his own country and language.

For England, in particular, this importance may have extended beyond Melusine's claim to fame as an ancestor of a number of European noble houses, including the family of England's own queen, Elizabeth Woodville, wife of Edward IV.[35] The translator may also have picked up on another significance of Melusine to England from his source text. Coudrette's original French version gives Melusine her own place in an insular British past. Not only is she an ancestor, but she is also a daughter of the Isles, having for her father "[t]he noble helmas, king of Albany," or Scotland (4365). This means that her genealogical line is part British, if not specifically English (though the two were not always differentiated).

This text also draws on another member of Melusine's family tree: King Arthur. Morris, speaking of the Valois kings' attempts to recover from the Hundred Years' War, gives Coudrette's visible interest in Arthurian legend and the particular British association he gives to Arthur (although there were also French connections for this figure) as proof that his *Melusine* version is "a composition that shows every indication of being a propagandistic work favoring the recently defeated English and their French partisan allies."[36] In particular, he examines Coudrette's prologue and an episode about the Bon Chevalier d'Angleterre, or the Good Knight of England, part of a quest for the treasure of Melusine's father that is protected by her sister Palestine.[37] In this episode, though many knights attempt it, the Good Knight, a member of Arthur's court whose ancestor is Tristan, is the only one Coudrette spends a significant amount of time on. However, he, too, fails the quest since the destiny of destroying the treasure's guardian monster belongs to Melusine's son, Geoffrey of the Great Tooth.

---

34   Somerset, "Professionalizing Translation," 150–1.
35   Philippa Gregory, David Baldwin, and Michael Jones, *The Women of the Cousin's War: The Duchess, the Queen, and the King's Mother* (New York: Touchstone, 2011): 55–56.
36   Matthew W. Morris, introduction to *A Bilingual Edition of Jean d'Arras's* Melusine, 41.
37   Morris, *Melusine,* 44–5.

Although the translator of *The Romans of Partenay* makes a concerted effort not to alter the story from his source text, he occasionally adds an extra word or two to the verses and notably does so when he translates these particular passages. Though fairly minor, these additions could connect to the translator's possible project of claiming the *Melusine* legend for England. The first change comes in the translation of the original prologue, which is included following the translator's own. In both the French and the Middle English, the narrator presents the tales of King Arthur's court as stories of a past that are beloved by his contemporary readers. The French states:

> Les choses de long temps passees,
> Plaisent quant ilz sont recordees,
> Mays qu'ilz soient bonnes et belles,
> Trop plus que ne font les nouvelles.
> Ne parlon tant du roy Artuz
> Qui voult esprouver les vertuz
> De nobles chevaliers et gens?[38]
> [The things of long ago
> Are pleasant when they are remembered,
> Provided that they are good and beautiful,
> Even more than new things are.
> Don't we speak so much of King Arthur
> Who wanted to prove the virtues of noble knights and people?] (13–19)

This passage is already laudatory in the French. But the Middle English translator adds his own admiration for Arthur, as well as a foreshadowing of his own project. He translates it as:

> Thinges of long time passyd in contre
> When rehersid is, pleasith hertes fre;
> Auncion thinges wich ben good and fayre,
> As to speke of king arthure debonayr
> How he wold preue his vertu and manhede
> With noble knightes and peple worthi. (98–103)

---

38   French quotations come from Coudrette, *Le Roman de Mélusine, ou, Histoire de Lusignan*, ed. Eleanor Roach (Paris: Librairie des Méridiens, 1982); line numbers follow in parentheses. The author wishes to thank Karl Steel and Stephanie Grace Petinos for their assistance in translating.

The word "debonayr" is a French cognate, but the original line uses no such adjective to describe Arthur. The rhyming phrases "in contre" and "hertes fre" are also added. These could have been from another manuscript, but the variations that Eleanor Roach has provided in her French edition do not include such words, suggesting that they were deliberate additions and leaving a greater question concerning their purpose.[39]

On one hand, all three of these additions, which come at the end of a verse, provide rhyme. This explains "debonayr," a rhyme word for "fayre," which does have a French equivalent in "belles." But neither "in contre" nor "hertes fre," though rhyming with each other, have any basis in the original. These words seem at first to be chosen at random, yet when considering the translator's possible project, they gain new meaning. This first phrase, "in contre," of course, reappears in the mother tongue passage (6573). Its use suggests King Arthur's roots in the translator's own land and his importance as an English hero. The repetition of "in contre" later, then, shows Melusine has similar associations with England, suggesting that her legend is another past event that would be enjoyable to listeners in the translator's homeland.

The other Arthurian passage, the Good Knight of England episode, which is part of the romance's conclusion, furthers this connection between the two traditions and reveals Melusine's link to the British Isles in an explanation of her origins. It does not just present her as part of Arthur's world but also sets her up to replace him by pitting one of her vast number of sons—and so herself as a matriarch—against one of his own men. Geoffrey of the Great Tooth, though known for his martial prowess (and burning down a monastery with one hundred monks, including his brother, inside), can succeed in this quest and win the treasure of his maternal—and Scottish—grandfather only because of his bloodline, the one qualification that the otherwise worthy English knight does not have. The French lines read:

> Douleur fut que le chevalier
> D'Engleterre, preux et legier,
> N'avoit esté de son lignage.
> Si estoit il de hault parage:
> De la lignie Tristram estrait,
> Ainsi que l'istoire retrait. (6551–6)
> [A pity it was that the knight
> Of England, proud and rash,
> Hadn't been of his lineage.

---

39   Coudrette, *Le Roman de Mélusine*, 107.

> Yes, he was of high parentage:
> From the line of Tristan he stemmed,
> Thus the history related.]

The narrator acknowledges that Tristan is a fairly impressive ancestor; the knight is still "de hault parage" [of high parentage]. But being of Tristan's line is not enough; only Helmas's own descendant, that is, his daughter's son (so there is descent through the female line) can achieve this quest.

In this episode, as in the other passage, the translator of *The Romans of Partenay* takes liberties with the wording. The narrator states, "Full heuy it was that this goodly knyght / Off Englande had noght be off that line ryght / He descended was off full hy parage, / Off Tristram hys line cam of natiuite / As the history rehersith hys linage" [A shame it was that this good knight of England was not of the proper lineage; he was descended of noble parentage, born of the line of Tristan, as the history tells us his lineage was] (6005–9). Comparing the translation with the original, it is clear that the Middle English retains French words in the cognates "parage," "line," and "linage." But one word is unique to the translation: "natiuite." Again, Eleanor Roach's list of manuscript variations shows that there is no mention of nativity or birth in the surviving copies of the French, so this is likely the translator's own invention.[40] And while rhyme may have also been a consideration for this change, the simple words "he" and "be" do not seem to warrant this specific choice. Furthermore, birth or its equivalent does not specifically come into play in the original. It is the translator alone, then, who links birth and geographic affiliation with this word "natiuite", similar to what he did with "birth naturall" and the French language in the "Prologue" (8). So, while it seems unusual in its immediate context, considering the work as a whole, there could be a rationale for this addition.

The Good Knight of England passage in particular would likely have meaning for an English audience since it concerns an English person and relates to the Arthurian tradition. This connection—even if Arthur and Tristan are adumbrated by Melusine—could further explain the translator's desire to put this text in his mother tongue. Another literary project, contemporaneous with this translation, and possibly influenced by Trevisa's suggestion of a "need" for historical sources, does the same to her rival: Caxton's printing of *Le Morte Darthur*. Though Malory frequently calls his source a "Frenshe book"—and so this text is another vernacular-to-vernacular translation—it is Caxton, through his paratextual apparatus, who places Arthur in a discussion about language,

---

40   Coudrette, *Le Roman de Mélusine*, 325.

using the concept of the mother tongue, just as the translator of *The Romans of Partenay* and the vernacularity debate participants do (726).[41]

Aside from printing Trevisa's *Dialogue and Epistle*, Caxton does not engage in a discussion of Biblical translation. Nevertheless, as a translator as well as a printer, the translation process has an interest for him, as previously shown.[42] He also utilizes the mother tongue trope in his preface to Malory. He states:

> And also [Arthur] is more spoke of beyonde the see, moo bookes made of his noble actes than there be in Englond; as wel in Duche, Ytalyen, Spaynysshe, and Grekysshe, as in Frensshe [...] it is a mervayl why he is no more renomed in his owne contreye, sauf onelye it accordeth to the Word of God, whyche sayth that no man is accept for a prophete in his owne contreye [...] And many noble volumes be made of hym and of hys noble knyghtes in Frensshe, which I have seen and redde beyonde the see, which been not had in our maternal tongue. But in Walsshe ben many and also in Frensshe, and somme in Englysshe, but nowher nygh alle.[43]
>
> [And so (Arthur) is more spoken of beyond the sea, and more books made of his noble acts than there are in England, as much in Dutch, Italian, Spanish, and Greek, as in French [...] it is astounding that he is not better known in his own country, save only that this accords with the Word of God, which says that no man is accepted for a prophet in his own country [...] And many great volumes are made of him and his noble knights in French, which I have seen and read beyond the sea, which cannot be had in our maternal tongue. In Welsh there are many and also in French, and some in English, but nowhere near (the same number).]

Though Caxton makes a nod to both French and Welsh, another vernacular language that was spoken in the British Isles, only English, in his estimation, is "our maternal tongue," that is, the mother tongue particular to both himself and to his readers, suggesting, as the Middle English translator does, a kinship between them. For his own part, he denies any familiarity with insular French and therefore the idea of it as another English vernacular, claiming that he read French Arthurian literature "beyonde the see," not in England, even though he could have done so there as well.

---

41   Quotations from Sir Thomas Malory come from *Malory: Complete Works*, ed. Eugene Vinaver (Oxford: Oxford University Press, 1971); page numbers follow in parentheses.

42   Caxton, *History of Jason*, 1.

43   "Caxton's Preface," in *Malory: Complete Works*, XIV.

Like the "First Seiþ Bois" author, Caxton wants his material—in this case, the secular legend of King Arthur, not the Bible—in his mother tongue, just as it is in other vernaculars. While this material has lower stakes than the devotional texts of the vernacularity debate in the early fifteenth century, there is what Patricia Clare Ingham calls "'a sovereign fantasy': [which] allow[s] nobles to repudiate their dynastic ties to their French cousins and (in the wake of the Hundred Years War) to claim an insular heritage."[44] Caxton's use of the trope, which is somewhat ironic, considering that this is still a translation from French, indicates that he believes Arthur belongs to the English people (despite actually being Welsh). And his printing seems to have a cultural significance in putting Arthur's stories back in the language of "his owne contreye," a phrase Caxton uses not once, but twice, making the mother tongue and his subject belong to a specific location, perhaps to broaden the audience for his printing in England.[45] This is not unlike how the translator of *The Romans of Partenay* repeats "in contre" (6573). Although there is not likely direct intertextuality between this work and Caxton's, they do share in common the drawing of this parallel between language and nation and therefore perhaps the treatment of these legendary figures as well.

Looking at what Caxton does with the concept of the mother tongue could help explain the project of the translator of *The Romans of Partenay* in using the language of the vernacularity debate. While the translator does not directly state that he wants the *Melusine* story in his own language as it is in others, this could be the case, since Melusine's continental popularity was great. Morris states that "translations in other tongues attest to the universal appeal of the romance of *Mélusine*" and lists the places in Europe where it spread.[46] Like Arthur—and perhaps vernacular Bibles as well—Melusine's legend had a wide circulation throughout Europe. The translator may have been thinking along the same lines as Caxton and the author of "First Seiþ Bois" in wanting to have this text written in the language of his own land, especially with Melusine's connections to it. Certainly, he is concerned with the accessibility for readers whose native language is English, as the mother tongue passage shows (6572). Unfortunately, particularly with the first page of the manuscript missing, his attitudes towards Melusine as a figure—as well as the greater circumstances of his commission—can never be known for certain. But this comparison with

---

44   Patricia Clare Ingham, *Sovereign Fantasies: Arthurian Romance and the Making of Britain* (Philadelphia: University of Pennsylvania Press, 2000), 6.

45   Caxton, "Preface," xiv.

46   Matthew W. Morris, introduction to *A Bilingual Edition of Coudrette's Mélusine, ou, Le Roman de Parthenay* (Lewiston, NY: Edwin Mellen Press, 2003), 5, 3.

other projects could imply that the translator's goal in putting this particular text into his mother tongue and discussing his process in such detail was to make the legend England's own, if not to the exclusion of other vernacular versions (the translator at one point expresses a wish for a facing-page translation), then at least to match them (6590–1).

The translator's emphasis on the mother tongue thus suggests that he wants to create literature in a language unique and familiar to England, especially considering the changing roles of the English and French languages. It also gives a new significance to the Melusine legend in that country. Although Melusine's immense popularity was certainly reason enough to have her legend translated, having a prologue and an epilogue placing *The Romans of Partenay* within the vernacularity debate, and thus paralleling biblical translation, distinguishes—or at least tries to distinguish—this particular poem from other translations at the time as being of a higher value and importance—the one exception being, of course, the legend of Arthur, which also claims that significance. Viewing *The Romans of Partenay* in this context, therefore, shows that ways to think about translation, particularly connections among language, birth, and country in the image of the mother tongue, extended beyond the vernacularity debate. It also demonstrates that, during the Middle Ages, the issues of translation and the meaning of language more generally were not limited to clerics and scholars, but were matters of interest to a broader literary population: the whole "contre" (5673).

CHAPTER 9

Melusine and Luxembourg: A Double Memory

Pit Péporté

Melusine has become a topos of collective memory across many parts of Europe, but scholars have often overlooked that her story itself is a medium of dynastic memory. In fact, the romance of Melusine and its later adoptions and adaptations illustrate how the content and the symbolism of a *lieu de mémoire* transform over time and space as it gains importance for a changing set of communities. One way to explore these continuities and discontinuities is through the connection of Melusine and Luxembourg,[1] not only because Melusine has become a central point of reference to the medieval past in the grand duchy of Luxembourg, but also because the original romance's intertextual references to the medieval Luxembourg dynasty[2] are key for understanding its political purpose.

The first version of Melusine's story was composed by Jean d'Arras under the patronage of Jean, Duc de Berry, the second son of King Jean II of France and the ruler of a border zone in the wars with the English crown.[3] Duc Jean had first been made count of Poitou by his father, but he had to relinquish the county to the English in the aftermath of the battle of Poitiers (1356). His father then gave him the neighboring duchy of Berry as his appanage, but Jean

---

1 This contribution recapitulates and updates a series of ideas previously explored in Pit Péporté, *Constructing the Middle Ages: Historiography, Collective Memory and Nation-Building in Luxembourg*, National Cultivation of Culture 3 and Publications of CLUDEM 34 (Leiden: Brill, 2011), 75–108.

2 For the past two centuries, the dynasty has mainly been referred to in historiography as the House of Luxembourg. However, the male ancestor of the dynasty was Duke Waleran III of Limburg and the so-called House of Luxembourg was technically a minor branch of the ducal House of Limburg. Members of the dynasty favored this view until the reign of Charles IV. See Péporté, *Constructing the Middle Ages*, 143–152. Thereafter most sources refer to the dynasty as the House of Bohemia. On the latter see Evamarie Clemens, *Luxemburg-Böhmen, Wittelsbach-Bayern, Habsburg-Österreich und ihre genealogischen Mythen im Vergleich* (Trier: Trierer Wissenschaftlicher Verlag, 2001).

3 On Jean de Berry see Françoise Autrand, *Jean de Berry: L'art et le pouvoir* (Paris: Fayard, 2000).

managed to retake the county of Poitou in the 1370s.[4] The siege and conquest of the mighty and strategically well-positioned castle of Lusignan in the summer of 1374 had proven a lengthy and costly affair.[5] It is generally accepted that the political point of Jean d'Arras' romance was to legitimize the Duc de Berry's ownership of Poitou in general and of Lusignan in particular.[6] The story not only tells how Melusine founded the Lusignan dynasty, but it also presents Jean de Berry implicitly as her descendant and therefore the legitimate successor of the Lusignan counts. Melusine suggested a fictive counter-argument to the English claims over Poitou, once a core Angevin possession, for the return of which the English crown negotiated repeatedly. In the early 1390s, at the time of the negotiations between Charles V of France and Richard II of England, Jean d'Arras composed the romance of Melusine. She also appeared in Jean de Berry's fabulous *Book of Hours*, written and decorated around 1414, when Henry V of England once more demanded the return of Poitou to the English crown.[7]

In his romance, Jean d'Arras mixes fact and fiction in a way that creates an entertaining tale while still suggesting a certain degree of veracity to its medieval audience. It is not the frame story of Melusine and Raimondin that is central to this end, but the stories of their many sons, which also fill the largest part of the romance. Here, the author plays with the well-known achievements of the House of Lusignan in the East. He has Melusine's sons set out to conquer Armenia and Cyprus, alluding to generally known facts, not least since King Peter I of Cyprus's tour of Europe (1362–64) and the celebration of his military feats in Guillaume de Machaut's *Prise d'Alexandrie* (post 1369) had boosted once more the family's fame.[8] In addition to these crusading adventures in Outremer, some sons are made to stay in Europe. Antoine and Renaud first ride to Luxembourg, from whence Renaud continues to Bohemia.[9] In both cases, they save the local princesses from the hands of some evildoer, marry them, and found local dynasties.

---

4   Autrand, *Jean de Berry*, 125–150.
5   Autrand, *Jean de Berry*, 137–138.
6   Donald Maddox and Sara Sturm-Maddox, "Introduction," in Jean d'Arras, *Melusine or The Noble History of Lusignan*, trans. Donald Maddox and Sara Sturm-Maddox (University Park: Pennsylvania State University Press, 2012), 3–16, at 12.
7   Autrand, *Jean de Berry*, 150.
8   Maddox and Sturm-Maddox, "Introduction," 11.
9   Jean d'Arras, *Mélusine. Roman du XIVe siècle*, ed. Louis Stouff (Geneva: Slatkine, 1974), 157; hereafter Stouff. *Mélusine,* ed. and trans. Jean-Jacques Vincensini (Paris: Le Livre de Poche, 2003), 262.

Again, the author subtly interweaves fact with fiction. Both Luxembourg and Bohemia had seen a princely heiress marry an outsider: Ermesinde of Luxembourg married Waleran of Limburg in 1214,[10] and Elisabeth of Bohemia married John of Luxembourg in 1310.[11] In the romance as in real life, the princess of Bohemia marries someone who has set off from Luxembourg. To give his account additional force, Jean d'Arras adds a few subtleties. All of Melusine's sons are slightly disfigured. Antoine in Luxembourg is marked by what looks like a lion's paw on his cheek. He also carries the lion as his heraldic emblem.[12] So had Waleran of Limburg, whose descendants in Luxembourg bore the animal on their coat of arms.[13] Renaud was disfigured by having only one eye. His historic model, John, who became king of Bohemia, was known for his blindness in later age, a condition that first started in one eye and only spread to both after a couple of failed medical procedures.[14] Renaud is further described as fighting Saracens in Bohemia, possibly a reference to King John's Baltic crusades.[15] These two stories of Antoine and Renaud are of crucial importance,

---

10   On Waleran, see Michel Richartz, "Waleran de Limbourg (ca.1165–1226): le devenir d'un grand politique entre Meuse et Rhin" (master's thesis, University of Liège, 1999). On his wife Ermesinde, see Michel Margue, "Ermesinde. Notice biographique," in *Ermesinde et l'affranchissement de la ville de Luxembourg: Etudes sur la femme, le pouvoir et la ville au XIIIe siècle*, Publications du Musée d'Histoire de la Ville de Luxembourg, Publications du CLUDEM 7, ed. Michel Margue (Luxembourg: CLUDEM and Musée d'Histoire de la Ville de Luxembourg, 1994), 23–41.

11   See Michel Pauly, ed., *Die Erbtochter, der fremde Fürst und das Land: Die Ehe Johanns des Blinden und Elisabeths von Böhmen in vergleichender europäischer Perspektive*, Publications du CLUDEM 38 (Luxembourg: CLUDEM, 2013).

12   Stouff, *Mélusine*, 171.

13   Jean-Pierre Kauder, "La légende de Mélusine: Contribution à l'histoire de la fée poitevine," in *Gymnase Grand-Ducal d'Echternach: Programme publié à la clôture de l'année scolaire 1903–1904* (Luxembourg: V. Bück, 1904), 32. See also below.

14   Michel Margue, "La fée Mélusine: Le mythe fondateur de la Maison de Luxembourg," in *Bestiaires d'Arlon: Les animaux dans l'imaginaire des Gallo-Romains à nos jours*, ed. André Neuberg (Bastogne: Ed. Musée en Piconrue, 2006), 133. John's blindness is well attested and became widely known after Froissart had mentioned it; see Jean Froissart, *Chroniques*, ed. Kervyn de Lettenhoven, *Oeuvres de Froissart* (Brussels: V. Devaux, 1867–1877), 5:55.

15   Michel Margue, "La fée Mélusine." N.B. This essay does not argue that each protagonist in the romance stands solely for one specific historical precedent. The figure of Renaud can also be linked to a count of Bar of the same name; see Péporté, *Constructing the Middle Ages*, 78. On some of the other sons, see Maddox and Sturm-Maddox, "Introduction," 10–11.

since they represent the link between Melusine and the book's patron. Jean de Berry's maternal grandfather was no other than King John of Bohemia, who had inherited the county of Luxembourg from his father and after his marriage to Princess Elisabeth was given the crown of Bohemia.[16] Since the romance suggests that the dynasties of Luxembourg and Bohemia both descended from Melusine, the Duc de Berry must thus have been doubly related to her.

Although patrilineal descent was considered prime in this age, Jean de Berry had several reasons to stress his maternal ancestry. First, his paternal Valois ancestors were disqualified on two grounds. The origin myth of the kings of France had been well-established for many centuries and traced their lineage back to the Trojans.[17] Building Melusine into this mythos might have appeared too artificial. The counts of Luxembourg, however, owned no such myth, while the kings of Bohemia had made use of one that shows striking similarities to the story of Melusine.[18] Probably as important was that the patron's direct Valois ancestors had achieved little chivalric glory in the recent past. In fact, Jean de Berry's father, King Jean II, had spectacularly lost the battle of Poitiers against the Black Prince in 1356, ending up in English captivity. It came to cost the dynasty dearly and directly affected the royal princes; in the early 1360s, Jean de Berry had to spend time in England as a hostage.[19]

This leads to the second reason for implicitly stressing Berry's maternal grandfather. By so doing, Jean de Berry hoped to profit from the king of Bohemia's *realpolitik* approach to everyday

---

16 On John of Bohemia see Raymond Cazelles, *Jean l'Aveugle: Comte de Luxembourg, Roi de Bohême* (Bourges: Tardy, 1947); Michel Margue and Jean Schroeder, ed., *Un itinéraire européen: Jean l'Aveugle, comte de Luxembourg, roi de Bohême. 1296–1346,* Publications du CLUDEM (Brussels: Credit communal; Luxembourg: CLUDEM, 1996).

17 Colette Beaune, "L'utilisation politique du mythe troyen à la fin du Moyen Âge," Publications de l'École française de Rome 80/1 (1982): 331–335; see also Colette Beaune, *Naissance de la nation France* (Paris: Gallimard, 1993), 29–39.

18 In this Bohemian myth of origin, Libuše, like Melusine one of three sisters and endowed with supernatural powers, married a ploughman with whom she founded the city of Prague and the Přemyslid dynasty of Bohemian dukes and kings. The story of Libuše was spread from the twelfth century. See Vit Vlnas and Zdenek Hojda, "Tschechien: 'Gönnt einem jeden die Wahrheit'," in *Mythen der Nationen: Ein Europäisches Panorama,* ed. Monika Flacke (Munich: Koehler & Amelang, 1998), 502–507. See also Patrick J. Geary, *Women at the Beginning: Origin Myths from the Amazons to the Virgin Mary* (Princeton, NJ: Princeton University Press, 2006), 35–39.

19 Autrand, *Jean de Berry,* 126–129.

government,[20] he had fostered a chivalric image through his persona.[21] A regular jouster, he also tried to emulate Arthur's Round Table in Prague.[22] More lasting was his patronage of the poet Guillaume de Machaut, who in his *Jugement du roy de Behaigne* [Judgment of the King of Bohemia] presented him as an Arthurian king, generous to his guests and expert on all matters courtly.[23] His chivalric image was cemented by his death in battle. He was one of the few late medieval kings to fall on the battlefield and represented the most prominent casualty on the field of Crécy (1345), where he supported his ally, the King of France, with a contingent of knights. Like his predecessor counts of Luxembourg, King John held good connections to the royal court in Paris under both Capetians and Valois, a political alliance that resulted in several marriages and a financially profitable military treaty.[24]

News of John's death quickly spread in a series of eulogies to the fallen knights of Crécy.[25] It then made its way into the chronicles. Although Froissart might have initially considered John's charge as, quite literally, blind foolishness,[26] his account of John's death was quickly and lastingly interpreted as

---

20   See for instance Winfried Reichert, "Johann der Blinde als Graf von Luxemburg,'" in *Johann der Blinde: Graf von Luxemburg, König von Böhmen. 1296–1346. Tagungsband der 9es Journées lotharingiennes. 22.-26. Oktober 1996. Centre Universitaire de Luxembourg*, ed. Michel Pauly, PSH 115; Publications du CLUDEM 14 (Luxembourg: Institut grand-ducal, 1997), 169–196.

21   See Michel Margue, "Jean de Luxembourg, prince idéal et chevalier parfait: Aux origines d'un mythe," *Mediaevalia Historica Bohemica* 5 (1998): 11–26; Péporté, *Constructing the Middle Ages*, 163–178.

22   Peter of Zittau, *Chronicon Aulae Regiae*, Fontes Rerum Bohemicarum 4, ed. Josef Emler (Prague: Nadání Františka Palackého, 1882), 252.

23   Guillaume de Machaut, *Le Jugement du roy de Behaigne*, ed. James I. Wimsatt and William W. Kibler (Athens, GA: University of Georgia Press, 1988). On the poet and his patron, see Nigel Wilkins, "A pattern of patronage: Machaut, Froissart and the houses of Luxembourg and Bohemia in the fourteenth century," *French Studies* 37 (1983): 257–284; Péporté, *Constructing the Middle Ages*, 163–169.

24   On John of Bohemia's relations with the French crown, see Margue and Schroeder, *Un itinéraire européen*, 51–86.

25   Examples include Jehan de Batery, *Li dis des VIII blasons*, ed. Adolf Tobler, *Jahrbuch für romanische und englische Literatur* 5 (1864): 211–225; Peter Suchenwirt, "Von hern Friedreichen dem Chreuzzpekch," in *Peter Suchenwirt's Werke aus dem vierzehnten Jahrhunderte: Ein Beitrag zur Zeit- und Sittengeschichte*, ed. Alois Primisser (Vienna: Wallishausser, 1827), 43–8; Jaap Tigelaar, "Dese es van Behem coninck Jan. Een onbekende ererede over Jan de Blinde, graaf van Luxemburg, koning van Bohemen (1296–13466)," *Queeste* 10 (2003): 146–161.

26   Péporté, *Constructing the Middle Ages*, 174–75.

a heroic feat.[27] Guillaume de Machaut could build on this resounding fame, now presenting his former patron as the example of an ascetic knight-errant,[28] a topos also taken up by Machaut's protégé Eustache Deschamps.[29] Along with his chivalric image, King John had managed to succeed in his dynasty's imperial ambitions, having his son Charles IV elected Holy Roman Emperor, who in turn managed to pass on the crown to his descendants. Emphasizing his Luxembourg ancestry thus held much more ideological and political potential for Jean de Berry than stressing merely his royal French blood. The attachment, though, might have been even more personal. Unlike his brothers, he tried to emulate his maternal grandfather.[30] He took over the king's two possessions in France: the Hôtel de Nesle in Paris and the castle of Mehun-sur-Yèvre. He also hired the king's trusted poet, Guillaume de Machaut, to compose the *Fonteinne amoureuse* [*The Fountain of Love*] for his consolation while in English captivity.[31]

Second, the alleged genealogical connection between Lusignan and Luxembourg worked well because the coats of arms of both houses are strikingly similar. As mentioned with reference to Antoine, Melusine's sons bore the arms of a red (gules) lion on a barry of white (argent) and blue (azure). Late medieval readers knowledgeable about heraldry must have recognized the coats of arms worn by the Lusignan kings of Cyprus, which happened to be identical to those worn by the counts of Luxembourg. This similarity, though, appears as pure coincidence from today's point of view. The Lusignan lion—which seemed not to have been worn by all family branches—might have derived from the arms of Poitou accorded by Richard the Lionheart during the Third Crusade.[32] The Luxembourg lion, on the other hand, had its origins in the duchy of Limburg and entered its coat of arms as a reference to the Limburg ancestry of its counts.

---

27 Jean Froissart, *Chroniques*, ed. Kervyn de Lettenhoven, Oeuvres de Froissart (Brussels: V. Devaux, 1867–1877), 5:54.

28 See especially Guillaume de Machaut, *Le Confort d'Ami*, ed. and trans. Robert Barton Palmer (New York: Garland, 1992).

29 Eustache Deschamps, Balade CCCX, ed. le marquis de Queux de Saint-Hilaire, *Œuvres complètes de Eustache Deschamps*, Société des anciens textes français (Paris: Firmin Didot, 1880), 2:310–314; see especially lines 177–206.

30 Autrand, *Jean de Berry*, 44.

31 Autrand, *Jean de Berry*, 60. One can even speculate if Guillaume de Machaut would have been hired to write the book of Melusine, had he not died in 1377.

32 Jean Bertholet, *Histoire Ecclésiastique et Civile du Duché de Luxembourg et Comté de Chiny*, 8 vols. (Luxembourg: André Chevalier, 1741–1743), 3:429–430; others prefer an Armenian origin, see Jean-Claude Loutsch, *Armorial du Pays de Luxembourg* (Luxembourg: Ministère des arts et des sciences, 1974), 27, n. 1.

While the white and blue barry seem to have represented the original arms of Lusignan and the lion a later addition, the lion came first in the Luxembourg case and the barry represents an added brisure to identify its bearers as the younger branch of the Limburg dynasty. The romance used the heraldic parallel to strengthen its claim of an existing dynastic connection between Lusignan and Luxembourg, referring to it implicitly, such as when Antoine, with the lion's paw on his cheek and the red lion on his shield, becomes the ruler of Luxembourg. A medieval readership might have accepted the similarity as proof of an ancient, probably forgotten familial link, as have many historians since.[33]

The romance itself guides the reader's gaze to Jean de Berry's maternal ancestry by focusing on a matrilineal genealogy.[34] The central protagonist is the female Melusine, who endows her descendants with particular skills and decides their fate, unlike her weak and ultimately deceitful husband, Raimondin. Despite her strong temperament and her fearsome appearance, she is the story's true hero. She rouses the reader's sympathy when giving her husband a second chance, when unable to avoid his betrayal, and when returning to nourish her young children, while it was her husband's misdeed that led to the decline of their progeniture for the following seven generations. Likewise, all of Melusine's sons gain their princely titles through marriage. Again, it is the wives providing their husbands' political success. In the same vein, Jean de Berry aimed to profit from his mother's pedigree. It is also his maternal grandfather, John, who links him with the two other patrons who are mentioned in the text: his sister, Marie de Bar, and their cousin Josse of Moravia.[35]

---

33   See discussion below.

34   The same point has been made by Angela Florschuetz, *Marking Maternity in Middle English Romance* (New York: Palgrave Macmillan, 2014), 155–59. Basing her reading solely on the literary content, Florschuetz, however, sees this matrilineal genealogy as negatively connoted, expressed by Melusine's monstrous appearance and the ill fate of her descendants in the long run (167–85).

35   "Si requier a mon Createur qu'il lui plaise que mon tresnoble et redoubté seigneur le vueille prendre en gré et aussi sa tresnoble seur Marie, fille du roy de France, duchesse de Bar et marquise du Pont, ma tresredoubtee dame, et le noble marquis de Morave, cousin germain de mon dit seigneur, qui a fait requerre qu'il lui veulle envoier ceste histoire" (Vincensini, *Mélusine*, 810) ["I ask my Creator to grant that my most noble and respected lord may find it to his liking, and also his very noble sister Marie, daughter of the King of France, Duchess of Bar and Marchioness of Pont, my very respected lady, and the noble Marquess of Moravia, my lord's first cousin, who has asked that this story be sent to him as well" (Maddox and Sturm-Maddox, *Melusine*, 227)]. The two other patrons may have had very similar political intentions as their relative the Duc de Berry. See Péporté, *Constructing the Middle Ages*, 77–80. See also Margue, "La fée Mélusine," 131–33.

Although the references to John of Bohemia in *Mélusine* are all rather oblique and implicit, their sheer quantity across different narrative layers demonstrates that Jean d'Arras' romance needs to be seen as a medium of dynastic memory, adapting, contributing, and continuing the memory of King John of Bohemia, while serving as a piece in its patron's grander scheme to legitimize his hold on the county of Poitou.

The suggested dynastic connection between Lusignan and Luxembourg that underpins the tale of Melusine has often been misunderstood. Some authors have even seen the reference to Luxembourg in the romance as referring to the lords of Luxembourg-Ligny, rather than the main branch of the Luxembourg family.[36] Meanwhile, certain historians and literary scholars have been speculating for some time about a real dynastic link between the families of Lusignan and Luxembourg. The argument for this link was spearheaded by Jean-Claude Loutsch and has since been accepted by several other scholars.[37] Loutsch sees Melusine as a reminder of a common ancestry of several dynasties that can be connected to the counts of Barcelona in the early eleventh century. One apparent expression of this connection is the barry that these families carry in their coat of arms, families that include those of Foix, Looz, Bliescastel, and, of course, Lusignan and Luxembourg. Furthermore, several members of these families seem to have carried a dragon on their crest; the dragon—according to Loutsch—symbolizes an age-old common ancestry and demonstrates that the memory of these common roots predate Jean d'Arras' romance. Furthermore, the genealogical connection was established by women, some of whom were called Ermesinde, thus alluding to a possible real-life model on which Melusine was based.[38] One is meant to conclude that Melusine indeed carries

---

36 See for instance Donald Maddox, "Configuring the Epilogue: Ending and the Ends of Fiction in the *Roman de Mélusine*," in *Melusine of Lusignan: Founding Fiction in Late Medieval France*, ed. Donald Maddox and Sara Sturm-Maddox (Athens, GA: University of Georgia Press, 1996), 267–288, at 286, n. 22.

37 Jean-Claude Loutsch, "Le cimier au dragon et la légende de Mélusine," in *Le cimier mythologique, rituel, parenté des origines au XVIe siècle. Actes du 6ᵉ colloque international d'héraldique La Petite-Pierre 9–13 octobre 1989*, ed. Académie International d'Héraldique (Brussels, 1990), 181–204. Michel Pastoureau in particular gave Loutsch's argument credibility when he endorsed it in *Une histoire symbolique du Moyen Âge occidental* (Paris: Seuil, 2004), 242. See also Martin Nejedlý, *Středověký mýtus o Meluzíně a rodová pověst Lucemburků* (Prague: Scriptorium, 2014), 271–74; and Céline Berry, "Les Luxembourg-Ligny, un grand lignage noble de la fin du Moyen Âge" (PhD diss., Université Paris Est Créteil, 2011), 651–52.

38 See above.

a dynastic memory, but one that seemingly stretches back to the early eleventh century.

Despite its outward beauty and ingenuity, Loutsch's argument seems far-fetched at second glance. First, although Loutsch followed other authors who revealed a real dynastic connection between the families of Lusignan and Luxembourg, a common ancestry of the counts of Luxembourg and the lords of Lusignan can only be established through the marriages of three women across six generations.[39] A genealogy elaborated in such a way looks a little tendentious, especially when considering that the entire higher nobility of Western Europe can be dynastically connected in one way or another. Second, Loutsch cannot provide a pattern for how the dragon crest or the heraldic barry was passed on, nor why it was adopted by some and not by others of these related dynasties. Again, there seems some randomness at play. Third, the heraldic elements that seem to refer to an early eleventh century connection only appear for most dynasties in the second half of the thirteenth century. This seems like a long span of time, especially since the author does not explain why some distant matrilineal connections should have been kept in such prominent memory over this period; nothing points to their having been particularly prestigious, as would have been a Carolingian ancestry. All in all, Loutsch's arguments seem to rest on shaky ground.

One of the essay's elements, though, deserves some additional attention. Among the prime witnesses for Loutsch's theory figure the counts of Ligny and St. Pol,[40] who from the late fifteenth century carried a crest on their helmet showing a winged dragon in a tub, often referred to as a Melusine.[41] There is

---

39   A first proponent of the thesis was Eleanor Roach. See the appendices in her edition of Coudrette, *Le roman de Mélusine, ou, histoire de Lusignan* (Paris: Klincksieck, 1982). See also Péporté, *Constructing the Middle Ages*, 80–81.

40   In the late thirteenth century, the younger son of Count Henry v of Luxembourg, Waleran, became lord of Ligny through marriage, thus establishing a secondary branch of the House of Luxembourg. Although of minor importance at first, this branch came to fame in the fifteenth century when its members inherited the county of St. Pol; they were then closely allied to the dukes of Burgundy, and many of them were appointed to the Order of the Golden Fleece. Among the branch's best-known scion is a certain John of Luxembourg, whose men captured Joan of Arc at the siege of Compiègne. The branch kept its epithet "of Luxembourg," probably stressing it the more after the main branch of imperial fame had died out with the death of Emperor Sigismund in 1437. The name was eventually passed on through the female line to lords nowadays remembered in the Parisian *Palais de Luxembourg*, seat of the French senate, with its famous gardens. See Berry, "Les Luxembourg-Ligny."

41   Loutsch, "Le cimier au dragon," 197.

no proof, however, that the crest with the dragon had been called a Melusine before the success of the romance around 1400. In fact, it seems as if during most of the fourteenth century the dragon on the crest was neither winged nor sitting in a tub.[42] In the second half of the fourteenth century, the crest of the counts could even take a different shape altogether and represent two griffons.[43] It seems more likely, therefore, that the counts of St. Pol reinterpreted one of their crests as a reference to Melusine in the wake of the romance's spread and popularity. They could profit doubly from labelling their crest as a Melusine. The crest could serve as a token of their links to the main branch of the family, especially after the latter died out in 1437, reminding their environment of the prestigious imperial dynasty. In this context the crest would also take up the role Melusine had played in the romance as reference to the family's perfect knight, John of Bohemia. In addition, the crest could help the counts of St. Pol style themselves as the inheritors of the Lusignans and their crusading successes, especially so within the Order of the Golden Fleece, the name of which many consider to contain the connotation of the crusades.[44]

Melusine continued to be a symbol of a dynastic memory beyond the medieval period, even if the principal medium from the sixteenth century onward became historiography. The humanist scholar Conrad Vecerius (ca.1487–1527) was born in Luxembourg but spent his life outside his native land, serving the emperors Maximilian I and Charles V as well as Pope Clement VII. He referred to Melusine in his biography of Henry VII, Roman Emperor and Count of Luxembourg, indicating that some considered Henry a descendant of hers.[45] Vicerius himself sees this as an empty fable. But his publication served as inspiration to Estienne de Chypre de Lusignan (1537–1590), bishop of Limassol and a descendant of Lusignan kings of Cyprus, who pursued genealogical research on sixty-seven noble dynasties in the service of François

---

42   Berry, "Les Luxembourg-Ligny," 651. The exact date of when this should have happened is in doubt.

43   Berry, "Les Luxembourg-Ligny," 652.

44   D'A. Jonathan D. Boulton, "The Order of the Golden Fleece and the Creation of Burgundian National Identity," in *The Ideology of Burgundy: The Promotion of National Consciousness, 1364–1565*, Brill's Studies in Intellectual History 145, ed. D'A. Jonathan D. Boulton and Jan R. Veenstra (Leiden: Brill, 2006): 21–97.

45   Conrad Vecerius, *De rebus gestis impertoris Henrici VII libellus* (Hanau: Secerius, 1531), fol. C iii r. This text has been edited and translated in Myriam Melchior and Claude Loutsch, *Humanistica Luxemburgensia: la Bombarda de Barthélemy Latomus, les Opuscula de Conrad Vecerius*, Collection Latomus 321 (Brussels: Latomus, 2009). For the passage on Melusine, see 190–195.

de Luxembourg-Piney, who had inherited some titles from the counts of St. Pol.[46] Unlike Vecerius, Estienne took the romance as proof that the House of Luxembourg—of which his patron claimed membership—derived from his own House of Lusignan.[47] Like Loutsch four centuries later, he cited the crest as additional proof, since it was apparently worn by "all members" of the Houses of Luxembourg and Lusignan.[48] Erudite Luxembourg-based historians in the seventeenth and eighteenth century show awareness of these genealogical theories, albeit without delving into detail, nor actually believing in their veracity.[49]

When Luxembourg City's authorities decided to mark the 1050th anniversary of the city's foundation,[50] they commissioned a monument to Melusine to be set right below the walls of the historic urban core. Her monument, designed by artist Serge Ecker, shows a stylized, life-size figure, half woman, half fish, sitting on a large slab on which passersby can join her. It is one of few figurative statues in the old town joined only by four other life-size, freestanding statues, and it remains the only one to represent a figure of medieval origin, even though that period provided the country with its supposed founder, Count Siegfried, and its best-known national hero, John of Bohemia.[51] This

---

46   Estienne de Chypre de Lusignan, *Les Genealogies de soixante et sept tresnobles et tres-illustres maisons, partie de France, parti estrágeres, yssuës de Meroüée, fils de Theodoric 2. Roy d'Austrasie, Bourgongne, &c.* (Paris: Guillaume Le Noir, 1586).

47   "La maison de Luxembourg, selon nostre opinion & beaucoup d'autres, est sortie de celle des Lusignans" ["The house of Luxembourg, which in our opinion and that of many others, is out of that of the Lusignans" (eds.)], De Chypre de Lusignan, *Les Genealogies*, fol. 99r.

48   De Chypre de Lusignan, *Les Genealogies*, fol. 100v.

49   "So sind auch etliche, so den Ursprung von der Fabel der Gauklerin Melusinae herbringen und Lusenburg nennen" ["There are also a few, who trace the origin to the fable of the imposter Melusine and call it Lusenburg"], writes Eustache of Wiltheim, *Kurzer und schlichter Bericht und Beschreibung des Hauses, Schlosses und Landes Luxemburg sammt dessen Fürsten und Herren Ursprung und Herkommen was sich auch bei deren Regierung im gemelten und anderen ihren Landschaften verlaufen und zugetragen*, ed. and trans. Jacques Grob, *Hémecht* 6 (1900), 90; see also Bertholet, *Histoire Ecclésiastique et Civile*, 1:429–430 and 3:3.

50   Unlike the millennium in 1963, this anniversary was celebrated with only little pomp. In either case, the anniversary is invented: not the foundation of the city is remembered—it had never been "founded"—but the possible date of the acquisition of the rock of Luxembourg by Count Siegfried. On the historical context, see Michel Margue and Michel Pauly, "Saint-Michel et le premier siècle de la ville de Luxembourg," *Hémecht* 39 (1987): 5–83.

51   See Péporté, *Constructing the Middle Ages*, chapters 1, 4, and 5.

statue is the latest step in Melusine's development as an important, yet multi-faceted *lieu de mémoire* in Luxembourg.

It would be tempting to suggest continuity between the dynastic memory of Luxembourg as found in the medieval romance and the emergence of Melusine in Luxembourg's collective memory as happened over the past two centuries, yet there is little proof of it. Some early modern authors hint at a local tale of Melusine, linking an old tower to her story,[52] but they provide neither the exact content of that tale, nor an estimate of how well it was known among the population. The first reference to the current Luxembourgian version of Melusine's story provides the late eighteenth century as its *terminus ante quem*.[53] That story may thus be linked to Melusine's re-emergence across Europe during the onset of Romanticism. The basic form of that tale resembles Jean d'Arras' framework story. Luxembourg's supposed founder, the tenth-century Count Siegfried,[54] stumbles upon Melusine on the banks of the local river Alzette. Enchanted by her beauty, Siegfried asks for her hand, which she grants him on condition of not being disturbed on Saturdays. They build a mighty castle overlooking the place where they first met. After a while the count is roused by jealousy and, peeking through the keyhole in the door to her chamber, he discovers her secret: bathing in a tub, Melusine is half woman and half fish.[55] Melusine then vanishes, never to be seen again.

---

52   Vecerius, *De rebus gestis*, fol. C iv r. See also *Cartulaire de la ville de Luxembourg anno 1632*, Archives Nationales de Luxembourg A-XV-12, f 16: "la tour de la ville appellée la tour de Melusine, maintenant demolie et redigée en autre Bastimen" [the city tower called the tower of Melusine, now destroyed and incorporated into another building (eds.)]. On the archaeological interpretation, see Isabelle Yegles-Becker, "Fouilles archéologiques au 11 rue de la Boucherie. Un site d'habitation dans la Vieille Ville de Luxembourg du 8ᵉ au 13ᵉ siècle," in *Aux origines de la ville de Luxembourg*, Dossiers d'Archéologie du Musée National d'Histoire et d'Art VII et du Service des Sites et Monuments Nationaux, ed. John Zimmer (Luxembourg: Musée national d'histoire et d'art, 2002), 282.

53   Théodore de la Fontaine (1787–1871) claims to have heard a local version in his childhood. Gaspar-Théodore-Ignace de la Fontaine, "Légendes Luxembourgeoises," *PSH* 6 (1850): 120.

54   Péporté, *Constructing the Middle Ages*, ch. 1.

55   In the medieval representations of Melusine the fishtail was rare; see François Eygun, *Ce qu'on peut savoir de Mélusine et de son iconographie* (Poitiers: Oudin, 1951), 5 and 41. It established itself in most nineteenth- and twentieth-century depictions, finding its origin maybe in some twin-tailed representations of her, or some cross-pollination from tales of mermaids, also growing in popularity around that time. See Frederika Bain's contribution to this volume for a discussion of the evolution of sirenic iconography.

The first two written forms of this story appear shortly after 1840, coincidentally written by foreign authors visiting the country. The first was Theodor von Cedersolpe, an officer in Luxembourg's Prussian garrison,[56] who collected local lore in a small booklet.[57] The first plotline was joined by short poems about Melusine's later reappearance to soldiers in the fortress. The second author was the fake Belgian nobleman Louis l'Evêque de la Basse-Moûturie,[58] who included the tale in his "picturesque" travel book of the country.[59] Over the following decades, the topic proved a staple for the first local romantically inclined literary authors, some of whom were also the first to use the local vernacular for literary purposes. The local version of Melusine quickly established itself as part of folklore;[60] attachment to it went along with rising patriotic sentiment, itself reflected in the language used by the different poets.[61] The story line changed little in that process. In some cases, it was mixed with other folkloric tales.[62] Further variances include Melusine vanishing into the castle rock,[63] while in others she jumps into the river;[64] in most versions she later

---

56   According to the stipulations of the Congress of Vienna (1815), Luxembourg was an independent grand duchy ruled by the Dutch monarch. It also joined the German Confederation (*Deutscher Bund*), which controlled its strategically located fortress through a Prussian-dominated garrison.

57   Theodor von Cederstolpe, *Sagen aus Luxemburg* (Luxembourg: G. Michaelis, 1843).

58   See Jules Vannérus, *Le chevalier l'Evêque de la Basse-Moûturie et son itinéraire du Luxembourg germanique* (Luxembourg: Bourg-Bourger, 1929), 1–3.

59   Louis le Chevalier l'Evêque de la Basse-Moûturie, *Itinéraire du Luxembourg germanique, ou voyage historique et pittoresque dans le Grand-Duché* (Luxembourg: V. Hoffmann, 1844), 60–64.

60   Antoine Meyer, "Melusina," in *Oilzegt-Kläng* (Liège: H. Dessain, 1853), 85–90; Nicholas Steffen, *Mährchen und Sagen des Luxemburger Landes* (Luxembourg: V. Bück, 1855), 10–19; Friedrich Albrecht, *Melusina: Luxemburgische Sage aus dem zehnten Jahrhundert* (Wismar and Luxemburg: Hinstorff, 1859); Nicolas Gredt, *Sagenschatz des Luxemburger Landes* (Luxembourg: V. Bück, 1883), 47–48; Nicolas Welter, *Siegfried und Melusine* (Berlin: Concordia, 1900); Nicolas Welter, *Aus alten Tagen: Balladen und Romanzen aus Luxemburgs Sage und Geschichte* (Luxembourg: M. Huss, 1900).

61   For a more detailed account, see Péporté, *Constructing the Middle Ages*, 103–105.

62   Peter Klein interweaves the story of Melusine with a Faustian story also featuring Count Siegfried. Peter Klein, "Siegfried und Melusina," in *Gedichte aus dem Nachlasse*, ed. Ernst Koch (Luxembourg: V. Bück, 1856), 101–122; on the latter story see Péporté, *Constructing the Middle Ages*, 51–53.

63   See for example Meyer, "Melusina," 90.

64   See for example Cederstolpe, *Sagen aus Luxemburg*, 13.

reappears in different shapes to soldiers of the local garrison,[65] while in some she is supposed to fly above the city in times of danger.[66]

Melusine became part of Luxembourg's myth of origin at a time when national sentiment was developing among the country's elites. The grand duchy's *de jure* independence following the Congress of Vienna in 1815 was given substance in the 1840s. After the capital's elite had stayed loyal to the Dutch crown during the Belgian Revolution (1830–1839),[67] it demanded a larger degree of autonomy, granted by the monarch in a new constitution (1841), which then paved the way for Luxembourg's own institutions of government. Alongside these political developments, the educated and political elites started to reinterpret the past along national lines in their historiographical and literary works.[68] The foundation of a learned historical association and the expansion of the history curriculum in schools were of fundamental importance to the creation and spread of national history. In the emerging national master narrative, the "first count of Luxembourg," as Count Siegfried was considered by early modern historians, was no longer merely the founder of a dynasty, but also became founder of a country and nation. The local tale of Melusine was a way in which this historiographical topos found a playful and romantic expression in literature. While historical scholarship dealt with the nation's alleged foundation in sometimes rather technical discussions about the count's genealogy, the stories of Melusine could cloak the same events in a romantic setting full of enchanting detail and without boring their audience with dry intricacies. The end of the nineteenth century also saw the appearance of visual depictions of the water fairy.[69] In 1885 the artist Michel Engels depicted her as the sole figure worthy of approaching the throne of the allegory of the fatherland, making her represent the nation's medieval origins, while also setting her

---

65   The first author to do so was Cederstolpe, *Sagen aus Luxemburg*, 5–9; most other authors add this as an epilogue. Generally, Melusine takes the appearance of a large snake.

66   See for example Gredt, *Sagenschatz*, 48.

67   Belgian historiography sees 1831 as the Revolution's endpoint; the Dutch crown, however, only agreed to the Belgium's territorial demands in 1839, leading to the partition of Luxembourg and the recovering of Dutch control over what remained of the grand duchy.

68   Pit Péporté, Sonja Kmec, Benoît Majerus, and Michel Margue, *Inventing Luxembourg: Representations of the Past, Space and Language from the Nineteenth to the Twenty-First Century*, National Cultivation of Culture 1 (Leiden: Brill, 2010).

69   The earliest depictions can be found in the satirical magazine *D'Wäschfra*, which used her in 1870; see *D'Wäschfra. Humoristisch-satyrisches Wochenblatt*, 9 July 1870 and 22 October 1870. Here, Melusine stands as an allegory of the Luxembourg City and the grand duchy, respectively.

in contrast with Luxembourg's supposed foreign rulers of the early modern period.[70] In the early 1890s her bas-relief adorned a stone console of the newly constructed wing of the grand-ducal palace.[71]

As a female founding figure in both the medieval romance and in Luxembourg's nineteenth century media, Melusine was represented as a fertile woman, not least because Luxembourg supposedly emerged from her union with Siegfried.[72] To add weight to this idea, many authors stress how bare or empty the land was before the meeting of the two figures and how quickly it became civilized thereafter.[73] Her fertility had a direct impact on her depiction. From 1918, one scene became increasingly popular in the visual arts: Melusine bathing in the river before her meeting with Siegfried.[74] Rare are the poets or artists who did not stress her physical qualities. Some also play with her siren-like appearance and stress how Siegfried was first seduced by her voice.[75] Unlike Jean d'Arras, more recent authors and artists generally leave her undressed, thus underlining her attractive features and the signs of her fecundity.[76]

By the mid-twentieth century, Melusine had become so entrenched a motif that the figure easily spread to an array of different media. First, she was used as a foil in satire that mocked the existing body of literature on her theme.[77]

---

70   Michel Engels, "Allegorie de la Patrie," Musée National d'Histoire et d'Art. On that specific piece of art, see Péporté et al., *Inventing Luxembourg*, 79–82.

71   See Margue, "La fée Mélusine," 132.

72   Franz Binsfeld and Jules Kruger, *Melusin. Oper an drei Akten no enger National-So* (Luxembourg: P. Linden, 1951), 37–38.

73   See for instance Richard Friedmann, "Festspill fir de Millenaire vun der Stât Letzebuerg" (Unpublished, 1963, Archives Nationales du Luxembourg DH 098), or Sus Hierzig, *Zou Lëtzebuerg stong d'Sigfriddsschlass: Eng al Geschicht nei erzielt a mat Biller* (Echternach: Phi, 1983), 9. Although an attractive literary idea and common among historians until the mid-twentieth century, its historic veracity has since been severely doubted. From today's point of view it seems that the historic *Siegfried* bought his real estate on a spot that was economically thriving. See Margue and Pauly, "Saint-Michel."

74   See for instance Michel Heiter, "Mélusine, Nymphe de l'Alzette," *Le Grand Almanach* (Barbert, 1918); Auguste Trémont, "Mélusine se baignant au pied la citadelle," *Luxembourg Illustré* 22 (1929): 337. A quasi-exhaustive number of visual depictions have been gathered by Laura Kozlik, "Entre Vierge et pute nationale. Regard critique sur l'iconographie de Mélusine au Luxembourg," in *Not the girl you're looking for: Melusina rediscovered. Objekt+Subjekt Frau in der Kultur Luxemburgs*, ed. Danielle Roster and Renée Wagener (Luxembourg: CID-femmes, 2010), 39–54.

75   Muriel Moritz and Lex Roth, *Melusina* (Luxembourg, 1996). See Sonja Kmec, "Le miroir éclaté: Essai sur la recherche mélusienne," in *Not the girl you're looking for,* 20.

76   See for instance Meyer, "Melusina," 86; Albrecht, *Melusina,* 60.

77   Félix Servais, *Boutade sur le conte de Mélusine* (Luxembourg, 1898).

Next came plays and books, particularly aimed at children.[78] Increasingly she was used on logos and advertising posters, not least during Luxembourg's millennium festivities of 1963, which celebrated Count Siegfried's acquisition of the rock of Luxembourg, when she decorated posters, calendars, and ashtrays.[79] Her earlier symbolic charge perdured. She was held up as a symbol of the purported age-old national origins, an idea that was meant to bolster national independence. This symbolic function emerged particularly during moments of heightened patriotism, such as after the liberation from Nazi occupation during World War II, when poets celebrated how the nation had prevailed,[80] or during the large-scale celebrations in 1963, which tried to root the nation in a millennial tradition while heralding Luxembourg's part in the European integration process and its supposed supranational future.[81] But from the 1970s her symbolism became more complex.

As the patterns of national identification in Luxembourg have changed, so have the depictions of Melusine. The tradition of using her for satirical purposes was taken up by some left-leaning authors to accuse Luxembourg of social conservatism and backwardness.[82] While some nationalist writers had used her in the mid twentieth century to stress the country's uniqueness and to buttress the standing of the Luxembourgish language, she has recently been held up by cosmopolitan authors as a symbol of Luxembourg's traditional multilingualism.[83] Her hybrid character represents a point of identification for multilingual authors, such as those who founded the crossborder literary association *Mélusine* in 2006.[84] Since the late 1980s another tradition has stressed her gender

---

78   The first one was Lucien Koenig, *D'Melusina-So* (Luxembourg: Letzeburger Nationalunio'n, 1937); more recent examples include Corinne Kohl-Crouzet and Maxime Blanco, *Mélusine et ses metamorphoses* (Luxembourg: FGIL, 2014).

79   See for example Kozlik, "Entre Vierge et pute nationale," illustrations 3, 4, 5, 15, 16 and 17.

80   Michel Stoffel, *La Clef de Mélusine* (Paris: G. Blanchong & Cie, 1944); Franz Binsfeld, *Hémechtslant, meng Gottesburech: Rosengen àus zèit a geshicht* (Luxembourg: Worré-Mertens, 1944), 10.

81   On the millennium celebrations, see Péporté, *Constructing the Middle Ages*, 60–64.

82   See for example Roger Manderscheid, "elfter ausflug – in die welt der legenden zu melusino und melusina," in his *Ikarus, dreißig Ausflüge und ein Absturz* (Luxembourg: Binsfeld, 1983). See also his *die dromedare: stilleben für johann den blinden* (Luxembourg: Lochness, 1973), 9–10.

83   See for example Gerd Heger, Jhemp Hoscheit, Paula de Lemos and Véronique Schons, *Mélusina* (Echternach: Phi, 1999).

84   See Sarah Lippert, "Hybride (National-)Symbole und Multilingualität: Mehrsprachige Melusinenfigurationen in der zeitgenössischen Literatur Luxemburgs," in *Philologie und Mehrsprachigkeit*, ed. Till Dembeck and Georg Mein (Heidelberg: Universitätsverlag Winter, 2014), 361.

for feminist purposes, celebrating her as a strong female figure.[85] At the same time, the principal media of her memory in Luxembourg were increasingly geared towards children, ranging from comic books and illustrated versions of her story[86] to dedicated websites,[87] audiobooks with songs,[88] and soft toys.[89] In 1998 her name was given to a film production company that specialized in animated films for children,[90] while in 2012 her story represented the basis for one of the most popular children's movies the country has (co-)produced so far.[91] Although constantly adapted to modern media, the invented tradition of Melusine is in all cases meant to provide those media with a particularly Luxembourgian character.

This idea of rooting oneself in local tradition emanates most strongly from the ways in which Melusine has been used in Luxembourg's capital. While the discourses of the nation and the capital often overlap in a small country like Luxembourg, particularly if country and capital share the same name, Melusine has nonetheless increasingly been given the role of the city's mascot. She profits here from the fact that, since the seventeenth century, Count Siegfried has been seen as the founder and builder of the town of Luxembourg.[92] Unsurprisingly, local clubs, businesses, and authorities have adopted Melusine readily as their emblem. The local scuba diving club, founded in the "millennium year" of 1963, has been using her as its logo.[93] In 1984 one of the city's best-known nightclubs named itself *Melusina*. But her boom properly took off in the early 2000s. The company *Oberweis*, one of the city's best-known bakers and chocolatiers, has produced a range of Melusine

85   One of the two branches of the soroptimist-movement in Luxembourg named itself af-
      ter her. See also her use in the publication Danielle Roster and Renée Wagener, ed., *Not
      the girl you're looking for: Melusina rediscovered. Objekt+Subjekt Frau in der Kultur Luxem-
      burgs* (Luxembourg: CID-femmes, 2010).

86   Marina Herber and Lex Roth, *Melusina* (Luxembourg: Editions Binsfeld, 2014).

87   http://aroundthestory.com/story/iframe/31 (accessed March 17, 2016)

88   Nadine Kauffmann and Pascal Schumacher, *D'Sünchen vu Lëtzebuerg* (Luxembourg: Potti
      Productions, 2005) [Audio CD]; Sonja Lux-Bintner and Asya Sergeeva, *D'Melusina, der
      Uelzecht hiert Kand* (Luxembourg: Lux-Bintner, 2016) [Audio CD].

89   See the toys made by designer DeeDee and her Popupstudio, http://www.popupstudio
      .eu/product-tag/melusina/ (accessed Aug. 2, 2016).

90   http://www.melusineproductions.com/ (accessed March 17, 2016)

91   *D'Schatzritter an d'Geheimnis vum Melusina*, dir. Laura Schroeder (Luxembourg and Ger-
      many: Lucil film et al., 2012).

92   Péporté, *Constructing the Middle Ages*, 47.

93   See the website of the Sub Aqua Club: http://www.sacl.lu (accessed March 17, 2016).

pralines.[94] Luxembourg's City Tourist Office used her as one of its emblems for about a decade and still mentions her on its history web page.[95] In 2007 it organized a spectacle called *Meluxina* during summer nights, with music and lights projected onto the old castle rock. The City's history museum redesigned its permanent exhibition in 2006, now opening with her story.[96] The culmination of this process has certainly been the decision to mark the city's supposed 1050th anniversary with the statue of Melusine, as detailed above.

Looking at Melusine through the perspective of memory reveals that she first represented a medium of a dynastic memory before becoming a *lieu de mémoire* herself in many parts of Europe, not least in the grand duchy of Luxembourg. In the first case, she was used to remind a noble audience of a supposed dynastic connection between the Houses of Lusignan and Luxembourg, a connection that Jean de Berry hoped would bolster his claims over Poitou. He chose to link Lusignan and Luxembourg not only because the similarities in heraldry rendered his proposition plausible, but also because he hoped to profit from the existing prestige of the Luxembourg dynasty, not least from the chivalric aura of one of his ancestors, King John of Bohemia. Later humanist authors propagated this fictive dynastic connection for a wider audience, though the implicit references to John of Bohemia in the original romance proved too obscure and insignificant to be upheld in memory after the king had lost his fame across most of Europe.

In the grand duchy of Luxembourg, Melusine has since the 1840s been amalgamated into the nation's foundation myth. The original framework story was tweaked by lore and poets to fit the topography of the country's capital. In this context, she symbolizes the nation's venerable roots in a distant, mysterious past, an idea expressed through ever-diversifying types of media. Over the past ten years, Melusine has seen an immense resonance in Luxembourg. In this process it is remarkable that her memory completely overshadows that of her local husband, Count Siegfried. Siegfried's memory seemed too fixed to be reinvented and reapplied to changing contexts, while Melusine, because of her gender, foreign origin, and fictive nature, could be accommodated by traditionalists and feminists, by nationalists and cosmopolites, by professional advertisers and artists of all sorts.

---

94   Oberweis ceased production of Melusine chocolates in 2014. The original idea was developed by Monique Oberweis, who also asked the artist Ger Maas to draw an aquarelle painting to decorate the box. The principal target customers were tourists in search for an "authentically" Luxembourgish gift. The author wishes to thank Jeff Oberweis for having shared this information by e-mail.

95   http://www.lcto.lu/en/info/presentation/history (accessed March 17, 2016).

96   Sonja Kmec, "'Luxembourg: Une ville s'expose.' Nouvelle exposition permanente du Musée d'histoire de la Ville de Luxembourg," *Forum* 266 (2007): 42–44.

PART III

Theoretical Transformations: Readings and Refigurations

∵

CHAPTER 10

Youth and Rebellion in Jean d'Arras'
Roman de Mélusine

Stacey L. Hahn

Celia M. Lewis contends that Jean d'Arras' *Roman de Mélusine* may have been considered appropriate reading for young adults of the late fourteenth and early fifteenth centuries.[1] In addition to the physical evidence backing this assertion, such as the marks of children's handwriting and names written in the margins of two of the manuscripts, Lewis argues that the thematic content of the romance, which focuses on Melusine's teenage sons, offers many lessons in knightly conduct that would have been instructive and of great interest to medieval youths.[2] The lack of promiscuous, erotic overtones common to other prose romances, and the fact that the romance was written during a period when conduct books for knights, women, and children were popular, give further credence to the idea that Jean's *Mélusine* would be suitable, edifying reading material for young and old alike.[3] In fact, the driving force behind much of the romance revolves around youth and the dilemmas it poses for both males and females throughout the course of the romance.

Not only does a crisis at the age of puberty launch Melusine into the human world, but a similar crisis on the part of her future husband, Raymond, also exiles him from courtly society, making the union between them both possible and necessary. Once Melusine and Raymond have firmly established their household and resolved the issues of their youth, their sons begin to mature, each one facing new challenges as he strives to make his way in the world. As the new generation takes over from the old, more crises ensue as issues relating to childish exuberance, or *chaude colle*—whether inspired by sibling rivalry, revenge or youthful ignorance and lack of experience—propel events to their

---

1   "Acceptable Lessons, Radical Truths: *Mélusine* as Literature for Medieval Youth," *Children's Literature* 39 (2011): 1–32.

2   The romance was considered a conduct book as early as 1900. See Jules Léon Baudot, *Les Princesses Yolande et les Ducs de Bar de la famille des Valois* (Paris: Picard 1900).

3   According to Louis Stouff, Jean d'Arras' patron, the Duke of Berry, who commissioned the *Roman de Mélusine*, had at least seven conduct books in his library. *Essai sur Mélusine: Roman du XIVe siècle par Jean d'Arras* (Paris: Picard, 1930), 120.

inevitable conclusion. Conflicts relating to the vagaries of youth frame the action at the beginning of the romance and continue to influence the course of events through to the end. Jean's work is original for the way in which it compresses into one family youthful behaviors that in other romances would be spread across a whole society. The large number of children involved, and the individualized portrait each child receives, make the romance fertile ground for the analysis of medieval conceptions of childhood. An examination of the work's structure reveals a highly organized and coherent program of education.

The *Roman de Mélusine* emphasizes the youth of its protagonists by carefully designating the approximate age of each child as his or her adventures unfold. Jean also separates children into two distinct age groups, which implies an awareness that a gap in aptitude exists between younger and older children. Readers first encounter the majority of main characters between the ages of fourteen and seventeen. These characters include Melusine and her sisters, who are fifteen at the time of their expulsion from Avalon, and Raymond, who is fourteen or fifteen when he leaves his family in order to serve his uncle, Count Aimery. Urien and Guyon set off on their adventure to the Near East at ages seventeen and fifteen, respectively, while Eudes, who stays home, is sixteen. Eude's son, Bernardon, is fifteen or sixteen when Geoffrey and Thierry set off with him for Montserrat to attend Raymond's funeral. Upon marriage, Hermine is fifteen or sixteen, and Aiglentine around fifteen.

The second group of children includes those between the ages of a little less than six weeks and ten, many of whom are Melusine's grandchildren, and who represent the promise of a future generation. The Count of Alsace's daughter Melide, who will one day marry Antoine's first son Bertrand, is two at the time of the count's assault on Luxembourg; the Lady of Valbruyant's daughter is eight or nine years of age, and her son around ten, when they are introduced to Geoffrey Big Tooth. During the campaign against the Caliph of Bagdad and the Great Karamen, Urian bids his wife, Hermine, and his five-year-old son, Hervé, farewell. After the war has been won, Geoffrey sails to Armenia to meet his four-year-old nephew, Remond, and shortly thereafter meets Urian's son, Griffon, who is not yet six weeks old. Horrible killed two of his wet nurses before the age of three and by age seven had slain two squires. At the time of Raymond's betrayal of Melusine, Remonnet is not yet three and Thierry is barely two. The births of Lohier and Olliphar are briefly mentioned in the context of their future accomplishments as a means of extending the glory of the Lusignan clan to the next generation. As demonstrated by these examples, the attempt to be specific, if not exact, regarding the children's ages reflects not only a concern on the part of the author to paint a truthful account of the past but also to emphasize the youth of the protagonists. By separating young people into two distinct age groups, Jean distinguishes between older youths, who engage with the outside world through the process of maturation, and children, who remain dependent upon their elders and represent an untapped source of human capital.

Arriving at a precise definition of childhood in the Middle Ages is difficult in that there is no consensus regarding the exact organization of the life cycle, which could be divided into periods of three, four, five, six, or seven, depending on the basis of division (whether it conforms, for example, with the four seasons or the seven planets).[4] According to Phyllis Gaffney, "Medieval notions about human age were based less on annual progression from year to year than on a person's progression through chronological phases."[5] Nicholas Orme asserts that the stages of youth were commonly divided into three phases designated by the Latin terms: *infantia* [infancy], *pueritia* [childhood], and *adolescentia* [adolescence]. According to this schema, infancy spans the ages from birth to seven, childhood the ages of seven to fourteen, and adolescence ages fourteen to twenty-eight.[6] Isabelle Cochelin finds the subdivision between *infantia* and *pueritia* rare and would characterize *pueritia* as one period, ranging from birth to age fourteen or fifteen, the age of majority. She further specifies that *adolescentia* "was always to be found in adulthood, and clearly distinguished from childhood."[7] Gaffney indicates that the term *adolescentia*, often used interchangeably with *iuventus*, could designate teenagers as well as men in their late thirties.[8] She also states that the term *enfant* in the Middle Ages "has a much wider definition than in modern French, and can refer to a person aged anything between birth and thirty, as well as meaning 'child' in the sense of offspring, and a young warrior."[9] James A. Schultz in his study of German literature rejects the notion that the medieval concept of *adolescentia* corresponds with our modern conception of adolescence as a distinct stage

---

4   Phyllis Gaffney, *Constructions of Childhood and Youth in Old French Narrative* (Burlington, VT: Ashgate, 2011), 31–33.

5   Gaffney, *Constructions of Childhood*, 31.

6   Nicholas Orme, *Medieval Children* (New Haven: Yale University Press, 2001), 6–7.

7   Isabelle Cochelin, "Adolescence Uncloistered (Cluny, Early Twelfth-Century)," *Medieval Life Cycles: Continuity and Change*, ed. Isabelle Cochelin and Karen Smyth, International Medieval Research 18 (Turnhout: Brepols, 2013), 147–182, at 169.

8   Gaffney, *Constructions of Childhood*, 37.

9   Phyllis Gaffney, "The Ages of Man in Old French Verse Epic and Romance," *The Modern Language Review* 85, no. 3 (July 1990): 570–582, at 572.

of life, characterized by "generational conflict and identity formation."[10] He does not find children in medieval romance to be particularly rebellious or in conflict with their parents. He asserts, instead, that conflicts arise as medieval youths, who are born with a set nature, confront cultural values in opposition to theirs.[11]

Scholars seem to be divided regarding the question of whether *adolescentia* represents a distinct stage of childhood, an intermediary stage between childhood and adulthood, or the beginning of adulthood.[12] While there has been much debate regarding whether medieval European cultures recognized a period of adolescence or puberty during the teenage years as distinct from childhood, the *Roman de Mélusine* makes it very clear that the deciding events in the lives of its main characters occur between the ages of fourteen and seventeen. These are the active years when romance protagonists leave home in order to gain self knowledge through adventure and leave their mark on the world. The question now becomes whether one should refer to these individuals as children, adolescents in the modern sense, or young adults.[13] This argument shall refer to them using the neutral term "youths," keeping in mind that Jean d'Arras is targeting a specific age group. The younger children fall into the general category of *pueritia*, who, according to Roman law, cannot speak with legal authority. These children play passive roles, but are important as signifiers of dynastic continuity.

---

10   James A. Shultz, "Medieval Adolescence: The Claims of History and the Silence of German Narrative," *Speculum* 66, no. 3 (1991): 519–539, at 521.

11   Schultz, "Medieval Adolescence," 525.

12   Cochelin, "Adolescence Uncloistered," 167–168.

13   Another way to characterize youths is to look at the terms used to describe them. The four Lusignan children who set off on adventure are described as *enfant, bachelier, damoiseau,* and *jeunes hommes,* but once they marry, they take on the titles of their deceased fathers-in-law, whose roles they fully assume, indicating that marriage confers upon them the status of adulthood. The same is true for the maidens they marry, who are designated as *pucelle* and *damoiselle* until marriage turns them into a countess, duchess, or queen. The childhoods of these characters are short-lived, as they become parents shortly after they marry. Here, marriage marks the period of majority for both maidens and knights. A further indication of the break between childhood and maturity may be seen in the change in Raymond's name. Early on he is referred to in the diminutive as "Raymondin;" then, beginning with the mobilization of Antoine and Renaud to Luxembourg, when the boys ask for their parents' permission to embark on their mission to rescue Crestienne from the Count of Alsace's unwanted attentions, he is referred to as "Raymond." It is not clear what precipitated this change, except that in contrast to the earlier mobilization of Urian and Guyon, the boys ask permission of both parents and not just Melusine, thus implying Raymond's growth in authority. This change occurs well after Raymond's marriage.

Regardless of whether adolescence in the modern sense is anachronistic when applied to the Middle Ages, authors from antiquity to the medieval period have offered definitions of youth that reflect characteristics often associated in modern times with teenagers. Aristotle and St. Paul, two authorities mentioned in Jean's prologue, make comments on youth. Aristotle characterizes childhood as a turbulent time marked by violent passions and lack of judgment. Youths are overly confident in themselves and act excessively and vehemently. They have exalted notions because they have not been humbled by life or learned life's limitations.[14] St. Paul associates childhood with folly and lack of knowledge.[15] An examination of depictions of youth in verse and prose romance reveals *démesure* [immoderation] to be a common characteristic, especially in the *chansons de geste*. Heroes of romance typically experience love and all of the confusion, hope, and despair it entails for the first time. In most instances a knight is improved through love service. At the age of majority, usually at age fifteen, the protagonist of romance leaves home in order to prove himself and in so doing becomes a productive member of society. Youth can also represent a period of self-discovery with its failures and triumphs. Following the norms of accepted gender roles, young men must leave the comfort of the home in order to demonstrate their merit, often engaging in feats of valor as a test of manhood, while young women are faced with the challenges of love, marriage, and childbirth.

The *Roman de Mélusine* exposes the latent dangers, both physical and moral, of stumbling blocks in the life of a maturing adult, which occur both diachronically, from generation to generation, and synchronically, across a single generation of the Lusignan clan, and in doing so demonstrate through both positive and negative outcomes the ramifications of youthful indiscretions. As with most romances that cover a spectrum of generations, often beginning with parents or grandparents in whom a certain flaw is detected, the *Roman de Mélusine* begins with the story of Melusine's fairy mistress mother, Presine, and her marriage to the mortal King Elinas of Scotland, who was a widower at the time of their meeting. The misfortune which harrows this couple introduces the theme of sibling rivalry and how it can disrupt family relations.

After the death of his first wife, Elinas goes hunting and, seized by a terrible thirst, approaches a fountain where Presine enchants him with her song. He soon falls in love with her and they agree to marry, provided that he adhere to a solemn oath, namely, that if they have children, Elinas shall never attempt to see her during her lying-in period after childbirth (*gesine*): "Se vous me vouléz

---

14   Aristotle, *Rhetoric,* Book II. 12.

15   1 Corinthians 13.11.

prendre a femme et jurer que se nous avons enfans ensemble que vous ne met-tréz ja peine de moy veoir en ma gesine ne ne feréz par voye quelconques tant que vous me voiéz, je suiz celle qui obeiray a vous comme loyal moillier doit obeir a son espoux" ["if you wish to take me as your wife, you must swear that, if we have children together, you will never in any way undertake to see me in childbed. Then I shall obey you as a loyal wife must obey her husband"].[16] If Eli-nas complies with this pact, all will go well and Presine will obey her husband as a loyal spouse. All does go well until Mataquas, Elinas's eldest son from his prior marriage, who is described as bearing enmity against Presine ("la haioit moult" [he greatly despised her] [128]), sees his three newborn half-sisters and urges his father to go see them. In his excitement over the birth of his chil-dren Elinas enters Presine's chamber, having forgotten his oath. Presine is then forced to obey the strictures of their pact by quitting her husband with her three daughters in tow, never to see him again. Although no particular reason is given for Mataquas' hatred for Presine, one may assume that several factors are at play. First, Mataquas, as Elinas's eldest son and heir, feels threatened by the birth of any siblings that could contest his claims to inheritance. The law of primogeniture, however, precludes any serious threat his half-sisters might pose. The threat could be psychological, inspired by a child's presumed prefer-ence for his biological mother and jealousy regarding his father's great affec-tion for his second wife and children. Mataquas could also be disturbed by Presine's influence over his father and her fairy nature, a fact that is confirmed by the birth of triplets, which was considered taboo during medieval times. As a result of Presine's banishment, Elinas goes mad with grief and the gov-ernment of his lands falls into the hands of Mataquas. In this way, Mataquas has craftily prepared the way for his own succession, usurping all rivals in his father's affections.[17] This act of sibling rivalry will be repeated with respect to

---

16   Jean d'Arras, *Roman de Mélusine, ou la noble histoire de Lusignan. Roman du XIVe siècle*, ed. Jean-Jacques Vincensini (Paris: Librairie Générale Française, 2003), 128. When page numbers are given, English translations are from *Mélusine; or, the Noble History of Lusig-nan*, trans. Donald Maddox and Sara Sturm-Maddox (University Park: Pennsylvania State University Press, 2012), here 23. When page numbers are not given, translations are the editors'.

17   E. Jane Burns views this episode as an effort to link the Lusignan family to Alexander the Great in light of Aimon de Varenne's romance *Florimont* where Mataquas, son of Elinas, is the grandfather of Alexander the Great. "Magical Politics from Poitou to Armenia: Mé-lusine, Jean de Berry, and the Eastern Mediterranean," *The Journal of Medieval and Early Modern Studies* 43, no. 2 (Spring 2013): 275–301, at 290.

Raymond and his brother the Count of Forez, and yet again between Geoffrey Big Tooth and Fromont. Thus, the theme of sibling rivalry has been introduced through the actions of Mataquas.

Forced into exile on the Isle of Avalon with her daughters, Presine takes them daily to a mountain from whose summit she shows them Scotland, the land that should have been theirs if Elinas had not betrayed her and laments: "Filles, veéz vous la le païs ou vous fustes neez et ou vous eussiéz eu vostre partie, ne feust la faulseté de vostre pere qui, vous et moy, a mis en grant misere sans fin jusques au jour du hault juge qui punira les maulz et essaucera les biens!" (132) ["There you see the land where you were born and where you would have had your share of the inheritance, were it not for the treachery of your father, who placed you and me in such great misery that it will not end until the day when the High Judge punishes the wicked and rewards the good"] (24). By crying and blaming her misery and that of her daughters on Elinas, Presine portrays her husband in negative terms, setting the scene for their subsequent act of vengeance.

In sympathy for their mother, Melusine hatches a plan with her sisters Palestine and Melior to imprison their father within the mountain of Brumblerio in order to avenge his "desloyauté" and "faulseté" [disloyalty and falsity] with a punishment they feel fits his crime.[18] Although Melusine and her sisters believe they are motivated by "amour de vrayes filles a [nostre] mere" [the love of true daughters to their mother] (132) in righting a wrong, Presine is furious when she learns what they have done and metes out a separate punishment to each of them. Melusine will take the form of a serpent from the waist down on Saturdays. Should she marry a man who promises never to seek her out on Saturdays nor speak of it to anyone, she will live the rest of her days as a mortal woman and die a natural death. If her husband betrays her trust, she will revert to serpent form until Judgment Day. Melior must guard a sparrow hawk in Greater Armenia until a noble knight keeps vigil there for three days, asking any boon of her except for her love (*marriage*) or sexual favors. Palestine will guard her father's treasure within Mount Canigou until a knight of her lineage uses the treasure to conquer the Holy Land and set her free. The punishments are so extreme that none of the daughters fulfill the conditions within the span of the romance and perhaps for all time.

---

18   The female siblings act in concert against their father, a variation on the ancient myth of sons rebelling against the father.

As Catherine Gaullier-Bougassas has demonstrated, the relationship between Presine and her daughters is problematic.[19] Unlike Melusine, who protects and forgives Geoffrey the heinous crime of killing his brother and the monks at Maillezais, Presine lacks motherly affection and punishes each of her daughters for having enclosed their father within the mountain of Brumblerio. She invokes a malediction upon each of them, without giving them the possibility to repent. Presine describes Elinas in such negative terms that, as Gaullier-Bougassas suggests, she seems almost to incite her daughters to carry out a vengeance that she appears to live out vicariously through them.[20]

The punishment Melusine and her sisters inflict on their father, by taking the law into their own hands and distributing justice as they see fit, although unlawful, reflects a possible revolt against the patriarchal system and the suffering it inflicts on their mother and by extension all women. Melusine and her sisters act upon that injustice and naturally side with their mother, as they have no experience of men or the outside world. Melusine's naïveté with regard to her father's guilt and her mother's true feelings reflects her lack of experience in matters of the heart and of the patriarchy. Like Perceval in the *Conte du Graal*, Melusine and her sisters exhibit the quality of *nice* or simplicity, a lack of knowledge that generates chaos when a child's perception of the world clashes with that of the adult. Presine accuses her daughters of being "faulses et mauvaises et tresameres et dures de cuer" [false, wicked, bitter and hardhearted] and of exhibiting "faulx et orguilleux couraige" [false and arrogant behavior] (134). In their *demesure* Mélusine and her sisters have deprived their mother of her one source of joy as she grieves over the fate of her husband.

Regardless of whether the daughters' punishments are merited, the expulsion of the sisters by their mother from the safety of Avalon, the isle of women, thrusts them into the harsh reality of men and marriage. Unlike Melusine's sons, who decide on their own to leave the family and set off on adventure, Melusine and her sisters are pushed out of the childhood nest by their mother in order to follow the destiny she prescribes for them. Their fates, like her own, will be isolation, loneliness, and exclusion, for it is the destiny of these women to be subject to men, who either seem incapable of holding fast to their promises, as is the case with Melusine and her mother, or incapable of achieving the tasks necessary for Palestine and Melior to be relieved of their punishments.

---

19   Catherine Gaullier-Bougassas, "La fée Présine: une figure maternelle ambiguë aux origines de l'écriture romanesque," in *550 Jahre deutsche Melusine-Coudrette und Thüring von Ringoltingen/550 ans de Mélusine allemande-Coudrette et Thüring von Ringoltingen*, ed. André Schnyder and Jean-Claude Mühlethaler (Bern: Peter Lang, 2008), 111–128.

20   Gaullier-Bougassas, "La fée Présine," 118.

Lewis suggests that Melusine's punishment "implies the extent to which women must accept and internalize the rule of patriarchal hierarchy."[21] Lewis also interprets the tail, a phallic symbol, as a concrete manifestation of Melusine's presumptuous assumption of masculine authority. Fairy magic and the prophetic powers conferred on fairies cannot alter the destiny of women, which is to be subject to men. Melusine's supernatural capabilities are acceptable only in so far as they serve the patriarchy through the uniquely feminine function of fertility that gives rise to material goods, such as land acquisition, fortress building, child-bearing, and maternal warmth, all of which further the well-being of men. As part of the terms of marriage, Presine agrees to obey her husband, thus acknowledging female submission in marriage: "je suiz celle qui obeiray a vous comme loyal moillier doit obeir a son espoux" (128) ["Then I shall obey you as a loyal wife must obey her husband"] (23). Melusine's difficult task will be to learn the lesson of obedience as a consequence of living in the human world.

Raymond's childhood resembles Melusine's in that he, too, commits a parricide that forces him to go into exile. Raymond, however, kills his uncle Aimery during a boar hunt by accident and not with the intent to do harm. Raymond retraces to a certain extent a path already traversed by his father, Hervé de Léon, at the same age. Both father and son unwittingly commit homicide and flee rather than face the consequences of their acts. Hervé killed the King of the Bretons's nephew in self-defense. The King's nephew was led to believe by persons jealous of Hervé that the king intended to dispossess him and make Hervé his heir in his stead. The impulsive youth believes the rumors and lies in wait to kill the unarmed Hervé, who is horrified to learn, when he removes the attacker's helmet, that he has just killed the King's nephew. Like his father before him, Raymond flees upon killing Aimery, believing that circumstantial evidence would prove he purposely committed homicide and condemn him as a murderer.

Fortunately, soon after his self-imposed exile, Hervé meets a lady, presumably a fairy mistress, who helps him restore his lost patrimony. When she leaves, Hervé marries the Count of Poitiers' sister and establishes a family, of which Raymond is a son. Raymond's destiny will echo that of his father. Not only will Melusine supply the exiled Raymond with a kingdom extracted from her fairy magic, just as a fairy mistress provided a kingdom for Hervé, but she will see to it that Raymond corrects Hervé's failure to restore his reputation and patrimony by sending Raymond on a mission to Brittany to avenge the treason

---

21   Lewis, "Acceptable Lessons," 20.

committed against his father.[22] He does so by seeking out Josselin de Pont de Léon, the only living member of the group of conspirators who plotted against his father. With the help of Melusine's knowledge of the past, Raymond challenges Josselin at court before the King of the Bretons and both exculpates his father and wins back his inheritance in a judiciary duel against Josselin's son, Olivier. This adventure, which occurs shortly after the birth of Urian, serves as a rite of passage, as if by proving himself in battle Raymond affirms his worthiness to be a father and shepherd of his people. Rather than keep the land he won, Raymond generously gives it to his uncle's sons, Alain and Hervé (his father's namesake), and establishes a priory. The episode highlights Raymond's prowess, concern for family honor, and piety. His successful completion of the adventure sets an example of princely conduct for his firstborn son to follow.

Unless the main character is female, detailed depictions of girlhood are rare in medieval literature, since most medieval works of fiction focus on boys, with females playing a secondary, supporting role. The depiction of Melusine's girlhood, mentioned first and juxtaposed with Raymond's, emphasizes her central role and, as befits her gender, her upbringing differs from his. Melusine and her sisters are raised as exiles in the fairy, feminized world of Avalon, separated from their father and male rule. Raymond's upbringing follows the older tradition of the *chansons de geste* in which a young man leaves his family in order to be raised by an uncle. Coudrette's later verse version of the tale, written in 1401, gives a more detailed account of Raymond's family background, indicating that Raymond's father, although wise and noble, was too poor to raise him and his numerous siblings adequately. Like Melusine, Raymond is singled out as one of three, the youngest of three elder siblings of the same gender, as opposed to the eldest of three, as is the case for Melusine.[23] Raymond's uncle, Count Aimery, who is much esteemed for his knowledge of astronomy and the seven liberal arts, plays the role of a loving foster parent. His erudition and ability to predict the future, based on astrology, contrasts sharply with Presine's innate gift of prophecy based on her fairy nature. This reinforces the stereotype that female intelligence is based on intuition or nature and that men

---

22   Before sending Raymond on his mission to Brittany, Melusine tests his fidelity to their marital oath, most likely as a way to avoid being betrayed, as was her mother. Raymond stays true to his promise and does not reveal Melusine's identity when queried about her origins twice by Count Bertrand of Poitiers and a third time by his brother, the Count of Forez. Melusine praises him twice for keeping the secret and warns him of the consequences should he betray her.

23   E. Jane Burns points out that Jean de Berry, who commissioned the work, was himself the youngest son. "Magical Politics," 294.

acquire knowledge through science and tradition. In Coudrette's version of the romance, Raymond is described as more learned than his male siblings, which may explain the affinity between nephew and uncle. As parents, Raymond and Melusine bring together in their marriage two disparate forms of nurture, one based on fairy magic and the other on formal education.

The exceptionally fertile union between Melusine and Raymond produces ten sons, eight of whom bear strange mother-marks as vestiges of their mother's fairy nature. Unlike their parents, the Lusignan children are raised by both parents in an initially stable and loving home. Melusine's sons exhibit a gamut of behaviors, ranging from diabolical to saintly, with variations in between. The great care with which the narrator differentiates each child indicates that they are meant to represent types whose behavior, when compared and contrasted, serves a didactic function, conveying lessons on appropriate and inappropriate conduct. Douglas Kelly has drawn attention to the three celibate sons, whom he describes as "especially unusual morally and socially."[24] At the diabolical extreme is Horrible, who has committed four homicides by age seven, while his saintly counterpart is the martyred Fromont. Both Horrible and Fromont perish, since Geoffrey Big Tooth slays Fromont in a fit of rage and Melusine recommends that Horrible be put to death as a precaution against his incipient violence. Of the remaining eight children, six bear mother-marks, and five of them—Urian, Guyon, Antoine, Renaud, and Geoffrey Big Tooth—set out on adventure and accomplish great deeds, while the two youngest sons, Thierry and Remonnet, who are free of mother-marks, do not pursue adventures abroad since they will be heirs. Eudes, Melusine's second son bearing mother-marks, for whom Melusine has arranged a marriage, also remains peacefully at home. These children will, however, demonstrate prowess like their heroic brothers' when they join forces to defend their elder brothers during the campaign against the Count of Freiburg and the Duke of Austria. With the exception of Horrible and Fromont, all of Melusine's sons engage in some form of chivalry that serves to glorify the Lusignan dynasty.

Rather than detract from Melusine's progeny, the mother-marks that appear on her sons' faces set the Lusignans apart from other lineages and distinguish them as fierce and formidable warriors. The firstborn Urian has one red and one blue eye and enormous ears; one of Guyon's eyes is higher than the other; Antoine bears a lion's paw that grows fur and sharp nails on his left cheek; Renaud has only one eye; Geoffrey was born with one large tooth jutting out of

---

24   Douglas Kelly, "The Domestication of the Marvelous in the Melusine Romances," in *Mélusine of Lusignan: Founding Fiction in Late Medieval France*, ed. Donald Maddox and Sara Sturm-Maddox (Athens, GA: University of Georgia Press, 1996), 32–47, at 34.

his mouth; a tuft of fur grows on Fromont's nose; and Horrible possesses three eyes. These marks are talismans of strength, wonder, and exemplary prowess. The most extraordinary warrior of them all, Geoffrey Big Tooth, sports the most notable mother-mark. In fact, Geoffrey's boar's tooth stands out most prominently in medieval iconography, which attests to the fascination this physical anomaly held for the medieval audience. Some of the mother-marks, like the lion's paw on Antoine's cheek and Geoffrey's boar's tooth, recall ferocious animals. Renaud's blemish mimics the terrifying man-eating Cyclops. Four of the sons have defects relative to eyes. In the context of children's literature, the mother-marks would be memorable attention-grabbers and elicit strong emotional responses. If one may extrapolate from the present to the Middle Ages, the defects of the Lusignans may have thrilled medieval youth much in the same way that modern day action heroes like Batman and Spiderman, whose identification with creatures normally considered repulsive, like bats and spiders, delight and amuse children today.[25]

As Lewis has observed, "Neither the tone nor the events of [Jean d'Arras'] narrative implies that physical deformity forcibly signifies a character's danger to his or her society."[26] In fact, any mention of the deformities is couched either in terms of awe or is mitigated with qualifying statements. When discussing Urian's facial features in the context of war, Hermine exclaims "Amis, "bontéz vault mieulx que beautéz" (348) ["Goodness is worth far more than beauty, my friend!" (87)], suggesting that prowess and valor outweigh good looks. She reiterates this as she muses further, "qu'elle dit a soy mesmes que, se il avoit le visaige plus contrefait.c. foiz que il n'a, si est il tailliéz pour sa bonté et pour sa prouesse d'avoir la fille du plus hault roy du monde a amie" (348) [She told herself that even if his face were a hundred times more distorted than reported, he would nonetheless be ideally suited, in terms of goodness and prowess, to have the daughter of the world's most exalted monarch as his beloved] (87).

Similarly, the citizens of Luxembourg marvel at Antoine's and Renaud's facial defects that give them an air of pride and ferocity. These blemishes are compensated for by the comeliness of their bodies and noble bearing:

> "Dieux, dist ly uns a l'autre, comme veéz la deux fiers hommes et qu'ilz sont a ressoingnier. Cil n'est pas saiges qui a telz gens prent noise ne debat." Et moult ont grand merveille de la joe Anthoine et, en vérité, ce estoit

---

25   Other heroes of the later Middle Ages like Richard the Lion-Hearted, who is described as a Saracen-eating cannibal, are portrayed in outrageous fashion, perhaps indicative of a trend.

26   Lewis, "Acceptable Lessons," 13.

une estrange chose a veoir, mais la grant beauté qui estoit ou remenant de lui faisoit oublier cela, et aussi il ne lui messeoit pas granmant. (482)

["My God," said one to another, "look at those two proud men: how fearsome they look—no one would dare pick a fight with them!" Everyone was amazed by Antoine's cheek, which was indeed a strange thing to see, but the great beauty of the rest of his body made one forget it, and it really wasn't all that unbecoming.] (126)

The mother-marks in no way prevent the Lusignans from marrying desirable, noble, and eligible maidens. Although Melusine's sons are fully human, the marks represent emblems of inherited fairy nature that endow them with exceptional prowess.

The depiction of the Lusignan brothers follows both a chronology and hierarchy, with the two elder brothers, when paired, taking the lead and mentoring the younger siblings. Urian and Guyon set off on adventure as part of the maturation process as soon as an opportunity presents itself. Urian is seventeen and Guyon fifteen. Although close in age, they are separated in birth order by Eudes, who does not set off on adventure. The bond between the brothers is carefully illustrated and, following the romance tradition, imitates strong ties between other romance siblings, such as that between Gauvain and Gaheriet, and Lionel and Bohort in the Prose *Lancelot*: "Moult amoient ly uns l'autre Uriiens et Guyon [...] et tous jours s'entretenoient compaignie Uriiens et Guyon" (294–296) [Urian and Guyon were very fond of each other [...] and the two of them were always together] (71). When two Poitevin knights return from Jerusalem, recounting how the sultan of Damascus is laying siege to Famagusta because the King of Cyprus refuses to let the sultan marry his daughter and only heir, Urian takes the initiative and proposes that he and Guyon come to her aid. Urian sees this venture as an act of charity, a means to gain renown abroad and to conquer land so as to increase the patrimony of their remaining siblings, since their younger brothers' inheritance would be quite reduced if Urian and Guyon claimed the land, as is their right, under the law of primogeniture. As Carolyne Larrington has observed in her study of medieval siblings, "Brothers will either learn to negotiate equitable shares of the kingdom or else they will destroy one another."[27] Urian and Guyon willingly agree to forfeit their share of the inheritance in exchange for support from their parents in funding their excursion. Here, the brothers act altruistically and harmoniously by renouncing

---

27   Carolyne Larrington, *Brothers and Sisters in Medieval European Literature* (Rochester, NY: York Medieval Press, 2015), 115.

the inheritance to which they are entitled, thus serving as a model of brotherly love for their younger siblings.

Besides providing her children with the material goods and soldiers necessary for their voyage, Melusine appoints four barons to watch over them and delivers to them the first of her *chastoiements*, designed to guide them in their future endeavors:

> Enfans, je vous encharge que en tous les lieux que vous seréz que tous les jours vous oÿéz le service divin tout premierement que vous faciéz autre chose. Et en tous voz affaires reclaméz l'aide de vostre Createur et le servéz diligemment et améz et creniéz comme vostre Dieu et vostre Createur, et nostre mere saincte Eglise soustenéz et soiéz si vrais champions encontre tous ses malveullans. Et aidiéz et conseilliéz les vefves et les orphelins, et honnouréz toutes dames et confortéz toutes pucelles que on vouldroit desheriter desraisonnablement. Améz les gentilz hommes et leur tenéz compaignie, soyéz humbles et humains au grant et au petit. (304–306)
>
> [My children, wherever you may be, you are to attend mass every day before you do anything else, and call on your Creator for help in all your endeavors. Serve Him diligently, and love Him and fear Him as your God. Uphold our Holy Mother Church and champion her against all evildoers. Give aid and counsel to widows and orphans, honor all women, and protect maidens from anyone who might seek to disinherit them without reason. Esteem men of honor and keep company with them. Be humane and humble toward both rich and poor.] (74)

Melusine's admonitions follow a specific order and hierarchy. First and foremost, her sons are to serve God and Church. Next, they are enjoined to respect and aid women. She then gives them practical advice on how to treat their peers and govern those who serve them. Urian and Guyon fulfill the two prescriptions mentioned above, for not only do the Lusignans prevent the King of Cyprus's daughter Hermine from being wed to the sultan of Damascus against her will, but they also engage in a full-fledged holy war against the Saracens, who are depicted as enemies of Christ.

The fates of Urian and Guyon closely parallel one another: both battle on behalf of kings, who are themselves brothers, each one having a daughter who is the sole heir of his realm. Urian, as the elder and hence more responsible brother, demonstrates his prowess first through various victories on land and sea and by killing the Sultan of Damascus, who began the altercation. Through the granting of a boon Urian agrees to marry Hermine, the King of Cyprus' daughter. It is imperative that Hermine marry because her father is dying of a poisoned wound inflicted by the sultan during battle, thus leaving her and her kingdom even more vulnerable to attack without a viable male suzerain to defend them. The literary device of the boon casts a positive light on the marriage, making it appear altruistic rather than self-interested.[28] Once Urian is married, Guyon distinguishes himself by defending the King of Cyprus' brother, the King of Armenia, who is besieged by pagans wishing to avenge the death of the sultan. As was the case with the King of Cyprus, the King of Armenia dies, leaving his daughter, Florie, in a vulnerable position, unable to defend her inheritance. Knowing of his imminent death, the King of Armenia addresses a letter to Urian, asking him to enjoin Guyon to marry his daughter and assume governance of his kingdom. Even though Florie appears to have fallen in love with Guyon, the literary device of the letter reinforces the notion that the Lusignans' motives for marriage are not mercenary. The king's letter addressed to Urian acknowledges the elder son's position of authority over his younger brother.

Inspired by the exploits of their elder brothers, yet considering themselves less worthy, Antoine and Renaud also set off on adventure when the occasion arises. Following a pattern set by their brothers, the opportunity for adventure comes from outside and requires a trip abroad. Antoine and Renaud follow Melusine's directive given in her first *chastoiement* to protect maidens from those seeking to disinherit them by defending the orphan Crestienne of Luxembourg against the King of Alsace, who threatens to marry her against her will. As was the case with Urian and Guyon, Melusine supplies her sons with the necessary equipment and men to carry out their mission successfully, in addition to two guardians to see to their well-being. She also gives them advice in the form of a second, slightly shortened *chastoiement*.[29]

Antoine and Renaud recapitulate the adventures of their predecessors with slight variations. The elder, Antoine, takes the initiative and makes most of the strategic military decisions; he vanquishes the King of Alsace, although he does not kill him, but rather delivers him to Crestienne to do with him what she will. Most probably because the King of Alsace is Christian, Crestienne and Antoine make peace with him and the two households become allies. Antoine

---

28   The altruism of the brothers and Raymond becomes a *leitmotif*, repeated every time that a kingdom is either conquered or secured. The final flourish of these activities is the founding of an abbey or priory.

29   In her second *chastoiement*, Mélusine excludes earlier advice concerning the protection of women, placing greater emphasis on principles of good civic behavior and military strategy.

agrees to marry the orphan Crestienne through a boon, and once the elder brother is married, Renaud makes a name for himself by defending Frederick, the King of Bohemia, who is the King of Alsace's brother, and who has a daughter as his sole heir, named Aiglentine. The Christian-defense motif is introduced once more, since Frederick's enemies are pagans. King Frederick dies in battle from a wound inflicted by Selodus, the King of Cracow, which Renaud avenges. The Duke of Alsace, seeing that his niece Aiglentine has become an orphan, appeals to Antoine, asking that he allow Renaud to marry her, which he does. Both pairs of sons gain fame and fortune through their prowess and ability to work harmoniously for shared principles, with the elder son in a position of authority, protecting and guiding the younger. All four sons fight on behalf of the Church by defeating two separate groups of adversaries, the Saracens, associated with the Middle East, and a second group of pagans, associated with Eastern Europe. Antoine and Renaud improve, perhaps, on their brothers by making a friend out of their adversary the Duke of Alsace, whose daughter Melide will become the future wife of Antoine's son.

Despite her fertility, Melusine has the uncanny ability to regulate her pregnancies. The births of Melusine's last two sons, the two that bear no mother-marks and hence attest to her progress towards attaining humanity through her marriage with Raymond, occur after Urian, Guyon, Antoine, Renaud, and Eudes have married and established their kingdoms.[30] Once the elder children have been provided for, Melusine can prudently give birth to two more sons, thus ensuring that they will have a secure future with sufficient land to support them. Up until this point, Urian, Guyon, Antoine, and Renaud, in spite of the mother-marks, have conducted themselves with the utmost honor. They have successfully negotiated the pitfalls of adolescent exuberance and sibling rivalry by focusing their energy on altruistic aims, the defense of maidens and upholding the Christian faith.

Geoffrey Big Tooth, Melusine's sixth son, recognized as "le plus fier et le plus courageux et le plus hardy de tous les autres" (552) [the hardiest, fiercest, and most daring of the lot] (148) will demonstrate his superiority over his elder brothers by surpassing them in several ways. He initiates his first adventure without any outside prompting by determining on his own to impose order on his father's vassals in Ireland who refuse to pay tribute. In this way Geoffrey follows in Raymond's footsteps by righting wrongs done in his own realm. He subdues Claude de Scion and Claude's brothers, who wreak havoc on Ireland through

---

30   For a discussion of mother-marks and Melusine's gradual evolution toward human nature, see Douglas Kelly, "The Domestication of the Marvelous."

robbery and unlawfully holding people for ransom, just as Raymond made sure that Josselin de Pont de Léon paid for the death of the King of the Bretons's son, which resulted in Hervé's exile. The Scion brothers are hanged for their crimes, as were Josselin and Olivier in Brittany. Geoffrey demonstrates justice both by adhering to the letter of the law in punishing the Scion brothers and also by showing mercy to the Lady of Valbruyant. Next, Geoffrey flies to the defense of Urian and Guyon, who are threatened in the Near East by pagans seeking to avenge the deaths of their relatives and allies previously killed by the Lusignans. Like his brothers before him, Geoffrey asks his parents to support his military campaign with ships and supplies, which they do, provided he return within a year.[31]

In the Near East, Geoffrey surpasses his brothers in chivalry, takes command of operations, and puts a definitive end to Saracen aggression by arranging a long-lasting truce. Going above and beyond his brothers in piety, Geoffrey makes a pilgrimage to the Holy Sepulchre in Jerusalem and demonstrates superior diplomatic powers by earning the esteem of the Sultan of Damascus. Geoffrey's final show of valor, which exceeds the exploits of any of his brothers heretofore, is his combat with the giant Gardon, a supernatural foe, in Geurande, another of his father's holdings. The giant, like the Scion brothers, exacts tribute from Raymond's subjects. Geoffrey makes short shrift of the giant and sends his decapitated head to Raymond as a trophy of his victory. In the adventures illustrated above, Geoffrey recapitulates both the exploits of his father, by upholding law and order in his father's ancestral lands, and of his brothers, by engaging in combat abroad against the Saracens. He goes one step further by battling the mythical giant. Geoffrey proves his mettle on three levels and in three spaces: on the home front, on foreign soil, and at the supernatural locus of the giant, an outer, mythical realm that recalls Melusine's fairy nature.

After having proved his merit and achieved more honor than any member of his lineage, Geoffrey immediately thereafter falls from grace by killing his brother Fromont and the monks at Maillezais in a fit of rage. Rupert Pickens has commented on the abrupt, unexpected, and violent rift that erupts suddenly between the brothers: "Although Geoffrey is foolhardy and often callous, nothing in his character and nothing in Jean's plot—not any form of antimonasticism, not a hint of hatred for his brother—anticipates such an effusion of cruelty."[32] If one considers the Lusignan brothers as exemplars of youthful

---

31   Melusine does not provide Geoffrey with guardians as she did for her other sons; however, Geoffrey did have a tutor named Philibert of Montmoret accompany him and witness his exploits during the campaign in Ireland.

32   Rupert Pickens, "The Poetics of Paradox in the *Roman de Mélusine*," in *Mélusine of Lusignan*, 48–75, at 60.

behavior on a broad scale, ranging from good to evil, Geoffrey's treatment of Fromont parallels that of Cain and Abel, the first and most notorious set of brothers. Indeed, no thorough examination of brotherly relations can occur without taking these two figures and other examples of fraternal hatred into account, especially since the author takes great pains to individuate each son. The context of the Hundred Years' War with its political turmoil and civil strife, sometimes pitting families against each other, would warrant an examination of brotherly enmity.

Earlier the narrator made a distinction between the monastic life and chivalry as indicated in the following quotation: "Et ot Melusigne les deux ans après, deux filz de quoy le premier ot a nom Fromont et ama moult l'eglise, car bien le monstra a la fin car il fu rendu moine a Malierés [...] Et ly autre filz qu'elle ot, l'an ensuivant, ot a nom Thierry et fu moult bachelereux" (552) [As for Melusine, over two years' time she gave birth to two more sons. The first of them, Fromont, was deeply devout, as was apparent when he eventually became a monk at the abbey of Maillezais [...] The son born the following year, Thierry, was a devotee of chivalric pursuits] (148). Fromont and Thierry follow two divergent paths: the monastic life and chivalry. With the exception of Fromont and Horrible, all of Melusine's sons choose chivalry. The knight who best embodies that chivalry up to this point is Geoffrey, for he has restored order to his father's lands in Ireland and Guérande, helped his brothers Urian and Guy subdue the Saracens, and slain the giant Gardon. Just as Cain and Abel represent two divergent lifestyles as evidenced by their separate burnt offerings in Genesis, Geoffrey berates Fromont for having chosen the monastic life over chivalry.[33] It appears that jealousy or anger at Fromont's rejection of Geoffrey, by choosing to follow a separate path, impels him to commit a crime of passion. It may also be attributed to pride, a quality Melusine warned against in her first *chastoiement*: "Sur toutes chose je vous deffend orgueil" (310) ["Above all I forbid you to succumb to pride"] (75).[34] Carolyne Larrington ascribes the act to several possible factors, among them, an ancient aristocratic belief that "a clerical calling was somehow unmasculine and unworthy," Fromont's privileging of the monastic brotherhood over blood ties, and Fromont's rejection of chivalry, which "damages his brother's sense of himself at a level which

---

33 Cain, who was a farmer, offered the fruits of the earth whereas Abel, a shepherd, made the blood sacrifice of a sheep. When God preferred Abel's burnt offering over Cain's, Cain slew his brother out of jealousy. For a discussion of Cain and Abel and other examples of fraternal hatred in the Middle Ages, see Larrington, *Brothers and Sisters*, 104–128.

34 Melusine herself, as noted above, is chastened by Presine for demonstrating "orgueilleux couraige."

provokes an excessive and infantilized rage."[35] Jean-Jacques Vincensini views the act in mythological terms as reflecting one of three patterns of heroic excess defined by George Dumézil. According to Vincensini, Geoffrey evinces all three patterns as part of the hero's civilizing function. This would entail violence against warriors (Geoffrey's murder of his uncle), violence against women, and finally, violence against holy figures as embodied in Fromont.[36] One could also view the episode as the consequence of original sin or even *translatio imperii*, the concept that civilizations rise to great heights only to fall apart when excellence has been achieved. The notion of *translatio imperii* would certainly have resonated with Jean's audience and patron, the Duke of Berry, who commissioned the work in order to glorify a dynasty that had lost its luster but to which he wanted to attach himself.

Like many romance heroes, Geoffrey is both superior to his peers and deeply flawed. In his defense, unlike Raymond and Hervé, who run away from the scene of the homicides they committed, Geoffrey assumes responsibility for the murders and makes restitution during his lifetime. He does not perform the penance right away, however, but will do so after he kills the giant Grimaut and discovers his family origins at King Elinas's tomb. Geoffrey's adventure at the tomb of his ancestor distinguishes him from his brothers in that he is predestined to accomplish this feat. The discovery of one's origins and name at a tomb is a common theme found throughout romance. This adventure will mark a turning point for Geoffrey and set him apart from his brothers. Urian, Guyon, Antoine, and Renaud follow the heroic pattern of the more archaic *chansons de geste* figures, who triumph in war but who engage in very little introspection. Even their love relationships seem more perfunctory than heartfelt. Their interests lie principally in making a name for themselves, conquering land, and carrying out complicated military campaigns. Their wives, as heiresses, have value insofar as they further these goals. According to Gaffney, the duty of the epic hero is "crystal-clear, and there is no doubt whatever about his goal and ultimate victory."[37] The medieval epic hero, sure of himself, rarely undergoes a period of personal struggle and self-discovery. Gaffney further specifies that "they act as members of a lineage, and their role is to assist their elders in ancestral feuds, avenging wrongs perpetrated against their kinsmen."[38] Geoffrey

---

35   Larrington, *Brothers and Sisters*, 117–119.

36   See also "La dent de la mère: Geoffrey ou les vertus de l'inquiétant merveilleux," in *Ecriture et réécriture du merveilleux féerique: Autour de Mélusine*, ed. Jean-Jacques Vincensini and Matthew Morris (Paris: Classiques Garnier, 2012), 157–175.

37   Gaffney, *Constructions of Childhood*, 140.

38   Gaffney, *Constructions of Childhood*, 99.

shares many traits of the epic hero but like the hero of romance, part of his quest involves unearthing family origins and forging an identity. Indeed, Geoffrey will not be capable of true penance or self-realization until he comes to terms with his own identity.

One of the direct consequences of Geoffrey's killing of Fromont is the disclosure of family secrets, which unravels family ties. Until the murder, Melusine and Raymond manage to cloak the truth regarding the youthful indiscretions that brought them together in their marriage of convenience. By killing Fromont, Geoffrey forces Raymond to speak out against Melusine and expose his anxieties regarding her fairy nature. Tied up in these truths is sibling rivalry, for it is the Count of Forez who, by inciting Raymond's jealousy regarding Melusine's Saturday absences, pushes his brother to betray his marital pact and spy on Melusine during her bath. It is very likely that the Count's own jealousy triggered what becomes a chain reaction of tragedy that will result in his own death at the hands of the avenging Geoffrey. The Count may also be overtly expressing fears about Melusine that Raymond himself shares but is bound by his oath not to reveal. The incident creates a permanent rift between the brothers, and Raymond's hatred for his sibling becomes so strong he regrets not having slain him.

Geoffrey's act of adolescent pique in killing Fromont forces him to separate from both mother and father, thus giving him the space to construct his own identity. Raymond associates the murder with Melusine's serpent nature and subsequently denounces her publicly, thus breaking his vow, which results in Melusine's banishment from the realm and her permanent transformation into a serpent. Raymond also turns against Geoffrey, threatening to kill him. Now that Geoffrey's ties with both mother and father have been severed, he can embark on his adventure against the giant Grimaut that will allow him to explore the mysteries of the past and come to terms with both his and their crimes.[39]

In order to do this, Geoffrey must return to the scene of his mother's crime by literally going underground to unearth family mysteries as he battles the monstrous giant Grimaut within the mountain of Brumblerio, where his grandfather was imprisoned by Melusine and is now buried in a tomb next to

---

39 Raymond's denunciation of Melusine can also be read as an attempt to break free from her dominance and assert his independence. Melusine often plays the role of mother to Raymond and one can observe his growing independence and authority as the text progresses. Melusine's dominance, however, is not without precedent, as many female heroines, Isolde and Guenevere among them, take the initiative and influence others to do their bidding.

a statue of Presine. At the tomb Geoffrey reads an inscription that informs him of his mother's lineage, and by extension his own, thus establishing Melusine's noble origins and throwing doubt on Raymond's claim that she is diabolical in nature. This giant represents, perhaps, an emblem of parental power that must be reckoned with and slain in order for Geoffrey to bring to the surface and expose the mystery of his maternal lineage and Melusine's similar revolt against her father and the patriarchal order. In many ways, Geoffrey's rejection of the priestly order mirrors Melusine's primal outrage against her father, in as much as Elinas represents the patriarchy. Geoffrey's rash act of burning the monks at Maillezais and his brother along with them, a manifestation of *démesure*, mirrors Melusine's headstrong decision to entomb her father within Mount Bromblerio and Raymond's impulse to kill his brother, kill Geoffrey, and condemn Melusine to her fate by denouncing her. Geoffrey recapitulates and brings to a head the latent violence that simmers within his family.

It is interesting that Presine, seen earlier to adhere to the patriarchal code, reigns over this underworld and has initiated Geoffrey's journey into it. Donald Maddox identifies this scene as a specular encounter, that is, a turning point in romance narrative where the protagonist is forced to confront his own selfhood and, in doing so, gains new insight into his identity.[40] For Maddox, the process of individuation or identity formation implies a psychic transition from the Imaginary Order embodied in the mother, with whom the protagonist severs ties, to the Symbolic Order of the father, who represents law, language, and social institutions.[41] This transition does not necessarily imply a rejection of the Imaginary Order but rather an integration of the two orders.[42] Once Geoffrey embraces his paternal and maternal origins and sees himself as part of an illustrious lineage, a path to redemption opens as he brings his behavior into conformity with social mores and the special destiny to which his inheritance entitles him. He is now a part of the social order, the continuity and reputation of which he has a duty to uphold. Both Raymond and Geoffrey make pilgrimages to Rome to repent of their crimes and Melusine, in her final address or *chastoiement*, preaches a lesson of forgiveness, which will help reconcile father and son.

A final irony of the romance arises from the parallels between Melusine and the young women who marry her sons. As stated earlier, unless a woman is the main protagonist, little attention is paid to the upbringing of female characters

---

40   Donald Maddox, *Fictions of Identity in Medieval France* (Cambridge: Cambridge University Press, 2000), 3.

41   Maddox, *Fictions of Identity*, 196.

42   Maddox, *Fictions of Identity*, 266, n. 89.

in medieval romance, as they usually play secondary, supporting roles. Such is the case regarding the four heiresses, Hermine, Florie, Crestienne, and Aiglentine, who marry into the Lusignan family and bear a striking resemblance. As motherless daughters and the sole heirs of distant kingdoms under attack, they fall into the category of women whom Melusine in her initial *chastoiement* says her sons must protect. Not only are the maidens motherless, but three of their fathers also conveniently die as casualties of war and the fourth has already died, thus precipitating the military campaign to Luxembourg.[43]

The narrator uses binary symmetry to contrast the maidens in sets of two, just as he contrasted the adventures of Urien and Guyon with those of Antoine and Renaud. For example, Hermine and Crestienne are pursued by unwanted suitors, which serves as the initial pretext for war. As soon as Urien and Antoine, the eldest of the two pairs of siblings, liberate the maidens, Guyon and Renaud rescue the maidens' feminine counterpart (Hermine's cousin Florie and the Duke of Alsace's niece, Aiglentine). In spite of the similarity of the circumstances in which the maidens find themselves, as with the male protagonists, Jean d'Arras makes a point of diversifying their personalities. Aiglentine expresses filial piety by hesitating to marry too soon after her father's death. Crestienne is perhaps the most independent, as she refuses to marry the Duke of Alsace, whom she finds unpalatable because of his age and a previous marriage. Florie falls deeply in love with Guyon, and Hermine graciously sends tokens of esteem in the form of a brooch and a ring to her defenders. In contrast to Melusine, who is depicted as a courtly woman conversant in matters of state and governance, and who is in complete charge of her household, the maidens are relegated to a secondary role, dependent upon their Lusignan champions for protection and sustenance as it is deemed inappropriate for women to rule well in their own right, as evidenced by the King of Alsace's statement to his barons: "car terre qui est en gouvernement de femme, c'est petit de chose" (534) [for a land under the governance of a woman is of little value] (142). Like Melusine, the maidens enter into marriages of convenience and shortly thereafter bear sons, thus reflecting the empire building to which Jacques Le Goff alludes when he says that Melusine incarnates the social ambitions of the chivalric class.[44]

---

43 The King of Cyprus dies slowly of a poisoned wound, the King of Armenia dies from an unknown cause, the King of Bohemia is killed by an arrow shot from the bow of an enemy king, and the Duke of Luxembourg's death leaves his daughter vulnerable to marriage with an unwanted suitor.

44 Jacques Le Goff and Emmanuel Le Roy Ladurie, "Mélusine maternelle et défricheuse," *Annales: Economies, Sociétés, Civilisations* 26 (1971): 587–622.

There is much evidence to support the thesis that the *Roman de Mélusine* may have been intended for an audience that included both adults and children. Jean d'Arras takes special pains to mention the exact ages of his youthful protagonists, who include young women as well as small children and who range from fourteen to seventeen years of age. Special attention is paid to family dynamics, particularly sibling rivalry and parent-child relations. The romance focuses on youth, for as soon as one child matures, the action moves on to a younger sibling. The variety and range of behaviors from one generation to the next, from mother to daughter, father to son, and among siblings both married and celibate, makes it particularly apt for the instruction of children. Within the spectrum of youthful behavior, there are lessons to be gleaned from both positive and negative examples. The romance demonstrates what harm may come to society when youths act on impulse, by taking the law into their own hands (Melusine, her sisters, and Geoffrey), while at the same time illustrating the great benefits a family can reap when siblings act harmoniously for the common good.

The romance emphasizes the importance of family dynamics and how fatal flaws such as sibling rivalry, *démesure,* and pride can carry over from one generation to the next and intensify over time. The problem of sibling rivalry is first posed by Mataquas, who engineers the removal of his stepmother in order to claim possession of his father's realm. He does so without any negative consequences to himself. Similarly, Raymond's brother, the Count of Forez, levels suspicion against his sister-in-law that causes Raymond to break his vow, thus ending his marriage, which unleashes Raymond's hatred and Geoffrey Big Tooth's vengeance. Raymond, as an adult, manages to exercise self-control and refrains from violence. Geoffrey, however, confronts the Count at his castle and causes him to fall to his death from the roof as he attempts to escape Geoffrey's wrath. Sibling rivalry comes to the fore once more when Geoffrey kills his brother Fromont along with the monks at Maillezais. This leads to an almost deadly altercation between father and son that is mollified by Melusine's third and final *chastoiement* where she pleads on Geoffrey's behalf: "Et ne chaciéz point vostre filz Gieffroy de vous, car il fera un tresvaillant homme (698)" [Do not send Geoffrey away, for he will become a very worthy man] (193). Once Geoffrey realizes the gravity of his crime, he repents and makes peace with his father.

At the opposite extreme, the two pairs of elder brothers serve as an example of brotherly love and harmony. After renouncing their share of the inheritance, Urian and Guyon set off on adventure, not only to make a name for themselves, but to acquire land abroad so that their younger brothers will have a greater share of the estate. Inspired by their example, Antoine and Renaud follow suit.

The two pairs of brothers work in tandem, with the elder brother taking the initiative, often deciding the fate of the younger, who is happy to comply. After proving their mettle on the battlefield, all four sons marry and found dynasties that extend the reach of the Lusignan empire. Brotherly harmony increases at the end of the romance when six of the brothers unite in a common cause to defend the King of Alsace, and all eight of them join their father in Montserrat for a final celebration. Most of the youths follow the model of the epic or *chanson de geste* hero who fights on behalf of family, church, and country with an ultimate goal in mind. Sure of themselves, they undergo no defining moment of transformation. Only Geoffrey undergoes the specular encounter at the tomb of his ancestor, which sets the stage for his rehabilitation and reintegration into courtly society. Presine prepared the adventure for Geoffrey alone, the child with the potential for the greatest good and the greatest harm. Geoffrey embodies both positive and negative attributes, and his change of heart ends the romance on a hopeful note.

Although Melusine's ultimate redemption remains a mystery, her civilizing influence and the content of her *chastoiements* provide many lessons that would be pertinent to children. The prologue and epilogue which frame the tale create a theoretical basis for interpretation, lending it an air of authenticity and seriousness that invites the reader to ponder the material with care. The greater portion of the romance narrates detailed descriptions of military exploits on sea and land, exotic venues, lessons on strategy, and encounters with giants and the Saracens, all of which could appeal to children. There are many amusing comic scenes, for instance in Geoffrey's combat with the giant Grimaut, after which his colossal head is drawn by six oxen and sent home as a trophy. Kevin Brownlee has commented on the comic elements of the peephole scene that "de-eroticize Melusine's composite body" with her serpent's tail as thick as a herring barrel and its "playful splashing."[45] Raymond's punishment of traitors in his ancestral lands and Geoffrey's lack of tolerance for lawlessness in Ireland teach lessons on civics. The mythological, fantastic nature of the tale allows children to explore thorny questions of violence and hatred safely, provided that those who commit heinous crimes repent, reform, and go on to lead productive lives in the aftermath. Horrible's brazen cruelty and execution teach children the lesson that no one is immune from the letter of the law, not even family members. Indeed, Melusine's command to extinguish Horrible may reflect objectivity rather than lack of maternal sentiment. Despite

---

45   Kevin Brownlee, "Melusine's Hybrid Body and the Poetics of Metamorphosis," in *Melusine of Lusignan*, 76–99, at 82.

Melusine's fairy nature and her sons' mother-marks, the overriding Christian message of Melusine's farewell speech and her sons' defense of Christendom make clear that her fairy nature is wholly circumscribed within socially accepted mores. Geoffrey's fall from grace and redemption demonstrates the power of grace and sends a message of hope to those who have gone astray. Jean d'Arras' narrative represents the devastation that the rebelliousness of youth can create, but resolves that rebelliousness within suitable boundaries.

CHAPTER 11

The Promise of (Un)Happiness in Thüring von Ringoltingen's *Melusine*

Simone Pfleger

Die Jungfrauw sprach: ‚Reymund / du solt mir zum ersten schweren bey Gott unnd seinem Leichnam / daß du mich zu einem Ehelichen Gemahel nemmen / und an keinem Sambstag mir nimmer nachfragen / noch mich ersuchen wöllest / weder durch dich selbs / noch jemand anderem günnen / gehelen / verschaffen / noch dich lassen darauff weisen / daß du mich denn immer ersuchst / wo ich sey / was ich thu oder schaff / sondern mich den gantzen Tag unbekümmert lassen wöllest.'[1]

[The maiden spoke: "Reymund, swear to me by God and his dead body that you will take me as your lawful spouse and that you will neither ask after my whereabouts nor look for me yourself or through somebody else. Do not let anybody convince you to look where I might be or what I might do, but you should leave me alone the entire day."][2]

These words uttered by Melusine, the central character in Thüring von Ringoltingen's *Melusine*—originally published in 1456, which he translated into German from Coudrette's *Le Roman de Mélusine* published around 1401 in verse form—set the stage for a tale that presents a wide range of tensions, transformations, and transgressions epitomized by Melusine's Christian values, her aristocratic lineage, her stunning beauty, her love story, and her marriage.[3]

---

1 Thürung von Ringoltingen, *Melusine – In der Fassung des Buchs der Liebe (1587)* (Stuttgart: Reclam, 1991), 14. Page numbers follow in parentheses.

2 Unless otherwise indicated, all translations are the author's.

3 Although Melusine's physical appearance, the love story, and her marriage with Reymund are important aspects that set into motion the shifts and changes in the narrative, Melusine's moral and ethical standards, which are heavily influenced by her religiousness, function as the connector to all these other motifs. From the very first encounter between Reymund and Melusine, it becomes apparent that she perceives being a good Christian not only to be a desirable trait, which she emphasizes when meeting Reymund for the first time, but also to be an attribute that communicates to him what kind of values she upholds and cherishes. She further insists that Reymund must swear by God when promising not to see her on Saturdays, in order to convey his integrity and sincerity.

To all of this must be added a genealogy of broken marriage oaths as well as the conflict with the reality of her shape-shifting nature as a woman who gives birth to eight sons who all display physical abnormalities: one or three eyes instead of two, hairy marks, or deformed mouth and ears, and one of whom even kills his brother. Through its asynchronicity, Thüring's narrative foregrounds the relationship between Reymund's "Eyd und Trew an ihr [Melusine]" [oath and faith in her (Melusine)] (14), and the notions of personal as well as genealogical "groß leyd und jammer" [great pain and sorrow] (14). It is clear that *Melusine* is not simply a story about secrecy, broken promises, and violations of contracts, but also about the destabilization and transgression of normative ideas of happiness.

What follows is a queer[4] reading of Thüring's narrative, in particular of the protagonists Reymund and Melusine, exploring the promise of (un)happiness that is embedded in Reymund's marriage oath as well as Melusine's secret. As a point of departure, the interpretation will be based on the theoretical framework developed by Sara Ahmed in *The Promise of Happiness*, a provocative and innovative approach to the notion of happiness as a social good, and a critique of the correlation between happiness and the virtuous life within a (hetero) normative economic, cultural, and political framework.[5] The examination pivots on the implications of the marriage promise, the mystery of Melusine's absence on Saturdays, and the significance of female corporeal malleability in dialogue with Ahmed's concept of happiness. The investigation will reveal and concomitantly destabilize and transgress the heteronormative narrative of personal and genealogical happiness, which traditionally centers on the idea of proximity. While traditional wedlock implies that happiness ensues from the physical, emotional, and spiritual closeness of the partners, Melusine's corporeal hybridity, its secret, and the necessity of Reymund's absence on Saturdays prevent conventional nearness. Rather, the marriage oath functions as a disruptive force that does not exclusively extend a promise of normatively conceived happiness and joy and, in so doing, points to what is at stake when over-valorizing such norms: that is, the possibility of nontraditional happiness or unhappiness as an alternative way of being in the world.

Thüring von Ringoltingen's *Melusine* is a genealogical narrative of three generations: Melusine's parents, Melusine and her sisters, and Reymund and

---

4 The term *queer* is used here as an umbrella term to refer to any "identities and behaviors [that are] seen as out of the ordinary, unusual, odd, eccentric." Brett Beemyn and Mickey Eliason, *Queer Studies – A Lesbian, Gay, Bisexual, and Transgender Anthology* (New York: New York University Press, 1996), 5.

5 Sara Ahmed, *The Promise of Happiness* (Durham: Duke University Press, 2010).

Melusine's sons. The reader is introduced to Melusine and Reymund when the latter accidentally kills his uncle and then, when wandering distraught around the woods, meets the "Edle Jungfraw" [noble maiden] (12) Melusine. She helps him to disguise his involvement in the death and promises to give herself to him as his wife under one condition: that Reymund will not "an keinem Sambstag [...] nimmer nachfragen" [not ask on any Saturday] (14) where Melusine is and what she is doing. Under oath—Reymund must "schweren bey Gott unnd seinem Leichnam" [swear by God and his dead body] (14)—she requires him to leave her "den gantzen Tag unbekümmert" [alone all day] (14). After the birth of their ten sons, Reymund's brother mocks him about Melusine's absence on Saturdays, insinuating that she is cheating on her husband, and he urges Reymund to investigate her whereabouts. Spying on her through a hole in the door of her bathroom, he observes Melusine's lower body, half snake, half woman, when he sees her sitting in a large marble bath tub in complete solitude. When provoked by the news of the death of one of his sons at the hands of one of his brothers, Reymund levels accusations at Melusine, publicly revealing her secret: "O du böse Schlang unnd schendtlicher Wurm" [Oh you evil snake and nefarious worm] (86). He breaks his promise, which in turn causes Melusine great unhappiness and forces her subsequent disappearance—she jumps out of a window, and flies away in her hybrid corporality—and also catapults Reymund, and the entire family, into despair and deep misery.

Adding to a long-standing tradition of critical scholarly engagement with *Melusine* by scholars such as Jan-Dirk Müller, Lorainne Daston, Gerhild Scholz Williams, and many others,[6] Thüring's text serves as an example of Ahmed's "unhappy archives": "an alternative history of happiness [...] considering those who are banished from it."[7] In *The Promise of Happiness*, Ahmed inquires how queer forms of subjectivity are foreclosed by a seemingly universal framework of normativity, and supports her ideas through readings of various twentieth- and twenty-first century texts.[8] She points to gaps and fissures that open between the promise and the feeling of happiness, and how traditional narratives

---

6 See Lorraine Daston, "The Nature of Nature in Early Modern Europe," *Configurations* 6, no. 2 (1998): 149–172 and Gerhild Scholz Williams, *Defining Dominion: The Discourses of Magic and Witchcraft in Early Modern France and Germany* (Ann Arbor: University of Michigan Press, 1995).

7 Ahmed, *The Promise of Happiness,* 17.

8 Ahmed applies her theoretical concept to literature and films alike and offers a reading of primary texts by Rita Mae Brown, James Gunn, Radclyffe Hall, Toni Morrison, and Virginia Woolf and films like *If These Walls Could Talk 2* (2000), *Bend it Like Beckham* (2002), and *Children of Men* (2006).

of compulsory and hegemonic normativity regarding class, race, gender, and sexuality dismiss, devalue, and illegitimize certain types of individuals. These figures—the feminist killjoy, the unhappy queer, and the melancholic migrant—discursively construct happiness outside of the "narrowing of horizons."[9] They defy the necessity to reiterate and affirm the correlation between happiness and economic, socio-political, and cultural normalcy.

What allows for an alternative—and, as Ahmed's theoretical concepts suggest, potentially queer and unhappy—reading of Thüring's text is the revelation of Melusine's hybrid body on Saturdays and the promise of Reymund's absence as part of the marriage oath. These two aspects in the relationship between Melusine and Reymund are crucial for the destabilization and deconstruction of Melusine's representation of traditional heteronormativity. Since Melusine is described as one of "drey gar schöne[r] Jungfrauwen / Hochgeboren / unnd Adelicher gestalt" [three very beautiful maidens, high-born and of noble character] (11), Reymund initially does not notice her because of his desperate state of mind after killing his uncle. She epitomizes an array of normative "Adeliche Tugend[en]" [aristocratic virtues] (12) and standards of traditional femininity: beauty, virginity, nobility, and devotion. Melusine assures Reymund during one of their initial conversations that she is "von Gottes Gnaden / und warlich ein gut Christen Mensch sey / denn [sie] glaub[t] alles das / das ein Christen Mensch sol halten und glauben" [by the grace of God truly a good Christian, because she believes everything that a Christian ought to uphold and believe] (13). She recites the Christian creed as an act of affirmation of her words. She claims that she will bring Reymund "Gut / Ehr / Glücks unnd Gelts" [land, honor, happiness and money] (12), all of which will allow him to become "glückhafftiger / mächtiger unnd reicher" [happy, powerful and rich] (12).

Based on the narrator's description of Melusine and her own words, her and Reymund's happiness appears to be associated with her physical appearance, her virtues, and her ability to influence her husband's life. If he keeps his promise, he will be rewarded with emotional well-being as well as socio-political and financial success. In this sense, she personifies what Ahmed calls a happy object: it is not one that "causes pleasure," but one that "affects us in a good way with joy."[10] This way of being affected is crucial in one's evaluation of "how bodies turn toward things"[11]—and the term *turn* is to be understood in regard

---

9   Ahmed, *The Promise of Happiness*, 61.
10   Ahmed, *The Promise of Happiness*, 23.
11   Ahmed, *The Promise of Happiness*, 23.

to Edmund Husserl's phenomenology.[12] According to Husserl, human beings are directed or oriented toward material things or other beings in the world from a standpoint that allows them to enter into a dialogue between body and object or subject. Through this dialogic relationship, the perceiver is capable of acquiring an alternative understanding of the world of objects and subjects as well as the importance of their material appearance and their influence on the human body.

Reymund's emotional distress and his "grosse Jämmerliche klag" [great miserable lament] (11) almost prevent him from noticing Melusine and the two other women standing at the fountain in the woods. In accordance with Ahmed's phenomenological approach toward happiness, and specifically toward happy objects, Melusine can be read as a happy object toward which Reymund directs or orients his sight; in other words, he *turns* toward her. Inviting her to move closer, she enters what Ahmed refers to as his "bodily horizon."[13] Both assume a particular spatial orientation: indeed, they *turn* to each other in the Husserlian sense in order to assume an orientation or a proximity that, in turn, shapes their bodies. If, as Ahmed suggests, happiness "can be described as *intentional* in the phenomenological sense (directed toward objects), as well as being *affective* (having contact with objects),"[14] then the protagonists' happiness hinges on their orientation to and contact with one another.

Combining Husserl's phenomenological line of theorizing with a reconceptualization of heteronormative happiness, Ahmed's notion of the happy object, which elicits a sense of joy and contentment as one *turns* toward it, serves as the central idea for the understanding the relationship between Reymund and Melusine. Indeed, their physical proximity not only becomes crucial for the initial construction of the female character as a happy object, but it also sets up a threat to the condition of the marriage oath which transforms Melusine into the figure of the Other:[15] the Ahmedian unhappy queer. This is a figure which society might render strange or atypical based on its own set of norms

---

12 Ahmed derives her concept from Edmund Husserl's phenomenological approach as presented in *Ideas: General Introduction to Pure Phenomenology* (1913, rpt. New York: Routledge, 2002) that elaborates on the ideal and essential structures of consciousness.

13 Ahmed, *The Promise of Happiness*, 24.

14 Ahmed, *The Promise of Happiness*, 24. Emphasis in original.

15 Various feminist scholars, such as Monique Wittig in "One Is Not Born a Woman" and Luce Irigaray's approach in *Speculum of the Other Woman*, critique the existence of a binary system that reaffirms hegemonic power relations in order to create *otherness* between individuals of a social system. Wittig, "One is Not Born a Woman," *Feminist Issues* 1, no. 2 (Winter 1981): 47–54 and Irigaray, *Speculum of the Other Woman*, trans. Gillian C. Gill (Ithaca, NY: Cornell University Press, 1985).

and values, yet is a figure that urges the reader to reconsider casting moral judgment upon Otherness.[16] Since Melusine requires Reymund's promise neither to question nor seek her whereabouts on Saturdays "weder durch [ihn] selbs / noch jemand andere[n]" [neither he himself nor anybody else] (14) and to leave her "den gantzen Tag unbekümmert" [the entire day untroubled] (14), Melusine reorients herself away from her husband. As she intentionally creates a distance between herself and Reymund, she ceases to exist within his bodily horizon during the time of her transformation. In the phenomenological sense, this distance between Reymund and Melusine transforms their happiness, a consequence which is neither intentional nor affective. If considering that happiness is causal to and contingent on the primary premise of the proximity to the happy object, then it can be deduced that a reorientation away from the happy object results in the person's becoming aimless (directed away from objects) and remote (being at distance with objects). This distance, in turn, causes unhappiness.

Working against socio-political and cultural rules and regulations of fifteenth-century society, Melusine reorients herself against rather than toward Reymund on Saturdays, leaving the realm in which she is expected to operate. This motif of Melusine's distance once a week—stepping out of the hierarchical domestic order to reside in a place that shall not be visited by anybody; not only away from her husband but also from society—creates a juxtaposition that underlines her queer nature and her causal relationship to unhappiness.

This ambiguity provides the basis for the relationship between her and Reymund and for the marriage oath, which plays a crucial role in the construction of happiness. Akin to Ahmed's argument that "happiness is promised through the proximity to certain objects"[17] and "[f]or the promise to be happy [...] one who promises must [...] keep the promise,"[18] Melusine addresses these two Ahmedian conditions for normative happiness in her speech: the close presence, or rather the lack of absence, of Melusine in Reymund's life as well as the husband's intent to keep his promise.

Considering the first stipulation—the proximity of Melusine and Reymund in each other's lives—the oath's purpose to establish and secure the couple's happiness already signals a promise of unhappiness because it requires Reymund "an keinem Sambstag [...] nimmer nachfragen / noch [ihr] ersuchen"

---

16   Ahmed, *The Promise of Happiness*, 88–90.

17   Ahmed, *The Promise of Happiness*, 29. Ahmed's use of the term *object* is not limited to the meaning of objects as being inanimate things or material goods, but also includes, for instance, "the family as a happy object" (21).

18   Ahmed, *The Promise of Happiness*, 30.

[neither to ask nor to look for her on any Saturday] (14). If, according to Ahmed, happiness is contingent on the closeness of a happy object—in this case, Melusine—then her recurring absence on Saturdays and the necessity of remaining "den gantzen Tag unbekümmert" create not only spatial but also emotional distance between Reymund and Melusine. This signals a potential source of unhappiness, or rather a form of nontraditional happiness that exists outside of the normative social structures of early modern marriage and family life.

In this sense, the couple's mutual happiness is conditional on Reymund's ability to keep his oath and to acknowledge and accept Melusine's absence one day per week. Otherwise he "solt [sie] warlich verlieren / und [sie] nimmermehr gesehen / und es wirdt darnach [seinen] Kindern und Erben fast mißgehen / und werden abnemmen an Land und Leuten / an Ehr und an Gut" [should truly lose her and never see her again, and his children and heirs will suffer and will lose land and people, army and estate] (14). This explicit vision of his future, presented in a commentary by the narrator that follows Melusine's speech, allows for the assertion that the text hints early on at personal as well as genealogical despair. The promise of happiness turns into the condition of impossibility.

Furthermore, the necessity of absence and her conscious acts of alienation also serve as a foil for the destabilization of her initial presentation of heteronormativity, since Melusine is only capable of functioning within a social realm that continuously marginalizes her. Thüring's depiction of Melusine constructs both her identity and corporality on the pillars of the most significant hegemonic patriarchal institutions of that time: the Catholic Church. In highlighting her devotion to religion, she affirms her unquestioned faith in a God "der alle ding vermag" [who is almighty] (13), and she defines her body as "natural"[19] and Christian. If understood literally as well as metaphorically, Melusine's claim "von Christlichem Blut [zu] kommen" [to be of Christian blood] (13) insinuates a genealogical connection to Jesus Christ[20] and a body with all the human features necessary for blood to course through her veins. In so doing, she affirms and solidifies her faith in God, the almighty unfathomable Creator.

---

19   The quotation marks are to suggest that this notion is inadequate, and based on a process of socialization rooted in the essentialist distinction between "natural" and "normal" and "unnatural" and "not normal" as representations of hegemonic discursive framework.

20   Hildegard Elisabeth Keller notes that Melusine's alterity and "latente Doppelnatur" [latent double nature] parallel Jesus Christ's "Mensch- und Gottnatur" [man and God-nature]. "Berner Samstagsgeheimnisse: Die Vertikale als Erzählformel in der *Melusine*," *Beiträge zur Geschichte der deutschen Sprache und Literatur* 127, no. 2 (2005): 208–238.

Akin to Ahmed's observation of the denial of queerness in literature in order to avoid "the 'promotion' of the social value of queer lives, or an attempt to influence readers to become queer,"[21] Thüring appears to adhere to an analogous principle. Even though he portrays a non-human and thus queer Melusine[22] who, to the contemporary reader, operates outside of socio-politically and culturally constructed and accepted norms and hierarchies, Thüring nonetheless uses her as an agent to highlight as well as promote the values of Christianity as the means to both individual and collective happiness. It is precisely her queerness that does not allow her character to initiate the crucial transformation of body and soul that will turn her into a complete human being with a mortal soul without the aid of dying in a Christian marriage.

In her speech, Melusine explicitly emphasizes the connection between "Leib unnd Seel" [body and soul] (88). She relates happiness to dying a "natural" or "normal" Christian death, she "wer natürlich gestorben / als ein ander Weib [...] und wer [ihre] Seel von [ihr]em Leib gewißlich zu der ewigen freuden kommen" [would have died naturally, like any other wife [...] and her soul would have surely departed her body to receive eternal joy] (88). However, her hybrid body chains her soul to her body—"nun so muß mein Leib unnd Seel zu dieser stund hie in leyden unnd pein / bleiben biß an den Jüngsten Tag" [now in this very hour, my body and soul must remain here until Judgment Day] (88)—and she is forced to accept both physical as well as spiritual agony and suffering until Judgment Day. Her future personal as well as genealogical unhappiness functions, as Ahmed points out, "to secure a moral distinction between good and bad lives."[23] In this sense, Thüring establishes a discursive framework that links happiness with corporal "normalness" and Christianity; queerness must be overcome in order to live a fulfilled and happy life.

However, Ahmed urges her reader to develop "an active disbelief in the necessary alignment of the happy with the good, or even in the moral transparency of the good itself."[24] With this in mind, the initial encounter at the fountain already implies that Melusine, phenomenologically and discursively, turns against the traditional, normative image of women. Her partial omniscience regarding Reymund's involvement in the accident with his uncle—"ich weiß deine noht und klage / und das ungefell / das dir zu dieser stund an deinem Herren und Vettern widerfahren ist" [I know about your misfortune and lament and the tragedy that happened to your lord and cousin in this hour]

---

21   Ahmed, *The Promise of Happiness*, 88.

22   A similar argument can be made about her mother and her sisters as well.

23   Ahmed, *The Promise of Happiness*, 89.

24   Ahmed, *The Promise of Happiness*, 89.

(12)—evokes the impression that she is not like other women. She possesses a certain power that allows her to be other or more than just human, or, in the words of Lorainne Daston, something "non-natural." In her article, Daston proposes four different non-natural types: "supernatural, preternatural, artificial, unnatural."[25]

In keeping with Daston's categories, Gerhild Scholz Williams classifies Melusine as a preternatural being and argues that she, "wie die ganze Schöpfung, gehorcht wiederum der Gewalt und dem Willen Gottes" [like God's entire creation, obeys in turn the power and the will of God].[26] In this vein, her type of alterity—a form of being different or Other—remains within the discursive framework of human understanding and thus makes her interactions with natural people possible.

Examining Melusine's Otherness from a different discursive angle, Daston's categorization of the female character as preternatural is reminiscent of a queer-theoretical approach toward subject identity. As one of its primary goals, queer theory explores the tensions and contradictions of heteronormativity and queerness which circulate in contemporary discourse. Michael Warner points out in *The Trouble with Normal* that the term "queer" draws attention to the stigmatized aspects of daily life which trouble socially constructed normalcy.[27] As a conceptual approach, queer is a strategy of questioning, destabilizing, and disturbing the positions and practices of traditional hegemony. As a label—a semantic marker—it can reference and affirm fixed identities and practices that are not hegemonic.

Thus, a queer individual can be understood as one who, as social scientist Richard Jenkins notes, defies society's practice of "attempt[ing] to impose concepts that are too straight-edged on [a person's] messy reality."[28] Crucial in this portrayal of queer individuals is that their existence is a necessary factor in the construction, stabilization, and perpetuation of heteronormativity within the

---

25   Daston, "The Nature of Nature," 153. According to Daston's theory, these four terms also define *ad negativo* what is natural, since early modern Europeans did not think in dichotomous concepts, such as "nature versus nurture, nature versus culture" (153), but rather positioned the natural in opposition with the supernatural.

26   Gerhild Scholz Williams and Alexander Schwarz, "Wundersame Dynastie: Interdikte und Verträge in Jean d'Arras' *Melusine*" in *Existentielle Vergeblichkeit*, ed. Anne Betten, Hartmut Steinecke, and Horst Wenzel (Berlin: E. Schmidt, 2003), 40.

27   Michael Warner, *The Trouble with Normal: Sex, Politics, and the Ethics of Queer Life* (Cambridge, MA: Harvard University Press, 2000).

28   Richard Jenkins, *Rethinking Ethnicity: Arguments and Explorations* (London: SAGE, 2008), 26.

social realm. Thus, Melusine's alterity constructs her as a hybrid being who strives for and partakes in cultural and social rituals, but who will forever remain an Other, an unhappy queer.

Melusine epitomizes a corporal hybridity that Thüring presents to the reader through the eyes of Reymund, who spies on Melusine in her private space one Saturday:

> sie war oberhalb dem Nabel ein schön Weiblich Bild / und von Leib und Angesicht gantz schön / aber von dem Nabel hinab war sie ein grosser langer und ungehewrer Wurmschwantz / als blaw Lasur / und mit weisser Silberfarb tröpfflich unter einander gesprengt / als denn ein Schlang gemeinlich gestallt ist
>
> [she was above the navel a beautiful woman with a stunning body and facial features, but below the navel she had a monstrous, long worm tail with a blue glaze and silvery white spots as is common for snakes] (71)

While her non-human features are described as disturbing, grotesque, or "ungehewrer" [monster], the human parts of her body still reflect beauty and attractiveness.

In regard to Melusine's hybrid corporal identity, Kevin Brownlee insists that her physical monstrosity—the aforementioned worm tail with blue glaze and silvery white spots—depicts "Melusine as a female fairy monster [that] is de-eroticized, while Melusine as courtly human lady is re-eroticized."[29] While grounding his analysis in the binary oppositions of privacy and court, monster and lady, fairy and human in order to construct her as an erotic being, he does not take into account the act which reveals her hybrid body to both Reymund and the reader.

In keeping with what Albrecht Classen titles the "voyeur motive,"[30] the look upon Melusine through a peephole as she sits in her bathtub with her snake tail does not, as Brownlee claims, de-eroticize her. Rather, the scene highlights a phallocentric hegemony that allows Reymund to exercise power. He drills a hole in to the door with his sword, which can also be interpreted as a highly phallic object that penetrates the boundaries Melusine has erected to protect

---

29   Kevin Brownlee, "Melusine's Hybrid Body and the Poetics of Metamophosis," in *Melusine of Lusignan: Founding Fiction in Late Medieval France*, ed. Donald Maddox and Sara Sturm-Maddox (Athens, GA: University of Georgia Press, 1996), 76–99, at 84.

30   Classen, "Love and Fear of the Foreign: Thüring von Ringoltingen's *Melusine* (1456): A Xenological Analysis," *Daphnis* 33, no. 1–2 (2004): 97–113.

her secret.[31] By piercing the door, Reymund assumes a type of physical agency that contrasts, or complements, the authority of the marriage oath.[32]

Assuming a position of social and cultural power when watching Melusine, Reymund's act appears to reiterate the concept of the male gaze, specifically one of looking and being looked at, which Laura Mulvey claims defines and asserts gender-based binary structures.[33] In regard to Thüring's *Melusine*, Mulvey's concept not only speaks to Classen's proposed "voyeur motive," but it also serves as the basis for an analysis of the female character representing an Ahmedian unhappy queer. By looking at her, Reymund turns his wife into an object of display, and in so doing exposes and affirms her queer corporality not only to his own eyes, but also to the readers'.

This presentation of Melusine's body is further emphasized when Thüring's text appears as part of a collection of stories in the *Buch der Liebe* (1587), published by one of the most important printers and publishers in the sixteenth century, Sigmund Feyerabend.[34] Created 131 years after the publication of Thüring's text, 22 commissioned woodcarvings that are included in the book not only serve as a visual confirmation of the artist's interpretation many years later, but they are also included in the Reclam version of *Melusine* available today. Hence, an unbiased interpretation of the text—completely disregarding the images during the reading process—can be deemed impossible when the working basis of analysis is the Reclam edition which uses a woodcarving of Melusine as its cover picture. In this sense, the images are worth including in the analysis of the narrative because they visualize selected scenes.

---

31   Maria Frangos argues in "'The Shame of All Her Kind': A Genealogy of Female Monstrosity and Metamorphosis from the Middle Ages Through Early Modern" (PhD diss., UC California, Santa Cruz, 2008) that Reymund's sword takes on a double function: it is a cutting instrument as well as a phallic object used to pierce the iron door to Melusine's chamber (75).

32   Despite being an oral promise, rather than a written contract, medieval society nonetheless assigned a high degree of power and authority to the marriage oath based on the fact that it was a commitment made in front of a priest, a congregation, and God.

33   Mulvey suggests that women are objectified in many Hollywood movies of the 1950s and 60s because of the spectators' identification with the male protagonist's gaze. Integrating psychoanalytical Freudian and Lacanian theories into her concept of the male gaze, she establishes a highly gendered system that interprets the position of the spectator as phallocentric, sadistic, and voyeuristic. Mulvey, "Visual Pleasure and Narrative Cinema," *Screen* 16, no. 3 (1975): 6–18.

34   See Thomas Veitschegger, *Das 'Buch der Liebe' (1587): ein Beitrag zur Buch- und Verlagsgeschichte des 16. Jahrhunderts: mit einem bibliograpgischen Anhang* (Hamburg: Verlag Dr. Kovač, 1991). See Albrecht Classen's contribution to this volume for a discussion of Feyerbrand's collection, specifically the series of woodcuts illustrating the *Melusine* narrative.

The frame of the image is oval-shaped, and appears to insinuate the peep-hole incident. Melusine, placed in the center of the picture,[35] wears only a type of hat with a veil that is typical for courtly women of that time, while the rest of her upper body is bare. Her left arm is crossed in front of her chest in a way that covers part of her breasts. The transition from human torso to snake tail happens just below her pelvis, so that the image does not have to expose her human genitalia. The snake tail loops and coils a few times, underlining its length and—cut with great precision by the artist—its many scales.

The portrayal of Melusine partially covering her breasts is reminiscent of sculptures and paintings of ancient goddesses: of women covering some parts of their bodies, epitomizing classic beauty.[36] With this in mind, the woodcut appeals to these ideals of flawless and quintessential corporal perfection. The depiction of Melusine presents both Reymund and the reader with ambiguity and an antagonistic struggle between experiencing desire for Melusine—as well as a desire to look at her—and feeling revulsion "da er nun diese greußli-che und gar frembde Geschöpff an seinem Gemahel sahe" [since he saw only this horrifying and completely strange being in the stead of his wife] (71). In this sense, she becomes a queer object of display: namely, one that is desirable, but one deemed "unnatural" due to her non-human, hybrid corporality.

Mocked and insulted by his brother, Reymund cannot resist the temptation to inquire into her whereabouts. Knowingly and willingly ignoring the prom-ise he made to Melusine, he also publicly denies her ambivalent corporality as both desirable and repulsive. He reveals her to be a "böse Schlang unnd schendtlicher Wurm / der Samen noch all [ihr] Geschlecht thut nimmer gut" [vicious snake und a nefarious worm whose seed is detrimental to the entire lineage] (86). In identifying and, in so doing, transforming her from a happy object into an unhappy queer, Reymund's public humiliation ultimately makes an alternative (and potentially queer) happiness in *Melusine* impossible. Had

---

35   The background of the wood carving also depicts Melusine's two sisters, Meliora with her castle and her "Sperber," and Palentina on the mountain with the invincible monster. While these two figures hold significance for both the narrative and the overall picture, they will not be discussed in further detail. Classen discusses this image in his contribu-tion to this volume.

36   The representation in the *Buch der Liebe* appears to be similar the idealized female hu-man body, which, based on the standards for ancient Greek sculptures, is curvy and lush, with full hips and smaller, firm breasts. In particular, the description of Aphrodite of Kni-dos in Christine Mitchell Havelock's *The Aphrodite of Knidos and Her Successors: A His-torical Review of the Female Nude in Greek Art* (Ann Arbor: University of Michigan Press, 1995) bears a resemblance to the woodcarving (11–13).

he kept his wife's hybridity and queerness "heimlich und verschwiegen [...]
so hette es nicht geschadt" [secret and discreet [...] it would not have harmed
(her)] (87). Not only would she not have suffered any misery, but his "grosse
verrätherey unnd falschheit / falsche Zung / und zornige grimmige Rede" [im-
mense betrayal and falsity, lies, and furious speech] (87) also affect Reymund's
happiness. She tells him, "so muß es dir an Leib und Gut / an Glück unnd an
Selde / unnd sonderlich an deinen Ehren mißgehen" [your body and health,
your happiness and your soul, and especially your honor must suffer] (87),
pointing out the gravity and magnitude of his actions.

If, according to Ahmed, "[u]nhappiness might involve feelings that get directed in a certain way, and even give the narrative its direction,"[37] Reymund's
announcement of his wife's hybridity and queerness causes unhappiness and
is necessary for the narrative to advance toward Melusine's unhappiness as a
logical consequence of his deed. In this sense, her queerness excludes her from
the socio-political and cultural realm, and it is ultimately and permanently affirmed as she undergoes her metamorphosis into a spirit of the air.

After instructing Reymund that he needs to perform certain tasks—kill his
son Horibel, divide the family estate among his sons in certain way, and pray
for her soul—she leaps toward the window and "schoß also zum Fenster auß /
unnd was zur stundt eines Augenblicks / under dem Gürtel widerumb ein fein-
dtlicher ungehewrer langer Wurm worden [...] [und] schoß durch den Lufft
schnelle" [leaped out the window, transformed from that moment on into a
hostile, monstrous, long worm from below the belt [...] and darted through the
air] (92) before she vanishes forever. This ultimate transformation and disappearance function in various different ways in the narrative: they affirm and
solidify Melusine's queer hybridity, and cause excruciating pain and sorrow
"daß in [Reymund] darnach nimmermehr kein Mensch frölich sahe / biß an
sein ende" [that nobody saw him (Reymund) happy henceforth until the day
he died] (93). This results in a redefinition and reappropriation of hope and
happiness in regard to the past, present, and future.

"Queer pessimism," as Ahmed points out, "matters as a pessimism *about* a
certain kind of optimism, as a refusal to be optimistic about 'the right things'
in the right kind of way."[38] This concept serves when looking at the murder of
Horibel. In an attempt to alleviate his grief and pain, one of the servants reminds Reymund of Melusine's last words. While the killing is not an optimistic
deed, in the sense that it brutally and unlawfully alters the genealogical order,

---

37   Ahmed, *The Promise of Happiness*, 89.
38   Ahmed, *The Promise of Happiness*, 160. Emphasis in original.

it is nonetheless "the right thing" to do. Hence, Horibel functions as a tool that opens the possibility to an alternative future, namely a hopeful and queerly (un)happy one.

Overall, an attempt has been made to represent what Ahmed herself set out to do with her work: open the existing scholarly discourse to different investigations and to embrace "the struggle against happiness as a necessity."[39] The focus of the investigation has been the relationship of the protagonists, Melusine and Reymund, and in particular the implications of the young man's marriage oath. The present reading extrapolates from the queer-theoretical, phenomenological approach to normative ideals of happiness conducted by Sara Ahmed in order to point to what is at stake when Melusine's female corporeal malleability and her absence on Saturdays disrupt traditional notions of marriage and heteronormative narratives of personal and genealogical happiness. Read through an Ahmedian lens, the narrative suggests that unhappiness destabilizes the coercive force of conventional happiness and potentially *turns* individuals toward alternative futures that allow for a queer way of being in the world.

While the analysis at hand focuses primarily on the construction of unhappiness between Melusine and Reymund, further investigation of different aspects, such as the examination of Melusine's parents as well as her son, need to be conducted to broaden the spectrum of implications of the term "(un)happy" in Thüring von Ringoltingen's *Melusine*. In this vein, narrative worlds of new and potentially queer possibilities can provide points of departure for readers not only to think about the subjects in the story world, but also to critically interrogate their own participation in the creation of a value system which equates heteronormativity with happiness. In lieu of excluding from the social order those individuals who do not follow the straight path of and to happiness but turn sideways, away, and around again, this present investigation of human interaction proposes a shift that will broaden the field of vision to recognize and respect precisely those who have decided to take a turn in a direction that has not been explored yet—a queerly unhappy or an unhappy queer one, so to speak.

---

39   Ahmed, *The Promise of Happiness*, 222.

CHAPTER 12

Half Lady, Half Serpent: Melusine's Monstrous Body and the Discourse of Romance

Angela Jane Weisl

In *Women's Power in Late Medieval Romance,* Amy N. Vines talks about the heroines of romance as models of "cultural, intellectual, and social authority."[1] In Vines's view, romances function didactically to teach women the operations of power as well as instruct men in the dangers of ignoring or rejecting female authority. Although *Melusine* is not one of Vines's examples, it is easy to see in this narrative an engagement with the dynamics of power, authority, and gender as they emerge in the courtly romance. At its most basic, the romance creates a rhetoric in which women acquire power within the erotic relationship: the power to consent or reject the lovers' advances, so often cast as the power to "save or spill," to give life or effect death. That this is metaphoric is obvious, and that this power is tenuous is equally clear; the Wife of Bath's contention that women most desire "sovereynetee / as wel over hir housbounde as over hir love / and for to been in maistrye him above"[2] [sovereignty over her husband and her love, and to have mastery over him] shows how little the sovereignty that romance offers is sustained once the legal and political discourses of marriage are enacted. Courtly romance is designed as a civilizing influence; the vast number of fights, battles, and jousts, often described in quite graphic terms, reveal both its connection to the epic whose narrative form it adopts, and how much the love, honor, and chivalry that inform the romance act as a force to contain masculine violence, both by elevation (through chivalric ideals) and distraction (love service). The courtly contexts of these stories show readers of romance that power dynamics—the cultural, intellectual, and social authority that Vines names—often extend from the erotic power of women in romance. Both because of the early romance writers' desire for female patronage and because of real conditions, women in romance often

---

1   Amy N. Vines, *Women's Power in Late Medieval Romance* (Woodbridge, Suffolk: D. S. Brewer, 2011), 3.

2   Geoffrey Chaucer, "The Wife of Bath's Tale," in *The Riverside Chaucer,* ed. Larry D. Benson (Boston: Houghton Mifflin, 1987). *Canterbury Tales* Fragment III, lines 1038–1040.

occupy positions of authority, whether as queens, princesses, or, sometimes, fairies or sorceresses. Melusine, in both Jean d'Arras' and Coudrette's versions and the Middle English translations of them, is a lightning rod for these power dynamics. The center of the romance and its genealogical and geographical purpose, Melusine is both the desired erotic object of the romance and the controller of its world, a world she herself builds. At the same time, the texts' anxieties about her power run rampantly against her, creating multiple hybridities in both Melusine's body and the text itself which destabilize and expose the courtly romance values at their center.

The figure of Melusine has a long history, medieval and contemporary. From the earliest legends to multiple continental European translations to her appearance in A. S. Byatt's *Possession* and the Starbucks™ logo, Melusine has shown a remarkable ability to endure, to speak to a range of audiences over a long span of time. To some extent, her form might account for her popularity. Clearly, the half human, half water spirit is a potent symbol of varying kinds of hybridity; as part of the medieval taxonomy of monsters, the melusine is often classified with other mermaids, echidna, and sirens.[3] At every level, Melusine produces a slippery form, from the micro-example of her hybrid body, to her complex and multi-vocal history made of competing histories and meanings, to her appearance in a variety of stories.

Textually she is best known from Jean d'Arras' *Roman de Mélusine* written ca.1393, something of a hybrid itself, offering both a romance plot and a chronicle narrative of the founding of the dynasty of Lusignan. If the text's political function appears to be a legitimization of Jean's patron, Jean de Berry's military appropriation of Lusignan, it simultaneously serves to legitimize that lineage by lending it prestige and authority through its foundational narrative. All the legitimation asked of the text is created through Melusine herself; after his responsibility for his lord's death early in the narrative, her husband, Raimondin, is incapable of doing anything. Melusine not only builds the place but also builds the generations (and returns to forsee their deaths, retaining

---

3   David Williams, *Deformed Discourse: The Function of the Monster in Mediaeval Thought and Literature* (Montreal: McGill and Queens University Press, 1996), 183–90. Williams points out that the melusine differs from other water spirits in her association with fountains rather than natural bodies of water, but that she shares with other ophidian earth/water hybrids the tendency to lure men to destruction and to give birth to monstrous offspring of varying kinds. His definition of melusines is drawn from Paracelsus, further discussed in Melissa Ridley Elmes's contribution to this volume; but see also Ana Pairet's chapter "Polycorporality and Heteromorphia," in which she challenges the definition of hybrid as it applies to Melusine. Frederika Bain offers a useful overview of the evolving depiction of biform women across the medieval period in her chapter, "The Tail of Melusine."

her connection to the genealogy so important in the narrative). She also does all the work to make sure the genealogy operates the way it is meant to, such as requesting that Horrible, the violent and dangerously disruptive son, be killed. For all her embodiment of the text's goals, she is still constructed as monstrous, at least in part because these roles diverge from the kinds of power allowed women in the text's other genre, the romance.

While women's power in romance is not simply limited to the erotic, Melusine seems to extend her authority well beyond convention. She is a builder of cities and a producer of sons. She embodies both private and public productivity; in a sense, she inhabits all textual roles, undoing the normative gender assumptions of romance and the institutions it upholds. Her power is erotic, economic, productive, and social; more importantly, it renders Raimondin passive. While romance antecedents certainly show this to be conventional within the love service—examples abound, from Marie de France's "Lanval" to the many stories of Lancelot and Guenevere—Melusine never restores Raimondin to any form of masculine authority. As a result, she becomes a monstrous gender hybrid, made visual in the dichotomy between her beautiful feminine body and her powerful serpent's tail.

Melusine's body figures the romance dichotomies represented in this text and its other medieval analogues, including Coudrette's French version (ca.1401) and the two Middle English translations from the sixteenth century. These texts are also hybrids, driven by multiple sets of assumptions that often conflict. Donald Maddox and Sara Sturm-Maddox, speaking speficially of Jean's text, although their observation applies equally to all versions, note:

> The fascination that the *Roman de Mélusine* holds for us modern readers lies in part in its complex play with the conventions of medieval fictional and historical writing [...] On a variety of levels, however, the text proposes an amalgam of disparate elements: of fiction, history, and genealogy, in its account of the founding of the illustrious dynasty of Lusignan and its innovate appropriation of Crusade narratives; of human and fairy, in the marriage of its two central protagonists; of human and monstrous, in the corporeal metamorphoses of its heroine and the grotesque marks borne by her progeny; of folk belief and Christianity; and of romance and epic conventions. The different components of the textual amalgam do not always seem to sit easily together, exacting the reader's vigilance and reflection in formulation of a response.[4]

---

4   Donald Maddox and Sara Sturm-Maddox, "Introduction: Melusine at 600," in *Melusine of Lusignan: Founding Fiction in Late Medieval France,* ed. Donald Maddox and Sara Sturm-Maddox (Athens, GA: University of Georgia Press, 1996), 1–11, at 2.

Maddox and Sturm-Maddox here offer an incisive reading of the narrative hybridities in *Melusine*; Melusine's hybrid body becomes a mirror of the text, as she, like the work itself, attempts to embody multiple competing discourses. All the "medieval fictional and historical" narrative assumptions that the authors name combine in Melusine herself. The text presents her as a hybrid body that deconstructs a series of binaries—between the animal and the human, the courtly and the erotic, the feminine and the masculine—ultimately putting forward a series of anxieties about identities that serve to define the woman in narrative practice and medieval life.

There is nothing new in saying that women in power make men anxious; this could be said now just as easily in the Middle Ages, but the notion of power in the text is as ambivalent as Melusine herself, anxious and celebratory, although the level varies between the different versions, with a greater sense of anxiety in the French than the Middle English adaptations. To the extent that the genealogical program serves to legitmize the power of a particular French family, this makes sense; the English version's stake in that side of the story being somewhat less, they are able to cast Melusine as a courtly ideal with an unfortunate body. That said, this dichotomy between legitimation and anxiety is what is distinct, possibly unique, about *Melusine*; that anxiety about female power and authority balances against the ways she embodies the values of the text (genealogy, authority, expansion, and growth), creating both an unresolvable center and unresolvable margins. Looking at the texts themselves, Melusine's complex position and the tensions it creates are represented on their pages; she is the titular figure in the romance, yet it is the stories of her sons and their destinies that occupy the center and the largest number of pages of the story. Her narrative might be said to be the frame or the margins—her backstory is revealed at the start in Jean's version and at the end in Coudrette's—and yet she is the preoccupying concern of the narrative and the critical tradition that follows. She demands the most attention while not occupying the most space.

Melusine's narrative presence and absence is another source of textual hybridity and, perhaps, anxiety; women in romance are often motivators for men's actions of varying kinds, and their presence can be both central and marginal. At one extreme lie Morgan le Fay and Guenevere in *Sir Gawain and the Green Knight*. Morgan's desire to frighten Guenevere to death is the motivation for all that takes place in the story, and yet each figure occupies very little textual space; as Sheila Fisher notes, "her agency appears to be the trick [...] that provides a seemingly *dea ex machina* ending for this intricately structured romance," adding, however, that most critics make very little of her, creating a "deliberate marginalization in the text."[5] Whether the source of men's quests or the motivations for their actions, other romance heroines are central to the text while still inhabiting these same margins. Melusine, however, resists this marginalization at the same time she embodies it, both exposing and challenging romance convention. Even as she sends her sons off to occupy their own narrative spaces, she remains the center of readers' interest and attention, an engagement that is produced by her inhabiting multiple roles.

Melusine appears in multiple forms within the narrative. She is the desired lady of courtly romance; she is the builder of cities and the founder of dynasties; she is an ideal wife and mother; she is a hybrid and, finally, a dragon. Occupying multiple forms and functions, she embodies a series of models of femininity that reflect both medieval practical reality and masculine anxiety, ultimately suggesting that it is the narrative function of the feminine to inhabit a series of dualities. In A. S. Byatt's novel *Possession*, Christabel LaMotte, a fictional poet writing a version of the Melusine story, converses with her niece Sabine de Kercoz:

> She said, in Romance women's two natures can be reconciled. I asked, which two natures, and she said, men saw women as double beings, enchantresses and demons or innocent angels.
> "Are all women double?" I asked her.
> "I did not say that," she said. "I said all men see women as double. Who knows what Melusina was in her freedom with no eyes on her?"[6]

Although Byatt and, by extension, Christabel are working with a different, post-medieval definition of romance, their articulation still proves helpful in interrogating Melusine's hybrid position within the medieval romance. After all, as Fisher and Halley note, "to write women" in the Middle Ages "was to refer not to women but to men—to desire not relationship with women, but the tradition of male textual activity, and, by extension, of male and social and political privilege."[7] Melusine's doubleness, therefore, is a function of masculine inscription, which sees her both as what it desires and what it fears.

---

5   Sheila Fisher, "Taken Men and Token Women in *Sir Gawain and the Green Knight*," in *Seeking the Woman in Late Medieval and Early Renaissance Writing*, ed. Shelia Fisher and Janet E. Halley (Knoxville, TN: University of Tennessee Press, 1989): 71–105, at 71.

6   A. S. Byatt, *Possession: A Romance* (New York: Vintage, 1991), 404.

7   Fisher and Halley, "The Lady Vanishes: The Problem of Women's Absence in Late Medieval and Renaissance Texts," in *Seeking the Woman*, 1–17, at 4.

Melusine is inherently productive: she builds castles, manors, monasteries; she produces an entire population of vassals for Raimondin; she controls water; she makes feasts and tournaments happen; and she gives birth to many sons, essentially assuring the preservation of the lineage, cities, and wealth she has created. While all these productions are lauded in the texts, once her body has been revealed, they become sources of anxiety because of their double association of magic and phallic power figured in her powerful tail. Melusine's productions are also hybrid; they are highly quotidian in themselves, but their origin is not. As Sara Sturm-Maddox notes, "In that series of trials and triumphs, there is of course much that is 'marvelous,' much that reminds the reader that Melusine is indeed different from mortals. Springs appear where there were none before; towers, fortresses, whole cities are built and populated overnight; fabulous wealth is displayed; children bearing strange marks are born to the couple."[8] Melusine combines domestic productivity and fertility with dynastic productivity; her actual increase in children is matched with the material increase of lands and goods that she brings to her marriage. While these productions add significantly to her courtly value in romance terms, they also constitute her outside the traditional roles assigned to heroines (as opposed to marginal figures like Morgan le Fay) in that genre.

In their first statement on medieval women and power, Mary Erler and Maryanne Kowaleski commented, "Contemporaries certainly acknowledged both the potential power that women could wield and the variety of female approaches to power"[9] as well as noting that

> Female motives in seeking power, as well as the ends to which this power was put, could of course vary widely. While the family dominates here also [...] we should not underestimate the frequency with which self-interest lay behind women's pursuit of influence [...] The presence of strong motivation or intensely desired end was in itself empowering because of the force and direction it gave to women's lives. On the other hand, medieval women may frequently have defined self-interest in terms of their relationships with men.[10]

---

8   Sara Sturm-Maddox, "Crossed Destinies: Narrative Programs in the *Roman de Mélusine*," in *Melusine of Lusignan*, 12–31, at 20.

9   Mary C. Erler and Maryanne Kowaleski, eds., "Introduction," in *Women and Power in the Middle Ages* (Athens, GA: University of Georgia Press, 1988), 1–17, at 11.

10   Ehler and Kowaleski, *Women and Power*, 10–11.

Even power itself emerges as a hybrid, a combination of influence, self-articulation, and ability. While the second may be the ineffable, Melusine in her bath with no eyes on her, Melusine moves between the other two; her influence may be seen in her ability to move Raimondin to follow her wishes, whether marrying her under the conditions she proposes, helping him fulfill his prophesy in Jean's version, or sending him off to reclaim his inheritance. She influences her sons' actions as well. Her power manifests as ability in her production of both children and cities. Melusine has none of Raimondin's passivity; her desires result in actions.

In using her influence to lure Raimondin, Melusine is certainly acting in self-interest, as his promise is designed to break the curse cast upon her by Pressine and allow her to die a mortal; this motivation and desired end define Melusine's self-interest in relation to her husband. However, like all elements of this work, any single reading is insufficient, as Melusine's power—constituted both by the male-constructed rules of *fin'amors* which place the lady over the man in love and by rules of political power which constitute power in those who control the largest amount of lands and numbers of people, and who find the means to retain and add to that power—is multiple and complex. The rules of love, designed originally to engage politically powerful female patrons, create another hybridity here: Melusine is both the object of the love game and its desired supporter. Ironically, she is Guenevere and Marie de Champagne (to borrow from Chrétien de Troyes' work) simultaneously.

However, Melusine seems once again to problematize the terms that seek to define her. Raimondin should be playing subservient as a part of his love service, but because it never ends—he really never claims any kind of masculine authority—the fictional relationships of courtly love are maintained even after consummation and marriage. Like many real medieval women, Melusine proves herself a highly competent administrator. To quote Sturm-Maddox, "the image of Melusine as fairy yields progressively to that of Melusine as mortal woman: devoted wife and mother, capable administrator of estates, bounteous *dame*."[11] In being both *seigneur* and *dame*, Melusine again appears to be playing all the parts, and her hybrid body emerges as a kind of hermaphroditic or intersex form, one that can wield both feminine and masculine force.

The positive qualities of Melusine's dynastic projects, however, are challenged by the increasingly deformed children she produces. While Melusine exercises the productive power desired of medieval women in the marriage economy, and takes on the domestic economy of Lusignan by creating both its

---

11   Sturm-Maddox, "Crossed Destines," 21.

royal family and the cities in which this family will live, she also foreshadows the destructive and dangerous currency of male anxiety about female power that is finally revealed in her serpent shape. Her sons' deformities play a peculiar role in the work; while Melusine's own serpent-body is the metaphoric anxiety at the center of the story, the first four of her sons, while obviously signals of their mother's hybridity, do not suffer from their own monstrosity in the same way. Indeed, they provide a kind of counter example; Melusine's monstrosity finally becomes the symbol of her inability to fit into the conventions of the courtly romance that likes its ladies young and beautiful, though her sons have no trouble as the heroes of their own courtly relationships. Douglas Kelly notes that while her last two sons are born without deformities, "the other brothers are not necessarily repulsive or even unattractive. Even the wives of the other brothers see the nobility of their spouses despite their disfigurement; at least, no one seems to object to it and some find excuses in the wonderful prowess the oddities seem to them to betoken."[12]

This difference clarifies the particular monstrous concerns in the narrative; the sons are not a product of physical deformity *per se*, but of Melusine's particular embodiment of narrative hybridity—her enacting, one might say, of both prowess and courtesy. It is the sons' presence—and no doubt also Melusine's other productivities—that cause the Count de Forez to urge Raimondin to spy on his wife. For the men in the text (though perhaps not its authors), women who are productive in both the domestic and public sphere become usurpers of governance. The real question isn't so much what Melusine is doing but that her husband exercise his right and demand to know. What he sees—Melusine's tail, with all its suggestions of phallic power—embodies the Count's concern; it replaces her female genitalia (understood in medieval medicine as essentially inside-out male ones) with an active phallus. Feminine on top (multiple textual illustrations show her with bared breasts and a stylish hat) and masculine if not male on the bottom, Melusine clearly embodies the anxiety that causes her to be spied on in the first place.

Medieval literature is rife with examples of bodies transforming into monsters. In the Melusine story, the dual transformation of the title character, first into the half woman/half snake and finally into a dragon, has a double function: it shows the potential for female power and male fear of that power. In discussing this transformation in the Middle English prose translation, Misty Urban notes, "Melusine's hybrid body [...] becomes fearsome because it figures

---

12   Douglas Kelly, "The Domestication of the Marvelous in the Melusine Romances," in *Melusine of Lusignan,* 34.

a type of feminine power—a protean ability viewed as particularly female, and specifically tied to a world at once natural and supernatural—that is creative, primal, regenerative, enormously persistent, and potentially destructive."[13] Through her transformations in the text, Melusine's hybrid body, as a source of power and desire, reflects the conventions of courtly romance back on themselves, showing the fine divide between the codified conventions of courtly behavior and their roots in violence and sexuality. Urban's observation that "the text uses Melusine's hybridity to dramatize the colliding claims of medieval misogyny and the gender ideology of the romance, which celebrates, even demands, a certain agency and fertility of its women"[14] is key here. The texts of *Melusine* are trapped in a desire to have things both ways; their desire for a beautiful courtly lady seems to spill into the textual desire for a robust genealogy. Melusine's agency and fertility, then, embody the text's values.

In courtly romance, intersections with the supernatural are unsurprising, yet in this story, Melusine is both real and surreal at the same time. In allowing the real and surreal world to interact, romance allows for the dissolution of boundaries, and thus the creation of reversals and hybridities that challenge and reflect the real in multiple ways. Raimondin himself crosses multiple borders throughout the text: gendered, genealogical, legal, and monstrous. Melusine first enters the story when Raimondin is lost in the forest and near death; in the Middle English poetic translation, he comes upon the "fontayn and well of thursty gladnesse" [the fountain and well of Glad Thirst] (*Romans of Partenay* line 323),[15] where he sees "Thre fair laydes of gret seignorie" [three fair ladies of great authority] (339), Ramondin doesn't know whether he encounters a "fantesie" as whether "he slepte or wakyd wel knew he nought" [he knew not whether he slept or waked] (358). Explaining his situation, he is amazed that the lady knows both his story and his name, declaring "I beleue noght that terrene boody sothlesse / of lusty beute may haue such richesse, / So moche of swetnesse, so moche of connyng / as in your gentil body is beryng" [I do not believe that any false earthly body of such tempting beauty could hold

---

13   Misty Urban, *Monstrous Women in Middle English Romance* (Lewiston, NY: Edwin Mellen Press, 2010), 51.

14   Urban, *Monstrous Women*, 51.

15   Quotations from the Middle English translation of Coudrette's poetic version are from *The Romans of Partenay, or of Lusignen, Otherwise Known as the Tale of Melusine*, ed. Walter W. Skeat (London: Early English Text Society/Kegan Paul, 1866); rpt. Elibron Classics, on demand. The title shows the textual uncertainties of the romance itself, which cannot determine what it is really about: whether the text is driven by its masculine imperative (the legitimation of Lusignan and Partenay) or by the feminine body of its protagonist.

such wealth, sweetness, and so much intelligence as your noble body bears]
(417–20). In fulfilling all elements of feminine perfection, Melusine must be a
fantasy, he implies, as a woman this ideal cannot be real, a sentiment he confirms by using the favorite buzz-word of romance when he says, "Fro you may
nought come but good *auanture*" ["nothing may come from you but good fortune," emphasis added] (416). Raimondin, of course, is right; for all her "wom-
anly noblesse" [womanly dignity], Melusine is indeed a fairy, although, oddly,
a Christian one. She assures him that "Y am, after god, your nexst frende trulye"
[I am, after God, your next true friend] (456) and that she believes "Ryght as
holy Catholike faith doth yeue" [rightly as the holy Catholic faith demands]
(462). This is, however, immediately followed by the spell that provides assur-
ance of her mystical form: "in marriage me wil be taking, / and that neuer, dais
of your leuing, / For no worde that man wyl unto you say, / ye shall not enquire
of me the Saturday" [if you will take me in marriage, you will never, until your
death, no matter what any man might say to you, ask to see me on a Saturday]
(487–90).

As they discuss the bargain, with Melusine telling Raimondin that he will
lose her, and that he and his heirs will also lose their lands if he breaks the
contract, the text reminds us that while Raimondin swears to the promise he
is being "forsworn." This scene is vital in understanding Melusine as double.
Before she even begins her literal transformations, she already inhabits multiple worlds; she is an ideal, Christian woman *and* a dark fairy luring the knight
into a potentially dangerous trap. Melusine, in preparation for their marriage,
instructs Raimondin to use Dido's trick with the cow hide to gain substantial
lands. He is successful, but if he gets the land, Melusine herself appears to people it, producing "knightes, ladies, And gentile wemmen fre, / clerkes, prelates,
Squiers at that ground, / Clothen, apparailled nobylly that stound" [knights,
ladies, and gentlewomen of rank, squires, clerks, prelates, and squires, all nobly
appareled, who stoodin that place] (772–5). These people "ben al yours" [are
all yours], Melusine assures Raimondin, ready to assume him as "lorde princi-
pall; / PARTENAY" [high lord of Parthenay] (781; 784–5).

Melusine's ability to produce—besides Raimondin's vassals, she serves a
lavish and rich wedding feast and hosts tournaments—continues throughout
their marriage. As she gives birth to each of her ten children, she undertakes
a concomitant building project, the city of Lusignan. During the building,
we are reminded, that, where Melusine is concerned, "merueles fautith non"
(1147)—that is to say, "no marvels are lacking."

This is the beginning of her campaign. As Urien is born, she builds a city;
after Oede, she makes the castle and town of Mel and Parthenay; after Guy's
birth, she founds Rochelle. She commemorates all important events, such as

Urien's and Oede's marriages, with building projects, including many churches and minsters. In doing so, Melusine combines domestic productivity and fertility with dynastic productivity; her actual increase in children is matched with the material increase of lands and goods that she brings to the marriage.[16] Like many real medieval women left in charge of the home while the knight was away, Melusine proves herself a highly competent *seigneur,* establishing Lusignan as a physical presence to be reckoned with, just as she creates the heirs to inhabit it. What is distinct about her resourcefulness isn't her overseeing of households and estates, but her doing so while Raimondin remains in the castle without other occupation. Contemporary readers may wonder what he has to do with himself if she is, essentially, both lord and lady. The text doesn't seem to be terribly concerned with this particular element of her power, just Raimondin's willingness to extend her authority so far that he never questions (or seems to wonder about) her Saturday activities. The positive qualities of her dynastic projects (and indeed, they are hers, as Raimondin does little besides some rejoicing in this entire section of the poem), however, are challenged by the deformed children she produces: Geoffrey with his "Grand Dent," Fromont with his wolf-skinned nose, and the apex, Horrible, with his three eyes. (The children she produces after Horrible seem to be fully human.) While Melusine enacts the productive power expected of medieval women, taking care of the domestic economy of Lusignan by creating its royal family and the cities in which they will live, her sons' mother markings foreshadow the hybridity that is finally revealed in her serpent shape.

Many medieval romance characters reveal monstrous forms, from the sorcerer who is turned into a serpent by his ward who hits him over the head with a book in *Bel Inconnu* to the heroic werewolves of *Guillaume de Palerne* and Marie de France's "Bisclavret." However, in *Le Roman de Mélusine*, the dual transformation of the title character, first into a half woman/half snake and finally into a dragon, works to locate another duality in the figure of Melusine. In *Monster/Beauty*, Joanna Frueh reminds readers that "monstrousness is an unnamed and implicit feminine condition [...] The Western tradition is populated by terrifically exciting female monsters, whose threat to men or male dominance is so great that they must be killed. Woman," she notes, "has been constructed as a hormonal and a sexual monster whose physical attractions lure man into the *vagina dentate*, where he will be emasculated." This monstrosity, however, is coupled with desirability: "monster/beauty's perceived

---

16   See Anna Casas Aguilar's contribution to this volume for a discussion of how Melusine's building projects take on a special resonance for readers of the Castilian translation of Jean d'Arras' romance, *Historia de la linda Melosina* (1489).

grotesqueness, based in taboo and the unconventional," is repellant and attractive at once.[17]

Melusine's allure is inseparable from her fairy identity, and when the Count de Foretz suggests to Raimondin that her Saturday absences are due either to illicit sex or illicit non-human identity, he implies that there is very little difference between them: "Now, fayre brother, wete it that the commyn talking of the peple is, that Melusyne your wyf every satirday in the yere is with another man in auoultyre / & so blynd ye are by her sayieng ye dare not enquire not knoweth wher she becommeth or gooth / and also other sayen, & make them strong that she is a spyryte of the fayrye" [now, brother, you should know that the common talk of the people is that Melusine, your wife, every Saturday of the year is with another man in adultery, and so blind are you by what she says that you dare not inquire to know where she goes or what becomes of her; and also others says and make a strong case that she is a spirit of the fairy].[18] Raimondin's response is symbolically sexual; he "toke his swerd, that was hard & tempered with fyn stele, and with the pounte of it dyde so moche that he perced the doore, and made a holl in it, and looked in that holl, and saw Melusyne" [(he) took his sword, which was hard and tempered, of fine steel, and with the point of it pierced the door and made a hole in it, and looked in that hole, and saw Melusine] (296). Here Raimondin crosses multiple boundaries; in piercing the door with his sword, he reinscribes masculine phallic power, violating his promise, her privacy, and the structures of courtly narrative (not to mention their bargain), which require his supplication to her. However, because of the poem's engagement in multiplicity, Melusine provides a striking double-image that reflects both her beauty and her power.

In Jean d'Arras' version, when Raimondin sees Melusine:

> Remond l'espee qu'il fist un peruis en l'uis, par ou il pot adviser tout ce quie setoit dedans la chamber, et voit Melusigne en la cuve, qui estoit jusques au nombril en figure de femme et pignoit ses cheveuls, et du nombril e naval estoit en forme de la queue d'un serpent, aussi grosse comme un tonne ou on met harenc, et longue durement, et debatoit de sa coue l'eaue tellement qu'elle la faisoit saillir jusques a lo voulte de la chambre.

---

17   Joanna Frueh, *Monster/Beauty: Building the Body of Love* (Berkeley: University of California Press, 2001), 19.

18   A. K. Donald, ed., *Melusine*, EETS es. 68 (London: Kegan Paul, Trench, Trübner & Co., 1895, rpt. Woodbridge, Suffolk: Boydell & Brewer, 2002), 296. Page numbers given in parenthesis.

[Raymond so twisted the sword, this way and that, that he made a hole in the door through which he could observe everything in the chamber. There he saw Melusine in the basin. Down to her navel, she had the form of a woman, gracefully combing her hair. But from the navel down, her body had the form of a serpent's tail. As big around as a barrel for storing herring, it was, and tremendously long. She lashed the water so forcefully with her tail that it made it splash all the way up to the vaulted ceiling of the chamber.][19]

The Middle English translation of Coudrette's poem offers a somewhat different image, albeit with a similar import. There Melusine "unto her nauell sewinger there full white / like As the snow A Faire branche upon, / The body well made, firke in ioly plite" [unto her navel (she) appeared as white as a fair branch upon the snow, her body well-made, disporting in a joyful manner] (lines 2801–4); her facie is "pre, fresh, clenly" [pure, fresh, unspoiled] and there is "Neuer non fairer ne more reuerent" [no one more lovely or pleasing] (2805–6). The stanza turns in its last line: "But A tail had beneth of serpent!" [but (she) had beneath the tail of a serpent!] (2807). The tail is both "orrible" [horrible] and "siluer And Asure" [silver and azure], and as it "Strongly the water there bete, it flashed hy" [as it (the tail) beat the water, it (the water) flashed high] (2801–2810). While Jean d'Arras attempts to emphasize the horror of the serpent's tale with the image of the herring barrel—both quotidian and perhaps humorous, but in either case allowing readers a specific visual measurement—Coudrette seems to dwell on Melusine's inherent beauty; the tail may be horrible but it is also jeweled, and the water flashes, language which, coupled with the more extended description of Melusine's beauty, suggests an image more arresting in its beauty than its terror. In either text, the image is at once feminine and erotic, monstrous and comic, phallic and powerful.[20] Jeffrey Jerome Cohen's work on monsters reminds readers that "a construct and a projection, the monster exists only to be read: the *monstrum* is etymologically that which reveals, 'That which warns,' a glyph that seeks a hierophant. Like a letter on the page, the monster signifies something other than itself: it is always a displacement, always inhabits the gap between

19   *A Bilingual Edition of Jean D'Arras's Melusine or L'Histoire de Lusignan,* ed. and trans. Matthew W. Morris, 2 vols. (Lewiston, NY: Edwin Mellen Press, 2007), 566–567. Hereafter Morris.

20   See Caroline Prud'Homme's contribution to this volume for further discussion of this scene, especially the implications in descriptions of Melusine's serpent tail.

the time of upheaval that created it and the moment into which it is received, to be born again.[21]

At this moment, Melusine is distanced from herself; it may be too contemporary to say she moves from character to symbol, and too extreme to suggest she moves from center to margin, but it is certainly a shift point in the work, the moment at which the possibility of the story being truly hers (or at least, her desired story) is removed. What Melusine wishes for—to break her mother's curse, to become a Christian and a human, and to be able to die—essentially becomes an impossibility in this moment, and at the revelation of her potential wholeness (as Christabel LaMotte suggests), the text takes it away. The conventions of romance, which have no place for a monstrous heroine, begin the process of driving her, not out of the story, but out of the heroine's position which she has occupied, albeit uncomfortably, to this point. Melusine, in this scene, is a readable text; she reveals (her true self) and warns (what is to come), but she is also symbol: her top half is the attractive fairy who won Raimondin at the fountain, the courtly heroine of the narrative, and the bottom half the land-producer and castle-builder whose power establishes the dynasty of Lusignan. This image, feminine and masculine, hideous and beautiful, appears at the moment when the text reveals its own terminologies and simultaneously undoes them.

Melusine here physically embodies the nexus of all the text's values. She is the source of all the modes of power represented in this romance: genealogical, courtly, erotic, constructive, productive. And at the moment of revelation, this knot is undone. Within the generic context of romance, the moment itself establishes Raimondin as both voyeur and phallic power, penetrating the liminal private feminine space; however, it simultaneously amplifies the projection of woman as Other. Because of her monstrous shape, Melusine literally enacts the romance role reversal which, pre-consummation, empowers the woman and elevates her over her desiring lover. Her snake-like tail provides a phallic image that equals or surpasses Raimondin's sword.

As Kevin Brownlee notes, "the first direct presentation of her hybrid body calls forth contrastively a more elaborate and intensive presentation of her human (courtly, erotic) body (and identity) than virtually anywhere else."[22] It is precisely the power of this form that prevents Raimondin from saying anything right away. Yet the gender fluctuations of this moment demonstrate

---

21   Jeffrey Jerome Cohen, "Monster Culture (Seven Theses)," in *Monster Theory: Reading Culture* (Minneapolis: University of Minnesota Press, 1996), 3–25, at 4.

22   Kevin Brownlee, "Melusine's Hybrid Body and the Poetics of Metamorphosis," *Yale French Studies* 86 (1994): 18–38, at 27.

Cohen's observation that "the difficult project of constructing and maintaining gender identities elicits an array of anxious response throughout culture, producing another impetus to teratogenesis. The woman who oversteps the boundaries of her gender role risks becoming a Scylla, Weird Sister, Lilith ("*die erste Eva,*" "*la mère obscure*"), Bertha Mason, or a Gorgon."[23] Whatever gender anxieties underlie the narrative prior to this moment, Ramondin's violation of Melusine's privacy, his breaking of their courtly agreement, and the vision of her hybrid body construct her as a monster, creating the textual point of no return. What comes between this moment and her final transformation serves primarily as delay of the inevitable.

When Geoffrey Big-Tooth irrationally burns the monastery of Maillezais that Melusine herself established, killing his brother Fromont, Ramondin finally reveals his discovery and moves the narrative towards Melusine's final transformation. The scene is somewhat ironic; just as she is about to become the dragon, Melusine espouses Christian values, suggesting that the monastery must have been engaging in sinful practices and that God's mercy may even allow Geoffrey to make penance and be absolved. Melusine has proved herself a good Christian throughout the text, which seems to find uproblematic her adoption of a religion that views her as, at best, outside its tenets and, at worst, demonic. As Erika Hess points out, "throughout the romance, Mélusine attends church regularly and participates in all of the standard Christian rituals. Her monstrous form does not seem to contradict her suitability for a Christian husband, yet those who base their judgment of Mélusine only on the most immediately apparent signs jump to the conclusion that her unusual behavior must be due to diabolical forces."[24]

The narrator of the poem asks the audience to accept another duality: that Melusine can simultaneously be a fairy who lacks a human soul and a good Christian. She has all the potential to achieve salvation and yet possesses qualities which ultimately render salvation impossible. Melusine espouses Christian doctrine, saying "Sachiez qu'il n'a si grant pechur du monde que Dieu ne soit plus grant pardonneur et plus debonnaire, quant le pecheur se repent et lui crie mercy de bon cuer et de bon voulenté" [Thou canst be sure that there is no sinner so great that He will not forgive in His infinite bounty, of that sinner willingly repents and sincerely asks for His mercy],[25] yet Ramondin refuses to view Melusine as Christian or see redemptive possibility in her, although the

23   Cohen, "Monster Theory," 9.

24   Erika E. Hess, *Literary Hybrids: Cross-Dressing, Shapeshifting, and Indeterminacy in Medieval and Modern French Narrative* (New York: Routledge, 2004), 29.

25   Morris, *A Bilingual Edition*, 596–7.

audience can. He can only see the demon, crying, "Hee, tres faulse serpent, par Dieu, ne toy ne tes fais ne sont que fantosme" [Ah! Sordid serpent! By God, thou and all of thy actions are naught but sorcery!].[26] His explicit juxtaposition of God's truth and Melusine's sorcery seems to unmake the words she has just uttered. While this isn't echoed in the Middle English poem, that version also creates its own equation that, because Melusine is a serpent, her "line" or "lineage" can do no good: "Ha, serpent! Thy line in lif no good shall doo! / Se here how A noble beginning, lo! [...] What Gaffray with long toth thy son hath don!" [Ah, serpent! Your line shall do no good in life! See from this noble beginning [...] what your son Geoffrey Great-Tooth has done!] (lines 3548-10). Both versions offer a hybrid, the Christian monster, simultaneously calling on sympathy and repulsion. The poem reminds the reader that "For therin gan do gret ill and sin plain. / Melusine Anon loste, neuer saw Again" [(Raimond) begain to feel great suffering and complaint, for Melusine, now lost, he would never see again] (3562–3). Melusine swoons with great sorrow, and after reviving cries "piteously," "Alas, alas, alas, Raimonde, this day! / ill saw I the euery times any! / Ill saw I the beaute of the, I say" [Alas, this day, Raimond! Ill (for me) that I ever saw you at all, ill that I saw your beauty] (3578–11); lamenting his "Werking amorous" "precious body" and "fair countennaunce" [dear, beloved body and fair face], she says, "Thy fals tonges unmesurabelnesse, / me put to paynes perdurability / that forthens neuer shall I depart me" [the immeasurableness of your false tongue has put me in never-ending torment, from which I shall never henceforth free myself], ending with "Neuer shal ye se my clere uisage plain" [never again shall you see my visage clearly (see me in this form)] (3595–6; 3599). Although it is her serpent form—her dark, erotic power—that causes their separation, the scene itself constructs Melusine as the wronged, betrayed lover, and Raimondin himself as the guilty party. At the point in the work where she least resembles the beautiful lady of courtly romance, she is most constituted in exactly that form, which is interestingly reflected in the many images of this textual moment that show Melusine flying out the window with a dragon's tail, her top half still human and clad in a very fetching hat.[27] Once again, Melusine's ability to embody a series of hybridities exceeds Raimondin's—and by extension, the narrative's—abilities to reconcile those hybridities.

---

26   Morris, *A Bilingual Edition*, 596–7.

27   See, for instance, the woodcuts accompanying the early printed edition of Thüring von Ringoltingen's translation (Basel, ca.1474) discussed in Albrecht Classen's essay in this volume.

Despite his earlier curse, Raimondin's language becomes increasingly erotically charged and courtly conventional as he loses her: "alas my love, now I have betrayed you ... the best and most loyal lady ever born"[28] and repeating "ma doux amy" [my sweet love] over and over as she delivers her final speech in human form from the liminal space of the windowsill. Raimondin cannot constitute Melusine in the Christian world, but he attempts to reincorporate her into the domestic space of their marriage. Just as he views her in romance terms as his lady, she transforms into her dragon form and flies away, returning at night to nurse her remaining sons. Brownlee notes that "Melusina is a discursive composite—a figure constructed out of a set of discourses in unstable contrast with each other: fairy-monstrous, courtly-erotic, maternal, political-foundational, fairy-Christian."[29] These serve to destabilize the "real" world of Lusignan and Poitou that she inhabits; her monstrous form reveals these conflicts to be located at its own center.

By simultaneously enacting self and Other, monsters become discursive composites that dissolve the linguistically and culturally constructed binaries that define civilization. As a romance, *Melusine's* particular constructed binaries include chivalry and violence, courtly love and erotic sexuality, all of which Melusine's body and transformation blur and destabilize. Cohen aptly notes:

> Monsters are our children. They can be pushed to the farthest margins of geography and discourse, hidden away at the edges of the world and in the forbidden recesses of our mind, but they always return. And when they come back, they bring not just a fuller knowledge of our place in history and the history of knowing our place, they the bear self knowledge, *human* knowledge—and a discourse all the more sacred as it arises from the Outside.[30]

When supposed oppositions reside in a single form, they reveal the essential hybridity of what the courtly world desires to keep separate. The "sacred discourse" that Melusine offers reflects the conventions and values of romance back on themselves, challenging the audience to determine what is truly human and what truly monstrous. Through her multiple changes, Melusine embodies the inevitable conflicts of the erotic and the natural, "the courtly and the Christian, the human and the monstrous,"[31] adding power and authority

---

28   Brownlee, "Melusine's Hybrid Body," 25.
29   Brownlee, "Melusine's Hybrid Body," 38.
30   Cohen, "Monster Theory," 20.
31   Brownlee, "Melusine's Hybrid Body," 19.

to the lineage of Lusignan while simultaneously legitimizing its conquest. If Cohen is correct that monstrous hybrids "ask us to reevaluate our cultural assumptions about race, gender, sexuality, or perception of difference, our tolerance towards its expression,"[32] Melusine calls to readers' attention the tensions in the understanding of female power, anxieties about difference, and fears of genealogical failure, while simultaneously portraying the fascination and desire for those same impulses. Within the world of the narrative, without Melusine, there is no Lusignan to conquer and legitimate; without her deformed sons, there is no stability and peace in Europe; without her prophesy, there is no knowledge of the future.

If the romance Other functions as a mirror thorough which the conventional world views itself, the mirror throws back a disturbing and complex picture. By constituting the self and the Other within the monstrous hybrid, *Melusine* elides the boundaries between what is civilized and what is visceral and experiential, between the ways the courtly world would like to see itself and the ways it is. As such, she embodies the inescapable liminality of romance, dramatically staging the unresolvable contradictions of a discursively hybrid text. Maddox and Sturm-Maddox say of *Melusine:* "while the work immediately gives more than an inkling of its qualities as a masterpiece of late medieval fiction, it also looms large as a medieval literary monster, a text unsettling on many accounts."[33] Cohen suggests that "The monster always escapes because it refuses easy categorization."[34] Melusine's power may exist less in her ability to build cities and produce children than in her ability, despite her inherently fragmentary nature and her uncontainability, to endure with such force.

---

32   Cohen, "Monster Theory," 20.
33   Maddox and Sturm-Maddox, *Melusine of Lusignan*, 1.
34   Cohen, "Monster Theory," 6.

CHAPTER 13

Passing as a "Humayn Woman": Hybridity and Salvation in the Middle English *Melusine*

Chera A. Cole

While it is also a politically motivated, dynastic history intended to increase the prestige of Jean, duc de Berry's family, *Melusine* can be read as a text about a fairy and her salvation. Woven into the narrative of the rise and decline of a great family is a concern for fairy's place within the spiritual hierarchy of medieval Christianity, with particular emphasis on the half-fairy, half-human soul.[1] The romance *Melusine* is an exploration of how closely one can be associated with evil and still be eligible for salvation. Fairy is linked closely with the demonic in this romance, and yet in no other romance is the fairy so concerned for the salvation of her soul. Close textual analysis of the English *Melusine* reveals that in her quest to attain salvation, it is her humanity that has the ability to save her.

As part fairy, part human, the mixed nature of Melusine's blood calls into question her eligibility for salvation. Melusine's options as a half fairy seem to be to achieve salvation by living as a human, or to live as a dragon until Judgment Day—but these are Melusine's options only after her transgression against her father and the punishment of her mother's curse.[2] Her mother Pressyne's stipulation that Melusine could only die as a "naturel & humayn woman" as the result of her husband's fidelity suggests that Melusine would not have been able to live a mortal life otherwise; however, this aspect of Melusine's curse offers the fate of living a human life that Melusine and her sisters forfeited when they imprisoned their father in the mountain. Pressyne tells them:

> For notwithstandyng the vnlawfulness of thy fader / bothe thou & thy
> sustirs he shuld haue drawen to hym, and ye should shortly haue ben out

---

1 See Richard Firth Green, *Elf Queens and Holy Friars: Fairy Beliefs and the Medieval Church* (Philadelphia: University of Pennsylvania Press, 2016) for a full discussion of the relationship between Christianity and the fairy realm in the Middle Ages.

2 Matilda Tomaryn Bruckner, "Natural and Unnatural Woman: Melusine Inside and Out," in *Founding Feminisms in Medieval Studies: Essays in Honor of E. Jane Burns*, ed. Laine E. Doggett and Daniel E. O'Sullivan (Cambridge: D. S. Brewer, 2016), 22–23.

© KONINKLIJKE BRILL NV, LEIDEN, 2017 | DOI 10.1163/9789004355958_015

of the handes of the Nymphes & of the fairees, without to retourne eny more.[3]

As a result of her mother's curse, Melusine's salvation is contingent upon how well she, as a fairy, can "pass" as human, and how well she can convince her human community that she is fully integrated into human society.[4] Melusine's ability to pass is dependent both on her behavior and her heritage: that is, her blood. The romance's concern for purity of blood, or lack of it, particularly among "races," surprisingly resonates with modern literary discussions on identity and race. The term "race" is a complicated one in both the medieval and the modern world: race in the medieval period is dynamic and the boundaries between people groups frequently overlap and blur. In the 2001 special edition of the *Journal of Medieval and Early Modern Studies*, "Concepts of Race and Ethnicity in the Middle Ages," several of the contributors observe that medieval understandings of "race" are closely knit with what are often considered "cultural" or "ethnic" markers—language, customs, and laws—rather than the color of one's skin.[5] Adding to the complexity of a medieval concept of race is the description of "monstrous races" in both travel writing and romances: giants, Cyclopes, dog-headed men, sciapods, and fairies, among others. Some of these creatures are so different from humans that they might even be considered different species according to modern parlance.[6] Melusine, first by being

---

3   A. K. Donald, ed., *Melusine compiled by Jean d'Arras. Edited from a unique manuscript in the Library of the British Museum*, Early English Text Society ES. 68 (London: Kegan Paul, Trench, Trübner and Co., 1895), 15. Page numbers hereafter given in parentheses.

4   The concept of "passing" as one gender or race other than one's own is outlined in Judith Butler, *Bodies That Matter: On the Discursive Limits of "Sex"* (New York: Routledge, 1993), 167–85. Suki Ali builds on Butler's idea by discussing the ways mixed-race people can "pass" as one race or another in *Mixed-Race, Post-Race: Gender, New Ethnicities, and Cultural Practices* (Oxford: Berg, 2003), 12–14.

5   Thomas Hahn, "The Difference the Middle Ages Makes: Color and Race before the Modern World," *Journal of Medieval and Early Modern Studies* 31, no. 1 (2001): 1–37; Robert Bartlett, "Medieval and Modern Concepts of Race and Ethnicity," *Journal of Medieval and Early Modern Studies* 31, no. 1 (2001): 39–56; William Chester Jordan, "Why 'Race'?" *Journal of Medieval and Early Modern Studies* 31, no. 1 (2001): 165–173. See also the *Race, Racism, and the Middle Ages* series hosted by The Public Medievalist, exploring issues of race in context of the medieval world at http://www.publicmedievalist.com/race-racism-middle-ages-toc/.

6   The descriptions of medieval monsters can call to mind modern "monsters," that is, aliens in science-fiction. Ian Lovecy observes that the supernatural in medieval texts often "performs the same function that bug-eyed monsters, Daleks, warp motion and curiously-inhabited planets perform in the fantasies of the modern age." Ian Lovecy, "Exploding the Myth of the

half human, half fairy, then by being half human, half serpent, is undeniably Other, whether it is by blood or by appearance.

When considering these monstrous races and the possibilities of "mixed-race" characters, Jeffrey Jerome Cohen argues that the questions asked in post-colonial theory can inform medieval studies, especially the idea of hybridity in race studies.[7] For example, applying Toni Morrison's observations about the role race plays in defining "Americanness" in American culture to medieval texts suggests that the presence of these marvelous races allows the writers and audiences the opportunity to construct a definition of "humanness."[8] Similarly, when discussing the way medieval artists portrayed black Africans—namely, the magus Balthasar or St. Maurice as a black presence in a tableau of white faces—Thomas Hahn postulates that these artists were appropriating the Other "to affirm the universality of the Same."[9] Just as these artists use the Other to promote

---

Celtic Myth: A New Appraisal of the Celtic Background of Arthurian Romance," *Reading Medieval Studies* 7 (1981): 3–18, at 14.

7   "Medieval monstrousness intimates an unthought epistemological limit to the widely influential postcolonial criticism derived from the study of English India, and suggests that an alliance might be usefully forged between medieval studies and what has been called borderlands theory. Derived mainly from Chicana/o studies, this growing body of work takes as its central figure not the all too literary hybrid, with his ambivalence, mimesis, and sly civility, but the provocative and proudly resistant *mestiza*, with her insistently embodied experience of that middle formed by the overlap among a multitude of genders, sexualities, spiritualities, ethnicities, races, cultures, languages." From "Hybrids, Monsters, Borderlands: The Bodies of Gerald of Wales," in Jeffrey Jerome Cohen, ed., *The Postcolonial Middle Ages* (New York: Palgrave, 2001), 85–104, at 85–6. The term *mestiza/o* refers to "mixed blood" individuals of Indian-Latino-White descent in Latin America. Chicana/o refers to *mestizos* living in the borderlands of Northern Mexico and the Southwest United States.

8   This question of how the presence of fairy can create a definition of humanness in the text is adapted from one of the observations made in Toni Morrison's *Playing in the Dark: Whiteness and the Literary Imagination* (Cambridge, MA: Harvard University Press, 1992). She writes, "Race, in fact, now functions as a metaphor so necessary to the construction of Americanness that it rivals the old pseudo-scientific and class-informed racisms whose dynamics we are more used to deciphering. [...] American means white, and Africanist people struggle to make the term applicable to themselves with ethnicity and hyphen after hyphen after hyphen" (47). According to Morrison, white American writers developed a definition of "Americanness" through the construction of an "Africanist presence," which refers to the roles and experiences white authors ascribed to characters of color. She argues that "Americanness" is defined by foregrounding the white experience over the "Africanist" experience. This method of defining one type of identity at the expense of another's has a wider application than just American literature and, as is the case for this essay, can be used to argue how the definition of "humanness" is made in contrast to "fairyness."

9   Hahn, "The Difference the Middle Ages Makes," 5.

the universality of Christian European values, so does *Melusine* appropriate the fairy Other to emphasize the primacy of the human race in medieval Christian cosmology. Despite her obvious hybridity, the narrative emphasizes Melusine's human side over that of her serpentine, fairy body, and in doing so, reassures audiences about humanity's central place in the Christian cosmic hierarchy. By posing the question of Melusine's salvation, this romance uses fairies to ask existential questions relevant to its medieval Christian audience.[10] As the romance chronicles Melusine's acceptance into human society (even if ultimately she is to be exiled from it), especially in courtly society, human society is depicted as both a privileged and desired place to be in the world—the "right" place to be.[11]

The tale of Melusine is compelling in part due to her strange hybridity. Stephen G. Nichols conflates Melusine's two types of hybridity, claiming that Melusine is monstrous as the result of her mixed parentage.[12] Nichols's claim would appear to be supported by medieval theorists. One explanation for the existence of monsters given in the twelfth century by Hildegard of Bingen was that hybrid offspring were the product of a mixing of seeds; thus, the human and fairy "seed" that mixed to result in Melusine, Melior, and Palatyne also resulted in their hybridity.[13] In the thirteenth century, Thomas Aquinas and Caesarius of Heisterbach also express concern for the spiritual condition of those who might be born as the result of mixed unions, particularly between human and demon.[14] Both seem to believe that, if a person were truly half demon,

---

10   Albrecht Classen argues that the presence of monsters allows authors and audiences to explore existential questions in "The Monster Outside and Within: Medieval Literary Reflection on Ethical Epistemology. From *Beowulf* to Marie de France, the *Nibelungenlied*, and Thüring von Ringoltingen's *Melusine*," *Neohelicon* 40 (2013): 521–42.

11   This is similar to Thomas Hahn's argument that Gawain often serves the role of reconciling the Other to the Arthurian court, which also indicates the primacy of the human court. Hahn, "Gawain and Popular Chivalric Romance in Britain," in *The Cambridge Companion to Medieval Romance*, ed. Roberta L. Krueger (Cambridge: Cambridge University Press, 2000), 218–234, see particularly 223–4.

12   Stephen G. Nichols, "Melusine Between Myth and History," in *Mittelalter – Neue Wege durch einen alten Kontinent*, ed. Jan-Dirk Müller and Horst Wenzel (Stuttgart: Hirzel, 1999), 217–240, esp. 223 and 228.

13   Tania M. Colwell, "Mélusine: Ideal Mother or Inimitable Monster?," in *Love, Marriage, and Family Ties in the Later Middle Ages*, ed. Isabel Davis, Miriam Müller, and Sarah Rees Jones (Turnhout: Brepols Publishers, 2003), 181–203, at 199. For further discussion on how hybridity was described and perceived in the late classical and medieval periods, see Ana Pairet's contribution to this volume.

14   Thomas Aquinas, *The Summa Theologiæ of Saint Thomas Aquinas: Latin-English*, Vol. 1, Prima Pars, Q. 1–64, trans. Fathers of the English Dominican Province (Scotts Valley, CA: NovAntiqua, 2008), Q.LI. Third Article, Reply Obj. 6, 611. Caesarius of Heisterbach,

that person would be damned irreparably, not simply victim to original sin as humans are but incapable of even being eligible for salvation.

One reason for this was the idea that demons, though they might desire happiness, were considered to be perverted in thought and too prideful to ask God for mercy.[15] Thomas Aquinas writes that "since the demon has a perverse and obstinate will, he is not sorry for the evil of sin."[16] In *Sidrak and Bokkus*, devils "mowen no mercy haue / Ne for pride þei mowen noon craue" [devils may have no mercy, and for pride they may ask for none].[17] That these ideas were included in *Sidrak and Bokkus* is an indication of how widespread this belief was. *Sidrak and Bokkus*, and its various incarnations, were enormously popular in the late Middle Ages, and the British Library contains manuscripts not only in English, but also French, Dutch, Danish, and Italian. *Sidrak and Bokkus* represents some of what theological knowledge would be available to the lay, non-specialist reader. Consequently, that Melusine and her sisters all express remorse about their sin, something that demons are said to be incapable of doing, becomes all the more noteworthy. The sisters' remorse indicates that fairies—or at least half fairies—are capable of desiring redemption, a desire that hitherto was consigned to humans.

Another half-human character whose fate can be compared with Melusine's is Sir Gowther, the titular character of an early fifteenth-century romance, who is the son of a woman and a devil.[18] He leads a wicked life, with episodes similar to the wickedness of Melusine's sons Geoffray and Horrible. As an infant, Gowther killed nine wet nurses; as an adult, he tortured and killed friars and priests, raped women and slew their husbands, and led a raid on a convent, raping the nuns before burning them alive. When he is told of his true paternity, he is struck with remorse, after which Gowther seeks absolution from the Pope. The Pope assigns Gowther a humiliating penance:

> Wherser thu travellys, be northe or soth,
> Thu eyt no meyt bot that thu revus of howndus mothe

    The Dialogue on Miracles, trans. H. Von E. Scott and Charles Cooke Swinton Bland (London: Routledge, 1929), Chapter XII, 139–40.

15   Aquinas, *The Summa Theologiæ*, Q.LXIV, Articles 2 and 3, 739–43.

16   Aquinas, *The Summa Theologiæ*, Q.LXIV. Third Article, Reply Obj. 3, 743.

17   T. L. Burton, ed., *Sidrak and Bokkus: a parallel-text edition from Bodleian Library MS Laud Misc. 559 and British Library, MS Lansdowne 79*, 2 vols. (Oxford: Early English Text Society OS.311–312, 1998), 121, lines 2053–4.

18   Line numbers for *Sir Gowther* come from "Sir Gowther," in *The Middle English Breton Lays*, ed. Anne Laskaya and Eve Salisbury (Kalamazoo: Medieval Institute Publications, 1995), 274–295.

Cum thy body within;
Ne no worde speke for evyll ne gud,
Or thu reyde tokyn have fro God,
That forgyfyn is thi syn. (lines 295–300)

Gowther shall speak to no one and only eat what is brought to him by dogs, and do so indefinitely; he is to continue his penance until he has received a sign from God that his sin has been forgiven. By giving Gowther an ongoing penance, the Pope admits that he himself does not have enough authority to forgive Gowther's sin: a half demon can only be forgiven by God.[19] Even so, despite being half demon, the human part of Gowther has the capacity for repentance that makes him eligible for salvation. Similarly, the human part of Melusine and her sisters would have allowed the three half-fairy sisters both mortality and the eligibility for salvation. During the pronouncement of their individual curses, or penances, for the sin against their human father, their fairy mother states that their human blood is superior to their fairy blood, to the point of being transformative. In this way, the romance privileges the human condition over the fairy condition. That the sisters' penances are also ongoing suggests that their salvation lies beyond the bounds of human Christian authority. Half fairies, like half demons, must receive special dispensation from God in order to be forgiven.

The next indication in the narrative that there is some concern about the nature of Melusine's blood comes when Raymondin informs his cousin, the Earl of Poitiers, of his engagement to Melusine. The concern is not yet about whether Melusine's blood is human, but whether Melusine is noble enough to enter the Poitevin court. The Earl of Poitiers is understandably surprised to hear of Raymondin's sudden betrothal to an unknown, mysterious woman. In true romance fashion, Raymondin claims he has been commanded by love and begs his cousin not to take offence. The earl responds by asking after Melusine's lineage. The following exchange takes place:

"By my feyth," said Raymondyn, "ye demande of me a thing / to the whiche I can not gyue none ansuere, for neuer in my lyf I ne dide enquyre me therof." "Forsouthe," sayd the Erle, "it is grett meruaylle. Raymondyn

---

19 Dana M. Oswald explores Gowther's penance in *Monsters, Gender, and Sexuality in Medieval English Literature* (Cambridge: D. S. Brewer, 2010). She writes, "Despite the Pope's absolution, Gowther's forgiveness can only come from God because of the nature of his monstrous body. His case requires the very highest authority; a priest cannot confer this kind of transformation" (181).

taketh a wyf that he knoweth not, ne also the lynage that she commeth of." (48–9)

[By my faith," said Raymondin, "you demand of me a thing to which I can give no answer, for never in my life did I enquire thereof." "Forsooth," said the Earl, "it is a great marvel. Raymondin takes a wife whom he knows nothing of, nor of what lineage she comes."]

That Raymondin, the third son of the Earl of March, cousin to the Earl of Poitiers, would choose to marry without first enquiring after his potential wife's family and lineage is unthinkable, and reckless for the family's bloodline. Raymondin's response is that it is not his cousin who is marrying Melusine, but himself, and that he "alone shall bere eyther joye or sorowe for it" [(he) alone shall received either joy or sorrow for it] (49). He then assures the earl that he will be well-pleased with Melusine once he meets her. Her beauty, manners, and speech are enough to make her noble. Here two differing definitions of nobility are held in tension: Raymondin seems to be on the side that "manners make the man," or that virtue instead of rank indicates nobility; but for the earl, nobility is found in one's blood or family lineage.[20] Melusine partially fulfills the earl's definition through her noble paternity, but the definition offered by Raymondin allows for Melusine to further perform her nobility and pass as fully human.

Raymondin's assurances do not quench the earl's curiosity, however, and he continues to ask about Melusine's heritage while en route to the Fountain of Soyf for the wedding. It is not until the Earl of Poitiers sees the richness of the pavilions set up around the Fountain of Soyf, observes the graciousness and courtesy of her servants, and meets the bride himself that his qualms about Melusine's mysterious lineage are eased, though not entirely put to rest. She certainly demonstrates largesse enough to be noble: Melusine gives rich, extravagant gifts to all who come to the wedding, especially to Raymondin's extended family. Despite the agreement that "alle sayd that Raymondyn was gretly mightily and valiauntly marryed" (59), the Earl of Poitiers still presses Raymondin for information about Melusine's estate and parentage. At last, Raymondin tells the earl that Melusine is a "kyngis doughter," which reinforces his earlier claim that her comportment and manners are evidence of her good

20   John Scattergood, "'The Unequal Scales of Love': Love and Social Class in Andreas Capellanus's *De Amore* and Some Later Texts," in *Writings on Love in the English Middle Ages*, ed. Helen Cooney (Basingstoke: Palgrave Macmillan, 2006), 63–79, at 68 and 72; S. H. Rigby, *English Society in the Later Middle Ages: Class, Status and Gender* (Basingstoke: Macmillan, 1995), 199.

breeding (60). The earl admits that he was afraid he had not given Melusine the proper honor due her, should she be of higher nobility than he is. The narrator employs dramatic irony throughout this episode: the readers know that the answer to the earl's questions about Melusine's background is that she is only half human, and yet the earl is satisfied with the revelation of her social rank. Although the earl's concern is centered on nobility and class, the narrator uses the earl's anxiety about class to suggest theological concerns about miscegenation.

The inclusion of strange deformities or birthmarks on Melusine's children is another way the romance demonstrates a concern for the purity of blood. Eight of her ten sons display some curious feature or defect, to which "wherof they that sawe hym wondred, & moche were abasshed" [whereof they that saw him were struck with amazement, and were very surprised] (104).[21] The sons' abnormalities of enormous ears, red eyes, too many eyes or too few, tusks, and claws coming out of the face are marvelous to all except, perhaps, the reader, who alone knows that Melusine herself is somewhat monstrous. Though the sons, their father, and their father's people are not aware that they contain a drop of fairy blood, some critics claim that the sons' deformities are the result of traces of fairy blood in effect "polluting" the bloodline, pointing to Melusine's own serpentine form as proof of a polluting hybrid figure.[22] By employing dramatic irony, the author is sharing with the reader the knowledge that there *is* something unusual about Melusine and Raymondin's progeny, even if the people of Lusignan do not know at first why Melusine's sons are born with these deformities.

A common thread in studies of monstrosity in *Melusine* is that Melusine's monstrous hybrid body is hereditary.[23] Birthmarks, or as Douglas Kelly calls them, "mother-marks," were believed to be related to conception and

---

21   Donald, *Melusine*, 104. This line is found in the description of Anthony's birth, but it takes no stretch of the imagination to believe that each of Melusine's sons was greeted with similar amazement, especially as the sons' appearance elicits wonder in their later adventures.

22   Kelly, "The Domestication of the Marvelous in the Melusine Romances," in *Melusine of Lusignan: Founding Fiction*, ed. Donald Maddox and Sara Sturm-Maddox (Athens, GA: University of Georgia Press, 1996), 32–47, at 39; Catharine Léglu, "Nourishing Lineage in the Earliest French versions of the Roman de Mélusine," *Medium Ævum* 74, no. 1 (2005): 71–85, at 77–78; Ivy A. Corfis, "Beauty, Deformity, and the Fantastic in the *Historia de la linda Melosina*," *Hispanic Review* 55, no. 2 (1987): 181–193, at 190.

23   Gabrielle M. Spiegel, "Maternity and Monstrosity: Reproductive Biology in the *Roman de Mélusine*," in *Melusine of Lusignan*, 100–24; Jane H. M. Taylor, "Melusine's Progeny: Patterns and Perplexities," in *Melusine of Lusignan*, 165–84.; Colwell, "Mélusine: Ideal

pregnancy—usually caused by something the mother strongly desired or feared during pregnancy.[24] This concept explained why someone might have a birthmark vaguely in the shape of an apple, for example, but what Kelly and Catharine Léglu both go on to claim is that Melusine's particular otherworldliness resulted in her sons' unusual birthmarks. This idea is not held by Kelly and Léglu alone; Ivy Corfis, while discussing the Spanish version of *Melusine*, the *Historia de la linda Melosina*, says, "the other-worldliness of the mother has left a stigma on the sons [...] the fairy heritage of the sons can explain their physical appearance and defects."[25] Léglu supports the idea that the sons' deformities categorize them as belonging to those groups marked by Cain—traitors, peasants, and monsters—and Albrecht Classen claims that the birthmarks are all "faint traces of their monstrous origin."[26] However, such readings do not quite encompass the whole of the sons' circumstances. They are only one-quarter fairy and have no magical powers, suggesting that the "power" of fairy is diluted as it is mixed with human blood.[27] Their mother is half fairy, half human, and though she regularly takes the form of a half serpent, this was not always her form. Equating Melusine's serpentine hybrid form with her fairy heritage falsely categorizes fairy as visibly monstrous; further, ascribing the deformities of Melusine's sons to their mother's fairy nature ignores the fact that Melusine's visible monstrousness is not inherent but was bestowed upon her by an external source. Melusine's fairy blood may have something to do with her sons' deformities, but an equally possible cause is the sin she committed against her father by imprisoning him in a mountain, for which she is continually punished.

Mother," 181–203; Sylvia Huot, "Dangerous Embodiments: Froissart's Harton and Jean d'Arras's Melusine," *Speculum* 78, no. 2 (2003): 400–21; Dorothy Yamamoto, *The Boundaries of the Human in Medieval English Literature* (Oxford: Oxford University Press, 2000), 212–24.

24   Kelly, "Domestication of the Marvelous," 39; Léglu, "Nourishing Lineage," 78.

25   Corfis, "Beauty, Deformity, and the Fantastic," 190.

26   Léglu, "Nourishing Lineage, 78;" Albrecht Classen, "Love and Fear of the Foreign: Thüring's *Melusine* (1456), A Xenological Analysis," *Daphnis* 33 (2004): 97–113, at 107.

27   Stacey Hahn discusses the relationship between the power of fairy and the dilution of fairy blood in "Crime, Punishment and the Hybrid in Medieval French Romance: Robert the Devil and Geoffrey Big Tooth," in *Crime and Punishment in the Middle Ages and Early Modern Age: Mental-Historical Investigations of Basic Human Problems and Social Responses*, ed. Albrecht Classen and Connie Scarborough (Berlin: De Gruyter, 2012), 87–108, esp. 91–92.

Monstrous births were also attributed to the sin of the parents, particularly the sin of the mother.[28] Indeed, something may be "wrong" with the mother, though it may be her curse more than her fairy blood. That two of Melusine's younger sons are born without any deformity suggests that Melusine *was* successfully "passing" as human and that the effects of her curse were lessening.[29] However, this observation about the lessening of Melusine's curse as it correlates to the birthmarks evident in her offspring is complicated by inconsistencies in the English translation. The English text diverges from the French regarding the timeline of the sons' births: the list of Melusine's sons maintains that there was a two-year gap between Froimond and Horrible, but Horrible is listed as the tenth rather than the eighth son.[30] And yet, both the French and the English narratives say that Thierry/Theoderyk is born the year after Froimond.[31] Melusine in the French text later describes Remnont and Thierry as being ages three and two respectively; in the English text, Theoderyk is called her youngest son and the narrative describes both Theoderyk and Raymond as being young enough to still need Melusine's care after her departure from Lusignan.[32] The lack of ages given and the inconsistency of birth order in the English text suggests that Theoderyk and Raymond were born between Froimond and Horrible, and also that they would probably be in their teens at this point in the narrative. Even if only Theoderyk/Thierry was born between Froimond and Horrible, the fact that the birth of a son without deformities is followed by the birth of the son with the most deformities further complicates the idea that the effects of Melusine's curse on her offspring were lessening over time. If the physical appearance of Melusine's sons indicates the success

---

28   Jane Gilbert, "Unnatural Mothers and Monstrous Children in *The King of Tars* and *Sir Gowther*," in *Mediaeval Women: Texts and Contexts in Late Medieval Britain, Essays for Felicity Riddy*, ed. Jocelyn Wogan-Browne et al. (Turnhout: Brepols Publishers, 2000), 329–344, at 330; Clarissa W. Atkinson, *The Oldest Vocation: Christian Motherhood in the Middle Ages* (Ithaca: Cornell University Press, 1991), 91–92; John Boswell, *The Kindness of Strangers: The Abandonment of Children in Western Europe from Late Antiquity to the Renaissance* (New York: Pantheon Books, 1988), 338–39.

29   Hahn, "Crime, Punishment and the Hybrid," 105.

30   Donald, *Melusine*, 105. Jean d'Arras, *Melusine; Or, The Noble History of Lusignan*, trans. Sara Sturm-Maddox and Donald Maddox (University Park: Pennsylvania State University Press, 2012), 71 (hereafter Maddox). The difference in birth order given for Horrible may be the result of a scribal error as the English text uses Roman numerals to number Melusine's sons.

31   Maddox, *Melusine*, 147; Donald, *Melusine*, 246.

32   Donald, *Melusine*, 318, 322–3.

with which Melusine's passes as human, then the English version of the romance suggests that Melusine is unsuccessful.

And yet, Melusine may not be the sole "polluting" influence in her offspring. Jane Gilbert's essay on the paternity of the mixed-race children in
King of Tars and *Sir Gowther* raises the Aristotelian theory that although the
mother provides the matter for making a child, the father's seed determines
what form the child will take.[33] Following this reasoning, it would seem that
the sons of Lusignan are deformed as a result of their father's sin (that of
killing his uncle), rather than their mother's. Writing about the French and
German versions respectively, Miranda Griffin and Sarah Hillenbrand Varela
both discuss the bestial connections between Raymondin and the wild boar
involved with his uncle's death. According to Griffin and Varela, the tusk-like
giant tooth protruding from Geoffray's mouth indicates Raymondin's monstrous influence more than Melusine's, as both father and son are linked by
their outbursts of rage that result in Melusine's exile.[34] As Griffin goes on to
observe, although she may have a monstrous body, Melusine herself is not
depicted as a monster. The fact that the author chose a fairy heroine as a
founding mother, and that neither the half-fairy Degaré in *Sir Degaré* nor the
half-demon Gowther is monstrous in appearance, casts into doubt the theory
that fairy blood in itself was considered to be a polluting influence.[35] Rather,
monstrosity is a consequence of Melusine's or Raymondin's (or both parents')
sin, and a constant reminder of the conditions Melusine must meet to attain
spiritual salvation.

The scene in which Raymondin spies on Melusine in her bath on a Saturday is one the reader would expect to emphasize Melusine's hybrid, if not serpentine, nature. Raymondin sees Melusine combing her hair in the bath, for
all appearances a beautiful woman until he sees that she has the body of a
serpent. Her tail was "as grete & thykk as a barell" and so long that she made
it touch the ceiling (297). When discussing the same scene in the French version, Kevin Brownlee writes that the description of Melusine's tail abruptly

---

33 Gilbert, "Unnatural Mothers," 330.

34 Miranda Griffin, "The Beastly and the Courtly in Medieval Tales of Transformation: *Bis-
    clavret, Melion,* and *Mélusine*," in *The Beautiful and the Monstrous: Essays in French Litera-
    ture, Thought, and Culture,* ed. Amaleena Damlé and Aurélie L'Hostis (Oxford: Peter Lang,
    2010), 139–150, at 149; Sarah Hillenbrand Varela, "Origins of Misfortune: Sympathetic
    Magic and the Transference of Animality in Thüring von Ringoltingen's *Melusine* (1456),"
    Neophilologus 99 (2015): 271–85, at 279.

35 Sir Degaré has a fairy father and a human mother. See "Sir Degaré" in *The Middle English
    Breton Lays,* ed. Laskaya and Salisbury, 101–29.

de-eroticizes Melusine as a woman: "She is portrayed not only as a monster, but as a somewhat comical monster."[36] This description serves to immediately emphasize the *non*-humanness of Melusine, but this emphasis is short-lived in the text. Raymondin's lament that he has betrayed her casts Melusine once again in courtly terms:

> "Now haue I fonde the ende of my Joye / and the begynnyng is to me now present of myn euerlastyng heuynes / Farwel beaute, bounte, swetenes, amyablete / Farwel wyt, curtoysye, & humilite / Farwel al my joye, al my comfort & myn hoop / Farwel myn herte, my prows, my valyaunce, For that lytel of honour whiche god had lent me, it came thrugh your nobless, my swete and entirely belouyd lady." (298)
>
> ["Now have I come to the end of my joy, and to me now is present the beginning of my everlasting sorrow. Farewell, beauty, bounty, sweetness, amiability; farewell, wit, courtesy, and humility; farewell, all my joy, all my comfort and my hope; farewell, my heart, my prowess, my valiance. For that little honor which God had lent me came to me through your nobility, my sweet and entirely beloved lady."]

Raymondin continues for another dozen or so lines, describing Melusine's nobility, wit, excellence, and other virtues. As Brownlee rightly observes, Raymondin's lament serves to "intensify Mélusine's human side at the very moment that her corporeal identity has been most graphically presented in the text up until now."[37] Instead of shock, disgust, or revulsion at the sight of his wife's hybrid body—all of which might be expected reactions on Raymondin's part—Raymondin expresses remorse that he has betrayed her trust. Classen argues that Raymondin's failure to investigate or examine Melusine's hybrid nature or her origins is his inability to face the existential question of Melusine's Otherness.[38] While this is ultimately true, as Raymondin's fear of the Other results in his denunciation of Melusine later in the romance, Raymondin's lack of revulsion in this particular scene suggests the possibility that Raymondin *could* accept the Other, the hybrid fairy, into his life and his worldview, albeit temporarily. Alternatively, it could be that Raymondin is so familiar with Melusine in her human form and dependent on her wisdom

---

36 Kevin Brownlee, "Mélusine's Hybrid Body and the Poetics of Metamorphosis," *Yale French Studies* 86 (1994): 18–38, at 25.

37 Brownlee, "Mélusine's Hybrid Body," 26–7.

38 Classen, "Love and Fear," 111–5.

and power that, rather than being shaken by the experience of seeing her in a hybrid form, he denies what he has seen and focuses on her humanity. This can certainly be the case considering his emphasis on her humanity in his lament.

However, Raymondin's acceptance—or denial—of Melusine's hybridity comes to an end when he denounces Melusine upon seeing the wreckage left by Geoffray at the monastery of Maillezes:

> "By the feyth that I owe to god, I byleue it is but fantosme or spurut werke of this woman / and as I trowe she neuer bare no child that shal at thende haue perfection, For yet hath she broght none but that it hath some strange token // see I not the horryblenes of her son called Horryble, that passed not vii yere of age whan he slew two squyres of myn / and or euer he was thre yere old he made dye two gentyl women his nourryces, thrugh hys byttyng of theire pappes? / sawe I not also theyre moder of that satirday, whan my brother of Forestz to me brought euyl tydynges of her / in fourme of a serpent fro the nauel douward? / by god, ye / and wel I wote certayn / it is some spyryt, som fantosme or Illusyon that thus hath abused me / For the first tyme that I sawe her / she knew & coude reherce all my fortune & auenture." (311)

> ["By the faith that I owe to God, I believe it is but illusion or the spirit work of this woman, and I believe she never bore a child who may at the end come to perfection (that is, achieve salvation), for yet has she borne (no child) that did not have some strange mark. Do I not see the hideousness of her son called Horrible, who was not seven years of age when he slew two squires of mine, and before he was three years old he killed two gentlewomen, his nurses, by biting their nipples? Did I not also see their mother that Saturday, when my brother (the earl) of Forestz brought me evil tidings of her, in the form of a serpent from the navel downward? Yes, by God, and I know for certain it is some spirit, some phantom or illusion that has thus betrayed me, for the first time I saw her, she knew and could recite my fate and my future."]

Raymondin repeats his accusations to Melusine herself, declaring her a "fals serpente" [deceptive serpent], claiming that neither she nor her sons are anything but phantoms, and that "goode fruyte yssued neuer" ["good fruit" (ie., children) never issued] from her (314). Although he almost immediately recants his words, the damage has been done. Melusine must leave the court of Lusignan and fully take on the form of a serpent, or dragon, until the Last Judgment.

As Raymondin and Melusine weep that they must now be separated by the fulfillment of her curse, their barons lament that they "shal lese this day þe best lady that euer gouerned ony land / the moost sage / most humble / moost charytable & curteys of all other lyuyng in erthe" [shall lose this day the best lady who ever governed any land, the wisest, most humble, most charitable and courtly of all others living on earth] (314). Here, through the voice of the barons, the narrative emphasizes Melusine's virtues both as a Christian woman and as a ruler. As E. Jane Burns observes, Melusine "emerges in this narrative as an exceedingly capable and highly rational manager of estates, convents, long-range expeditions, and battles. All of these tasks require the expert use of her head and appear wholly unimpeded by her partly (and intermittently) animal body."[39] Once again the narrator humanizes Melusine, even on the verge of her transformation, by highlighting her social role—which she developed by performing humanity and passing as human—and how loved she is by the people of Lusignan.[40]

Melusine's path to redemption requires her assimilation into human society, despite her mixed fairy and serpentine nature. Judith Butler, Suki Ali, and Sara Ahmed all discuss how performance is part of how someone of mixed-blood can "pass" as one race or another.[41] In order to successfully pass as another race or gender, one needs to do more than dress the part; the way one behaves, moves, speaks, and interacts with others are all visible markers by which one claims a particular identity. For Melusine to successfully pass as human woman in medieval France, even a fictional one, this would include participating in courtly and Christian society. Melusine attempts to integrate into human society through the performance of certain rites of passage: namely, her marriage to Raymondin and her construction of the castle of Lusignan. The former marks her entrance into human society and the latter establishes her place and her authority in that society. These performances and participation in human society are necessary for Melusine's eligibility for salvation.

---

39   E. Jane Burns, "A Snake-Tailed Woman: Hybridity and Dynasty in the *Roman de Mélusine*," in *From Beasts to Souls: Gender and Embodiment in Medieval Europe*, ed. E. Jane Burns and Peggy McCracken (Notre Dame: University of Notre Dame, 2013), 185–220, at 205.

40   Brenda M. Hosington, "Mélusines de France et d'Outremanches: Portraits of Women in Jean d'Arras, Coudrette, and their Middle English translators," in *A Wyf Ther Was: Essays in Honour of Paule Mertens-Fonck*, ed. Juliette Dor (Liège: Dép. d'anglais, Université de Liège, 1992), 199–208, at 203.

41   Suki Ali, *Mixed-Race, Post-Race*, 12–14; Sara Ahmed, *Strange Encounters: Embodied Others in Post-Coloniality* (London: Routledge, 2000), 127.

Comprising six chapters in the romance, the wedding is described in immense detail, complete with feasting, jousting, and gift-giving. Most important is the ceremony itself, which takes place in a richly ornamented chapel filled with images of the crucifixion and of the Virgin Mary. Unlike the supernatural women in analogues to *Melusine* from Walter Map, Gerald of Wales, and Gervase of Tilbury, and even the fairy ancestress of Richard I, Melusine has no aversion to the crucifix or to the Eucharist.[42] All three of these writers include stories of supernatural women who hide their true nature by studiously arriving late to Mass and leaving before the Host is consecrated; but when forced to stay for the consecration of the Host, they vanish, usually by flying out of the window.[43] Melusine, however, passes "the Eucharist test," for not only does she attend mass sung by the bishop, but the bishop also blesses the wedding bed.[44] As James Wade observes, most fairies in literature are comfortable with Christian ritual, unlike demons, who cannot withstand swearing in the name of God or the presence of the Eucharist.[45] That Melusine participates in Christian ritual and even encourages her sons to keep the Christian faith counters the claim that fairies are demonic; rather, Melusine's behavior in these instances is more like a human than a demon.[46] These scenes of Melusine's engagement in Christian rituals and the blessing of the bed legitimize Melusine's marriage to Raymondin and thus remove any doubt of their marriage's validity in what is

42   The prologue to Melusine includes a discussion of other supernatural women, specifically mentioning the account described by Gervase of Tilbury. A recurring theme in these descriptions of otherworldly mistresses is their aversion to Christian rituals or symbols. Walter Map, *De Nugis Curialium* [*Courtiers' Trifles*], trans. M. R. James, ed. C. N. L. Brooke and R. A. B. Mynors (Oxford: Clarendon Press, 1983), 344–51; Gerald of Wales, *Giraldi Cambrensis Opera*. Vol. VIII, De Principis Instructione Liber, ed. G. F. Warner (London: Rolls Ser. 21.8, Kraus Reprint 1964), 310; S. E. Banks and J. W. Binns, ed. and trans., *Gervase of Tilbury: Otia Imperialia: Recreation for an Emperor* (Oxford: Clarendon Press, 2002), 664–69; B. B. Broughton, *The Legends of King Richard I Coeur de Lion: A Study of Sources and Variations to the year 1600* (Paris: Mouton & Co., 1966), 78–86.

43   Tania M. Colwell, "Reading *Mélusine*: Romance Manuscripts and Their Audiences, c.1380–c.1530" (PhD diss., Australian National University, 2008), 101; Gabrielle M. Spiegel, "Maternity and Monstrosity: Reproductive Biology in the *Roman de Mélusine*," in *Melusine of Lusignan*, 100–124, see 101–2.

44   Donald, *Melusine*, 54, 56–7. This phrase is borrowed from James Wade, *Fairies in Medieval Romance* (New York: Palgrave Macmillan, 2011), 31.

45   Wade, *Fairies in Medieval Romance*, 31–32.

46   Nichols, "Melusine Between Myth and History: Profile of a Female Demon," in *Melusine of Lusignan*, ed. Maddox and Sturm-Maddox, 137–64, at 145; Robert J. Nolan, "An Introduction to the English Version of *Melusine*: A Medieval Prose Romance" (PhD diss., New York University, 1971), 60, 106–36.

essentially a dynastic founding tale. These Christian details also highlight Melusine's positive relationship with Christianity and her attempts to "perform" as fully human.

If Melusine's wedding marks her entrance into human Poitevin society, then her construction of Castle Lusignan further establishes her position. Immediately after their wedding, Melusine oversees the construction of a castle on the land Raymondin received from his cousin, the Earl of Poitiers. Up until this point in the narrative, the Earl of Poitiers and the rest of his court have expressed curiosity, and perhaps a little suspicion, at Melusine's unknown origins. Melusine oversees the construction of the Castle of Lusignan, which is built in mere days. Melusine's magic, worked through her mysterious workmen "that no body knew from whens these werkmen were" [no one knew from whence these workmen came] (62), is the only way Castle Lusignan could have been built with such expediency. When it is finished, the Earl of Poitiers and his family, the Earl of Forestz, and other barons are invited to a great feast that includes the usual pastimes of jousting and dancing. Melusine then announces that the reason for the feast is to decide upon a name for the castle. Tania Colwell describes this construction and "baptism" scene as being a "watershed moment" in which Melusine is accepted into the Poitevin court.[47] In an exchange in which Melusine and the Earl of Poitiers both submit to the authority of the other, the Earl of Poitiers publicly acknowledges Melusine's wisdom and superiority, and thus her right to name the castle herself:

> "By my feyth, fayre Cousyn," said the Erle of Poiters, "we as in general sayen to you, as oure wylle is / that ye your owneself shall / as right is / gyue name to it [the castle]. For emong we alle is not so moch wyt as in you alone that haue bylded up & achyeuyd so strong and fayre a place as thesame is / and wete it, that none of us shall entremete hym to doo that ye spek of." (62)
>
> ["By my faith, cousin," said the Earl of Poitiers, "we as a whole say to you, that our will is that you yourself by right should give name to it (the castle), for there is not among us so much cleverness as in you, who have alone built and accomplished so strong and fair a place as this is. And be aware that none of us shall undertake to do that which you speak of."]

In this speech, the Earl of Poitiers allows Melusine a place in his court based not on her status as wife to his cousin Raymondin, but in her own right. When Melusine christens the castle Lusignan after her own name, the Earl of Poitiers

---

47   Colwell, "Reading *Mélusine*", 113–4.

approves, declaring that Lusignan is a fitting name because it is derived from Melusine's own name, which he says means "marvelous" in Greek, and also because the castle was marvelously made:

> "By my feyth," said the Erle, "the name setteth full wel to it for two causes, First bycause ye are called Melusyne of Albanye, whiche name in grek language is as moch for to say / as thing meruayllous or commyng fro grete merueylle, and also this place is bylded and made meruayllously." (64)
>
> ["By my faith," said the Earl, "the name fits it well for two reasons: first, because you are called Melusine of Albany, a name which in the Greek language means 'wonderful' or 'coming from a marvelous event,' and also this place was miraculously made."]

It is Melusine's name that is commemorated in the naming of the castle; here, Melusine secures her position in the human court in that a castle and a dynasty can be named after her. The more she integrates into human society, the closer she moves towards her goal of salvation. Melusine continues her enterprises by overseeing the construction of other castles, churches, and monasteries, as well as sponsoring her sons' crusades. In these ways Melusine "performs" humanity by taking part in rituals that mark her as part of human and Christian society, especially as one of the nobility.

But Melusine would not need to attempt to "pass" as human if it were not for her mixed blood, and the narrative focus is always on Melusine's hybrid nature. When it comes to defining a cultural identity or race, "people label themselves, and are labeled," and so the labels Melusine uses for herself must be considered alongside those assigned to her by others, characters and critics alike, when examining Melusine's identity and its salvific implications.[48] Throughout the narrative, Melusine herself elevates her human heritage above her fairy nature. In addition to saying that she is "of god" and a "Catholique" (31) when she first meets Raymondin, she also openly speaks of her lineage after Raymondin publicly denounces her fairy nature:

> "I wyl lete you knowe what I am & who was my fader, to thentent that ye reproche not my children, that they be not borne but of a mortal woman, and not of a serpent, nor as a creature of the fayry / and that they are the children of the doughter of kynge Elynas of Albanye and of þe queene Pressyne." (320)

---

48   Bartlett, "Medieval and Modern Concepts of Race and Ethnicity," 54.

["I will let you know what I am and who my father was, so that you cannot rebuke my children that they were born not of a mortal woman but of a serpent, or a woman of the fairy, for they are the children of the daughter of King Elinas of Albany and the queen, Pressine."]

Here Melusine claims her human paternity, not her fairy maternity, as her primary identity. She does this partly for her sons' sakes to ensure her children are classified as human. Her sons are the grandchildren of the former king and queen of Albany; it is her human heritage that Melusine leaves her children, not her heritage as a fairy. However, she also claims her human nature for her own sake. It was as a human woman that she had lived among them for so many years, and as a human woman she almost attained her desired salvation. The timing of her speech, spoken on the verge of her transformation, from the liminal location of the window, highlights her hybridity, yet Melusine's choice to claim her human heritage even as she is changing into a serpent is important.[49] For Melusine, the life of a human woman is preferred to that of a fairy, and she is sorry to be leaving human society. She is aggrieved not only because the human court of Lusignan is where she has made her family and her home, but also because it was only by living, and dying, as a human woman that she could have attained salvation for her soul. It is during this episode that Melusine's capacity for remorse and desire for redemption is most evident, thus distinguishing her from the demonic and associating her with humanity. And yet the transformation into a serpent is the result of her maternal heritage, ultimately establishing her identity as a fairy.

The romance of *Melusine* displays an interest in the purity of blood and the possibility of a fairy "passing" as human. Melusine herself expresses anxiety about which heritage her sons will be known for, demonstrating her own conflict regarding being a person of mixed fairy and human blood. The author, too, shows concern for the mixing of human and fairy blood through the descriptions of Melusine's sons' deformities. This concern for purity of blood implies a hierarchy that privileges one race over the others. Recent studies on mixed-race experiences highlight not only the injustice rooted in such a hierarchy, but also the ambiguities that come from being perceived as belonging to two races, such as someone who is "mixed" having difficulty integrating into either of the races, ethnicities, or cultures of which they are a part.[50] Regarding fairies, "race"

---

49   Brownlee, "Mélusine's Hybrid Body," 33–4.
50   Janice Gould, "The Problem of being 'Indian': One Mixed-Blood's Dilemma," in *De/Colonizing the Subject: The Politics of Gender in Women's Autobiography*, ed. Sidonie Smith and Julia Watson (Minneapolis: University of Minnesota Press, 1992), 81–89, at 83.

does not have to do with skin color, but rather the spiritual and supernatural qualities that make them inexplicably different and Other. Melusine's attempt to perform humanity is apparent to the reader through the use of dramatic irony; although the other characters in the romance are unaware that Melusine is of a different "race," the audience knows Melusine's mixed heritage and that she, half human and half fairy, can only "pass" as a human until her fairy lineage is revealed. The public denunciation of her fairy heritage triggers the other half of her fairy mother's curse, resulting in a forced transformation into a flying serpent for eternity, or until the day of judgment. The use of dramatic irony is integral for the narrative to explore the extent of, and the limits to, the soul's redemption from sin. The theological hierarchy here privileges the human race over all others, and being half human is not enough for Melusine to earn salvation on her own.

The romance demonstrates that Melusine's human heritage and attempts to pass as human are integral to her eligibility for salvation. Initially, Melusine's human blood would have won out over her fairy blood, making her human, mortal, with an immortal soul. Her sin of imprisoning her father somehow gives primacy to her fairy blood, which can only be countered through Melusine's marriage to a human husband who upholds the conditions laid out in her mother's curse. Melusine must successfully "pass" as human if she wants the human gift of salvation. The romance prioritizes Melusine's humanity first by stating that her human blood was superior to her fairy blood, then again by illustrating how Melusine performs humanity. In both cases, Melusine would have had to become human in order to attain salvation, suggesting that only humans are allowed redemption.

The romance's concern for both her salvation and how "human" she is suggests that Melusine's plight reassures the audience of the place humanity holds in the medieval Christian cosmos. In the hierarchy of spiritual beings, demons are too evil to desire mercy, and fairies might yearn for salvation, but only humans can have reconciliation with God as His prized creation. That Melusine and her mother both desire human society, that Melusine's salvation is dependent first on the superiority of her human blood inherited from her father, and then on the success with which she integrates into human society, demonstrates that in *Melusine,* for all of fairy's beauty and allure, humanity is the privileged race in this paradigm.

CHAPTER 14

Melusine and Purgatorial Punishment: The Changing Nature of Fays

Zoë Enstone

Laurence Harf-Lancner divided medieval romances involving fairies into two distinct categories: *conte mélusinien* and *conte morganien,* based on the two eponymous fairies Morgan le Fay and Melusine.[1] Michael Twomey identifies the main difference between these two types of romance as the attitude of the fairy towards her human love interest: "in 'Melusinian' narratives the fay's desire for a human male is beneficent, whereas in the 'Morganien' narratives the fay's desire is dangerous and destructive."[2] However, these terms belie the inconsistency of the two fays themselves within the various works in which they appear. An exploration of these two fairy types, and of magical women within romance more broadly, shows that this division is complicated, as an assumption of consistency of character and motivation is not necessarily applicable to these complex figures. Magical women in romance tend to defy such a straightforward categorization; a distinction between characters based on a single attribute blurs the impacts that particular authors, periods, and literary developments have on their presentation. The same characters can appear differently depending on the context; characters shift and develop across time, languages and texts. Furthermore, they can be considered in terms besides their attitudes to lovers; their fairy natures exist in conjunction with roles as mothers, wives, sisters, daughters, and rulers. Their motivations are more complicated and diverse than a binary in terms of romantic relationships would suggest; indeed, in a number of later romances, fairy women sometimes function as agents of punishment within a Christian context, thus acting with a motivation separate from (although potentially related to) their love interests. These punishments are not generally directed at their male lovers and would

---

1 Laurence Harf-Lancner, *Les Fées au Moyen Âge: Morgane et Mélusine ou la naissance des fées* (Paris: Champion, 1984).

2 Michael W. Twomey, "Morgain la Fée in Sir Gawain and the Green Knight: From Troy to Camelot," in *Text and Intertext in Medieval Arthurian Literature*, ed. Norris J. Lacy (New York: Garland Publishing, 1996), 91–115, at 103.

therefore indicate additional nuances within the representation of these characters not explained by Harf-Lancner's division.

Jean d'Arras' *Mélusine* heralds a change in depictions of the nature of fairy women, with Presine assuming the role of punisher in relation to her daughters' sins. However, the framing of the role of fairies within a Christian context seems the result of a more gradual Christian appropriation of fairy women within the romances over time. Earlier romances were often content to imagine the power of the fairies as merely Other in nature; as James Wade notes, as "beings neither angelic nor demonic, fairies constitute the ambiguous supernatural," and Helen Cooper remarks, "Although they were sometimes given a place in the divinely created order of beings, fairies sit very uneasily with a Christian context, and tend to be made the subject of works whose ideologies are oblique to orthodox piety."[3] Thus these figures are not contained within a straightforward Christian conception of good and evil, at least in their earlier iterations.

Indeed, their role and nature is questionable and in earlier works these fairies are often less amenable to Christian explication. For example, in Geoffrey of Monmouth's *Vita Merlini* [*Life of Merlin*] (ca.1150), Morgan le Fay is portrayed as a mysterious goddess-like figure, the head of a group of sisters who inhabit an island:

> quarum que prior est fit doctior arte medendi exceditque suas forma prestante sorores. Morgen ei nomen didicitque quid utilitatis gramina cuncta ferant ut languida corpora curet. Ars quoque nota sibi qua scit mutare figuram et resecare novis quasi Dedalus aera pennis.
>
> [The one who is first among them has greater skill in healing, as her beauty surpasses that of her sisters. Her name is Morgen, and she has learned the uses of all plants in curing the ills of the body. She knows, too, the art of changing her shape, of flying through the air, like Daedalus, on strange wings].[4]

Similarly, in the *Draco Normannicus* [*Standard of the Normans*] of Étienne de Rouen, written between 1167 and 1170, the author states that

---

3   James Wade, *Fairies in Medieval Romance* (Basingstoke: Palgrave Macmillan, 2011), 1; Helen Cooper, *The English Romance in Time: Transforming Motifs from Geoffrey of Monmouth to the Death of Shakespeare* (Oxford: Oxford University Press, 2004), 173.

4   Geoffrey of Monmouth, *Life of Merlin: Vita Merlini*, trans. Basil Clarke (Cardiff: University of Wales Press, 1973), 100–1.

Saucius Arturus petit herbas inde sororis;
Avallonis eas insula sacra tenet.
Suscipit hic fratrem Morganis nympha perhennis,
Curat, alit, refovet, perpetuumque facit.
[the wounded Arthur seeks after the herbs of his sister; these the sacred isle of Avallon contains. Here the immortal fay Morgan receives her brother, attends, nourishes, restores, and renders him eternal].[5]

These early portrayls of Morgan le Fay depict a figure who is immortal and inhabits a space that is separate from the world of the mortal characters of the text. In these examples fairies are associated with healing, but also shapeshifting; their powers do not seem to accord specifically with a Christian framework and they do not appear in the role of punishers at this juncture. The immortal aspect of Avalon seems unrelated to Christian ideas of heaven, hell, and eternity, perhaps instead drawing on Celtic myth, as several critics have commented; Maureen Fries, for instance, states that it is a "typical Celtic Otherworld."[6] Fairy power is not Christian power at this point, and where fairies do act to help or punish mortals, this appears to be as a result of their own inclination rather than as part of a divine plan.

However, later romances sought to incorporate fairies more clearly within a Christian context and therefore approach their Otherness more skeptically. The author of the thirteenth-century French *Lancelot*, part of the Vulgate Cycle, notes that it is fools who refer to Morgan le Fay as "la dieuesse" [the goddess].[7] As Cooper notes, "although fairies might perhaps exist, goddesses, in a Christian world, do not."[8] The author of the *Lancelot* is dismissive of the earlier

---

5   Roger Sherman Loomis, "King Arthur and the Antipodes," *Modern Philology* 38 (1941): 289–304, see particularly 290, n.7. Étienne de Rouen, *Le Dragon Normand et autres poèmes d'Étienne de Rouen*, ed. M. H. Ormot (Rouen: Société de l'histoire de Normandie, 1884), 112, lines 1161–4.

6   Maureen Fries, "Female Heroes, Heroines, and Counter-Heroes: Images of Women in Arthurian Tradition," in *Popular Arthurian Traditions*, ed. Sally K. Slocum (Madison, WI: Bowling Green University Popular Press, 1992), 5–17, at 13. See also Ferdinand Lot, "Nouvelles études sur le cycle Arthurien: Une source de la Vita Merlini, les Etymologiae d'Isidore de Séville," *Romania* 45 (1919) 1–22, at 14; Gertrud Schoepperle Loomis, "Arthur in Avalon and the Banshee," in *Vassar Mediaeval Studies*, ed. Christabel Forsyth Fiske (New Haven: Yale University Press, 1923), 3–25.

7   Alexandre Micha, ed., *Lancelot: Roman en Prose du XIIIe Siècle*, vol. 1 (Geneva: Droz, 1978–83), 275. Samuel N. Rosenberg, trans., "Lancelot, part III," in *Lancelot-Grail: The Old French Arthurian Vulgate and Post-Vulgate in Translation*, ed. Norris J. Lacy, vol. 2 (Oxford: Garland, 1993–6), 305.

8   Cooper, *English Romance in Time*, 186.

power attributed to fairies and gives his magical characters distinct origins for their abilities. Indeed, the two principal magical women of the Vulgate Cycle, Morgan le Fay and the Lady of the Lake, have both acquired their magic from the same source: their relationship with Merlin.[9]

Merlin's powers in this work are placed in a specifically Christian context, which means that the women's powers can be ascribed to a Christian source. Although he is described as the son of an incubus in earlier works such as the *Historia regum Brittaniae* [*History of the Kings of Britain*] (ca.1155),[10] the Vulgate Cycle is based on Robert de Boron's *Merlin*, which "drew upon Christian tradition by making the sire a devil in hell, motivated not merely by sexual desire but by a complicated plot to circumvent the mother's natural goodness and piety to create the Antichrist."[11] The plan is undermined by Merlin's baptism, but his powers are still ascribed to his demonic parentage (and the power of God). The magical women of the Vulgate Cycle therefore possess arcane knowledge and magical powers that derive from a Christian rather than otherworldly origin. Thus, the process of reconsidering the nature of fairy and an explanation of their otherworldly power is already underway before the creation of the *Melusine* texts. With a Christian basis for their power, their actions are included within a Christian morality much like the human characters, rather than being part of a separate order of magic and morality.

As Christian figures enacting punishment on behalf of God, these fairy women become part of a Christian scheme of salvation. However, establishing what the authors of romances may have drawn from contemporary Christian ideas of hell and purgatory is complicated by the diverse nature of the works. As Helen Cooper notes, "the romances themselves display a multiplicity of angles on Christianity. It is indeed misleading to speak of 'Christianity' as a single entity in this context [...] because the various texts connect with it in so many different ways."[12] Indeed, notions of hell and purgatory[13] developed

---

9   Micha, *Lancelot*, I, 301; Rosenberg, "Lancelot, part III," 311.

10   Geoffrey of Monmouth, *The History of the Kings of Britain: An Edition and Translation of the De gestis Britonum (Historia Regum Britanniae)*, ed. Michael D. Reeve, trans. Neil Wright (Woodbridge: The Boydell Press, 2007), 137–8.

11   Peter H. Goodrich, "The Erotic Merlin," *Arthuriana* 10 (2000): 94–115, at 97.

12   Helen Cooper, "Introduction," in *Christianity and Romance in Medieval England*, ed. Rosalind Field, Phillipa Hardman, and Michelle Sweeney (Cambridge: D. S. Brewer, 2010), XIII-XXI, XV.

13   Helen Phillips notes that purgatory could be seen as a period of time spent in hell, or part of hell rather than as a separate space. "Introduction," in *The Awntyrs off Arthure at the Terne Wathelyne*, ed. Helen Philips (Lancaster: Modern Spelling Texts, 1988), 1–21, at 4.

across the medieval period and were hugely influential on literature and art, generating various works on visions of hell and some specific descriptions of the punishments that might await.[14] Jacques le Goff's exploration of the development of the idea of purgatory in the twelfth and thirteenth centuries noted that it "was an elaboration of the Christian belief that certain sins could under certain conditions be redeemed after death" and that "each soul must spend a greater or lesser time in Purgatory depending on the gravity of the sins that must be expiated."[15] Katherine Clarke suggests that "earlier medieval conceptions of 'purgatorial punishments' and 'purgatorial fire' matured into a sense of a fixed location for purgatory as the *limus* of heaven, where elect souls resided between physical death and the day of the Last Judgment. In the schools and in popular tales and sermons, clerics developed and disseminated ideas about a tangible, spatial purgatory that took hold in the medieval imagination."[16] This tangible purgatory with its fiery punishments as well as hell and the tortures inflicted there resonate with the notion of sin and punishment in the works discussed in this chapter. There are points of correspondence between the imagery used in the punishment of particular sins, especially *luxuria*, but also in the way that some of the punishments are tied directly to a specific sin or duration of time, suggesting an atonement for the sin identified.

Along with the more general incorporation of fairies into a Christian reconception of magic as part of a wider gift from God, the nature of fairies' power is developed further in the French *Melusine* texts and later English romances as the fays in these works use their powers to identify and punish sin. These penalties include a Christian purgatorial language relating to punishment or make use of imagery that draws on consequences for sin. This change is especially apparent through the modifications that the authors make to their sources, which function as intentional developments in the roles of these fairy women. In particular, Malory's *Morte Darthur* reframes both Morgan le Fay and Nymue as agents of punishment, a development of their roles in the sources, and Tryamour in *Sir Laufal* by Thomas Chestre is similarly developed from her earlier incarnations.

---

14   See Eileen Gardiner, ed., *Medieval Visions of Heaven and Hell: A Sourcebook* (New York: Garland Medieval Bibliographies, 1993).

15   Jacques le Goff, *The Medieval Imagination*, trans. Arthur Goldhammer (Chicago: University of Chicago Press, 1985), 67, 70.

16   Katherine Clarke, "Purgatory, Punishment, and the Discourse of Holy Widowhood in the High and Later Middle Ages," *Journal of the History of Sexuality* 15, no. 2 (2007): 169–203, at 177.

The legend of Melusine was "known from folklore,"[17] as Jean-Jacques Vincensini notes, but became more widely popular after Jean d'Arras' and Coudrette's versions were produced in the late fourteenth and early fifteenth centuries. These romances were evidently read in England, as an English translation of Jean's narrative was made around 1500,[18] and there is, therefore, the prospect that *Melusine* had an impact on the development of fairies in later English romances. Given that Melusine cannot be proven as a direct source of the romances discussed, Christine Rauer's concept of analogues is particularly useful in discussion of this nature as the works do "present parallels."[19] *Sir Launfal* was written in the late fourteenth to early fifteenth century, surviving in a fifteenth-century manuscript, British Library MS Cotton Caligula A. ii, but was based on Marie De France's *Lanval* of the late twelfth or early thirteenth century and the Middle English *Sir Landevale* from the fourteenth century.[20] Sir Thomas Malory's *Le Morte Darthur* was composed in the mid to late fifteenth century and exists in a printed edition produced in 1485 by William Caxton and the Winchester Manuscript (London, British Library, MS Additional 59678). Malory drew on a range of sources to produce his work, including a number of French romances. According to Croft, Malory may have had access to a "single-volume compilation," given his repeated references to a mysterious "Freynshe booke" when speaking of his sources.[21] However, as Terence McCarthy has pointed out, often "he claims to be borrowing when he is being original" in order to add *auctoritas* to his narrative.[22] Both these English

---

17   Jean-Jacques Vincensini, foreword to *A Bilingual Edition of Jean D'Arras's Mélusine or L'Histoire De Lusignan*, by Jean d'Arras, trans. Matthew W. Morris (Lewiston, NY: Edwin Mellen Press, 2007), XIII. Hereafter, Morris.

18   A. K. Donald, ed., *Melusine: Compiled (1382–1394 AD) by Jean D'Arras, Englisht about 1500*, Part I, Early English Text Society ES. 68 (London: Kegan Paul, Trench, Trübner & Co., 1895).

19   Christine Rauer, *Beowulf and the Dragon* (Woodbridge: Boydell and Brewer, 2000), 10. According to Rauer, a source "presents distinctive parallels with the target text's phraseology and/or imagery," "demonstrably predates the target text," and "demonstrably circulated in the same historical and literary context as the target text." An analogue "presents parallels with the target text's phraseology and/or imagery," "cannot be shown to predate the target text; it is determined by a late or undetermined date of composition," and "cannot be shown to have circulated in the same historical and literary context [...] it is characterized by a different or undetermined historical and literary background."

20   Both works available in A. J. Bliss, ed., *Sir Launfal* (London: Nelson, 1960).

21   Thomas H. Crofts, *Malory's Contemporary Audience: The Social Reading of Romance in Late Medieval England* (Cambridge: D. S. Brewer, 2006), 17.

22   Terence McCarthy, "Malory and his Sources," in *A Companion to Malory*, ed. Elizabeth Archibald and A. S. G. Edwards (Cambridge: Boydell and Brewer, 1996), 75–96, at 78.

texts are part of a wider textual tradition and network of source texts, but are notable in their divergence from the source material in relation to the changes made in the roles of the fairy women. These alterations present a consistent development in the incorporation of fairy power into a Christian structure as seen in the French romances, but also suggests a broader change in the role and nature of fairies stemming from the influence of *Mélusine*.

Despite this reconfiguration of the nature of fairies, Jean d'Arras clearly also sought to position his characters within ongoing traditions of romance fairies. He followed works such as the *Vita Merlini* and Vulgate Cycle in his reference to Avalon as the natural environment of his fays. When she can no longer live with her husband, Presine takes her three daughters to Avalon, a magical island, "also called the Lost Isle, because none could ever find their way back to it, no matter how many times they'd been there, except by chance."[23] Morgan le Fay's early appearance in Geoffrey of Monmouth's *Vita Merlini* depicts her as one of eight sisters who rule over Avalon, and her accompaniment of a dying Arthur to Avalon is one of the points of consistency across works of an otherwise multifaceted figure. The other fairy figures discussed in this chapter are similarly incorporated into this wider fairy tradition through their links to Avalon. In the *Morte Darthur*, Nymue is one of the women who goes to Avalon with Morgan le Fay and Arthur at the end of the text, and although *Sir Launfal* gives Olyran as Tryamour's kingdom, a "jolif ile,"[24] other versions of the Lanval story give Avalon as the source and destination of the fay.[25] These references to Avalon demonstrate the Otherness exemplified by the fairies and the level of their power. Corinne Saunders has noted that "This parallel world [is] neither demonic nor divine," and that while theologians explained fairies as "demons, fallen angels who now inhabited the space between heaven and earth, with the power to tempt and harm," the romances were "more ambivalent about the powers of such creatures."[26] Thus the mentions of Avalon across the works under discussion do not align the characters with a particular moral inclination, but these references instead remind the reader of the literary nexus within which these figures have evolved and act as a reminder of the potential power of fairies.

---

23   Morris, *A Bilingual Edition of Mélusine*, 67.

24   Thomas Chestre, "Sir Launfal," in *Middle English Romances*, ed. Stephen H. A. Shepherd. (New York: W. W. Norton, 1995), 190–218, at 217, line 1022. Hereafter, Shepherd.

25   Shepherd, "Sir Launfal," 198, n.7.

26   Corinne Saunders, "Magic and Christianity," in *Christianity and Romance in Medieval England*, 84–101, at 86.

As Jean d'Arras' narrative develops, his intended positioning of the actions of his fays becomes clearer. The Christian framing of the punishment by fairies is initially demonstrated in the way in which Melusine's punishment by Presine is described. Melusine has imprisoned her father in retribution for his broken promise and her mother's suffering as a result of this betrayal. As a punishment for Melusine's actions, Presine decrees that Melusine will become a serpent below the waist each Saturday:

> Mais se tu treuves homme qui te veuille prendre a espouse, que il te convenance que jamais le samedy ne te verra, non qu'il te descuevre, ne ne le die a personne, tu vivras cours naturel comme femme naturelle, et mourras naturelment [...] Et se tu es dessevree de ton mary, saiches que retourneras ou tourment de devant, sans fin, tant que le Hault Juge tendra son siege.
>
> [But if you can find a man who will be willing to take you for his wife and will promise to never look upon you on Saturday—or if he should come upon you on that day and say nothing about it to anyone—you will live out the course of a normal life like a mortal woman and will die a natural death [...] And you may be certain that if your husband fails you, you will return to your previous torment without respite until that day that the Great Arbiter comes to sit in judgment.][27]

The language of this description, including the specific idea that this "torment" will only continue until Judgment Day, indicates that Presine is working within the limitations of Christian punishment. Presine gives Melusine specific details about the duration of her punishment and its conclusion, indicating the purgatorial nature of her intentions. At the end of Melusine's life she will have expiated her sin; however, this punishment may be extended to Judgment Day, the traditional end of purgatorial torment. Jean is careful to contextualize the power of the fairies within a specific Christian framework, noting "L'en treuve tant des merveilles, selon commune estimacion, et si nouvelles que humain entendement est contraint de dire que les jugemens de Dieu sont abisme sans fons et sans rive, et sont ses choses merveilleuses" [And in fact, so many things are found that are commonly considered extraordinary and astonishing that the human mind is forced to admit that the judgments of God are indeed unfathomable abysses].[28] He additionally refers to the religious context suggested

---

27   Morris, *A Bilingual Edition of Mélusine*, 70–1.
28   Morris, *A Bilingual Edition of Mélusine*, 52–3.

in similar stories by Gervase of Tilbury: "Et dit le dit Gervaise qu'il creoit que ce soit par aucuns meffaiz miseres que nulz n'en a congnoissance fors lui" [That same Gervais says also that he believes it was because of some misdeeds un-known to the world which displeased God that He secretly punished them with these afflictions, such that none have knowledge of it but He].[29] Thus Presine's punishment of Melusine is contained within the broader sense of a punish-ment from God; God is here presented as all-knowing and his agent, Presine, is able to formulate a fitting punishment for Melusine, such as the "unfathom-able" nature of punishment from God allows.

The punishment itself is also suffused with Christian connotations. Melu-sine's partial submersion in a bathtub at the point of the discovery by Ray-mondin and the split of her human and serpent halves resonates with a similar punishment enacted by Morgan le Fay in an episode in Malory's *Morte Dart-hur.* In both instances, a woman appears in a split form, punished below the waist by a fairy. Both works could be drawing on a well-developed tradition in Christian works describing hell and purgatory of sinners, as penance, being partially immersed in water, the specific depth depending on the nature of the transgression. Although the water itself does not form part of the punishment in Jean's *Melusine*, Melusine's discovery by Raymondin within a bath is the key image that represents her Saturday punishment. There are clear correlations between this immersion in water, the idea of baptism, and the fiery immer-sion that forms part of purgatory. As Helen Phillips has noted, "[p]urgatory, like baptism, cleansed the soul and helped it to escape Satan and his demons (Matt. 3.11 speaks of a baptism of water and a baptism of fire)."[30]

In Malory's *Morte Darthur,* this correspondence resonates all the more given the changes that Malory makes to his source material at this juncture. The nar-rative describes "a dolorous lady" imprisoned in a tower "that hath bene there in paynes many wyntyrs and dayes, for ever she boyleth in scaldyng watir" [a sad lady ... who has been there in pain for many days and winters, for she is ever boiling in scalding water].[31] Lancelot discovers that she has been placed there by Morgan le Fay and her confederate, the Queen of North Galys, "bycause she was called the fayryst lady of that contrey" [because she was known as the fair-est lady of the country].[32] As Molly Martin has noted, the woman becomes "an image not of threateningly superior beauty, but of vulnerability and inactivity.

29   Morris, *A Bilingual Edition of Mélusine*, 55–6.

30   Phillips, "Introduction," 4.

31   Thomas Malory, *The Works of Sir Thomas Malory*, ed. Eugène Vinaver, rev. P. J. C. Field, 3rd ed. (Oxford: Clarendon Press, 1990), 791.

32   Malory, *Works*, 792.

Though still a spectacle, the boiling woman highlights her captors' relative power and apparently does not diminish their beauty as she had previously."[33] This power indicates the fairies' and the woman's relative statuses within the text in terms of the nature of the punishment; the woman is punished through both the pain inflicted and through her removal from the chivalric world. This alternate space of punishment would also seem to resonate with the spatial and time-specific nature of purgatory.

There are two similar instances in Malory's French sources. The Prose *Tristan* gives this account taken from its source in the Vulgate *Lancelot,* but Morgan is not involved in this punishment in this version; it is, in fact, God who subjects the woman to "agony and torment" from which she is not permitted to escape, "il ne s'est pas encore vengiés d'un grant pechié que je fis ja" [for He has not yet avenged himself of a great sin I committed.][34] The second instance in the *Lancelot* occurs when Morgan subjects a woman who is her rival in love to a brutal punishment: "ele le mist en une tant felenesse chartre que il li estoit avis de jor et de nuit qu'ele fust en glace des les pies jusqu'a la çainture, en amont sambloit qu'ele fust en feu ardant" [she put her into a harsh prison, where she had the feeling day and night that she was standing in ice from the waist down and in a blazing fire above.][35] Malory may have combined these two instances, but it is also possible that he was influenced by the wider iconographic significance of this scene, drawing on Christian depictions of punishments in hell.

Although Myra Olstead has noted that the imprisonment of the woman in scalding water is "a motif that folklorists and Arthurian scholars recognize as unusual, if not, in fact, unique", both Olstead and Lucy Paton have noted another instance of Morgan le Fay enacting a similar punishment which suggests that Malory's episode is not the only occurrence.[36] In the Italian *Pulzella Gaia* [Merry Maiden] dating from the middle of the fourteenth century, Gawain fights against a serpent who defeats him and then transforms into a beautiful

---

33   Molly Martin, *Vision and Gender in Malory's* Morte Darthur (Cambridge: D. S. Brewer, 2010), 157.

34   Micha, *Lancelot: Roman en Prose du XIIIe Siècle,* II, p. 374; Roberta L. Krueger, trans., "Lancelot, part IV," in *Lancelot-Grail: The Old French Arthurian Vulgate and Post-Vulgate in Translation,* ed. Norris J. Lacy, vol. 3 (Oxford: Garland, 1993–6), 99.

35   Micha, *Lancelot: Roman en Prose du XIIIe Siècle,* vol. 1, 276; Samuel N. Rosenberg, trans. "Lancelot, part III," in *Lancelot-Grail: The Old French Arthurian Vulgate and Post-Vulgate in Translation,* ed. Norris J. Lacy, vol. 2 (Oxford: Garland, 1993–6), 305.

36   Myra Olstead, "Lancelot at the Grail Castle," *Folklore* vol. 76, no. 1 (1965): 48–57, at 48. See also Lucy Allen Paton, *Studies in the Fairy Mythology of Arthurian Romance* (Boston: Ginn & Company, 1903), 100.

woman who becomes his lover. He is warned not to reveal their relationship and when he does, breaking his promise, the maiden has to return to her mother, Morgan le Fay, who imprisons her in a dungeon "up to her waist in water"[37] in a partial fish-like state. Although the *Pulzella Gaia* predates Jean d'Arras' version of *Mélusine* (while potentially sharing the tale's source in oral tradition), it is possible that both Jean and the Italian author were drawing on a similar iconographic tradition when developing these episodes within their respective texts, a tradition which commonly depicts punishments in hell through the division at the waist and use of serpents.

There is a well-established background to the use of heat or water as a means of punishment, including the tenth-century *Fis Adamnáin* [*Vision of Adamnan*], preserved in *Lebor na hUidre* [*The Book of the Dun Cow*], the oldest surviving compilation of early Irish vernacular literature. This work features a "river of fire, its surface an ever-burning flame" which lies before one of the portals to heaven:

> Abersetus dan anim aingil ingaire in tsrotha sin derbas ocus niges anmand na nǽm din chutrumma chinad nos lenand, corroichet comglaine ocus comsoillse frietrochta rétland.
> [Abersetus is the angel's name who keeps watch over that river, and purges the souls of the righteous, and washes them in the stream, according to the amount of guilt that cleaves to them, until they become pure and shining as the radiance of the stars.][38]

The number of ablutions is related to the level of sin that needs to be purged. This theme of the punishment being proportional to the crime, but also developing to encompass specific body parts for specific sins, was common, stemming from the third-century Greek *Apocalypse of Paul* (extant in Greek, Syriac, Coptic, and Ethiopic) and its fifth- or sixth-century Latin translation, the *Visio Sancti Pauli* [*Vision of St. Paul*], which was well-known during the Insular period. The *Visio* influenced a number of Old and Middle English texts and is also preserved in an Old French version. As Theodore Silverstein notes, the *Visio*

---

37   Edmund G. Gardner, *The Arthurian Legend in Italian Literature* (London: J. M. Dent & Sons, 1930), 244.

38   Ernst Windisch, ed., *Irische Texte mit Wörterbuch*, 4 vols, vol. 1. (Leipzig: Hirzal, 1880), 180–1. C. S. Boswell, *An Irish Precursor of Dante: A Study on the Vision of Heaven and Hell Ascribed to the Eighth-century Irish Saint Adamnán, with Translation of the Irish Text* (London: David Nutt, 1908), 36; R. I. Best and Osborn Bergin, eds., *Lebor na hUidre* (Dublin: Royal Irish Academy, 1929), 71.

"became one of the chief formative elements in the later legends of heaven and hell."[39] While visiting hell, St. Paul sees a "fiery stream" in which sinners are punished to different levels according to their sins, "some up to their knees, some up to their navels, others to their necks, others still, up to their eyebrows." The archangel Michael, who acts as Paul's psychopomp, tells him that "Those in pain to their navels were adulterers who did not repent until the time of death."[40]

A similar punishment is meted out to the lustful in *Visio Tnugdali* [*Vision of Tnugdal*] (1149), which was extremely popular throughout the later Middle Ages.[41] Cormac Mac Cartaig, king of Desmond and Munster, is immersed to the waist in fire as an "expiation of a breach of his marriage vow."[42] The tropological significance of this demarcation at the navel is emphasized in John Mirk's *Festial* of the early fifteenth century, in which he describes an abbess who was "a clene woman of hyr body as for dede of lechery" [a woman whose body was pure of the act of lechery] but "had gret lust to talke þerof" [had great desire to talk (about it)] and is therefore punished above the waist while her lower half "schon as þe sonne" [shone like the sun].[43] A similar sentiment is expressed in King Lear's summation of women, which reflects the late medieval homiletic commonplace that *superbia* [pride] and *luxuria* [lust] are especially characteristic of the frailty of women:[44]

> Down from the waist
> They're centaurs, though women all above.
> But to the girdle do the gods inherit;
> Beneath is all the fiend's.[45]

---

39   Theodore Silverstein, ed., *Visio Sancti Pauli: The History of the Apocalypse in Latin Together with Nine Texts* (London: Christophers, 1935), 3.

40   Silverstein, *Visio Sancti Pauli*, 12–13.

41   See Thomas Kren, ed., *Margaret of York, Simon Marmion, and the Visions of Tondal* (Malibu: J. Paul Getty Museum, 1992).

42   Boswell, *Irish Precursor of Dante*, 222.

43   John Mirk, *Mirk's Festial: A Collection of Homilies*, ed. Theodor Erbe, Early English Text Society ES. 96, vol. 1 (London: Kegan Paul, 1905), 96–7.

44   Mireille Vincent-Cassy, "Péchés de femmes à la fin du Moyen Age," in *La condición de la mujer en la Edad Media. Actas del Coloquio Celebrado en la Casa de Velázquez, del 5 al 7 de noviembre de 1984. Madrid*, ed. Y.-R. Fonquerne and A. Esteban (Madrid: Universidad Complutense, 1986), 501–17.

45   William Shakespeare, *The Tragedy of King Lear*, in *The Oxford Shakespeare: The Complete Works*, ed. Stanley Wells and Gary Taylor (Oxford: Oxford University Press, 1998), IV.5.121-4. See also Frederika Bain's use of this passage in "Hybridity, Mutability, and the Accessible Other" in this volume.

Thus, a division at the waist appears relatively common in the depiction of punishments, especially for the sins of lust and lechery, particularly when the punishment is directed at women. There are, therefore, potential links between the notion of a physically divided punishment in religious works, especially in terms of a partial immersion in heat or water, and the use of this depiction in the romances, despite Olstead's claims of scarcity. It is possible that Malory's sources are making direct reference to this association, especially given that the punishment is delivered directly by God.

In relation to this instance in Malory's *Morte Darthur*, Malory's deviation from his source text in transferring responsibility for this torture from God to fairies is unusual. Malory's sources do not reveal the nature of the sin that the woman has committed to be punished in this manner by God; she claims that "l'achoisons por quoi g'i sui mise ne savrois vos ja ne vos ne autres par moi, devant que cil sera venus qui de ci me getera" [neither you nor anyone else will ever find out why I am here until the knight comes who will release me],[46] although in fact, no further information is forthcoming when Lancelot succeeds in this task. However, it seems likely that, in being immersed only to her waist, Malory's sources imply that her "great sin" is a sexual transgression. The reallocation of responsibility for the punishment to Morgan and the Queen of North Galys and the specific motivation of jealousy of her appearance would thus be a logical progression; Morgan's sexual advances towards knights, her lust, is being enacted through her repression of a potential rival.

The link between the fairy women and lust is explained through an ongoing assumption of women's frailty in relation to sexuality. Ruth Mazzo Karras notes that by the later Middle Ages, "lust was considered the woman's sin par excellence",[47] while Anke Bernau observes, "The trope of the extreme 'sexual sinner' is decidedly gendered, in keeping with beliefs surrounding female sexuality and carnality."[48] Ferrante describes the specific association of women with *luxuria* in terms of a putative physiological rationale: "woman was held to be more given to lust than man because she was thought to be, in her humors, more cold and wet."[49] Indeed, *Luxuria* was generally a feminine

46 Krueger, "Lancelot, part IV," 99; Micha, *Lancelot: Roman en Prose du XIIIe Siècle*, II, 374.

47 Ruth Mazo Karras, "The Regulation of Brothels in Later Medieval England", *Signs* 14 (1989): 399–433, at 400. See Richard Kieckhefer, "Erotic Magic in Medieval Europe," in *Sex in the Middle Ages*, ed. Joyce E. Salisbury (New York: Garland, 1991), 30–55, at 30.

48 Anke Bernau, "Gender and Sexuality," in *A Companion to Middle English Hagiography*, ed. Sarah Salih (Cambridge: Boydell and Brewer, 2006), 104–121, at 112.

49 Joan M. Ferrante, *Woman as Image in Medieval Literature: From the Twelfth Century to Dante* (New York: Columbia University Press, 1975), 6.

personification, often intertwined with a serpent, as in the carving of *Luxuria* in the Chapter House Vestibule of Salisbury Cathedral (ca.1260–80). The serpent or dragon is traditionally associated with the devil: "et proiectus est draco ille magnus serpens antiquus qui vocatur Diabolus et Satanas qui seducit universum orbem proiectus est in terram et angeli eius cum illo missi sunt" [And that great dragon was cast out, that old serpent, who is called the devil and Satan, who seduceth the whole world; and he was cast unto the earth, and his angels were thrown down with him].[50] In addition to this, serpents, "dragons and other monsters seem frequently to have exhibited an association with untrammelled sexuality within medieval written and visual culture."[51] In this context, the scene in Herrad of Hohenburg's *Hortus Deliciarum* [*Garden of Delights*] (1186-ca.1196), in which the lustful are punished in hell by both flames and serpents, is also notable.[52]

   This serpentine imagery is used in the appearance of Gaynour's [Guinevere's] mother in the late fourteenth century *Awntyrs off Arthure at the Terne Wathelyne,* in which the ghost of Gaynour's mother appears in grisly form to provide a warning of the dangers of sin and the potential punishments that await. She is described as "Serkeled with serpents [that sate] to the sides / To tell the todes theron my tonge wer full tere" [Circled with serpents that sat to the sides: / My tongue would be hard pressed to count the toads on it].[53] The role of the mother in this instance is not to impose the punishment, but to warn against the sin through the use of herself as an example of the repercussions of sins of this nature, as Barbara A. Goodman notes, using "strong sexual implications; indeed, according to her own report, her form is due to her sexual misconduct when alive."[54] This example demonstrates the transition between

50   *Biblia sacra iuxta vulgata versionem*, ed. R. Weber et al., 3rd ed. (Stuttgart, 1983); Richard Challoner, trans., *The Holy Bible: Translated from the Latin Vulgate* (Rockford, IL: Tan Books, 1989); Revelation 12.9.

51   Samantha J. E. Riches, "Virtue and Violence: Saints, Monsters, and Sexuality in Medieval Culture," in *Medieval Sexuality: A Casebook*, ed. April Harper and Caroline Proctor (London: Routledge, 2008), 59–80, at 60.

52   Herrad of Hohenbourg, *Hortus deliciarum*, ed. Rosalie Green et al., 2 vols (Leiden: Warburg Institue, 1979), I, 220, fol. 255r (pl. 146).

53   Shepherd, ed., "The Awntyrs Off Arthure at the Terne Wathelyne," in *Middle English Romances*, 219–242, at 223, lines 120–1. Helen Phillips, ed. *The Awntyrs off Arthure at the Terne Wathelyne* (Lancaster: Lancaster Modern Spelling Texts, 1988).

54   Barbara A. Goodman, "Women's Wounds in Middle English Romances: An Exploration of Defilement, Disfigurement, and a Society in Disrepair," in *Wounds and Wound Repair in Medieval Culture*, ed. Larissa Tracy and Kelly DeVries (Leiden: Brill, 2015), 544–570, at 565.

common depictions of punishments in hell or purgatory and the use of these punishments and images within the context of the romances, especially given the specific use of the serpents within this description.

Thus, the combination of partial immersion in water and transformation into a serpent or dragon from the waist down would have resonated with the punishment for sin for medieval readers, and more specifically with lust and sexuality, particularly in its focus on the division of the female form. This division of the body at this point into half a fish or serpent can also be considered in relation to mermaids and their overt sexuality. As Christina Weising notes: "Mermaids are sexual creatures. They symbolize the sinning woman descending from original sin and are the incarnation of temptation since antiquity and Homer's Odyssey."[55] Much has been written on the link of Melusine to the notion of the mermaid; as succinctly noted by Sophia Kingshill, "she is clearly a water spirit".[56] Thus the idea of a partial immersion in water or partial transformation from the waist down would have had a wider significance to authors of the romances discussed. This iconographic resonance of Melusine as a partial dragon or serpent has particular import when considering the punitive implication of Melusine's split serpentine form. The Christian connections between both the serpentine aspect and the partial immersion is apparent in Jean d'Arras' text through the notion of the purgatorial immersion reflecting the purification of baptismal water, and hinted at with Malory's replacement of God with Morgan and the Queen of North Galys. The serpent's association with sin and punishment is evident, linking Melusine through this split form with a range of meanings and connections associating her particularly with the devil and mermaids, and suggesting a sexual link to Melusine's punishment in terms of the imagery as well as the use of Presine as an agent of punishment on behalf of God.

Although neither Melusine nor the woman in Malory's *Morte Darthur* are being punished directly for lust, the symbolic division of the upper and lower half of their bodies serve a similar function in both instances. In each text,

---

55   Christina Weising, "Vision of 'Sexuality,' 'Obscenity,' or 'Nudity'? Differences Between Regions on the Example of Corbels," in *Sexuality in the Middle Ages and Early Modern Times: New Approaches to a Fundamental Cultural-Historical and Literary-Anthropological Theme*, ed. Albrecht Classen (Berlin: De Gruyter, 2008), 325–82, at 337.

56   Sophia Kingshill, *Mermaids* (Dorchester: Little Toller Books, 2015), 105. For a full discussion of the analogues of Melusine in art and myth, see Misty Urban, *Monstrous Women in Middle English Romance* (Lewiston, NY: Edwin Mellen Press, 2010), 59–68. Sabine Baring-Gould confidently classifies Melusine as a mermaid in *Curious Myths of the Middle Ages* (London: Rivingtons, 1876); see also Frederika Bain's contribution to this volume for a discussion of Melusine/mermaid parallels.

the punishment functions to render the woman temporarily unattractive or unobtainable to a love interest. In relation to Melusine, Kevin Brownlee has noted that her transformation and Raymondin's discovery of her form draws on contemporary literary traditions: "the voyeur gazing through a secret perforation in the door leading to a lady's bath is a stylized generic convention within the context of the late fourteenth-century French romance narrative."[57] Expectations of this convention are undermined, however, by the description of her portrayal as "a somewhat comical monster."[58] Thus Melusine is rendered as unattractive through the form that she takes in the gaze of Raymondin and becomes potentially less desirable as a wife, mother, and ruler. Although his initial concerns after his discovery dwell on the implications of his broken promise, Raymondin's later accusations reflect on her undesirable form: "Hee, tres false serpent" [Ah! Sordid serpent!].[59] Presine succeeds in punishing Melusine through the physical agony that she will endure as a serpent in her final transformation, but it is this initial emotional barrier that is perhaps most damaging. Melusine's first lament when Raymondin reveals her serpentine state relates to the impact on their relationship: "Las! Mon amy, or sont noz amours tornees en hayne, noz doulceurs en durté, noz soulaz et noz jjoyes en larnes et en plours, nostre bon eur en tres dure et infortuneuse pestilence" [Alas, my love! Now our love has changed to hatred, our gentleness to harshness, our comfort and joy to tears and weeping, our happiness to great misfortune and tribulation].[60] It is notable that although Melusine does not see Raymondin again while in her human form, the texts do note that she returns to care for her children. The transformation is thus specifically aimed at the destruction of her relationship with Raymondin.

In this punishment of division through enchanted water or serpent transformation, the fays are really focusing their punishment on a specific aspect: the women's relationships with men. In Malory's *Morte Darthur*, it is the sexual potential of Morgan's rival understood through Morgan's assessment of her beauty that is being addressed; Morgan is ensuring that she will not be able to act as competition for the affection of knights. It is only Lancelot, with his status as the best knight, who is finally able to rescue her after five years. And in the *Pulzella Gaia,* Morgan renders her daughter, who has already escaped a

---

57   Kevin Brownlee, "Melusine's Hybrid Body and the Poetics of Metamorphosis," in *Melusine of Lusignan: Founding Fiction in Late Medieval France,* ed. Donald Maddox and Sara Sturm-Maddox (Athens, GA: University of Georgia Press, 1996), 76–99, at 80.

58   Brownlee, "Melusine's Hybrid Body," 82.

59   Morris, *A Bilingual Edition of Mélusine,* 596–7.

60   Morris, *A Bilingual Edition of Mélusine,* 598–9.

fully serpent form once, unavailable to her lover through the dual punishment of imprisonment and transformation.

The shared punitive intention of the fays in these examples is perhaps also indicative of the changing role of the fairy, for the terms of the punishments they inflict, being purgatorial in nature, are thus part of a sanctified process of divine punishment. Sara Sturm-Maddox notes that "It would appear that God's secret judgements, hidden from mortals, are at least partially accessible to fairies, for Melusine is fully aware of her own fate."[61] As these texts are rooted within a Christian framework, the actions of the fays must be seen as ultimately subject to the will of God, especially given the purgatorial nature of the torture inflicted. Indeed, after her concern about the impact on their relationship, much of Melusine's distress at Raymondin's revelation of her Saturday form is caused by the implications that this has for her future, the "penance obscure" [dark penance][62] that she sadly informs Raymondin is now unavoidable: "Et les joyes que je y souloye avoir me seront peines, tribulacions et griefs penitences et pestilences" [And the joys I had here, will henceforth be naught for me but pain and suffering, great penance and affliction][63] as well as specifically stating "puis qu'il plaist a Cellui qui tout puet faire et deffaire" ['tis the will of Him who has the power to do and undo all things].[64] Thus Melusine and Presine, her mother, who has inflicted this punishment upon her, have a unique understanding of the nature of Melusine's condition. Their fairy or half-fairy nature allows them an insight into the disposition of their own souls that is not available to the humans of the text. For Melusine, this nature is not necessarily depicted positively, as Presine indicates that Melusine should have aspired to the potential human, rather than fairy, nature that her father might have offered her—perhaps indicating that fairies' inclusion within a Christian framework and as enactors of God's will is not the same as being part of humanity. This insight and almost God-like ability to inflict purgatorial torment may have suggested the replacement of God with Morgan and the Queen of North Galys in the section of the *Morte Darthur* involving Lancelot's rescue of the maiden. God's punishment of an unspecified sin in the source text gives way to a more petty jealousy, but retains the burning purgatorial punishment of the original.

---

61   Sara Sturm-Maddox, "Crossed Destinies: Narrative Programs in the *Roman de Mélusine*," in *Melusine of Lusignan*, 12–31, at 27.

62   Morris, *A Bilingual Edition of Mélusine*, 598–9.

63   Morris, *A Bilingual Edition of Mélusine*, 606–7.

64   Morris, *A Bilingual Edition of Mélusine*, 604–5.

Although Melusine is the recipient of punishment, she is also the agent of punishment within the text in a role that resonates with an instance in the *Morte Darthur*. Melusine leads her sisters in the imprisonment of their father "en la merveilleuse montaigne de Norhonbelande nommee Brumbloremllion, et de la n'ystra de toute sa vie" [in the enchanted mountain of Northumberland called Brumborenlion, from which he will never emerge],[65] particularly noting the "dolour" [misery][66] that he will suffer as retribution for breaking the promise that he would not see Melusine's mother while she was in childbed.[67] The mountain imprisonment is not unique to this work as a fairy punishment, as some Arthurian texts include Arthur's imprisonment in a mountain by Morgan le Fay as an alternative to his removal to Avalon.[68] However, the direct link between the perception of his sin and Melusine's role as a fairy agent of punishment suggests similarities to Merlin's imprisonment by Nymue in Malory's *Morte Darthur*.

Nymue and Merlin are linked through their relationship in a number of works, but in Malory's version, an unwilling Nymue is sexually pursued by Merlin and tolerates him only long enough to learn his magic before enacting an imprisonment as punishment. Malory makes substantial changes to this incident when compared to his potential source texts for this aspect of the *Morte Darthur*: the *Merlin*, the *Lancelot,* and the *Suite du Merlin*.[69] The French works are careful to explain the reasons for the imprisonment. In the *Merlin,* Nymue is described as being genuinely in love with Merlin and imprisons him out of a fear of losing him, whereas in the *Lancelot* or *Suite du Merlin*, she is described as being more calculated in her use of Merlin for education and cruel in her final imprisonment.

In the *Morte Darthur,* Nymue's actions are carefully established within the context of Merlin's motivation and pursuit of her, which is described as sinful: "allwayes he lay aboute to have hir maydynhode, and she was ever passynge

65   Morris, *A Bilingual Edition of Mélusine*, 68–9.
66   Morris, *A Bilingual Edition of Mélusine*, 70–1.
67   Morris, *A Bilingual Edition of Mélusine*, 65.
68   R. S. Loomis, "The Legend of Arthur's Survival," in *Arthurian Literature in the Middle Ages*, ed. R. S. Loomis (Oxford: Oxford University Press, 1959), 64–71, at 64–5
69   Rupert T. Pickens, trans., "Merlin," in *Lancelot-Grail: The Old French Arthurian Vulgate and Post-Vulgate in Translation*, ed. Norris J. Lacy, vol. 1 (Oxford: Garland, 1993–6), 281–3; Martha Asher, trans., "Suite du Merlin Part 1," in *Lancelot-Grail: The Old French Arthurian Vulgate and Post-Vulgate in Translation*, ed. Norris J. Lacy, vol. 4 (Oxford: Garland, 1993–6), 245–8; Samuel N. Rosenberg, trans. "Lancelot Part 1", in *Lancelot-Grail: The Old French Arthurian Vulgate and Post-Vulgate in Translation*, ed. Norris J. Lacy, vol. 2 (Oxford: Garland, 1993–6), 12.

wery of hym for cause he was a devils son" [he always made attempts to have her maidenhead (that is, seduce or rape her), and she was surpassingly weary of him because he was a devil's son].[70] By showing how much Nymue is harassed and also noting that Merlin has prior connections to evil through his parentage, Malory makes Merlin's imprisonment seem justified, as Hodges notes: "Malory takes care to make Nyneve's innocence clear [...] He persistently tries to seduce her against her will, clearly violating the code of chivalry Arthur has just announced."[71] Malory is also careful in the way that he describes how Merlin feels. He never claims that Merlin loves Nymue; therefore, as Holbrook maintains, "the traditional fatal love has diminished into patent lechery."[72] Merlin no longer falls into the category of a *fin'amor* lover, tested by his mistress with the expectation of a reward and then cruelly betrayed, as he appears in some of the French sources, but is a lecherous stalker who deserves his punishment. Nymue imprisons Merlin but does not harm him as in, for instance, the *Suite du Merlin* where her heartless nature is made explicit, as although she claims not to want to kill him, she actually devises a much crueler death for him to "avenge myself better."[73] The purgatorial aspect of Merlin's imprisonment in the *Morte Darthur*, the implication of suffering for a period of time until he is judged to have atoned for his sins, is emphasized through the discovery of his ongoing imprisonment later in the text: Bademagus "herde hym make a grete dole" [heard him express great sorrow] and Merlin reveals that "he might never be holpyn but by her that put hym there" [he might never be helped but by she who put him there].[74] Nymue retains control of Merlin's imprisonment for an indefinite amount of time and thus seems to act as an agent of God's punishment, albeit retaining some of the incomprehensible nature of God's wisdom that Jean d'Arras noted.

This potentially subversive action of Nymue's in removing an integral member of Arthur's court, and also eliminating the magical support that Merlin offers to Arthur in the development of his empire, is justified within the framework that Arthur and Merlin have developed. Nymue is, in fact, supporting the ideals and structure to which Arthur has bound his subjects. If Nymue is considered as a religious agent, this action is also justified, as she enacts a

---

70 Malory, *Works*, 126.

71 Kenneth Hodges, "Swords and Sorceresses: the Chivalry of Malory's Nyneve," *Arthuriana* 12 (2002): 78–96, at 83.

72 S. E. Holbrook, "Nymue, the Chief Lady of the Lake in Malory's Le Morte Darthur," *Speculum* 53 (1978): 761–77, at 770.

73 Asher, "Suite du Merlin Part 1," 260.

74 Malory, *Works*, 132.

punishment that is warranted in a Christian context. This role alters the sense of this imprisonment compared to Malory's sources, but is part of a broader reconsideration of Nymue, one demonstrated through the changes that Malory makes in a later episode in the *Morte Darthur* that also presents Nymue as a righteous agent of Christian punishment.

Nymue is instrumental in the retributive treatment of a lady called Ettarde. Ettarde's rejection of the love of a knight called Pelleas demonstrates the sin of pride: she "was so proude that she had scorne of hym and seyde she wolde never love hym thoughe he wolde dye for hir" [was so proud that she scorned him and said she would never love him, though he would die for her].[75] The text emphasizes the humiliation that Ettarde causes Pelleas in order to prevent him from pursuing her, as well as her cruel dismissal of him, despite his status as "a passynge good knyght of his body" [a surpassingly good knight]:[76] "she rebukyth me in the fowlyst maner [...] she woll nat suffir me to ete nother drynke. And allwayes I offer me to be her prisoner, but that woll she nat suffir me" [she rebuked me in the foulest manner [...] she would not allow me to eat or drink, and always I offered to be her prisoner, but she would not tolerate me].[77] Ettarde is clearly censored within the work for this demonstration of pride: "all ladyes and jantyllwomen had scorne of hir that she was so prowde" [all ladies and gentlewomen scorned her, because she was so proud].[78] Thus Nymue's intervention has a substantive basis in terms of her implementation of a Christian sense of morality, but also in terms of the expectations of the court and society.

This focus on Ettarde's sinful rejection of Pelleas is in contradiction to Malory's source, the *Suite du Merlin*, in which the lady, Arcade, does not love Pelleas because of his inferior lineage—"he was not of such birth that she should love him"[79]—but instead falls in love with Gawain. Arcade does not seem to be considered sinful in the way that Ettarde does, and it is Gawain's guilt at his actions that causes him to relinquish Arcade and convince her to marry Pelleas. Malory thus alters his version through the punishment that Nymue perpetrates, enchanting Ettarde so that she loves Pelleas "well nyghe she was nere

75   Malory, *Works*, 166.

76   Malory, *Works*, 169.

77   Malory, *Works*, 168.

78   Malory, *Works*, 166.

79   Martha Asher, trans., "Suite du Merlin Part 2," in *Lancelot-Grail: The Old French Arthurian Vulgate and Post-Vulgate in Translation*, ed. Norris J. Lacy, vol. 5 (Oxford: Garland, 1993–6), 6.

oute of hir mynde" [she was close to being out of her mind].[80] Although the text clearly states that it is Nymue who has used magic to change Ettarde's feelings, she tells Ettarde that it is "the ryghteuouse jugemente of God" [the righteous judgement of God].[81] The text does not specifically indicate that Nymue uses her magic to make Pelleas hate Ettarde rather than loving her, but when Pelleas claims "suche grace God hath sente me that I hate hir as much as I have loved hir" [such grace God has sent me that I hate her as much as I loved her], Nymue replies "thanke me therefore" [thank me for that].[82] The language that Malory uses in this instance clearly develops the link between the punitive actions of fays and Christian punishment, as Nymue's actions not only serve to punish the sin of pride but also advance her own interests, as the text notes that Nymue becomes Pelleas's lover herself, and they "loved togedyrs duryng their lyfe" [loved together during their life].[83]

Malory's *Morte Darthur* is not the only later medieval romance that makes these alterations and developments; a punishment associated with a specific sin and enacted by a fairy woman is also an integral component of *Sir Launfal* by Thomas Chestre. This work makes distinct alterations to its sources, Marie de France's *Lanval* and the Middle English *Sir Landevale,* to add the punishing fairy role. In *Sir Launfal*, Gwennere [Guinevere] makes advances to Sir Launfal, and when rejected accuses him of trying to seduce her as well as offending her through an unfavorable comparison to his lady. Sir Launfal is tried and required to produce his lady, with Gwennere declaring that she should be blinded if he is able to do this. When the lady Tryamour appears at the court to exonerate Launfal, she enacts this punishment on the queen: "Wyth that, Dame Tryamour to the Quene geth / And blew on her swych a breth / That never eft might sche se" [with that, Lady Tryamour went to the Queen and blew on her such a breath that she might nevermore see].[84]

As with Malory's depiction of Ettarde, the sinful nature of the recipient of the punishment is made clear and, as Dinah Hazell observes, the punishment is appropriate to Gwennere's actions: "[a]n obvious physical manifestation of Gwennere's moral and spiritual blindness."[85] This punishment is an addition to the sources and again shows the fairy lady in a punitive role. The sin of

---

80   Malory, *Works*, 172.
81   Malory, *Works*, 172.
82   Malory, *Works*, 172.
83   Malory, *Works*, 172.
84   Chestre, "Sir Launfal", 217, lines 1006–8.
85   Dinah Hazell, "The blinding of Gwennere: Thomas Chestre as Social Critic," *Arthurian Literature* xx (2003): 123–44, at 138.

Gwennere is made clear throughout the text; the initial description depicts her in stark contrast to the worthy Sir Launfal:

> But Syr Launfal lykede her noght-
> Ne other knyghtes that wer hende.
> For the lady bar los of swych word
> That sche hadde lemmannys under her lord,
> So fele ther nas noon ende.[86]
> [But Sir Launfal was not pleased with her—
> Nor were any other knights who were noble,
> For the lady revealed such a failure of her word
> That she had lovers concealed from her lord,
> So very many that there was no end (to them).]

Her promiscuity is identified before she is more broadly described as "fel" [wicked][87] and the full range of her anger at the rejection by Launfal explored: "Therefore the Quene was swythe wroghth [...] For wrethe syk sche hyr bredde" [therefore the Queen was so intensely angry that she made herself sick with wrath].[88] Peter Lucas notes that "the queen's anger receives greater emphasis than in *Landevale*,"[89] while Eve Salisbury comments that "Guenevere exhibits a threatening female libido that challenges not only the legal parameters of marriage but the entire social order."[90] Thus the fairy Tryamour's actions, much like the other fairies discussed, are justified within the Christian context of the work, as Lucas notes: "Only supernatural power can prevail against this evil human initiative."[91] Tryamour therefore works in a similar way to the other fairy ladies through her knowledge of the sin committed and the exacting of a suitable punishment. Gwennere, much like the lady in boiling water in Malory's *Morte Darthur,* will act as a visible reminder of the consequences of sin and will endure an ongoing punishment.

---

86   Chestre, "Sir Launfal," 191, lines 44–8.

87   Chestre, "Sir Launfal," 195, line 156.

88   Chestre, "Sir Launfal," 209, lines 700, 704.

89   Peter J. Lucas, "Towards an Interpretation of 'Sir Launfal' with particular reference to Line 683," *Medium Aevum* 39 (1970): 291–300, at 291.

90   Eve Salisbury, "Chaucer's 'Wife,' the Law, and the Middle English Breton Lays," in *Domestic Violence in Medieval Texts*, ed. Eve Salisbury, Georgiana Donavin, and Merrall Llewelyn Price (Gainesville: University Press of Florida, 2002), 73–93, at 86.

91   Lucas, "Towards an Interpretation," 293.

Through a consideration of the later medieval texts involving these fairy figures, it is evident that there is a change in the way that fairy women are portrayed in relation to the punishments that they enact on other characters and the Christian justification for these punishments. The actions of Melusine and Presine in Jean d'Arras' *Mélusine* precipitate a change in the nature of fays and a reworking of the source texts to include this revised role. There are particular resonances between the punishment of Melusine by Presine and Morgan le Fay and the Queen of North Galys' punishment of a beautiful woman in the *Morte Darthur*. These texts are connected by an iconographic significance in the punishments that the fairies inflict relating to the depiction of punishment in hell or purgatory. There are further associations between the changes made to Nymue in the *Morte Darthur* and Tryamour in *Sir Launfal* that give them the power to punish sin, especially Merlin's imprisonment for lust, Ettarde's broken heart as a consequence of pride, and Gwennere's lust and anger punished through blinding by Tryamour. Thus, Harf-Lancner's division of romances according to the attitude of the fay to her lover does not accommodate the changing role of fairy women in relation to the development of a religious punishing role. Although *Mélusine* cannot be considered a definite source or direct influence on later English romances, it would seem to exemplify a change in the depiction of fairy women, one that emerges in the alterations that Malory and Chestre make to their source texts to rework the Otherness of the figures of Morgan, Nymue, and Tryamor to promote a more obviously Christian version of events. A consideration of the changing nature of fairies thus reveals much about attitudes to the conflict between magic and religion that these authors attempted to negotiate in their works. The *Mélusine* texts provide a crucial turning point in the way in which this conflict is examined that continues through the later romances.

CHAPTER 15

Metamorphoses of Snake Women: Melusine and Madam White

Zifeng Zhao

Metamorphosis, a common term in biology, indicates the developmental change in the form or structure of an animal after its birth or hatching. In literature and art, the term usually indicates a transformation from human to non-human being, or vice versa. As Irving Massey has observed, despite its unclassifiable variety, literary metamorphoses always serve certain purposes: to "point [to] a moral, assist in structural differentiation, illustrate a theory of transmigration, or simply provide an escape."[1] Many literary works such as Ovid's *Metamorphoses* demonstrate that metamorphosis brings either positive or negative, but never neutral, attributes to the one who undergoes it. Notably, these works also show that the creature into which someone transforms often determines which qualities they assume.

Serpentine metamorphosis, as one can imagine, rarely brings a happy ending to heroes or heroines because of its association with the negative symbolism of snakes in many cultures. However, David Gallagher points out that the consequences of serpentine metamorphosis are mostly dependent on gender: snake women are prone to unhappy endings. For instance, according to Gallagher's observation, Cadmus's metamorphosis in Ovid's *Metamorphoses*, which gradually turns him into a serpent, is "a means of escaping the crisis he finds himself in."[2] In contrast, Serpentina in Hoffmann's *Der Goldne Topf* [*The Golden Pot*], a beautiful woman and a snake, represents sexual temptation and portrays a negative image.[3] These two serpentine metamorphoses suggest a potential mechanism of literary metamorphoses whereby a character's gender plays a significant role in deciding his or her destiny, even moreso than the type of creature into which he or she transforms.

---

1 Irving Massey, *The Gaping Pig: Literature and Metamorphosis* (Berkley: University of California Press, 1976), 17

2 David Gallagher, *Metamorphosis: Transformations of the Body and the Influence of Ovid's Metamorphoses on Germanic Literature of the Nineteenth and Twentieth Centuries* (Amsterdam: Rodopi, 2009), 274–275.

3 Gallagher, *Metamorphosis,* 277–283.

© KONINKLIJKE BRILL NV, LEIDEN, 2017 | DOI 10.1163/9789004355958_017

The European Melusine and her Chinese counterpart Madam White, two significant and popular figures in the literature and art of their cultures, exemplify this gender-specific mechanism of serpentine metamorphoses. The stories of both snake women have changed tremendously over time from their prototypes in folklore into numerous literary versions. Early works of Melusine in French by Jean d'Arras (1393) and in German by Thüring von Ringoltingen (1456) present her as a supportive wife and thoughtful mother despite her tragic ending. Melusine's serpentine nature contributes to her tragedy in Jakob Ayrer's drama *Von der schönen Melusina* (1598). By comparison, in the early Chinese work "The Legend of the Three Pagodas of West Lake" (1550), Madam White's image is closely connected with promiscuity and cannibalism. In later adaptations such as "Madam White Is Kept Forever under the Thunder Peak Pagoda" (1624), she is portrayed as a loyal wife but still associated with transgressions such as theft.

Apart from Melusine and Madam White's possible communal origins in Nāga, an Indian serpentine goddess,[4] it is arresting that Melusine and Madam White's images and stories share so much in common. On one hand, both metamorphoses suggest a fluid transformability between ambiguous dichotomies, such as between monstrosity and humanity, malevolence and benevolence, evil and good; on the other hand, they point to certain embedded mechanisms of the serpentine metamorphoses, in which the male authors of these two stories and their premodern societies play a significant role. A comparison of Melusine and Madam White demonstrates that the serpentine metamorphosis of women in both European and Chinese literature reflects how women of both cultures were influenced by masculine authority in premodern times. Their similar tales display the ambiguity of female power and patriarchal constraint, which increases over time under the pressure of political and religious ideologies.

Sarah Miller believes that the female body by itself is the key to the fluid characteristics of the metamorphosis of women, as its "ubiquity and necessity" demand an "intimate engagement" with not only sexuality and reproduction but also monstrosity: "The (corporeal) seepages of the monstrous female body [...] erode not only the boundaries of the discursive ideologies endowed with the task of translating monstrous signs, but also the very boundaries that

---

4   Misty Urban, *Monstrous Women in Middle English Romance* (Lewiston, NY: Edwin Mellen Press, 2010), 59; Josef Kohler, *Der Ursprung der Melusinensage: Eine ethnologische Untersuchung* (Leipzig: E. Pfeiffer, 1895), 1–10; Nai-tung Ting, "The Holy Man and the Snake-Woman: A Study of a Lamia Story in Asian and European Literature," *Fabula* 1 (1966): 145–191, esp. 145–147.

shape individual bodies and subjectivity itself."[5] Therefore, metamorphoses that allow serpentine female bodies to fluidly traverse between humanity and monstrosity, sexuality, and imposed transgressions of moral and religious standards such as theft or unchasteness are the expressive means by which to camouflage or promote certain male-dominated societies' intentions of oppressing femininity. To investigate these intentions, it is necessary to identify the changeable elements of snake women in Melusine and Madam White's stories, as they demonstrate how male authors have manipulated the female body of snake women.

Gervase of Tilbury's *Otia Imperialia* and "Li Huang" of *Boyizhi* (ca. 827AD/Tang Dynasty) are considered the earliest written versions of Melusine and Madam White, respectively. Both the western and eastern myths have underlying ancient roots and exerted great influences on later adaptations.[6] The conformities and deviations between them and their early modern versions point to three significant contrived elements regarding the serpentine metamorphosis: a specific time frame, religious context, and forced metamorphosis. These elements, as will be demonstrated, are closely connected with the female gender. Thus, examining these three elements will help to uncover how the mechanism of the serpentine metamorphosis in Melusine and Madam White's stories is used to constrain femininity.

Three elements added to the later versions appear outstanding regarding the serpentine metamorphoses in the two stories. First, in *Otia Imperialia*, the Melusine figure transforms into a snake but not according to a specific time, whereas both Jean d'Arras' and Thüring von Ringoltingen's versions set her serpentine metamorphosis on every Saturday.[7] The addition of a specific date also happens in "Three Pagodas" and "Thunder Peak Pagoda," where the protagonist

---

5 Sarah Miller, *Medieval Monstrosity and the Female Body* (New York: Routledge, 2010), 136–137.

6 For futher discussion of Melusine and Madam White's roots in European and Chinese mythologies respectively, see Urban, *Monstrous Women*; Kohler, *Der Ursprung der Melusinensage;* Claudia Steinkämper, *Melusine – von Schlangenweib zur "Beauté mit dem Fischschwanz": Geschichte Einer Literarischen Aneignung* (Göttingen: Vandenhoeck & Ruprecht, 2007); Jonathan Chamberlain, *Chinese Gods* (Hong Kong: Long Island, 1983); Pei-yi Wu, "The White Snake: The Evolution of A Myth in China" (PhD diss., Columbia University, 1969), 37.

7 Before the snake-woman figure of Gervase's story accepts her husband Reymundt's marriage proposal, she warns him about not seeing her nudity while she is bathing; otherwise, misfortune will strike. However, Reymundt eventually breaks his promise and his wife turns into a serpent and disappears. See Thüring von Ringoltingen's German translation of this story in *Melusine*, ed. Hans-Gert Roloff (Stuttgart: Philipp Reclam, 1991), 159. Hereafter, Thüring.

Xu encounters Madam White on the Qingming Festival, the day when people honor the deceased. Notably, Saturday, the original biblical Sabbath day,
and the Qingming Festival both have close connections with religious observance. Therefore, the second element refers to religious contexts. In *Melusine*,
the heroine and her family are clearly portrayed as devout Christians, building churches and chapels, teaching Christian doctrines, and fighting Saracens.
These two stories are rooted in Christian beliefs and practices. Nevertheless,
Gervase's story never gives any details about their religion, nor does his version
show any direct connection to Christianity. Similarly, the Taoist and the Buddhist abbots who imprison Madam White in later versions are nowhere to be
found in the earliest extant version.

The third factor missing in the early texts is forced metamorphosis. Here,
forced metamorphosis refers to a situation in which the heroines are transformed into serpentine beings against their will by external powers, such as a
curse or magic. In the two later adaptations, it is clearly stated that Melusine's
metamorphosis is the result of her mother's punitive curse, whereas the early text only introduces her as a transformable being. In "Three Pagodas" and
"Thunder Peak Pagoda," Madam White is also forced to turn into a white serpent
by Taoist or Buddhist magic before she is imprisoned in a pagoda. Interestingly,
in the text "Li Huang," her metamorphosis is not only intended but also simply
implied.[8] Thus, the early texts do not make an explicitly negative connection
between Melusine and Madam White's monstrosity and their female gender.

As suggested by the first two elements, both the early modern versions of
Melusine and Madam White's stories are enriched with references to religion,
the patriarchal doctrines of which play a significant role in hybridizing wom-
en with serpents, maternity with monstrosity, good with evil. Through investigation of these interrelated hybrid features, one can identify how the male
authors use religious doctrines to degrade and contain a suspect femininity.
Neither Jean's nor Thüring's text portrays Melusine as a purely evil creature.
In addition to her monstrous nature, by which she passes physical and mental
abnormalities down to her sons, she is also one of the founders of Lusignan,[9]
a loyal wife, and a caring mother. As many scholars have discussed, it is more

---

8   There is no single scene in this story that describes the snake woman's transformation. It only
    hints at it by telling readers that the ruins where Li Huang saw the snake woman's mansion
    used to be inhabited by a giant white serpent. See Shenzi Gu and Yongruo Xue, eds., "李黄,"
    in 博异志·集异志. (Shanghai: Zhonghua Shuju, 1980).

9   Donald Maddox and Sara Sturm-Maddox, "Introduction," in *Melusine; or, The Noble History of
    Lusignan*, trans. and ed. Donald Maddox and Sara Sturm-Maddox (University Park: Pennsyl-
    vania State University Press, 2012), 3–16, at 6.

specifically her Christian maternity and monstrosity that render her character paradoxical and ambiguous. On one hand, Christian maternity and humanity furnish Melusine with virtues and benevolence; on the other hand, her serpentine monstrosity serves as a reminder of her evil and sinful nature. These dichotomous features of Melusine's character and the Christian background of her story suggest a Christian *Kippfigur*, an ambiguous image of Mary and Eve.[10]

Scholars such as Gabriele Becker believe that women in medieval literature written by male authors are mostly portrayed according to images of Mary and Eve, who stand for very contrary characteristics.[11] For instance, Hubrath argues that Eve is presented as "Gegenfigur zu Maria" [a counter figure of Mary], which represents the negative side of femininity: "Attraktiv und sexuell verführerisch und zugleich verführbar, ungehorsam und sündig, wird Eva die Verantwortung für das Vorhandensein von Tod und Leid in der Welt übertragen" [Because of her being attractive and sexually seductive as well as seducible, disobedient and sinful, Eve is responsible for the existence of death and suffering in the world].[12] Hubrath's interpretation of Eve shows a clear association with Melusine. Eve, the first woman, is driven out of Eden because of her sin, committed at the instigation of a serpent. She is punished because she betrayed God, the father figure who created her. This similar plot can also be found in Melusine's story, as she is cursed for betraying her father. That she, her mother, and her sisters are in exile betrays an even closer similarity to the post-lapsarian Eve.

Melusine's image as an exemplary Christian wife and mother also triggers an immediate association with the Virgin Mary, who is considered in western European cultures to be "the embodiment of medieval ideal motherhood and wifedom."[13] Tania Colwell apotheosizes Melusine by comparing her with the Virgin Mary. Her analysis sheds light on the argument that Mary's "roles as nurse, teacher, sufferer, and intercessor or comforter/healer of others" perfectly

---

10   Regarding more discussion of the *Kippfigur* of Mary and Eve, see Silvia Gabriele Becker, *Aus der Zeit der Verzweiflung: Zur Genese und Aktualität des Hexenbildes* (Frankfurt am Main: Suhrkamp, 1977).

11   Becker, *Aus der Zeit der Verzweiflung*, 24–27.

12   Margarete Hubrath, "Eva: Der Sündenfall und seine Folgen im Mittelalter und in der Frühen Neuzeit," in *Verführer, Schurken, Magier*, ed. Ulrich Müller and Werner Wunderlich (St. Gallen: UVK-Fachverlag für Wissenschaft und Studium, 2011), 243–61, at 243.

13   Tania M. Colwell, "Mélusine: Ideal Mother or Inimitable Monster?," in *Love, Marriage, and Family Ties in the Later Middle Ages*, ed. Isabel Davis, Miriam Müller, and Sarah Rees Jones (Turnhout: Brepols, 2001), 181–203, at 184.

demonstrate that "Christian humanity" can be seen in Melusine's character.[14] There is no doubt that both Jean and Thüring portray Melusine as a supportive, loyal Christian mother who guides and teaches her husband and sons with Christian doctrines and thoughts. In addition to her spiritual guidance of her loved ones, she also builds numerous churches and chapels in their land in appreciation of God.[15]

Some scholars believe that Mary and Eve are more than counter figures in terms of their images. There is also an inner connection between these two Biblical females. For instance, Stica believes that Mary is the opposite or "parallel" to Eve: the latter "brought death to the human race" through her disobedience, whereas the former "brought salvation" by obedience. He points out that Irenaeus's works promoted "the ethical aspects of man's redemption" via the manifestation that Eve guides man into a sinful state, whereas Mary emancipates him from it.[16] Stica's argument suggests that Marian benefaction redeems Eve's wrongdoing. This observation may further the argument that the dichotomy of Melsusine's character enables her to incarnate the *Kippfigur* of Mary and Eve. Akin to Eve, Melusine's monstrosity, the punishment for her betrayal of her father, caused abnormality to her male offspring, but she eventually saved her last two sons from it. In order to achieve this final salvation, it appears that Melusine performs Marian acts as a path to redemption.[17]

As noted, Mary represents a perfect maternity and wifeliness that requires a woman to perform multiple auxiliary or subservient roles as a nurse, teacher, and comforter in addition to being an obedient helpmeet. In both Jean's and Thüring's texts, Melusine uses her magic to help her husband Reymundt rapidly build and expand the land of Lusignan. In addition to the ever-increasing construction of churches and chapels, she also guides him to the achievement of a Christian spiritual state by constantly reminding him of Christian doctrines and faith in God, and she never disobeys him. Melusine never fails to be a comforter for her husband and sons. For example, when Reymundt is upset by Melusine's monstrous secret, she returns home immediately from her business as soon as she becomes aware of his abnormal mental condition. According to the text, her consolation is always presented as soft and gentle, intended

---

14   Colwell, "Ideal Mother," 184–192.

15   Thüring, *Melusine*, 43.

16   Sandro Stica, "Sin and Salvation: The Dramatic Context of Hrotswitha's Women," in *The Role and Images of Women in the Middle Ages and Renaissance*, ed. Douglas Radcliff-Umstead (Pittsburgh: University of Pittsburgh Press, 1975), 3–27, at 4.

17   See Chera A. Cole's contribution to the volume for a discussion of Melusine's interrupted progress toward salvation.

to relax and calm her husband. She even tries to console him with Christian belief at their last moment together, when she sees Reymundt still saddened and infuriated by Goffroy's atrocity to his brother Freymund and the other monks.[18]

Melusine's role as a comforting wife does not exert a direct influence on her sons' normality, but she does serve her abnormal sons as an educator. Melusine often teaches her sons Christian moral ethics and reminds them of the imperative to follow God's will. In Jean's *Mélusine*, her indoctrination of Christianity appears even more often than in Thüring's. All episodes with respect to her sons' performance on battlefields or departure for administration start with her calling them before her and preaching Christian thoughts.[19] Here is one of the dialogues with Uriens and Goyt: "My Children, wherever you may be, you are to attend mass every day before you do anything else, and call on your Creator for help in all your endeavors. Serve him diligently and love Him and fear Him as your God."[20] Evidently, Melusine's preaching to her sons helps them find cure or compensation for the monstrosity passed down by their mother. Despite their physical or mental aberrance, all of them are welcomed by the nobility and the folk owing to their firm faith in God as well as their brave and triumphant performance in battles against pagans. Also, most of them end up acquiring titles of nobility and marrying courtly ladies. Firstborn Uriens becomes the King of Cyprus; the second son, Goyt, becomes the King of Armenia; and their younger brothers Anthoni and Reinhart turn out to be the Count of Luxembourg and the King of Bohemia, respectively. In addition to helping her abnormal sons, Melusine also manages to help her last two sons avoid inheriting monstrous features from her. Thus, it can be said that Melusine attempts to redeem her Eve-like wrongdoings and emancipate her male progeny from the negative results of her monstrous serpentine nature by undertaking benevolent actions of Marian salvation or redemption.

Melusine's representation of the *Kippfigur* of Mary and Eve contains some noticeable nuances. In the Biblical story, God, the father figure, casts the curse on the serpent, whereas Melusine and her sisters are punished by their mother. This mother-child relationship may reflect beliefs in education. As Murray has pointed out, the Bible and related biblical works were the major sources for

---

18   Thüring, *Melusine*, 88.

19   Stacey L. Hahn discusses these scenes of instruction in context of the rhetorical gesture of the *chastoiement*; see her chapter, "Youth and Rebellion," in this volume. Hahn also notes the tendency within Jean's text for observers not to interpret the "mother-marks" on Melusine's sons as any sign of abnormality.

20   Maddox and Sturm-Maddox, *Melusine; or, The Noble History,* 74.

people to find ideal "models of familial behavior" in medieval times.[21] Although most of these books concentrate on Christian marriage, some of them deal with children's enlightenment. For example, in the Book of Ecclesiasticus (also known as Sirach), an entire chapter teaches children to respect their parents.[22] In *Life of St. Anselm*, Eadmer showcases how a perfect child should behave by introducing the childhood of St. Anselm. Caesarius of Heisterbach's *Dialogue on Miracles* utilizes some collected stories to warn readers about the conflict between parents and children, as well as siblings and the consequences of such conflict.[23] In terms of the education of girls, both St. Jerome in *To Latea* and Bartholomaeus Anglicus in *De Proprietatibus Rerum* give some extremely misogynistic advice, which aims to remind readers that girls are born to be inferior to boys. In addition to pointing out that chastity and virginity are the most cherished virtues of girls, they also suggest that girls should be separated from boys from their early education, as they may have a negative influence on boys.[24] Nikki Stiller has also noticed this phenomenon of educational separation and argues in *Eve's Orphans: Mother and Daughters in Medieval Literature* that since girls' education is isolated and mostly given by mothers, who possessed positions secondary to men, they could only learn "passivity and subordination" from their mothers.[25]

As these books have shown, most of the biblical works from which medieval parents learned the method of educating children put women in a subordinate position to men from an early age. This may have affected women's role in teaching their children. According to Colwell, children of both sexes received most moral education from their mothers, although the education of boys and girls was separated and "fathers, tutors, and members of other courts were generally entrusted with the military and pragmatic training of their sons."[26] In addition to biblical works, manuals like Raymond Llull's *Doctrine d'enfant* were used in medieval Europe to guide women on how to teach their children moral standards. This explains why it is Melusine's mother who casts the curse on her three daughters, as it is the mother's responsibility to teach children, especially girls, how to behave morally and to correct their misbehaviors by administering punishment. Melusine similarly provides the moral education of her ten

---

21   Jacqueline Murray, *Love, Marriage, and Family in the Middle Ages: A Reader* (Peterborough: Broadview Press, 2001), 416.

22   Murray, *Love, Marriage, and Family*, 416–417.

23   Murray, *Love, Marriage, and Family*, 442–444.

24   Murray, *Love, Marriage, and Family*, 418–442; 447–449.

25   Marianne Hirsch, "Mothers and Daughters," *Signs* 7 (1981): 200–22, at 217.

26   Colwell, "Ideal Mother," 190.

sons. Most importantly, these books and doctrines reveal how Christianity at that time, on which both of the Melusine stories are based, has subordinated women to supportive roles for men, and can subsequently help the modern readers of *Melusine* understand the male authors' degradation of Melusine and her female nature by hybridizing her with a serpent.

Although one might read Melusine's Marian roles of wife and mother as indicating her good qualities, considering the mechanism of the *Kippfigur*, it is noteworthy that Melusine's representations of both Mary and Eve signify a requirement of women's service to men. The Marian actions, namely benevolence, offer Melusine the ability to keep her human form, prevent her offspring from obtaining abnormality, and possibly allow her to die as a mortal.[27] By contrast, the Eve-like behaviors and the monstrous nature referring to Eden's serpent, namely her betrayal of her father and her transformation into a serpent, emphasize the danger and supernatural power of femininity, which brings suffering and catastrophe to the men related to Melusine and thus provides a reason for the constraint of the snake woman and her femininity.

As demonstrated, both identities, Mary and Eve, woman and serpent, originate in Melusine's femaleness. Although the incarnation of the *Kippfigur* shows both the benevolent and malevolent characteristics of Melusine, these two dichotomous identities only serve to demonstrate the male authors' manipulation of Melusine's female and serpentine nature. Although Melusine is given opportunities to conduct benevolence to redeem her transgression, it is evident that the authors have decided never to set Melusine free from her monstrous feature, but rather want to seal her pathetic fate with eternal lamentation. Evidence supporting this argument can be found in a close analysis of the curse, namely the forced metamorphosis, which swiftly switches Melusine between the two identities. According to the curse, Melusine turns into a half-human, half-serpent creature every Saturday, and she will only be able to live and die like a human being if a man is willing to take her as his wife and promise not to see her on Saturdays.[28] That is to say, Melusine's salvation can solely be achieved through her marriage with a man. Therefore, the serpentine metamorphosis tied to her marriage can be read in the understanding of Melusine's position in her relationship with Reymundt.

The implications of Melusine's forced metamorphosis demonstrate that she is put in a subservient position in this marriage from the beginning to the end. At the point where Melusine meets Reymundt, she is already cursed for

---

27   Thüring, *Melusine*, 106.
28   Thüring, *Melusine*, 106.

her transgression. Like Eve, she has transgressed against her father, but, as a serpentine monster, Melusine also has much in common with the Eden serpent. The curse that turns her lower body into a serpent's tail every Saturday deprives Melusine of the ability to walk, much as God also took away the Eden serpent's ability to walk as punishment.[29] Her weekly transformation serves as a reminder of Melusine's sinful nature, underlying her monstrosity, which is also what Eve and the serpent represent. Thus, Melusine carries a sinful body into her marriage to Reymundt. She properly raises ten sons for him by preaching Christianity and saves them from the negative consequences of her monstrosity. Although it appears that she does not show any sign of approaching pure humanity, scholars such as Maddox and Sturm-Maddox as well as Douglas Kelly do believe that Dieterich and Raymond's normal physiognomy indicate that Melusine is gradually progressing to her "fully human state" or "real humanity" until the time when Reymundt breaks his oath, which happens after they were born.[30]

Although the text does not reveal whether Melusine is in fact progressing to a fully human state, it is clear that she eventually fails to achieve it, since she finally becomes a serpent or dragon and flies away.[31] Instead of acquiring real humanity, she only ends up embracing pure monstrosity. However, the hybridity of her two influences, Eve causing misfortune and the Virgin Mary bringing salvation, also illustrates the authors' perspectives towards her fate. By taking benevolent actions, she manages to redeem her husband and sons and, temporarily, herself from her Eve-like wrongdoings. It seems that Jean and Thüring intend to give Melusine a second opportunity to compensate for her evildoing

---

29   Henry Ansgar Kelly, "The Metamorphoses of the Eden Serpent during the Middle Ages and Renaissance," *Viator* 1 (1971): 301–327, at 304.

30   Maddox and Sturm-Maddox, *Melusine; or, The Noble History,* 7; Douglas Kelly, "The Domestication of the Marvelous in the Melusine Romances," in *Melusine of Lusignan: Founding Fiction in Late Medieval France,* ed. Donald Maddox and Sara Sturm-Maddox (Athens, GA: University of Georgia Press, 1996), 32–47, at 44.

31   H. Kelly, "The Metamorphoses," 304–305; Friedrich Kluge, *Etymologisches Wörterbuch der deutschen Sprache* (Berlin: De Gruyter, 1915), 806; Matthias Lexer, *Matthias Lexers mittelhochdeutsches Taschenwörterbuch* (Stuttgart: S. Hirzel, 1981), 329; Thüring, *Melusine,* 86. In biblical works such as Isidore of Seville's *Etymologies,* dragons are considered "the largest of the serpents." Interestingly, the Middle High German word "wurm," which Thüring uses in the text, also suggests the close connection between serpents and dragons. In Middle High German, "wurm" mostly refers to snakes, though the compound "wurmgarte," for example, most frequently refers to a swamp, maze, dark forest, though it can possibly indicate a pit of vipers, among other interpretations. But in most cases, a dragon-like creature that has short legs and tiny or no wings is referred as "lintwurm."

and to acknowledge her Marian acts of redemption, which allow her to stay in human form by maintaining a balance between her monstrosity and humanity. Nonetheless, all her efforts only serve to postpone the male authors' intention of completely destroying Melusine's dream of living as a normal human being. This harmony is easily broken by her husband's explosive accusation of Melusine's being a monster.[32] As pointed out, Melusine's femininity and monstrosity put her in a passive position throughout the story, where her transformation and fate, which she has no control over, are decided by her husband and the male authors.

Melusine, in both Thüring's and Jean's stories, receives a punishment that hybridizes her femininity with monstrosity after she transgresses against her father, namely the forced metamorphosis to turn her into a serpentine creature. As has been demonstrated, the transformation shows close parallels to Eve and the Eden serpent, which leaves Melusine in a vulnerable position in her marriage by imposing a punishment on her from the beginning of the story. She is given the opportunity to redeem herself and acquire pure humanity at her mortal death through her marriage to a noble man and by acting like the Virgin Mary, who embodies the perfect Christian maternity and wifeliness. However, she is not able to achieve salvation on her own. Even by putting herself into a subservient position to her husband and helping him, as well as his sons, accomplish success, she can only hope to keep herself from losing her humanity. Nevertheless, her remaining humanity, hanging by a thread, is easily eliminated through her husband's fault.

This dependence suggests that these two authors held negative perspectives toward their female characters, depicting them either as women who ought to be obedient, secondary, and naturally sinful, or as those who disobey men and are punished, to be put on the road of purgatory to redeem themselves from their imposed sins.[33] By inflicting the serpentine metamorphosis on Melusine, which governs the snake-woman's life from her acquiring monstrosity to completely losing her humanity, Jean and Thüring present a process of oppressing female power. They portray female power as monstrous, for which Christian doctrines, such as that expressed in Raymond Llull's *Doctrine d'enfant* and by Bartholomaeus Anglicus in *De Proprietatibus Rerum,* make suppression necessary. Likewise, Buddhist and Taoist thought play a similar role in the Chinese

---

32   Thüring, *Melusine,* 86.

33   Gerhild Scholz Williams and Alexander Schwarz, *Existentielle Vergeblichkeit: Verträge in der Mélusine, im Eulenspiegel und im Dr. Faustus* (Berlin: Erich Schmidt, 2003), 43–44. For a futher exploration of the idea that Melusine's curse is a purgatorial type of punishment, see Zoë Enstone's contribution to this volume.

male authors' attitudes toward the serpentine metamorphosis in Madam White's story.

Madam White is a snake woman originating in Chinese folklore who gradually evolves into one of the most popular and significant characters in Chinese culture through multiple adaptations in different genres of Chinese literature, including *zhiguai xiaoshuo* [tales of the miraculous], *chuanqi* [transmission of the strange], *huaben* [novella], and regional operas. This supernatural creature often appears in Chinese mythology and folklore and is able to turn itself into a captivating woman. In most literary versions, Madam White is depicted as a beautiful widow dressed in white who is transformed from a powerful snake spirit. Like Melusine, she marries an innocent and common man and desires to live as a human. However, Madam White is eventually defeated by a dominating male monk and imprisoned under a pagoda after being forced to revert to her original form: a white serpent. In earlier versions of the Madam White story, the serpentine creature is described as evil and dangerous, especially to men.

Similar to the *Kippfigur* of Virgin Mary and Eve, Madam White has a counter-figure that represents the opposite of her evilness and monstrosity: Nü Wa. Nü Wa is a serpentine goddess who shows strong connections with feminine characteristics such as female fertility and maternity and was worshipped in multiple cults throughout ancient China. This goddess is possibly the earliest combination of woman and snake in Chinese literature. Due to her symbolism of female fertility, Nü Wa has a positive and even savior-like image among the Chinese. In a later description of Nü Wa in Ying Shao's *Fengsu Tongyi* [*Comprehensive Meaning of Customs and Habits*], which is quoted in *Taiping Yulan* [*Imperial Readings of the Taiping Era*], the snake goddess is portrayed as the mother of mankind, who not only vitalizes the earth but is also put on a pedestal.[34]

Some scholars such as Pei-yi Wu suggest that Nü Wa is the reversed prototype of Madam White.[35] It is believed that the evil snake woman motif in Chinese literature originates from Nü Wa, as the serpentine goddess's image experienced a great degradation during China's societal transition from matriarchy to patriarchy after the Han Dynasty. Despite the disbelief triggered by the hardship of finding and reconciling Nü Wa's true identity, she and snakes

34   Fang Li, 太平御覽, ed. Yongchang Sun and Yulan Xiong (Shijiazhuang: Hebei Jiaoyu, 1994), 672.

35   Wu, "The White Snake," 155.

36   Edward H. Schafer, *The Divine Woman: Dragon Ladies and Rain Maidens in T'ang Literature* (Berkeley: University of California Press, 1973), 29.

remained significant figures in Han and pre-Han cults owing to "the new 'Con-fucian' insistence on euhemerization."[36] However, the worship and the posi-tive image of snakes in ancient China were gradually enfeebled "due to the contempt of some eminent and educated men for animalian gods" and "the increasing domination of masculinity in elite social doctrine."[37]

Along with this demotion in prestige, snakes and women accumulated negative impressions with the emerging practice of Taoism. Taoism, which advocates freedom and fluidity, became the strongest and most influential op-ponent to the strict dogmas of Confucianism.[38] The ultimate goal of practicing Taoism is to reach Tao, the state where Taoists can live as immortals in the world, which is divided into three elements: Heaven, Earth, and Man. Those who have reached Tao are called *zhenren*, or True Men. To reach this state, they need to practice magic and interact with nature, where, according to Taoist be-liefs, plants and animals can turn themselves into humans. These supernatural beings are called *yao*, or demons, who need to be eliminated, because they sap vitality from humans to keep themselves in human form and cause illness and adversity.[39] Thus the snake, which "due to its position in the Ten Celestial Stems as the Heraldic Animal of the North" represents "disasters and all sorts of evil," was naturally demonized in Taoism as well as Chinese mythology and became the most dreadful creature. At this point, the snake's image was completely cut off from its positive connection with Nü Wa.[40] Evil snake women in literature, such as Madam White, became the characteristic representation of the snake in Chinese culture.

Although the core of the plot stays almost unaltered in various versions, different personalities of Madam White and her authors' divergent perspec-tives on her are juxtaposed in the literature of different time periods. As the story of Madam White existed in oral tradition long before the appearance of its written versions, scholars generally believe that "Li Huang," a *zhiguai* narrative of *Boyizhi* [*Vast Records of the Strange*; ca.827 AD/Tang Dynasty] is considered the inspiration behind Madam White's story. "The Legend of the

---

37   Schafer, *Divine Woman*, 184–192.

38   Jacques Gernet, *A History of Chinese Civilization* (Cambridge: Cambridge University Press, 1996), 439.

39   Gernet, *A History*, 206–210; John Lagerwey, *China: A Religious State* (Hong Kong: Hong Kong University Press, 2010), 59–60; Ch'ing-k'un Yang, *Religion in Chinese Society: A Study of Contemporary Social Functions of Religion and Some of Their Historical Factors* (Berke-ley: University of California Press, 1961), 149–151; Wu, "The White Snake," 140.

40   Ong Hean-Tatt, *Chinese Animal Symbolism* (Selangor: Pelanduk Publications, 1993), 90–91.

Three Pagodas of West Lake," a story included in *Qingpingshantang huaben* [*The Tales of the Serene Mountain*] (1550), is the most developed of the later literary adaptations. In early versions, Madam White is often associated with evil. She is portrayed as a femme fatale who seduces innocent men and eats them alive without hesitation. Although appearing in human form, this snake spirit possesses absolutely no humanity. However, this demerit is progressively compensated for by the omission of her ferocity and the addition of benevolence as well as true affection for her husband, demonstrated in later versions such as "Madam White Is Kept Forever under the Thunder Peak Pagoda" in *Jingshitongyan* [*Stories to Caution the World*] (1624).

This compensation does not reflect the authors' positive perspectives towards Madam White, but rather a reconciliation with the writing style of new literary genres. Only in the eighteenth century do authors and readers start to have sympathy for Madam White's characters in plays such as Huang Tubi's *Thunder Peak Pagoda* (1738) and Fang Chengpei's *The Legend of Thunder Peak Pagoda* (1771). Nonetheless, the original plot of imprisonment under the pagoda after her transformation stays intact. The metamorphosis of Madam White as the key element of the prototypical plot is the unique method through which readers can trace the male authors' manipulation of the snake woman and their intentions, by investigating the nuances or changes these men have incorporated to scenes related to White's transformation.

Although both versions are categorized as demon stories, the plot of "Thunder Peak Pagoda" has been considerably expanded and varied compared to that of "Three Pagodas." In addition to added episodes, the story seems much less violent and more humanized. Patrick Hanan believes that this change is influenced by the development of vernacular short stories that occurred between 1550 and the 1620s in China. He argues that the brutal and "harsh" plots of the stories in *Sanyan* (the abbreviation of three collections of vernacular stories: respectively, *Stories to Enlighten the World, Stories to Caution the World,* and *Stories to Awaken the World*) originating from *Qingpingshantang huaben* are distinctively softened.[41] Wu further points out that, in the case of Madam White, a "more sympathetic treatment of the heroine" has been adopted. He notices that White is transformed from a cannibalistic and licentious monster into a woman "whose only fault is her attraction to the young man who is perhaps unworthy of her love."[42] Another minor but conspicuous change to one episode also indicates a likely influence.

---

41   Patrick Hanan, "The Early Chinese Short Story: A Critical Theory in Outline," in *Harvard Journal of Asiatic Studies* 27 (1967): 168–207, at 197.

42   Wu, "The White Snake," 37.

In "Thunder Peak Pagoda," Madam White is imprisoned by a Buddhist monk, instead of being defeated by a Taoist as in "Three Pagodas." The history of the introduction of Buddhism and its acclimatization in China helps explain its function in the story. According to Gernet, Buddhism penetrated China in the Han Dynasty (206 BC – 220 AD) after centuries of development influenced by Indian, Iranian, and Hellenistic cultures.[43] It was soon accepted as well as supported by the court and then gradually practiced more widely by commoners. Buddhism reached its peak of influence in the Northern Zhou (557–581 AD) and early Tang Dynasties (618–690 AD; 705–907 AD) and then gradually declined at court after the Song Dynasty (960–1279 AD). However, after centuries of acclimatization under the influence of Taoism and Confucianism, Buddhist contributions to Chinese culture, especially literature, are indelible. By the Ming Dynasty (1368–1644 AD), when "Thunder Peak Pagoda" was written, Buddhism appeared to have absorbed Taoist and Confucian ideas and advocated kindness, softness, and peace as well as abstinence.[44] This development within Buddhism can be linked to the rationale for the omission of cannibalism and licentiousness in "Thunder Peak Pagoda."

In the literature of this time period, antagonism toward Taoist priests was frequent in fiction, according to C. T. Hsia,[45] whereas Buddhism was embraced. This phenomenon can also be found in "Thunder Peak Pagoda," where the Taoist is not completely omitted but is rather portrayed as being overpowered by White, who in turn is defeated by Fahai, the Buddhist abbot. Another factor that showcases Buddhist ideas are the poems at the end of the story. One of them is written as the grand finale by the protagonist, Xu, who eventually embraces Buddhism and becomes a monk.[46]

Thanks to the widely accepted Buddhism in Ming novels, Madam White in "Thunder Peak Pagoda" is not portrayed as a monster that devours innocent people. She shows true affection for Xu and keeps herself loyal and chaste to her husband. However, this behavior, which is considered as the attribute of a good wife in traditional Chinese culture, does not save her from stigmatization and her final imprisonment. Due to the influence of Buddhism, Madam White's crimes are diminished from the lust of concupiscence and cannibalism to mere theft. Although the thefts that White commits are rooted in her

---

43   Gernet, *A History*, 211.

44   Kenneth Kuan Shêng Ch'en, *Buddhism in China: A Historical Survey* (Princeton: Princeton University Press, 1964), 436; Gernet, *A History*, 439.

45   Wu, "The White Snake," 63.

46   Menglong Feng, "白娘子永鎮雷峰塔," in 馮夢龍全集, ed. Tongxian Wei (Nanjing: Fenghuang, 1993), 445.

intention to attract and abet her love, Xu, they are also one of the reasons why the Taoist and the Buddhist monks decide to punish her. Nevertheless, since the theft was a crime according to the law and is not directly attributable to her serpentine nature, it can be argued that it is only a subordinate factor introduced to emphasize her heinousness. The true reason to punish Madam White needs to be further explored.

Akin to "Three Pagodas," the *raison d'être* for "Thunder Peak Pagoda" is to blame Madam White for her defiance of societal demands on women. These demands can be found in books prescribing women's behavior. They had been constantly published and well accepted by civilians since the Han Dynasty. In the late Ming Dynasty, which is also the time when "Thunder Peak Pagoda" was published, Wang Xiang edited a book called *Nüsishu* [*The Four Books for Women*], which is based on four earlier books of conduct literature for women. This popular book's main idea is to educate women to serve and obey their husbands unconditionally and to stay loyal and chaste. A book dating from Qing Dynasty (1644–1912 AD) named *Guimen Baoxun* [*Indoctrination of Married Women*], for example, has several chapters imposing onerous social requirements on women, including hiding their abilities and showing absolute obedience to their husbands.[47]

Madam White in "Thunder Peak Pagoda" acts in a manner very contrary to these demands. Although her husband, Xu, is depicted as a mediocre, law-abiding, somewhat submissive and cowardly person, he is perceived as a respectable civilian by the other characters. Madam White, on the other hand, is portrayed as a beautiful, smart, and resourceful woman who never bothers to hide her cleverness and power. Xu's ordinariness thus naturally triggers White's motive to help him become a better and more successful man by giving advice, or, more accurately, by speaking to and prompting him. Nevertheless, this action is treated by the author as her way of manipulating her husband, and her intelligence, accordingly, is distorted into craftiness. Every time that she tries to convince Xu of something or influence him, something bad comes after White or her husband. For example, Xu is imprisoned in jail after White talks him into marrying her. A Taoist who is later defeated by Madam White and a monk who finally imprisons her come to her after she tries to dissuade Xu from visiting Buddha. Xu, for his part, avoids confronting his employer after being informed that he has spied on his wife, and every time he encounters difficulties, he chooses to seek help or shelter from a superior figure such as Madam White, his sister, or the monk Fahai. Xu seems to be deficient when it comes to

47   Dalin Liu, 中国古代性文化 (Yinchuan: Ningxiarenmin, 1993), 136–137.

being a protective husband. In addition, after being told by the monk that his wife is a monster, and ignoring all her generosity and affection for him, he immediately denies their marriage and cites the monk's poem defaming Madam White in self-defense.[48]

However, from the author's perspective, Xu is still a victim of the serpentine monster. The cowardliness and ruthlessness of the inadequate husband are easily overshadowed by the author's shifting the emphasis from Xu's incapability to Madam White's lies and manipulation. For example, instead of calling attention to Xu's irresponsibility for not questioning his boss's sexual harassment of his wife, the author focuses instead on describing how White lies to her husband and maneuvers him into doing what she wants.

Although Madam White in "Thunder Peak Pagoda" is less violent and sexually predatory, she is still portrayed as possessing the characteristics of an evil monster that deserves eternal imprisonment. Similar to the function of cannibalism in the earlier vernacular version, theft is a crime introduced to worsen White's image, although the major evil is presented in her action of disobeying her husband, which goes against what the conduct books for women like *Nüsishu* and *Guimen Baoxun* require. Since the author's emphasis on White's promiscuity in "Three Pagodas" is used to warn women to keep chaste, it can be suggested that her disobedience to her husband in "Thunder Peak Pagoda" is introduced to caution women to suppress their talents and be absolutely submissive to their husbands. Women who do not follow the rules of the patriarchal society end up imprisoned like Madam White. In later versions of this story, White continues to appear as a snake woman who is imprisoned by a monk at some point because of her inborn sin of being a monster, even though she is benevolent and never kills.

In both the Western European and Chinese stories, the patriarchal ideologies of their respective religions are the key factor explaining the serpentine women with dichotomous features like Melusine and Madam White. Supernatural powers are given to these hybrid female creatures not to demonstrate their powerful femininity but rather their evil and threatening monstrosity that needs to be suppressed or controlled by men. In this case, serpentine metamorphoses are utilized by the authors as a justified tool to constrain them. In *Melusine*, the influence of Christian doctrine is predominant. The paradoxical combining of Mary and Eve as well as the Eden serpent in Melusine's character not only perfectly exposes the dichotomy of her humanity and monstrosity, but it also encapsulates the development of her character. With her betrayal of

---

48   Feng, "白娘子," 439.

her father, Melusine is cursed to become a hybrid monster and to pass down her monstrosity to her male offspring, most of whom are born with physical or mental abnormalities. By guiding and instructing her husband and sons with Christian doctrines and paying homage to Christianity by building churches and chapels, she achieves the salvation of humanity for her sons and husband. Nonetheless, despite her selfless work, the devotion of this snake woman who desires to become human is easily rendered futile not by her own, but by a man's mistake. This permanently isolates Melusine from humanity. These actions and results draw a picture wherein Melusine is reduced to being a supportive and subordinate figure whose man can and does facilely tarnish her contribution to his welfare.

The outgrowth of the monstrosity attributed to Madam White, transgressions such as cannibalism in "Three Pagodas" and theft in "Thunder Peak Pagoda," can be seen as one of the methods of degrading her character. In both adaptations, Madam White exhibits various disobedient behaviors and thus belongs to the morally abhorrent group. In "Three Pagodas," she is clearly portrayed as a cannibal and a promiscuous and unchaste wife, whereas in "Thunder Peak Pagoda" she is benevolent and loyal despite her thievery. But instead of supporting her husband blindly, Madam White has strong opinions and consistently attempts to manipulate her husband. All these actions that show femininity overpowering or resisting masculinity are portrayed as transgressions against the rules of patriarchal society and lead to her eternal imprisonment.

It appears that the forced metamorphoses of snake women are the results of transgressive actions. In Jean's and Thüring's texts, Melusine's first forced metamorphosis, into a serpentine monster and hybrid who is both human and monstrous, was imposed on her for her betrayal of her father. Likewise, the second forced metamorphosis occurs as a punishment that transforms her into a full monster. In a similar fashion, forced metamorphosis also functions as a punishment for Madam White because she disobeys moral and religious rules. She eventually is forced to turn into a white serpent before being imprisoned forever. In both cases, these imposed wrongdoings are embedded in the respective author's patriarchal conceptions concerning women's behavior. They are all linked more or less with acts of betrayal or disobedience.

Thus, in Melusine and Madam White's stories, the metamorphoses of snake women are utilized to warn women about the potential consequences of their behavior in rebellion against male authority. The serpentine metamorphosis, which starts on a specific religious date such as Saturdays (the Old Testament Sabbath) or the Qingming Festival, introduces a religious context embedded into the stories. The religious context not only promotes the development of the characters and plots but also popularizes religious thought through the interactions of characters of both genders. The final forced metamorphosis, which transforms heroines into pure monsters, is punishment for their imposed transgressions and also a warning for the audience. The transformation from woman to serpent (or vice versa) indicates changed forms as well as fates. Despite retellings, what has remained intact in their stories is a misogynistic prejudice that itself would eventually metamorphose into an obsolete vestige of patriarchy.

PART IV

Melusines Medieval to Modern

∵

CHAPTER 16

Goethe and *Die neue Melusine*: A Critical Reinterpretation

Renata Schellenberg

Goethe published his literary fairy tale *Die neue Melusine* [*The New Melusine*] as part of his last great prose work *Wilhelm Meisters Wanderjahre* [*Wilhelm Meister's Journeyman Years*] (1821/1829), a cryptic and complicated literary project that integrated various narrative modes and voices and which continues to evade conclusive interpretation by literary scholars.[1] He included *Melusine* in the *Wanderjahre* narrative as a digressive interlude contemplating the meaning of marriage and introduced the story within the novel with great pomp, noting that it was an exemplary story, the narrative value of which "die bisherigen weit übertrifft" [supersedes that of all others].[2] The material that Goethe presented to his readers was not entirely original, as he presented an adaptation of the medieval *Melusine* tale, a narrative with known authorship and a literary genesis that could be traced back to the work of Jean d'Arras in late fourteenth-century France.[3] Goethe readily acknowledged this literary precedent by referring to his own version as the "neue Melusine," alluding to his own creative transformation of the original tale and noting narrative

---

1 For more insight into *Wanderjahre* scholarship, as well as information on the various interpretations of the work, see Ehrhard Bahr, *The Novel as Archive: The Genesis, Reception, and Criticism of Goethe's Wilhelm Meisters Wanderjahre* (Columbia: Camden, 1998); Martin Bez, *Goethes "Wilhelm Meisters Wanderjahre": Aggregat, Archiv, Archivroman* (Berlin: De Gruyter, 2013); Jane K. Brown, *Goethe's Cyclical Narratives, Die Unterhaltungen deutscher Ausgewanderten and Wilhelm Meisters Wanderjahre* (Chapel Hill: University of North Carolina, 1975); Claudia Schwamborn, *Individualität in Goethes "Wanderjahren"* (Paderborn: Schöningh, 1997).

2 Johann Wolfgang von Goethe, *Sämtliche Werke: Briefe, Tagebücher und Gespräche*, ed. Henrik Birus, et al., 40 vols., Vol 10 (Frankfurt/Main: Deutscher Klassiker Verlag, 1985ff), 633. All subsequent references to the Frankfurt edition of Goethe's collected works appear as FA in parentheses, followed by the volume and page number. All translations are the author's.

3 Jean d'Arras, *Mélusine. Roman du XIVe siècle*, ed. Louis Stouff (Dijon: Publications de l'Université, 1932). See Melissa Ridley Elmes's suggestion in this volume that Goethe also drew heavily on alchemical traditions depicting Melusine in his adaptation of the tale.

changes he made in its customary composition. The transformation underlying Goethe's *Melusine* narrative is most fruitfully investigated by tracing the origins of the author's interest in the work, as well as by revealing some of the reasons Goethe engaged with this canonical text so late in his own literary career. In particular, the professional curiosities of Goethe's *Melusine* extend beyond matters of literature, exhibiting a conscious interplay of literary and scientific convention, ultimately suggesting that Goethe's interest in the Melusine topic may not have been based on medieval literary precedent at all.

Goethe's approach to literature in his later years was notoriously complex. His *Spätwerk* [later work] is defined by a cryptic style that is difficult to identify in singular, definitive terms and seemingly impossible to subsume within standard literary categorization.[4] Works written during this late phase are considered self-referential and intentionally solipsistic, difficult to read for those not familiar with Goethe's corpus of writings and unaware of the author's stated skepticism to literature in general.

Chronologically, his *Melusine* fairy tale belongs to this later period of Goethe's career. Although familiar with the content of the tale since childhood, Goethe began writing his own version in 1807, publishing portions of it in the popular *Taschenbuch für Damen* [*Paperback for Women*] in 1817 and 1819, before including it as an interpolated narrative in *Wilhelm Meisters Wanderjahre*, a lengthy prose work published in two separate versions towards the end of his life. The *Wanderjahre* framework is interesting as it places the *Melusine* tale within a critical context that conspicuously complicates its reading and popular reception. Considered a literary anomaly by most scholars, the *Wanderjahre* text refutes clear literary genre and concrete literary placement, an idiosyncrasy demonstrable through its complex narrative structure, its changing array of characters, and by the fact that in the 1829 version Goethe purposely omitted the "Roman" designation from the title. Curiously, within this inchoate work the *Melusine* tale is openly identified as a fairy tale, a formal classification that carries a set of its own complexities and which in the end does little to clarify its purpose within the *Wanderjahre* structure. All of these things suggest a rather intricate adaptation of the original *Melusine* narrative on Goethe's part, one that warrants careful reading and consideration.

---

4   See Peter Eichhorn, *Idee und Erfahrung im Spätwerk Goethes* (Munich: Alber, 1971); Annette Johanna Schneider, *Idylle und Tragik im Spätwerk Goethes* (Frankfurt am Main: Peter Lang, 2009); Hans Joachim Schrimpf, *Das Weltbild des späten Goethe; Überlieferung und Bewahrung in Goethes Alterswerk* (Stuttgart: Kohlhammer, 1956); Martin and Erika Swales, *Reading Goethe: A Critical Introduction to the Literary Work* (Rochester: Camden, 2002).

It is important to stress that within the German literary tradition, the *Märchen* [fairy tale] genre maintains a certain ambiguity in its terms of designation and literary categorization, and that clear demarcation of the genre is not always possible.[5] It also occupies special prominence within German literary circles, especially in the nineteenth century.[6] Scholars conventionally subdivide the genre in a twofold way, defining it according to genesis and composition as either a *Volksmärchen*, a recorded oral tale, or as a *Kunstmärchen*, a literary fairy tale conceptualized and authored by an identifiable writer. The relationship of the *Kunstmärchen* to the organic and more predominant oral fairy tale, the *Volksmärchen*, is, however, a known point of discussion among many literary scholars and has been traditionally problematic to define.[7] Some consider the simplistic *Volksmärchen* a mere reservoir of material for the more complex *Kunstmärchen* counterpart, and see the two genres as intertwined, with the oral version emerging as the substandard alternative.[8] Other scholars dispute the necessity of this subdivision, arguing that the differentiation is contrived, as all fairy tales rest on the premise of believability and the reader's willing acceptance of a fantastic fictional world that contradicts the experiences of real life.[9] As a consequence, some critics even contemplate the *Kunstmärchen* apart from its generic designation and view it simply as a modern

---

5 There are, for example, noted overlaps between the fairy tale and other literary genres that incorporate extraordinary elements, such as myths and fables. For a precise definition and more information on the genre see "Fairy Tales," *Merriam-Webster's Encyclopedia of World Religions*, ed. Wendy Doniger (Springfield: Merriam Webster, 1999), 772.

6 Jack Zipes has written on this topic, noting that Germans developed a "love affair" with the fairy tale genre in the nineteenth century and explaining that it became a key means of literary expression during the epoch. See Jack Zipes, "The Formation of the Literary Fairy Tale in Germany," *The Oxford Companion to Fairy Tales*, ed. Jack Zipes, 2nd, edition (Oxford: University Press, 2015), 246.,

7 The abiding debate revolves around the question of what constitutes a proper fairy tale ("das eigentliche Märchen"). Is it the simplistic oral narrative or the crafted written tale? For an extensive overview on the traditional scholarly debate, see the introductory chapter in Max Lüthi's *Märchen* (Stuttgart: Metzler, 1968), 1–6.

8 Hans-Heino Ewers, "Nachwort: Das Kunstmärchen – eine moderne Erzählgattung," in *Zauberei im Herbste: Deutsche Kunstmärchen von Wieland bis Hofmannsthal,* ed. Hans-Heino Ewers (Stuttgart: Reclam, 1987), 647–80, at 657.

9 Paul Wührl argues this point in his seminal study on the literary fairy tale *Das deutsche Kunstmärchen: Geschichte, Botschaft und Erzählstrukturen*, where he authoritatively states, "Das Kunstmärchen gibt es nicht" [The literary fairy tale does not exist], making this claim on the basis of the many similarities the two types of fairy tale share; Peter W. Wührl, *Das deutsche Kunstmärchen: Geschichte, Botschaft und Erzählstrukturen* (Baltmannsweiler: Schneider, 2003), 15.

mode of narration, one that constantly expands its peripheries by integrating new elements, asserting that this feature is especially conducive to appropriating the fantastic and supernatural elements of the basic oral fairy tale. In any case, there is considerable overlap between the two types of *Märchen* as both the *Volksmärchen* and the *Kunstmärchen* share this propensity for "das Wunderbare" [the wonderful], and intentionally include improbable and fantastic elements to engage the imagination of their readers. Petra Küchler-Sakellariou has argued this point in her study on the Romantic *Kunstmärchen*, noting that the reader's imagination does sometimes conflate the two types of *Märchen* in their appropriation of the obvious fiction of the fairy tale.[10]

Goethe's identification of his *Melusine* tale as a *Märchen* needs to be read in view of this larger discussion of genre, for it underscores some of the potential difficulties of the form, possibly indicating Goethe's own predicament of categorizing his *Melusine* narrative. However unintentional this may be, his use of the *Melusine* fairy tale within *Wilhelm Meisters Wanderjahre* does highlight some of the inherent difficulty of defining the *Kunstmärchen* genre in singular terms. In the *Wanderjahre,* the *Melusine* is both an oral and a written tale, thereby demonstrating some of the problems with its literary categorization.

This is, however, not the only issue. As Rosmarie Zeller writes, one of the determining qualities of the *Kunstmärchen* genre is its self-conscious nature that readily recognizes fantastic elements ("das Wunderbare") as part of its structure and makes these elements a theme of the narrative as a whole. There is consequently a natural narrative tension in the text between the fantastic and the probable ("das Wahrscheinliche").[11] As Zeller explains: "Das Kunstmärchen vergißt nie, daß es Wunderbares erzählt, und macht dadurch das Wunderbare zum Thema. Die Konfrontation von Wunderbarem und Wahrscheinlichem erfolgt auf verschiedene Weise" [The Kunstmärchen never forgets that it is narrating wondrous elements, thereby making das Wunderbare a theme of the story. The juxtaposition of these remarkable events with more probable events occurs in different ways].[12] Goethe's *Melusine* never employs its fantastic elements in quite such a way, and instead downplays their presence within the narrative.

---

10   Petra Küchler-Sakellariou, "Romantisches Kunstmärchen – Über die Spielarten des Wunderbaren in 'Kunst' und 'Volks'märchen," in *Phantasie und Phantastik; Neuere Studien zum Kunstmärchen und zur phantastischen Erzählung,* ed. Hans Schumacher (Frankfurt: Peter Lang, 1993), 43–75.

11   Rosmarie Zeller, "Das Kunstmärchen des 17. und 18. Jahrhunderts zwischen Wirklichkeit und Wunderbarem," *Zeitschrift für Literaturwissenschaft und Linguistik* 92 (1993): 56–74.

12   Zeller, "Das Kunstmärchen," 61.

In fact, one could argue that in Goethe's version of the *Melusine* tale, the fantastic elements within the narrative never truly come into play. They are undermined and rejected by the narrator who recounts the *Melusine* tale as a disappointing autobiographical episode, rather than as an incredulous narrative that suspends belief. The fairy tale is narrated from personal memory, rather from a script, and is set in a recent, experienced past, a probable context that comes to life through a narrator who is also a main character in the tale. Speaking, rather than acting, seems to be this character's specialty, for he is described within Goethe's *Melusine* primarily as a raconteur, as someone who possesses a certain "Redetalent," a propensity for speaking and storytelling (FA 10: 632). As Volker Klotz observes, the accuracy of his account should be immediately brought into question by the unreliability of the character, who, within the tale, proves to have little moral credibility and loyalty.[13] "Das Wunderbare" is depicted within this mundane framework as a failing and disappearing power that is massively beholden to a flawed human counterpart and which never comes to full realization within the narrative. This detail is important, for Goethe's modifications to (and especially the narrative interactions he created within) his *Melusine* tale highlight human agency in such a way as to dispute the entire notion that this story is to be read as a fairy tale at all, repositioning the text instead as an altogether different type of narrative.

It is known that Goethe assumed a flexible and creative approach to the *Melusine* narrative, as he appropriated materials from a variety of different sources to write his own version of the tale. Gonthier-Lois Fink has compared Goethe's finished *Melusine* to a "Kaleidoscope" of influences, noting that a flexibility of perspective is necessary to comprehend his assembly of literary sources in the text.[14] Goethe's initial encounter with the *Melusine* narrative occurred in a commonplace setting, without much excitement or intellectual intention. He learned of the tale in his youth in Frankfurt through a German chapbook (*Volksbuch*) adaptation, a copy he inadvertently found and bought together with other books. He remembered this occasion in his autobiography, noting that the *Melusine* text was a cheap and unremarkable edition which he purchased "für ein paar Kreutzer" [for a few Kreutzer (small coins)] (FA 10: 1206).

---

13   He observes: "Da erzählt ein Held, der keiner mehr ist, von Heldentaten, die keine gewesen sind" [A protagonist narrates who is no longer a protagonist, and he speaks of heroic deeds, that were no such thing]. Volker Klotz, *Das Europäische Kunstmärchen: Fünfundzwanzig Kapitel seiner Geschichte von der Renaissance bis zur Moderne* (Stuttgart: Metzler, 1985), 123.

14   Gonthier-Lois Fink, "*Die neue Melusine:* Goethes maieutisches Spiel mit dem Leser," *Euphorion* 107 (2013): 7–43, at 14.

Although not specified, this chapbook was most likely Thüring von Ringoltin-gen's translation of Jean d'Arras' tale, a version that was translated into German in 1456 and which was widely known to the German reading public in Goe-the's youth. Several different chapbook versions were circulating at the time, so it is difficult to know which exact version Goethe read.[15] A chapbook edition of the *Melusine* tale does, however, speak of its general accessibility, for these versions of the tale were cheap to acquire and easily found their way to all levels of the reading public. The quality of the *Volksbuch* edition is another matter, for these editions were designed simplistically with little regard for detail and external design. In the case of the *Melusine* narrative, this publication point matters, due to the famous iconography of the Bernhard Richel woodcuts associated with Jean d'Arras' fairy tale. As Lydia Zeldenrust explains, these images had a significant impact on the way this narrative was relayed by subsequent authors in their pan-European dissemination of the tale, affecting very precisely how Melusine was portrayed to readers.[16] It is not known whether Goethe saw these images or not, but they did attract other authors to engage with the Melusine narrative, thereby contributing to a continuation of creative interest in the medieval narrative.

Goethe's interest in the narrative eventually deviated from original medieval sources, as he actively looked to expand the legend, gradually including other elements that hitherto had not been associated with it. As indicated above, the process of writing his *Melusine* was decidedly long for Goethe, taking place sporadically over the course of more than two decades, so it is not surprising that the author would adapt his methodology over time and in line with other interests he was nurturing. Reference to the *Melusine* tale comes up numerous times within his work, starting with autobiographical reminiscences from the 1770s. In *Dichtung und Wahrheit* [*Poetry and Truth*], Goethe recorded an instance in Sessenheim in his youth when he recounted the tale to a group of friends. He vividly noted the context of narrating the fairy tale, stating: "Wir begaben uns in eine geräumige Laube und ich trug ein Märchen vor, das ich hernach unter dem Titel 'die neue Melusine' aufgeschrieben habe" [We

---

15   There were at least four different chapbook versions of the *Melusine* narrative circulating throughout Germany in the first half of the eighteenth century. For more on this see Paul Heitz and Frank Ritter, *Versuch einer Zusammenstellung der deutschen Volksbücher des 15. und 16. Jahrhunderts nebst deren späteren Ausgaben und Literatur* (Strassburg: Heitz, 1924), 125. See also Albrecht Classen's contribution to this volume for an overview of the circulation of German printed *Melusines*.

16   Lydia Zeldenrust, "Serpent or Half-Serpent? Bernhard Richel's *Melusine* and the Making of a Western European Icon," *Neophilologus* 100, no. 1 (2016): 19–41.

ventured to the shade of a tree and I narrated a fairy tale, which I have since recorded as "die neue Melusine"] (FA 14.1: 485). There is no preserved manuscript to attest to a particular version he may have used within this context and no documentation to indicate the creative amendments he may have made to the original medieval material. It is decisively known, however, that Goethe was persuaded not to preserve a written version of his tale at this time and that he willingly left it in oral form.[17] Subsequent references to the fairy tale were made in 1797 in a letter to fellow writer Friedrich Schiller, in which he noted his ongoing preoccupation with the material. At this time he appeared to consider the Melusine character as an elemental water creature, referring to her as an "undenisches Pygmäenweibchen" (FA 10: 1206), a type of miniature siren, bound to life in the water. This utterance is important as it indicates that Goethe was considering new and distinct elements for his narrative, incorporating folkloric imagery to the *Melusine* story and thereby loosening its association with the medieval literary source.

As Katharina Mommsen writes, although the title was left intact, Goethe indeed drew on a variety of sources in his *Melusine* tale, deliberately merging diverse literary traditions to create an innovative and free reinterpretation of Jean d'Arras' tale.[18] As she observes, the motif of the woman residing in a wooden chest (*Weibchen im Kasten*), the means by which Melusine is presented in Goethe's tale, is famously derived from the narrative frame of *1001 Nights*, as are the spendthrift characteristics of the narrator/barber character.[19] Most crucially, in his *Melusine* Goethe deviated from the customary characters by replacing the supernatural fairy world with a kingdom of dwarves and by making Melusine the princess of these miniature creatures, rather than retaining her appearance as a mermaid, water fairy, or serpent-like being. Within Goethe's narrative, the character of Melusine, moreover, self-identifies as the daughter of King Eckhard and positions herself as a person with a long and traceable literary lineage, ancestry that designates her as established nobility within a parallel mythological society. She is presented by Goethe in an intelligent light, as an articulate and self-aware character, fully cognizant of her heritage and historical provenance, stating: "Die Gestalt, in der du mich im

---

17 For more on this biographical episode, see Nicolas Boyle, *Goethe: The Poet and the Age*, Vol. 1 (Oxford: Oxford University Press, 1991), 100–4.

18 In her analysis, Mommsen identifies a miscellanea of influences on *Die neue Melusine*: *1001 Nights*, the chapbook *Der gehörnte Siegfried*, the *Cabinet des fées*, the *Heldenbuch* sagas, as well as work from the historian Herodotus; Katharina Mommsen, *Goethe und 1001 Nacht* (Bonn: Bernstein, 2006), 139.

19 Mommsen, *Goethe und 1001 Nacht*, 142–43.

Kästchen erblicktest, ist mir wirklich angeboren und natürlich: denn ich bin aus dem Stamm des Königs Eckwalds, des mächtigen Fürsten der Zwerge, von dem die wahrhafte Geschichte so vieles meldet" [The shape in which you saw me in the chest is my natural and rightful shape, for I am of the lineage of King Eckwald, the mighty king of dwarves, who is recorded by history] (FA 10: 646). Melusine's rank, however, cannot protect her from the predicament she must confront in Goethe's narrative, which is biological rather than social in nature, an existential quandary that affects her future and that of her kingdom. Melusine and her kingdom are quite literally disappearing, as their isolation from the real world results in self-annulment and the gradual diminishment of their already infinitesimal race.

The solution to overcoming this obstacle is not mythical, heroic, or indeed magical. Instead it is plainly biological, as Melusine needs to bond with a human counterpart and bear children to strengthen the dwarf bloodline. This intimate physical interaction will prevent the demise of her race and reinvigorate the dwarf world, reinstating the kingdom to its former glory. In his version of the fairy tale, Goethe preserves the notion of communication between two separate worlds, keeping intact the premise of an exotic intercultural contact and thereby maintaining aspects of the original narrative for the reader. The element of transgression is common to most versions of the *Melusine* tale, and it rests on the instance of exposing the truth about Melusine's hybrid body, with those in her most trusted vicinity breaking an oath of silence and revealing her ability to change shapes and occupy two levels of existence interchangeably.[20] Transformation is also a key theme in the tale, as Melusine is able to convert from one type of being to another, and in Jean d'Arras' account this conversion takes place between the body of a woman and that of a hybrid water creature which is half-serpent and half-human in appearance.[21] Goethe opts to retain this notion of change, but he chooses to use it in quite a different fashion. Rather than associating Melusine with a chthonic, monstrous form, Goethe's Melusine retains her physical beauty in both of her alternate forms. The change that he introduces to his tale has more to do with size rather than physical appeal and can be interpreted as a type of mobility, for his Melusine is able to move from her miniature world to the realm of humans and back.

More importantly, Goethe drew on a decidedly different Germanic source in his version of the story, abandoning elements found in Thüring's popular

20   For a helpful analysis of this, see Kevin Brownlee, "Mélusine's Hybrid Body and the Poetics of Metamorphosis," *Yale French Studies* 86 (1994): 18–38, at 21.

21   For more on Melusine's process of transformation in the original French prose romance, see Ana Pairet's contribution to this volume.

translation and rendering a story that was completely different from the one found in the chapbook edition.[22] He included materials that were recognizably old-Germanic in origin, a choice that diverged from the medieval literary prototype. This is made obvious through the inclusion of new information on Melusine's provenance. The King Eckwald lineage that Melusine professes to have is a clear reference to King Egwaldus from the *Heldenbuch Der gehörnte Siegfried* [*The Hero Book of the Horned Siegfried*], a popular folkloric text that had been republished in Germany in 1726 and which was widely read in the eighteenth century.[23] Egwaldus plays a vital role in this folk narrative, in which he is described as a brave soldier and formidable foe, someone who fights against size and even defeats the giant Wolfgrambär in battle.[24] Rather significantly, the provenance of elves is also explained in the appendix to this old Germanic narrative, a seemingly authoritative source that sheds light on the general history of elves, giants, and other mythological creatures. Here it is revealed that, chronologically, elves precede the human race, occupying a lineage much older and more established than all other living beings, making it clear they take historical and literary precedent to all other creatures.

Some critics argue that Goethe's inclusion of this Germanic material in the *Melusine* narrative had the specific purpose of augmenting the public's understanding of the fairy tale by incorporating elements not customarily used by other writers in their accounts of the *Melusine* tale.[25] Others claim this mythological addition was informed by Herder's work on cosmogony and his expansive study *Ideen zur Philosophie der Geschichte der Menschheit* [*Reflections on the Philosophy of the History of Mankind*].[26] In any case, familiarity with this old-Germanic material is helpful, for it provides a broader, if alternate, comprehension of Melusine's background.[27] The exact relationship that exists between Goethe's modified *Melusine* text and its medieval counterpart is

---

22 For more on this see Fink, *Die neue Melusine,* 21.

23 *Eine wunderschöne Historie von dem gehörnten Siegfried* (Braunschweig, Leipzig: np, 1726).

24 For more on this narrative content, see Clemens Friedrich Meyer, *Goethes Märchendichtung* (Heidelberg: Winters Universitätsbuchhandlung, 1879), 95–102.

25 Fink, *Die neue Melusine,* 39.

26 Monika Schmitz-Emans, "Vom Spiel mit dem Mythos: Zu Goethes Märchen 'Die neue Melusine,'" *Goethe Jahrbuch* 105 (1988): 316–32, at 323.

27 The popularity of the *Siegfried* saga would seem to guarantee this connection. German literary historian Heinrich Pröhle identified this tale in 1886 as one of the essential stories of the Rheinland region, publishing a compendium dedicated to the preservation of oral Volk traditions (*Rheinlands schönsten Sagen und Geschichten,* Berlin: Verlag Meidinger, 1886). Goethe's work on the *Melusine* material obviously precedes Pröhle's compilation,

not explained by the author, but any intertextual connection would presuppose a great deal of literary sophistication on the part of the reader, who could compare the two narratives and recognize Goethe's creative additions to the original.[28]

It should be noted that Goethe was not alone in nurturing literary interest in the *Melusine* story in the 1800s. Other authors had also discovered the narrative and throughout the long eighteenth century they created updated versions of Jean d'Arras' version of the tale. For the most part, these authors adhered to Thüring's translation and observed the conventional narrative format propagated through Jean's medieval work. As such, they retained the customary characters for their readers, enforcing a traditional interpretation of the plot by having it transpire between a human and a secret fairy world, keeping the narrative's basic premise of betrayal and lost love intact. Interestingly enough, one of the versions circulating during this time was a text by Friedrich Wilhelm Zachariä, who entitled his work *Zwei schöne Mährlein* [*Two Lovely Fairy Tales*], recounting the *Melusine* narrative as a fairy tale in verse.[29] His work was known to Goethe, who reviewed and rejected it publicly in the critical journal *Frankfurter Gelehrte Anzeigen* in 1772. In his review, Goethe scathingly dismissed the fairy tale, not on the basis of content, but on the manner in which it was narrated, finding Zachariä's mode of narration boring and ill-suited to the narrative itself. He accuses Zachariä of "Prätension" and "Affektation" [pretension and affectation], rejecting the author's text as a contrived literary endeavour,

---

but his intention may well have been the same, namely, to preserve a national literary heritage by reworking and repositioning certain recognizable themes within a corpus of his own writings.

28   In his late work Goethe often referred to a preferred type of reader, believing that astute attention was needed to understand his writings. On numerous occasions Goethe refers to the "careful," "thoughtful," "critical" reader, alluding to the fact that he is writing for a sophisticated audience capable of understanding his real authorial intentions. When concluding the *Wanderjahre*, for example, he was cognizant that the text was difficult, but stated: "Hier kommen also die Wanderjahre angezogen; ich hoffe, sie sollen bei näherer Betrachtung gewinnen; denn ich kann mich rühmen, daß keine Zeile drinnen steht, die nicht gefühlt oder gedacht wäre. Der *echte* Leser wird das alles schon wieder heraus fühlen und denken" [The *Wanderjahre* are now completed: I hope that upon better reflection they will gain favour, as I can profess that there is not a single line in it that has not been fully contemplated and felt. The real reader will be able to feel and think all of this] (FA 10: 853).

29   Friedrich Wilhelm Zachariä, *Zwey schöne neue Mährlein als 1) von der schönen Melusinen; einer Meerfey, 2) Von einer untreuen Braut, die der Teufel hohlen sollen* (Leipzig: In der Jubilatemesse, 1772).

claiming that its narration lacks the authenticity a real balladeer[30] would have employed in recounting the tale. This observation indicates that Goethe was critically engaged with the *Melusine* material many years before his own publication. It also shows that he was concerned as to how this medieval narrative was being appropriated and understood by contemporaries, some of whom, like Zachariä, appeared, in his view, to completely miss the mark in terms of its proper presentation to the German reading public.

Other authors were more successful with their attempts in revitalizing the tale, finding better critical reception with their interpretations of the *Melusine* narrative. Several Romantic authors utilized the *Melusine* figure to create stories that explored her dual mythical appearance, perpetuating her literary legacy while adapting her appearance to suit their own narrative needs.[31] Romantic author Ludwig Tieck published a version of the tale in 1800 entitled *Die sehr wunderbare Historie von der Melusina* [*The Very Wonderful Story of Melusina*],[32] in which he conscientiously preserved the medieval format and focused strictly on the content of the story as it was translated into German by Thüring von Ringoltingen in 1456.[33] Tieck modified the narrative by giving more emphasis to the personal betrayal suffered by Melusine, remaining within the parameters of the original tale by alluding to her character's disillusionment following the breakdown of her relationship with Raymond. As Boria Sax notes, Tieck focused particularly on the final lament of Melusine

---

30   Goethe uses the term "Bänklesänger;" see Johann Wolfgang von Goethe, "Zwei schöne neue Mährlein," *Goethes Werke, Vollständige Ausgabe letzter Hand,* vol. 33 (Stuttgart: Cotta, 1830), 47.

31   A prime example of the use of the Melusine character as a water spirit is Friedrich de la Motte Fouqué's novella *Undine*, published in 1811. In it the character of Undine marries a knight so she may gain a soul and become human. In his 1814 novella *Der goldne Topf* [*The Golden Pot*], Romantic writer E. T. A. Hoffmann engages with a similar theme of a marriage between human and mythical world. Here the character of Anselmus marries Serpentina, a hybrid serpent creature, to gain access to Atlantis. These are but two examples that show the popularity of the narrative in Romantic literary circles.

32   Ludwig Tieck, *Die sehr wunderbare Historie von der Melusina, Undinenzauber: Geschichten und Gedichte von Nixen, Nymphen und anderen Wasserfrauen,* ed. Frank Rainer Max (Stuttgart: Reclam, 1991), 46–78.

33   Thüring von Ringoltingen's translation popularized the tale with German readers, but he did not use Jean d'Arras' prose version. Instead, he translated the later version by Coudrette, a verse adaptation of Jean's tale. For more on the dissemination of the *Melusine* tale in the German-speaking world, see Friedmar Apel, *Die Zaubergärten der Phantasie: Zur Theorie und Geschichte des Kunstmärchens* (Heidelberg: Winter Universitätsverlag, 1978), 16–20.

and took poetic license to transform her final words to Raymond into verse, a literary adjustment that dramatizes her abandonment and vividly conveys her emotional distress for the reader.[34] The conventional interaction that occurs between human and animal (half-serpent) is consequently kept intact in Tieck's version, as is Raymond's betrayal of his original promise to Melusine. Goethe, however, changed the constellation entirely, not only by portraying Melusine in dwarf form, thereby asserting an old-Germanic template of characters, but also by abolishing the nobility of an earthly kingdom from his tale entirely. Goethe's *Melusine* is consequently not only an interspecies tale, but also a tale that transpires between characters who inhabit different moral and social codes and who find themselves migrating from one world of values to the other and back again.

The male human counterpart presented in Goethe's version of the *Melusine* narrative is especially surprising. He departs quite dramatically from any expectations one may have derived from the traditional narrative and exists separately from any association with Raymond, the male protagonist of the original *Melusine* tale. In the chapbook version of *Melusine,* an earthly kingdom meets a supernatural world, each with its own code of conduct, and the contest that occurs is between two clearly defined realms. Raymond, despite years of bliss and prosperity with Melusine, betrays her simple request to not observe her on a certain day of the week (Saturday), when she reverts to her half-serpent form. Persuaded to steal a glance, he becomes conscious of her full identity. Guilt, regret, and irrevocable loss ensue as a result of Raymond's preventable indiscretion.

Goethe's earthly character is similarly fallible, but he is not noble, aristocratic, or particularly enchanting. His presence is grounded in the mundane, and he behaves accordingly. He is a common barber and, contextually, a peripheral character in the larger *Wanderjahre* narrative, to which the *Melusine* tale ostensibly belongs. Within the *Melusine* fairy tale he is initially presented as someone of import, namely, the savior and the solution to Melusine's predicament of preserving her race and her kingdom. His course of action demonstrates, however, that this is not to be. There is a clear philosophical misalignment with the task presented to him, as the barber proves not to have the moral constitution to exercise proper (and helpful) agency within the fairy tale, dallying and disappointing everyone along the way until he ultimately abandons its magical world entirely. His dishonorable presence within the narrative and poor

---

34   Boria Sax, *The Serpent and the Swan: The Animal Bride in Folklore and Literature* (Blacksburg: The McDonald & Woodward Publishing Company, 1998), 121.

treatment of the Melusine character has led critics like Beate Otto to liken his character to that of a "Heiratschwindler,"[35] a type of gigolo, with no real moral center or credibility.

Within the narrative, the barber's character demonstrably fails to fulfill any expectations one may have of traditional fairy tale action or valor. Through his own admission, he does not recognize the magical world he narrates as particularly special, and he refuses to identify his as a wondrous or imaginative experience. He refers to the entire episode with Melusine rather nonchalantly as a "ziemliche[n] Umweg" [a considerable detour] (FA 10: 656), describing it as a mere distraction from his regular course of action, and noting no surprise or awe when remembering the remarkable nature of the event. Incidentally, his lack of incentive to participate, imaginatively and otherwise, in the fairy tale is a determining factor that makes him oddly unsuitable to the genre itself, because he so steadfastly refuses to transform into anything beyond what he currently is. This obstinacy appears contrary to a basic fairy tale ethos of mutability and change, as the barber's behavior allows the events of the tale to transpire on one egocentric, self-serving level alone. In Goethe's fairy tale there is, consequently, no real challenge, nor is there a reward, because the hero is simply too passive to exert himself to change or betterment.[36] Hans Geulen has written on the crass nature of this character, stating that the barber foregoes any possible transformation in the fairy tale, as he is incapable of seeing the experience apart from sexuality and the implicit physical interaction that occurs between him and Melusine, thereby reducing the entire episode to a disappointingly corporal level.[37]

As Jack Zipes explains, within the generic fairy tale this notion of transformation is vital, for it drives the narrative and justifies both the use and appearance of other extraordinary elements within the story. Transformation also brings about equilibrium between seemingly irreconcilable needs and allows

---

35   Beate Otto, *Unterwasser-Literatur: von Wasserfrauen und Wassermännern* (Würzburg: Königshausen & Neumann, 2001), 74.

36   Bruno Bettelheim has written on the traditional expectations placed on fairy tale heroes and notes the following: "Typical for [...] all true fairy tales, is that the child or adolescent hero has to meet fearful dangers and to engage in actions requiring great valor before he can gain his rewards. However the hero may have been threatened as the story unfolds, in the end he is rescued" (18). See "Fairy Tales as Ways of Knowing" in *Fairy Tales as Ways of Knowing: Essays on Märchen in Psychology, Society and Literature,* ed. Michael M. Metzger and Katharina Mommsen (Bern: Peter Lang, 1981), 11–21.

37   Hans Geulen, "Goethes Kunstmärchen *Der neue Paris* und *Die neue Melusine*: Ihre poetologischen Imaginationen und Spielformen," *Deutsche Vierteljahrsschrift für Literaturwissenschaft und Geistesgeschichte* 59, no. 1 (1985): 79–93, 89.

problematic inconsistencies within the narrative itself to be resolved. Zipes writes: "Fairy tales begin with conflict because we all begin our lives with conflict. We are all misfit for the world, and somehow we must fit in, fit in with other people, and thus we must invent or find the means through communication to satisfy as well as resolve conflicting desires and instincts."[38] In the case of Goethe's *Melusine,* the character of the barber is the ultimate misfit, for he is so patently ill-equipped in every possible way for the task presented to him. Rather significantly, he also *remains* ill-suited for the task throughout the fairy tale. He neither learns to accommodate his own needs, nor does he adapt any of his views to ameliorate the situation he is in. Instead, as an act of free will, he simply opts out of the narrative, relinquishing any personal responsibility he may have had to other characters and abandoning the fairy tale entirely to resume his ordinary, commonplace life. Having deserted the kingdom of the dwarves, the barber laconically notes the anti-climactic conclusion of this experience, stating: "Da stand ich nun wieder, freilich um so vieles größer, allein, wie mir vorkam, auch um vieles dümmer und unbehülflicher" [And there I stood, admittedly, as it seemed, to me much bigger in size, but also much stupider and much more unhelpful] (FA 10: 656).

This inalterability renders the barber a difficult and somewhat obtuse character, someone the reader can easily dislike. He is openly flawed and immature and seems bent on a self-destructive course of action that damages the essential fabric of the fairy tale. He also commits a multiplicity of errors. Unlike Jean d'Arras' Raymond, who commits two significant transgressions vis-à-vis Melusine and is punished accordingly, Goethe's male character errs continuously. His various transgressions repeatedly breach the trust he is meant to have with the princess through a series of insolent actions that expose him as possessing a poor character and being of weak insight. He disrespects their initial agreement by peeking into the chest and spying on the princess, viewing her in her authentic form and thereby betraying her confidence and privacy. He also cheats on her and spends her money with little concern for repercussions. At one point, he even exposes her secret existence as an elven princess by pointedly calling her out in public with a derogatory "Was will der Zwerg?" [What does the dwarf want?] (FA 10: 645), articulating her existence to be of lesser value than his own. The size aspect of their relationship is of metaphorical importance here, for despite the many gains to be had from a bond with the

---

38   Jack Zipes, *The Irresistible Fairy Tale: The Cultural and Social History of a Genre* (Princeton, NJ: Princeton University Press, 2012), 2.

princess and her kingdom, the barber cannot relinquish the impression that this relationship devalues him and he consequently sees everything in terms of reductive, negative size. He contemplates the entire institution of marriage as a loss and is unable to acquiesce to this type of union, noting:

> Dabei hatte ich jedoch leider meinen vorigen Zustand nicht vergessen. Ich empfand in mir einen Maßstab voriger Größe, welches mich unruhig und unglücklich machte. Nun begriff ich zum erstenmal, was die Philosophen unter ihren Idealen verstehen möchten, wodurch die Menschen gequält sein sollen. Ich hatte ein Ideal von mir selbst und erschien mir manchmal im Traum wie ein Riese.
>
> [I unfortunately had not forgotten my previous condition. I sensed within me the measure of my previous size, which made me restless and unhappy. But (through this) I came to comprehend what philosophers understand as their ideal, that which torments the human mind. I too had an ideal of myself and came to think of myself as a giant.] (FA 10: 655)

It is interesting to observe that in the interactions shared between Melusine and the barber, Goethe conflates two different versions of the *Melusine* tale. In a moment of drunken stupor the barber, arguing with Melusine and wanting more wine, shouts out to her "Wasser ist für die Nixen!" [water is for mermaids] (FA 10: 645). This comment, construed as a derision, is seemingly a reference to Melusine's secret background, marking an open betrayal of her hidden identity. This is a curious utterance as there is no context for this information, for nowhere in Goethe's narrative is there mention of Melusine's being a mermaid, nixie, or other type of aquatic creature. Critics like Ellis Dye note that this reference may be a playful gesture on the part of the author to remind his readers of the composite and collective nature of the text.[39] Whatever Goethe's intent may be here—and critics do agree that this comment is not mere sloppiness on part of the author—the "Nixe" comment draws attention to the inherent heterogeneity of the Melusine literary figure, a character inspired by and composed from a variety of different sources. As Monika Schmitz-Emans argues, it might be precisely this complexity of being that motivated Goethe to take on the *Melusine* narrative in the first place, for the Melusine character

---

39   See Ellis Dye, *Love and Death in Goethe: One and Double* (Rochester: Camden, 2004), 117.

seems to espouse the very essence of literary fabrication and creativity, asserting her own unique set of criteria within the text.[40]

In view of the many creative additions made to this tale, some of which are
baffling and make little logical sense, it is difficult to determine Goethe's exact
authorial intent. Overall it seems that, for him, the attraction of the tale rests
on the quality of interaction that transpires between different worlds, as well
as on the general possibility of transformation, aspects of the medieval narrative he kept and utilized in his own adaptation. It is known that the genre of
the fairy tale in general appealed to Goethe as an author, for he believed that it
stimulated the mind, encouraging acts of imagination that were conducive to
the creation of good thought. In his autobiography he reflected on the relative
benefits of the genre and wrote: "Das leerste Märchen hat für die Einbildungskraft schon einen hohen Reiz, und der geringste Gehalt wird vom Verstande
dankbar aufgenommen" [Even the most vacuous fairy tale is a great stimulus
to the imagination, and its most negligible content is gratefully accepted by
one's reason] (FA 14.1:360). This reflective stance is duly manifested in the
main *Wanderjahre* text through the comportment of the barber, who deliberately pauses to gather his thoughts prior to his recounting of the *Melusine* tale.
Although never identifying the *Melusine* narrative as a fairy tale per se, the
barber adopts a reflective stance before telling the story; he becomes solemn
and organizes his thoughts, gathering as it were the requisite contemplative
remove to tell the tale and giving the fairy tale an appropriately thoughtful
context. His manner of narration is justified in the following manner: "Sein
Leben ist reich an wunderlichen Erfahrungen, die er sonst zu ungelegener Zeit
schwätzend zersplitterte, nun aber durch Schweigen genötigt im stillen Sinne
wiederholt und ordnet. Hiermit verbindet sich denn die Einbildungskraft und
verleiht dem Geschehenen Leben und Bewegung" [His life is full of wondrous
experiences which he dispenses through chatter at the most inopportune
times, rather than ordering them through silence and with quiet disposition.
By committing to the latter, one engages the imagination and imbues life and
momentum to that which has happened] (FA 10: 632).

Goethe seemed to have recognized a general propensity in the fairy tale genre that was capable of organizing and incorporating incongruities into a larger,

---

40   She writes: "Das 'Melusinen' Märchen etabliert seine eigene Ordnung, die sich zunächst
      einmal als ein Verstoß gegen konventionelle Sinngefüge präsentiert, als implizite Au-
      flehnung gegen Stimmigkeits-Postulate" [The Melusine fairy tale establishes its own set
      of order, which can be perceived as a breach against conventional logical structures and
      as an implied revolt against all presumptions of coherence], "Vom Spiel mit dem Mythos,"
      322.

cohesive narrative whole. Drawing on these advantages of the genre, notably its elasticity and symbolic potential, he was known to develop his own fairy tales for decades, carefully editing the subject matter to suit complex narrative purposes. He was also known to interpolate the fairy tales into other works he was writing, incorporating them into the context of a larger prose framework, so they could serve a greater reading objective than mere entertainment and offer an alternate means with which to engage with the overall content of the text.

Critics have identified this common feature in all three of Goethe's fairy tales. In addition to *Die neue Melusine,* there is *Das Märchen,* which became part of the framed narrative *Unterhaltungen deutscher Ausgewanderten [Conversations of German Refugees]* (1795), and *Der neue Paris [The New Paris],* which was integrated into his autobiography *Dichtung und Wahrheit* (1811–1831). All of these fairy tales can be read independently, but placed within the larger narrative they help the reader access the overriding context of the book, providing a text within a text and an alternate literary structure through which to ponder the larger narrative framework. There is an implicit chronological order between at least two of the fairy tales themselves, as Goethe indicated when reflecting on their writing in his *Dichtung und Wahrheit*: "Es [Die neue Melusine] verhält sich zum neuen Paris wie ungefähr der Jüngling zum Knaben" [(Die neue Melusine) relates to Der neue Paris, the same way a youth relates to a boy] (FA 14.1: 485). *Der neue Paris* is even subtitled a *Knabenmärchen,* a puerile fairy tale appropriate to the fantasy of a young mind, leaving no doubt as to the intended readership. *Die neue Melusine,* on the other hand, was consciously presented as a more serious narrative, intended for more mature readers, containing material that had been significantly edited and revised over the years and reflecting a process of growth and maturation on the part of the author.

Goethe's prolific literary activity is but one aspect of his creative work and should be understood accordingly. Throughout his life he nurtured a keen interest in science, engaging in a careful observation of nature while pursuing projects in an array of scientific disciplines. A known empiricist, he published research in diverse fields, including botany, zoology, osteology, mineralogy, and color theory, basing his work consistently on observation, experiment, and fact.[41] His scientific writings consequently comprise a large part of his overall

---

41 For more on Goethe's scientific method, see Hugh Barr Nisbet, *Goethe and the Scientific Tradition* (London: Institute of German Studies, 1972); David Seamon, and Arthur Zajonc, eds., *Goethe's Way of Science* (New York: SUNY Press, 1998); and Roger H. Stephenson *Goethe's Conception of Knowledge and Science* (Edinburgh: Edinburgh University Press, 1995).

corpus of writing and regularly appeared alongside other works, demonstrating the author's concurrent dedication to literature and science. Goethe himself valued his scientific work immensely, placing it ahead of anything he had produced in the field of literature.[42] Regrettably, the scientific aspect of Goethe's work tends to be overlooked by scholars who focus solely on his literary texts, even though there is substantial evidence showing considerable overlap between his scientific and literary writings and suggesting that the two should be read in conjunction, as they purposely inform each other.[43] The *Melusine* narrative is a project that would benefit from such an analysis, as it illustrates some of Goethe's key scientific points, reflecting principles found in his unorthodox methodology of science.

Melusine's miniature shape and provenance are two narrative elements—both innovations by Goethe to the medieval narrative—that point to a possible overlap with this scientific theory. One of the key concepts underlying all of Goethe's scientific work was, notably, the notion of the *Urphänomen,* the archetype, the essential but symbolic form that underlies all phenomena, giving shape and purpose. Goethe believed that this archetype was common to all living beings and, more importantly, that it could be visible to the discerning human eye, which, with some effort, was capable of detecting this binding commonality in the natural world. By carefully observing a natural (physical) phenomenon, one could trace it to its original, but abstract, archetype. Recognition of the archetype was, however, predicated on visibility and on a willingness to see the interconnectedness of disparate phenomena in the natural world, an engaged observation that Goethe qualified as "Anschauung" in his

---

42   There is a famous 1828 statement in which Goethe asserts that his scientific research
       with color theory was his most significant achievement. In his conversations with Ecker-
       mann he claimed: "Auf alles, was ich als Poet geleistet habe, bilde ich mir gar nichts ein
       [...] Daß ich aber in meinem Jahrhundert in der schwierigen Wissenschaft der Farben-
       lehre der einzige bin, der das Rechte weiß, darauf tue ich mir etwas zugute" [I do not
       hold much to what I achieved as a poet [...] But that I am the only one in my century who
       knows what is right in the difficult field of color theory, that is rewarding] (FA 36: 216).

43   John A. McCarthy, *Remapping Reality: Chaos and Creativity in Science and Literature* (*Goe-
       the, Nietzsche, Grass*) (Amsterdam: Rodopi, 2006); Dorothea-Michaela Noé-Rumberg,
       *Naturgesetze als Dichtungsprinzipien: Goethes verborgene Poetik im Spiegel seiner Dich-
       tungen* (Freiburg: Rombach, 1993); Peter Sachtleben, *Das Phänomen Forschung und
       die Naturwissenschaft Goethes* (Frankfurt/Main; New York; Paris: Peter Lang, 1987); Jost
       Schieren, *Anschauende Urteilskraft: Methodische und philosophische Grundlage von Goe-
       thes naturwissenschaftlichem Erkennen* (Bonn: Parerga, 1998).

own scientific writings (FA 23.1: 13). *Anschauung* required concentration and a sophistication of attention on the part of the observer, who would commit to this type of mental inquiry and persist in viewing the phenomenon in a two-fold way, both as *Phänomen* and *Urphänomen*. This type of perception saw the outside world as necessarily harmonious and, rather significantly, in terms of the interactions it nurtured, rather than in terms of the separate and isolated phenomena it contained. Goethe recognized that this perspective necessitated a particular type of person and a particular type of intellect, and in 1807 he had to concede the overall rarity of that dedication, noting that "eine aufrichtige, reine, belebende Teilnahme [ist] selten" [a genuine, pure, and invigorating participation is seldom] (FA 24.1: 389). Within Goethe's *Melusine* narrative, the failure of proper participation is made obvious through the barber character, who can neither commit to Melusine nor understand the governing complexities of her world, remaining therefore genuinely imperceptive to everything that transpires around him.

In his science, Goethe valued the act of seeing as the most viable means with which to garner knowledge, maintaining a causal link between sight and insight and believing that proper use of the former was conducive to the latter. He pursued optical studies with the intention of asserting this point and developed a comprehensive color theory that argued for a better and more intelligent visual comprehension of the world. He wrote:

> Jedes Ansehen geht über in ein Betrachten, jedes Betrachten in ein Sinnen, jedes Sinnen in ein Verknüpfen, und so kann man sagen, daß wir schon bei jedem aufmerksamen Blick in die Welt theoretisieren. Dieses aber mit Bewußtsein, mit Selbstkenntnis, mit Freiheit, und um uns eines gewagten Wortes zu bedienen, mit Ironie zu tun und vorzunehmen, eine solche Gewandtheit ist nötig, wenn die Abstraktion, vor der wir uns fürchten, unschädlich, und das Erfahrungsresultat, das wir hoffen, recht lebendig und nützlich werden soll.
>
> [Every look converts to an observation, every observation turns into a perception, and every perception becomes a connection, and one can say that with each attentive view of the world we theorize. To attempt to do this with self-awareness, self-knowledge, freedom and, to use a bold world, with irony, such skillfulness is necessary, if we are to make the abstraction, which we fear, and the result, for which we hope, vibrant and useful]. (FA 23.1:14)

In its own short format, Goethe's *Die neue Melusine* also places special emphasis on acts of seeing. This is obvious at the basic narrative level as the first transgression committed by the barber consists of his peeking in the box entrusted to him and seeing Melusine in her miniscule form. The *topos* of seeing is, rather significantly, dealt with in Goethe's *Melusine* as an act of non-seeing as well, through the depictions of willful ignorance that the barber displays and his inability to see the many benefits of a relationship with Melusine in her kingdom.

Form is a prevalent theme in Goethe's *Melusine* too, with both Melusine and the barber converting from large human form to a more miniature format. His narrative closely explores the perceived incompatibility of these two differently sized and shaped worlds. Goethe had recognized expertise in the field of morphology as he discovered the intermaxillary bone in 1784, making a definitive contribution to the field.[44] The notion of morphology which he developed during his scientific career rested more on mobility, however, than on the perception of concrete shape, for Goethe was intent on tracing the appearance of phenomena back to their origins, back to the invisible *Urphänomen*. As he emphatically stated in his studies on morphology: "Die Gestalt ist ein bewegliches, ein werdendes, ein vergehendes. Gestaltenlehre ist Verwandlungslehre" [Form is (something that is) moving, becoming, disappearing. The study of form is the study of transformation] (FA 24.1: 349). The onus is entirely on the outside observer to make the connections and to see the implicit unity that exists in a multiplicity of forms and which is constantly changing. Flexibility of understanding and perspective are vital elements to the process as a whole.

These scientific utterances may seem obscure, but they bear relevance for many of Goethe's late literary writings, not only because of their chronologic overlap (and the possible influence they may have had on his writing of fiction), but also because they may well elucidate some of the general intentions underlying the author's literary writing. As noted above, many scholars have drawn on Goethe's scientific writings to gain better understanding of the author's late literary work. They believe that this scientific model provides the cohesive framework with which to make sense of some of the author's more unconventional writings.

The novel *Wilhelm Meisters Wanderjahre*, to which the Melusine fairy tale belongs, has been particularly rich in such analyses, its amorphous and unconventional structure proving to be rewarding material for many non-literary

---

44   See George A. Wells, "Goethe and the Inter Maxillary Bone," *The British Journal for the History of Science* 3, no. 4 (1967): 348–61.

interpretations.[45] Unfortunately, among this prolific non-literary *Wanderjahre* research there has not been much focus on *Die neue Melusine* itself, as critics continue to read it primarily as an anomalous and aggregate fairy tale rooted within a literary tradition. The complexity of the Melusine material, with its size-shifting mythological characters, flawed narrator, errant human behavior, intimate physical interactions, bad decision-making, and other intrinsic narrative developments, speaks to a broad intellectual realm and a more inclusive consideration than conventional literature can perhaps offer. Goethe's commitment to the Melusine narrative and his significant redevelopment of its central themes suggests that he understood the potential of the text, but viewed the material beyond the qualities of a fantastic or mythological narrative alone. Providing a different direction for the original narrative, Goethe's many reformulations do little to elucidate plot and clarify authorial intent. Instead, they exploit the medieval tale's connotative qualities in order to give an alternative intelligibility to this world, playing on its very literariness to make the point that an entirely different inquiry may be necessary to truly understand the Melusine storyline.

---

45   Citing but a sample of the available scholarship on the matter, see Azzouni Safia, *Kunst als praktische Wissenschaft: Goethes Wilhelm Meisters Wanderjahre und die Hefte "Zur Morphologie"* (Cologne: Böhlau, 2005); Günter Sasse, *Auswandern in die Moderne: Tradition und Innovation in Goethe's Roman Wilhelm Meisters Wanderjahre* (Berlin: De Gruyter, 2010); Alfred Gilbert Steer, *Goethe's Science in the Structure of the Wanderjahre* (Athens, GA: University of Georgia Press, 1979).

CHAPTER 17

"Listening Down the Hall": An Epistemological Consideration of the Encounter with Melusine in the Germanic Literary Tradition

Deva F. Kemmis

The emphasis on the role of the eyes as the primary organ of the epistemological endeavor has a long history, particularly prominent in the European Enlightenment.[1] Listening, as a key element in the epistemological process, is often overshadowed in this history.[2] The encounter between human being and the figure of Melusine, seen in her mythological predecessors and variations as siren, water sprite, undine, nixie, selkie, nymph, or mermaid,[3] is a compelling site to examine the larger epistemological dynamic between sight and hearing, because within the history of the motif, the human being in the encounter often gains access to knowledge outside of human scope. The question of

---

1 Susanne Kord, "Ancient Fears and the New Order: Witch Beliefs and Physiognomy in the Age of Reason," *German Life and Letters* 61, no. 1 (2008): 61–78. Albert Borgmann discusses this in terms of the etymology and history of the word "focus," which as he notes took on a relation to the optical in the writings of Johannes Kepler; Borgmann, *Technology and the Character of Contemporary Life: a Philosophical Inquiry* (Chicago: University of Chicago Press, 1987), 197.

2 Herder's argument as to the medial and therefore key role that hearing plays among the senses in the invention and use of human language is an important exception. Johann Gottfried Herder, *Abhandlung über den Ursprung der Sprache* (Stuttgart: Reclam, 1966), 57–62.

3 For a history of nixie figure in world literature see Elisabeth Frenzel, *Motive der Weltliteratur: Ein Lexikon dichtungsgeschichtlicher Längsschnitte* (Stuttgart: Alfred Kröner Verlag, 1988), 774–788, and for an account of the motif in the Germanic tradition see Jakob Grimm, *Deutsche Mythologie* (Göttingen: Edwin Redslob, 1835), 244, 275–278. For a comprehensive classification of the nixie motif in world mythologies see Stith Thompson, *Motif-index of Folk-literature; a Classification of Narrative Elements in Folktales, Ballads, Myths* (Bloomington: Indiana University Press, 1955); see esp. Sirens, Vol. 1, p. 369; Water Sprites, Vol. 2, p. 31; Marvels, Vol. 3, F200-F399; Mermaids, Vol. 5, p. 371. See also Linda Phyllis Austern and Inna Naroditskaya, *Music of the Sirens* (Indianapolis: Indiana University Press, 2006), especially Leofranc Holford-Strevens, "Sirens in Antiquity and the Middle Ages," 16–52.

© KONINKLIJKE BRILL NV, LEIDEN, 2017 | DOI 10.1163/9789004355958_019

interest here is: By which epistemological avenue does this knowledge come?[4] In a twentieth-century poetic realization of the encounter with the water nymph, Ingeborg Bachman's "Undine Geht" [Undine Goes] (1961), it is not the eyes that play the central role in the epistemological character of the knowledge transfer, but the ears. Specifically, the posture of *attentive listening* that precedes the encounter with this later Melusine iteration indicates a state of readiness that leads to a moment of extraordinary awareness for the human being in that text, in which the epistemological experience is transformational.[5] On the poetological level, the representation of the encounter between human and water nymph is read here as symbolic of the dialogue between reader and text, which likewise may give rise to a moment of exceptional awareness for the reader.[6]

Bachmann's narrative poem gives full voice to the archetypal water woman, and in so doing both echoes the Melusine of the medieval sources (along with those who precede her in myth, saga, literature, and legend), and opens new vistas of inquiry surrounding the figure, particularly with respect to the poetology of the encounter. Within the larger framework of the literary and mythological tradition, Bachmann's water nymph speaks directly to numerous strands in the history of the motif that have come before her, and the reverberations of the Melusine legendary in particular are striking. At these sites of intertextuality, Bachmann's text takes part in the larger Germanic Melusine literary tradition by reflecting and refracting essential moments in Thüring von Ringoltingen's iteration of the French source material, *Melusine* (1456), the foundational text for German-speaking audiences of the Melusine legend and, through the subsequent chapbook, source for the numerous European variants that secured Melusine's popularity and legacy across the continent.[7]

---

4 See Deva Kemmis Hicks, "'On the Verge of Hearing': Epistemology and the Poetics of Listening in the Human-Nixie Encounter in Germanic Literature" (PhD diss., Georgetown University, 2012) for a fuller discussion including Goethe's "Der Fischer" (1779), Kafka's "Das Schweigen der Sirenen" (1917), and Johannes Bobrowski's "Undine" (1964).

5 See Albert Borgmann's elaboration of *focal occasions* in "Cyberspace, Cosmology, and the Meaning of Life," *Ubiquity* 8, vol. 7 (2007).

6 For the purposes of this chapter, poetological is defined as the level on which the interaction between text, author, and reader is thematized. Aristotle's theory of *anagnorisis* as developed in the *Poetics* is foundational. Ronald Murphy's exposition of realization theory serves as a present-day elucidation of Aristotle's approach to aesthetics; see *The Owl, the Raven and the Dove: The Religious Meaning of the Grimms' Magic Fairy Tales* (New York: Oxford University Press, 2002).

7 See Albrecht Classen's contribution to this volume for a discussion of the printing history of Thüring's *Melusine*.

Not all encounters between a human being and mythological water woman in Germanic literature have a clear epistemological character.[8] What is here termed the epistemological moment, however, accompanies the diverse traditions in at least one major work, and is generally recurrent in the various works that articulate the tradition in literature. The encounter in Germanic literature is not of a homogenous nature, but the epistemological nature of the encounter is a salient feature that emerges from the varied traditions and one read here as a unifying thread. This conceptual framework underlies the exploration of both the moment of epiphany in the texts and of the possibility for a similar transformation for the reader at the poetological level.[9]

The figure of the mythological water woman is generally considered to have first appeared in the Germanic tradition in the thirteenth-century Middle High German *Das Nibelungenlied* [*Song of the Nibelungs*] (ca.1200),[10] approximately 2000 years after Homer's account of Odysseus and the sirens and well into the history of the literary motif. The nixies appear in Adventure 25 of the *Nibelungenlied*, when the Burgundians, on their way to visit Kriemhild in Etzel's kingdom, run into a serious obstacle: the water of the Danube has risen and they have no way to cross. Stuck for the moment and searching for the ferryman, King Gunther's knight Hagen hears splashing in the water and stops to listen. Described by the poet alternately as "merewîp" [mermaid], "wîsiu wîp" [wise woman], and "diu wilden merwîp" [the wild mermaids], the water nixies are bathing in the river when Hagen, after becoming curious about the

---

8   See for instance *Kinder- und Hausmärchen, gesammelt durch die Brüder Grimm* (München: Winkler-Verlag, 1956), nos. 79, and 181, which feature malevolent nixies absent any clear epistemological interest.

9   This theoretical grounding rests on Hans-Georg Gadamer's hermeneutic approach to art as initially articulated in *Wahrheit und Methode: Grundzüge einer philosophischen Hermeneutik* (Tübingen: J. C. B. Mohr, 1975) and further developed in his late essays on aesthetics, specifically "Dichtung und Mimesis," in *Gesammelte Werke: Ästhetik und Poetik I: Kunst als Aussage* (Tübingen: J. C. B. Mohr [Paul Siebeck], 1993), 80–86, and "Über den Beitrag der Dichtkunst bei der Suche nach der Wahrheit" in *Gesammelte Werke*, 70–79.

10   Joyce Tally Lionarons, "The Otherworld and its Inhabitants in the Nibelungenlied," in *A Companion to the Nibelungenlied*, ed. Winder McConnell (Columbia: Camden House, 1998), 153–171, at 168. Lionarons has argued that the Icelandic sagas and the *Edda* contain references to possible early relatives of the mythical water woman or prophetess, generally, but that the figure comes from no discernible tradition. Ulrich von Zatzikhoven's *Lanzelet* features mermaids, or fairies from the sea (*meerfiene*), and has been dated approximately to 1195–1200, very close to the first appearance of the *Nibelungenlied*.

splashing sound and then listening for a moment, becomes aware of them.[11] In short order, the nixies give Hagen what he wants: a way across the river; but more importantly, they prophesy the future, and the knowledge they impart to Hagen arguably alters the course of events to the epic's tragic end.

These few lines in the *Nibelungenlied*, a tiny, fleeting moment in proportion to the work as a whole, deserve nonetheless to be seen as foundational to the flowering of water nixies in their diversity in future Germanic texts. These lines provide an important textual site for a discussion about the encounter between the mythical and the human in literature as a figuration of the larger epistemological confrontation between the ear and the eye. Though these passages in the *Nibelungenlied* are thought to represent the first known textual instance of the water nixie in German literature, in the broader realm of Germanic literature and myth, the mythological water woman and related motifs were evident in contemporary writings, as well as in artistic depictions and oral tradition.[12]

Several early Germanic manuscripts portray sirens or other mermaid figures in woodcarvings; the figures are also found adorning church panels and ceilings in the early medieval period.[13] One notable example from literature from the early medieval period is the figure of Grendel's mother in the second battle sequence of the heroic *Beowulf* (lines 98–113). She is referred to in Anglo-Saxon as a *nicor* [sea monster] and *mere-wīf* [mermaid], among other designations.[14] Grendel's mother lives in the waters of a primordial mere, and in this respect the figure bears some resemblance to the siren or other versions of the

11   The stealing of clothing speaks to the swan maiden legend, in which the man who steals the swan maiden's clothing is bound to them. Sometimes the reverse holds true. Found in the *Poetic Edda* in the Germanic tradition, the legend also appears in Russian and Slavic mythology. In the *Edda*, Valkyries also assume the shape of the swan maiden at times. See Grimm, *Mythologie*, 244, 275, and Frenzel, *Motive der Weltliteratur*, 776. For an introduction to the swan maiden legend and related motifs in world folklore, see Barbara Fass Leavy, *In Search of the Swan Maiden* (New York: New York University Press, 1994), 11–32.

12   See Edward R. Haymes, *The Nibelungenlied: History and Interpretation* (Urbana: University of Illinois Press, 1986). Haymes finds sources for epics of this period in much earlier oral tradition, not an approach agreed to by all scholars. See Winder McConnell for a discussion of the diverse scholarly approaches to the poem in his introduction to *A Companion to the Nibelungenlied*, 1–18.

13   Beatte Otto, *Unterwasser-Literatur* (Würzburg: Verlag Königshausen & Neumann, 2001), 26–34.

14   *Nicor* is related to Old High German *nichus* and New High German *Nixe*. See Grimm, *Deutsche Mythologie*, 244, 275–278.

motif, but she is also situated firmly in a biblical tradition.[15] A fear-inspiring figure that more closely resembles beasts in other epics, such as the Gorgons, Medusa, giants of the *Edda,* and other female monsters in classical and Germanic
mythology, Grendel's mother as a matter of portrayal does not seem to stem
from the water nixie tradition. The designations used to describe her—one of
them the same term used for the water sprites in the *Nibelungenlied* (*merewîp*),
in Anglo-Saxon (*mere-wīf*)—indicate a linguistic commonality, and from this
perspective the figure ought to be included in a discussion of Germanic female
water figures, particularly as she is one of the few that textually predate the
Nibelungenlied's nixies.[16] Finally, the Icelandic heroic sagas and the writings of
the *Edda* corpus also reference mythical figures related to the water nixie, from
swan maidens to goddesses who personify the waves.[17]

In later eras, the motif of the mythological water woman found extensive
treatment, both in primary texts and corresponding secondary literature. The
most well-known tradition to emerge is the legend of Melusine, with influence
and reverberations in literature and culture to the present day. Melusine goes
on to have a rich history in Germanic literature; her tale or versions of it are
told by, among others, Hans Sachs, Martin Luther, Goethe, Achim von Arnim,
E. T. A. Hoffmann, and Wilhelm Raabe.[18] Melusine is the name of one of the
main characters of Theodor Fontane's 1899 novel *Der Stechlin*; a version of her
story is told by Ludwig Tieck in his *Sehr wunderbare Historie von der Melusina*
[*The Very Wonderful Story of Melusina*] (1800) and Georg Trakl's poem *Melusine* (1909, 1912). The nature of the encounter between the water woman and

---

15   That Grendel's mother is one of a number of beasts who are of Cain's lineage is made
       explicit in *Beowulf.* Nixie or mermaid figures appear in the Latin bestiaries from roughly
       the eighth century through the early modern period. See Holford-Stevens, "Sirens," 29–37.
       In these catalogues, the nixie figure is set apart from the monsters, also apart from the an-
       gels and other heavenly beings, often situated in the center of the constellation of beasts,
       emerging from the water. See also Otto, *Unterwasser-Literatur,* 29–31.

16   As *Beowulf* has been interpreted as a text characterized by the traditions of both the an-
       cient Germanic and emergent Christian religions, perhaps the figure of Grendel's mother
       likewise combines elements of the old and new orders. See Friedrich S. J. Klaeber, "The
       Christian Coloring," *Beowulf,* 3rd ed. (Lexington: Heath, 1950).

17   See the *Poetic Edda,* (Codex Regius) Introduction and HH1. The first manuscript of the
       Edda (Codex Regius), the collection now housed in Iceland, most likely a copy of a now-
       lost original, is dated ca.1280; Snorri Sturluson's prose *Edda* was composed ca.1220. Ear-
       lier oral traditions are very difficult to date.

18   See Renata Schellenberg's chapter in this volume, "Goethe and *Die neue Melusine,*" for a
       discussion of how Goethe distinctly reworks the European myth within German fairy tale
       traditions.

mortal man in Thüring von Ringoltingen's late medieval work, in combination
with his French sources, is critical for understanding later works that feature
Melusine and her mythological variants, and here serves as the point of reference for an examination of the epistemological nature of the encounter in
Ingeborg Bachmann's short story "Undine Geht."

In Bachmann's narrative poem, the story of the encounter between human
and water nymph is told for the first time entirely from the nymph's point of
view. Bachmann's eponymous water nymph, by name an Undine,[19] narrates
this internal monologue, in which she explains why she is leaving the human
world and returning to the water. While this text has generally been read as a
literary response to Friedrich de la Motte Fouqué's 1811 novella *Undine* and
the twentieth-century drama by Jean Giraudoux, *Ondine* (1939),[20] Bachmann's
protagonist speaks for the figure of the mythical female water nymph from
varied traditions and is not confined to Fouqué's Undine.[21] That Bachmann has
given her Undine a voice is significant in several respects, given the prevailing silence of nixie figures in the last nearly two hundred years of the motif's
history, particularly when compared to the prophesying characteristic of the
nixies in earlier classical and medieval texts.[22]

The term Undine, from Latin "little wave," originated with the early modern
philosopher Paracelsus, whose treatise influenced poets and writers who take

---

19   For a thorough analysis of the undine motif in literature, see Ruth Fassbind-Eigenheer,
      *Undine, oder die nasse Grenze zwischen mir und mir: Ursprung und literarische Bearbeitun-
      gen eines Wasserfrauenmythos, von Paracelsus über Friedrich de la Motte Fouqué zu Inge-
      borg Bachmann* (Stuttgart: Heinz, 1994).

20   See Fassbind-Eigenheer, *Undine*, 123, 136.

21   Fouqué's *Undine* is thought to have stemmed largely from two sources: Paracelsus's *Liber
      de Nymphis, Sylphis, Pygmaeis et Salamandris et de Caeteris Spiritibus* (ca.1566) and the
      Melusine legend, originally recorded as *Roman de Mélusine* by Jean d'Arras (1393). A third
      source may have been Christian August Vulpius' novel *Die Saal-Nixe* (1795), as identified
      by both Fassbind-Eigenheer and by Andreas Kraß in *Meerjungfrauen: Geschichten einer
      unmöglichen Liebe* (Frankfurt am Main: Fischer Verlag, 2010), 165–205.

22   Exceptions to the silence of the nixie figure in German literature since the early Romantic
      period are the Lorelei figure in Clements Brentano's ballad "Zu Bacharach am Rheine"
      (1801) and in his novel *Godwi* (1801), among several others, including Goethe's revision
      of the Melusine legend in his *Die neue Melusine*, in Book 3 of *Wilhelm Meisters Wander-
      jahre* (1821). The theme of the sirens as silent is best known from Kafka's 1917 fragment
      Das Schweigen der Sirenen, discussed below. Another important example of this literary
      trend, in which the sirens or nixie figures are discussed but not heard from directly, is
      Rilke's "Die Insel der Sirenen" (1908), in which the reader can nearly hear the song of the
      sirens. In this lyric as well it is the silence and not the song that is thematized and which
      forms the strongest impression.

up the undine theme in eighteenth- and nineteenth-century texts.[23] The literary tradition stemming from Paracelsus's sixteenth-century work opens in the Germanic context with Goethe's brief mention of the Undine in the scene in Faust's study in *Faust* (1808), in which Faust summons the four spirits of the earth, naming Undine as the water spirit, only to be subsequently rejected by the earth spirit.[24] The next major work to feature the undine figure is Fouqué's 1811 novella, *Undine*.[25] The undine figure found its greatest resonance in the German *Romantik*, particularly in the late romantic period. E. T. A. Hoffmann, a friend and collaborator of Fouqué's, fascinated by the legend of the undine, wrote an opera of that name with Fouqué,[26] and mentions the undine in a number of works.[27] The undine figure was the inspiration for the magical half maiden, half snake, Serpentina, in *Der goldne Topf* [*The Golden Pot*].[28]

Bachmann's twentieth-century version of the legend begins with the accusation, "You people! You monsters! You monsters named Hans. With this name that I can never forget."[29] Undine's monologue is a retelling of her relationship with Hans, which is at once an account of this Undine and her relationship

---

23 Paracelsus, *Liber de Nymphis, sylphis, pygmaeis et salamandris et de caeteris spiritibus*, trans. Henry E. Sigerist (Baltimore: Johns Hopkins Press, 1941). See Melissa Ridley Elmes's contribution to this volume for a discussion of Paracelsus's use of Melusine. See also Fassbind-Eigenheer, *Undine*, 15–63, Renate Böschenstein, "Undine oder das fließende Ich," in *Verborgene Facetten: Studien zu Fontana* (Würzburg: Königshausen & Neumann, 2006), 176–223, or Andreas Kraß's history of the undine figure in German literature, "Undine: Nymphe und Verführerin III," in *Meerjungfrauen*, 289–344.

24 This scene draws directly on Paracelsus's account, naming the four elementals that represent the four elements of earth, water, air, and fire.

25 It is in Fouqué's version that an important element of the water nymph legend becomes explicit, namely the matter of the soul. See Andersen's *Little Mermaid* (*Den lille havfrue*, 1837), in which the mermaid gains access to a soul but loses her voice.

26 *Undine: Zauber-Oper*, first performed in Berlin in 1816. The music was written by E. T. A. Hoffmann and lyrics by Fouqué. The scenery was designed by the well-known Berlin architect Karl Friedrich Schinkel.

27 See Fassbind-Eigenheer, *Undine*, 109–116, or Kraß, *Meerjungfrauen*, 310.

28 See Kraß's chapter on the undine figure and the work he cites as Fouqué's main source, Christian August Vulpius's *Die Saal Nixe*, which has a similar plot and essentially identical character names, although the constellation is different. Vulpius's novel appeared in 1795, well before Fouqué's work. The striking similarities of name and plot form the basis of Kraß's argument that Fouqué drew heavily from this little-known source. Kraß, *Meerjungfrauen*, 166–168.

29 Bachmann, "Undine Geht," in *Werke 2. Erzählungen* (München: Piper & Co. Verlag, 1978), 253–265. References from this text will hereafter be given in parenthesis. The irony of Bachmann's Undine calling Hans a monster has been well-noted.

with a man or men named Hans and an account of the relationship between water nymph and human being in the various literary and mythological strands associated with the broader archetype.[30]

Bachmann's "Undine Geht" is thus immediately and purposefully intertextual: it takes up a dialogue with the texts that have come before and, through its use of the internal monologue, presents an entirely new aspect to the textual history surrounding Undine specifically and the water nymph motif more broadly.[31] Situated very differently from other texts of the Germanic tradition that feature this figure, "Undine Geht" directly takes up the discourse about the female supernatural in literature and myth, and specifically the water-dwelling female.[32]

Bachmann's text follows the encounter between Undine and Hans through several of its cycles. The language Undine uses to tell her story is cyclical, fragmentary, and repetitive; it does not proceed in a chronological or linear fashion and resists translation into a plot summary.[33] When Undine's monologue is coaxed into a more linear structure, her own account of her relationship with Hans follows roughly this pattern: Undine and Hans meet in a clearing (*die Lichtung*), greet each other, are together, something goes wrong, and she returns to the water, only to one day rise to the surface and begin again.

Strikingly, the meeting place in this story does not speak to the traditions in either the Giraudoux or Fouqué text, two of the likely *Ur* sources for

---

30　See C. G. Jung's "Über die Archetypen des kollektiven Unbewussten," in *Gesammelte Werke*, 20 vols. (Stuttgart: Racher, 1958–1994), 9:1–34, or "Über den Archetypus mit besonderer Berücksichtigung des Animabegriffs," in *Von den Wurzeln des Bewusstseins* (Zurich: Racher, 1954). Jung's reading of the symbolism of the nixie figure is as a symbol for the primordial anima and the role of water as symbolic of the unconscious. The water nymph for Jung symbolizes a knowledge-bringer, among many other attributes of the anima.

31　See Bakhtin's concept of addressivity in M. M. Bakhtin, "The Problem of Speech Genres," in *Speech Genres and Other Late Essays*, trans. Vern W. McGee, ed. Caryl Emerson and Michael Holquist (Austin, TX: University of Texas Press, 1986), 60–102. For an influential theoretical framework by which to understand the role of the image of the female supernatural in literature and myth and its influence in the cultural realm from a feminist perspective, see Silvia Bovenschen, *Die imaginierte Weiblichkeit. Exemplarische Untersuchungen zu kulturgeschichtlichen und literarischen Präsentationsformen des Weiblichen* (Frankfurt: Suhrkamp, 2003).

32　See Anna-Lisa Baumeister's essay in this volume, "Woman, Abject, Animal," in which she locates specular moments in certain late twentieth-century Viennese works that evoke the discovery of Melusine at her bath.

33　Karen R. Achberger, "Undine Goes," in *Understanding Ingeborg Bachmann* (Columbia: University of South Carolina Press, 1995), 74–95.

Bachmann's Undine; rather, it more powerfully recalls the Melusine tradition, in which the clearing is a central topos for the mortal man/fairy union. Though the clearing as motif has a secure place throughout legend, saga, and fairy tale as marker of the numinous,[34] where the otherworldly woman should always be looked for and will often be found, particularly near a fountain,[35] Bachmann's use of the clearing as the central meeting place for Undine and Hans, whether in the forest clearing or in the clearing of Hans's living room, provides an un-canny reminder of Melusine and Raymond, who themselves have repeated the pattern of their own legend of origin by meeting in the clearing. More than that, Bachmann's choice of the clearing as meeting place points to the phe-nomenological potential of the clearing, a place that is often marked by truth.[36] In the case of Thüring's Melusine, this clearing is the site where Melusine's extraordinary knowledge is first revealed: she is aware of what has befallen Raymond before they even meet.[37]

There are numerous variations to this pattern of encounter that provide glimpses of Hans and Undine in different settings, both in rural and forested landscapes and in urban scenes: she refers to visits to the theater, drinking Pernod, a train station, and the great boulevards. Their story exists in differ-ent temporal dimensions; they meet in the present day, as evidenced by the gadgets and references to science and modern life which punctuate her ac-count, but these encounters also exist in the past of the undine legend, as seen in the meetings in the clearing and the other appearances of the mythologi-cal, which underscore that this Undine speaks for supernatural water women more broadly.[38]

---

34   For the role of the forest as site of the numinous, see Jack Zipes, for instance "Who's Afraid of the Brothers Grimm? Socialization and Politization through Fairy Tales," in *A Critical Journal of Children's Literature* 3, vol. 2 (Brooklyn: Lion and the Unicorn, 1979).

35   For a discussion of the function of fountains in the meeting of the fairy woman with her lover, see Misty Urban, "Magical Fountains in Middle English Romance," in *The Nature and Function of Water, Baths, Bathing, and Hygiene from Antiquity through the Renais-sance*, ed. Cynthia Kosso and Anne Scott (Leiden: Brill, 2009), 427–52.

36   See Martin Heidegger on the clearing as an ontological enclosure for truth recognition. A clearing, *Lichtung*, from German *Licht* (light), is for Heidegger a place of disclosure, an activity fundamentally related to truth. See "Die Frage nach der Technik," in *Vorträge und Aufsätze*, Teil III (Tübingen: Verlag Günther, 1967), 5–36, or "Dichterisch wohnet der Mensch," in *Vorträge und Aufsätze*, Teil I (Tübingen: Verlag Günther, 1967), 61–78.

37   Thürung von Ringoltingen, *Melusine – In der Fassung des Buchs der Liebe* (1587) (Stutt-gart: Reclam, 1991), 12.

38   Achberger, "Undine Goes," 89.

Undine's monologue is internal, but she speaks both to and about Hans using alternately the informal singular and plural second-person forms of address with him ("Ihr" and "Du") as well as referring to him in the third person. She is telling their story to herself, to him, and to the others who came before him on the human side of the encounter. The name Hans likely refers to the knight figure in Giraudoux's *Ondine*, called Ritter Huldebrand in Fouqué's text.[39] In the course of both plots, the knight falls in love with and marries Undine and the pair leaves the wood to live in his castle. In both cases, the knight ends up breaking a promise to Undine,[40] which sends her back to the water and ultimately results in his death.[41]

Huldebrand's and later Hans's broken promises to Undine also recall the Melusine legendary, as the broken promises in each text precipitate the water nymph's leaving the world of men, albeit within different very temporal frameworks. The structural element of the water nymph leaving the world of men on the textual level, yet remaining on the poetological level, is central to both Bachmann's narrative and the Melusine legend. Bachmann's iteration, with its internal direct voicing of the water nymph, provides a modern aesthetic insight into Melusine's own act of final leaving the family home, with the visible footprint she leaves on the windowsill that accompanies it as the sole evidence of her prior presence there, and her the cry of pain the sole explanation:

> But let me be very clear, you monsters, and degrade you, I will never come again, follow your gestures to come along, your invitations to a glass of

---

39 "Ja, diese Logik habe ich gelernt, dass einer Hans heißen muss, dass ihr alle so heißt, einer wie der andere, aber doch nur einer" [Yes, I've learned this logic, that one must be called Hans, that you're all called Hans, one the same as the other, but still only one]. Bachmann, "Undine Geht," 253.

40 The broken-taboo theme is important for texts featuring water nymphs, going back to Jean d'Arras' *Melusine*, but it functions differently in the Undine legend. For the importance of the taboo/transgression in the Melusine myth, see Gerhild Scholtz Williams, "Magic and the Myth of Transgression: *Melusine de Lusignan* by Jean D'Arras (1393)," in *Defining Dominion: The Discourses of Magic and Witchcraft in Early Modern France and Germany* (Ann Arbor: University of Michigan Press, 1995), 21–45. In contrast to the Melusine variations, the consequences in this tradition are more severe: the result of the broken taboo is the death of the human and the forced return of the water nymph to the water.

41 Giraudoux's drama departs from Fouqué's at several important junctures, but in both texts the knight breaks a promise to Undine and dies as a result. In Fouqué's version, it is a promise not to mistreat her near the water lest her powerful uncle or other water-kin seek vengeance; in Giraudoux, Hans is unfaithful with Bertha, his former fiancée.

wine, a trip, a visit to the theater. I will never come again, never say *Yes* again and *You* and *Yes*. (254)

In Bachmann's iteration, Undine's monologue signals clearly that, for her, too, there will be an end. Undine's speech stakes out a position of finality: this is her story, and after her story ends, she will go. Undine's leaving is an aural reification of Melusine's watery footprint left on the windowsill, and her explanation for why she has to go, the narrative itself, can be read as giving voice to Melusine's cry as she circles the castle in despair.

Buttressed by the narrative poem's title, the intention of Undine's language with respect to its content is clear, but the form of the language—poetic, cyclical, and very difficult to separate into a linearity—stakes out a different position. When Undine says she will never again say *you* and *yes* and *you*, she is already saying them again, continuing the cycle of encounter with Hans. This inability to disconnect is emphasized by the otherwise redundant *you* (*Du*). She cannot help but say that word again, which is a way of naming him, reinforcing their connection. This tension between signaled intent and content of her language courses through the text.

Moreover, the form of Bachmann's language evokes the sound of waves in its cyclical and repetitive nature. The reader hears both Undine's thoughts as she expresses them and the sound of water as if rising from the text. The messages that each brings, in form and content, are divergent. The wave-like acoustic that is a hallmark of Bachmann's language in this text also echoes human breath in its autonomic quality. The waves and the reader's own breathing draw the story forward. Both, however, are in tension with Undine's stated intention that this story will come to an end.[42] This tension points to the opaque history of the motif of the encounter between the human and the mythical in its origins, an encounter that cannot be fixed textually in one moment in the past, nor predicted with any certainty to end.

The dual nature of Undine's language can also be read as a means by which to understand Undine as essentially connected in this text, not able to be either in one world—the world of a story which ends—or another, the world of a story which does not end. On the poetological level, in which the reader hears both the rhythm of water and human breath, no ending is possible, and

---

42   This tension has been explored by Achberger, among others, in terms of the tension between *melos* and *logos*, music and speech ("Undine Goes," 85–90), especially between this text as a kind of feminine writing and what is seen in certain feminist scholarship as the male narrative style, dominated by the analytic tradition of logical oppositions.

Undine is necessarily connected to this level as well. This is her language that comes as if in waves.

Although Undine inhabits both realms in this text and resists being placed firmly in one realm or the other, she refers to her life in the water as if it is a separate existence. She refers therefore either to a time not represented in the text, before a first encounter with Hans, or to the way she sees herself, which is distinct from the world of men. The text as a whole does not support this view, but in terms of the intention of the content of language Undine uses, this is her view of her own life.

Undine refers to how she was condemned to love and when she came freely out of love, she had to return to the water. She portrays the water as the element lacking the human accomplishments of planning, domesticating, building. Undine sets up a distinction here in terms of consciousness and activity that reflect an awareness of the future between the natural realm, which in this text is the watery realm, and the human realm. This distinction also harkens to Melusine, who comes from a more natural realm and returns to it after her confrontation with Raymond compels her exile.

Undine's description of the human realm as the realm in which time is present and understood—where time is reified—serves an important role in this text. It is one of the contrasting features that Undine identifies to differentiate one realm from the other. In order to draw this distinction, Undine must herself be aware of time in some way and thus connected to the human realm, in which an awareness of the forward motion of time is central. The awareness of time that Undine reveals in her description sets her firmly in both realms; she may see herself as primarily connected to the natural realm, but her description belies that distance. Further, the use of language is a conscious activity for Undine: she is putting the language down in a confessional manner, as she says. The monologue itself speaks to a conscious activity, as she has stated that once she is done with this monologue, she will return to the water, revealing a consciousness about the activity she is undertaking. Finally, Undine takes part in the very oppositional categories of analysis that she ascribes to the human realm, categories she herself employs to differentiate the two, which reminds the reader of the tension between the stated intent of her language in terms of its positioning and the way in which the language functions to communicate.

This thematization of the temporal is important because Undine ascribes both the awareness of time and its nature as linear to the human realm. Although Undine's speech relies on the categories that she ascribes to humanity, the one characteristic of the human understanding of time that Undine has so far pointed out—its nature as forward-moving, hence the need for planning and building—is a feature that Undine's language, at both the textual and the poetological levels, does not partake of. Although there is an awareness of time on Undine's part in order to ascribe it to humanity, her monologue, as noted above, is circular, repetitive, and fragmentary. It is not possible to turn this monologue into something with a beginning and an end; it resists chronological order.

In this one respect, there is a gap between Undine and the human realm as she has described it. The human conceptualization of time as linear and forward-moving is not something the text or Undine's narrative supports. Although Undine remains always connected to both realms in this text, the temporal aspect is one site that may reveal something about Undine's nature with much more credibility than the bulk of her own assertions, which are often undermined by her particular use of language.[43] Specifically, this gap points the reader to the circuitous nature of the encounter between human and mythical.

The moment of meeting between Hans and Undine, in its different versions and dimensions, comprises the bulk of the monologue, and despite the cyclical nature of the account, there are significant points of overlap in the structure of those moments of encounter. Sound signals the moment of encounter between Undine and Hans. In this description of their meeting, the second in the text, while Hans is busy with wives and children and newspapers, looking through the bills and turning the radio up loud, Undine says:

> and to hear, despite all that, the sound of mussels, and the weathervane, and then, again, later, when it's dark in the houses, to stand, to secretly open the door, to listen down the hall, into the yard, into the alleyways, and then to hear it clearly: the sound of pain, the cry from far away, the uncanny music. Come! Come! Come just once! (255)

In Undine's description of the encounter, which this time takes place in the clearing of Hans's home, the key element is the way in which Hans is listening, and then hears the note of pain, the call from far off.[44] The role of audial

---

43   Undine's characterization of the world as divided in a temporal sense works against the reader's experience of the text, allowing for an opening in which the reader may understand the world as connected.

44   These lines, among others, are thought to have been inspired by Hans Werner Henze, close friend to Bachmann, who wrote an opera entitled "Undine" (1957). Bachmann and Henze lived together in Italy in the years before "Undine Geht" was published and it is considered likely that their respective work on the Undine material influenced the other. See discussion in Fassbind-Eigenheer, *Undine,* 126–133, or Achberger, "Undine Goes," 86–89.

awareness as antecedent to the encounter with Undine is salient in this passage. The sound that Hans hears, the note of pain from far off, has not only carried over many cycles of their meetings, as the narrative suggests, but it also carries with it an older cry still. This call of pain evokes Melusine's cry as she circles the castle, the *cri du Mélusine*. The call from far off in Undine's narrative gives voice to the serpentous footprint on the windowsill, all that was left of Melusine in the medieval legend, still and now again borne by its uncanny music to the human ears that listen for her.

Hans's posture from one encounter to the next also bears commonalities. He is twice described as listening. In the encounter above, in which the living room transforms into the clearing, the precipitous factor seems to be the emotional state that Hans is in: empty, with nothing useful to think of, lost. Both postures, listening and at a loss, signal a readiness in Hans for Undine to appear. Undine points to Hans's divided state as the time she really loves him. Undine's call to Hans, "der Ruf zum Ende" [the call to the end], does not come randomly. There is a time for Undine to come, (*dann war es Zeit für mich*), and that time comes about by way of how Hans is at those moments: he is quiet, empty, and listening for something.

Of note in this encounter, which is at once every encounter that takes place at Hans's home as the clearing, is that Hans as listener is the causal agent, the force that sets the encounter with Undine in motion. The emphasis on the acoustic and on the human posture of listening that precedes the encounter is set very firmly at this point in the text. In these descriptions, the sounds that precede the moment of encounter between Hans and Undine are sounds of nature, often connected with water: the gust of wind, the note of seashell, Undine's laughter rippling the water. These sounds characterize the moments before the encounter.

Undine comes when Hans is ready, calls on him, and tells him what to think, be, and say—but what is that? Hans is moved by the incomprehensibility of the institutions and order that mark human life, and the idea that he secretly nurtures, the great and unpractical idea in which time and death burn brightly, is the idea that Undine charms (*hervorgezaubert*) out of Hans, but not in the sense of seducing; rather, she magically brings it forth, *conjures* it from him. The kernel that seems to hold Hans's great idea together is that there is disorder at the heart of the ordering of human life, and in the center of that disorder stand death and time.

Through Undine's portrayal of the human understanding of time, an understanding that is future-oriented, her representation of her encounters with Hans, which take place in the past tense, and the descriptions of herself, which take place in the present tense, the reader becomes aware of the text as source, as giving rise to these three representations of time. The text works at odds with this delineation, suggesting by its own structure that there is another understanding of time at work—a fourth conception in which time is circular. This notion of time, embodied by the structure of the text itself, is cast into sharp relief by the ways in which it departs from the three temporal voices Undine uses. When the reader notices that difference—a structural possibility that emerges with particular force in this passage in which time is thematized—she becomes aware of the text as its own voice and hence becomes aware of herself as reader. The independent conception of temporality that the text evokes provides a structural possibility for a moment of exceptional awareness on the poetological level, a moment in which the role of time is central.

> But I have taught you with a look, when everything is complete, bright, and raging—I've said to you: there is death in it. And: there is time in it. And at the same time: Go, death! And: stand still, time! (258)

When Undine addresses death and time directly, banishing death and telling time to stand still, the core of Hans's idea emerges: the fear of death, and the role of time as that which carries mortals toward death. The reader glimpses what Undine helps Hans to be, think, and say, which was elusive earlier in this passage: that mortals long for time to stop, for death to go. The awareness of death and the inevitable flow of time are what Hans must recognize and say; and the reader, brought to awareness of herself as reader at this point in the short story, may here likewise experience a longing for time to stand still, for death to go, which is an acknowledgment of mortality. To recognize, as Undine says, that there is death in it and that there is time in it, is to be face to face with the fact of human mortality.

In Undine's description, Hans secretly wishes for this, the destruction of all order, which is death, but only with her help could he be, think, and speak what he wanted. For Hans wishes for both: for death, and for death to be banished. For Undine to banish death and tell time to stand still, both entities have to be present at once, and they are, as she states. Undine's bringing Hans to an awareness of the inevitability of death and time and the desire to be free of them opens the epistemological possibility for a moment of extraordinary awareness for the reader. The form of Bachmann's language in its evocation of waves reinforces this possibility by inviting the reader to hear the water, in which there is always danger.

After Undine says these words to Hans, his spirit has turned toward her; his voice is completely slow, truthful, and saved, and freed from everything. In seeing the wish for death and for death to go, for time to stand still, Hans is changed, at least momentarily. This passage confirms the sense from earlier descriptions of the initial encounter between Undine and Hans that when he doesn't understand or can't think of what use he is, in this case that his spirit is not meant for any use, that is when she loves him most and when their love thrives. Another message that radiates from this passage is the idea that Undine teaches Hans something about his life that he didn't know before. Her confirmation of death and time followed by her command for death to flee and time to stand still has a strong effect. His reaction to these words, to her commands, signals that this has been a moment of exceptional quality. This is a transformational moment for Hans that results from his encounter with Undine, but specifically it is the acknowledgment of the role of death and time in human life that gives rise to the possibility for Hans.

It is in this moment of the text that something more of Undine's supernatural vision can be glimpsed. Undine, moments after conjuring (*hervorgezaubert*) Hans's impractical idea of the world, in which death and time appeared and burned bright, shows him those forces and commands them to retreat. She does not tell Hans the future outright, although later in the text she alludes to what is to come for both of them. Her power of vision seems to lie rather in her ability, through words, to tell the defining forces in human life—death and time—to retract for a moment. In that moment in which death, once acknowledged, is told to go and time, once acknowledged, is told to stand still, Hans's spirit is changed, his voice is changed. He is momentarily transformed. It is not a change that endures; Hans and Undine go through the cycle again and again, but the force of the encounter changes him in that moment.

Likewise, the reader may experience that moment of awareness and the wish for death to go, for time to stand still. This is brought about both structurally, in the way that the text suggests a different conception of time than the temporalities at work in Undine's monologue, and by the thematization of death and time in this passage and the resulting possibility for the acknowledgment of the role of time with respect to human mortality, and in turn the life-defining nature of mortality.

How is the reader to understand Undine's call for death to flee and for time to stand still? In what way can Undine stop time and banish death? In one respect: as literature. It is as literature, in one of its aspects understood as the transmission of knowledge, that Undine as text can banish death and stand time still for a moment.[45] Moreover, this text as part of the history of the motif

---

45   *Poetic Edda*, "Sayings of the High One" (Hávamál), 34–35, Stanza 80. Other poems in the *Eddic* corpus point to the well as source of knowledge, including the poetic Hávamál and Snorri's *Gylfaginning*.

of the encounter between human and mythical water women participates in the transcendence of art over death. It is in this poetological aspect that Bachmann's narrative gives voice to Melusine, among those who came before her and those who will come after. Undine as art has banished death and stood time still, and the reader is afforded a moment to glimpse that.[46]

In "Undine Geht," the reader sits outside the text but becomes aware of time and the text as separate through its representation of time. The reader becomes aware of a different possibility for understanding time, and this awareness brings with it the need to acknowledge the role of time in terms of death. Death and time must be acknowledged, and once they are, the text as art may banish death for a moment, may stand time still for a moment. This cannot happen without the reader, this is an activity, a dialogic structure that is itself constitutive of the possibility for epiphanic awareness.

In the final part of her monologue, Undine is leaving:

> Bent over the water, close to giving up. The world is already dark, and I can't find the seashell necklace. There won't be any more clearing. You different from all others. I am under water. Am under water. (252)

In these lines, Undine makes good on her claims from the beginning of the text, now in the present tense: she is bending over the water, and then she is in the water. The reader is alerted to Undine's movement from land to water because she says the world is already dark and she cannot clasp the seashell

---

46   Bachmann said of the Undine figure, "Die Undine ist keine Frau, auch kein Lebewesen, sondern, um es mit Büchner zu sagen, 'die *Kunst*, ach die Kunst'. Und der Autor, in dem Fall ich, ist auf der anderen Seite zu suchen, also unter denen, die Hans genannt werden" ["Undine isn't a woman, nor is she a creature, rather, as Büchner put it, 'art, oh, art.' And the author, in this case me, is to be found on the opposite side, therefore among those named Hans"]. Bachmann, *Wir müssen wahre Sätze finden: Gespräche und Interviews*, 46. Interview conducted November 5, 1964. Bachmann here quotes Georg Büchner's Drama "Dantons Tod." Gadamer's theory of aesthetics is helpful here, pointing out that there is a possibility for the audience to dwell with the artwork in a way that is transformational, and specifically that poetic language plays a critical role in the hermeneutic possibility for a different way of seeing, or, more radically put, of being, for the reader, in the space and time taken up by the aesthetic experience. This conceptual framework is illustrative for both the moment of epiphany for Hans, at the textual level, and of the possibility for a similar transformation for the reader at the poetological level. Hans-Georg Gadamer, *Gesammelte Werke: Ästhetik und Poetik I: Kunst als Aussage* (Tübingen: J. C. B. Mohr [Paul Siebeck], 1993), 80–86, and "Über den Beitrag der Dichtkunst bei der Suche nach der Wahrheit," 70–79.

necklace.[47] This becomes explicit in the next line: she is under water (*bin unter Wasser*). Undine uses the future tense to say there will be no more clearing, hence no more encounters. She refers to Hans as "you different from all others" (252), and then she is underwater.

Undine repeats the last line without a subject, which reinforces the fragmentary and poetic form of language. This formal characteristic has coursed through the text but emerges in particular when Undine speaks in the present about herself, and it becomes more pronounced as the story closes.[48] Bachmann's language becomes poetry by the end of the text. It transforms from a lyrical short story to an ending that no longer resembles prose at all, and this passage heralds that change. The hybrid nature of this short story shifts to a wholly poetic work at its close.

The language begins to strongly resemble waves in this final section: the lines roll forward, echoing human breath. The reader is carried forward by the autonomic quality of the narrative. The reader hears the water in the poetry, which is not unique to this section of the text, but what is significant about the accoustic nature of the poetological experience in this section is that the reader *hears* Undine leaving. The sound of the water moving is the sound of Undine slipping under water. The reader experiences Undine's leaving directly:

> Nearly silent
> nearly still
> hearing the call.
> Come. Just once.
> Come. (263)

In these final lines, the phrases are short and appear as two poems instead of lines of prose. The language of the text, Undine's last lines, transforms fully into poetry. This call is the same call that Undine describes the first time the clearing has been transformed into Hans's home, when he is listening down the hall: the call from far off, which is at once Undine's voice and the cry of pain as Melusine leaves. It is the voice of the mythological water woman as she leaves the world of men.

These lines enact a different kind of ending than the one Undine promised from the beginning. Who is calling to whom in the end? There is no answer about who made the call or whether it was heard. The call is the ending, and

---

47   This is a reference to Fouqué's *Undine*, in which Undine attempts to give Bertalda a seashell necklace, which Huldbrand flings back into the water.

48   See Achberger "Undine Goes," 89.

because the call assumes an answer, even though the text does not provide an answer, the ending becomes a beginning, or another moment that precedes the clearing. The reader cannot know with certainty what happens, but the language signals the ongoing nature of the encounter.

Bachmann's text, mainly prose in this short story, is the prose of a poet, and her language betrays its poetic moorings constantly. Music radiates from Bachmann's text: it is present in this iteration of the legend despite the fact that this Undine does not sing.[49] She gives voice to the water nymph whose own voice has rarely been heard, through her words, but the text itself provides the music that is at the center of the mythology of the sirens, Melusine, and the mermaids. The water-dwelling women in each text are characterized by singing or speaking; in different ways, all of them participate in the tradition of the Homeric siren motif, and this unifying thread makes the self-imposed silencing of Bachmann's Undine so disturbing.

This apparent contradiction of the silent or silenced siren, the possibility of which asserts itself poetically at the end of Bachmann's text, was treated by Franz Kafka half a century earlier in his 1917 fragment *Das Schweigen der Sirenen* [*The Silence of the Sirens*]. Kafka retells the encounter of Odysseus and the sirens, albeit with striking departures. In Kafka's version, Odysseus stops his ears with wax and instead of hearing the sirens, he sees them. Kafka suggests the possibility that the sirens' silence is more powerful and deadly a weapon than their singing, which turns the encounter on its head in several respects.

Similar to Kafka's apparent contradiction of a siren who is silent, what appears to be the final silencing of Ingeborg Bachmann's siren in "Undine Geht" is only a momentary silence which prompts an immediate reaction: the call to return.[50] The distance between what Undine states as her wish at the outset of the text—the speechlessness that Kafka describes, an ending—and what the

---

49   For discussion of the role of music in "Undine Geht," see Karen Achberger, "Music and Fluidity in Bachmann's 'Undine Geht,'" in *Fictions of Culture: Essays in Honor of Walter H. Sokel*, ed. Steven Taubeneck (New York: Peter Lang, 1991), 309–320.

50   Much of the secondary literature reads a real silencing of the Undine figure in this text. See for instance Sara Lennox, "Bachmann and Wittgenstein," in *Modern Austrian Literature* 18, no. 3–4 (1985): 239–259, and Kraß, *Meerjungfrauen*, 337. Fassbind-Eigenheer sees only a temporary silencing of Undine, which in her reading equates to the artist's inspiration. In Fassbind-Eigenheer's analysis, the inspiration must always come to an end, leaving the artist bereft, but underlies the circular nature of the text and the ending; *Undine*, 169–172. This article suggests a reading which sees the ending as a renewal of the cycle between both Undine and Hans at the textual level, and between reader and text at the poetological level.

voice of the text supports, in particular the last lines, reveal the ongoing nature of the cycle between Hans and Undine at the textual level, and between reader and text at the poetological level. There is no ending, only another wave of encounters. Undine leaves but nearly hears the call, and whether the call stems from Hans, Undine, the reader, or the tradition of otherworldy water women who came before her, the cycle of encounters renews itself.

At the close of the text, the reader, listening to the wave-like music of Bachmann's language as Undine returns to the water, hears the call for her to return in the final lines. This is at once Undine's own call and a poetic instantiation of Melusine and her predecessors who left the world of men long before. This aesthetic footprint is none other than the *cri du Mélusine*, the wailing of Melusine as she flies from the castle, leaving only her watery footprint on the sill and the sound of her despair. Listening to the water, but no longer able to hear the call, the reader herself may be the one calling. It is the poetological footprint that stays present; it endures.

CHAPTER 18

Woman, Abject, Animal: Refigurations of Melusine in Frischmuth, Jelinek, and EXPORT

Anna-Lisa Baumeister

> Raymond do er düse grüsenlich und frömde geschöpfte an synem
> gemachel sach, do wart er gar sere betrübet und von allem synem gemüte
> bekümbert und erschrak uß der achte von düser geschickt und stund also
> von forcht und in sorgen, das im der sweiß von not ußgieng.
>
> [Raymond, as he saw this gruesome and foreign creature in his wife,
> was distraught and worried with all of his mind, and was incredibly star-
> tled at this fate, and thus stood in fear and in sorrow, sweating in distress.]
> (81, lines 17–21)

This scene from Thüring von Ringoltingen's *Melusine* (1456) leaves ample
room for interpretation. There are, first of all, questions to be asked about
Raymond's reaction. Is he simply surprised, or is he scared? Does his worry
(*Sorge*) arise out of genuine concern for his wife, who has undergone a mysterious metamorphosis? Or is he rather troubled that he has broken his promise
never to visit her in the bath on a Saturday? Does his sweating have to do with
the fact that he has come to mistrust Melusine, following his brother's (now
shown to be false) allegation that she may be cheating on him? There is also
the question of the meaning of Melusine's animal body. How monstrous, in
fact, is she? Thüring von Ringoltingen describes Melusine as a horrifying and
foreign creature ("düse grüsenlich und frömde geschöpfte," 81, line 17). And
yet, her worm-tail is detailed in admiring terms: it bears a blue glaze and is
speckled with round silver drops (81, lines 11–13). Is Melusine's animality to
be understood as a literal transgression of species boundaries? Or should it be
understood metaphorically, as the emergent alterity of the female form under
an unwitting male gaze?

In diverse ways, various figures in twentieth-century feminist art, literature, and theory have responded to and drawn upon the interpretive ambiguity of the Melusine bathing scene.[1] In this context, critically approaching

---

1 See Caroline Prud'Homme's discussion on medieval and early modern textual interpretations of this scene in her chapter, "Mermaid, Mother, Monster, and More," in this volume.

Melusine's nimality and Raymond's reaction to it allows for the negotiation of ontologies of sex, gender, and species. Take, for instance, Simone de Beauvoir's well-known evaluation of the Melusine figure. In her foundational work *The Second Sex*, Beauvoir turns to the woman-serpent hybrid as one way of answering her guiding question, "what is a woman?"[2] On a critical register, Beauvoir detects in the Melusine tale an androcentric "mythology of the absolute Other" in which the gazed-upon woman is reduced to a "static idol," a "mystery" to ponder.[3] A nymph's animality, writes Beauvoir, must be understood as a feature that is "profoundly anchored in men."[4] The revealed animality of women found in the Melusine tale, along with many others, evidences the entrenched and traditional association of women with nature. More positively, though, Beauvoir ends her chapter on myth with the suggestion that much hinges on the contemporary relation to the figure of the Melusine going forward. She invites her reader to imagine a "Melusina, no longer under the burden of fate unleashed on her by man alone, Melusina, rescued."[5] In that it approaches the Melusine figure critically, as a lens onto androcentric power structures, and positively, as a vehicle for the subversion of these same structures, Beauvoir's reading is paradigmatic of the complex status of Melusine in twentieth-century feminist art, literature, and theory. Here Melusine remains irreducibly ambiguous, her legacy both potentially disempowering and potentially liberating.

A modern retelling of the Melusine tale appears in the work of three feminist authors or artists in late twentieth-century Vienna: Barbara Frischmuth, Elfriede Jelinek, and VALIE EXPORT. Each author or artist, working within distinct media (the short story, the novel, and the short film), presents a contemporary feminist encounter with the alterity of the abject female body that reenacts some combination of the fundamental elements of the mythical Melusine scene: the bath or bathroom setting, the male gaze through the peephole, the onlooker's unsettled reaction, or Melusine's human-animal hybridity. Uniting the three works under discussion are certain thematic commonalities that underlie these three encounters, though each exhibits a different evaluative stance toward the Melusine figure and her cultural status. Frischmuth, in her 1982 short story "Adder" ["Otter"], interprets Raymond's reaction as one of disgust, and so reflects debates about the role of

---

2 Simone de Beauvoir, *The Second Sex*, trans. Constance Borde and Sheila Malovany-Chevallier (New York: Knopf, 2010), 3.

3 Beauvoir, *The Second Sex*, 269–272.

4 Beauvoir, *The Second Sex*, 175.

5 Beauvoir, *The Second Sex*, 274.

embodiment and affect in the modern constitution of sex, gender, and species. Jelinek revisits the Melusine myth as a site for the cultural production of
sexed bodies in modern societies. In her 1983 novel *Die Klavierspielerin* [*The
Piano Techer*], Melusine resurfaces as a pornographic commodity—a sexualized identity internalized by adolescent girls and peddled in exotic forms,
including the "dragon lady," at local peep shows. EXPORT's 1973 short film
Mann & Frau & Animal [*Man & Woman & Animal*] similarly invokes pornographic narrative conventions in its approach to the Melusine figure, though
with the result that these conventions are undermined in the act of their repetition. By depicting the discovery of Melusine in the bath as the voyeuristic
encounter with a grotesque, animal-like vagina, EXPORT's film provides an
experience of alterity that goes beyond established aesthetic categories, such
as the threatening and the beautiful, as well as established ontological categories, such as sex and species.

Frischmuth effectively transposes the medieval setting of castles, knights,
thermal springs, and heavy wooden doors into modern times. Her unnamed
male protagonist, an urban "fat cat," uses a chair to peek through a window
above the bathroom door where his favorite prostitute, Adder, is taking a bath.
This voyeuristic moment echoes the discovery scene in Thüring von Ringoltingen's retelling of the Melusine tale. In that version, Raymond is frightened
at the sight of Melusine's hybrid body ("er gar zůmal erschrak" [he was very
especially frightened], 81, line 14) and regretful of his voyeurism in light of
Melusine's innocence ("sü ist from und aller schande unschuldig" [she is innocent of all disgrace], 81, line 36). In Frischmuth's altered retelling, the male
protagonist reacts with disgust:

> Die Versuchung war groß, er widerstand ihr nicht. Durch die Oberli-
> chte—er hatte sich einen Stuhl geholt—konnte er auf sie herunterblick-
> en, wie sie in der schaumgefüllten Wanne kauerte und dann die nackten
> Füße auf deren Rand legte, um mit dem Oberkörper tiefer einzutauchen.
> Es waren weiße, wohlgeformte Beine, und auch an den Füßen fiel ihm
> nichts auf, erst als sie die Zehen spreizte und die Häute, die sich zwi-
> schen ihnen spannten massierte, glaubte er zu wissen, was es mit ihrem
> Geheimnis auf sich hatte. Ihm war klar, dass es kindisch war, dass einem
> das als erwachsenem Menschen nicht passieren durfte, dennoch ekelte
> es ihn.
>
> [The temptation was great, he did not withstand it. Through the tran-
> som window—he had taken a chair—he could look down on her. How
> she squatted in the foam-filled tub and how she then put the naked feet
> on the rim, so she could plunge deeper into the water with her upper

body. They were white, well-formed legs, and neither could he discover anything unusual about the feet. Only when she splayed her toes and started to massage the webbing that was stretched between them, did he believe he knew something of her secret. To him it was clear, that it was childish of him, that, being an adult human, this shouldn't happen. Even so, it disgusted him].[6]

That her voyeuristic male protagonist's reaction at the sight of Adder's massaging the webbing between her feet is one of disgust, rather than of fright or guilt, is the most immediate marker of Frischmuth's critical transformation of the medieval *Melusine* tale. In this passage, the phenomenon of disgust is given three distinct features. First, disgust is experienced as something powerful, beyond control, "natural" rather than "cultural." The protagonist sees his disgust as something "childish" that overcomes his adult human self. Second, considering that it stems from the visibility of a minor imperfection (the small webbing between the toes) on an otherwise perfectly conventional female body, disgust is felt as something of an overreaction, an "even so." This feature is in a way in tension with the first, pointing as it does beyond the explanation of disgust as a powerfully "natural" or inborn reaction to threatening attributes. Rather, disgust is rendered a matter of context. Finally, the phenomenon of disgust is seen to have a decisive impact on the life of the disgusted observer: from this moment on, nothing will be as it was before. The next morning, Adder will leave the protagonist's home, but her impression upon him will remain. In this way, Frischmuth figures disgust not as a merely passive perceptual reaction, but as a performative activity.[7]

Winfried Menninghaus, in his extensive analysis of disgust in Western history, demonstrates the extent to which the disgusting is gendered.[8] Surveying a wide range of texts since the mid-eighteenth century, Menninghaus concludes

---

6 Barbara Frischmuth, "Otter," in *Undinenzauber: Geschichten und Gedichte von Nixen, Nymphen, und anderen Wasserfrauen*, ed. Frank R. Max (Stuttgart: Reclam Verlag, 1991), 400–410, at 408. Translations into English are the author's. Hereafter, page numbers will be given in parentheses.

7 For a discussion of disgust as a constitutive performative activity (figured in terms of abjection), see Julia Kristeva, *Powers of Horror: An Essay on Abjection*, trans. Leon S. Roudiez (New York: Columbia University Press, 1982). For a treatment that focuses on the bodily affective dimension of disgust, as something below or beyond its cultural coding, see William Ian Miller, *The Anatomy of Disgust* (Cambridge, MA: Harvard University Press, 1997).

8 Winfried Menninghaus, *Disgust: The Theory and History of a Strong Sensation*, trans. Howard Eiland and Joel Golb (Albany: State University of New York Press, 2003), 7.

that "the disgusting has the attributes of female sex and old age."[9] For Menninghaus, the *vetula* or "disgusting old woman" is the epitome of the disgusting, possessing "repugnant defects of skin and form, loathsome discharges and even repellent sexual practices."[10] Whether or not she is depicted as particularly old, Melusine, as a shape-shifting, physically defective, sexually promiscuous female, fits the modern category of the disgusting that Menninghaus describes. Frischmuth's retelling of the Melusine myth reflects this emergence of a modern aesthetic wherein the gazed-upon female body appears disgusting. As a prostitute—someone engaged in "repellent sexual practices"—with webbed toes—displaying "defects of skin and form"—Adder personifies modern disgust with the female body.

By making visible the process of abjection through which the sense of disgust registers in her male protagonist, Frischmuth's take on the category of the disgusting becomes a critical one. Her story shifts attention from the female body as a site of visual allure and discovery to the abjectifying structural conditions of modern society that support the production of disgust in the first place. Three such conditions, each at play in Frischmuth's version of the Melusine myth, are especially worth addressing here: the male gaze, the bathroom setting, and the process of female animalization.

In Frischmuth's retelling, the male protagonist's specific *way of looking* is a constitutive element in the abjection of Adder's body. Frischmuth's narrative breaks with the idea that the protagonist's look is an innocent, merely passive form of observation. This break takes place on several levels. For one, "Adder" presents the reader with a glimpse of the power relations that precipitate the protagonist's coming to view his recurrent prostitute in the way he does. In both the medieval Melusine tale and Frischmuth's short story, the male protagonist's gaze is framed literally and narrowly. In Thüring von Ringoltingen's version, Raymond's view is defined by the edges of a sword-cut hole in the door; he "machte mit synem swert ein loch durch die türe" [made with his sword a peephole in the door] (81, line 5).[11] In Frischmuth's version, the protagonist's

---

9   Menninghaus, *Disgust*, 7. Menninghaus traces the history of disgust in European aesthetic theory ranging from Lessing and Kant to Nietzsche, Bataille, and Kristeva. He understands the disgusting as a distinctively modern aesthetic category that negates the beautiful, being the "absolute other of the aesthetic" (7). Grounded in the unique role of the disgusting in modern aesthetics, Menninghaus proposes a new approach to literature as a "processing of the disgusting" (11).

10   Menninghaus, *Disgust*, 7.

11   See Caroline Prud'Homme's contribution to this volume for an examination of this discovery-in-the-bath scene in several premodern versions of *Melusine*, which take varying stances toward the heroine's unexpected shape.

view is defined by a transom window. Just as the sword-cut hole may be taken to represent a kind of androcentric power, the height of the transom window literally causes the protagonist to "look down" on Adder (408). The way the gaze is framed marks the relation of power in which the male and female characters are set.

Moreover, the guilty secrecy of Raymond's look becomes, in Frischmuth's retelling, the hallmark of an inherent asymmetry. Neither Melusine nor Adder shows any sign of awareness that they are being watched. This pairing of heightened awareness and lack of awareness establishes a one-sided relationship between viewer and viewed. One is subject, the agent of inspection; the other object, the site of inspection. This asymmetry is foregrounded in Frischmuth's story, with the effect that her protagonist actively interprets what he sees, passing judgment on the merits of Adder's body: "[t]hey were white, well-formed legs, and neither could he discover anything unusual about the feet" (408). His evaluative gaze, as it pans along Adder's legs, equates "whiteness" and "well-formedness" with the "nothing unusual" that he at first associates with her feet. Here the aesthetic norm sources from the viewing subject, not the gazed-upon object. In this way, the dominant social formula whereby standards of beauty track positions of power is in evidence in the form of looking itself.

Laura Mulvey was among the first to address the way in which Western frameworks of visual storytelling reflect gendered hierarchies precisely in the way that they enact certain androcentric modes of gazing. According to Mulvey, many of the characteristic cinematic elements of Hollywood films (including camera angles, lighting, and editing) foist a masculine voyeuristic perspective upon audiences. As a result, viewers of such films, regardless of gender, are led to adopt a "male gaze" in relation to the female bodies that appear on screen, which are simultaneously objectified and eroticized.[12] Along similar lines, Frischmuth's retelling of the Melusine tale exposes the function of the male gaze in Western literary narrative. Frischmuth shows how a certain anticipation of embodied abnormality is inherent to the male gaze in its secrecy. "[N]either," the text reads, "could he discover anything unusual about the feet" (408), suggesting that the protagonist's look involves the expectation that something *ought to be* unusual. In this way, the male gaze, as inscribed in Frischmuth's narrative, can be said to function as a self-fulfilling prophecy: seek the unusual, and the disgusting you shall find.

Another crucial condition—historically linked to the abjection of women and a common feature in both Thüring von Ringoltingen's *Melusine* and

---

12   Laura Mulvey, "Visual Pleasure and Narrative Cinema," *Screen* 16, no. 3 (1975): 6–18.

Frischmuth's retelling of it in "Adder"—is the bathroom setting. In the fifteenth-century tale, Melusine is observed nude and enclosed in her bath, separated from the observer by a wooden door (81, line 5). In Frischmuth's story, Adder is seen nude and bathing through the transom window above the locked bathroom door. In each case, the female body is revealed within a clearly defined bathroom setting distinct from other areas of the narrative's setting. Indeed, bathrooms, especially bathrooms occupied by nude women, have traditionally been seen as abject spaces. "I always remember," Mary Douglas writes, "how unrelaxed I felt in a particular bathroom," which held the "engraved portrait of Vinogradoff, the books, gardening tools, the row of gumboots [...] the impression destroyed repose."[13] In her classic anthropological examination of spaces of pollution and impurity, Douglas notes how it is traditionally only in the bathroom—where excrement and other fluids are disposed of and skin and hair are grated and plucked—that the human body is allowed a degree of permeability and disintegrity that is denied to it in other spaces. This singular function explains why the bathroom, more so than other distinct spaces, must be clearly differentiated from other rooms, and why it is jarring when a bathroom contains elements usually reserved for other rooms, such as books and painted portraits. Douglas rejects the idea that a biologically grounded concern for hygiene lies beneath the widespread ritualization of bathing practices, and the associated prevalence of bathroom-related taboos, in human societies. Instead, she understands the spatial definition of bathrooms, and the restriction of bathroom-associated practices to such settings, primarily as a manifestation of the need to organize and uphold the boundaries of the modern human subject.

In a similar vein, Julia Kristeva remarks how *"corporeal waste*, menstrual blood and excrement, or everything that is assimilated to them, from nail-parings to decay, represent—like a metaphor that would have become incarnate—the objective frailty of symbolic order."[14] For Kristeva, the broad cultural import of the bathroom rests not so much on a generalized concern for hygiene as on the inherent instability or "objective frailty" of conventional society and the power structures that support it ("the symbolic order"). On a micro level, those bodily functions confined to the bathroom would in turn represent the instability of the modern subject itself. Accordingly, when a (proto-typically male) observer registers disgust at the sight of (proto-typically

---

13   Mary Douglas, *Purity and Danger: An Analysis of Concept of Pollution and Taboo* (London: Routledge & Kegan Paul, 1966), 12.

14   Julia Kristeva, *Powers of Horror: An Essay on Abjection*, trans. Leon S. Roudiez (New York: Columbia University Press, 1982), 70.

female) hair, menstrual blood, nail clippings, or other bathroom-associated bodily traces, this can be understood, following Kristeva, as the gazing subject's attempt to reinforce their position of power and avoid the threat of their own destabilization through rendering abject the body (or trace of a body) at the other end of their gaze.

The commonality of the bathroom setting—regarded through the critical lens afforded by both Douglas and Kristeva—therefore facilitates further interpretation of the peeping gaze of the male protagonists in both *Melusine* and "Adder," along with the other Austrian feminist works considered below.[15] From this vantage, it is not enough to say that, in gazing at their female targets as they do, the male protagonists have violated any taboo regarding the concealment of nudity or that they have broken any promise made to the women themselves. If the bathroom is understood as a ritualized space of abjection, then the deeper meaning behind such stolen looks lies in the fact that the male observers have thereby been exposed to the frailty of human subjectivity in concrete form. Both Melusine and Adder, in shedding dead skin and hair as in physically attending to the previously hidden parts of themselves, have,

---

15 It should be noted that the intention here is not to make any ahistorical claim about the role of the male gaze in the constitution of human subjectivity. The point is rather that Frischmuth's emphasis on the bathroom setting amplifies an element in the Melusine myth that bears the trace of early-modernity. Architecturally circumscribed bathrooms within one's living space (as opposed to free-standing outhouses or latrines set away from the home) became common among European nobility at the time of the First Crusade but were only a standard amenity within castles and homes of many sizes by the late Middle Ages. Interestingly, in this period of the bathroom's history, the nudity of the same or opposite sex in itself was not yet subject to taboo, though the discharge and disposal of bodily fluids (especially female bodily fluids) appears to have been. Indeed, women and men often bathed together. See Françoise Bonneville, *The Book of the Bath*, trans. Jane Brenton (New York: Rizzoli, 1998), esp. 34. Connecting this with the Melusine myth, Georges Vigarello observes that, as the culture of late medieval France continued to develop, there was an increasing level of suspicion towards bathing, to the point of its being laden with taboos by the Baroque era. Fueling this suspicion was the emergence of two still-recognizable paradigms concerning the human body: the ideal of bodily stability and, directly connected with this, rising anxieties about bodily frailty and penetrability. "The skin," writes Vigarello about the attitude in evidence by the sixteenth and seventeenth centuries, was "seen as porous, and countless openings seemed to threaten, since the surfaces were weak and the frontiers uncertain" (9). Vigarello, *Concepts of Cleanliness: Changing Attitudes in France since the Middle Ages* (Cambridge, UK: Cambridge University Press, 2008). It was during the late Middle Ages that the beliefs emerged that it was during bathing especially that the body was weakened and made vulnerable to potentially damaging metamorphoses, and even that bathing could result in pregnancy.

in this interpretation, revealed the instability and porosity of human bodily boundaries—a revelation that is profoundly unsettling to the men who observe them. In an important sense, this suggests that the disclosure of the abnormality of Melusine's body, or of Adder's, is, taken on its own, not the bombshell that it may seem. Rather, it is only because this disclosure is set in an occupied and in-use bathroom—a setting available to the male gaze only under the guise of secrecy—that this abnormality has the abject, disgust-inducing, and subjectivity-destabilizing quality that it does.

A final abjectifying structural condition apparent in both the fifteenth-century *Melusine* tale and its contemporary Austrian feminist retellings, though with a different function in each case, is the process of female animalization.[16] By calling her heroine "Adder" [Otter], Frischmuth reiterates the serpentine dimension of the medieval Melusine myth and, even more explicitly, plays on the myth's legacy of reception, especially within nineteenth-century literary Romanticism. More specifically, giving the name Adder to her central female character connects Frischmuth's story to the Melusine figure in the work of German Romantic poet Eduard Mörike. In his literary fairy tale, "The Story of Lau, the Beautiful Water Nymph," the character Lau is said to act "more venomously than an adder" [giftiger als eine Otter].[17] Lau's body, in turn, is said to be "in all respects like that of a beautiful, normal woman, with one exception; between her fingers and toes she had webbing" [ihr Leib war allenthalben wie eines schönen, natürlichen Weibes, dies eine ausgenommen dass sie zwischen den Finger und Zehen eine Schwimmhaut hatte].[18] Parallels between Mörike's and Frischmuth's versions of the Melusine tale become clear: both replace the blue-glazed "worm tail" in Thüring von Ringoltingen's version [wurms schwantz von blawer lasur (81, lines 11–12)] with webbing between fingers and/or toes, and both introduce this webbing as a flaw disrupting what would otherwise be perfectly normal beauty. Given these parallels, the critical feminist perspective in evidence in Frischmuth's retelling should be taken as primarily directed not against the medieval Melusine myth per se, but rather

---

16   For an analysis of Thüring von Ringoltingen's *Melusine* in light of contemporaneous concerns about the magical transference of animality among human beings (and specifically the magical transformation of women into animals), see Sarah Hillenbrand Varela, "Origins of Misfortune: Sympathetic Magic and the Transference of Animality in Thüring von Ringoltingen's *Melusine* (1456)," *Neophilologus* 99, no. 2 (2015): 271–285.

17   Eduard Mörike, *Die Historie Von Der Schönen Lau – The Story of Lau, the Beautiful Water Nymph*, trans. Stan Foulkes, ed. Peter Schmid (Ebenhausen Bei München: Langewiesche–Brandt, 1997), 8–9.

18   Mörike, *Die Historie Von Der Schönen Lau*, 7.

against the myth's modern reception, and its appropriation within androcentric romantic narrative conventions especially.

As Claudia Steinkämper has shown, the many refigurings of the Melusine tale within German Romanticism shared a common positioning of Melusine as a certain kind of absolute Other. Within this romantic framework, argues Steinkämper, Melusine is transformed from a mysterious "beauty with a fish tail" to the static archetype of the femme fatale.[19] Characteristically, Romantic interpreters such as Mörike often blend Melusine with various other mythological figures such as the undine, the siren, and the water nymph, thereby foregrounding her categorical distinctness from male protagonists and from humanity more generally. In this context, Melusine's specifically non-human dimensions become increasingly important. The overriding lesson or moral message conveyed by Romantic versions of the Melusine tale is that, even if Melusine seems at first sight to perfectly match established standards of human beauty, it must in the end be recognized that her radical and internalized non-human Otherness places her in the category of the aesthetically dangerous and the erotically just-out-of-reach.[20] This is especially clear in Mörike's version: here Melusine's ultimate and inescapable animality, visible in the webbing between her fingers and toes, becomes a metaphor for Otherness itself.

Feminist scholarship has long treated the animalization of women in modern cultural history as an especially powerful mode of women's objectification. Carol Adams, for one, has examined how placing women and non human animals in close conceptual proximity (even identity) has traditionally fueled and reinforced the idea that women are naturally inferior to men (intellectually, physically, and otherwise), which has in turn justified the exclusion of women and non human animals alike from various male-dominated social and political institutions and activities.[21] This is precisely the mechanism at work in Mörike's "The Story of Lau." While in Thüring von Ringoltingen's work Melusine's human-animal hybridity arguably marks what is first and foremost a physiological difference (though a striking one) between herself and her male

---

19   Claudia Steinkämper, *Melusine – vom Schlangenweib Zur »Beauté mit dem Fischschwanz«:*
      Geschichte einer literarischen Aneignung (Göttingen: Vandenhoeck & Ruprecht, 2007),
      345.

20   But see Melissa Ridley Elmes's contribution to this volume, in which she argues that
      alechmical uses of Melusine inspired by the works of the early modern philosopher Paracelsus were of greater influence on German and English Romantic portrayals than the
      literary tradition.

21   Carol J. Adams, *The Sexual Politics of Meat: A Feminist-Vegetarian Critical Theory*, Twentieth Anniversary Edition (New York: Continuum, 2010), 69.

observer, in Mörike's text Lau's hybrid body marks not just physical alterity but also moral and intellectual alterity. That is, the disclosure of Lau's animality is primarily taken as evidence of her immorality and irrationality. Acting "more venomously than an adder," Lau is seen, despite her apparent beauty, to be poisonous, incapable of either empathy or principled action. Compared with the medieval Melusine, who is revealed to be half animal in the most visceral sense, the animalization of Lau's externally visible body is evidenced only in the details of her hands and feet. But Lau's internalized animalization is more extensive and penetrating than the medieval Melusine's, and it is this internal determination that, in the Romantic iteration of the myth, marks the true extent of Melusine's Otherness.

Frischmuth's retelling makes the modern tendency toward female animalization especially visible. Moreover, by attending to the male protagonist's disgusted reaction to the animalized female form he observes, she assigns an affective significance to the female animal body that goes beyond the mere metaphorical meaning it had received in Romantic versions of the Melusine myth. In this way, she restores something of the appreciation for embodied physicality that was present in Thüring von Ringoltingen's version. Not only is Adder animalized by virtue of the webbing between her toes, but her status as an animal being is also reflected in the fact that the male protagonist reacts to the sight of her in his own less-than-human way. On beginning to feel disgust at the sight of Adder's webbing through the transom window, the protagonist reflects that "this shouldn't happen to an adult human" (148), establishing that his disgusted reaction is linked to a certain deviation from humanity. Adams's critical analysis of the animalization of women in the modern Western cultural imagery provides a way of understanding how these two modes of animalization are both connected and deeply problematic. Her ethical concern with women's animalization, explains Adams, does not derive from any objection to the alignment of women with non human animals per se, but rather from the fact that non human animals tend, in modern Western culture, to hold very low social status.[22] In that Frischmuth's male protagonist reflects upon his own loss of humanity, the reader can detect what is really at stake in his disgust. Disrupted by what he sees, the protagonist steadies himself simultaneously in opposition to the observed animal-like woman and in opposition to his own animal-like reaction, thereby drawing upon a fiction of clear boundaries: between sexes on the one hand, and species on the other.

Frischmuth's short story, playing on Mörike, critically addresses the animalization of women that Adams and others have elsewhere observed, revealing

---

22   Adams, *The Sexual Politics of Meat*, 4.

in the process the evaluative mechanism that generates both disgust and ab-jection. The twist to her treatment of animalization, however, lies in the fact that the very disgust that in one sense separates the protagonist from Adder's supposed animality also reminds him of his own animal self, thus establishing corporeal meaning across the narrative. Frischmuth excises from the Melusine myth the internalized gender essentialism that it holds in its romantic restag-ing. At the same time, she positions the body (male and female) as a physi-cal site of narrative action. In other words, Frischmuth does not deprive her protagonists of their animality. In Frischmuth's retelling, Melusine stands at the intersection of the abjectifying process of gendered animalization and the recuperative reminder that human beings remain, after all, animal creatures. Ultimately, the male protagonist's discovery of Adder's animal body stands for an encounter with alterity beyond established notions of gender and human animality.

Some of the Melusine figures in Jelinek's *The Piano Teacher* take the form of strippers. Their bathrooms are rotating stages on which they are watched not through a single improvised peephole, but by many eyes from the privacy of individual booths. The show proceeds as follows:

> A black-haired woman assumes a creative pose so the onlooker can look into her. She rotates on a sort of potter's wheel. First she squeezes her thighs together, you see nothing; but mouths fill with the heavy waters of anticipation. Then she slowly spreads her leg as she moves past several peepholes.[23]

As with Frischmuth's "Adder," Jelinek's novel thematizes the male gaze. But be-yond merely featuring a gazing scene within in her narrative, Jelinek exposes and dwells upon what she sees as the basic ingredients of the Melusine figure's mysterious appeal. The fact that at first "you see nothing" is a calculated part of the show. The male gaze is shown to be a constituent part of the sex industry, the mystery of what it gazes upon designed and commodified. Frischmuth's Adder was indeed an image of women's becoming eroticized, objectified, and exploited. But any sense of ambiguity and allure still associated with the Mel-usine figure in Frischmuth's version is supplanted in Jelinek's version with the radical deconstruction of a cultural myth that repeats and justifies gendered oppression.

---

23   Elfriede Jelinek, *The Piano Teacher*, trans. Joachim Neugroschel (New York: Grove Press, 2004), 53. Hereafter, page numbers will be given in parentheses.

If in Frischmuth the Melusine figure stands for an encounter with alterity, the authenticity of such an encounter with Otherness is radically challenged in Jelinek's account. For "[n]o deformed woman is ever hired here. Good looks and a good figure are the basic requirements. Each applicant has to undergo a thorough physical investigation: No proprietor buys a pig without poking her" (53). In its appearance, the stripping platform mimics Melusine's bathroom as a space of visual discovery whereby a female body is revealed to concealed male eyes. However, due to its commodified, purpose-built presentation, the platform is not the space of bodily instability and potential transformation that the closed-off bathroom had been. Instead, Melusine's bathroom becomes the opposite of this: it changes from a site of gender instability, as in Frischmuth, to a site for the re-inscription of gendered bodily norms and calculated sexual affects.

Not only are the objects of the gaze in the stripping scene within Jelinek's novel pre-selected and inspected, the peep-show is sustained by an army of abjected cleaners, all of them female: "[t]he booth smells of disinfectant. The cleaning women *are* women, but they don't look like women. They heedlessly dump the splashed sperm of these hunters into a filthy garbage can" (52). In the twentieth-century Vienna that Jelinek presents, the process of female abjection reaches beyond the Melusine figure herself to those mechanisms of social and economic abjection—in the work of the cleaning women—that take place outside the limelight. And yet, precisely because their invisibility tracks their sex-industrial necessity, these mechanisms are shown to constitute relations of sex and gender all the more deeply and pervasively. In this way, Jelinek addresses how a certain commodified mystification of female sexuality precedes and then overwrites lived reality, to the extent that cleaning women "don't look like women" (52).

In one sense, there is no parallel for Melusine's alterity in Jelinek's taking up of the myth. Her women do not have the bodily abnormalities found in Thüring von Ringoltingen and Frischmuth. In another sense, the instrumentalization of Melusine's alterity is apparent throughout *The Piano Teacher*, particularly in the way gazed-upon female bodies are fetishized, exoticized, and commodified. After the first stripper leaves the platform, "a dragon lady with dyed red hair now thrusts her chubby backside into view" and "massages herself with her right hand, which has blood-red claws" (52). With the appearance of the "dragon lady," Jelinek's novel connects the image of the worm-tailed woman on the other side of the peephole with racialized myths of the femme fatale prevalent in Western orientalist fantasies. Inhabiting the stereotypical image of the "sexually aggressive dragon lady," the stripper embodies what Jane Caputi and Lauri Sagle call a "white racist projection" onto Asian women that "originated and continues under conditions of sexual slavery and serves to disguise and legitimate that slavery."[24] The way the "dragon lady" is depicted evokes animality in a way similar to the descriptions of Melusine and Adder, with the dyed red hair and blood-red, claw-like nails. But here these animal-like characteristics are framed as artificial outgrowths of the gendered marketplace that is the strip club rather than manifestations of a more or less internal female-animal nature. Here female animalization appears as a predictable mechanism of commodified sexual objectification, one that goes hand-in hand with racialized and gendered suppression. Hence, the animalized female presents no real danger to the paradigmatically male observer's subjectivity, nor does she elicit any reaction of disgust in him, as she had in Frischmuth's version. Rather, she is gazed upon and consumed from the safe distance of the peeping booth, which the gazer exits once he has achieved what he has already paid for.

Though the peepshow is one of its most important narrative locations, the real setting of *The Piano Teacher* is the vexed lifeworld of the novel's protagonist, 38-year-old Erika Kohut, a piano teacher at a prestigious Viennese music conservatory. Erika is an avid reader, and one of the novel's central themes is how processes of storytelling, within society and within the individual, underlie the formation of sexuality and gender. From an early age, through the stories she both reads and tells herself, Erika has internalized various myths of femininity, especially the idea that women must be mysterious, even and perhaps especially to themselves. In the novel, the effect of such myths is always at once ideological and physiological. Even before Erika was born, "her pregnant mother had visions of something timid and tender. Then, upon seeing the lump of clay that shot out of her body, she promptly began to mold it relentlessly in order to keep it pure and fine. Remove a bit here, a bit there" (23). The novel subverts traditional notions of female preservation and upkeep; Erika's fineness, musicality, and mysteriousness are treated not as expressions, but as the physiological instantiation, in Erika's life, of gendered cultural fantasies.

In her approach to Erika as in her approach to the "dragon lady," Jelinek underscores the way in which female animalization sustains dominant myths of femininity. Frequently in the novel, Erika is figured in animalized terms, and she is often placed in associative proximity with maritime animals in particular. She is "in the pink of health—a well-nourished fish in her mother's amniotic fluid" (56). Jelinek's prose might be called post-mythological: it recalls the mythological imagery of the fish-woman hybrid, but with a critical,

---

24   Jane Caputi and Lauri Sagle, "Femme Noire: Dangerous Women of Color in Popular Film and Television," *Race, Gender & Class* 11, no. 2 (2004): 99–111, at 101–102.

deflationary twist. Erika's female-animal body is deprived of any power or mystique, her animality thoroughly domesticated. Erika is "a weary dolphin, listlessly preparing to do her final trick" (58). A woman's animality, in this understanding, is a locus of her commodification. A woman's body is material to be consumed, property to be purchased, meat to be eaten. In line with Carol Adams's analysis of the sexual politics of meat, Jelinek's prose draws suggestive parallels between the routinized violence against non human animals in evidence in many present-day industrialized societies and the sexualized violence against women also and not accidentally in evidence within them. So, while Erika bears comparison to fish and birds, late in the novel the central male protagonist/antagonist, Walter, takes violent revenge on both Erika and the non human animals he finds around him, in the aftermath of his emasculated humiliation at Erika's hands:

> He will avenge himself unbelievably on the defenseless animals in the park. They've got flamingos and other exotic spawn, creatures that have never been seen here. And these creatures demand to be ripped apart. Walter Klemmer is an animal lover, but too much is too much, and an innocent party must be forced to believe him. (250)

If Melusine's animality is surprising to Raymond, Erika's animality has long been a prescribed and expected element of what it means to be a woman. No stand-in for her alterity, Erika's animality instead justifies Walter's violence against her and the feminized animals in the park, while also justifying the violence Erika enacts toward herself.

Much of Erika's difficulty in life derives from the fact that she is incapable of *living* the prescribed gender roles that, in their mythic form, she has long internalized: "[s]he simply cannot submit" (14). The tension between feminine myth and lived reality becomes painful when Erika compares her womanhood to that of other women. During such moments of painful self-comparison, the novel frequently employs the bathroom as that ritualized space where gender norms penetrate the female body—where feminine myths are performed and become physiological. "In other homes," Jelinek writes, distinguishing Erika's childhood bathroom-experience from more typical others, "hot steaming water hisses into bathtubs. A girl mindlessly tries a new hairdo. Another girl picks the right blouse for the right skirt" (57–58). Other girls Erika's age "are well versed in feminine movements! Femininity pours from their bodies like small, clean brooks" (58). Whereas others seem to master the performance of their femininity effortlessly, Erika fails to master her role. She thus resorts to blunt force. From an early age, she locks herself into bathrooms to attempt transforming herself into a "woman," as others do. She "feels solid wood in the place where the carpenter made a hole in any genuine female" (51). So she cuts herself into a woman, using her father's razor and shaving mirror. Even as a teenager, "[w]ith little information about anatomy and with even less luck, she applies the cold steel to and into her body, where she believes there ought to be a hole" (86). In her bathroom, and in her own brutal way, Erika parodies the production of gendered identities taking place in other girls' and women's bathrooms. Though she fails to live her femininity outside the bathroom as other women do, she succeeds in producing those features she understands as characteristic of female biology: above all the "hole," a "feminine mystique," and the bleeding genitalia.

Feminist literary theorists have long examined the effect of an androcentric literary canon and of androcentric narrative techniques, including the universalized male gaze, on the self-understanding of female readers. Judith Fetterly summarizes this effect as a "powerlessness which results from the endless division of self against self."[25] Patrocinio P. Schweickart has argued that "androcentric literature is all the more efficient as an instrument of sexual politics because [...] it draws her into a process that uses her against herself."[26] For a woman to engage with the Melusine myth, in this account, requires a certain schizophrenia in reading. Such a woman must attempt to reconcile identifying, on the one hand, with Raymond peeping on Melusine, and, on the other hand, with Melusine herself being peeped upon. The female reader, caught between these two poles of identification, therefore both adopts the male gaze and likens herself to the female subject that is gazed upon. Along these lines, rather than reading Erika's self-cutting psycho-pathologically (as, for instance, a symptom of an underlying sadomasochism), the behavior can instead be read as the illustration of Jelinek's vision of the complex relation in which contemporary women stand to themselves. As Erika's story exemplifies, a central component of this relation is its paradoxical structure.

Erika is both perpetrator and victim of injury, both subject and object of inspection. She secretly attends the peepshow. Here, her desire is to renounce identification with the female strippers and smoothly inhabit the position of Raymond the onlooker: "[n]othing fits into Erika, but she, she fits exactly into

---

25   Judith Fetterly, *The Resisting Reader: A Feminist Approach to American Fiction* (Bloomington: Indiana University Press, 1978), XIII.

26   Patrocinio P. Schweickart, "Reading Ourselves: Toward a Feminist Theory of Reading," in *Gender and Reading: Essays on Readers, Texts, and Contexts*, ed. Elizabeth A. Flynn and Patrocinio P. Schweickart (Baltimore: Johns Hopkins University Press, 1986), 31–62, at 42.

this cell" (51). The coin-operated peepshow booth is the male inversion of the women's bathroom, and in it Erika sheds her publically feminized role as female stage performer at the piano: "Erika doesn't want to act, she only wants to look. She simply wants to sit there and look. Look hard" (52). Her perspective takes on a meta-male gaze: she looks at women being looked at by men. For Erika, this mode of looking is an exercise in self-inspection. Later, she tries repeating it at home in the bathroom—the only lockable room in the apartment she shares with her mother. There, literally mirroring the male gaze by inspecting her naked self in her long-deceased father's shaving mirror, Erika is frustrated to encounter the limits of what she can see:

> The man must often feel (Erika thinks) that the woman must be hiding something crucial in that chaos of her organs. It is those concealments that induce Erica to look at ever newer, ever deeper, even more prohibited things. She is always on the lookout for a new incredible insight. Never has her body—even in her standard pose, legs apart in front of the shaving mirror—revealed its silent secrets, even to its owner! (108)

The myth of an elusive feminine mystery, so much at play in Melusine's bathroom discovery scene, has left its mark in Erika's self-conception. She never doubts that her body contains "silent secrets," even as she again and again fails to commune with them. In Jelinek's novel, there is no recuperation of this failure, no lesson learned. Rather than coming to abandon or even to challenge the myth of feminine mystery, Erika sees the fact that she fails to discover anything mysterious about herself as itself part of the mystery, thereby strengthening the hold of the myth upon her and perpetuating the fraught tension between it and her lived reality.

By the end of *The Piano Teacher*, Erika's lifelong inability to fully conform to gender norms while nonetheless being entirely beholden to them has established the conditions for a tragic ending. Erika is brutally raped by Walter, who understands his action to be justified in light of Erika's by-then deeply abject status in his eyes. Though she has privately lived with a realization of it since she was a child, Walter cannot tolerate the fact that Erika, as has become apparent to him step-by-step in their time together, is "neither object nor subject."[27] In a bathroom scene leading up to the rape, Walter registers his disgust with Erika's abject, animalized body:

---

27   Kristeva, *Powers of Horror*, 3.

Klemmer keeps repeating—senselessly, because he was understood the first time—that Erika stinks so horribly that the whole small room reeks of her, it's disgusting [...] She should leave town, so his young, fresh nostrils won't have to smell that peculiar, repulsive stench, that animal emanation of putrescence. (246)

In such scenes, Jelinek's novel provides a dark picture of the status of the Melusine myth and its constituent narrative elements in contemporary times. *The Piano Teacher* both exhibits the social construction of the animalized female body and suggests that certain patterns of commercialized sexual violence, reinforced by the male gaze, may in fact surround the figure of the half-serpent, female-animal hybrid.

One question to be taken from Frischmuth's retelling is: What is the precise relationship between Raymond's "horror" and Melusine's animal body? Is her body to be read as an instance of culturally coded abjection, or as instance of the experience of alterity? In the 1973 short film *Man & Woman & Animal* (*Mann & Frau & Animal*), the visual artist and experimental filmmaker VALIE EXPORT offers her own answer. Here she explores the relation of sex and species by employing the Melusine-inspired imagery of a woman in a bathtub who, under the gaze of a secret spectator, transforms into a monstrous animal. EXPORT's understandings of sex and gender are anti-essentialist. "We must assume," she declares in a 1985 interview, "that there is no such a thing as the woman's natural body because images, projections and codes cover the woman entirely."[28] Nevertheless, EXPORT's work is sometimes read to offer an alternative picture of female sexuality beneath its being overwritten, an assertion of its ultimate independence from male-dominated conventions. Hence, Martine Beugnert suggests that the animal body, in EXPORT's film, is more than a product of androcentric body politics. "The animal" in *Man & Woman & Animal*, she claims, "is more than a metaphor [...] The animal is there."[29] The question this precipitates—basic to any feminist interpretation of the Melusine myth in any of its guises—is whether and, if so, to what extent representations of female animality can represent the de-essentialization of sex and gender, rather than their re-naturalization?

---

28   Quoted in Anja Zimmermann, *Skandalöse Bilder – Skandalöse Körper: Abject Art vom Surrealismus bis zu den Culture Wars* (Berlin: Reimer Verlag, 2001), 123.

29   Martine Beugnert, "EXPORTs Werden: Mann & Frau & Animal," in *EXPORT LEXICON: Chronologie der bewegten Bilder bei VALIE EXPORT*, ed. Sylvia Szely (Vienna: Sonderzahl Verlagsgesellschaft, 2007), 15.

FIGURE 18.1 *Bathtub featured in VALIE EXPORT's* Mann & Frau & Animal (*1973*)

The roughly eight-minute-long film is divided into three parts. Part one opens with a mundane scene: an empty bathtub, shot in black and white. EXPORT's hand-held camerawork, erratic cutting and panning, and the undetermined rustling noise in the background give the scene an uncanny "home movie" feel. This deliberately plays upon an aspect of conventional filmmaking that Mulvey associates with Hollywood cinema generally: "conditions of screening and narrative conventions give the spectator an illusion of looking in on a private world."[30] EXPORT aligns her audience with Raymond's transfixed gaze. The camera's shakiness contrasts with its apparent immobility in the bathroom. The perspective is locked on the bathtub, confined by its own narrow frame. For the first three minutes, the viewer sees nothing other than the empty bathtub, the drain, the water faucet, and shower head and hose extending from it.

EXPORT's establishing shot makes experienceable the anticipation that arises in the absence of action. One of the elements that Jelinek identifies as essential to the peep show—that one at first "sees nothing"—is taken up by EXPORT to dramatic effect. These opening minutes of *Man & Woman & Animal* visualize the making of mystery. In his analysis of cinematic conventions, Pascal Bonitzer remarks on the importance of holes as markers of gender and

---

30   Mulvey, "Visual Pleasure and Narrative Cinema," 10.

power: "the keyhole for the secret look of the voyeur," "the drain of the bath tub," and "the gaping sex" are "always dramatic in cinema."[31] In an androcentric order, the female sex is coded as mysterious, as what Luce Irigaray calls "a hole-envelope that serves to sheathe and massage the penis in intercourse: a non-sex, or a masculine organ turned back upon itself."[32] It is precisely this sexed cultural nexus—the association of peepholes, bathtubs, and the female sex—that EXPORT addresses in her short film.

In many ways, EXPORT satisfies the cinematic urges that she parodies. After the three-minute opening shot, a nude, masturbating woman appears in the bathtub—it is in fact the artist herself. Mirroring the standards of mainstream pornography, in this second part of the film the female body is not presented as a whole but in its parts: a face is never shown, and isolated body parts are investigated in color and in close detail. Jelinek also thematizes this pornographic technique of fragmentation when she writes that Erika, closely examining her genitals in the shaving mirror, wants "to look at ever newer, ever deeper, even more prohibited things. She is always on the lookout for a new and incredible insight" (108). In Yann Lardeau's account, the specifically pornographic male gaze, in its fragmentedness, imports the investigative perspective of dissective science into film and is accordingly driven by a certain desire for omnipotence. The pornographic gaze is "obsessed with truth, obsessed to become acquainted with the knowledge of everything."[33] EXPORT's employment of the close-up mimics these and other porno-cinematic attempts to appropriate the female body in pieces.

Ultimately, however, the viewer of *Man & Frau & Animal* is denied such appropriation. On several levels, EXPORT subverts the conventions she invokes. Her breasts remain covered, and the visibility of her tattoo (a characteristic garter belt on her left thigh) personalizes the image despite its fragmentation. A second shot closes further in on the vulva and exposes the female genitalia in detail. Rather than presenting a mere "lack," the vulva-shot shows complex raw matter: female secretion, menstrual blood, and tangled pubic hair—all elements in excess of the clinical image of conventional pornography. Under the spectator's gaze, the same vulva then transforms into a sort of animal. Its pulsing lifting and lowering recalls a breathing organism; the movement of

---

31   Pascal Bonitzer, *Le Champ Aveugle: Essais Sur Le Réalisme Au Cinéma* (Paris: Cahiers du cinéma, 1999), 31.

32   Luce Irigaray, *This Sex Which is Not One*, trans. Catherine Porter and Carolyn Burke (Ithaca, NY: Cornell University Press, 1985), 23.

33   Yann Lardeau, "Le sexe froid: Cinéma et pornographie," in *Théories du cinéma*, ed. Antoine de Baecque and Gabrielle Lucantonio (Paris: Cahiers du cinéma, 2001), 140.

slime and blood within it emphasize its vibrant materiality. EXPORT pairs the close-up with an unexpected soundtrack: an indistinct, animal grunting to accompany the vulva's movement. Beugnert describes the effect as a grotesque one: at this point the spectator confronts "the grotesque face of a becoming animal. Not only the metaphorical evocation of sexual drive, but a monstrous being."[34] EXPORT's disorienting animal-vulva scene co-opts the mission of the pornographic closeup, setting it to a new purpose. No longer is it a means of safely packaging an isolated part of the female body. Here the object of inspection is turned from sexually fetishized meat to living, breathing animal flesh.

In her audience, EXPORT's film-assemblage may stir laughter, surprise, and disgust all at once. Following Beugnert's above remark, this combination of affect can be summed up in the notion of the grotesque. As Justin D. Edwards and Rune Graulund point out, the grotesque explodes easy aesthetic categorization: in fact, it characteristically juxtaposes seemingly incompatible categories like the comic and the tragic, the threatening and the ridiculous. The grotesque emerges "where disgust mixes with laughter."[35] Precisely therein, they argue, lies its queer, empowering potential. To Edwards and Graulund, the grotesque has, in literary history especially, served as the demarcation of the human species. It comes in "hybrid forms that disrupt the borders separating what is acceptable within the categories 'human' and 'non-human.'"[36] Mary J. Russo, attending to the role of the female body in Western discourses of the grotesque, emphasizes its power to unsettle notions of sex and gender. According to Russo, the grotesque, when applied to women, inverts the male idealization of female static beauty. The female grotesque body is the evolving body; it is "open, protruding, irregular, secreting, multiple, and changing."[37] EXPORT's film can be understood as foregrounding the female grotesque as a way to recover the female body in its animality and materiality without appeal to myths of femininity or preconceived categories of sexual difference.

The first part of *Man & Woman & Animal* treats the central narrative convention that underlies the modern reception of the Melusine myth: the secret male gaze into a bathroom setting. Part two confronts these conventions with the jarring reality of grotesque female animality. EXPORT's grotesque animal-vulva de-essentializes female sexuality by exploding the categories through which this part of the female body is normally represented. Building on these steps, the

---

34   Beugnert, "EXPORTs Werden," 15.

35   Justin D. Edwards and Rune Graulund, *Grotesque* (Abingdon, UK: Routledge, 2013), 4.

36   Edwards and Graulund, *Grotesque*, 39–40.

37   Mary J. Russo, *The Female Grotesque: Risk, Excess, and Modernity* (New York: Routledge, 1994), 8.

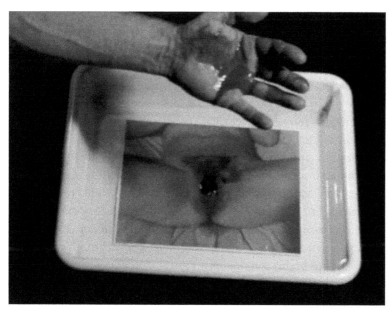

FIGURE 18.2 *Scene from VALIE EXPORT's* Mann & Frau & Animal (*1973*)

film's third part depicts an androcentric attempt to pacify these feminist gestures by rendering the scene that has just ended into a static, easily possessed representation. The viewer is shown a male hand allowing drops of its own blood to fall onto a still-developing photograph of a female sex organ. The blood colors parts of the photograph red, along with the developing fluid in which it bathes.

This third part of the film may be taken as an appraisal of the history of Melusine's mythologization. As with the image of abject, violently sexualized female-animal hybridity that appears near the end of *The Piano Teacher*, here EXPORT's film points to the way in which a certain male possession of and violence toward the female body continues to frame any cinematic approach to the female body. *Man & Woman & Animal* thus leaves the viewer with two distinct but connected visions of the female-animal body: the one of materiality in its upheaval, the other of the apparently inevitable attempt for male reappropriation.

It is worth noting that Thüring von Ringoltingen's depiction of Raymond's discovery of Melusine bathing—one of the centerpieces of the version of the Melusine tale that remains most influential in the German-speaking context— remains ambiguous in its key points. Both the exact nature of Melusine's hybrid body and Raymond's reaction to it cannot be clearly discerned. And yet, such narrative ambiguity provides excellent fuel for contemporary debates about the constitution of sex and gender in Western history and society. In its recent interpretive history, the Melusine figure has been read variously as an exemplar of the essentialist mythical association of women with animality (as in Beauvoir), and as a positive emblem of female sexual difference.[38] Each in their own way, Frischmuth, Jelinek, and EXPORT retell the Melusine myth and unpack its bearing on the lives of contemporary women.

The Melusine figure that Frischmuth's "Adder" responds to is not so much Thüring von Ringoltingen's but Melusine in her taking up by the German Romantics, for whom her physical difference is more internal than external. Adder's "webbing" is primarily a metaphor for her Otherness. Channeling Raymond, the male protagonist reacts to what he sees with disgust, with an embodied, affective reaction that recalls to him his own unstable boundaries. In this way, Frischmuth addresses how, in the modern, post-mythical world, affective responses can disclose relations of power that remain constitutive for dominant gendered norms and myths. Melusine, in Frischmuth's retelling, marks the space of this bodily remainder.

Jelinek's *The Piano Teacher*, published a year later than "Adder," presents a darker, more cynical take on the same theme. Here there are at least two Melusine figures. There is the commodified sex worker, the fetishized stripper or "dragon lady" at the other end of the peephole. And there is the protagonist, Erika, who locks herself in the bathroom to pierce holes in her animal body under the gaze reflected in her father's shaving mirror. In Jelinek, traces of the Melusine tale reach into every area of modern life: into language, consciousness, the structure of desire, and the sex industry. Melusine's abjection plays out in sexual exploitation, imperial fantasies, and in child's play. In particular, Jelinek addresses the normative violence that operates through the myth of the secretly observed female animal, and the depth to which this is internalized, by women and men alike, in contemporary society.

Similar to Jelinek, EXPORT thematizes androcentric attempts to appropriate the Melusine figure symbolically. The violence of representation is exhibited in the third and final part of her short film, where Melusine has become flattened into a photographic image, bath-developed and blood-colored by a male hand. Not succumbing to cynicism, however, the impression that EXPORT's viewers are left with is that an encounter with the female grotesque *cannot* be fully encoded or written over by androcentric norms. EXPORT's Melusine is queer, at once monstrous and comic, defying easy categorization. Her defining

---

38   See, for example, Ulrike Junk, "'So müssen Weiber sein': Zur Analyse eines Deutungsmusters von Weiblichkeit am Beispiel der *Melusine* des Thüring von Ringoltingen," in *Der frauwen buoch: Versuche zu einer feministischen Mediävistik*, ed. Ingrid Bennewitz (Göppingen: Kümmerle Verlag, 1989), 327–352.

feature is that, in the belligerence of her animality, she escapes appropriation by narrative conventions, be they literary or porno-cinematic. Drawing upon the subversive potential that has accompanied the Melusine myth since medieval times, *Man & Woman & Animal* prompts an encounter with what may in the end be an unaccountable sexualized animal alterity. In this way, the gaze EXPORT invites viewers to take towards Melusine may reflect the gaze that Derrida, in his famous essay on animality, calls out by name: "[a]s with every bottomless gaze, as with the eyes of the other, the gaze called 'animal' offers to my sight the abyssal limit of the human: the inhuman or the ahuman, the ends of man [...] [a]nd in these moments of nakedness, as regards the animal, everything can happen to me."[39]

---

39   Jacques Derrida, *The Animal That Therefore I Am*, trans. Marie-Louise Mallet (New York: Fordham University Press, 2008), 12.

CHAPTER 19

How the Dragon Ate the Woman: The Fate of Melusine in English

Misty Urban

Despite her enormous popularity on the Continent, the figure of the cursed, prophetic, serpent-tailed fairy ancestress virtually disappears from the English cultural imagination after 1500. Four versions of the French *Roman de Mélusine* which came to rest in Britain attest to some readership or at least interest in the story, and two late Middle English translations exist: British Library MS Royal 18 B.ii, an English prose translation of the French romance dated ca.1500, and the *Roman de Parthenay*, a translation of Coudrette's verse account, held by Trinity College, Cambridge, R 3.17.[1] But despite an entry in the stationer's register for 1510, only fragments remain from an English version of *Melusine* printed by Wynkyn de Worde.[2] Lack of further evidence for this or other printings suggests that the romance fell prey to what A. S. G. Edwards calls the "surprising [...] failure of works popular in later manuscripts to get any purchase on the sensibilities of print audiences."[3] Two mentions of Melusine in sixteenth-century English prose allude to her as a well-known

---

1 Tania M. Colwell identifies the fourteen remaining manuscripts and fragments of the French romance in "Fragments of the *Roman de Mélusine* in the Upton House Bearsted Collection," *Library: The Transactions of the Bibliographical Society*, 13, no. 3 (2012), 279–315. The four MSS in British libraries include BL MS Harley 4418, BL MS Cotton Otho D.II, the UHB fragments, and the Clumber MS belonging to the library of the 7th Duke of Newcastle (282). John Ashton, in his 1890 collection *Romances of Chivalry* (see n.31), identifies five printed versions of the prose *Melusine* in the British Museum library, three in German and two in Spanish. These MSS attest to the story's existence, but not its readership.

2 A. W. Pollard and G. R. Redgrave, *A Short Title Catalogue of Books Printed in England, 1475–1640*, 2d ed., ed. W. A. Jackson, F. S. Ferguson, and Katharine F. Pantzer, 3 vols. (London: Bibliographic Society, 1976–1991), 2:28. These fragments, retained in the Bodleian Library, are described by Tania M. Colwell in "The Middle English Melusine: Evidence for an Early Edition of the Prose Romance in the Bodleian Library," *The Journal of the Early Book Society for the Study of Manuscripts and Printing History* 17 (2014): 254–282.

3 A. S. G. Edwards, "Books and Manuscripts," in *The Oxford Handbook of Medieval Literature in English*, ed. Elaine Treharne and Greg Walker (Oxford: Oxford University Press, 2010), 30.

figure of danger,[4] an association much less emphasized in the Continental cir-
culations of her tale in which, as previous chapters in this volume attest, she
continued to be a fruitful literary and artistic subject into the early modern
period and beyond. Mermaids and melusines persisted in Irish folklore, and
the mermaid or selkie wife surfaced in Welsh, Scottish, and Cornish legends
documented in the nineteenth century.[5] But until Edward Yardley's *Melusine
and Other Poems* published in 1867, the character of Melusine takes a hiatus
from English literature for more than three centuries. Charting the long with-
drawal of the fairy-serpent-woman, her gradual return, and the virtual explosion of Melusine analogues in popular culture of recent decades reveals an
ongoing metamorphosis of Melusine in the English cultural imagination that
cycles from fascination and fear back to fascination with her multivalent and
multitudinous forms.

Several speculations might be offered for Melusine's early expulsion from
the English literary imagination, if not the legend and folklore of Great Britain.
Romance narratives in early modern England continued their strong interest
in the marvelous and the otherworld, but in the form of an increasingly well-
defined and popular fairy realm that Richard Hutton says peaked in popularity
between 1560 and 1640.[6] The fairy Melusine and her family do not feature in
this English other-realm. Instead, characters like Oberon, Robin Goodfellow,
and the other elvish creatures made familiar to modern readers through works
like Shakespeare's *A Midsummer Night's Dream* (ca.1590) served the purpose
of reflecting on and tweaking the English social and political world, a realm
they preferred to upset or amuse themselves with rather than enter.[7] Melusine
in the original prose romance by Jean d'Arras (ca.1393) is raised on Avalon,
but in the Arthurian legends delivered to English readers by Malory's *Le Morte*

---

4   Wilfrid Holmes in *The Fall and Evill Successe of Rebellion* (1537) refers to the "mystical
    nymph" Melusine in his catalogue of influential but also destructive women, and Richard
    Hyrd's translation of Juan Luis Vives' *Instruction of a Christian Woman* (1529) ranks *Mélusine*
    among a list of French romances that represent dangerous reading. See Misty Urban, *Mon-
    strous Women in Middle English Romance* (Lewiston, NY: Edwin Mellen, 2010), 45.

5   Gregory Darwin, "On Mermaids, Meroveus, and Melusine: Reading the Irish Seal Woman and
    Mélusine as Origin Legend," *Folklore* 126, no. 2 (2015), 123–41.

6   Richard Hutton, "The Making of the Early Modern British Fairy Tradition," *The Historical
    Journal* 57, no. 4 (2014): 1135–56.

7   It might be worth noting that Melusine's absence from the fairy world continues into the
    Victorian period; for example, she does not appear in Nicola Brown, *Fairies in Nineteenth
    Century Art and Literature* (Cambridge, UK: Cambridge University Press, 2001). Possibly, her
    half-serpent or near-dragon form gave her less in common with the dainty, pretty, often mis-
    chievous fairies the Victorian imagination produced.

D'Arthur, printed in 1485, Avalon is claimed by the powerful if treacherous enchantress Morgan, a British dispossession of her French contemporary. Though
the daughter of King Elynas of Albanie, taken for Scotland and situated in the
prose romance near Northumbria, Melusine's British descent does not give her
any special claim on her audience, despite moves made by the Middle English
poetic translator to emphasize her ancestry.[8] Gerald of Wales popularized the
myth that a Melusine figure was ancestress to the house of Anjou, and Elizabeth Woodville's mother Jacquetta of Luxembourg hailed from the Counts of
St. Pol, who similarly recognized Melusine as their founding matriarch. But
the Tudor monarchs cultivated associations with the native, British figure of
Arthur rather than a shape-shifting French fairy, suggesting that, aside from
the matter of her complex body, Melusine's national and cultural associations
might account for her failure to capture an English readership.[9]

At the same time, Melusine's liminal, changeable form held a dangerous
charge for early modern readers. While the monstrous or supernatural gave
medieval authors a metaphorical language for grappling with the dangerous
influence of that established inferior, woman,[10] late medieval English literature typically required that its biform women be altered or reduced for tran-
scription into legible political and social systems.[11] A "broad reimagining of the
feminine in the early modern period" reinforced the separation of and distinction between positive, passive female characters and active, evil ones.[12] Changing the medieval use of *monstra* to indicate marvels or wonders, early modern
writers apply the term "monstrous" to any upset in the boundaries outlined by
God and nature. This usage is amply illustrated by the reformist preacher John
Knox in his *First Blast of the Trumpet Against the Monstrous Regiment of Wom-
en*, in which he rails that "it is more than a monster in nature that a woman

8   See Jennifer Alberghini's chapter, "Matriarchs and Mother Tongues," in this volume.

9   The naming of Henry VII's firstborn son as Arthur is frequently taken as evidence of his
     Arthurian identification, extended and elaborated by Henry VIII's self-integration into
     the Winchester Round Table.

10   *Monstrous Women in Middle English Romance* makes this claim, specifically in its chapters
     on Melusine, and the idea is shared by Johanna Ludwikowska in "Uncovering the Secret:
     Medieval Women, Magic, and the Other," *Studia Anglica Posnaniensia* 49, no. 2 (2015):
     83–104, at 84–5.

11   So argues Eve Salisbury in "Lybeaus Desconus: Transformation, Adaptation, and the
     Monstrous-Feminine," *Arthuriana* 24, no. 1 (Spring 2014): 66–85. Salisbury uses the term
     monstrous-feminine as defined by Barbara Creed in *The Monstrous-Feminine: Film, Femi-
     nism, Psychoanalysis* (New York: Routledge, 1993).

12   Richard Hillman and Pauline Ruberry-Blanc, eds., *Female Transgression in Early Modern
     Britain: Literary and Historical Explorations* (Burlington, VT: Ashgate, 2014), 4–5.

shall reign and have empire above man," and that "this monstriferous empire of women" [ie., the reign of Mary Tudor] is a sign of how far England has fallen from God's grace.[13] Surviving seventeenth-century ballads and broadsides such as "The carless curate and the bloody butcher" attest to the popularity of a tune identified as "Oh women, monstrous women," which either inveighs against specific forms of female misbehavior or attests to the monstrous nature of women more generally.[14] The character of Moll Cutpurse in Middleton and Dekker's *The Roaring Girl* (1611) is, more specifically, a "monster" because she dresses in male attire.[15] Despite the period's fascination with hermaphroditism and the female transvestite,[16] gender-confusing figures like Shakespeare's Viola and Spenser's Britomart are conquered by heterosexual impulses and safely repatriated into marriage at the end of their tales, their transgressiveness repaired as they become sorted into the clearly-marked category of "woman." No such repatriation is possible for Melusine, who remains knitted to the serpentine form she is doomed, because of male betrayal, never to shed.

Melusine's disappearance as a named character is made more curious by the fact that her archetype, the ovidian-female or piscine-female hybrid, fairly litters the landscape of early modern European literature, visual art, and architecture. Tara Pedersen argues that the "profound incoherence" represented by the irreconcilable animal and human bodies of the mermaid provides a site of epistemological and ontological creation, a mechanism of knowledge production.[17] The significance she finds in the mermaid figure, however, seems divorced from the specific political and cultural meanings attached to Melusine by the medieval romance, and the serpent-tailed female body in the literary works of Elizabethan England slides easily into a sinister presence. In Book I of Spenser's *Faerie Queene* (1590), the Redcrosse Knight encounters a

---

13   Marvin A. Breslow, ed., *The Political Writings of John Knox* (Washington, DC: The Folger Shakespeare Library, 1985), 38 and 42.

14   "The carless curate and the bloody butcher" (Printed for William Gilbarton, 1662, and available through Early English Books Online) tells the story of a licentious curate who endears himself to a butcher's wife, with predictably violent results.

15   In Thomas Middleton and Thomas Dekker's *The Roaring Girl*, ed. Jennifer Panek, Norton Critical Edition (New York: W. W. Norton & Co., 2011), Moll is, in addition to monstrous (p. 17), a "varlet," a "mock," a hermaphrodite, and "a monster with two trinkets" (p. 37).

16   Linda Woodbridge notes both trends in *Women and the English Renaissance: Literature and the Nature of Womankind, 1540–1620* (Chicago: University of Illinois Press, 1984); she refers both to the "cherished [...] symbol of the hermaphrodite" and "the strange paradoxical dragon that is Women and English Renaissance" (8).

17   Tara E. Pedersen, *Mermaids and the Production of Knowledge in Early Modern England* (Burlington, VT: Ashgate, 2015), 1–16.

figure named Errour, an "ugly monster plaine, / Halfe like a serpent horribly displaide, / But th'other halfe did womans shape retaine, / Most lothsom, filthie, foule, and full of vile disdaine." Errour, who nurses her malformed progeny with poisoned milk and vomits poisoned books and papers, represents moral miseducation as well as physical vileness.[18]

Later, Milton's Sin in *Paradise Lost* (1667) is "woman to the waist, and fair, / But ended foul in many a scaly fold / Voluminous and vast, a serpent armed / With mortal sting," and ringed with hell-hounds that bark invisibly from her womb. Sin, born of Satan and through incestuous union with him the mother of Death, could hardly find a more terrible aspect than that of a "double-formed," "snaky sorceress."[19] While Raymondin's first sight of his fish-tailed wife instills regret that he broke his promise to her, the sisters Sin and Errour provoke horror and shame, their bodies a physical manifestation of a moral transgression. Thus the sixteenth century might be identified as the point where the beneficent fairy-born serpent-woman morphs into a figure of baleful significance in English literature. First shedding her importance as a political and dynastic figurehead, as documented by E. Jane Burns,[20] Melusine's story next loses its emotional potency as a fable of betrayal and fall from fortune as, for English audiences at least, her serpent tail is sharply redefined as an outright threat and the dragon becomes a figure of Otherness, of monstrosity, of abjection that must be vanquished by a St. Margaret, a Redcrosse Knight, or St. George.

When Melusine does begin to resurface in English literary works of the nineteenth century, her first forays come, again, from the Continent, and she returns in the form of that enduringly fascinating folkloric figure, the supernatural wife.[21] This theme preoccupies the Romantics, as evidenced by Goethe's "Die neue Melusine," La Motte Fouqué's *Undine*, the Little Mermaid of

---

18   Hugh MacLean and Anne Lake Prescott, eds., *Edmund Spenser's Poetry*, A Norton Critical Edition, 3d ed. (New York: W. W. Norton, 1993), I.i.14–20.

19   John Milton, *Paradise Lost*, ed. Alastair Fowler, 2d ed. (Harlow, UK: Pearson Education, 1998), II.650–3, 741, 724.

20   "A Snake-Tailed Woman: Hybridity and Dynasty in the *Roman de Mélusine*," in *From Beasts to Souls: Gender and Embodiment in Medieval Europe*, ed. E. Jane Burns and Peggy McCracken (Notre Dame: Notre Dame Press, 2013), 185–220. Also E. Jane Burns, "Magical Politics from Poitou to Armenia: Mélusine, Jean de Berry, and the Eastern Mediterranean," *Journal of Medieval and Early Modern Studies* 43, no. 2 (2013): 275–301.

21   It might be noted that Melusine remained in use as a proper name, most famously in the case of Ehrengard Melusine von der Schulenberg (1167–1743), mistress to George I, who bestowed her legendary name on one of their daughters, Petronilla Melusine (1693–1778). Melusina Fay Peirce (1836–1923) was a reformer and early feminist active in the northeast United States.

Hans Christian Andersen fame, and the tales of supernatural wives told by the Grimm brothers, which follow the pattern of Melusine's union with Seigfried of Luxembourg.[22] Unlike the dynastic mother and able administrator portrayed by Jean d'Arras, the supernatural wife in these tales is a private asset who marries, aids, and then typically parts from her human husband under duress. Like their medieval predecessors in Walter Map and Gervase of Tilbury, these Romantic spirits figure the unassimilated nature of the foreign wife and the more problematic Otherness of woman. Her association is rarely of lasting benefit to her spouse, and she is rarely admired as a figure of virtue.

This is especially true of the serpent woman who rears her head in John Keats's "Lamia," in which female desire, not male treachery, ultimately dooms the lovers. Recalling the ancient Greek demon-woman with that name, Keats describes his heroine as "some penanced lady elf, / Some demon's mistress, or the demon's self," who longs, not for a human soul, but for the human love of a Corinthian youth.[23] This "doubtful tale from faery land" enshrines the moral that passionate love can only survive in private, for once exposed to public view and inquisition, "all charms fly / At the mere touch of cold philosophy."[24] As proof, the Lamia's illusory human form collapses into her serpent aspect when pierced with the gaze of the seer Apollonius, and the shock of her transfiguration proves fatal to her beloved Lycius. Like her medieval counterpart, the Lamia inherits her ovidian form as the consequence of a curse, but Keats's poem exhibits less sympathy toward its tortured heroine than Jean d'Arras does toward his Melusine, shows more unease with her serpentine aspect, and seems ambivalent about her motives for masquerading as human.

A supernatural female who endangers the mortal she loves is likewise the theme of Sir Walter Scott's "Mermaid" ballad. The "syren" who bears Macphail away for a passionate interlude beneath the sea finds her seduction thwarted

---

22 See Pit Péporté's contribution to this volume for a discussion of Melusine's Luxembourgian ties. Renata Schellenberg discusses Goethe's Melusine in her contribution to this volume.

23 Keat's sources and use of the legend are discussed in *The Norton Anthology of English Literature*, 8th ed., Vol. D: The Romantic Period, ed. Jack Stillinger and Deidre Shauna Lynch (New York: W. W. Norton & Co., 2006), 909–925. Quoted material from 1.55–6 and 1.186. Philostratus, in telling the original tale, suggests his Lamia feeds on people; that touch seems not to survive into Robert Burton's 1621 version in the *Anatomy of Melancholy*, which appears to be Keats's source (p. 909). See Diane Purkiss, *At the Bottom of the Garden* (New York: New York University Press, 2001), 26. See Melissa Ridley Elmes's contribution to this volume for a discussion of how Keats's poem draws on figurations of Melusine surviving in alchemical rather than literary traditions.

24 Keats, "Lamia," 2.8, 5, 229–30.

FIGURE 19.1 *Julius Hübner, Die schöne Melusine (1844), oil on canvas; 67 x 98 cm, Inv. No.: MNP FR 499, Collection: The Raczyński Foundation at the National Museum in Poznań*

not by philosophy but by his steadfast love for the fair (and fully human) maid of Colonsay.[25] In both tales, the serpent-woman is a figure of seductive glamor, but her hybrid form hints at female deceptiveness and her charged eroticism poses a distinct threat to the hero's intellect and values, much like the female-faced serpent threaded throughout medieval depictions of the Garden of Eden.[26] Unlike a Melusine who showers her earthly husband with wealth and fortune, these Romantic superstitions instead threaten their male targets with destruction and loss.

When English literature and art of the modern era calls Melusine forth by name, it is usually to favor one resonance of the medieval story over the others. Nineteenth-century portrayals of Melusine in the visual arts, like Julius Hübner's 1844 oil portrait *Die schöne Melusine* [The Fair Melusine], tend to distill the narrative to the moment of Raymondin's staggering discovery that his beloved wife has an alternate form. The transformed Melusine in her bath, unknowingly inspected by her husband, proves illegible to male epistemological schema, a revelation of the slippery line between ontological categories

---

25   Sir Walter Scott, *Minstrelsy of the Scottish Border,* 3 vol., 2d. ed. (Edinburgh: James Ballantyne, 1803), 306–320.

26   Burns, *Beasts to Souls,* 197–205.

and simultaneously a threat to them. But the focus on the vulnerable and nude female body, in contrast to Raymondin's fully-clothed and often armed form, emphasizes the mutual betrayal, creating a visual diptych that balances the husband's comprehension of his wife's terrible secret with the wife's violation of her private space, as if the two horrors are equivalent. In this, portrayals like Hübner's painting take a small step away from Sin and Errour toward emphasis on the human aspect of the serpent-woman that Continental iterations of Melusine more readily retain.

In her English literary re-emergence in the later nineteenth century, Melusine forfeits something of her supernatural and dynastic powers and transforms again into a fable about the complex dynamics of marriage. The Reverend Sabine Baring-Gould's account of Melusina devotes most of the chapter to Melusine's fantastical appearances, legendary analogues, and reports of mermaid sightings; the story itself serves as a brief but poignant sketch of a talented and capable wife whose devotion to her husband's well-being is repaid by breach of promise.[27] It is likely that Baring-Gould's collection, first published in 1866, had more of an influence than Walter Skeat's edition of the Middle English *Romans of Partenay*, published by the Early English Text Society in the same year, on Edward Yardley's 1867 verse narrative "Melusine." Yardley's wandering knight meets a damsel who promises to be "a consort meek, / Devoted, frank, affectionate, and true" (VI.5–6) if allowed one day a week in seclusion. Not gossip but mere suspicion over "woman's freakish ways" (XII.2) drives Raymond to break down her chamber door and behold his wife "[a]bove as fair as woman e'er can be, / But ending in a serpent from the waist" (XVII.3–4). She begs one last embrace before "her half-woman's form becomes a snake's: / Then from the room the wretched serpent glides" (XXII.6–7).[28] For both Baring-Gould and Yardley, Melusine represents a fascinating antique tale, but in terms of moral relevance she offers little beyond a platitude on the dangers, in older times when spirits inhabited the edges of the world, of marrying a woman of unknown family and lineage.[29] The symbolic Otherness of her altered form is muted in favor of, in Baring-Gould, a natural history of the mermaid, and in Yardley a tale of failed romance.

---

27   Sabine Baring-Gould, *Curious Myths of the Middle Ages* (Boston: Roberts Brothers, 1894), 343–393.

28   Edward Yardley, "Melusine," in *Melusine and Other Poems* (London: Longmans, Green, and Co., 1867), 1–13. Part and line numbers given in parentheses.

29   "And ages now since she was seen have past [sic]," Yardley concludes in XXIII.8, attesting to a dwindling relevance of her tale borne out by the 350-year interval between the English translation of the prose romance and his poem. Extending Baring-Gould's catalogue, Gillian M. E. Alban discusses the heritage of the serpent woman in *Melusine the Serpent Goddess in A.S. Byatt's* Possession *and in Mythology* (New York: Lexington Books, 2003).

John Ashton, in his 1890 collection *Romances of Chivalry*, embraces the story of Melusine as an exemplar of late medieval romance, and is the first to question why she disappeared. He blames a waning of interest in the genre of prose romance at the turn of the seventeenth century.[30] Ashton suggests that the value of medieval romances to his audience lies in their "wonderful insight into the manners and customs of our own country, centuries ago" (VII) though he calls the romance of *Melusine* merely a "charming *fabliau*," "one of the prettiest, and daintiest, of the fanciful tales of the so-called middle ages" (1) written for the entertainment of the Duchesse de Bar (2).[31] While Ashton's translation hews closely to British Library MS Royal 18 B.ii, and sometimes quotes large chunks of late Middle English from it, he follows the pattern set by Yardley and Baring-Gould in focusing on the central romance between a doomed fairy and her well-intentioned but ultimately human spouse.

Ashton retains his source's treatment of Melusine's prophetic abilities, Catholic faith, and the wise counsel that accounts for Raymondin's subsequent political success, but his scattered remarks frame the story within late-Victorian beliefs about the proper roles of man and wife. He notes, for instance, that Melusine, "quite properly, and womanlike [...] intended her wedding day to be *the day* of her life" (38), which explains her extensive preparations. In her building endeavors, he observes that Melusine "took upon herself the ordering of every thing, and, from a business point of view, seems to have regarded Raymondin as simply a sleeping partner" (48). Likewise the distinguishing marks on Melusine's sons are not marvelous but quite the opposite: "She was unfortunate in her progeny; they were all, in some way or other, malformed" (49) and, apart from Geffray the Great-Tooth's destruction of the Abbey of Maillières, their adventures are excised. Instead, the moment of greatest drama is the dinner at which his brother makes troubling insinuations to Raymondin,

---

30   John Ashton, *Romances of Chivalry: Told and Illustrated in Fac-Simile* (London: T. Fisher Unwin, 1890), v. Page numbers follow in parentheses.

31   Ashton mentions Skeat's edition of the *Romans of Parthenay;* A. K. Donald's edition of the English prose romance *Melusine* would issue from the Early English Text Society five years later. In his introduction to *Melusine,* Ashton admits to finding "no record of its ever having engaged the attention of any of our early printers" (6), a surprising fact not only because of its popularity in other languages but because "[a]t first sight it would seem that this Romance was indebted to England for its very inception" (9), given the involvement of the Earl of Salisbury in providing source material. He also observes that the Lusignans "furnished Kings to Jerusalem and Cyprus" and footnotes a mention of the death in 1884 of a Russian officer claiming both the name Lusignan and the crown of Cyprus, through which it is possible that something of the family and its history might have come to the attention of English readers (1).

THE MYSTERY OF MELUSINE DISCOVERED.   [*Frontispiece*.

FIGURE 19.2 *Melusine discovered at her bath, from John Ashton's Romances of Chivalry* (*1890*)

"who had hitherto taken his wife's hebdomadal absences with perfect calm-
ness" (50) but who now, "like a man [...] determined to know the worst" (52)
is moved to spy upon his spouse, and "then [...] made the discovery of the
awful effects of his wife's fairy origin, and of the expiation she was doomed to
undergo" (53). Ashton's Raymondin, exhibiting a more modern sensibility, is
shocked less by the violation of his oath than by the visible manifestation of
his wife's cursed form.

When confronted with Melusine's changed shape, Ashton's confidence
as a narrator also changes. He adheres to his source's matter-of-fact treatment of Melusine's final and most remarkable transformation along with the

observation that, due to her husband's "revelation of her dual existence [...]
she would have to resume her fairy shape of half serpent, half woman, and
linger about in that guise until the day of judgment" (63). Of her final transformation and the eponymous footprint, he wryly footnotes, "A serpent's foot
must have been remarkable" (63). Though he retains her testamentary speech
documenting her descent from the King of Albanie, Ashton does not use this
to make a case for Melusine's insular origins and therefore her relevance for
British readers. He likewise makes little of the concluding marvels reported
by Jean d'Arras, though he does note the legend of the *cri de Melusine* and the
"Melusine cakes" sold at fairs, depicting a woman half-serpent in form (64–8).

Instead, Ashton ends his "Melusine" with a peculiar appeal to the story's
truth-value: "Can any one doubt the truth of the story after this? Reader, do
you?" (79). While in some respects his question echoes the gesture of medieval
storytellers to persuade their audiences of the truth of their tale, Ashton, like
Baring-Gould, reduces the marvels of Melusine to a fireside ghost story or a
wonder tale. Although he brings the full complexity if not length of her medieval tale to the attention of his modern audience, Ashton avoids any attempt
to gloss or organize Melusine's many meanings and proceeds directly to Sir
Isumbras. He attempts no interpretation of the story beyond noting its interest
as a historical document capturing the culture and attitudes of an earlier age.

Inclusion in Ashton's volume did not herald a comeback for Melusine into the
realm of English literature. Instead, artistic renditions continued to separate the
dragon from the woman, though in John Waterhouse's *Circe Invidiosa* (1892),
the one is a shadow of the other, and the dragon hints at a suppressed power the
enchantress might unleash at any time.[32] Only the full flowering of the Romantic
impulse not just to encounter the supernatural but to investigate the truth-ori-
gins behind the stories leads to a resuscitation of Melusine that holds anything
close to the novelistic scope and complexity of Jean d'Arras' romance.

Charlotte Haldane's *Melusine, or Devil Take Her!* (1936) also focuses on the
tragic love story. Like the poets of the previous century, Haldane reads Melusine's difference as a metaphor for belonging to a different world, though in
this case a more literal one: she casts Melusine as a follower of the so-called
Old Religion, a pagan practice demonized by medieval Christian authorities.[33]

---

32   The author wishes to thank Tina Boyer for drawing her attention to this remarkable image.

33   Charlotte Haldane, *Melsuine, or Devil Take Her! A Romantic Novel* (London: Arthur Barker,
      1936). Haldane's interpretation of an Old Religion as foundation for the European witch
      draws much from Margaret Murray's claims in *The Witch Cult in Western Europe* (1921,
      rpt. Oxford University Press, 1962) and *The God of the Witches* (1931, rpt. Oxford Univer-
      sity Press, 1970). Page numbers given in parentheses.

Pressine's meeting with Elynas of Albany and Melusine's grooming to ensnare Raymond are part of an economic and political strategy of survival cultivated by this religion's leaders. Melusine's "curse" is not magical but an obligation to conduct services—the Black Sabbath—and this function legitimizes her Saturday absences while literalizing the fantastic elements of the medieval tale. Melusine's high place in the ritual requires her to don a serpent crown and a dress made of viper's scales, which can only be made to fit after bathing herself in oil, and it is in the midst of this process that Raymond surprises her in the infamous betrayal scene. His subsequent accusation is not so much that she is a fairy, demon, or serpent, but rather that her affiliation with the "Black Arts" has led to perversion in her sons (241). Her failure to enforce her husband's adherence to their marital vow compels Melusine's expulsion, and Haldane's description of the departure scene is highly original. Melusine walks proudly into the Great Hall wearing her regalia, "the red-gold Serpent's crown," and "clad from neck to feet only in the dark shimmering snake-skin" (265–6). She makes her farewells, reveals her lineage, and then dives out the window into the moat of Merment, though she is said later "to have flown in the form of a great Serpent from Merment Castle to Lusignan, to have alighted on the Postern Tower there and crashed it to the ground" in a lightning strike (293). Later, another huge thunderstorm serves as explanation for Melusine's noisy reappearance around Lusignan to announce Raymond's death.

Haldane's mode of novelistic realism treats Melusine, as do the medieval versions, as a real historical character rather than a wonder tale,[34] but her interpretation, though it provides an intriguing practical explanation for the more marvelous elements of the story, hugely reduces Melusine's agency and power. Melusine's enclosure of her father in the mountain of Bramblehoe is neither an act of patriarchal rebellion nor revenge for her mother's suffering, but rather a girlish prank that goes horribly wrong when the old man suffers a heart attack. Her prophetic knowledge is largely the work of an invented figure called Owain the Wanderer, a descendant of ancient druids and a high-ranking officer of the vague and secret organization the Old Religion is depicted as having. The construction of marvelous castles and abbeys is completed under Owain's direction, not Melusine's, and as the adventures of her other sons

---

34 Haldane opens the story in 1116, and her endnotes reference the historical facts: the castle of Lusignan was founded in the tenth century by Hugues II (le Bien-Aimé) (309), and she cites Leo Hoffrichter as her source for the information that Geffrai au Grand Dent is a native Poitevin hero and rebel who really did burn down the abbey of Maillezais in 1232 (315). She acknowledges as her source A. K. Donald's edition of the Royal MS 18 B.II, published by the Early English Text Society in 1895.

beside Geffray are highly summarized, the medieval Melusine's dynastic power and empire-building functions are much reduced. The character Haldane creates is predominantly a satisfied and busy wife and mother who devotedly loves her husband and children and is broken-hearted to part from them. The novel completes its domestication of the character by reuniting Melusine at the end with her sisters, Melior and Palatine, in the castle of their birth. As she alchemized her subject from half-serpent to entirely human, Haldane muted Melusine's metaphorical and political significance. The book's reprinting in 1978 by Arno Press as part of its Lost Race and Adult Fantasy series suggests the story was thought to hold no more than a niche appeal as a curious medieval antiquity.

Still, Haldane's reworking opened doors to further recoveries. William Matthews excerpted a few pages of the English prose *Melusine* in his 1963 collection *Later Medieval English Prose,* making the work visible to academic audiences. Robert Nolan's 1971 dissertation marked the first scholarship on the English prose romance, mainly concerned with philological, textual, and originary aspects.[35] In a move away from Haldane's realism, British author Lynne Reid Banks, in her young adult novel *Melusine* (1988), uses the myth as a provocative metaphor for the splintered self that abused children develop as a coping mechanism to protect them from trauma. And in her collection *Mermaid Tales from Around the World,* American author Mary Pope Osborne keeps to the tradition Ashton observed of turning medieval romances into chapbooks for children, and makes Melusine her lead story. Both treatments receive Melusine as little more than a folkloric figure, a solidly Othered representation and essentially indecipherable symbol, the contours of her dragon and human aspects uneasily conjoined. Like late medieval audiences, it seems modern audiences also find something explanatory in the serpent-tailed woman, but the form is most often a metaphor for women's secret and occasionally hostile power.

In her novel, Reid Banks departs from Jean d'Arras' established history and instead invokes a legend local to the Vendée region about a "shadowy mythological figure" whose "origins [are] lost in the mists of antiquity," "a woman by day and a snake by night" (72). A guidebook read by the young protagonist, Roger, "suggests that [Melusine] is a direct descendant of the serpent in the Garden of Eden" and therefore "the embodiment of both good and evil,"

---

35   William Matthews, ed., *Later Medieval English Prose* (New York: Appleton-Century-Crofts, 1963). Robert J. Nolan, "An Introduction to the English Version of *Melusine*," PhD diss., New York University, 1971.

an incongruity manifested in her dual form (145).[36] Suggestions scattered throughout the book associate snake imagery with the young daughter of the Chateau de Bois-Serpe, where Roger and his family are vacationing. Here her form alludes to non-normative sexuality, for the young girl Melusine turns into a snake to escape her father's sexual molestation. In snake form she comes to Roger for protection, and in snake form she, Laocoön-style, ultimately attacks her father and, in a reversal of the romance narrative, throws him out the window (184). The trajectory of this hybrid Melusine moves toward the achievement of full humanity rather than transformation into a barely human figure, for after this final violent confrontation she molts her snakeskin and the next time Roger encounters her, "Melusine had emerged from her snake self, she was all human now, and that shedding had taken away the snake look she had had, leaving her almost supernaturally new and beautiful" (197). She ends the story as a fully human, self-governing, financially independent young woman, though when Roger meets her again "[t]here was a wildness about her, an untamed, animal side—still" (244). In this story, the woman-snake is an anomaly to be rejected, a curse that is happily escaped once the betraying male is removed.

Pope Osborne introduces Melusine as "the most popular of all medieval legends," one that "the noble families in France down to the humble peasantry believed in [...] implicitly." While she suspects that Melusine was created and "originally told as explanations of certain historical phenomena,"[37] she follows Yardley, Ashton, and Matthews in condensing the political and genealogical romance into a love story, with emphasis on Raymond's betrayal. In the moment of discovery, when Raymond finds his wife alone in the bath with "the entire lower half of her body [...] changed into the huge blue tail of a fish," "[o]ddly enough, his horror of losing his beloved wife was greater than his horror at discovering her astonishing fish tail" (4). The resulting confrontation plays out as if the two were a wealthy modern couple alone in their suburban mansion, and then, "with a wail of agony, Melusine rushed out of her house, leaving her footprint on the last stone that she touched" (4). An accompanying illustration shows Geoffrey the Great Tooth studying a flagstone with the imprint of a bare human foot, toes clearly delineated. Thereafter, the castle and fountain of Lusignan stood empty, "haunted by the ghost of the vanished countess who

---

36   Lynne Reid Banks, *Melusine: A Mystery* (New York: Harper & Row, 1988). Page numbers given in parentheses.

37   Mary Pope Osborne, *Mermaid Tales from Around the World* (New York: Scholastic, 1993). Pope Osborne draws for her source on Gwen Benwell and Arthur Waugh's *Sea Enchantress: The Mermaid and her Kin* (New York: Citadel Press, 1961) and on Baring-Gould.

was half human and half fish" (5). Unlike medieval versions of the story, which explain Melusine's prophetic power and resources by associating her with the realm of fairy, or Haldane's and Reid Banks's modern treatments, which depict her as fully human, Pope Osborne's doubled Melusine recalls the supernatural wife of the Romantics, signaling the general indecipherability of women, who retain some hidden aspect that cannot be fully articulated or understood in the language of a patriarchal world.

This idea of Melusine as a metaphor for the doubled nature of women—or the coincident existence of two very different impulses, desires, selves—is most fully explored in A. S. Byatt's *Possession: A Romance*, the book which brought Melusine—six hundred years after the composition by Jean d'Arras—to English bestseller lists. The character Christabel LaMotte, Victorian poet and author of the "fairy epic" *Melusina*, tells her young cousin that "men saw women as double beings, enchantresses and demons or innocent angels" (404). Are all women double? her cousin inquires, and Christabel answers, "I said all men see women as double. Who knows what Melusina was in her freedom with no eyes on her?" Romance, LaMotte says, is the only mode in which "women's two natures can be reconciled" (404).[38] She refers to the narrative genre of romance, for the book's action shows what women, and sometimes men, sacrifice for and in erotic relationships.

Melusine's interpretations throughout *Possession* are as varied as her viewers. She is explained as a symbol of "self-sufficient female sexuality," a revenant water goddess, sister to the Breton sorceress Dahud (also a subject of Christabel's poetry), a "watery being," "the vestigial memory of an other world where women were powerful," and a symbol of hard-won female autonomy, with her marble bath, her private secrets, and her one day a week of seclusion.[39] Christabel identifies with the heroine of her novel in that she too feels herself a shapeshifter, French and English, and in that she has fought for her small freedom against family and society, much like Melusine's plea for weekly seclusion.[40]

---

38   A. S. Byatt, *Possession: A Romance* (New York: Vintage, 1991). Page numbers in parentheses.

39   Byatt, *Possession*, 19, 266, 379.

40   At the point of her identification with Melusine's two nationalities, LaMotte is pregnant, having escaped to her Breton relations to have her baby in secret (377); she speaks of her rebellion on 208 and her resistance to Ash on 213. LaMotte's insistence on intellectual independence parallels Melusine's plea for one day a week of solitude, a permission she has to fight for, but her remark to Ash—"I cannot let you burn me up" (213)—while reference to the convention of lust/love/passion as a fire, plays against the Aristotelian-inspired medieval idea that men are governed by the fiery element and women the watery. If Ash is a fire, then he is in more danger from a watery being like Melusine/LaMotte than she is from him.

Most poignantly, the poetess identifies with her transformed subject when she calls herself "an old witch in a turret" in her last letter to her lover, the poet Randolph Ash: "I have been Melusina these thirty years. I have so to speak flown about and about the battlements of this stronghold crying on the wind of my need to see and feed and comfort my child, who knew me not" (544). Ellen Ash's interpretation of Melusina, in LaMotte's poem, is far more cold and less compassionate: "She is beautiful and terrible and tragic, the Fairy Melusine, inhuman in the last resort" (135).

Alone of the modern resurrections of Melusine, Byatt's fairy woman comes closest to capturing and holding in balance the many conflicting and sometimes ambivalent resonances that one can trace in the medieval Melusine's body. As in Pope Osbourne's telling, when the mermaid's fish scales sparkle in the sunlight at the moment of discovery, Melusine's finned tail and its "argent scale" are in LaMotte's poem almost inexpressibly beautiful.[41] Yet she figures in her changeable body the heart of a great mystery: the unknowability of the beloved, the unknowability of self, the limits of language to capture the full plenitude of human sensation, and likewise its power to shape and confine, to constrict and exclude. Melusine's betrayal by male authority parallels the experience of many of Byatt's female characters—Christabel, Ellen Ash, Beatrice Nest, even Val and Maud Bailey—in that their current world allows them insufficient space and license to exercise the full power of their talents and capabilities.

The fishtail as signification of female Otherness, of the mystery and illegibility of the not-male, persists in the portrait of Melusine offered by historical novelist Philippa Gregory, who references Melusine in her Cousin's War series (2009–15), which retells the English Wars of the Roses through the eyes of various female characters. Instead of employing the medieval legend of the fairy foundress, fecund mother, political advisor, and empire-builder who consolidates a far-reaching dynasty, Gregory transforms her Melusine into a forsaken mermaid whose magical heritage explains Elizabeth Woodville's and her mother Jacquetta of Luxembourg's talent for witchcraft. To other figures in the novels, Melusine is an inimical legend, suggesting something tainted or not quite human in the power and influence of Edward's Queen, but to Elizabeth Woodville, Melusina is a protectress and a source of power. She sings to warn the family of a death; she is an advisor, and she carries out Elizabeth's

---

41   Pope Osborne, *Mermaid Tales*, 4; Byatt, *Possession*, 135. One might contrast here the medieval romance, which tries to make this image legible to readers using a rather mundane analogy: Melusine's tail is "as grete & thykk as a barell" in the prose version (Donald, *Melusine*, 297).

curses.[42] But when Gregory retells the legend itself—retaining touches more reminiscent of the later, Luxembourgian versions of the story than the French-inspired medieval legends cherished by the Counts of St. Pol—it is as a lament for the burden of women living in a world shaped by men, a fable "that all women are creatures of a divided nature," a reminder that men can never really understand or trust this dualism and so will always betray the women they love.[43] As Gregory herself said of her choice of the legend, "The story of Melusina [...] came to signify for me the difficulty that women have living in a man's world—almost as if women are beings of another element."[44]

Thanks to the work of Byatt and Gregory, Melusine has returned in force to the English popular imagination as an expression of a powerful womanhood that can be both creative and destructive at the same time. A vindictive Melusine prevails in Claire Delacroix's novella "An Elegy for Melusine" (2004), as the bitter, exiled fairy protagonist achieves a final revenge not on the husband who betrayed her but on the visiting noblewomen who, unlike her, are able to successfully masquerade as medieval noblewomen, wives, and mothers.[45] In the ubiquitous logo for the Starbucks™ corporation, the threatening form of the mermaid-siren, shorthand for female mystery and dangerous allure, has been glamorized into an extravagantly coiffed and elegantly curved royal damsel.[46] A villainous Melusine appears among the cast of the Final Fantasy video game franchise, while in other digital arts she is presented as a figure of enchantment, for example in an artwork by Alexandra V. Bach, in which the mermaid tail represents the woman's imaginative capabilities.[47] A similarly romanticized reading prevails in the logo for the fantasy imprint Melusine Muse Press,

---

42   Philippa Gregory, *The White Queen* (New York: Simon & Schuster, 2009); see 265, 275, 308, 313, 344, 351, 361, and 365 for mentions of Melusine.

43   Gregory, *White Queen*, 1, 62, 145.

44   Gregory, "On Melusina, and on Women in Love," *The Globe and Mail,* August 25, 2009, updated August 23, 2012, http://www.theglobeandmail.com/arts/books-and-media/on -melusina-and-on-women-in-love/article4284481/.

45   Claire Delacroix, "An Elegy for Melusine," in *To Weave a Web of Magic* (New York: Berkley Books, 2004), 269–362. *Melusine* is the title of Sarah Monette's fantasy novel (New York: Ace Books, 2005), but in her invented world Melusine is a city populated by magical figures not including a serpent woman.

46   Steve M., a staff writer for the Starbucks website, describes the siren logo as a "storyteller," a "muse," and a guide, as well as "a seductive mystery." Steve M., "So, Who is the Siren?," Starbucks.com, January 5, 2011, http://www.starbucks.com/blog/so-who-is-the-siren.

47   Alexandra V. Bach, "Melusine," DeviantArt, posted December 10, 2008, http:// alexandravbach.deviantart.com/art/Melusine-105973544.

while the literary magazine *Cleaver* cleverly uses the image of a siren with a chopping knife to advertise the literary punch of its contents.[48]

While the appearance of the mermaid figure is perhaps not any more prolific in our own time than in the early modern period, the return of Melusine offers a productive way of thinking about her embedded metaphors, one reminiscent of the many interpretive possibilities of the medieval legend and yet with the potential to reflect present ideas about women, the body, the nature of the human, and the workings of power. Janelle Elyse Kihlstrom, founding editor of the online literary magazine *Melusine, or Woman in the 21st Century*, explains that in designing her publication she was "intrigued by the notion of an archetypal feminine power that must draw on some measure of solitude and seclusion, even in the midst of an active and involved social, sexual, procreative and maternal life."[49] While modern readers of Gregory's novels can appreciate the medieval use of a supernatural ancestress to endow a lineage with authority, contemporary women can access Melusine more directly as an image of personal empowerment, representing a universal aspect of modern female experience in a world where the privileged gender is still male.

At the same time, Melusine's figuration as what critic Barbara Creed calls the "monstrous-feminine" persists in contemporary film, keeping alive the spectacle of horror that Melusine's suprahuman body presents.[50] In his 2007 film *Beowulf*, director Robert Zemeckis endows actress Angelina Jolie, playing the role of Grendel's mother, with a computer-generated tail that, along with her watery element, makes her character reminiscent of Melusine. Louis Leterrier's 2010 remake of *Clash of the Titans* imagines the mythical character of Medusa as woman to the waist and from the navel downward imbued with a long, thrashing tail that concludes with a deadly stinger. While she retains her hissing hair and lethal gaze, this Medusa's sinuous body and her loud cry as she attacks make her more a sister to Melusine than the Greek Gorgons, touching on whatever vein of the unconscious that the serpent woman uses to embody heroic threats and masculine fears. Interestingly, in *Clash of the Titans,* Melusine's gifts of prophecy, wisdom, and dynasty-building are bestowed upon the character of Io, who becomes the hero Perseus's wife and mother of

---

48   Melusine Muse Press at http://melusinemusepress.blogspot.com/; see the submissions page for *Cleaver* magazine online at http://www.cleavermagazine.com/opportunities/.

49   Janelle Elyse Kihlstrom, e-mail message to author, June 13, 2015. Used by permission.

50   Barbara Creed, *The Monstrous-Feminine: Film, Feminism, Psychoanalysis* (New York: Routledge, 1993).

his children, neatly separating the dual nature of the serpent-woman into the early modern categories inherited by our own time.[51]

The category collapses again, however, in what might so far be the closest reunion of the dragon and the woman on the screen of a blockbuster film: Disney's 2014 live-action *Maleficent*, which re-envisions the supernatural fairy enchantress of the Sleeping Beauty legend into a figure much like Melusine.[52] With horns on her head highly reminiscent of the headdress Melusine wears in late medieval and early modern woodcuts, the fairy Maleficent otherwise appears human in form save for a pair of wings, of which she is deprived in the course of the movie by a false lover. The Maleficent of this film harbors strongly protective maternal instincts and is a powerful enchantress with un-limited resources who can physically transform her kingdom at will and who is its recognized ruler. While male betrayal is a prevalent motif, the emotional charge of the narrative rests on the way that the two central female characters lift the curse on each other: Maleficent herself breaks the curse of the death-like sleep she laid on Aurora, and an awakened Aurora consequently restores her wings to Maleficent, who in a film moment highly evocative of Melusine's final exit transforms into a winged creature, exits the castle that entraps her by shattering a stained-glass window, and then flies about the parapets, scream-ing, as she sends the malicious King Stefan to his death.

While the film transfers the medieval Melusine's latent serpent form into Maleficent's dragon sidekick, the echoes of Melusine embedded into the nar-rative and into the character's physical form signal, at last, a return to the cultural imagination of an aerially equipped supernatural female figure who can rule, guide, instruct, build, fight wars, and expand kingdoms. It would be inaccurate to suggest that the film embraces Melusine's full complexity; this character, after all, does not seek or deceive a husband, nor order the mur-der of a three-eyed son. But in understanding that the dragon and the woman can go together—can in fact be manifestations of the same entity, capable of an immense power that may be employed as she wishes, and not always to destructive ends—modern English-speaking audiences finally have avail-able a metaphor that begins to capture the full complexity coded into the medieval Melusine narrative, one lost in the subsequent centuries. Further, in re-imagining that the conclusion to a story about a supernaturally gifted dragon-woman might be integration rather than expulsion, modern audiences

---

51   *Beowulf,* directed by Robert Zemeckis (Paramount Pictures, 2007); *Clash of the Titans,* directed by Louis Leterrier (Warner Bros., 2010).

52   *Maleficent,* directed by Robert Stromberg (Walt Disney Pictures, 2014).

have the chance to return to circulation a symbol that rejects flattened or split depictions of women's nature to embrace a set of more complex connotations that can re-signify formerly Othered, marginalized, or monstrous figures into a coherent and cohesive cultural whole.

CHAPTER 20

Melusines Past, Present, and Future: An Afterword

Tania M. Colwell

In the 1340s, scholar and royal translator Pierre Bersuire recounted a local Poitevin legend about the fairy of Lusignan. In so doing he gave name to Melusine, a metamorphic fairy-serpent whose tragic tale has enchanted audiences for over six hundred years. Following the publication of Jacques Le Goff and Emmanuel Le Roy Ladurie's seminal essays on the fairy's place in medieval and early modern French culture in 1971, a gradual but increasingly steady flow of studies has explored the colorful Melusine legend.[1] In their contributions to the *Annales* journal, Le Goff and Le Roy Ladurie identified a range of important historical, literary, and mythic themes illuminating the cultural valence of the Melusine legend in premodern France. Core among those themes were motifs which have continued to inform contemporary investigations into the Lusignan fairy in both her French and transnational incarnations. In particular, Melusine's role as dynastic founder and loving matriarch, her serpentine transformations, and her identification with the vitality of water have remained central to reinventions, representations, and analyses of the hybrid fairy over the centuries. However, as Ladurie observed of early modern reiterations of the myth, and the essays in *Melusine's Footprint* elucidate, Melusine's reincarnations have not simply repeated existing story patterns, but have responded acutely to contemporary concerns across space and time.[2]

Ground breaking scholarship of the Melusine story has often focused exclusively on the medieval origins and developments of the metamorphic fairy's tale. As a result, the deep mythic structural underpinnings of the fairy's evolution and historical function, Melusine's transformations across early

---

1　Jacques Le Goff and Emmanuel Le Roy Ladurie, "Mélusine maternelle et défricheuse," *Annales Économies, Sociétés, Civilisations* 26 (1971): 587–622. Important earlier studies include Léo Desaivre, "Le mythe de la mère Lusine (Meurlusine, Merlusine, Mellusigne, Mellusine, Mélusine, Méleusine). Étude critique et bibliographique," in *Mémoires de la Société de statistique, sciences, lettres et arts du département des Deux-Sèvres*, 2nd ser., 2 (1882): 81–302; Louis Stouff, *Essai Sur Mélusine: Roman du XIVe siècle par Jean d'Arras* (Paris: Picard, 1930); and François Eygun, *Ce qu'on peut savoir de Mélusine et de son iconographie* (Puiseaux: Pardès, 1951).

2　Le Roy Ladurie, "Mélusine maternelle et défricheuse," 605 (Le Roy Ladurie's contribution to this essay was entitled "Mélusine ruralisée," 604–22).

iconographic and print media, her status within medieval folk, fairy, and demonological cultures,[3] and more recently the problematic status of Melusine
in early English culture[4] have all been sensitively examined. Edited collections
have featured prominently among these endeavors, offering scholars the opportunity to interrogate the Melusine story thematically; thematic foci have
included Melusine's status as a dynastic legend, cross-cultural correspondenc-
es between Celtic and Romance myth, the fairy *merveilleux*, and the myth's
afterlife in European culture.[5] *Melusine's Footprint* joins this invaluable corpus
of scholarship but is distinguished from it in innovative ways. While it shares

---

3 Jean-Jacques Vincensini, *Pensées mythiques et narrations médiévales* (Paris: Champion, 1996);
   Laurence Harf-Lancner, *Les fées du Moyen Âge: Morgane et Mélusine: la naissance des fées* (Geneva: Droz, 1984); see also Harf-Lancner's *Le monde des fées dans l'Occident médiéval* (Paris:
   Hachette, 2003), and, on iconography, Harf-Lancner's articles "La serpente et le sanglier: les
   manuscrits enluminés des deux romans français de Mélusine," *Le Moyen Âge: Revue d'histoire
   et de philologie* 101 (1995): 65–87, and "L'illustration du *Roman de Mélusine* de Jean d'Arras
   dans les éditions du XVᵉ et du XVIᵉ siècle," in *Le livre et l'image en France au XVIᵉ siècle*, ed. Nicole
   Cazauran, *Cahiers V.L. Saulnier* 6 (1989): 29–55; Hélène Bouquin, "Les aventures d'un roman
   médiéval: éditions et adaptations de *L'Histoire de Mélusine* de Jean d'Arras (XVᵉ–XIXᵉ siècles)"
   (PhD diss., École nationale des chartes, 2000); Françoise Clier-Colombani, *La fée Mélusine au
   Moyen Âge: images, mythes et symboles* (Paris: Le Léopard d'Or, 1991); Pierre Gallais, *La fée à la
   fontaine et à l'arbre: un archétype du conte merveilleux et du récit courtois* (Amsterdam: Rodopi,
   1992); Myriam White-Le Goff, *Envoûtante Mélusine* (Paris: Klincksieck, 2008); Gerhild Scholz
   Williams, *Defining Dominion: The Discourses of Magic and Witchcraft in Early Modern France
   and Germany* (Ann Arbor: University of Michigan Press, 1995).

4 Misty Urban, *Monstrous Women in Middle English Romance* (Lewiston, NY: Edwin Mellen
   Press, 2010); Jan Shaw, *Space, Gender and Memory in Middle English Romance: Architectures
   of Wonder in Melusine* (New York: Palgrave, 2016).

5 *Melusine of Lusignan: Founding Fiction in Late Medieval France*, ed. Donald Maddox and Sara
   Sturm-Maddox (Athens, GA: University of Georgia Press, 1996); *Mélusines continentales et
   insulaires*, Actes du colloque international tenu le 27 et 28 mars 1997 à l'Université Paris XII
   et au Collège des Irlandais, ed. Jeanne-Marie Boivin and Proinsias MacCana (Paris: Champion, 1999); *Écriture et réécriture du merveilleux féerique: autour de Mélusine*, ed. Matthew
   Morris and Jean-Jacques Vincensini (Paris: Classiques Garnier, 2012); *Mélusine moderne et
   contemporaine*, ed. Arlette Bouloumié with Henri Béhar (Angers: L'Âge d'homme, 2001);
   Melusine: Atti del Convegno (Verona, 10–11 novembre 2006), ed. Anna Maria Babbi (Verona:
   Fiorini, 2009). See also *Melusine: actes du Colloque du Centre d'études médiévales de l'Université de Picardie Jules Verne, 13 et 14 janvier 1996*, ed. Danielle Buschinger and Wolfgang
   Spiewok (Greifswald: Reineke-Verlag, 1996); and *550 Jahre deutsche Melusine—Coudrette
   und Thüring von Ringoltingen: Beiträge der wissenschaftlichen Tagung der Universitäten Bern
   und Lausanne vom August 2006*, ed. André Schnyder and Jean-Claude Mühlethaler (Bern:
   Peter Lang, 2008).

with collections edited by Arlette Bouloumié and Anna Maria Babbi the desire to trace the shifting permutations of the legend within and beyond the medieval period well into the modern, it is only the second collection in over twenty-five years to disseminate all of its contributions in English.[6] Given the growing popularity in Anglophone culture of various hybrid female figures attested in the introduction, an English-language volume examining the metamorphic afterlife of the Melusine figure is more than timely.

This is not to suggest that the collection centers on Anglophone Melusines—far from it. *Melusine's Footprint* illustrates the breadth of scholarship and critical approaches which are emerging to enrich understandings of Melusine's evolution across time and place. Responding to widening interest in the Melusine tale type's global resonances, the volume includes new considerations of how the mythic figure has been conceptualized and re-interpreted in English culture, along with fresh investigations into the cultural function of and metamorphoses experienced by Melusine and her tale across western and central Europe and beyond to imperial China.[7] As well as probing the varied role of Melusine as cultural metaphor, several contributors raise questions about the transnational networks which shaped late medieval and early modern literary and iconographic production across Western Europe, a growing area of investigation with implications for understanding early literature beyond the Melusine romances.[8] The collection contributes significantly to intersecting scholarly debates about the status of Melusine as a hybrid fairy and the epistemological potential inherent in her changeable form. These essays implement new critical and historically sensitive lenses to offer important

---

6   *Melusine of Lusignan*, ed. Maddox and Sturm-Maddox (1996) was the last volume entirely in English.

7   For interest in the global resonances of the Melusine tale type, see essays in *Mélusines continentales et insulaires*, ed. Boivin and MacCana, and *Melusine*, ed. Babbi; also Gregory Darwin, "On Mermaids, Meroveus, and Melusine: Reading the Irish Seal Woman and Melusine as Origin Legend," *Folklore* 126 (2015): 123–41. For a modern interpretation which intersects with Anna-Lisa Baumeister's chapter in this volume, see Markus Hallensleben, "Rewriting the Face, Transforming the Skin, and Performing the Body as Text: Palimpsestuous Intertexts in Yoko Tāwada's 'The Bath'," in *Beyond Alterity: German Encounters with Modern East Asia*, ed. Qinna Shen and Martin Rosenstock (New York: Berghan, 2014), 168–89.

8   Lydia Zeldenrust, "Serpent or Half-Serpent? Bernhard Richel's *Melusine* and the Making of a Western European Icon," *Neophilologus* 100, no. 1 (2016): 19–41; Tania M. Colwell, "The Middle English Melusine: Evidence for an Early Printed Edition of the Prose Romance in the Bodleian Library," *The Journal of the Early Book Society for the Study of Manuscripts and Printing History* 17 (2014): 254–82; and, for instance, Martha Driver, *The Image in Print: Book Illustration in Late Medieval England and its Sources* (London: British Library, 2004).

re-evaluations of the medieval romance heroine, and participate in new conversations about the role of fairies within late medieval Christian discourses such as those led by Corinne Saunders and Richard Firth Green.[9] Contributions pursuing Melusine's reception in German culture extend studies of the medieval fairy's salvific potential into other metaphysical realms, and striking analyses of modern multimedia reinterpretations of tropes essential to the Melusine myth illustrate the way animal hybridity has remained an enduring motif reflecting anxieties about feminine subjectivity and sexuality. Indeed, moving away from earlier scholarly concerns with the demonological qualities of the mythic figure, *Melusine's Footprint* underlines the deep significance of shapeshifting women within and across nations and continents, illustrating how tensions arising from feminine agency could cut across cultural frontiers in surprisingly similar textual, visual and material ways.[10] *Melusine's Footprint* thus brings essays building on distinctive literatures, disciplines and approaches into productive dialogue with each other. Thematic and conceptual intersections between essays produce new insights into the ways audiences past and present have explored and adapted the Melusine myth in idiosyncratic and yet, often, consistent ways. The collection also models new critical approaches which offer ways to refine analyses of how Melusine taps into shared human experiences and concerns across time. As a whole, the volume not only sheds new light on melusines past and present, but it also suggests important new directions for future Melusine research.

The introduction identifies the important function of polymorphic Melusine figures as cultural metaphors articulating anxieties about feminine performance of gender, sexuality, and authority; Chera Cole, Ana Pairet and

---

9   Corinne Saunders, "Magic and Christianity," in *Christianity and Romance in Medieval England*, ed. Rosalind Field, Phillipa Hardman and Michelle Sweeney (Cambridge: Brewer, 2010), 84–101, and her *Magic and the Supernatural in Medieval English Romance* (Woodbridge: Brewer, 2010); Richard Firth Green, *Elf Queens and Holy Friars: Fairy Beliefs and the Medieval Church* (Philadelphia: University of Pennsylvania Press, 2016). See also Sara Sturm-Maddox's "Alterity and Subjectivity in the *Roman de Mélusine*," in *The Court and Cultural Diversity*, ed. Evelyn Mullally and John Thompson (Woodbridge: Brewer, 1997), 121–29 and her "Configuring Alterity: Rewriting the Fairy Other," in *The Medieval Opus*, ed. Douglas Kelly (Amsterdam: Rodopi, 1996), 125–38.

10   See for instance, Stephen Nichols, "Melusine Between Myth and History: Profile of a Female Demon," in *Melusine of Lusignan*, ed. Maddox and Sturm-Maddox, 137–64; several essays in this collection explore how Jean d'Arras attempts to ameliorate the demonic qualities of his heroine. See also Marie-Geneviève Grossel, "Fée en deçà, démone au-delà: remarques sur les aspects inquiétants du personnage mélusinien," in *Mélusine*, ed. Buschinger and Spiewok, 61–76.

Simone Pfleger point out that ontological tensions arising from Melusine's nature as fairy-human hybrid also contribute to this potent mix. Such tensions
typically emerge between heteronormative ideals and expectations on the one
hand, and performance and representation on the other.[11] In this light, contributors ask how people over time have grappled with the possibilities and
problems, desires and fears, embodied by the Melusine character's anomalous
expression of gender, sexuality, and humanity. Angela Weisl's reflection on
the early French and English Melusines, for instance, illustrates how the fairy
is multiply hybrid, by birth, by form, and by gender: Melusine's troubling appropriation of masculine authority is inscribed punitively on her fairy-human
body by her monstrous transformations. Anna Casas Aguilar reads Melusine's
secular and spiritual construction work within the medieval Castilian translations as a material discourse which metaphorically expresses disquiet about
the fairy's performance of gender and her essential alterity. Acknowledging
scholarly arguments about the ways the Melusine romance affirmed the expansionist aims of the Castilian queen Isabel at the end of the fifteenth century, Aguilar convincingly positions diegetic uncertainty regarding Melusine's
building projects in relation to contemporary ambivalence toward the Spanish
monarch's far-reaching powers.

Exploring questions about power, gender, and feminine nature within the
context of marital relations, Zoë Enstone argues that Melusine's punitive monstrous transformation renders the fairy's body inaccessible as a desirable object to her husband. In this way, Melusine's serpentine metamorphosis both
reflects and contests norms of power and sexuality within medieval marriage.
Complementing Enstone's observations and extending iconographic analyses
of Melusine's hybridity elsewhere,[12] Frederika Bain's analysis of serpentine imagery in the premodern romances also foregrounds concerns about blended
ontologies and masculine access to the feminine object. Identifying a pictorial
movement away from the depiction of Melusine with a serpentine tail toward
an aesthetic which privileged a piscine or sirenic tail, Bain argues that this
iconographic shift effectively transformed Melusine into an 'accessible Other.'

---

11   As Angela Weisl pertinently notes in her contribution, expressions of such tensions with-
      in early figurations of the metamorphic and/or hybrid woman have generally been in-
      scribed by male authors, and by extension, artists and musicians.

12   Joanna Pavlevski, "Une esthétique originale du motif de la femme serpent: recherches on-
      tologiques et picturales sur Mélusine au XVe siècle," in *L'Humain et l'animal dans la France
      médiévale (XIIe–XVe s.): Human and Animal in Medieval France, (12th–15th c.)*, ed. Irène
      Fabry-Tehranchi and Anna Russakoff (Leiden: Brill, 2014), 73–94; Clier-Colombani, *La
      fée Mélusine*.

the piscine tail, especially in its bifurcated aspect, modulated the disturbing hermaphroditic sexuality of the serpent woman into a sexuality that was more open, more accessible and so less threatening to the male subject, even as the female object remained Other. Collectively, essays by Weisl, Casas Aguilar, Enstone, and Bain point in new ways to how the Melusine metaphor and metaphors within the Melusine romances were adapted to articulate perennial concerns about feminine agency, sexuality, and alterity in the medieval and early modern periods.

Melusine's Footprint highlights that discourses expressing anxieties about feminine gender, sexuality, and nature in polymorphic and monstrous terms were not unique to premodern Europe. Zifeng Zhao's comparative analysis of Thüring von Ringoltingen's 1456 German adaptation of the *Roman de Parthenay* and the Madam White tales in imperial China demonstrates how serpentine transformation warned (female) audiences against transgressing gendered norms in vastly different geographic and temporal zones. Zhao's essay identifies additional commonalities between the ways religio-patriarchal frameworks in early German and Chinese cultures imposed dichotomous Eve-Mary types on female subjects such as Melusine and Madam White. As Misty Urban illustrates, A. S. Byatt also uses her nineteenth-century poet, Christabel LaMotte, to interrogate this familiar structure for *Possession*'s modern audiences.[13] LaMotte observes that women continue to be seen by men as either angels or demons, and questions the independent subject identity of Melusine away from the male gaze: who would she have been, or wanted to be, given a room of her own?

The intersections between the essays considered thus far underscore Melusine's capacity to speak to intercultural concerns far removed from the political-dynastic motivations of the medieval romances' earliest patrons and audiences. In so doing, the volume elucidates the legend's transcultural resonance and ready transmission across and beyond Europe. Indeed, the transnational depth of the metamorphic water fairy is indicated at the outset in the introduction's review of early oral and textual sources and analogues across Celtic, Greek, Sumerian, and American cultures, as well as by evidence of imperial Chinese variants of the figure.[14] Crucially, as Zhao explains, one of the

---

13 For a critique of Byatt's use of the Melusine tale to articulate contemporary concerns, see Jan Shaw, "The Tale of *Melusine* in A. S. Byatt's *Possession*: Retelling Medieval Stories," in *Storytelling: Critical and Creative Approaches*, ed. Jan Shaw, Philippa Kelly, and L.E. Semler (Basingstoke: Palgrave Macmillan, 2013), 222–37.

14 For the distinction between sources, analogues and parallels, see Zoë Enstone's neat explanation of Christine Rauer's definitions of these categories in this volume.

folkloric sources for both European and Asian incarnations of the dynamic fairy may well have been the ancient Indian serpent woman Nāga. Such potential points of shared origin indicate the importance of a global focus when assessing the cultural value of the Melusine fairy and her metamorphic sisters, and open the door to further investigations of the hybrid icon beyond the European continent.

While Zhao's contribution makes an important start to this world project in the collection, *Melusine's Footprint* also sheds further light on the legend's transnational resonance across Western Europe, illustrating how the fairy was adopted by and adapted to local cultural dynamics. The Castilian translations analyzed by Casas Aguilar and Caroline Prud'Homme are notable in this regard, both for their idiosyncrasies and their relationship to wider romance production in late medieval Europe. In effect, editorial principles used by the Castilian translators to align the *Roman de Mélusine* with audience expectations of local *libros de caballerias* toward the end of the fifteenth century are mirrored to some extent in contemporary French romance manuscripts.[15] The translation's deflection of attention away from the fairy qualities of Jean d'Arras' leading female figures in favor of their courtly characteristics[16] echoes those late fifteenth- and early sixteenth-century copies of the French prose and poetic romances which considerably heighten Melusine's courtly, affective qualities and depict her as a tragic romance heroine.[17] Interestingly, the Castilian romances' emphasis on masculine agency in the establishment of alliances and dynasties also recalls the way the later fifteenth-century copy of the *Roman de Mélusine* currently in Madrid sharpens its focus on Raymondin as the central founder of

---

15   On the Spanish translations, see also Ana Pairet in this volume, and Pairet's "Intervernacular Translation in the Early Decades of Print: Chivalric Romance and the Marvelous in the Spanish *Melusine* (1489–1526)," in *Translating the Middle Ages*, ed. Karen L. Fresco and Charles D. Wright (London: Ashgate, 2012), 86–101.

16   Prud'Homme's observation that fairies are identified with vampires in the Spanish editions consulted does however raise questions about the transmission of myths between central-east Europe and the Iberian peninsula. Coupled with the Czech (and French) tradition recalling the *cri de Mélusine* discussed in the introduction, a vampiric association indicates an interesting point of departure for a new strand of Melusine/monstrosity studies.

17   Tania M. Colwell, "Reading *Mélusine*: Romance Manuscripts and their Audiences, *c.* 1380–1530," (PhD. diss., Australian National University, 2008), 237–50; and Colwell's "Gesture, Emotion, and Humanity: Depictions of Mélusine in the Upton House Bearsted Fragments," in *The Inner Life of Women in Medieval Romance Literature: Grief, Guilt, and Hypocrisy*, ed. Jeff Rider and Jamie Friedman (New York: Palgrave Macmillan, 2011), 107–27.

Lusignan.[18] However, as tempting as it may be to associate the Madrid prose Melusine of Jean d'Arras with the first Castilian edition of 1489, Lydia Zeldenrust has drawn on iconographic evidence to point to a Lyonnais French edition as a likely source text.[19] Nonetheless, such affinities raise important questions about the transnational circulation of and relationships between chivalric and romance literature across Europe at the turn of the sixteenth century.

Zeldenrust's own contribution to the present volume attends to questions about transnational romance circulation very keenly. Her analysis of Melusine's hybridity within the little-known Middle Dutch translations of Jean d'Arras' prose romance reveals that these printed works are themselves hybrid cultural artifacts. A complex network of influences including prose and poetic sources, as well as possibly manuscript and printed copies of romances in both French and German, collectively produce a new Melusine work in which a textual and visual emphasis on Melusine's own physical hybridity is entirely apposite. Pit Péporté's condensed yet comprehensive review of the myriad ways the hybrid fairy has been appropriated from the Middle Ages onward for a range of dynastic, nationalist and, more recently, civic purposes persuasively identifies Melusine as a *lieu de memoire* herself within Luxembourgeois culture.[20] If Melusine's fecundity remains a prevailing motif shaping portraits of her as a semi-naked water fairy in Luxembourg, her eternal malleability is illustrated by her use as a symbol to denote both regional distinctiveness and transculturality. These essays underscore the extent to which Melusine's hybridity has remained central to popular imaginings of the tale in this northwestern pocket of Europe since the Middle Ages. This point is emphasized by Zeldenrust's observations concerning the use of woodcuts depicting the bathing fairy to advertise an early printed translation of the Dutch romance in the 1490s and the presence of a Melusine weathervane atop Het Toreken in Ghent. Considered alongside the near-contemporary production of a French poetic manuscript in nearby Bruges, in which Melusine's feminine qualities are visualized alongside her monstrous form in several scenes,[21] the question of why the fairy's *hybridity* embedded itself deeply within early Dutch and Luxembourgeois culture is worth further investigation: to what extent might a sustained interest in Melusine's hybridity relate to the multicultural nature of this small

---

18   Colwell, "Reading *Mélusine*," 177–83.

19   Zeldenrust, "Serpent or Half-Serpent?," 28.

20   For the use of Nora's *lieu de mémoire* in relation to the Melusine myth, see also Tania M. Colwell, "Patronage of the Poetic Melusine Romance: Guillaume l'Archevêque's Confrontation with Dynastic Crisis," *Journal of Medieval History* 37 (2011): 215–29, at 229.

21   Paris, Bibliothèque nationale de France, MS français 24383, fols. 19r, 23r, and 30r.

but influential region of northwestern Europe, from the later fifteenth and six-teenth centuries to the present day?

With the exception of France and Luxembourg, European fascination with the Melusine figure has nowhere been more consistently evident than in Germany.[22] Complementing recent studies exploring the fairy's function as a marvel within the economy of medieval romance,[23] essays in this collection offer new perspectives on Germanic reincarnations of Melusine, illustrating how German thinkers over time have been particularly attentive to the rich potential of the myth as a framework for thinking through mystical and epistemological questions. Since Thüring von Ringoltingen rendered Coudrette's poetic Melusine romance into prose in 1456, German-language writers and artists have been instrumental in engaging with the fairy's plurality to interrogate relationships between the human, the divine, and the natural world. Prud'Homme and Albrecht Classen each draw attention to Thüring's own textual and iconographic play with the fairy's hybridity, Classen noting further that the 1587 *Buch der Liebe* compilation locates the bathing hybrid Melusine pictorially on the margins between civilized society and the wilderness of nature. Melissa Ridley Elmes explains that decades earlier, the philosopher Paracelsus had also reflected on the status of the watery spirit-beings called melusines in the natural world. Ridley Elmes traces the evolution of melusines in Paracelsus's thought, from their role as sources of enlightenment in his mystical theology to the philosopher's understanding of the hermaphroditic Melusine within the symbolic alchemical creation of Primordial Man—the archetype for longevity which was predicated on the split and then unification of man's essential natures. By elucidating the ways in which Paracelsus integrated melusines into his cosmology, Ridley Elmes's sheds new light on how the amorphous figure of Melusine offered this thinker a creative conceptual lens through which to interpret divine creation.[24]

---

22   For the persistence of the tradition in French literature, see Bouquin, "Les aventures d'un roman médiéval."

23   See essays in the second half of *Écriture et réécriture du merveilleux féerique*, ed. Morris and Vincensini; more generally on the *merveilleux* in French literature, see Christine Ferlampin-Acher, *Merveilles et topique merveilleuse dans les romans médiévaux* (Paris: Champion, 2003); Ferlampin-Acher's *Fées, bestes et luitons: croyances et merveilles* (Paris: Presses de l'Université de Paris-Sorbonne, 2002); and Francis Dubost, *Aspects fantastiques de la littérature narrative médiévale* (*XIIᵉ-XIIIᵉ s.*). *L'autre, l'ailleurs, l'autrefois*, 2 vols. (Paris: Champion, 1991).

24   Jonathon Hughes attempts to argue that alchemists at the Yorkist court of Edward IV and Elizabeth Woodville similarly appropriated Melusine, but his discussion is highly speculative. See Jonathon Hughes, *Arthurian Myths and Alchemy: The Kingship of Edward IV* (Stroud: Sutton Publishing, 2002).

The potential for the shapeshifting Melusine to inspire philosophical insight is further reflected in contributions examining modern Germanic culture by Renata Schellenberg and Deva F. Kemmis. Schellenberg analyzes *Die Neue Melusine* in light of Goethe's scientific interests in the natural world and use of the fairy tale genre as a way to inspire and structure metaphysical thought. Schellenberg reveals that Goethe used his Melusine figure to illustrate how insight into the complexity and unity of the world required careful optical perception and a willingness to identify connections between seemingly disparate and paradoxical elements of existence. In her exploration of Ingeborg Bachmann's "Undine Geht" of 1961, Kemmis privileges hearing and attentive listening to Bachmann's watery nymph as the conduits through which wisdom is conveyed, rather than literal sight and perception. In this Kemmis adapts and extends Goethe's Neoplatonic conception of vision as the means to attain truth to the sphere of aurality. Given the dramatic significance of speech and aurality in the medieval Melusine romances, a point debated by Laurence Harf-Lancner and Christine Ferlampin-Acher, the sustained application of Kemmis' sensory model to an analysis of the romances' metaphysical significance would prove highly stimulating.[25]

Collectively, these studies of Germanic engagement with Melusine illustrate an enduring interest in the way encounter with the hybrid, metamorphic Other can produce a transformative experience in which the viewer/listener attains insight and wisdom.[26] In this regard, Germanic traditions elaborate the metaphysical and epistemological potential central to the original French medieval Melusine romances, whereby encounter with the marvelous fairy offers Raymond the opportunity to re-envisage his world and attain enlightenment. As Rupert T. Pickens has noted, it is the paradox inherent in the shapeshifting marvel and the knowledge she implicitly articulates which poses the intellectual and intuitive challenge to the human observer in the French romances.[27] Whereas Paracelsus, Goethe, and Bachmann embrace the paradox

---

25 Harf-Lancer argues that Raymondin's verbal breaking of his oath to Melusine to a listening audience is the act which triggers their tragic separation in the *Roman de Mélusine*, whereas Ferlampin-Acher insists on Raymond's visual transgression as the point of no return. Harf-Lancner, *Les fées au Moyen Âge*, 173–74; Ferlampin-Acher, *Merveilles et topique merveilleuse*, 113–16.

26 Urban cites Tara Pedersen, who likewise argues that the ontological incoherence of hybrid creatures stimulates the creation of knowledge. See Urban, "How the Dragon Ate the Woman: The Fate of Melusine in English," p. 371, n. 17.

27 Rupert T. Pickens, "The Poetics of Paradox in the *Roman de Mélusine*," in *Melusine of Lusignan*, 48–75.

of the Melusine figure in their conceptualization of the truth immanent in the world, those who encounter a melusine are often constrained by logic and convention to a superficial and less-than-fully realized understanding.

In contrast with Melusine's status in continental traditions, *Melusine's Footprint* illustrates how the hybrid fairy has occupied an ambivalent position in Anglophone culture. Jennifer Alberghini's analysis of the concerted efforts made by the Middle English translator of Coudrette's poetic romance to integrate Melusine into a specifically English literary heritage suggests the extent to which the French romance was considered a literary Other by late medieval contemporaries.[28] As Urban explains, Melusine enjoyed a problematic political and cultural status in late medieval England, not least as a result of Elizabeth Woodville's identification with her Luxembourg mother's mythic ancestor. Ridley Elmes and Urban each note how the German mystical and international Romantic movements contributed to a revival of Melusine figures in British literature. These depictions often remained hesitant about the transformative figure, emphasizing the deception implicit in the hybrid form and the threat to masculinity posed by her serpentine sexuality. Nonetheless, Urban's contribution reveals that the decades following second wave feminism have witnessed the return of a polymorphic Melusine in innovative new interpretations. Contrasting with premodern tendencies to soften Melusine's hybridity, young adult fiction has endowed the fully serpentine character with an apotropaic role, while the metamorphic, aerial Maleficent, who sits at the heart of a Hollywood fantasy film exploring women's protective and destructive qualities, strikingly revels in her alterity. Perhaps, as Urban suggests, Anglophone audiences have begun to re-envision a definition of femininity that advances beyond an identification as not-masculine, and therefore monstrous. Speculation that the revived, modern Melusine(s) may once again act as "a metaphor that begins to capture the full and glorious complexity" of womanhood essential to the medieval continental romances offers hope that socio-cultural attitudes toward the spectrum of women's agency may slowly be turning.[29]

Drawing on a range of philological, iconographic, philosophical, historical, and feminist approaches, essays discussed thus far underline the broad transcultural resonance of Melusine's tale across time and space. Importantly, they illustrate how the hybrid fairy responded flexibly to distinctive local intellectual and cultural environments, and they further highlight how those local environments shared interrelated universal concerns about the nature of

---

28   See Prud'Homme's contribution for additional observations on the textual shifts applied to the Middle English prose and poetic translations.

29   See the conclusion of Urban's chapter, "How the Dragon Ate the Woman."

feminine agency and sexuality, woman's purity and hybridity, and mystical desires to understand the nature of truth and creation. These essays suggestively point to further cross-cultural research exploring the global reach of Melusine tales across non-European cultures. They also prompt scholars to continue investigations into the intersecting cultural networks shaping later medieval literary production, and to explore creatively how the Melusine figure can continue to respond to shifting gendered ideals and expectations

Melusine's Footprint offers a provocative challenge to scholars of the hybrid fairy to develop and apply new critical approaches to medieval and modern iterations of the tale. Building on postcolonial models of hybridity and race articulated by Jeffrey Jerome Cohen, contributions by Pairet and Cole urge scholars to resist conflating medieval concepts of hybridity, monstrosity, and bodily metamorphosis when analyzing the early Melusine romances. Arguing that these three concepts occupied distinctive discourses in the Middle Ages, Pairet proposes that Melusine's periodic metamorphoses be analyzed less as the inevitable product of Presine's curse on a hybrid daughter and more in terms of a broader theme of transformation as process within the romances. Pairet's call to direct attention to the processual, rather than asynchronous, nature of change challenges audiences to focus more laterally on Melusine's experience and, by extension, that of humankind to penetrate to the deeper existential meanings within the tale. Cole's emphasis on analytical precision underwrites her analysis of fairies as natural members of God's world who are capable of attaining salvation, but who are nonetheless identified as inferior and other to humanity. Cole's analysis reveals how the fictional fairy Other was deployed to explore late medieval spiritual anxieties, suggesting that Melusine ultimately affirms sinful humanity's potential for redemption, even at the expense of her own salvation.

In her examination of fairies and penance, Enstone traces the position of the French Melusine romances within the literary evolution of the relationship between fairies and God. Arguing for the romances' pivotal role in literary portraits of fairies implementing divine punishments, Enstone, with Cole, contributes to current reassessments of the changing status and function of fairies in the Christian fabric of medieval romance.[30] Individually, these essays apply sensitive conceptual models to the Melusine romances which illuminate distinctive aspects of the fairy's nature, her transformations, and her existential

---

30   In addition to studies by Saunders and Green cited above, see, for instance, James Wade, *Fairies in Medieval Romance* (New York: Palgrave Macmillan, 2011) and Joanna Ludwikowska, "Uncovering the Secret: Medieval Women, Magic and the Other," *Studia Anglica Posnaniensia* 49 (2014): 83–103.

role within a Christian economy. Collectively, they introduce important new questions about the way medieval discourses shaped early understandings of the Melusine figures and their analogues, and prompt renewed attention to the categories of fairy, hybridity, monstrosity, and metamorphosis within and across the literatures of medieval Europe.

This collection highlights how discourses of the family and instruction intersect to produce another valuable, yet underutilized framework through which to analyze the Melusine romances and late medieval prose more broadly. Alberghini observes that the English translator of Coudrette retains verses extolling the moral benefit of the tales of great deeds and men for his Anglophone audiences. Not only does this comment rationalize the translation project, but it also creates incentive for audiences to engage with this Anglicized exemplary tale. Stacy Hahn explores similar questions through the themes of youth and rebellion, illustrating how the romances articulate a range of moral codes, behaviors, and family relationships relevant to late medieval audiences. Such instructional paradigms are fruitful for exploring the reception of the Melusine tales, and manuscript studies have shown how fifteenth-century patrons, book producers, and audiences routinely aligned the Melusine romances with and alongside practical, theoretical, and conceptual works designed to educate their youthful (and perhaps not-so-youthful) audiences.[31] Hahn's focus on domestic relationships is taken up by Classen in his recent assessment of the important role that kinship and family networks, such as those evident in Thüring's Melusine romance, played in the development of the early modern prose novel.[32] The ease with which literary tropes and forms travelled across borders in the period suggests that a domestic and didactic framework, such as Hahn employs in her analysis of the popular *Roman de Mélusine*, might similarly offer a productive opportunity to reassess the evolution of French prose from the fifteenth into the sixteenth century.

Contributors to *Melusine's Footprint* also introduce innovative modern critical approaches to medieval and modern hybrid Melusines through the lenses of queer and transgressive sexualities. Pfleger applies Sara Ahmed's queer

---

31   Celia M. Lewis, "Acceptable Lessons, Radical Truths: Mélusine as Literature for Medieval Youth," *Children's Literature* 39 (2011): 1–32; Jean-Jacques Vincensini, "Aristote dans les prologues de Mélusine (Jean d'Arras, Coudrette et Thüring von Ringolingen): du contexte culturel à la valeur herméneutique," in *550 Jahre deutsche Melusine*, ed. Schnyder and Mühlethaler, 305–25; Colwell, "Reading *Mélusine*," 255–74.

32   Albrecht Classen, "Family and Kinship in Early Modern German Prose Novels: Thüring von Ringoltingen's *Melusine* and the Anonymous *Fortunatus*," *Orbis Litterarum* 70 (2015): 353–79.

critique of happiness to Thüring's German romance, suggesting that the fairy's weekly metamorphosis and isolation are modes of queerness which challenge romance hetero-norms of marital bliss whereby the female subject remains accessible to the husband. Intersecting with Enstone's study, this thought-provoking reading responds to modern visions of the world liberated from traditional marital and sexual values and offers a productive new framework within which to position the medieval tale. With Pfleger, Anna-Lisa Baumeister draws on Mulvey's understanding of the male gaze as constitutive of a heteronormative aesthetic to analyze twentieth-century Viennese literary and film adaptations of tropes central to the Melusine story. Whereas the male gaze conventionally renders the female subject abject, Baumeister argues that filmic feminine subversion of sexual norms, signaled by VALIE EXPORT's close-up shot of a woman stimulating her own genitalia, renders the female subject grotesque and bestial. The resultant queering of the feminine from the male viewpoint echoes the transgressive potential inherent in Melusine and her monstrous form, highlighting the inextricable relationship between the masculine viewpoint on the one hand, and womanhood and animal alterity on the other. Taken together with essays by Pairet, Cole, Enstone, and Hahn, these contributions introduce and apply new or undervalued critical lenses to analysis of the Melusine story and its tropes over time. Whether they refine and enrich historical insights into the romances and their place in late medieval culture, or challenge us to radically rethink the conceptual frameworks applied in the first instance, they represent some of the creative approaches to new research available to Melusine studies.

A theme that emerges quietly throughout the collection, and which is crystallized in the trope of Melusine's footprint, that tangible yet textual reminder of the Lusignan fairy's multiform existence, is the significance of material culture in the propagation, circulation, and reception of the Melusine legend across time. The Middle Ages saw an abundance of multivalent hybrid women in church architecture, as Bain observes, and Péporté notes that the Lusignan fairy herself occupied an important place as a winged dragon in heraldic crests at the same time that tableaux of the fairy-dragon and her offspring were created for competing dynastic, political and spiritual ends by members of the mid-fifteenth-century Burgundian court.[33] Alongside the hybrid statue of Melusine on the tanner's guild tower in Ghent, described by Zeldenrust, Classen draws attention to the striking premodern German tradition of *Lüsterweibchen* chandeliers, where busts of women are suspended from candle frames by

---

33   Colwell, "Reading *Mélusine*," 310–20.

stag antlers, which look uncannily like the dragon wings attributed to Melusine in manuscripts and printed editions. The embeddedness of the Melusine motif in German culture is further attested by Bain, who observes that hybrid women with piscine tails were integrated into Germanic heraldic discourse with the name *melusina* by the seventeenth century. As Péporté illustrates, modern Luxembourg has enjoyed the creation and promotion of hybrid melusines in a range of visual and material media, while mermaids and Melusine figures are used commercially across the world, whether via the Starbucks logo found globally or as a brand of wedding boutiques in Burgundy. Interestingly, this last example explicitly draws on its namesake's fairy heritage to aspirationally, if heteronormatively, associate a fairy-tale wedding and dress with domestic bliss. In this way, it illustrates the enduring identification of Melusine with her traditional role as wife and mother.[34]

The wealth of material melusines which have survived across time prompt a reconsideration of how the hybrid fairy has been produced, reinterpreted, and examined. Certainly, textual re-creation and analysis will remain critical indices of the tale's reception history. However, as evidence of material melusines accrues, perhaps one can ask not only how the non-textual, visual, and multi-dimensional iterations of the myth reflect personal or collective reception, but also how they work to *shape* past and present responses and understandings. If, as Alfred Gell suggested, objects and images have agentive potential, how might we analyze Classen's stunning chandeliers to understand their creative role in the reception process?[35] To what extent might the Ghent tanners have identified Melusine with the Virgilian advice she gives Raymond about marking the site of their future dynastic home with the seemingly endless strip of hart's hide, and how did Melusine in turn enhance the prestige of the guild?[36] Alternately, if the Lusignan tableau at Philip the Good's Feast of the Pheasant banquet was intended to evoke the crusading exploits of Melusine's sons, might the dragon's setting amongst an array of chivalric, marvelous, and spiritual emblems have complicated the serpentine figure's potential demonic associations? Tracing not just the meaning of these material melusines but also their active role in circulating and shaping the myth of the hybrid fairy opens up an exciting new interdisciplinary avenue for Melusine research.

---

34   Mélusine Création is a wedding boutique located in Dijon and Besançon (http://www
        .creation-melusine.com/; accessed July 20, 2017).

35   Alfred Gell, *Art and Agency: An Anthropological Theory* (Oxford: Clarendon Press, 1998).

36   For resonances with Dido's foundation of Carthage, see Jean-Jacques Vincensini, "De la
        fondation de Carthage à celle de Lusignan: *engin* de femmes vs prouesse des hommes,"
        Sénéfiance 42 (1998): 581–600.

Collectively, *Melusine's Footprint* draws together scholarship offering fresh conceptual insights and new methodological approaches which significantly enrich the study of the mythic water fairy. Exploring the Lusignan fairy's legacy in innovative ways, essays adopt an array of interdisciplinary frameworks to interrogate Melusine's capacity to endure over time. As contributors enter into a mutually productive dialogue about different facets of the Melusine tradition, audiences are also alerted to the broader implications such discussions have for understanding the historical, cultural, and intellectual circumstances framing particular iterations of the metamorphic fairy. Essays exploring the transnational dimensions of Melusine simultaneously draw attention to the intercultural networks shaping literary production and transmission across late medieval and early modern Europe. The contours of these networks remain shadowy and demand further attention. New critical frameworks informing analyses of Melusine in her medieval and modern incarnations highlight the way the changeable fairy—and feminine Other more broadly—consistently offers a productive epistemological trope through which to interrogate human existence, enlightenment, and redemption. Juxtaposed with these revelations are analyses of the fairy's hybridity which underline the abjection and abnegation to which agentive womanhood and feminine sexuality have been consistently subject across cultures over time. The tensions between these persistent threads are visually invoked by images of the hybrid Melusine, particularly those depicting Melusine nursing her sons, which survive from the earliest manuscripts onward.

And yet, such images increasingly privilege the fairy's maternal, feminine qualities at the expense of her monstrosity, in an effort to render the Melusine figure more accessible to her changing audiences. Indeed, Melusine's protean ability to accommodate change over time and space, across media, and for divergent audiences illustrates the magnetism and continued cultural value attached to this ambivalent mythic figure. *Melusine's Footprint* thus establishes cross-cultural and interdisciplinary dialogues that will stimulate new investigations into melusines past, present, and future within inclusive critical frameworks. In so doing, these dialogues will also prompt further inquiry into the diverse cultural imaginations which have represented woman as both a problematic entity whose potential must be contained and as a complex, amorphous, yet nurturing being through whom wisdom and insight may be attained.

Selected Bibliography

Editions and Translations of *Melusine*

d'Arras, Jean. *A Bilingual Edition of Jean d'Arras's* Mélusine *or* L'histoire de Lusignan. Edited and translated by Matthew W. Morris. Lewiston, NY: Edwin Mellen Press, 2007.

d'Arras, Jean. "Histoire de la belle Mélusine (Geneva: Steinschaber, 1478)." In *Incunabula: The Printing Revolution in Europe 1455-1500. Unit 64: Romances. Part II.* 1st ed. Edited by Lotte Hellinga. Reading, UK: Research Publications International, 2011.

d'Arras, Jean. *Melusine; or, The Noble History of Lusignan.* Translated by Donald Maddox and Sara Sturm-Maddox. University Park: Pennsylvania State University Press, 2012.

d'Arras, Jean. *Mélusine; ou, la noble histoire de Lusignan.* Edited by Jean-Jacques Vincensini. Paris: Librairie Générale Française, 2003. (Edition of Paris, Bibliothèque de l'Arsenal, MS 3353)

d'Arras, Jean. *Mélusine: Nouvelle édition conforme à celle de 1478, revue et corrigée.* Edited by Charles Brunet. Paris: P. Jannet, 1854.

d'Arras, Jean. *Mélusine: Roman du XIVe siècle.* Edited by Louis Stouff. Dijon: Bernigaud et Privat, 1932. Reprint, Geneva: Slatkine, 1974.

d'Arras, Jean. *Le Roman de Mélusine; ou, l'Histoire des Lusignan.* Translated by Michèle Perret. Paris: Stock, 1979.

Corfis, Ivy A., ed. *Historia de la linda Melosina.* Madison: The Hispanic Seminary of Medieval Studies, 1986. (Edition of the Toulouse 1489 and Seville 1526 printed editions)

Coudrette. *A Critical Edition of Coudrette's* Mélusine *or* Le Roman de Parthenay. Edited and translated by Matthew W. Morris. Lewiston, NY: Edwin Mellen Press, 2003.

Coudrette. *Le roman de Mélusine; ou, histoire de Lusignan.* Edited by Eleanor Roach. Paris: Klincksieck, 1982. (Edition of Carpentras, Bibliothèque municipale, MS 406)

Coudrette. *The Romans of Partenay or of Lusignen, otherwise known as the Tale of Melusine.* Edited by Walter W. Skeat. Early English Text Society OS. 22. London: Trübner & Co., 1866. (Edition of Cambridge, Trinity College, MS R.3.17)

Donald, A. K., ed. *Melusine compiled (1382–1394 A.D.) by Jean d'Arras, Englisht about 1500.* Early English Text Society ES. 68 London: Kegan Paul, Trench, Trübner & Co., 1895. (Edition of British Library Royal, MS 18 B. II)

Kuiper, Willem, ed. "Meluzine: Leeu 1491." In *Bibliotheek van Middelnederlandse Letterkunde: nieuwe digitale reeks.* Amsterdam: Leerstoelgroep Historische Nederlandse Letterkunde, 2008–16.

Ringoltingen, Thüring von. *Melusine.* Basel: Bernhard Richel, 1474.

Ringoltingen, Thüring von. *Melusine.* Edited by Karin Schneider. Berlin: E. Schmidt, 1958. (Edition of Copenhagen, Kongelige Biblioteket, Bibl. Thottiana 2° 423)

Ringoltingen, Thüring von. *Mélusine et autres récits.* Edited by Claude Lecouteux. Paris: Champion, 1999.

Ringoltingen, Thüring von. *Melusine – In der Fassung des Buchs der Liebe (1587).* Edited by Hans-Gert Roloff. Stuttgart: Reclam, 1991.

Primary Sources

Albrecht, Friedrich. *Melusina: Luxemburgische Sage aus dem zehnten Jahrhundert.* Wismar and Luxemburg: Hinstorff, 1859.

Babinet, Jérémie. *Mélusine, Geoffroy à la Grand'Dent: légendes poitevines.* Paris: Techener, 1847.

Banks, Lynne Reid. *Melusine: A Mystery.* New York: Harper & Row, 1988.

Binsfeld, Franz and Jules Kruger. *Melusin: Oper an drei Akten no enger National-So.* Luxembourg: P. Linden, 1951.

Bliss, A. J., ed. *Sir Launfal.* London: Nelson, 1960.

Boswell, C. S., trans. *Fis Adamnáin: An Irish Precursor of Dante: A Study on the Vision of Heaven and Hell Ascribed to the Eighth-century Irish Saint Adamnán, with Translation of the Irish Text.* London: David Nutt, 1908.

Byatt, A. S. *Possession: A Romance.* New York: Vintage, 1992.

Cartulaire de la ville de Luxembourg anno 1632. Archives Nationales de Luxembourg A-XV–12.

Caxton, William. "Caxton's Preface." In *Malory: Complete Works,* edited by Eugène Vinaver, XIII–XV. Oxford: Oxford University Press, 1971.

Cederstolpe, Theodor von. *Sagen aus Luxemburg.* Luxembourg: G. Michaelis, 1843.

Challoner, Richard, trans. *The Holy Bible: translated from the Latin Vulgate.* Rockford, IL: Tan Books, 1989.

Chaucer, Geoffrey. *The Romaunt of the Rose.* In *The Riverside Chaucer,* edited by Larry G. Benson, 685–767. Boston: Houghton Mifflin, 1987.

Chaucer, Geoffrey. "The Wife of Bath's Tale." In *The Riverside Chaucer,* edited by Larry D. Benson, 105–122. Boston: Houghton-Mifflin, 1987.

Chestre, Thomas. "Sir Launfal." In *Middle English Romances,* edited by Stephen H. A. Shepherd, 190–218. New York: W. W. Norton, 1995.

Chypre de Lusignan, Estienne de. *Les Genealogies de soixante et sept tresnobles et tresillustres maisons, partie de France, parti estrágeres, yssuës de Meroüée, fils de Theodoric 2. Roy d'Austrasie, Bourgongne, &c. Auec le blason & declaration des armoyries que chacune maison porte.* Paris: Guillaume Le Noir, 1586.

Delacroix, Claire. "An Elegy for Melusine." In *To Weave a Web of Magic,* 269–362. New York: Berkley, 2004.

Eine wunderschöne Historie von dem gehörnten Siegfried. Braunschweig, Leipzig: np, 1726.

"First Seiþ Bois." In *The Earliest Advocates of the English Bible: The Text of the Medieval Debate*, edited by Mary Dove, 143–149. Exeter: University of Exeter Press, 2010.

Friedmann, Richard. *Festspill fir de Millenaire vun der Stât Letzebuerg.* Unpublished, 1963, Archives Nationales du Luxembourg DH 098.

Frischmuth, Barbara. "Otter." In *Undinenzauber: Geschichten und Gedichte von Nixen, Nymphen, und anderen Wasserfrauen*, edited by Frank R. Max, 400–410. Stuttgart: Reclam Verlag, 1991.

Froissart, Jean. *Oeuvres de Froissart.* Edited by Kervyn de Lettenhove. 25 vols. Brussels: V. Devaux, 1867–1877.

Geoffrey of Auxerre. "Sermo XV." In *Super Apocalypsim*, edited by Ferruccio Gastaldelli, 186–7. Rome: Edizione di Storia e Letteratura, 1970.

Gervase of Tilbury. *Otia imperialia: Recreation for an Emperor.* Edited and translated by S. E. Banks and J. W. Binns. Oxford: Clarendon Press, 2002.

Goethe, Johann Wolfgang von. *The Collected Works: From My Life. Parts One-Three.* Edited and translated by Thomas P. Saine and Jeffrey L. Sammons. Princeton, NJ: Princeton University Press, 1987.

Goethe, Johann Wolfgang von. *Sämtliche Werke: Briefe, Tagebücher, und Gespräche*, edited by Henrik Birus, et al. 40 vols. Frankfurt am Main: Deutscher Klassiker Verlag, 1998.

Gredt, Nicolas. *Sagenschatz des Luxemburger Landes.* Luxembourg: V. Bück, 1883. Reprint, Luxembourg: Institut Grand-Ducal, 2005.

Gregory, Philippa. *The White Queen.* New York: Simon & Schuster, 2009.

Haldane, Charlotte. *Melsuine, or Devil Take Her! A Romantic Novel.* London: Arthur Barker, 1936.

Heger, Gerd, Jhemp Hoscheit, Paula de Lemos, and Véronique Schons. *Mélusina.* Echternach: Phi, 1999.

Heitz, Paul and Frank Ritter. *Versuch einer Zusammenstellung der deutschen Volksbücher des 15. und 16. Jahrhunders nebst deren späteren Ausgaben und Literatur.* Strasburg: Heitz, 1924.

Herber, Marina and Lex Roth. *Melusina.* Luxembourg: Editions Binsfeld, 2014.

Herrad of Hohenbourg. *Hortus deliciarum.* Edited by Rosalie Green, Michael Evans, Christine Bischoff, and Michael Curschmann. 2 vols. London: Warburg Institute, 1979.

Isidore of Seville. *Etymologiae XI.* Edited and translated by Fabio Gasti. Paris: Les Belles Lettres, 2010.

Lacy, Norris J., ed. *Lancelot-Grail: The Old French Arthurian Vulgate and Post-Vulgate in Translation*, 5 vols. Oxford: Garland, 1993–6.

Lüthi, Max. *Märchen.* Stuttgart: Metzler, 1968.

Machaut, Guillaume de. *Le Confort d'Ami*. Edited and translated by Robert Barton Palmer. London: Garland, 1992.

Machaut, Guillaume de. *Le Jugement du roy de Behaigne*. Edited by James I. Wimsatt and William W. Kibler. Athens, GA: University of Georgia Press, 1988.

Malory, Thomas. *The Works of Sir Thomas Malory*. Edited by Eugène Vinaver, revised by P. J. C. Field. 3rd ed. 3 vols. Oxford: Clarendon Press, 1990.

Man & Frau & Animal. Directed by VALIE EXPORT. 1973. Vienna: Arge Index, 2004.

Map, Walter. *De nugis curialium: Courtiers' Trifles*. Edited by M. R. James, revised by C. N. L Brooke and R. A. B. Mynors. Oxford: Clarendon Press, 1983.

Micha, Alexandre, ed. *Lancelot: Roman en Prose du XIIIe Siècle*. 9 vols. Geneva: Droz, 1978–83.

Mirk, John. *Mirk's Festial: A Collection of Homilies*. Edited by Theodor Erbe. Early English Text Society ES. 96, vol. 1. London: Kegan Paul, 1905.

Monmouth, Geoffrey of. *Life of Merlin: Vita Merlini*. Translated by Basil Clarke. Cardiff: University of Wales Press, 1973.

Monmouth, Geoffrey of. *The History of the Kings of Britain: An Edition and Translation of the* De gestis Britonum (Historia Regum Britanniae). Edited by Michael D. Reeve, translated by Neil Wright. Woodbridge: The Boydell Press, 2007.

Ovid. *Metamorphoses: A New Translation*. Translated by A. D. Melville. Oxford: Oxford University Press, 1998.

Paracelsus. "A Book on Nymphs, Sylphs, Pygmies, and Salamanders, and on the Other Spirits." Translated by Henry E. Sigerist. In *Four Treatises of Theophrastus von Hohenheim, Called Paracelsus*, edited by Henry E. Sigerist, 223–253. Baltimore: Johns Hopkins Press, 1941.

Phillips, Helen, ed. *The Awntyrs off Arthure at the Terne Wathelyne*. Lancaster: Lancaster Modern Spelling Texts, 1988.

Pope Osborne, Mary. *Mermaid Tales from Around the World*. New York: Scholastic, 1993.

Pröhle, Heinrich. *Rheinlands schönsten Sagen und Geschichten*. Berlin: Verlag Meidinger, 1886.

Raymo, Robert R., Ruth E. Sternglantz, and Elaine E. Whitaker, eds. *The Mirroure of the Worlde: A Middle English Translation of the Miroir de Monde*. Toronto: University of Toronto Press, 2003.

Rouen, Étienne de. *Le Dragon Normand et autres poèmes d'Étienne de Rouen*. Edited by M. H. Ormot. Rouen: Société de l'histoire de Normandie, 1884.

Shakespeare, William. "The Tragedy of King Lear (1610): The Folio Text." In *The Oxford Shakespeare: The Complete Works*, 2d ed., edited by John Jowett, William Montgomery, Gary Taylor, and Stanley Wells, 1153–1184. Oxford: Oxford University Press, 1998.

Shepherd, Stephen H. A., ed. "The Awntyrs Off Arthure at the Terne Wathelyne." In *Middle English Romances*, 219–43. New York: W. W. Norton, 1995.

Silverstein, Theodore. *Visio Sancti Pauli: The History of the Apocalypse in Latin Together with Nine Texts*. London: Christophers, 1935.

"Sir Degaré." In *The Middle English Breton Lays*, edited by Anne Laskaya and Eve Salisbury, 101–129. Kalamazoo, MI: Medieval Institute Publications, 1995.

"Sir Gowther." In *The Middle English Breton Lays*, edited by Anne Laskaya and Eve Salisbury, 274–295. Kalamazoo, MI: Medieval Institute Publications, 1995.

Trevisa, John. "Dialogue Between the Lord and the Clerk on Translation (Extract) and the Epistle to Thomas, Lord Berkeley, on the Translation of Higden's Polychronicon." In *The Idea of the Vernacular*, edited by Jocelyn Wogan-Browne, et al., 130–138. University Park: Pennsylvania State University Press, 1999.

Valentinus, Basilius. *Les douze clefs de philosophie de frere Basile Valentin [...] plus l'Azoth, ou, Le moyen de faire l'or cachû des philosophes: traduction françoise*. Edited by Jean Gobille and Clovis Hesteau Nuisemen. Paris: Pierre Moët, 1660.

Vecerius, Conrad. *De rebus gestis impertoris Henrici VII libellus*. Hanau: Secerius, 1531.

Weber, R., et al., eds. *Biblia sacra iuxta vulgata versionem*. 3rd ed. Stuttgart: Deutsche Bibelgesellschaft, 1983.

Welter, Nicolas. *Aus alten Tagen: Balladen und Romanzen aus Luxemburgs Sage und Geschichte*. Luxembourg: M. Huss, 1900.

Welter, Nicolas. *Siegfried und Melusine*. Berlin: Concordia, 1900.

Windisch, Ernst, ed. *Irische Texte mit Wörterbuch*. 4 vols. Leipzig: Hirzel, 1880.

Woolverton, Linda. *Maleficent*. Directed by Robert Stromberg. Burbank, CA: Walt Disney Pictures, 2014.

Yardley, Edward. "Melusine." In *Melusine and Other Poems*, 1–13. London: Longmans, Green, and Co., 1867.

Zachariä, Friedrich Wilhelm. *Zwei schöne Mährlein als 1) von der schönen Melusinen: einer Meerfey, 2) von einer untreuen Braut, die der Teufel hohlen sollen*. Leipzig: In der Jubilatemesse, 1772.

Zittau, Peter of. *Chronicon Aulae Regiae*. Edited by Josef Emler. Fontes Rerum Bohemicarum 4. Prague: Nadání Františka Palackého, 1882.

Secondary Sources

Abulafia, David. *The Discovery of Mankind: Atlantic Encounters in the Age of Columbus*. New Haven, CT: Yale University Press, 2008.

Aguirre Castro, Mercedes. "Scylla: Hideous Monster or Femme Fatale? A Case of Contradiction between Literary and Artistic Evidence." *Cuadernos de Filología Clásica: Estudios griegos e indoeuropeos* 12 (2002): 319–328.

Ahmed, Sara. *The Promise of Happiness*. Durham: Duke University Press, 2010.

Alban, Gillian M. E. *Melusine the Serpent Goddess in A.S. Byatt's* Possession *and in Myth*. Lanham: Lexington Books, 2003.

Alban, Gillian M. E. "The Serpent Goddess Melusine: From Cursed Snake to Mary's Shield." In *The Survival of Myth: Innovation, Singularity and Alterity*, edited by Paul Hardwick and David Kennedy, 23–43. Newcastle-upon-Tyne: Cambridge Scholars Publishing, 2010.

Almqvist, Bo. "The Mélusine Legend in Irish Folk Tradition." In *Mélusines continentales et insulaires: actes du colloque international tenu les 27 et 28 mars 1997 à l'Université Paris XII et au Collège des Irlandais*, edited by Jeanne-Marie Boivin and Proinsias MacCana, 263–279. Paris: Champion, 1999.

Andersen, Jørgen. *The Witch on the Wall: Medieval Erotic Sculpture in the British Isles* Copenhagen: Rosenkilde and Bagger, 1977.

Apel, Friedmar. *Die Zaubergärten der Phantasie: Zur Theorie und Geschichte des Kunst-märchens*. Heidelberg: Winter Universitätsverlag, 1978.

Ashton, John. *Romances of Chivalry: Told and Illustrated in Fac-Simile*. London: T. Fisher Unwin, 1890.

Autrand, Françoise. *Jean de Berry: L'art et le pouvoir*. Paris: Fayard, 2000.

Bahr, Ehrhard. *The Novel as Archive: The Genesis, Reception, and Criticism of Goethe's* Wilhelm Meisters Wanderjahre. Columbia: Camden, 1998.

Ball, Phillip. *The Devil's Doctor: Paracelsus and the World of Renaissance Magic*. New York: Farrar, Strauss, and Giroux, 2006.

Baquedano, Laura. "Toulouse, 14 juillet 1489: la première impression de l'*Historia de la linda Melosina*." *Atalaya: Revue d'études médiévales romanes* 13 (2013). Accessed August 29, 2017. http://atalaya.revues.org/1140.

Baquedano, Laura. "'Paz, amor e buena ventura': Les mots, la sagesse et la subtilité des femmes au service de la paix dans *l'Historia de la linda Melosina* à la fin du XVe siè-cle." *E-Spania* 20, n. 20 (February 2015). DOI: 10.4000/e-spania.24089.

Baring-Gould, Sabine. *Curious Myths of the Middle Ages*. Boston: Roberts Brothers, 1894.

Bartlett, Robert. "Medieval and Modern Concepts of Race and Ethnicity." *Journal of Medieval and Early Modern Studies* 31, no. 1 (2001): 39–56.

Basse-Moûturie, Louis le Chevalier l'Evêque de la. *Itinéraire du Luxembourg ger-manique, ou voyage historique et pittoresque dans le Grand-Duché*. Luxembourg: V. Hoffmann, 1844. Reprint, Luxembourg: J.-P. Krippler-Muller, 1980.

Batery, Jehan de. *Li dis des VIII blasons*. Edited by Adolf Tobler. *Jahrbuch für romanische und englische Literatur* 5 (1864): 211–225.

Baudot, Jules Léon. *Les Princesses Yolande et les Ducs de Bar de la famille des Valois*. Paris: Picard, 1900.

Beaune, Colette. "L'utilisation politique du mythe troyen à la fin du Moyen Âge." *Publications de l'École française de Rome* 80/1 (1982): 331–355.

Beaune, Colette. *Naissance de la nation France*. Paris: Gallimard, 1993.

Beauvoir, Simone de. *The Second Sex*. Translated by Constance Borde and Sheila Malovany-Chevallier. New York: Knopf, 2010.

Becker, Gabriele. *Aus der Zeit der Verzweiflung: Zur Genese und Aktualität des Hexenbildes*. Frankfurt am Main: Suhrkamp, 1977.

Beemyn, Brett and Mickey Eliason. *Queer Studies: A Lesbian, Gay, Bisexual, and Transgender Anthology*. New York: New York University Press, 1996.

Benwell, Gwen and Arthur Waugh. *Sea Enchantress: The Mermaid and her Kin*. New York: Citadel Press, 1961.

Bernardini, Silvio. *The Serpent and the Siren: Sacred and Enigmatic Images in Tuscan Rural Churches*. Translated by Kate Singleton. Siena: San Quirico d'Oricia, 2000.

Bernau, Anke. "Gender and Sexuality." In *A Companion to Middle English Hagiography*, edited by Sarah Salih, 104–121. Woodbridge: D. S. Brewer, 2006.

Berry, Céline. "Les Luxembourg-Ligny, un grand lignage noble de la fin du Moyen Âge." PhD diss., Université Paris Est Créteil, 2011.

Bertholet, Jean. *Histoire Ecclésiastique et Civile du Duché de Luxembourg et Comté de Chiny*. 8 vols. Luxembourg: André Chevalier, 1741–1743. Reprint, Brussels: Ed. culture et civilisation, 1973, and Bastogne: Éd. Musée en Piconrue, 1997.

Bettelheim, Bruno. "Fairy Tales as Ways of Knowing." In *Essays on Märchen in Psychology, Society, and Literature*, edited by Michael M. Metzger and Katharina Mommsen, 11–21. Bern: Peter Lang, 1981.

Bez, Martin. *Goethes Wilhelm Meisters Wanderjahre: Aggregat, Archiv, Archivroman*. Berlin: De Gruyter, 2013.

Bildhauer, Bettina and Robert Mills, eds. *The Monstrous Middle Ages*. Toronto: University of Toronto Press, 2003.

Binsfeld, Franz. *Hémechtslant, meng Gottesburech: Rosengen àus zèit a geshicht*. Luxembourg: Worré-Mertens, 1944.

Bishop, Paul. *Analytic Psychology and German Classical Aesthetics: Goethe, Schiller, and Jung*. Vol. 2. New York: Routledge, 2009.

Bloomer, Kent and Charles W. Moore. *Body, Memory, and Architecture*. New Haven, CT: Yale University Press, 1977.

Boivin, Jeanne-Marie and Proinsias McCana, eds. *Mélusines continentales et insulaires: Actes du colloque international tenu les 27 et 28 mars 1997 à l'Université Paris XII et au Collège des Irlandais*. Paris: Champion, 1999.

Bonneville, Françoise. *The Book of the Bath*. Translated by Jane Brenton. New York: Rizzoli, 1998.

Boulenger, George Albert. *The Snakes of Europe*. 1913. Reprint, London: Forgotten Books, 2013.

Boulton, D'A. Jonathan D. "The Order of the Golden Fleece and the Creation of Burgundian National Identity." In *The Ideology of Burgundy*, edited by D'A. Jonathan D. Boulton and Jan R. Veenstra, 21–97. Leiden: Brill, 2006.

Bouquin, Hélène. "Éditions et adaptations de l'*Histoire de Mélusine* de Jean d'Arras (XVe-XIXe siècle): Les aventures d'un roman médiéval." PhD diss., École nationale des chartes, 2000.

Boyle, Nicolas. *Goethe: The Poet and the Age.* Vol. 1. Oxford: Oxford University Press, 1991.

Brooks, Peter. *Body Work: Objects of Desire in Modern Narrative.* Cambridge, MA: Harvard University Press, 1993.

Brown, Jane K. *Goethe's Cyclical Narratives,* Die Unterhaltungen deutscher Ausgewanderten *and* Wilhelm Meisters Wanderjahre. Chapel Hill: University of North Carolina, 1975.

Brownlee, Kevin. "Melusine's Hybrid Body and the Poetics of Metamorphosis." *Yale French Studies* 86 (1994): 18–38.

Bruckner, Matilda Tomaryn. "Natural and Unnatural Woman: Melusine Inside and Out." In *Founding Feminisms in Medieval Studies: Essays in Honor of E. Jane Burns,* edited by Laine E. Doggett and Daniel E. O'Sullivan, 21–31. Cambridge, UK: D. S. Brewer, 2016.

Burns, E. Jane. "Magical Politics from Poitou to Armenia: Mélusine, Jean de Berry, and the Eastern Mediterranean." *Journal of Medieval and Early Modern Studies* 43, no. 2 (2013): 275–301.

Burns, E. Jane. "A Snake-Tailed Woman: Hybridity and Dynasty in the *Roman de Mélusine*." In *From Beasts to Souls: Gender and Embodiment in Medieval Europe,* edited by E. Jane Burns and Peggy McCracken, 185–220. Notre Dame: University of Notre Dame, 2013.

Buschinger, Danielle. "Thüring von Ringoltingen, adaptateur du roman français de Coudrette." In *550 Jahre deutsche Melusine – Coudrette und Thüring von Ringoltingen. Beiträge der wissenschaftlichen Tagung der Universitäten Bern und Lausanne vom August 2006,* edited by André Schnyder and Jean-Claude Mühlethaler, 47–62. Bern: Peter Lang, 2008.

Butler, Judith. *Bodies That Matter: On the Discursive Limits of "Sex."* New York: Routledge, 1993.

Butterfield, Ardis. *The Familiar Enemy: Chaucer, Language, and Nation in the Hundred Years War.* Oxford: Oxford University Press, 2009.

Canon, Christopher. "From Literacy to Literature: Elementary Learning and the Middle English Poet." *PMLA* 129, no. 3 (2014): 349–364.

Cazelles, Raymond. *Jean l'Aveugle: Comte de Luxembourg, Roi de Bohême.* Bourges: Tardy, 1947.

Chamberlain, Jonathan. *Chinese Gods.* Hong Kong: Long Island, 1983.

Charles, Leen and Marie Christine Laleman. *Het Gent Boek.* Zwolle Waanders, 2006.

Ch'en, Kenneth Kuan Shêng. *Buddhism in China: A Historical Survey.* Princeton, NJ: Princeton University Press, 1964.

Cirlot, Jean. *Dictionary of Symbols*, 2nd ed. Translated by Jack Sage. Mineola: Dover Publications, 1971. Reprint 2002.

Clarke, Katherine. "Purgatory, Punishment, and the Discourse of Holy Widowhood in the High and Later Middle Ages." *Journal of the History of Sexuality* 15, no. 2 (2007): 169–203.

Classen, Albrecht. *Childhood in the Middle Ages and the Renaissance: The Results of a Paradigm Shift in the History of Mentality*. Berlin: De Gruyter, 2005.

Classen, Albrecht. *The Forest in Medieval German Literature: Ecocritical Readings From a Historical Perspective*. Lanham: Lexington Books, 2015.

Classen, Albrecht. "Love and Fear of the Foreign: Thüring von Ringoltingen's *Melusine* (1456). A Xenological Analysis." *Daphnis* 33, no. 1–2 (2004): 97–113.

Classen, Albrecht. "The Monster Outside and Within: Medieval Literary Reflection on Ethical Epistemology from *Beowulf* to Marie de France, the *Nibelungenlied*, and Thüring von Ringoltingen's *Melusine*." *Neohelicon* 40 (2013): 521–42.

Clemens, Evamarie. *Luxemburg-Böhmen, Wittelsbach-Bayern, Habsburg-Österreich und ihre genealogischen Mythen im Vergleich*. Trier: Trierer Wissenschaftlicher Verlag, 2001.

Clier-Colombani, Françoise. "Le beau et le laid dans le *Roman de Mélusine*." In *Le beau et le laid au Moyen Âge*, 81–103. Aix-en-Provence: Presses universitaires de Provence, 2000.

Clier-Colombani, Françoise. *La fée Mélusine au Moyen Âge: Images, mythes, et symboles*. Paris: Le Léopard d'Or, 1991.

Cohen, Jeffrey Jerome. *Hybridity, Identity, and Monstrosity in Medieval Britain: On Difficult Middles*. New York: Palgrave MacMillan, 2007.

Cohen, Jeffrey Jerome. *Monster Theory: Reading Culture*. Minneapolis: University of Minnesota Press, 1996.

Colwell, Tania M. "Mélusine: Ideal Mother or Inimitable Monster?" In *Love, Marriage, and Family Ties in the Later Middle Ages*, edited by Isabel Davis, Miriam Müller, and Sarah Rees Jones, 181–203. Turnhout: Brepols Publishers, 2003.

Colwell, Tania M. "The Middle English Melusine: Evidence for an Early Printed Edition of the Prose Romance in the Bodleian Library." *The Journal of the Early Book Society for the Study of Manuscripts and Printing History* 17 (2014): 254–82.

Cooper, Helen. *The English Romance in Time: Transforming Motifs from Geoffrey of Monmouth to the Death of Shakespeare*. Oxford: Oxford University Press, 2004.

Cooper, Helen. "Introduction." In *Christianity and Romance in Medieval England*, edited by Rosalind Field, Phillipa Hardman, and Michelle Sweeney, XIII–XXI. Cambridge, UK: D. S. Brewer, 2010.

Corfis, Ivy A. "Beauty, Deformity, and the Fantastic in the *Historia de la linda Melosina*." *Hispanic Review* 55 (Spring 1987): 181–193.

Corfis, Ivy A. "Empire and Romance: *Historia de la linda Melosina.*" *Neophilologus* 82 (1998): 559–575.

Cowling, David. *Building the Text: Architecture as a Metaphor in Late Medieval and Early Modern France.* New York: Oxford University Press, 1998.

Creed, Barbara. *The Monstrous-Feminine: Film, Feminism, Psychoanalysis.* New York: Routledge, 1993.

Crofts, Thomas H. *Malory's Contemporary Audience: The Social Reading of Romance in Late Medieval England.* Cambridge, UK: D. S. Brewer, 2006.

Darwin, Gregory. "On Mermaids, Meroveus, and Melusine: Reading the Irish Seal Woman and Mélusine as Origin Legend." *Folklore* 126, no. 2 (2015): 123–41.

Daston, Lorainne. "The Nature of Nature in Early Modern Europe." *Configurations* 6, no. 2 (1998): 149–172.

Debaene, Luc. *De Nederlandse volksboeken: Ontstaan en geschiedenis van de Nederlandse prozaromans, gedrukt tussen 1475 en 1540.* Antwerp: De Vlijt, 1951. Reprint, Hulst, 1977.

De la Fontaine, Gaspard-Théodore-Ignace. "Légendes Luxembourgeoises." *PSH* 6 (1850): 115–120.

Delcourt, Denyse. "Métamorphose, mystère et féminité: lecture du *Roman de Mélusine* par Jean d'Arras." *Le moyen français* 33 (1993): 85–106.

De Rachewiltz, Siegfried. *De Sirenibus: An Inquiry into Sirens from Homer to Shakespeare.* New York: Garland Publishing, 1987.

Denison, Christina Pollock. *The Paracelsus of Robert Browning.* New York: The Baker and Taylor Company, 1911.

Derrida, Jacques. *The Animal That Therefore I Am.* Translated by Marie-Louise Mallet. New York: Fordham University Press, 2008.

Désaivre, Léo. "Le mythe de la mère Lusine (Meurlusine, Merlusine, Mellusigne, Mellusine, Mélusine, Méleusine). Étude critique et bibliographique." In *Mémoires de la Société de statistique, sciences, lettres, et arts du département des Deux-Sèvres.* 2nd series. Vol. 2, no. 1 (1882): 81–302.

Deyermond, Alan D. "La *Historia de la linda Melosina*: Two Spanish Versions of a French Romance." In *Medieval Hispanic Studies. Presented to Rita Hamilton*, edited by Alan D. Deyermond, 57–65. London: Tamesis, 1976.

Deyermond, Alan D. "The Lost Genre of Medieval Spanish Literature." *Hispanic Review* 43 (1975): 231–259.

Dodds, Jerrilyn. *Architecture and Ideology in Early Medieval Spain.* University Park: Pennsylvania State University Press, 1989.

Douglas, Mary. *Purity and Danger: An Analysis of Concepts of Pollution and Taboo.* London: Routledge & Kegan Paul, 1966.

Dubost, Francis. *Aspects fantastiques de la littérature médiévale (XIIe-XIIIe siècles): L'Autre, l'Ailleurs, l'autrefois.* Paris: Champion, 1991.

Duijvestein, Bob. "Der niederländische Prosaroman von Meluzine: eine Orienterung." In *Melusine: Actes du Colloque du Centre d'Études Médiévales de l'Université de Picardie, 13–14 janvier 1996*, edited by Danielle Buschinger and Wolfgang Spiewok, 37–50. Greifswald: Reineke-Verlag, 1996.

Dye, Ellis. *Love and Death in Goethe: One and Double*. Rochester: Camden, 2004.

Edwards, Justin D. and Rune Graulund. *Grotesque*. Abingdon, UK: Routledge, 2013.

Erler, Mary C. and Maryanne Kowaleski, eds. *Women and Power in the Middle Ages*. Athens, GA: University of Georgia Press, 1988.

Ewers, Hans-Heino. "Nachwort: Das Kunstmärchen – eine moderne Erzählgattung." In *Zauberei im Herbste: Deutsche Kunstmärchen von Wieland bis Hofmannsthal*, edited by Hans-Heino Ewers, 647–80. Stuttgart: Reclam, 1987.

Eichhorn, Peter. *Idee und Erfahrung im Spätwerk Goethes*. Munich: Alber, 1971.

Eygun, François. *Ce qu'on peut savoir de Mélusine et de son iconographie*. Poitiers: Oudin, 1951. Reprint, Puisaux: Pardès, 1987.

Fang, Chengpei. "雷峰塔傳奇." In 皖人戲曲選刊：方成培卷, ed. Dongliang Jia, 1–166. Hefei: Huangshan Shushe, 2008.

Faral, Edmond. "La Queue de Poisson des Sirènes." *Romania* 74 (1953): 433–506.

Feng, Menglong. "白娘子永鎮雷峰塔." In 馮夢龍全集, ed. Tongxian Wei, 418–446. Nanjing: Fenghuang, 1993.

Ferlampin-Acher, Christine. *Merveille et topique merveilleuse dans les romans médiévaux*. Paris: Champion, 2003.

Fernández-Armesto, Felipe. *The Canary Islands After the Conquest. The Making of a Colonial Society in the Early Sixteenth Century*. New York: Oxford University Press, 1992.

Ferrante, Joan M. "Public Postures and Private Maneuvers: Roles Medieval Women Play." In *Women and Power in the Middle Ages*, edited by Mary C. Erler and Maryanne Kowaleski, 213–29. Athens, GA: University of Georgia Press, 1988.

Ferrante, Joan M. *Woman as Image in Medieval Literature: From the Twelfth Century to Dante*. Durham, NC: Labyrinth, 1985.

Fetterly, Judith. *The Resisting Reader: A Feminist Approach to American Fiction*. Bloomington: Indiana University Press, 1978.

Fink, Gonthier-Lois. "*Die neue Melusine*: Goethes maieutisches Spiel mit dem Leser." *Euphorion* 107 (2013): 7–43.

Fisher, Sheila and Janet E. Halley, eds. *Seeking the Woman in Late Medieval and Early Renaissance Writing*. Knoxville, TN: University of Tennessee Press, 1989.

Flores, Nona C. "'Effigies Amicitiae … Veritas Inimicitiae': Antifeminism in the Iconography of the Woman-Headed Serpent in Medieval and Renaissance Art and Literature." In *Animals in the Middle Ages*, edited by Nona C. Flores, 167–95. New York: Garland, 1996.

Florschuetz, Angela. *Marking Maternity in Middle English Romance: Mothers, Identity, and Contamination*. New York: Palgrave Macmillan, 2014.

Frangos, Maria. "The Shame of All Her Kind': A Genealogy of Female Monstrosity and Metamorphosis from the Middle Ages Through Early Modernity." PhD diss., University of California – Santa Cruz, 2008. Ann Arbor: UMI, 2008.

Freiberg, Jack. *Bramante's Tempietto, the Roman Renaissance, and the Spanish Crown.* Cambridge, UK: Cambridge University Press, 2014.

Friedman, John Block. *The Monstrous Races in Medieval Art and Thought.* Cambridge, MA: Harvard University Press, 1981.

Fries, Maureen. "Female Heroes, Heroines, and Counter-Heroes: Images of Women in the Arthurian Tradition." In *Popular Arthurian Traditions*, edited by Sally K. Slocum, 5–17. Madison, WI: Bowling Green University Popular Press, 1992.

Frontón Simón, Miguel Àngel. "*La historia de la linda Melosina*: Edicion y estudio de los textos españoles." PhD diss., Universidad Complutense de Madrid, 1996.

Fröschle, Hartmut. *Goethes Verhältnis zur Romantik.* Würzburg: Königshausen & Neumann, 2002.

Frueh, Joanna. *Monster Beauty: Building the Body of Love.* Berkeley, CA: University of California Press, 2001.

Fox-Davies, Arthur Charles. *The Art of Heraldry: An Encyclopedia of Armory.* London: T. C. and E. C. Jack, 1904.

Gaffney, Phyllis. *Constructions of Childhood and Youth in Old French Narrative.* Burlington, VT: Ashgate, 2011.

Galderisi, Claudio. "Mélusine et Geoffroi à la grand dent: Apories diégétiques et réécriture romanesque." *Cahiers de recherches médiévales* 2 (1996): 73–84.

Gallagher, David. *Metamorphosis: Transformations of the Body and the Influence of Ovid's* Metamorphoses *on Germanic Literature of the Nineteenth and Twentieth Centuries.* Amsterdam: Rodopi, 2009.

Gardiner, Eileen, ed. *Medieval Visions of Heaven and Hell: A Sourcebook.* New York: Garland Medieval Bibliographies, 1993.

Gardner, Edmund G. *The Arthurian Legend in Italian Literature.* London: J. M. Dent & Sons, 1930.

Gaullier-Bougassas, Catherine. "La fée Présine: une figure maternelle ambiguë aux origines de l'écriture romanesque." In *550 Jahre deutsche Melusine – Coudrette und Thüring von Ringoltingen. Beiträge der wissenschaftlichen Tagung der Universitäten Bern und Lausanne vom August 2006*, edited by André Schnyder and Jean-Claude Mühlethaler, 111–128. Bern: Peter Lang, 2008.

Gaullier-Bougassas, Catherine. *La Tentation de l'Orient dans le roman médiéval: sur l'imaginaire médiéval de l'Autre.* Paris: Champion, 2003.

Geary, Patrick J. *Women at the Beginning: Origin Myths from the Amazons to the Virgin Mary.* Princeton, NJ: Princeton University Press, 2006.

Gernet, Jacques. *A History of Chinese Civilization.* 2nd ed. Cambridge, UK: Cambridge University Press, 1996.

Geulen, Hans. "Goethes Kunstmärchen *Der neue Paris* und *Die neue Melusine*: Ihre po-etologischen Imaginationen und Speilformen." *Deutsche Vierteljahrsschrift für Literaturwissenschaft und Geistesgeschichte* 59, no. 1 (1985): 79–93.

Gilbert, Jane. "Unnatural Mothers and Monstrous Children in *The King of Tars* and *Sir Gowther*." In *Medieval Women: Texts and Contexts in Late Medieval Britain: Essays for Felicity Riddy*, edited by Jocelyn Wogan-Browne, et al., 329–44. Turnhout, Belgium: Brepols, 2000.

Giudicini, Giovanna. "The Political and Cultural Influence of James V's Court on the Decoration of the King's Fountain in Linlithgow Palace." In *Art and Identity: Visual Culture, Politics, and Religion in the Middle Ages*, edited by Sandra Cardarelli, Emily Jane Anderson, and John Richards, 167–192. Newcastle-upon-Tyne: Cambridge Scholars Publishing, 2011.

Goodman, Barbara A. "Women's Wounds in Middle English Romances: An Exploration of Defilement, Disfigurement, and a Society in Disrepair." In *Wounds and Wound Repair in Medieval Culture*, edited by Larissa Tracy and Kelly DeVries, 544–71. Leiden: Brill, 2015.

Goodrich, Peter H. "The Erotic Merlin." *Arthuriana* 10 (2000): 94–115.

Green, Richard Firth. *Elf Queens and Holy Friars: Fairy Beliefs and the Medieval Church*. Philadelphia: University of Pennsylvania Press, 2016.

Gray, Ronald D. *Goethe the Alchemist. 1952*. Reprint, Cambridge, UK: Cambridge University Press, 2010.

Gregory, Philippa, David Baldwin, and Michael Jones. *The Women of the Cousin's War: The Duchess, the Queen, and the King's Mother*. New York: Touchstone, 2011.

Griffin, Miranda. "The Beastly and the Courtly in Medieval Tales of Transformation: *Bisclavret, Melion*, and *Mélusine*." In *The Beautiful and the Monstrous: Essays in French Literature, Thought, and Culture*, edited by Amaleena Damlé and Aurélie L'Hostis, 139–150. Oxford: Peter Lang, 2010.

Gu, Shenzi and Yongruo Xue. "李黃." In 博异志.集异记. Shanghai: Zhonghua Shuju, 1980.

Hahn, Thomas. "The Difference the Middle Ages Makes: Color and Race before the Modern World." *Journal of Medieval and Early Modern Studies* 31, no. 1 (2001): 1–37.

Hanan, Patrick. "The Early Chinese Short Story: A Critical Theory in Outline." *Harvard Journal of Asiatic Studies* 27 (1967): 168–207.

Harf-Lancner, Laurence. *Les Fées au Moyen Âge: Morgane et Mélusine: la naissance des fées*. Geneva: Droz, 1984.

Harf-Lancner, Laurence. "L'illustration du *Roman de Mélusine* de Jean d'Arras dans les éditions du XVe et du XVIe siècle." In *Le livre et l'image en France au XVIe siècle*, edited by Nicole Cazauran, *Cahiers V.L. Saulnier* 6, 29–55. Paris: Presses de l'Ecole normale supérieure, 1989.

Harf-Lancner, Laurence. *Métamorphose et bestiaire fantastique*. Paris: Collection de l'Ecole Normale Supérieure de Jeunes Filles, 1985.

Harf-Lancner, Laurence. "La serpente et le sanglier: les manuscrits enluminés des deux romans français de Mélusine." *Le Moyen Âge: Revue d'histoire et de philologie* 101, no. 1 (1995): 65–87.

Hassig, Debra. *Medieval Bestiaries: Text, Image, Ideology*. Cambridge, UK: Cambridge University Press, 1995.

Havelock, Christine Mitchell. *The Aphrodite of Knidos and Her Successors: A Historical Review of the Female Nude in Greek Art*. Ann Arbor: University of Michigan Press, 1995.

Hean-Tatt, Ong. *Chinese Animal Symbolism*. Selangor: Pelanduk Publications, 1993.

Hess, Erika E. *Medieval Hybrids: Indeterminacy in Medieval and Modern French Narrative*. New York: Routledge, 2003.

Hierzig, Sus. *Zou Lëtzebuerg stong d'Sigfriddsschlass: Eng al Geschicht nei erzielt a mat Biller*. Echternach: Phi, 1983.

Hillenbrand Varela, Sarah. "Origins of Misfortune: Sympathetic Magic and the Transference of Animality in Thüring von Ringoltingen's *Melusine* (1456)." *Neophilologus* 99, no. 2 (2015): 271–285.

Hillman, Richard and Pauline Ruberry-Blanc, eds. *Female Transgression in Early Modern Britain: Literary and Historical Explorations*. Burlington, VT: Ashgate, 2014.

Hirsch, Marianne. "Mothers and Daughters." *Signs* 7 (1981): 200–222.

Hodges, Kenneth. "Swords and Sorceresses: The Chivalry of Malory's Nyneve." *Arthuriana* 12 (2002): 78–96.

Holbrook, S. E. "Nymue, the Chief Lady of the Lake in Malory's *Le Morte Darthur*." *Speculum* 53 (1978): 761–77.

Holford-Strevens, Leofranc. "Sirens in Antiquity and the Middle Ages." In *The Music of the Sirens*, edited by Linda Phyllis Austern and Inna Naroditskaya, 16–51. Bloomington: Indiana University Press, 2006.

Hong, Pian, and Huasan Zuo, ed. "西湖三塔记."In 中国古代通俗小说集成：清平山堂话本.风流悟, 17–24. Beijing: Huaxia, 2012.

Hosington, Brenda. "Melusines de France." In *A Wyf Ther Was: Essays in Honour of Paule Mertens-Fonck*, edited by Juliette Dor, 199–208. Liège: Dép. d'anglais, Université de Liège, 1992.

Hosington, Brenda. "From Theory to Practice." *Forum for Modern Language Studies* 35 (1999): 408–420.

Hubrath, Margarete. "Eva: Der Sündenfall und seine Folgen im Mittelalter und in der Frühen Neuzeit." In *Verführer, Schurken, Magier*, edited by Ulrich Müller and Werner Wunderlich, 243–261. St. Gallen: UVK - Fachverlerlag für Wissenschaft und Studium, 2011.

Hudson, Anne. "The Debate on Bible Translation, Oxford 1401." *English Historical Review* 90 (1975): 1–18.

Huet, Marie-Hélène. *Monstrous Imagination*. Cambridge, MA: Harvard University Press, 1993.

Huot, Sylvia. "Dangerous Embodiments: Froissart's *Harton* and Jean d'Arras's *Melusine*." *Speculum* 78, no. 2 (2003): 400–420.

Husserl, Edmund. *Ideas: General Introduction to Pure Phenomenology. 1931.* New York: Routledge, 2002.

Hutton, Richard. "The Making of the Early Modern British Fairy Tradition." *The Historical Journal* 57, no. 4 (2014): 1135–56.

Irigaray, Luce. *This Sex Which is Not One*. Translated by Catherine Porter and Carolyn Burke. Ithaca, NY: Cornell University Press, 1985.

Jacobi, Jolande, ed. *Paracelsus: Selected Writings*. Translated by Norbert Guterman. Princeton, NJ: Princeton University Press, 1951.

Jalabert, Denise. "De l'art oriental antique à l'art roman: Recherches sur la faune et la flore romane. II. Les sirènes." *Bulletin monumental* 95 (1936): 433–71.

James, M. R. *The Western Manuscripts in the Library of Trinity College, Cambridge: A Descriptive Catalogue*. Cambridge, UK: Cambridge University Press, 1900–4.

Jenkins, Richard. *Rethinking Ethnicity: Arguments and Explorations. 1997.* London: SAGE, 2008.

Jose, Laura. "Monstrous Conceptions: Sex, Madness and Gender in Medieval Medical Texts." *Comparative Critical Studies* 5, no. 2–3 (2008): 153–163.

Jung, Carl. *Mysterium Coniunctionis*. Translated by Gerard Adher and R. F. C. Hull. Princeton, NJ: Princeton University Press, 1977.

Jung, Carl. "Paracelsus as a Spiritual Phenomenon." In *Alchemical Studies*, translated by R. F. C. Hull, 109–188. Princeton, NJ: Princeton University Press, 1967.

Kappler, Claude-Claire. *Monstres, démons, et merveilles à la fin du Moyen Âge*. Paris: Payot, 1980.

Kauder, Jean-Pierre. "La légende de Mélusine: Contribution à l'histoire de la fée poitevine." In *Gymnase Grand-Ducal d'Echternach: Programme publié à la clôture de l'année scolaire 1903–1904*, 1–66. Luxembourg: V. Bück, 1904.

Keller, Hildegard Elisabeth. "Berner Samstagsgeheimnisse: Die Vertikale als Erzählformel in der *Melusine*." *Beiträge zur Geschichte der deutschen Sprache und Literatur* 127, no. 2 (2005): 1–29.

Kelly, Douglas. "The Domestication of the Marvelous in the Melusine Romances." In *Melusine of Lusignan: Founding Fiction in Late Medieval France*, edited by Donald Maddox and Sara Sturm-Maddox, 32–47. Athens, GA: University of Georgia Press, 1996.

Kelly, Henry Ansgar. "The Metamorphoses of the Eden Serpent during the Middle Ages and Renaissance." *Viator* 1 (January 1971): 301–332.

Kieckhefer, Richard. "Erotic Magic in Medieval Europe." In *Sex in the Middle Ages*, edited by Joyce E. Salisbury, 30–55. London: Garland, 1991.

Kingshill, Sophia. *Mermaids*. Dorchester: Little Toller Books, 2015.

Klein, Peter. "Siegfried und Melusina." In *Gedichte aus dem Nachlasse*, edited by Ernst Koch, 101–122. Luxembourg: V. Bück, 1856.

Kline, Daniel T. "Medieval Children's Literature: Problems, Possibilities, Parameters." In *Medieval Literature for Children*, edited by Daniel Kline, 1–11. New York: Routledge, 2003.

Klotz, Volker. *Das Europäische Kunstmärchen: Fünfundzwanzig Kapitel seiner Geschichte von der Renaissance bis zur Moderne*. Stuttgart: Metzler, 1985.

Kmec, Sonja. "'Luxembourg: Une ville s'expose': Nouvelle exposition permanente du Musée d'histoire de la Ville de Luxembourg." *Forum* 266 (2007): 42–44.

Kmec, Sonja. "Le miroir éclaté: Essai sur la recherche mélusienne." In *Not the Girl You're Looking For: Melusina Rediscovered. Objekt+Subjekt Frau in der Kultur Luxemburgs*, edited by Danielle Roster and Renée Wagener, 17–35. Luxembourg: CID-femmes, 2010.

Koenig, Lucien. *D'Melusina-So*. Luxembourg: Letzeburger Nationalunio'n, 1937.

Kohl-Crouzet, Corinne and Maxime Blanco. *Mélusine et ses metamorphoses*. Luxembourg: Fédération Générale des Instituteurs Luxembourgeois, 2014.

Kohler, Josef. *Der Ursprung der Melusinensage: Eine ethnologische Untersuchung*. Leipzig: E. Pfeiffer, 1895.

Kok, Ina. *Woodcuts in Incunabula Printed in the Low Countries*. Houten: Hes and de Graaf, 2013.

Kozlik, Laura. "Entre Vierge et pute nationale: Regard critique sur l'iconographie de Mélusine au Luxembourg." In *Not the Girl You're Looking For: Melusina Rediscovered. Objekt+Subjekt Frau in der Kultur Luxemburgs*, edited by Danielle Roster and Renée Wagener, 39–54. Luxembourg: CID-femmes, 2010.

Kristeva, Julia. *Powers of Horror: An Essay on Abjection*. Translated by Leon S. Roudiez. New York: Columbia University Press, 1982.

Küchler-Sakellariou, Petra. "Romantisches Kunstmärchen – Über die Speilarten des Wunderbaren in 'Kunst' und 'Volks'märchen." In *Phantasie und Phantastik: neuere Studien zum Kunstmärchen und zur phantastischen Erzählung*, edited by Hans Schumacher, 43–75. Frankfurt am Main: Peter Lang, 1993.

Larrington, Carolyne. *Brothers and Sisters in Medieval European Literature*. Suffolk, UK: York Medieval Press, 2015.

Lecouteux, Claude. "La structure des légendes Mélusiniennes." *Annales Économies, Sociétés, Civilisations* 33 (1978): 294–306.

Léglu, Catherine. "Nourishing Lineage in the Earliest French Versions of the *Roman de Mélusine*." *Medium Aevum* 74, no. 1 (2005): 71–85.

Le Goff, Jacques. *The Medieval Imagination*. Translated by Arthur Goldhammer. Chicago: University of Chicago Press, 1985.

Le Goff, Jacques. *Time, Work, and Culture in the Middle Ages*. Chicago: Chicago University Press, 1980.

Le Goff, Jacques and Emmanuel Le Roy Ladurie. "Mélusine maternelle et défricheuse." *Annales Économies, Sociétés, Civilisations* 26, no. 3–4 (May-August 1971): 587–622.

Leighton, Gerald Rowley. *The Life-History of British Serpents and Their Local Distribution in the British Isles*. Edinburgh: William Blackwood and Sons, 1901.

Le Roy Ladurie, Emmanuel. "Mélusine Down on the Farm: Metamorphosis of a Myth." In *The Territory of the Historian*, 203–220. Chicago: University of Chicago Press, 1979.

Lewis, Celia M. "Acceptable Lessons, Radical Truths: *Mélusine* as Literature for Medieval Youth." *Children's Literature* 39 (2011): 1–32.

Lippert, Sarah. "Hybride (National-)Symbole und Multilingualität: Mehrsprachige Melusinenfigurationen in der zeitgenössischen Literatur Luxemburgs." In *Philologie und Mehrsprachigkeit*, edited by Till Dembeck and Georg Mein, 359–79. Heidelberg: Universitätsverlag Winter, 2014.

Longnon, Jean, Raymond Cazelles, and Millard Meiss. *Les Très Riches Heures du Duc de Berry*. Chantilly: Musée Condé, 1969.

Looze, Laurence de. "*'La fourme du pié toute escrite'*: Melusine and the Entrance into History." In *Melusine of Lusignan: Founding Fiction in Late Medieval France*, edited by Donald Maddox and Sara Sturm-Maddox, 125–36. Athens, GA: University of Georgia Press, 1996.

Loutsch, Jean-Claude. *Armorial du Pays de Luxembourg*. Luxembourg: Ministère des arts et des sciences, 1974.

Loutsch, Jean-Claude. "Le cimier au dragon et la légende de Mélusine." In *Le cimier mythologique, rituel, parenté des origines au XVIe siècle. Actes du 6e colloque international d'héraldique La Petite-Pierre 9–13 octobre 1989*, edited by Académie Internationale d'Héraldique, 181–204. Brussels: Académie Internationale d'Héraldique, 1990.

Ludwikowska, Johanna. "Uncovering the Secret: Medieval Women, Magic, and the Other." *Studia Anglica Posnaniensia* 49, no. 2 (2015): 83–104.

Maddox, Donald. *Fictions of Identity in Medieval France*. Cambridge, UK: Cambridge University Press, 2006.

Maddox, Donald and Sara Sturm-Maddox, eds. *Melusine of Lusignan: Founding Fiction in Late Medieval France*. Athens, GA: University of Georgia Press, 1996.

Margue, Michel. "Jean de Luxembourg, prince idéal et chevalier parfait: Aux origines d'un mythe." *Mediaevalia Historica Bohemica* 5 (1998): 11–26.

Margue, Michel. "*La fée Mélusine: Le mythe fondateur de la Maison de Luxembourg*." In *Bestiaires d'Arlon: Les animaux dans l'imaginaire des Gallo-Romains à nos jours*, edited by André Neuberg, 129–137. Bastogne: Ed. Musée en Piconrue, 2006.

Margue, Michel and Michel Pauly. "Saint-Michel et le premier siècle de la ville de Luxembourg." *Hémecht* 39 (1987): 5–83.

Margue, Michel and Jean Schroeder, eds. *Un itinéraire européen: Jean l'Aveugle, comte de Luxembourg, roi de Bohême 1296–1346*. Publications du CLUDEM. Brussels: Crédit communal; Luxembourg: CLUDEM, 1996.

Markale, Jean. *Mélusine; ou, l'androgyne*. Paris: Retz, 1983.

Martin, Molly. *Vision and Gender in Malory's* Morte Darthur. Cambridge, UK: D. S. Brewer, 2010.

Massey, Irving. *The Gaping Pig: Literature and Metamorphosis*. Berkeley: University of California Press, 1976.

McCarthy, John. *Remapping Reality: Chaos and Creativity in Science and Literature (Goethe-Nietzsche- Grass)*. Amsterdam: Rodopi, 2006.

Melusine: Actes du colloque du Centre d'Etudes médiévales de l'Université de Picardie-Jules Verne, 13 et 14 janvier 1996. Greifswald: Reineke Verlag, 1996.

Menninghaus, Winfried. *Disgust: The Theory and History of a Strong Sensation*. Translated by Howard Eiland and Joel Golb. Albany, NY: State University of New York Press, 2003.

Meyer, Antoine. "Melusina." In *Oilzegt-Kläng*, 85–90. Liège: H. Dessain, 1853.

Meyer, Clemens Friedrich. *Goethes Märchendichtung*. Heidelberg: Winters Universitätsbuchhandlung, 1879.

Miles, Margaret. *A Complex Delight: The Secularization of the Breast, 1350–1750*. Berkeley: University of California Press, 2008.

Miller, Sarah. *Medieval Monstrosity and the Female Body*. New York: Routledge, 2010.

Miller, William Ian. *The Anatomy of Disgust*. Cambridge, MA: Harvard University Press, 1997.

Mommsen, Katharina. *Goethe und 1001 Nacht*. Bonn: Bernstein, 2006.

Mörike, Eduard. *Die Historie Von Der Schönen Lau: The Story of Lau, the Beautiful Water Nymph*. Translated by Stan Foulkes, edited by Peter Schmid. Ebenhausen bei München: Langewiesche–Brandt, 1997.

Moritz, Muriel and Lex Roth. *Melusina*. Luxembourg: Editions Saint-Paul, 1996.

Morris, Matthew W. "Jean d'Arras and Coudrette: Political Expediency and Censorship in Fifteenth-Century France." *Postscript* 18–19 (2009): 35–44.

Morris, Matthew and Jean-Jacques Vincensini, eds. *Ecriture et réécriture du merveilleux féérique: Autour de Mélusine*. Paris: Classiques Garnier, 2012.

Morrison, Toni. *Playing in the Dark: Whiteness and the Literary Imagination*. Cambridge, MA: Harvard University Press, 1992.

Müller, Catherine M. "Pour une poétique de la dénomination dans *Mélusine* de Jean d'Arras et de Coudrette." *Le Moyen Âge: Revue d'histoire et de philologie* 107 no. 1 (2001): 29–48.

Mulvey, Laura. "Visual Pleasure and Narrative Cinema." *Screen* 16, no. 3 (1975): 6–18.

Mustard, Wilfred. "Siren-Mermaid." *Modern Language Notes* 23, no. 1 (January 1908): 21–4.

Nejedlý, Martin. *Středověký mýtus o Meluzíně a rodová pověst Lucemburků*. Prague: Scriptorium, 2014.

Nisbet, H[ugh] B[arr]. *Goethe and the Scientific Tradition*. London: Institute of German Studies, 1972.

Nolan, Robert J. "An Introduction to the English Version of *Melusine*." PhD diss., New York University, 1971.

Noé-Rumberg, Dorothea-Michaela. *Naturgesetze als Dichtungsprinzipien: Goethes verborgene Poetik im Speigel seiner Dichtungen*. Freiburg: Rombach, 1993.

Orchard, Andy, ed. and trans. "Liber monstrorum." In *Pride and Prodigies: Studies in the Monsters of the* Beowulf-*Manuscript*. Toronto: University of Toronto Press, 1995.

Orme, Nicholas. "Children and Literature in Medieval England." *Medium Aevum* 68, no. 2 (1999): 218–46.

Orme, Nicholas. *Medieval Children*. New Haven, CT: Yale University Press, 2001.

Oswald, Dana M. *Monsters, Gender, and Sexuality in Medieval English Literature*. Woodbridge, Suffolk: Boydell & Brewer, 2010.

Otto, Beate. *Unterwasser-Literatur: von Wasserfrauen und Wassermännern*. Würzburg: Königshausen & Neumann, 2001.

Pagès, Amédée. *La poésie française en Catalogne du XIIIe siècle à la fin du XV*. Toulouse: Privat-Didier, 1936.

Pairet, Ana. "Histoire métamorphose et poétique de la réécriture: les traductions espagnoles du *Roman de Mélusine* (XVe–XVIe siècles)." In *Mélusine moderne et contemporaine*, edited by Arlette Bouloumié and Henri Béhar, 47–55. Paris L'Age d'Homme, 2001.

Pairet, Ana. "Intervernacular translation in the early decades of print: Chivalric romance and the marvelous in the Spanish *Melusine* (1489–1526)." In *Translating the Middle Ages*, edited by Karen L. Fresco and Charles D. Wright, 86–101. London: Ashgate, 2012.

Paré, Ambroise. *On Monsters and Marvels*. Translated by Janis L. Pallister. Chicago: University of Chicago Press, 1982.

Pastoureau, Michel. *Une histoire symbolique du Moyen Âge occidental*. Paris: Seuil, 2004.

Pavlevski, Joanna. "Une esthétique originale du motif de la femme-serpent: recherches ontologiques et picturales sur Mélusine au XVe siècle." *L'Humain et l'animal dans la France médiévale (XIIe–XVe s.): Human and Animal in Medieval France, (12th–15th c.)*. Leiden: Brill, 2014.

Pavlevski, Joanna. "Naissances féériques et fondation de lignée dans *La Noble Histoire de Lusignan* et *Le Roman de Parthenay* de Coudrette." *Questes* 27 (January 2014): 125–52.

Pearson, Terry. "The Mermaid in the Church." In *Profane Images in Marginal Arts of the Middle Ages: Proceedings of the VI Biennial Colloquium Misericordia International*, edited by Elain C. Block and Frédéric Billiet, 105–21. Turnhout, Belgium: Brepols, 2009.

Pedersen, Tara E. *Mermaids and the Production of Knowledge in Early Modern England*. Burlington, VT: Ashgate, 2015.

Péporté, Pit. *Constructing the Middle Ages: Historiography, Collective Memory, and Nation-Building in Luxembourg*. National Cultivation of Culture 3. Leiden: Brill, 2011.

Péporté, Pit, Sonja Kmec, Benoît Majerus, and Michel Margue. *Inventing Luxembourg: Representations of the Past, Space, and Language from the Nineteenth to the Twenty-First Century*. National Cultivation of Culture 1 and Publications of CLUDEM 34. Leiden: Brill, 2010.

Pickens, Rupert. "The Poetics of Paradox in the *Roman de Mélusine*." In *Mélusine of Lusignan: Founding Fiction in Late Medieval France*, edited by Donald Maddox and Sara Sturm-Maddox, 48–75. Athens, GA: University of Georgia Press, 1996.

Pillard, Guy. *La déesse Mélusine: mythologie d'une fée*. Hérault: Maulévrier, 1989.

Pinto-Mathieu, Elisabeth. *Le roman de Melusine de Coudrette et son adaptation dans le roman en prose de Thüring von Ringoltingen*. Göppinger: Kummerle, 1990.

Poirion, Daniel. *Le merveilleux dans la littérature française du Moyen Âge*. Paris: Presses Universitaires de France, 1982.

Rauer, Christine. *Beowulf and the Dragon*. Woodbridge: D. S. Brewer, 2000.

Rautenberg, Ursula. "New Books for a New Reading Public: Frankfurt *Melusine* Editions from the Press of Gülfferich, Han and Heirs." In *Specialist Markets in the Early Modern Book World*, edited by Richard Kirwan and Sophie Mullins, 85–109. Leiden: Brill, 2015.

Rautenberg, Ursula. *Zeichensprachen des literarischen Buchs in der frühen Neuzeit: die Melusine des Thüring von Ringoltingen*. Berlin: De Gruyter, 2013.

Richards, Robert J. *The Romantic Conception of Life: Science and Philosophy in the Age of Goethe*. Chicago: Chicago University Press, 2002.

Richartz, Michel. "Waleran de Limbourg (ca.1165–1226): le devenir d'un grand politique entre Meuse et Rhin." Master's thesis, University of Liège, 1999.

Riches, Samantha J. E. "Virtue and Violence: Saints, Monsters, and Sexuality in Medieval Culture." In *Medieval Sexuality: A Casebook*, edited by April Harper and Caroline Proctor, 59–78. New York: Routledge, 2008.

Rivera, Isidro J. "The *Historia de la linda Melosina* and the Construction of Romance in Late Medieval Castile." *MLN* 112 (1997): 131–146.

Roach, Eleanor. "La tradition manuscrite du *Roman de Mélusine* par Coudrette." *Revue d'histoire des textes* 7 (1977): 186–221.

Roster, Danielle and Renée Wagener, eds. *Not the Girl You're Looking For: Melusina Rediscovered. Objekt+Subjekt Frau in der Kultur Luxemburgs*. Luxembourg: CID-femmes, 2010.

Ru, G. "*La traduction nééerlandaise de Jean d'Arras.*" Master's thesis, University of Ghent, 2008.

Russo, Mary J. *The Female Grotesque: Risk, Excess, and Modernity*. New York: Routledge, 1994.

Sachs, Eleanor. "Some Notes on a Twelfth-Century Bishop's Mitre in the Metropolitan Museum of Art." *The Bulletin of the Needle and Bobbin Club* 61, no. 1–2 (1978): 3–52.

Sachtleben, Peter. *Das Phänomen Forschung und die Naturwissenschaft Goethes*. Frankfurt am Main: Peter Lang, 1987.

Salisbury, Eve. "*Lybeaus Desconus*: Transformation, Adaptation, and the Monstrous-Feminine." *Arthuriana* 24, no. 1 (Spring 2014): 66–85.

Saneba, Magalie. "Savoirs féminins et fééériques au Moyen Âge: Le cas de Mélusine dans les romans de Jean d'Arras et de Coudrette." *Analyses: Revue de critique et de théorie littéraire* 10, no. 1 (2015): 117–39.

Saporiti, Sonia. *Myth and Symbol: A Psychoanalytic Study in Contemporary German Literature*. Newcastle-upon-Tyne: Cambridge Scholars Publishing, 2013.

Sasse, Günter. *Auswandern in die Moderne: Tradition und Innovation in Goethes Roman Wilhelm Meisters Wanderjahre*. Berlin: De Gruyter, 2010.

Saunders, Corinne. "Magic and Christianity." In *Christianity and Romance in Medieval England*, edited by Rosalind Field, Phillipa Hardman, and Michelle Sweeney, 84–101. Cambridge, UK: D. S. Brewer, 2010.

Saunders, Corinne. *Magic and the Supernatural in Medieval English Romance*. Woodbridge: D. S. Brewer, 2010.

Sax, Boria. *The Serpent and the Swan: The Animal Bride in Folklore and Literature*. Blacksburg: The McDonald & Woodward Publishing Company, 1998.

Schafer, Edward H. *The Divine Woman: Dragon Ladies and Rain Maidens in T'ang Literature*. Berkeley: University of California Press, 1973.

Schnyder, André and Jean-Claude Mühlethaler, eds. *550 Jahre deutsche Melusine – Coudrette und Thüring von Ringoltingen. Beiträge der wissenschaftlichen Tagung der Universitäten Bern und Lausanne vom August 2006*. Bern: Peter Lang, 2008.

Schorbach, Karl. "Eine Buchanzeige des Antwerpener Druckers Geraert Leeu in niederländischer Sprache (1491)." *Zeitschrift für Bücherfreunde* 9 (1905): 139–48.

Schwamborn, Claudia. *Individualität in Goethes Wanderjahren*. Paderborn: Schöningh, 1997.

Seamon, David and Arthur Zajonc, eds. *Goethe's Way of Science*. Albany, NY: State University of New York Press, 1998.

Shaner, Mary E. "Instruction and Delight: Medieval Romances as Children's Literature." *Poetics Today* 13, no. 1 (1992): 5–15.

Shull, Donald Marshall. "The Effect of the Theory of Translation Expressed in the Anonymous *Romans of Partenay* (T.C.C. MS R.3.17) Upon the Language of the Poem." PhD diss., University of North Carolina at Chapel Hill, 1984.

Spiegel, Gabrielle M. "Maternity and Monstrosity: Reproductive Biology in the *Roman de Melusine*." In *Melusine of Lusignan: Founding Fiction in Late Medieval France*, edited by Donald Maddox and Sara Sturm-Maddox, 100–124. Athens, GA: University of Georgia Press, 1996.

Stanesco, Michel. "La fée amante et le chevalier: de l'interdit premier au rite sacrificiel." In *Transgression et contestation*, edited by Russell King, 3–12. University of Nottingham: Nottingham Modern Languages Publications Archive, 2000.

Steer, Alfred Gilbert. *Goethe's Science in the Structure of the* Wanderjahre. Athens, GA: University of Georgia Press, 1979.

Steffen, Nicholas. *Mährchen und Sagen des Luxemburger Landes*. Luxembourg: V. Bück, 1855.

Steiner, Rudolf. "Goethe's Secret Revelation, Part III: *The New Melusine* and *The New Paris*." Lecture, March 2, 1905. Accessed August 30, 2017. http://wn.rsarchive.org/Lectures/GA053/English/UNK2014/19050302p01.html.

Steinkämper, Claudia. *Melusine – vom Schlangenweib Zur »Beauté mit dem Fischschwanz«: Geschichte einer literarischen Aneignung*. Göttingen: Vandenhoeck & Ruprecht, 2007.

Stephenson, Roger H. *Goethe's Conception of Knowledge and Science*. Edinburgh: Edinburgh University Press, 1995.

Stica, Sandro. "Sin and Salvation: The Dramatic Context of Hrotswitha's Women." In *The Role and Images of Women in the Middle Ages and Renaissance*, edited by Douglas Radcliff-Umstead, 3–22. Pittsburgh: University of Pittsburgh Press, 1975.

Stoffel, Michel. *La Clef de Mélusine*. Paris: G. Blanchong & Cie, 1944.

Sturm-Maddox, Sara. "Crossed Destinies: Narrative Programs in the *Roman de Melusine*." In *Melusine of Lusignan: Founding Fiction in Late Medieval France*, edited by Donald Maddox and Sara Sturm-Maddox, 12–31. Athens, GA: University of Georgia Press, 1996.

Swales, Martin and Erika Swales. *Reading Goethe: A Critical Introduction to the Literary Work*. Rochester: Camden, 2002.

Taylor, Jane H. M. "Melusine's Progeny: Patterns and Perplexities." In *Melusine of Lusignan: Founding Fiction in Late Medieval France*, edited by Donald Maddox and Sara Sturm-Maddox, 165–184. Athens, GA: Georgia University Press, 1996.

Temkin, C. Lilian, trans. and ed. "Seven Defensiones, the Reply to Certain Calumniations of His Enemies." In *Four Treatises of Theophrastus von Hohenheim, called Paracelsus*, edited by H. E. Sigerist, 1–41. Baltimore: The Johns Hopkins University Press, 1941.

Tieck, Ludwig. *Die sehr wunderbare Historie von der Melusina*. In *Undinenzauber: Geschichten und Gedichte von Nixen, Nymphen, und anderen Wasserfrauen*, edited by Frank Rainer Max, 46–78. Stuttgart: Reclam, 1991.

Ting, Nai-tung. "The Holy Man and the Snake-Woman: A Study of a Lamia Story in Asian and European Literature." *Fabula* 1 (January 1966): 145–191.

Urban, Misty. *Monstrous Women in Middle English Romance*. Lewiston, NY: Edwin Mellen Press, 2010.

Van Duzer, Chet. *Sea Monsters on Medieval and Renaissance Maps*. London: British Library, 2013.

Vannérus, Jules. *Le chevalier l'Evêque de la Basse-Moûturie et son itinéraire du Luxembourg germanique*. Luxembourg: Bourg-Bourger, 1929.

Vigarello, Georges. *Concepts of Cleanliness: Changing Attitudes in France Since the Middle Ages*. Translated by Jean Birrell. Cambridge, UK: Cambridge University Press, 1988.

Vincensini, Jean-Jacques. "La dent de la mère: Geoffrey ou les vertus de l'inquiétant merveilleux." In *Ecriture et réécriture du merveilleux féerique: Autour de Mélusine*, edited by Jean-Jacques Vincensini and Matthew Morris, 157–175. Paris: Classiques Garnier, 2012.

Vincent-Cassy, Mireille. "Péchés de femmes à la fin du Moyen Age." In *La condición de la mujer en la Edad Media: Actas del Coloquio Celebrado en la Casa de Velázquez, del 5 al 7 de noviembre de 1984. Madrid*, edited by Y.-R. Fonquerne and A. Esteban, 501–17. Madrid: Universidad Complutense, 1986.

Vines, Amy N. *Women's Power in Late Medieval Romance*. Woodbridge, Suffolk: D. S. Brewer, 2011.

Vlnas, Vit and Zdenek Hojda. "Tschechien: 'Gönnt einem jeden die Wahrheit'." In *Mythen der Nationen: Ein Europäisches Panorama*, edited by Monika Flacke, 502–527. Munich: Koehler & Amelang, 1998.

Wade, James. *Fairies in Medieval Romance*. New York: Palgrave Macmillan, 2011.

Walter, Philippe. *La fée Mélusine: le serpent et l'oiseau*. Paris: Imago, 2008.

Warner, Michael. *The Trouble with Normal: Sex, Politics, and the Ethics of Queer Life*. Cambridge, MA: Harvard University Press, 1999.

Wear, Andrew. *The Western Medical Tradition*. Cambridge UK: Cambridge University Press, 1995.

Weir, Anthony and James Jerman. *Images of Lust: Sexual Carvings on Medieval Churches*. London: B. T. Batsford Ltd., 1986.

Weissberger, Barbara F. *Isabel Rules: Constructing Queenship, Wielding Power*. Minneapolis: University of Minnesota Press, 2003.

Wilkins, Nigel. "A Pattern of Patronage: Machaut, Froissart, and the Houses of Luxembourg and Bohemia in the Fourteenth Century." *French Studies* 37 (1983): 257–284.

Williams, David. *Deformed Discourse: The Function of the Monster in Mediaeval Thought and Literature*. Montreal: McGill and Queens University Press, 1996.

Williams, Gerhild Scholz. *Defining Dominion: The Discourses of Magic and Witchcraft in Early Modern France and Germany*. Ann Arbor: University of Michigan Press, 1995.

Williams, Gerhild Scholz and Alexander Schwarz. "Wundersame Dynastie: Interdikte und Verträge in Jean d'Arras' *Melusine*." In *Existentielle Vergeblichkeit*, edited by Anne Betten, Hartmut Steinecke, and Horst Wenzel, 35–66. Berlin: E. Schmidt, 2003.

Wogan-Browne, Jocelyn, Nicholas Watson, Andrew Taylor, and Ruth Evans, eds. *The Idea of the Vernacular: An Anthology of Middle English Literary Theory, 1280–1520*. University Park: Pennsylvania State University Press, 1999.

Woodbridge, Linda. *Women and the English Renaissance: Literature and the Nature of Womankind, 1540–1620*. Chicago: University of Illinois Press, 1984.

Wu, Pei-yi. "The White Snake: The Evolution of a Myth in China." PhD diss., Columbia University, 1969.

Wunder, Jennifer N. *Keats, Hermeticism, and the Secret Societies*. New York: Routledge, 2016.

Yamamoto, Dorothy. *The Boundaries of the Human in Medieval English Literature*. Oxford: Oxford University Press, 2000.

Yang, Ch'ing-k'un. *Religion in Chinese Society: A Study of Contemporary Social Functions of Religion and Some of Their Historical Factors*. Berkeley: University of California Press, 1961.

Zeldenrust, Lydia. "Serpent or Half-Serpent? Bernhard Richel's *Melusine* and the Making of a Western European Icon." *Neophilologus* 100, no. 1 (2016): 19–41.

Zhong, Maosen, ed. 女四书 女孝经. Beijing: Zhongguo Huaqiao, 2012.

Zipes, Jack. "The Formation of the Literary Fairy Tale in Germany." In *The Oxford Companion to Fairy Tales*, edited by Jack Zipes, 239–51. Oxford: Oxford University Press, 2015.

Zipes, Jack. *The Irresistible Fairy Tale: The Cultural and Social History of a Genre*. Princeton, NJ: Princeton University Press, 2012.

Index

Lightning Source UK Ltd.
Milton Keynes UK
UKHW02f0226100218
317653UK00004B/127/P